MW01001271

PREFACES TO
SHAKESPEARE

PREFACES TO
SHAKESPEARE

Tony Tanner

WITH A FOREWORD BY
STEPHEN HEATH

THE BELKNAP PRESS OF HARVARD UNIVERSITY PRESS
Cambridge, Massachusetts · London, England
2010

Prefaces by Tony Tanner copyright © 1992–1996 by the Literary Estate of Tony Tanner

Originally published by Everyman Library, an imprint of Alfred A. Knopf, Random House

Foreword by Stephen Heath copyright © 2010 by the President and Fellows of Harvard College

Printed in the United States of America

Library of Congress Cataloging-in-Publication Data

Tanner, Tony.

   Prefaces to Shakespeare / Tony Tanner ; with a foreword by Stephen Heath.

     p.   cm.

   Includes bibliographical references.

   ISBN 978-0-674-05137-9 (cloth : alk. paper)

   1. Shakespeare, William, 1564–1616 — Criticism and interpretation.   2. Prefaces.

I. Title.

PR2976.T26   2010

822.3′3—dc22   2009044556

CONTENTS

ROMANCES   677

FOREWORD

When Everyman's Library decided on an edition of the complete plays of Shakespeare, they asked Tony Tanner to write introductions to its seven volumes. He relished the challenge this involved and went to work with characteristic enthusiasm. The result was a set of substantial pieces made up of a series of accounts of the individual plays in each volume, preceded by initial discussion of topics and issues relating to the volume's particular dramatic mode (tragedy, comedy, history, romance). It is these introductions that are now brought together by Harvard University Press in recognition of their value as a contribution to the understanding and enjoyment of Shakespeare. Tanner, indeed, had always envisaged that they would make a book (while recognizing that, given their length, they might have to be published as more than one book); they were written with the intention that taken together they would provide an extended introduction to reading Shakespeare.

Tanner's life was spent as a teacher of English and American literature in the University of Cambridge, England. American writers and writing were his first and abiding interest, and his numerous books and essays made him a key figure in American literary studies. His range was wider still, and there were books on Joseph Conrad as well as Thomas Pynchon, Jane Austen as well as Henry James, along with ambitious works of comparative literature—on adultery and the novel, and on the literary myths and imaginings of Venice. It was late, however, in what was to be the last decade of his life, that he came to write on Shakespeare; but then this was after years of reading and thought during which he had gained a comprehensive familiarity with Shakespeare's work. The first Everyman's Library volume, containing the four major tragedies, appeared in 1992; the last, the romances, in 1996, just two years before Tanner's untimely death in 1998. In one short, intense period of time, he had written on all the plays and achieved a critically informed and stimulating presentation of Shakespeare's dramatic world.

Tanner was not a professional Shakespearian and he always insisted, overly modestly, that what was at stake in the introductions was not strictly scholarly. Modesty aside, he was well able to find his way around the mass of Shakespeare scholarship and had no difficulty in gathering and using what was directly relevant and illuminating. His learning was substantial: it could be called upon for the discussion of tragedy and revenge from the Greeks onwards, or for the understanding of the nature of Elizabethan theatre, or for an investigation of the sources of Shakespeare's historical knowledge. As a student at Cambridge, he had been taught by two Shakespeare critics, A. P. Rossiter and Philip Brockbank, and he took from the latter especially what he described as a complex, ironic humanism. This indeed is the underlying manner of his introductions, with their lack of dogmatism and their refusal to bind Shakespeare in what Henry James called the 'shackles of theory' (James was one of Tanner's touchstone authors, and this was a phrase he often invoked). It is not that Tanner was unaware of, or uninterested in, contemporary theoretical developments; simply, for him theory was to be approached as a potential source of local ideas and concepts that could at times help to crystallize a moment of reading, or suggest a fitting way of expressing an insight his reading had given him, or take his writing on this or that play in new directions. Much more important for the introductions is the considerable knowledge Tanner possessed of other Shakespeare critics, old and new (Dryden and Stanley Cavell, for instance, or Coleridge and Frank Kermode, along with a host of others); he engages constantly in dialogue with these critics, taking up their views and interpretations, opening up for his readers multiple perspectives on the Shakespearean critical tradition.

The practice of literary criticism for Tanner was one of immersion in an author's work, and nowhere is this more evident than in his writing on Shakespeare. His was never criticism *at a distance;* in an age of academic caution and guarded theoretical correctness, Tanner never held back from what might be called a *warmth* of reading, a fundamental generosity of response to the texts with which he was dealing. He thought of himself, in fact, much less as a critic than as an *appreciator:* the task was that of reading, writing, and teaching in enjoyment of literature, in admiration, as he put it, of literature's capacity 'to replenish and revivify our vision of the world'. That capacity is Shakespeare's supremely, and it is what Tanner was intent to bring out and help us appreciate. He looks carefully at what is going on in the plays and does so through a close attention to language, drawing out from Shakespeare's words the complex meanings of the plays and exploring the varied responses they provoke.

Edward Said, a longtime friend of Tanner's, spoke of 'the human heart' of a text, which is exactly what counted for Tanner, and counted for him as he was writing these Shakespeare introductions. Tanner's Shakespeare is at once historically specific and humanly contemporary. The plays speak to us, whether in the theatre or on the page, and the critic as appreciator must make them live for us in all their profound humanity. These days, often for good reason, we have lost faith in any appeal to 'the common reader'; what Tanner's introductions propose, however, is a *common pursuit of reading,* involving us in sharing with him as much as possible of the richness of Shakespeare's dramatic world.

The introductions can be read for the discussion of this or that play, as well as for their treatment of tragedy, comedy, history, or romance; they can be read through together as a series of long essays—meditations, explorations, interpretations—and as the interrelated chapters of the large work on Shakespeare that Tanner had wished to produce. There are many ways of using them, and many different readers for them, whether students, teachers, or non-academics. Tanner's critical humanism is inclusive, not exclusive, and his style is one of a clarity and a humour, an enthusiasm and a sheer vitality that never loses sight of its responsibility to Shakespeare and to the engagement of his readers in a dialogue of understanding and learning and valuing the reality of the achievement of the plays.

PREFACES TO
SHAKESPEARE

COMEDIES

O if it prove,
Tempests are kind, and salt waves fresh in love!
(*Twelfth Night,* III, iv, 395–6)

Where a river meets the sea, there is a strange point at which the fresh water of the river suddenly gives way to the salt water of the sea (or, if you are
coming in, salt water becomes fresh). The actual place of the transition may
change according to whether the sea is at the full—in which case it pushes
the river back—or ebbing—when the river runs further out. But, either
way, the transition is relatively sudden—now this, now that; here salt, here
fresh. In this, it differs from the usual gradualisms which mark natural
changes—the acorn becoming the tree; the calf becoming the bull; the girl
growing up, the man growing old. Because of this prevailing gradualism,
we have the saying—nature does not make leaps. But it does. Now salt,
now fresh. It seems rather mysterious—but it *is* part of nature. Natural
magic.

Tennyson notes this phenomenon, and used it for his own purposes in
In Memoriam:

> There twice a day the Severn fills;
>   And salt sea-water passes by,
>   And hushes half the babbling Wye,
> And makes a silence in the hills.
>
> The Wye is hush'd nor moved along,
>   And hush'd my deepest grief of all,
>   When fill'd with tears that cannot fall,
> I brim with sorrow drowning song.
>
> The tide flows down, the wave again
>   Is vocal in its wooded walls;
>   My deeper anguish also falls,
> And I can speak a little then.
>   (XIX)

Tennyson is using the natural phenomenon to project—and perhaps to understand—the fluctuations in his own grief. Sometimes it is silenced and 'bottled up' and the tears 'cannot fall'—as when the powerful sea blocks the outward flow of the river. But sometimes his grief finds a degree of tearful release and articulation—as when the river is allowed to run out some distance into the ebbing sea. The natural phenomenon provides an analogue—and perhaps, in part, an explanation—for his moods. Now salt; now fresh. Now you cry; now you don't. Shakespeare, as I shall suggest, uses it somewhat differently.

The sea, even more for the Elizabethans than for us, is always a potential place of tempest and shipwreck; of lostness, confusion, and destruction; of chaos, disappearance, and death. By contrast, the river, flowing calmly and containedly between its 'wooded walls', bespeaks the peace, order, and reassuring familiarity of a known and stable land. The paradigmatic movement of Shakespearian comedy is out and away from just such a stable place, onto or into just such a sea-realm (literal or metaphorical), back to a land haven. But there is something unusual and unprepared for about that third movement. It is not just a 'return'—it is a 'catastrophe', which means literally a *sudden* turn (used by Ben Jonson of comedies and tragedies alike). Characters can seem to be in direst extremities and confusion—all at sea, as we say—when lo!, they find themselves in calm, clear, fresh water. So much, I have suggested, may be justified by a strange, natural phenomenon. But for Shakespeare's characters—the lucky and deserving ones—tempests do not just calm down but 'are kind', and they find themselves in 'salt waves fresh in love'. Another element has been added, another perspective opened up; nature is turning benignly, magically, metaphoric. It is not exactly supernatural, but it is as if a mysterious power and force has supervened. Now salt, now fresh *in love*.

In the anonymous letter attached to the second Quarto of *Troilus and Cressida,* the unknown writer asserts (of Shakespeare's work): 'So much and such savored salt of witte is in his Commedies, that they seeme (for their height of pleasure) to be borne in that sea that brought forth *Venus.*' Venus means sex, and sex is 'the height of pleasure', and that, says our enthusiastic friend, is the kind of pleasure we get from Shakespeare's comedies. At first sight, it might seem rather odd to conflate wit and sex in this way; but a little consideration yields the recognition that he is in the right of it. They are inextricable in Shakespearian comedy, and—think only of the erotically suffused sparring of Beatrice and Benedick—our commentator is probably spot on in suggesting that the two saltinesses spring from the same source. And the salt waves of sexual desire (often producing an insatiable thirst) can—it is another deeply natural mystery—turn into the refreshing, fresh water of love. Venus is always rising—though, of course, her native element may wreck and drown you.

The sea, and tempests and shipwrecks, recur in Shakespearian comedy literally from first to last. So much was a familiar theatrical plot device. Indeed, a French critic writing in 1641 complained that 'authors make tempest and shipwreck at will', though he did see that 'the sea is the most fitting scene for great changes, and . . . some have called it the theatre of inconstancy'. More than a thousand years earlier (AD 523), in the *Consolation of Philosophy* of Boethius, the figure of Philosophy adopts the role of Fortune and speaks for her:

> Must I only be forbidden to use my right? . . . The sea hath right sometime to fawn with calms, and sometime to frown with storm and waves. And shall the insatiable desire of men tie me to constancy, so contrary to my custom? This is my force, this is the sport which I continually use. I turn about my wheel with speed, and take a pleasure to turn things upside down . . .

The sea/Fortune/inconstancy—this is the element man must move in, and at a basic level it is always a matter of sink or swim. In *The Two Gentlemen of Verona,* the character all too aptly named Proteus cries out near the end: 'O heaven, were man/But constant, he were perfect!' (V, iv, 109–10). But only heaven is 'perfect'. Here in the sublunary world, we have forever to struggle in the sea of inconstancy, an inconstancy, as Shakespeare so often demonstrates, that is both within and without us. But, even here, it is a matter of more and less—and to make the point, Shakespeare will present us with heroines of such constancy as to merit the description 'heavenly true' (Desdemona, but applicable to many others), affording us at least glimpses and intimations of a world beyond change.

And, although many of his characters have to undergo tempest, shipwreck, near drowning, and sea-changes, there is invariably that coming back to a land haven, or some equivalent. The end of Shakespearian comedy (perhaps all comedy) is characterized by at least some of the following 're-' words. I apologize for the list, but it does have some cumulative point: return (which implies a previous dislodgement or flight); restoration (after displacement, exile or usurpation); recognition, which includes clarification and unravelling (after confusion, tangles, darkness); reconstitution and re-assemblage (after a disordering and scattering); remedy (for sickness); re-lease (after constraint, repression); reversion (after inversion, and perhaps perversion); revitalization (of lost energies); replenishment and refreshing (for emptiness and desiccation); recovery (of someone/something missing or lost); reunion (after separation); resolution (of problems and uncertainty); reconciliation (where there was discord and enmity); reordering (of actual or potential chaos); rebirth (after seeming death); renewal (after stagnation); regeneration (superseding blocked generation); and—perhaps—redemption (of sins). I leave the explicitly religious possibility until last for a reason. As Northrop Frye often pointed out, there is a clear parallel between the structure of romantic comedy and the central myth of Christianity: 'The framework of the Christian myth is the comic framework of the Bible, where man loses a peaceable kingdom, staggers through the long night-mare of tyranny and injustice which is human history, and eventually re-gains his original vision.' Or, in terms of my very simple model—land—sea experience—back (somewhat miraculously) to fresh water and harbour; and Eden—history—Paradise—may be felt, as sequences, to be in some (tenuous or distant) way homologous or isomorphic. There is, indeed, often some feeling, some flickering, some hint, of the supernatural, the supernal, the other-worldly, even the expressly religious at the end of some of Shake-speare's romance comedies (this of course includes the Last Plays). And yet, I shall want to suggest, it is a feeling—an experience—generated from *within* nature. (Venus rising can seemingly attain almost angelic heights.) There are no *trans*cendental (or transcendentalizing) words in my list. The prefix 're-' simply means 'back' or 'again'. Not, that is, 'up' or 'beyond'. Though getting or coming back, and happening or doing again, may not be either simple or easy. More likely it will happen suddenly and strangely. As when the salt wave is, again, fresh.

> *Valentine.* She shall be dignified with this high honor—
>   To bear my lady's train, lest the base earth
>   Should from her vesture chance to steal a kiss,
>   And, of so great a favor growing proud,
>   Disdain to root the summer-swelling flow'r,
>   And make rough winter everlastingly.
>   (*The Two Gentlemen of Verona,* II, iv, 157–62)

This preposterous conceit, used by Valentine to claim his lady's superiority over any other woman, is an extreme example of the foolish hyperboles often employed by young men in Shakespeare's comedies in their would-be gallant rhetoric. Quite rightly, Proteus protests—'What braggardism is this?' But in this bit of absurd 'braggardism', Shakespeare, in his own inscrutable way, has incorporated what is in effect a glance back at the very origins of comedy. One of the most ancient of dreads was that spring might not return, that the 'base earth' would, precisely, 'make rough winter everlastingly'. All the laments and nightmares throughout literature about wastelands and periods of protracted sterility are, in effect, echoes or elaborations of that primal fear. There was, correspondingly, a great joy when the 'summer-swelling' flowers did, after all, duly appear. Many rituals and festivities grew up both to awaken and revive the forces of fertility still sleeping in the 'base earth', and to celebrate the feelings of renewal which accompanied the liberation of energies after the long hibernation of 'rough winter'. Comedy comes out of these seasonal celebrations of nature's periodicity, the alternation of the seasons, the succession of generations. (Hesiod's personification of harvest-bloom and feasting, Thalia, became the muse of Comedy.) These archaic feelings were clearly still fresh and strong in (still primarily rural) Elizabethan England. Here is part of the song announcing Summer's approaching death, in Nashe's *Summer's Last Will and Testament*:

> Fair Summer droops, droop men and beasts therefore;
> So fair a summer look for never more.
> All good things vanish, less than in a day,
> Peace, plenty, pleasure, suddenly decay.
>   Go not yet away, bright soul of the sad year;
>   The earth is hell when thou leav'st to appear.

This pageant (written during the plague years of 1592–4, when Shakespeare was writing his early comedies) contains the famous lines:

> Brightness falls from the air,
> Queens have died young and fair,
> Dust hath clos'd Helen's eye.
> I am sick, I must die;
>   Lord, have mercy on us.

The threat of 'rough winter everlastingly', the 'hell' which is the absence of summer and the end of the 'summer-swelling flower', that falling from the air of brightness—none of these are forgotten in Shakespeare's comedies which, one way or another, always bear what Henry James called 'the dark smudge of mortality'.

Shakespeare lived through a time when there were increasing attacks —from Puritans and city authorities—on both the great church festivals (vestiges of Catholicism) and rural folk festivals (too pagan and disorderly). The Puritan triumph over festivals was completed in 1644, when they were officially banned. Nevertheless, a great number of festivals persisted throughout Shakespeare's lifetime, such as those marking moments in the agricultural year—Plough Monday, sheep-shearing, rush-bearing, hop-picking, nutting, bringing in the may, harvest-home etc.: in addition there were all kinds of primitive folk dramas related to (elaborations of) festival—mummer plays, Robin Hood plays, morris dances, wooing games, mock battles as between Carnival and Lent, and other pastimes, revels, and pageants: not to mention fairs and wakes, christenings, weddings, and funerals. (It is in these rurally-based games and plays that we find the figure—so important for Shakespeare—of the clown, which then meant simply 'peasant'.) Shakespeare refers to many of these festivals and festival activities in a variety of ways—sometimes alluding to them, sometimes incorporating bits of them in a different context, sometimes elaborating and transforming some of their structural features and principles for the theatre, which was, after all, a kind of festival, albeit a self-conscious one, with the crucial difference from actual festivals that it was completely scripted and controlled (traditional festivals could become anarchic and chaotic, as in the ancient saturnalia or the Lord of Misrule feasts). Shakespeare's interest in (and very likely youthful familiarity with) festivals was searching and profound: in festival and in 'festivity' itself—as an ineradicable human compulsion, need, and desire; as both a social and socializing resource *and* a potential problem (some festivals were *very* disorderly—for instance, brothels and theatres sometimes got pulled down!); as an ambivalent phenomenon which somehow draws on and enacts some of our deepest feelings about the relationship of man and nature. We should not be surprised if some of his comedies turn out to be not only a sort of sophisticated festival themselves, but also dramatic inquiries into the nature of festival. 'Festivals' about festivals, in other words. Or, perhaps better, plays about playing—in every sense.

There are, needless to say, books exclusively on the subject of Elizabethan festival and Shakespeare. The most comprehensive, and one of the very best, is François Laroque's *Shakespeare's Festive World*. He traces festival's roots in an archaic sense of time and the cosmos, and stresses the qualitatively differentiated time of the countryside and the agricultural calendar linked to natural cycles, as opposed to the homogenous, quantitative clock-time of the town. (John Kerrigan says that, with the introduction of the fob-watch into Elizabethan England, 'clock time invaded men's lives'. 'There's no clock in the forest' Orlando reminds Rosalind.) He shows how Shakespeare manages to contrive the coexistence of the cyclical time of festival and the linear time of theatrical representation. Reminding us of the great urban and commercial boom affecting Elizabethan England, he says:

> Yet the town/country opposition still lay at the heart of the whole phenomenon of festivity, for even if it was through the towns that festivals were developed, embellished, and enriched, essentially the festival was the product of a rural civilization whose seasonal rhythms and magico-religious beliefs were linked with the mysteries of natural fertility. Furthermore, for Shakespeare's contemporaries, the countryside (whether cultivated or fallow or forest), lying *extra muros,* beyond the town walls, was still the object of ancient beliefs and deep-rooted fears. The forest, linked with royal privileges, was the domain of hunting, wildness and the sacred, as is testified by the ballads and legends of Robin Hood, [and] the wealth of iconographic variants on the grotesque theme of the *homo sylvarum* . . .

The forest stands with the sea as a crucial part of the topography of Shakespeare's comedies.

Laroque makes two particularly important points, as I see it, about the two-wayness, and the two-sidedness of festival. Thus: at some times, flowers, plants, etc., were gathered and arranged indoors—'these were ritual gestures that moved from the outside inwards, betokening a twofold desire: to overstep boundaries and to appropriate nature'. At other times, the town/countryside relationship was reversed, and people headed out to disport themselves in the fields and woods. Again, there was the 'beating of the bounds' during which people toured the parish, and, at certain points, the children were beaten to impress on their memories the boundaries and frontiers of different plots of land, and paths, and so on—a kind of conse-

cration of property. But on May Day and Midsummer Day, people were allowed to 'commit crimes against the vert'—that is, they could steal flowers,
timber and trees from forests and parks. 'This provides us with a particularly striking illustration of the ambivalence of the festival: sometimes it
served as a solemn ratification of boundaries, points of reference, and dividing lines; at other times it gave a community licence to transgress those
boundaries and abolish those dividing lines.' Ratifying and transgressing
boundaries and dividing lines of all kinds—not least those of gender and
rank—are matters at the very centre of Shakespeare's comedies.

Festival is holiday, and holiday is precisely not workday, though it takes
place within the awareness of the inevitable and necessary return to the so-
brieties and exigencies of the everyday world. It was a (limited) time of liberty and release, an outflowing of energies and vitalities usually held down,
or kept in, by awe, deference, and respect (or the police). And some of the
energies which started to flow were akin to the juices which went into those
swollen summer flowers. Laroque quotes from an interesting anonymous
piece called *The Passionate Morrice* (1593), to this effect:

> Liking will not be long a dooing; and love that followes is but little,
> whereby he brings no great harme; but al the mischieefe comes with de-
> sire, which swells the affections, and predominates over love and liking;
> he makes the misrule, and keeps the open Christmas; he desires the
> sporte, and maintains the pastime, so that, though he be long in comming,
> and staies but little in his Lordship, yet the remembrance of his jolitie is
> not forgotten a long time after.

Swelling flowers, swelling affections—there is something inherently tu-
mescent in comedy ('the height of pleasure' at least one spectator found
it, remember). And, of course, all (or most) of the mischief—almost anywhere—*does* come from desire—here importantly differentiated from love
and liking—which may indeed 'stay but little' in the desirer but can have
results 'not forgotten a long time after'. Undoubtedly, there was intoxication and a degree of sexual promiscuity at festival times, though surely not
as much as the fevered imaginations of the Puritans pruriently conjured up.
(In this connection, see the invaluable *Anatomie of Abuses* by the Puritan
Phillip Stubbes, which gives the most vivid, not to say high-temperature,
accounts of contemporary festivals that we have.) Here is a characteristi-

cally balanced comment by C. L. Barber (whose magisterial *Shakespeare's Festive Comedy* remains the best single book on Shakespearian comedy) on the Misrule festivals: 'The instability of an interregnum is built into the dynamics of misrule: the game at once appropriates and annihilates the mana of authority. In the process, the fear which normally maintains inhibition is temporarily overcome, and the revellers become wanton, swept along on the freed energy normally occupied in holding themselves in check.' To the authorities, revellers might easily become rebels, even revolutionaries, and in their eyes you couldn't always tell a revel from a riot. There is no doubt that some festivals could release forces of destruction, as well as those of procreation. François Laroque is at some pains to remind us 'just how great the ravages caused by festivity can be', as, he maintains, Shakespeare's comedies sometimes reveal. But, more importantly, those comedies are, says Laroque, like 'the upside-down festival world characterized by all the ambiguities and metamorphoses of desire'. In this sense, they certainly are 'borne in that sea that brought forth Venus'.

One last point about festival, which I take from Barber. He quotes one of Phillip Stubbes' descriptions of a Maypole ('stinking idol'—Stubbes) festival which, as Barber points out, serves, perhaps inadvertently, 'to bring out how completely all groups who lived together within the agricultural calendar shared in the response to the season'. Then he quotes this very revealing comment from the Puritan castigator:

> I think it convenient for one friend to visit another (at some-times) as opportunity and occasion shall offer itself; but wherefore should the whole town, parish, village, and country keep one and the same day, and make such gluttonous feasts as they do?

As Barber acutely comments—'clearly Stubbes assumes a world of isolated, busy individuals, each prudently deciding how to make the best use of the time'. The Puritan distrust of pleasure and appetitive excess is familiar; but, as important, is this inability to appreciate the instinct of a community to experience itself *as* a community—the sociality and bonding power of festival. Now think of those crowded last scenes of Shakespeare's comedies, and you realize how important the communalizing, harmonizing, integrating instincts were for him.

Finally, I just want to suggest that perhaps the greatest influence of festival on Shakespeare was on his comic imagination. If ever language went on holiday and enjoyed a carnival time it is in his comedies—in the awareness, always, that holidays have to end.

> I am transformèd, master, am not I?
> (*The Comedy of Errors,* II, ii, 196)

There are three explicit invocations of the name of Ovid in Shakespeare's plays (*The Taming of the Shrew, Titus Andronicus, As You Like It*—four, if you include 'Ovidius Naso' in *Love's Labor's Lost*). He names one character 'Proteus', and allows one other—the future Richard III—to boast that he will 'add colors to the chameleon,/Change shapes with Proteus' (3 *Henry VI,* III, ii, 191–2). Joan de Pucelle is accused by York of giving him a witch-like look 'as if with Circe she would change my shape', while the bemused Duke, confronting the identity confusion in *The Comedy of Errors,* says 'I think you all have drunk of Circe's cup' (V, i, 271). The word 'metamorphis'd' in the same play is given by the OED as the earliest known usage of the word. 'Metamorphosed' occurs twice in *The Two Gentlemen of Verona,* and nowhere else in Shakespeare. All this by way of indicating that the influence on Shakespeare of Ovid's *Metamorphoses* is there from the start (as it was on very many Renaissance writers and artists. To give just one, relevant, contemporary example, the evil shape-shifter Archimago, so crucial in Spenser's *Fairy Queen,* is able to take 'As many forms and shapes in seeming wise,/As ever *Proteus* to himself could make'). The somewhat more pertinent point to note is that all these very *specific* references to Ovid and his main work, occur in Shakespeare's earliest plays. Subsequently, the influence is diffused. Or rather, it is opened out and deepened, as Shakespeare engages in repeated dramatic explorations of the phenomenon of 'transformation' at all levels and in every part of life (the word—and cognates like 'translate'—occur from first to last: more generally, 'change'—word and phenomenon—is everywhere). It is almost as if Shakespeare is 'transforming' specifically Ovidian *Metamorphoses* to get down to the very heart of the mystery of metamorphosis—the metamorphosing drive in nature—itself.*

---

* Less specific allusions to, and borrowings from, stories in Ovid, are to be found throughout Shakespeare. One way or another, he nods to tales from almost every book of the *Metamorphoses*—in addition to the early references to Proteus and Circe: the

John Lyly, an important precursor of Shakespeare, was, according to Jonathan Bate (in his admirable book, *Shakespeare and Ovid*), the first writer to introduce Ovidianism into English drama. His plays abound in Ovidian metamorphoses—see, for example, *Love's Metamorphosis* from the 1580s. Shakespeare allows only one literal metamorphosis—'O Bottom, thou art changed!'—in his drama, and here (in *A Midsummer Night's Dream*) it takes place in the atmosphere of an archaic form of folk drama which is set in the larger context of his own much more sophisticated play; as if Shakespeare was not only looking back to one of his own drama's crude antecedents, but saying something about Ovidian literalism—and perhaps literalism itself. (Shakespeare put his Ovidianism into his language—which does, at times, become a magic realm of metamorphosis and metaphoric transformations.) And, of course, Bottom's metamorphosis is—unOvidianly—reversible. In Lyly's *Gallathea* (1585), two girls dressed as boys (for self-protective disguise) fall in love. This awkwardness is resolved when the goddess Venus agrees to metamorphose one of them into a boy, saying she has already done it to Iphis, a character in a story in Ovid. A number of girls dress up as boys in Shakespearian comedy—and since they were already boy-actors dressed up as girls, this allows Shakespeare enormous scope for all kinds of receding ironies, from sexual *double entendres* and ambiguities, to searching and unsettling probes into the nature and boundaries of gender identity. These boy-girl-boys may also problematically arouse the desire of a member of their own sex (Viola and Olivia in *Twelfth Night*). But the problems have to work themselves out *in* nature—there are no divinely ordained gender alterations (nor, I would maintain, divinely ordained anything else). All Shakespeare's main comic lovers are transformed by desire in some way—for the better (a love which ennobles and spiritualizes), for the worse (a lust which degrades and bestializes), and Shakespeare is clearly fascinated at all the changes and transformations which can be occasioned and precipitated by aroused desire. But the changes are *within*—psychological, emotional,

Golden Age; Phaeton; Acteon; Narcissus and Echo; Pyramus and Thisbe; Ceres and Proserpina; Arachne and her tapestries; Medea; Baucis and Philomel; Hercules and the shirt of Nessus; Orpheus; Venus and Adonis; Ajax and Ulysses; Hecuba; the philosophy of Pythagoras; and so on. Jonathan Bate gives all the details, and it is his informed opinion that 'approximately 90 per cent' of the mythological references in Shakespeare come, or could come, from Ovid.

spiritual. Ovidianism, we may say, is internalized. As the Doctor warns
Conrad's Marlow before he sets out for Africa (in *Heart of Darkness*)—'the
changes take place inside, you know'.

In his famous *Oration on the Dignity of Man* (1486)—a seminal Renaissance declaration—Pico della Mirandola has God say this to Adam:

> 'We have made thee neither of heaven nor of earth, neither mortal nor
> immortal, so that with freedom of choice and with honor, as though the
> maker and molder of thyself, thou mayest fashion thyself in whatever
> shape thou shalt prefer. Thou shalt have the power to degenerate into the
> lower forms of life, which are brutish. Thou shalt have the power, out of
> thy soul's judgment, to be reborn into the higher forms, which are divine.'
> O supreme generosity of God the Father, O highest and most marvelous
> felicity of man! To him it is granted to have whatever he chooses, to be
> whatever he wills . . . Who would not admire this our chameleon? Or
> who could more greatly admire aught else whatever? . . . It is man who
> Asclepius of Athens, arguing from his mutability of character and from
> his self-transforming nature, on just grounds says was symbolised by Pro-
> teus in the mysteries.

It is hard to imagine a more exhilarating, celebratory prescription for that
stress on 'self-fashioning' which is such an important feature of the Renaissance (see Stephen Greenblatt's *Renaissance Self-Fashioning*). But when
'this our chameleon' turns out to be, for example, Richard III, then man's
seemingly miraculous self-transforming powers seem less obviously to be a
matter for unequivocal delight and self-congratulation. If a man really *can*
become anything, then he may easily become nothing, or certainly no one
certain stable knowable thing. Richard himself (in his nightmare before
Bosworth) ends in a state of terminal identity fragmentation and dispersal.
He just doesn't know who he is. Ovid's evocation of an endlessly flowing
world, in which 'nothing is permanent' and 'all things are fluent . . . wandering through change', opened up all kinds of possibilities of release and
emancipation from all manner of restricting, blocking, rigidifying forms of
constraint and arrest. Flexibility, suppleness, 'fluency', openness and willingness to change, are essential virtues in Shakespearian comedy—indeed,
it is just those fixed and fixated figures who, locked up in themselves, cannot and will not change—Shylock, Malvolio, Jacques—who resist, and are

unapt for, assimilation into the harmonizing reintegrations of the comedies' conclusions. That aspect of the Ovidian precedent was all for the good,
and invaluable for Renaissance humanism. (Montaigne, whose first pleasure in books was 'reading the fables of *Ovids* Metamorphosies', and who
revealed himself in his essays to be *'ondoyant et divers'*, is another important
influence for Shakespeare. It seems likely that the only surviving copies of
books owned by Shakespeare himself are an annotated edition of the *Metamorphoses* and a copy of Montaigne's *Essais*. 'Perhaps too convenient' says
Bate.)

But there were distinctly less desirable sides to what Golding (transla-
tor of the *Metamorphoses*), rather nicely called 'Ovid's dark philosophie of
turned shapes'. Ovidian change just goes on and on—indeed his Pythagoras argues that change itself provides the only constant principle; there is no
Christian belief in, or hope for and aspiration towards, a realm beyond or
above 'mutability'. A living metaphor for this belief in, or aspiration for,
permanence is marriage, with a related stress on the importance of the virtue of chastity. Marriage and chastity, of little interest to Ovid, are of supreme importance in Shakespeare. Then again, there is a lot of very real
violence in Ovid—people are dismembered and raped in good earnest: in
Shakespearian comedy there is often the sinister threat of real violence, but
it is, as Bate says, invariably forestalled, and those threatening it converted
or expelled. William Carroll (in his very valuable book, *The Metamorphoses
of Shakespearian Comedy*) sums up the ambivalence felt by Renaissance writers, concerning the metamorphosing power of self-fashioning. Following
Mirandola, they celebrated it:

> but they also feared this power, not only because it seemed fundamentally
> a chaotic energy, and not only because they might sink down the scale of
> being, but also because no matter what the nature of their transformation
> —self-controlled or random, higher or lower, celestial or bestial—man's
> essential identity is put at risk . . . In this respect, the whole idea of meta-
> morphosis is subversive, for it undermines the traditional belief in a sta-
> ble, fixed, and ordered self upon which much of western thought, and in
> particular ethics, rests.

And one final consideration about metamorphoses—they may be generated from within, and they may be caused by some mysterious outside force:

it is one thing for a girl to resolve to simulate a man, or for a prince to determine to prove a villain; and quite another to wake up and find yourself a cockroach—or an ass. But every kind of metamorphosis, all aspects of the phenomenon are brought into focus by Shakespeare's eye which, as we often come to feel, seems to have missed nothing.

While at school (as a pupil, or, as one legend has it, briefly as a master), Shakespeare was almost certainly exposed to the 1550 edition of *Andria,* by Donatus, a fourth-century grammarian. It contained, among many other things, a theory of, a formula for, comedy. Thus: 'Comedy ought to be five-parted, the first of which unfolds the argument' (or in another version 'contains either the peril, the anguish, or some trouble'); 'the second completes the same. The third has the increment of turbations and contentions' (or 'brings on the perturbations, and the impediments and despair of the desired thing'); 'the fourth seeks a medicine for the perturbations' (or 'brings a remedy for the impending evil') 'and is a preparation for the catastrophe, which the fifth demands by right for itself. (See T. W. Baldwin, *Shakespeare's Five-Act Structure;* Martin Herrick, *Comic Theory in the Sixteenth Century.*) As we might expect, Shakespeare was clearly an attentive student. Comedy is related to what Henry James called our 'precious capacity for bewilderment'. Not only do we slip on banana skins, which can be funny enough; but we also get things wrong—hopelessly, sometimes indeed 'catastrophically', wrong, which can be far funnier (and, of course, more serious). And there are times, of course, when we simply don't know what on earth is going on. Donatus stressed that there should always be 'something towards error' (*'aliquid ad errorem'*) in comedy; and two important Italian plays of the Renaissance (both known to Shakespeare) are the anonymous *Gl'Ingannati* (*The Deceived*) and Ariosto's *Suppositi* (translated as *Supposes* by Gascoigne who explained in a Prologue: 'But understand, this our Suppose is nothing else but a mistaking or imagination of one thing for another'). Deceptions can be intentional tricks; 'supposes' can be innocent misapprehensions. Both contribute to (are essential for) what another grammarian-theorist, Evanthius, called 'the forward progress (or growth) of the confusions (or turmoils)' (*'incrementum processusque turbarum'*). Whether or not Shakespeare needed to learn all this in school may be doubted, but it is absolutely pertinent to his comedies, the first of which was, indeed, a 'Comedy *of Errors*'. And what he certainly did study—

and what Donatus and Evanthius are theorizing from—is Roman New Comedy.

This means, effectively, the plays of Plautus (254–184 BC) and Terence (186–159 BC). These are translations, imitations, and adaptations of Athenian New Comedy which, unlike the Old Comedy of Aristophanes with its ironic concern for the myths and conduct of the whole city-state, concentrated on domestic concerns, sexual rivalry, marriage settlements, money-making, household discords and reconciliations. It emphasized the separation of town from country, and its background, instead of farming (Old Comedy), is trade, with a lot of business trips, and related journeying and travelling. The (bourgeois) family is the dominant social unit, and the comedy comes from all those things which can hinder or threaten its smooth running and self-perpetuation—obstructive fathers, shrewish wives, wayward sons, disobedient daughters, all variously aided and abetted, or foiled and thwarted, by clever servants and wily slaves. Identification and misidentification; worries, uncertainties and confusions concerning birth, name, and status; the disguises, trickeries, and dissimulations often required to pursue a prohibited love affair or outwit a tyrannical master—such things are the very meat of New Comedy: not surprisingly perhaps, it made extensive use of twins and doubles, and developed the dramatic technique of the 'double plot'—resources and devices calculated to accelerate the 'forward progress of the confusion'. Shakespeare based his first comedy on a play by Plautus (of which more in due course), and his Roman-Italian borrowings play a decisive role in many of his subsequent comedies. (On this, as on much else, see Leo Salingar's admirable and helpful book, *Shakespeare and the Traditions of Comedy*.)

These Roman plays are visibly contrived, almost ostentatiously artificial, even mechanical and tending towards an almost mathematical abstraction in that they offer the spectacle of problems being set and then solved (they were thus very popular among the law students at the Inns of Court). In this, they are at a far remove from the primitive semi-improvizations of folk games, and even further from the unpredictable frolics of festival. Different again were the rambling medieval romance narratives which informed the popular drama which had been in existence probably from the fifteenth century. These meandering stories characteristically told of chivalric love, painful separation, long-suffering heroines (calumniated queens were very popular), prolonged searchings, and miraculous reunions. The humour of

New Comedy tended towards the sharpness of satire; to this, Shakespeare added the sweetness of romance (and, perhaps some intimations of mystery from the miracle plays). He also used the tighter forms of New Comedy to give a more urgent and compact shape to these romances, as well as to harness, contextualize, and control the festive impulse. We should add to these dominant influences on the young Shakespeare—morality and miracle plays and interludes (a pervasive influence on his history plays as well); and courtly entertainments, masques and revels and mythological pageants. (Leo Salingar points out that Shakespeare is much more drawn to the great house and the court in his comedies, than to the bourgeois world of craftsmen, tradesmen and shopkeepers. In almost every concluding scene there is a prince figure—not present in New Comedy—arbitrating, arranging, or just overseeing the appropriate reconciliations and reunions.) One more writer must be mentioned—Boccaccio. Leo Salingar sees him as an absolutely crucial influence, for the following reasons:

> The stories transmitted to Shakespeare by Boccaccio and his followers are remarkable, not so much for their air of reporting actualities . . . but for their internal balance and rationality, for the authors' skill in propounding a quandary in practical conduct and then showing its resolution by means of an exact system of moral equivalences, an exchange of gifts or actions or speeches which is symmetrical and at least logically satisfying. In Boccaccio such concern with ethical symmetry is a guiding artistic principle . . . but it is present in all the stories which interested Shakespeare, and, together with the writers' sober attention to the realities of civic life, must have made the Italians' stories stand out from the other moralistic or ramblingly romantic fiction available to him.

In sum, in Shakespeare's comedies, there is an extraordinary confluence of classical, medieval, renaissance, and folk traditions and influences. With his astonishing assimilatory alchemy, he produced out of this unprecedented synthesis Mozartian miracles still capable of inducing a ravishing delight.

One other factor should be taken into consideration as we approach the individual plays. In Shakespeare's childhood, it was still the case that plays and performances of all kinds took place in social spaces not primarily intended for that purpose—the court, great halls and houses, universities, inn-yards; or the church, church-yard, street, market square, and other public places. In 1576 (Shakespeare was twelve), James Burbage built the first permanent playhouse in England, intended solely for the drama. It was called simply the Theatre—as well it might be, since there was no other. Others soon followed, of course—the Swan, the Globe (Shakespeare's main theatre), the Rose, the Fortune, and so on. Shakespeare's lifetime saw quite unparalleled theatrical activity in London, with up to five companies performing plays every day except Sunday; and, it has been reckoned, some two thousand new plays appearing between 1590 and 1642 (when the theatres were closed). The main point here is, that when Shakespeare started writing plays (let's say, around 1588), 'the theatre', a place devoted *exclusively* to dramatic performances and plays, was a new kind of social space which had, as it were, been inserted into the community. Clearly any young playwright was going to be fascinated by the relation of the theatre space to the other social spaces which contained it, and on which it now directly, or indirectly, impinged. Drama was make-believe, but the Theatre was real. How did it react with the other realities around it which, one way or another, it reflected or represented? If Shakespeare puts a play within a play, he is not anticipating Pirandello, but rather exploring the implications and possibilities of a relatively new fact of social life. And another—related— thing. Until some time around the middle of the sixteenth century, the performers in all kinds of plays and performances—aristocratic, religious, popular—were amateurs or part-time players. From around the 1540s, we start to find full-time professional actors. So as well as a new kind of social space, here was a new social being—for a professional actor was a man of no certain rank, no recognized role, no accredited function, dedicated exclusively to simulation and masquerading. Yet he, too, was real. What was the relation between that real man and the role(s) which he assumed? And between the actor and the non-acting spectators? Shakespeare was himself, of course, a professional actor, so we should not be surprised to find him fascinated by such questions, and their dramatic possibilities—leaving us, perhaps, finally not entirely certain where acting starts and stops.

THE PLAYS

There is no available certainty, nor complete editorial agreement, concerning either the date of composition of the first four comedies or the sequence in which they were written. There is a general consensus that they were

written between 1592 and 1594, and I have retained the sequence preferred
by E. K. Chambers.

 ## THE COMEDY OF ERRORS (1589–94)

It is remarkable that Shakespeare's (possibly) first comedy opens with an
old man under sentence of death, so that the long shadow of mortality falls
over all that follows. The Syracusian Egeon submits, without hope, to the
sentence passed on him for having entered Ephesian waters. The Duke of
Ephesus, explaining this harsh punishment, speaks of 'enmity and discord'
between 'our adverse towns', leading to 'rancorous outrage', 'intestine jars';
and invokes 'law' and 'rigorous statutes' while specifically excluding 'all
pity from our threat'ning looks'. He evokes a little world in which all the
normal, nourishing 'traffic' between two geographically related places has
been blocked—trade replaced by violence, communication by contestation,
love by law, and pity by 'penalty'. All the normal life-maintaining, life-
enhancing, circulations and modes of meeting and exchange, have gone,
somehow, fatally awry. It offers an opening glimpse of a world of sterility,
oppugnancy, and death. This is the *start*. It is just such a world that comedy
conspires to break up and uncongeal, by restoring the normal channels of
communication and relationship to their proper flowings, leading to the re-
establishment of a better appreciated amity and concord. That is all to
come.

Asked to explain why he has risked coming to Ephesus (given the mortal
interdiction on Syracusians), Egeon gives a long narrative account of how
he lost his wife and one of his sons in a shipwreck—a common danger for
travelling merchants such as he; of how, years later, his remaining son 'became inquisitive/After his brother' and set out in 'quest of him'; of how he,
Egeon, grown old, has since spent five years roaming through Asia and
Greece searching for him—and, at last, had to try Ephesus. 'I hazarded the
loss' he says—loss of family, loss of remaining son, finally loss of life. Haz-
arding loss is an important willingness, bravery if you like, in the world
of comedy, where, it may be said, 'nothing venture, nothing gain' is an operative rule, and losing is often a necessary prelude to finding. Egeon's
story—voyage, calamity, loss, quest and so on—is archetypal romance material; but material which, one way and another, Shakespeare will draw on

throughout his writing career; for the theme of the broken family—members variously separated, scattered, believed lost—and the ensuing desolation, searching, and final reunion, is one to which he returned time and time again. Egeon stands there, a true figure of pathos—the old patriarch, utterly alone, bereaved, bereft. His life could be ransomed for a 'thousand marks', but since he is friendless in a hostile city, this seems to offer no reprieve. The Duke feels a certain amount of sympathy for him, but stresses that 'we may pity, though not pardon thee'; that he 'may not disannul' the laws; and that the 'passed sentence may not be recalled'. It is still an iron world—inflexible, intransigent, obdurate. But this is still only the first scene; so far, we have romance threatening to end in tragedy. It remains to be seen if, and how, comedy can 'disannul' law.

The 'comedy' begins with the next scene, and Shakespeare has based this comedy on the *Menaechmi* by Plautus—during the Renaissance, one of the most popular, and often adapted, Roman plays (and, itself, taken from an ancient Greek play—thus justifying Bullough's observation that 'it is interesting to find Shakespeare, in what may be his first comedy, going back to the classical source of modern drama'). How Shakespeare transforms this source is so important and illuminating with regard to all his comedies (and comedy-romances) that a brief summary of the Plautus play is necessary. The play opens with a soliloquy by 'Peniculus, a Parasite', foregrounding a concern with appetite and greed, riches of the table and the market. The comedy arises from the mistakes and misunderstandings—errors and 'supposes'—which are occasioned by the arrival of one of a pair of identical twin brothers (the Menaechmi of the title) in a town, Epidamnum, where, as the Prologue or Argument explains, 'th'other dwelt inricht, and him so like,/That Citizens there take him for the same'. The first brother is actively searching for this long-lost second brother, but has, of course, no idea that he has finally arrived in his home town. (This is exactly the root situation Shakespeare takes over.) Act I shows us the wealthy resident brother having a row with his shrew of a wife. Out of patience with her, he resolves to give one of her cloaks to his favourite courtesan (Erotium), with whom he plans to have dinner—and whom he unambiguously prefers ('I never looke upon thee, but I am quite out of love with my wife'). The other, newly arrived, brother appears in Act II, and, to his amazement, is knowingly approached by the courtesan's servant, and then by Erotium herself. He thinks they are mad, but he goes along with them, accepts their hospitality, and pretends to be whoever they think he is. In Act III he is given, mistakenly of course, the cloak his brother had taken from his wife, and then a gold chain is also thrust upon him. Fine by him—'Do not all the gods conspire to loade mee with good luck?' Not so fine for his brother, who, in Act IV, is taxed by his wife about the cloak, and by Erotium concerning both cloak and gold chain, and ends up by being 'everie way shut out' by both of them. Act V sees the confusion ever more deeply confounded, until pretty well everybody thinks that everybody else is 'starke mad'—and then the twin brothers appear on stage together for the first time, and the source of all the errors is revealed—'I never saw one man so like an other; water to water, nor milke to milke, is not liker then he is to you' (bear in mind this 'watery' image of similitude). So then follow joyful reunions and happy endings, with the resident Menechmus concluding the play by saying that he would willingly sell his shrewish wife 'but I thinke no bodie will bid money for her'.

The Plautus play is basically a farce, with hilarious misunderstandings proliferating from one root cause—mistaken identity. Now, it is true that the phenomenon of twins or identical siblings (or rather, *almost* identical siblings—it is important that nature does not produce *exactly* interchangeable replicas) touches a deep human nerve. For some reason—think about it—the phenomenon is funny. Pascal noted that 'Two faces that are alike, though neither of them excites laughter in itself, make me laugh when together on account of the likeness.' It must have something to do with the spectacle of *difference*—which makes me *me*—almost disappearing into *sameness*—which would make me indistinguishable from everybody else. But identical twins are not only funny; they are, as folk-tales bear out, slightly uncanny—'with all the divisible indivisibility that traditionally mysterious relationship implies' (Leah Scragg). Clearly, the phenomenon can raise questions about the nature and stability of identity, and it certainly fascinated Shakespeare. But Plautus really does nothing with it—apart from exploiting its obvious potential for identities mistook. His characters are more like ciphers or types—irascible merchant, bemused stranger, nagging wife, amiable whore, parasitical parasite, and so on. They have no significant inner experience; they do not learn; they do not change. Indeed, nothing really changes: matters get tangled up—then, with sudden facility, straightened out. The mercantile life of the city of Epidamnum goes on as before after barely a ripple.

Shakespeare takes exactly the same root situation, including many of the incidents and details—such as the courtesan and the gold chain; but, with his changes and amplifications, he produces an infinitely richer play. All his changes are, in different ways, significant. He does away with the Parasite —parasitism and self-interested greed is not, here, part of his interest. He reduces the role of the courtesan (there is no comedy in casual adultery for Shakespeare); and, more importantly, greatly enlarges the role of the wife, who, while still shrewish, is also complex, articulate, and sympathetic. (He also gives the wife a sister which, in the event, makes possible the expression of a kind of romantic love completely absent in Plautus.) Indeed, it may be said that, in general, the main characters have an emotional and even moral dimension, an inner life, which is entirely foreign to Plautus' mercenary knock-abouts. An apparently slight structural shift is, perhaps, even more interesting. Plautus starts his play with an emphasis on the resident brother, who has the larger part in the play—the, as it were, foreign brother only arrives in town after the local domestic scene has been set. Shakespeare reverses this. We see the newly arrived, traveller brother first, trying to make sense of a new and strange town; so that, as Harry Levin put it, 'we experience what goes on from the alien's point of view'. Concomitantly, of the two brothers, *he* now has (much) the larger part. And *we* have much more 'strangeness'.

Shakespeare raises the stakes—and multiplies the possibilities for comic confusion—by doubling-up on identical twins, adding the two Dromios as servants of the brothers Antipholus. Whatever else, this gave him a longer play; for, while at 1777 lines it is his shortest, it is in every way larger than the *Menaechmi*. But the more significant amplification is the addition of the framing romance narrative concerning the sad, sentenced Egeon; his lost and sundered family; and its final rediscovery and reunion. There is no trace of this in Plautus, whose play shows no interest at all in the *family* as such. For Shakespeare, it is to be a central concern. One more change—and this perhaps the most interesting of all. Shakespeare changed the city in which the action is set from Epidamnum to Ephesus. Why?

Not surprisingly, it was Geoffrey Bullough (in his *Sources*) who first suggested a cogent reason for the move. The name Epidamnum suggested bad

luck to the Romans, and thus perhaps suitable enough for a place where everything seems to go wrong. Ephesus was better known to the Elizabethans, as a great port and the capital of Roman Asia; and—more to the
point—'renowned for its Temple of Diana and as the place where St Paul
stayed two years (Acts 19)' (Bullough). Acts 19 refers to the 'curious arts'
(sorcery, exorcism and so on) which Paul found were practised in the city
when he arrived. Shakespeare develops the hint. Whereas in the Plautus
play, Messinio warns his master that Epidamnum is 'full of Ribaulds, Parasites, Drunkard Catchpoles, Cony-Catchers and Sycophants . . . Curtizans',
in Shakespeare's play Antipholus of Syracuse says apprehensively:

> They say this town is full of cozenage:
> As nimble jugglers that deceive the eye,
> Dark-working sorcerers that change the mind,
> Soul-killing witches that deform the body
>   (I, ii, 97–100)

There are no *actual* witches and sorcerers in this Ephesus; it is still very
much a merchants' (and, from what we see, honest merchants') town. But
as the characters grope their way further and further into the fog of misap-
prehension, Shakespeare wants them to *feel* that there must be some sorcery
and witchcraft—a kind of weird magic—in the air, as they believe themselves either being driven, or simply going, mad. They experience a far
deeper sort of mental estrangement and disorientation than in Plautus,
where people simply believe that other people seem to have gone a bit
dotty.

   Bullough suggests, convincingly, the relevance of another Pauline reference. In his Epistle to the Ephesians, Paul writes: 'Wives, submit yourselves
unto your own husbands, as unto the Lord. For the husband is the head of
the wife, even as Christ is the head of the Church . . . Husbands, love your
wives . . . let every one of you in particular so love his wife even as himself;
and the wife see that she reverence her husband' (5: 22, 25, 33). Paul was
concerned about domestic harmony and unity. In his play, Shakespeare inaugurates what will be a continuing, vital debate about 'marriage', and the
most appropriate relationship between man and wife, throughout his work.
Indeed, in no play is it more seriously examined than in *The Comedy of Errors*. And Ephesus was also the place of the great Temple of Diana. Here

again, Shakespeare makes a crucial change. Instead of a temple and Diana, we have a priory and an Abbess. That this Abbess turns out to be the long-lost wife of Egeon and the mother of the Antipholus brothers serves to contribute decisively to that atmosphere of wonder, strangeness, and possible improbability with which Shakespeare chooses to end his play, as the far-flung family is, seemingly miraculously, reunited. It is a far cry from the rueful joke about his unsellable wife with which Menechmus concludes the Plautus romp.

The priory and the Abbess do not mean that Shakespeare has simply Christianized the Roman world of Plautus—though it is as important for his comedies as it is for his tragedies that Christianity supervened between the ancient classical models and his own practice. Antipholus of Syracuse refers to himself as a Christian, but he comes to Ephesus where the paganism of the antique Mediterranean world seems to cohabit with the religion brought there by St Paul. This enables Shakespeare to draw on, and combine, both pagan and Christian language to create a far more complex feeling than would be generated by an orthodox rehearsal and deployment of the one discourse or the other. Although, as Gunnar Sorelius has demonstrated, 'Shakespeare uses biblical language more strikingly in this his most classical comedy than anywhere else', the pagan world is still vibrantly, resonantly there. It is a case of simultaneity and fusion rather than any supplanting conversion—a pagan-Christian perspective offers much greater depth than either would separately afford. From the start, Shakespeare is a great includer and amalgamator, a capacious gatherer-in. (Thus here, he *adds* romance to comedy; just as he will soon add comedy to history.) An unprecedented richness ensues.

The comic part starts with Antipholus of Syracuse, just arrived in Ephesus, handing over his money (a thousand marks—ironically, exactly the sum which would ransom his father, of whose presence in the city Antipholus has, of course, not the slightest idea) to his servant Dromio for safe-keeping. 'Go bear it to the Centaur, where we host' (I, ii, 9) are his first words; and even here there is an anticipatory sign if we care to read it. The centaur was, of course, half man and half horse, posing, among other things, questions about the boundary between the human and the animal—questions which will be raised, in other forms, throughout; for this is, in part, an Ovidian play, with possibilities of metamorphosis very much in the air.

(We soon learn that the other Antipholus, of Ephesus, lives at a house called 'the Phoenix', I, ii, 75—a self-transcending bird, pointing to higher forms; while, when later a group heads off for a good dinner in town, they repair to 'the Tiger' inn—unmistakably all animal. The courtesan, incidentally, lives in a house called 'the Porpentine'—i.e. porcupine—an animal known for its prickles; which is perhaps all that need be said about that bit of no-menclature. Shakespeare is having his fun, but even with these house and inn signs, he is glancing at one of his most serious themes: how far from, near to, the beasts are these people—are *we*?) Dismissing his servant, Dro-mio, Antipholus S. (for convenience) indicates his immediate intentions: 'I will go lose myself, / And wander up and down to view the city' (I, ii, 31–2). Put like that, it sounds like a simple resolve to go for a random meander in the strange port. But the opening phrase returns with renewed force in his next speech, a short soliloquy which effectively adumbrates the central is-sues of the play. A departing merchant politely says: 'I commend you to your own content'; and Antipholus:

> He that commends me to mine own content
> Commends me to the thing I cannot get.
> I to the world am like a drop of water
> That in the ocean seeks another drop,
> Who, falling there to find his fellow forth,
> Unseen, inquisitive, confounds himself.
> So I, to find a mother and a brother,
> In quest of them, unhappy, lose myself.
>
> (I, ii, 33–40)

'Con*tent*'—in his separated, isolated state, he cannot be happy: '*con*tent'—he doesn't yet know what is in him, what he contains. It is what, crucially, he has to find out; what the action of the play will reveal to him. Then he likens himself to 'a drop of water'. A drop of water does not, I suppose, have much 'content' (either way), and certainly suggests degree zero iden-tity; but this water drop proves to be the master image of the play. In Plau-tus, the image also occurs—but simply to stress similitude, apparent indis-tinguishability. When the two twins are finally on stage together, a witness comments: 'I never saw one man so like an other; water to water, nor milke to milke, is not liker than he is to you'. Shakespeare is doing more. Dissolving, melting, various forms of liquefaction—such processes are often invoked by Shakespearian characters to articulate a felt, or feared, loss or blurring of identity; a weakening sense of the separate, independent self. As when Antony confronts his own impending erasure, and compares himself, implicitly, with a cloud which rapidly loses its shape and form and becomes 'indistinct / As water is in water' (*Antony and Cleopatra,* IV, xiv, 9–11). (Ovid is full of figures, admittedly invariably women—Cyane, Byblis, Egeria, who dissolve into rivers, fountains, waters and so on; as Sorelius puts it—'diminution by dissolution is one of the persistent events in the *Metamorphoses*'.) But Antipholus is also using the metaphor in a positive sense; he has become like a drop in the ocean, *but* in an attempt to 'find his fellow forth'—this is accepting the risks of dissolution in the interests of relationship. The bravery of the drop of water daring the engulfing ocean. It is, exactly, losing to find—and what is to be lost is no less than the self. Now, of course, one of the most famous of Christ's exhortations is: 'For whosoever will save his life shall lose it: and whosoever will lose his life for my sake shall find it' (Matthew 16:25; repeated in slightly different forms in Mark 8:35, and Luke 9:24). It is the basic Christian promise, and produces an ethics which extends from the small self-sacrifices of unselfishness to literal martyrdom. This play is emphatically not a Christian allegory, but that central Christian idea is refracted and diffused throughout. So that when Antipholus says again—'I [will] lose myself', the repetition has much greater resonance and potential implication than his first use of the word, which merely suggests not knowing one street from another. Both the Antipholus brothers (and the Dromios), like the father and mother before them, will have to lose their selves—experience a loss of identity—in order to find themselves, *and* their necessary, complementing and completing others. And, thereby, a healed and better life. After this soliloquy, the Ephesian Dromio enters to summon Antipholus, incomprehensibly, home to dinner. More worryingly, he denies knowledge of the money which Antipholus is sure he just recently gave him to look after. He is beaten for his pains, and a puzzled Antipholus is left in the beginning of his amazement. The comedy of errors is under way.

However, the next Act shows us Adriana, the wife of Antipholus of Ephesus (E. for convenience), in confidential conversation with her sister, Luciana. Luciana and the conversation itself are very much Shakespeare's addition to Plautus, and the whole scene serves to initiate that prolonged debate about the nature of marriage—the correct behaviour of husbands and wives—which is a serious concern of the play. Adriana is fretful and angry at her husband's unexplained absence, and spiritedly complains that husbands have more 'liberty' than wives. Luciana, unmarried, more demurely and conventionally counsels patience, accepting male superiority, and boundedness and boundaries in general:

> Why, headstrong liberty is lashed with woe.
> There's nothing situate under heaven's eye
> But hath his bound, in earth, in sea, in sky.
> The beasts, the fishes, and the winged fowls
> Are their males' subjects, and at their controls . . .
> [Men] Of more preeminence than fish and fowls,
> Are masters to their females, and their lords;
> Then let your will attend on their accords.
>
> (II, i, 15–25)

Adriana is scornful of this orthodox compliance and 'fool-begged patience', on the reasonable grounds that it is easy for a woman to be meek if she doesn't have a grievance, or, come to that, a husband. Luciana's views are, in part, validated by the play; and for all we know, they might have been, in part, Shakespeare's own. But only in part. For while Shakespeare undoubtedly honours and reveres his Cordelias and Desdemonas, he has a good deal of sympathy with Adriana's 'headlong liberty' even though, or perhaps just because, it all too often procures its own lashing 'woe'. A woe we soon witness, as Adriana succumbs to a fit of anguished melancholy, prompted by feelings of resentment and neglect:

> His company must do his minions grace,
> Whilst I at home starve for a merry look:
> Hath homely age th' alluring beauty took
> From my poor cheek? Then he hath wasted it.
> Are my discourses dull? Barren my wit?
> If voluble and sharp discourse be marred,
> Unkindness blunts it more than marble hard.
> Do their gay vestments his affections bait?
> That's not my fault; he's master of my state.
> What ruins are in me that can be found,

By him not ruined? Then is he the ground
Of my defeatures. My decayed fair
A sunny look of his would soon repair.
But, too unruly deer, he breaks the pale,
And feeds from home; poor I am but his stale.
                              (II, i, 87–101)

There is perhaps a touch of plangent self-pity there, but Luciana's dismissive, summary criticism—'Self-harming jealousy!'—is entirely inadequate. The lines are heartfelt, at times even moving, and bespeak a serious conception, based on experience, of the kind of vital symbiotic relationship a marriage can be. Adriana certainly has a case to make.

The seriousness continues when, accompanied by her sister, Adriana goes out into the town looking for her husband. She runs into Antipholus S. whom, of course, she takes to be her own Antipholus E. The man, understandably enough, shows no signs of knowing her. And this occasions a very articulate, and important, lament:

How comes it now, my husband, O how comes it,
That thou art then estranged from thyself?
That, undividable, incorporate,
Am better than thy dear self's better part.
Ah, do not tear away thyself from me;
For know, my love, as easy mayst thou fall
A drop of water in the breaking gulf,
And take unmingled thence that drop again
Without addition or diminishing
As take from me thyself, and not me too.
How dearly would it touch thee to the quick,
Shouldst thou but hear I were licentious,
And that this body, consecrate to thee,
By ruffian lust should be contaminate!
Wouldst thou not spit at me, and spurn at me,
And hurl the name of husband in my face,
And tear the stained skin off my harlot brow,
And from my false hand cut the wedding ring,
And break it with a deep-divorcing vow?
I know thou canst, and therefore see thou do it.

> I am possessed with an adulterate blot.
> My blood is mingled with the crime of lust;
> For, if we two be one, and thou play false,
> I do digest the poison of thy flesh,
> Being strumpeted by thy contagion.
> Keep then fair league and truce with thy true bed,
> I live distained, thou undishonorèd.
>
> (II, ii, 120–47)

Now, there is something comic in the *situation*—a wife addressing a torrent of reproach to a bewildered man who doesn't, as it were, know her from Eve. But the sentiments expressed are of the utmost seriousness (and the verse has a corresponding passionate energy and kinaesthetic power which would not be out of place, I venture to say, in many of Shakespeare's later, greater plays—particularly those which touch on sexual infidelity. This is true of quite a lot of the poetry given to Adriana; as, for example, when, referring to her husband, she asks her sister what she has observed of 'his heart's meteors tilting in his face', IV, ii, 6—one of those astonishing Shakespeare images which, I find, leave one both speechless and haunted). The drop of water image is there again, you will notice, though with another turn. Once you've let fall a drop of water into the sea, you can't get it out again, at least, not as it was. The theme is the indissolubility of the marriage bond, and one of the texts behind it, again, is Paul's Epistle to the Ephesians: '. . . a man shall leave his father and mother, and shall be joined unto his wife, *and the two shall be one flesh*' (5:31—my italics). The two-in-oneness achieved, or achievable, in the marriage tie, was a crucial notion for Shakespeare. He writes in 'The Phoenix and the Turtle', at around this time:

> So they loved, as love in twain
> Had the essence but in one;
> Two distincts, division none:
> Number there in love was slain.
> . . .
> Property was thus appalled,
> That the self was not the same;
> Single nature's double name
> Neither two nor one was called.

I will just say here that the two-in-one-ness of marriage, which somehow preserves difference in unity (which is how number is 'slain'), is, for Shakespeare, the ideal of a true relationship; while the two-in-one-ness suggested by identical twins (it points to a narcissistic effacement of difference—just glanced at in the final scene: 'Methinks you are my glass and not my brother') is very much the wrong model for relating. And the experience that 'the self was not the same' is undergone, has to be undergone, by those figures in Shakespearian comedy who variously emerge from the self to achieve, or rediscover, a true relationship. When Adriana asks Antipholus S. 'how comes it,/That thou art then estranged from thyself?' she is being much more pertinent, and prescient, than she can possibly know. For that is just what is about to happen to him. *And,* in a different way, to her errant husband as well.

The feeling of self-estrangement, and possible transformation, immediately takes hold of this Antipholus and Dromio:

> *D.S.* I am transformèd, master, am not I?
> *A.S.* I think thou art in mind, and so am I.
> *D.S.* Nay, master, both in mind and in my shape.
> *A.S.* Thou hast thine own form.
> *D.S.* No, I am an ape.
> *A.S.* If thou art changed to aught, 'tis to an ass.
> (II, ii, 196–200)

The Ovidian moment, with the Shakespearian difference. They do *not* experience a change in shape and form, but something is happening in their minds. Dromio, as perhaps befits a servant, has a traditional (English) rustic-superstitious explanation for what is happening:

> This is the fairy land. O spite of spites!
> We talk with goblins, owls, and sprites;
> If we obey them not, this will ensue:
> They'll suck our breath, or pinch us black and blue.
> (II, ii, 190–93)

We will encounter fairy land, and a man transformed to an ass, in a later Shakespeare comedy. Here, Antipholus has the more relevant response

to this seeming strangeness of being known to women (because of their
names) whom they have never seen.

> What, was I married to her in my dream?
> Or sleep I now, and think I hear all this?
> What error drives our eyes and ears amiss?
> Until I know this sure uncertainty,
> I'll entertain the offered fallacy.
>   (II, ii, 183–7)

Awake, asleep; sane, mad; right, wrong?—the important point is that,
whatever is the case, he is both willing and determined to 'entertain the offered fallacy'. He thus shows himself to be a good candidate for positive
metamorphosis. He repeats this resolve when Adriana insists that he comes
back to dinner with herself and Luciana:

> Am I in earth, in heaven, or in hell?
> Sleeping or waking, mad or well-advised?
> Known unto these, and to myself disguised?
> I'll say as they say, and persever so,
> And in this mist at all adventures go.
>   (II, ii, 213–17)

It is this resolve to plunge into the 'mist' which is the saving, or rather the
making, of this Antipholus. Mist, like water, like dream, is an area in which
boundaries blur and identities dissolve—as William Carroll puts it: 'metamorphosis thrives in unstable regions, and it takes some courage to step into
"this mist"'. He will gain his reward.

   Once Adriana has her 'husband', as she thinks, securely back within the
house, she orders the doors to be locked and no one allowed entrance. This
leads to one of the central scenes of inversion, or subversion, of the play.
The local Antipholus, of E., at last puts in an appearance for the first time
(Act III), and finds that he is barred from his own house, denied access to
his own wife. This is a visible image of the sort of topsy-turvydom which is
beginning to spread outwards from the initial mistakes of identity—the
stranger is within, the familiar is without; the outsider is inside, the insider
outside. Antipholus E. is, understandably, both angry and bemused. He is

starting *his* experience of self-estrangement, displacement and dislocation, which will take him, as it will his brother, to the edge of a kind of madness or mania—from which he too will emerge a new, or renewed, man. (For Antipholus S. the experience mainly concerns spiritual or mental strangenesses; for his brother, it is more a matter of a series of domestic and social goings-wrong.) The comic errors begin to multiply.

Inside the house, Antipholus S. is suddenly and powerfully smitten by the sister, Luciana, and thus he addresses her:

> Less in your knowledge and your grace you show not
> Than our earth's wonder, more than earth divine.
> Teach me, dear creature, how to think and speak:
> Lay open to my earthly-gross conceit,
> Smoth'red in errors, feeble, shallow, weak,
> The folded meaning of your words' deceit.
> Against my soul's pure truth why labor you
> To make it wander in an unknown field?
> Are you a god, would you create me new?
> Transform me, then, and to your pow'r I'll yield.
>
> (III, ii, 32–40)

This is Ovidianism refracted through Revelation ('And he that sat upon the throne said, Behold, I make all things new', 21:5). The vocabulary is laced with Christian terms—grace, soul—and projects the idea of being purified of the error-prone grossness of man's earthly condition. Just as he calls her 'my sole earth's heaven, and my heaven's claim'. (Note, incidentally, Shakespeare's first use of the word 'folded'—concealed, hidden; it was to become a crucial word for him.) But he also shifts into a pagan key which, perhaps unconsciously, reveals more wariness or ambivalence about Luciana's female attractions.

> O train me not, sweet mermaid, with thy note,
> To drown me in thy sister's flood of tears.
> Sing, siren, for thyself, and I will dote;
> Spread o'er the silver waves thy golden hairs;
> And, as a bed I'll take them, and there lie,
> And, in that glorious supposition, think

> He gains by death that hath such means to die.
> Let Love, being light, be drownèd if she sink!
>   (III, ii, 45–52)

Perhaps she promises, not redemption but (admittedly delicious) drown-ing—not a saviour but a siren. (It offers yet another extension of the mo-tif of entering water—to find, or to lose.) By the end of the scene, he has decided to 'trudge, pack, and begone'—flee the possible danger. Luciana (who, of course, thinks he is her brother-in-law and has given him no en-couragement) is, he says:

> Possessed with such a gentle sovereign grace,
> Of such enchanting presence and discourse,
> Hath almost made me traitor to myself.
> But, lest myself be guilty to self-wrong,
> I'll stop mine ears against the mermaid's song.
>   (III, ii, 165–9)

It is, of course, the time-honoured Ulysses strategy, and for Antipholus, it represents a defensive, self-retractive instinct coming into play. Deciding that 'There's none but witches do inhabit here' (III, ii, 161), he wants to leave Ephesus—get out of the 'mist' as it were. But that will not prove so easy.

In the same scene, Dromio reveals that he, too, has had a disturbing en-counter with a strange woman—the 'kitchen wench', called Luce rather than Luciana, and (on account of her kitchen work) 'all grease', not 'grace'. Dromio's account of this encounter offers an amusing parody of the Pe-trarchan, etherialized discourse of love which we have just heard from his master. Famously, with earthy humour, he describes her very large body in terms of contemporary geography—'I could find out countries in her'—thus Ireland is 'in her buttocks' and so on. (Curiously, this topographical tour of the female body provides the only occasion, in all his plays, on which Shakespeare refers to 'America'.) It all points to the extremely physical and corporeal element in the relationship between the sexes. Dromio, too, is be-ginning to feel that sense of self-estrangement which seems to be spreading. 'Do you know me, sir? Am I Dromio? Am I your man? Am I myself?' The important point about his encounter—apart from its amusingness—is that

it threatens a *downward* transformation: 'she would have me as a beast—
not that, I being a beast, she would have me, but that she, being a very
beastly creature, lays claim to me . . . She had transformed me to a curtal
dog, and made me turn i' th' wheel.' (III, ii, 86–9, 151). Grease, not grace.
Metamorphosis can go either way. Revelation *and* Ovid. Remember that
the whole play takes place under the signs, as it were, of 'the Centaur'
and 'the Phoenix' and 'the Tiger'. Are these people going up—or down?
Experiencing a change in the self can be an unnerving—and risky—business.

From here on, the confusion becomes worse confounded—or better, from
the point of view of comedy. It is comic, as the errors and perplexedness of
other people can be (in this play, almost uniquely, the division between
complete knowledge for the audience, and total ignorance and oblivious-
ness for the participants, is maintained until about a hundred lines from the
end. There is here no plotter or 'practicer' on stage—no Richard III, Don
John, Iago, Iachimo; no Rosalind, Portia, Viola, Helena, Hamlet, Oberon,
Prospero—mediating between us and the characters). But there are potentially serious results as well. Relationships are threatened, and the sense of
individual isolation increased, as assumptions cease to be shareable, and
mutuality fades and fails. The trust on which the commerce of the city depends is threatened, as promises are seemingly broken, words not kept,
contracts not honoured, goods not delivered, debts not paid. *Apparently,*
that is. For this is a world in which appearances become increasingly unreliable. There is the sense of a small community moving towards chaos—
and a corresponding increase in the explosions of rage and violence (more
of the tiger than the phoenix for a while). The Antipholus brothers move
towards a condition of complete paranoia—Antipholus S. becomes convinced that he is in a town of 'fiends' and 'witches'; and Antipholus E. is
bundled away and locked up as, as it were, certifiably insane (premonitory
shades of the treatment of Malvolio). By the time he has broken free, and
the other Antipholus taken refuge in the priory, the turmoil is total. Well
might the Duke say—'I think you all have drunk of Circe's cup' (V, i, 271);
and well may Adriana cry out—'I long to know the truth hereof at large'
(IV, iv, 144).
    At this point, the 'unfolding' begins; for once the twins are seen *together,*
errors are explained, and clarification spreads rapidly. It is a dazzled mo-

ment for the onlookers, who seem to be seeing double and begin to wonder which is which, and who is who, and, indeed, what is what? Individual identity itself seems to shimmer unsteadily. Ontology wobbles. The Duke reasons:

> One of these men is genius to the other;
> And so of these, which is the natural man,
> And which the spirit? Who deciphers them?
>   (V, i, 333–5)

This is, perhaps, the main question of the play; a question which, in one 'deciphering' way and another, Shakespeare never stopped asking—which, what, finally *is* the 'natural' man; which and what the 'spirit'?

But before all that happens, Shakespeare has reintroduced the romance element, or the frame narrative, and this deserves some comment. There has been, throughout the day of the play, a constant awareness of time (and much bantering about it), as we move inexorably towards five o'clock, the appointed hour for the execution of Egeon. Everything and everyone converges on this place and this time, which occasions the first 'recognition' as Egeon sees what he takes to be his lost son, Antipholus E. But it is the wrong Antipholus who, understandably, does not recognize his father. This provokes a lament of true pathos from the father:

> O, grief hath changed me since you saw me last,
> And careful hours with time's deformèd hand,
> Have written strange defeatures in my face.
> . . .
> Now know my voice! O, time's extremity,
> Hast thou so cracked and splitted my poor tongue
> In seven short years, that here my only son
> Knows not my feeble key of untuned cares?
> Though now this grainèd face of mine be hid
> In sap-consuming winter's drizzled snow,
> And all the conduits of my blood froze up,
> Yet hath my night of life some memory;
> My wasting lamps some fading glimmer left
>   (V, i, 298–301, 308–16)

Time's deforming and 'defeaturing' hand works more slowly than the 'magic' or 'miracle' of metamorphosis. But 'time's extremity' is as powerful a force as there is in Shakespeare's world, and it is a crucial point, both here and in all that is to come, that time can prove to have a *re*forming, a *re*featuring hand, as well. As Egeon soon discovers when the Abbess appears.

The Abbess, just prior to her final appearance, has taken the chance to trick Adriana into confessing her own shrewishness, for which the Abbess blames the 'madness' of Adriana's husband:

> And thereof came it that the man was mad.
> The venom clamors of a jealous woman
> Poisons more deadly than a mad dog's tooth.
>   (V, i, 68–70)

Adriana accepts the way she has been manoeuvred into self-accusation—quite meekly: 'She did betray me to my own reproof' (V, i, 90). But it is an important last touch—bearing in mind Shakespeare and 'shrews'—that her erstwhile critical sister now speaks up in her defence. Thus Luciana:

> She never reprehended him but mildly,
> When he demeaned himself rough, rude, and wildly.
> Why bear you these rebukes and answer not?
>   (V, i, 87–9)

Adriana may have to curb her tongue a little; but rough, rude Antipholus will have to mend his ways—reform, indeed—to become a proper husband.

And now the Abbess can reclaim *her* husband—old Egeon—along with their two lost sons, who now stand before them. The family is thus magically, 'miraculously' reunited; and what better site for such a wonder than the precincts of the priory or abbey (Temple). (It is interesting that when Antipholus E. now offers to pay the ransom for his father's life, the Duke answers: 'It shall not need; thy father hath his life' (V, i, 391). Such effortless remission was not possible at the start; but in the new atmosphere of mercy and reconciliation, inflexible sentences can melt away—the comedy has finally worked to 'disannul' the law.) The Abbess, Emilia as wife and

mother, invites all into the abbey—nobody locked out this time, everybody
included in:

> And all that are assembled in this place,
> That by this sympathizèd one day's error
> Have suffered wrong, go, keep us company,
> And we shall make full satisfaction.
> Thirty-three years have I but gone in travail
> Of you, my sons, and till this present hour
> My heavy burden ne'er delivered.
> The Duke, my husband, and my children both,
> And you the calendars of their nativity,
> Go to a gossips' feast, and joy with me
> After so long grief such nativity.
>
> (V, i, 397–407)

By now, the Antipholuses and the Dromios have sorted themselves out,
identities have been re-secured, names are properly affixed, people are seeing straight again, and on all sides, relationships are being established, re-
affirmed, and rediscovered—'traffic', in every sense, is beginning to flow
again between Syracuse and Ephesus. The Abbess summons them all to a
new christening, or 'gossips' feast' (gossip, from 'godsibb'—godparent or
sponsor at a baptism), to celebrate 'such nativity'. This is not birth, but *re-*
birth—she says she has been 'in travail' for thirty-three years for this second
delivery of her children (the insistence by Antipholus S. at the beginning
that 'In Ephesus I am but two hours old', II, ii, 149, unknowingly suggests
that this is a place where he might be 'born again'). This is, then, effectively
the rebirth and renewal of the whole community. There is nothing of all
this in Plautus, and if this is indeed Shakespeare's first comedy, it is truly
remarkable how many of the themes and preoccupations of his later work
he here, thus early, broached—how promptly, as it were, he staked out his
dramatic territory.

✳ THE TAMING OF THE SHREW (1590–3)

> For she is changed as she had never been.
>
> (V, ii, 115)

Adriana could be 'shrewish', though not without provocation—'My wife is shrewish *when I keep not hours*' admits Antipholus (my italics). But she is shown to be, throughout, a serious and devoted wife, if prone to possessive jealousy. In *The Taming of the Shrew,* Shakespeare gives us a woman who appears to be a total shrew—shrewish all the way down, as they say; seemingly, the most unprepared and unsuitable candidate for marriage and wifely responsibilities (and feelings) that could be imagined. (I might say here that Brian Morris, in his excellent Arden edition, argues that *Shrew* is the earlier play—indeed, perhaps Shakespeare's *first* play. His arguments are quite persuasive, and one thing is undeniable. Adriana is a much more complex, more intellectually and emotionally advanced character than the relatively primitive Kate, who is, it has to be said, not very intelligent; though, importantly, shown to be more 'educable' than her sister.)

'Shrew', as a word, has an interesting history. The word for a mouse-like animal, wrongly thought to be venomous, it was applied to the devil up to the fourteenth century (and is indeed related to an old German word which meant 'devil'—*schrawaz*). It was also used to refer to a malignant person of either sex. By the sixteenth century it was reserved for women (Morris finds the first use in this sense in Chaucer), by which time it meant pretty much what we mean by it today, though it still carried suggestions of something evil and malevolent, if not diabolic. Shrews are, apparently, very aggressive, and go in for 'squeaking matches'; they have a reputation for irascibility and noise—'a particularly scolding and complaining note' in the words of an expert on shrews, quoted by Morris (for the Romans, it was a 'noise of ill-omen'). Why something as small as the shrew should be used to figure something as, presumably, large as the Devil, one can only speculate. Women, notoriously, have a dread of mice and mice-like creatures, though whether that horror was shared by the dames of sixteenth-century rural Warwickshire, I have no idea. It probably has to do with fast little scurrying, squeaking, things which can get anywhere, and with the combination of smallness and aggression (not unfamiliar from the human realm) with what can apparently be unbearable *noise*. We perhaps need a rural account.

Writing in 1607, the Rev. Edward Topsell said of the shrew: 'It is a ravening beast, feigning itself gentle and tame, but, being touched, it biteth deep and poysoneth deadly. It beareth a cruel minde, desiring to hurt anything, neither is there any creature that it loveth, or it loveth him, because it is feared of all'. And Gilbert White, in his matchless *Natural History of Selborne,* writes: 'It is supposed that a shrew mouse is of so baneful and deleterious a nature that, wherever it creeps over a beast, be it horse, cow, or sheep, the suffering animal is afflicted with cruel anguish, and threatened with the loss of the use of the limb'. Shakespeare must have known this country lore. Be that as it may, Kate is called a 'shrew' at least ten times, and 'devil' nearer fifteen, while her noisiness and aggression are constantly remarked and displayed; so there can be little doubt about what type of woman she is meant to be—at least in the eyes of everyone around her. Which might not be the fairest—and certainly not the final—verdict.

There are, effectively, three different worlds represented in the play—all, of course, occupying the same stage space. Here again, from (what might be) the very beginning, we can see Shakespeare pursuing mutually enriching, mutually ironizing, genres and modes. The Induction (a device he never used again) is set, undoubtedly, in his own rural Warwickshire. The main story is rooted in familiar folk-tales and fabliaux concerning the subjugation or taming of an overbearing shrewish wife. (Leah Scragg records that there are over four hundred versions still extant, and she gives as a typical example *A Merry Fest of a Shrewde and Curste Wife, Lapped in Morrelles Skin, for Her Good Behavyour* (c. 1550). Morrell is a horse, and his owner kills and flays him so that he can enclose his shrewish wife in the skin, after he has beaten her unconscious. This way, she quickly learns deference and obedience, as who wouldn't. Petruchio employs, on the whole, less violent and subtle methods, and it could be said that his efforts are aimed at releasing Kate from a 'beastly' condition, not returning her to one.) The sub-plot, wonderfully interwoven with the main story, takes us into the sophisticated, complex world of Italian comedy. The specific source was Gascoigne's *Supposes* (1566), which was a version of Ariosto's *I Suppositi* (1509)—a source Shakespeare specifically refers to in his play, a self-conscious acknowledgment of theatrical precedent. Gascoigne explained the title: 'But understand, this our Suppose is nothing else but a mistaking or imagination of one thing for an other. For you shall see the master supposed for a servant, the servant for the master: the freeman for a slave, and the bondslave for a freeman: the stranger for a well known friend, and the familiar for a stranger'. This is the world of Roman New Comedy; a world of misunderstanding—errors—disguise, deception, subterfuge, and intrigue. Just so, Shakespeare's sub-plot is a world of 'counterfeit supposes' (V, i, 115), in which one character, multiplying manufactured identities for plotting purposes says:

> I see no reason but supposed Lucentio
> Must get a father, called 'supposed Vincentio'
> (II, i, 400–401)

All this plotting is occasioned by the contest between a number of suitors for the hand of Bianca, Kate's apparently mild and angelic sister. Both plots are about wooing and courtship: but, while Petruchio has recourse to his own kind of 'counterfeiting', his 'blunt' and 'peremptory' approach is in marked contrast to the Italianate intriguing practised by the others. It is also, in part, the contrast between conventions of realism and romance, which runs through the play. Brian Morris comments: 'Contrasts of social and dramatic convention of this kind are the staple of the play's development, and they comment ironically one on the other, refusing to allow any single attitude to love and marriage to go unchallenged.' Where Italian Classical comedy was contextualized by Romance in *The Comedy of Errors,* here it intermingles with folk-tale and rural tradition. Long before Ezra Pound's specific injunction, Shakespeare always 'made it new'.

The Induction is only 282 lines, yet it is one of the richest and most compacted pieces in Shakespeare's comedies. It seems to set up a 'frame' situation, so that we will have a play-within-the-play, but, somehow, somewhy, Shakespeare does not complete the frame. It centres on Sly, the tinker, and involves two scenes. First, a 'rural alehouse', where he gets drunk and falls asleep. A local Lord, returning from hunting 'with his train', decides to 'practice on this drunken man' (another 'practicer'—or director on stage), and arranges for Sly to be transported to his mansion where he will be made to believe, when he wakes up, that 'he is nothing but a mighty lord'. Itinerant actors or players arrive, and the Lord arranges that they shall perform a play, both for 'lord' Sly, and the Lord and his house (and, of course, us). Scene two is set in a bedroom in the Lord's house, where Sly wakes up and is convinced that he is, indeed, an amnesiac lord, and settles down to watch the 'pleasant comedy' which he is told has been arranged for him—on doctors' orders. This play turns out to be *The Taming of the Shrew.* The theme of the beggar transported into luxury can be found in the *Arabian Nights,* and the poor man who wakes up and thinks he is in heaven is another old folkloric subject. But, given this basic motif, it is amazing how many themes and issues Shakespeare touches on, or anticipates, in this relatively short Induction.

I should, perhaps, mention here the existence of a play, published anonymously in 1594, entitled *The Taming of a Shrew* (my underlining). Shakespeare's play only appeared in print in the Folio of 1623, and there have been ongoing arguments—which need not concern us—as to whether *A Shrew* was a 'first shot' by Shakespeare, or—more likely—some kind of inadequate reconstruction of Shakespeare's play by others. I don't think much should be made of the shift between definite and indefinite article (on the lines that Shakespeare was offering *The* definitive article): the plays are very similar in outline, theme, and scenic detail—though *A Shrew* is detectably the cruder play. The important difference concerns Sly, and the framing situation. In Shakespeare's play, Sly slides off into silence and, apart from a moment at the end of the first scene, when he nods off, and wishes it was all over, he is never heard from again. One *can* justify this, and say that, with the disappearance of Sly, the play-within-the-play becomes simply *the* play, scaffolding jettisoned; and we, as audience, are brought one step nearer to the depicted events. That is—rather than looking at X looking at Y (us looking at Sly looking at Kate), we watch Y (Kate) direct (the now irrelevant Sly forgotten). I can see this as a plausible case, and, personally, I am quite happy with the play as we have it. But in *A Shrew,* Sly interrupts the 'play' on four occasions, and, more importantly, the play ends back with him at the alehouse—frame completed. Distinguished editors, from Bullough to Morris, think that, for a variety of reasons, the text we have is defective, and that Shakespeare's play almost certainly included Sly's interruptions, and the completion of the frame back at the alehouse at the end. That ending is certainly potentially important, and I will return to it.

But now let us consider Shakespeare's Induction, just about twice as long as the one in *A Shrew*—and much more interesting. It opens with the Hostess of the alehouse—the shrew?—fiercely upbraiding the drunken Sly. A note of struggle and discord between the sexes is immediately struck. Then the Lord enters, accompanied by his retinue and dogs—affectionately named (Merriman, Clowder, Silver, Bellman, Echo—not yet time for Lear's Tray, Blanche and Sweetheart). This is very much rural England, and will make the shift to the bourgeois, merchant world of Padua in the 'play' all the more marked. Seeing Sly, drunkenly asleep, the Lord comments: 'O monstrous beast, how like a swine he lies.' He has undergone a downward transformation—humans into beasts (swine if Circe had anything to do with it): it is very much Ovid's world. The Lord decides to 'practice' on him, and simulate an upward transformation—like a magician, or a play-wright:

> What think you, if he were conveyed to bed,
> Wrapped in sweet clothes, rings put upon his fingers,
> A most delicious banquet by his bed,
> And brave attendants near him when he wakes—
> Would not the beggar then forget himself?
>   (37–41)

In the event, the beggar does, finally, *not* forget himself—which may be taken to indicate that some people are unapt for metamorphosis, or that there are limits to the metamorphosing art. This is the case with Sly: it won't be true of Kate. The Lord continues with making the arrangements to carry out his plan. He really *is* like a stage director, specifying the decor, supervising the props and trappings, and, in particular, giving very detailed instructions as to how people are to 'act'. His page, Bartholomew, is to have the crucial role of pretending to be 'lord' Sly's loving wife. This is how he is to do it:

> Tell him from me—as he will win my love—
> He bear himself with honorable action
> Such as he hath observed in noble ladies
> Unto their lords, by them accomplishèd.
> Such duty to the drunkard let him do
> With soft low tongue and lowly courtesy,
> And say, 'What is't your honor will command
> Wherein your lady and your humble wife
> May show her duty and make known her love?'
> And then, with kind embracements, tempting kisses,

And with declining head into his bosom,
Bid him shed tears, as being overjoyed
To see her noble lord restored to health
Who for this seven years hath esteemèd him
No better than a poor and loathsome beggar.
And if the boy have not a woman's gift
To rain a shower of commanded tears,
An onion will do well for such a shift,
Which in a napkin being close conveyed
Shall in despite enforce a watery eye.

(109–128)

Now, of course, this is exactly how a boy playing a part in an Elizabethan play (by Shakespeare, among others) would be prepared—dressed up as a woman, and then told how to simulate the emotional states of a mature woman (not easy, surely, for a young lad, who no doubt had recourse to the onion trick and other stratagems). So we may fairly say that here Shakespeare (a theatre professional, after all) is, effectively, showing himself at work. And a boy into a woman is a theatrical equivalent of tutoring and changing an unbearable shrew into just such an obedient, courteous, *quiet,* loving wife as young Bartholomew is ordered to impersonate. The whole process of the coming drama of transformation is here anticipated, to be this time, of course, managed by Shakespeare himself. And where the Lord fails—Sly remains the same old Sly—Shakespeare will succeed. Superior magic. Just watch me do it—the Induction seems to say.

When Sly wakes up in the Lord's bedroom, and the servants duly enact their allotted, pampering roles, he thinks they are mad (as Kate will think Petruchio is). 'What, would you make me mad? Am I not Christopher Sly . . . now by present profession a tinker? Ask Mariam Hacket, the fat ale-wife of Wincot.' Wincot was a village near Stratford, so we know that Shakespeare is, as it were, close to home. In addition to wine and delicacies, the servants offer him music (but, in time, lutes will be broken); hunting (Petruchio will take that over); and paintings:

Dost thou love pictures? We will fetch thee straight
Adonis painted by a running brook
And Cytherea all in sedges hid,

Which seem to move and wanton with her breath
Even as the waving sedges play with wind.
. . .
We'll show thee Io as she was a maid
And how she was beguilèd and suprised,
As lively painted as the deed was done.
. . .
Or Daphne roaming through a thorny wood,
Scratching her legs that one will swear she bleeds,
And at that sight shall sad Apollo weep,
So workmanly the blood and tears are drawn.

(49–60)

This is Ovid plain, or rather Ovid illustrated (it is a good example of *ek-phrasis*—a verbal description of a work of art). All the examples are from the *Metamorphoses,* and, indeed, Jonathan Bate is of the opinion that 'what is laid out here is almost a programme for Shakespeare's subsequent Ovidianism'. (This is continued in the play: Ovid is mentioned by name in the first scene, line 33—one of only four times in Shakespeare; and when Lucentio is smitten by Bianca he says:

O yes, I saw sweet beauty in her face,
Such as the daughter of Agenor had, [i.e. Europa]
That made great Jove to humble him to her hand
When with his knees he kissed the Cretan strond.

(I, i, 167–70)

In Ovid's account, Jove changed himself into a bull; Lucentio, with less scope, turns himself into a schoolmaster.) Here, there, and everywhere, metamorphosis of one kind or another (from change of clothes, roles, identities, to some deep inner change in the self) is in the air. It might be pointed out that the Ovidian illustrations do not offer particularly felicitous examples of the results of love—Adonis killed by a boar; Io changed to a heifer; and bleeding, crying Daphne turned into a laurel. Ovidian metamorphosis is, invariably, a brutal, and 'brutalizing', business; Shakespeare wants to find a better way. Sly, deciding to go along with the 'play' in which he finds himself, tells his 'wife' to undress and come to bed; he is, he makes clear—

'it stands so'—ready for it. Shakespeare, with his boy-girl figures (not to mention his boy-girl-boy characters), often delights in taking us to the very borders of so-called sexual normality, allowing us to feel the dangerous, exciting edge of imminent and proximate deviance. (Just in case we were feeling complacent and too much at ease in our sexual identities.) Bartholomew makes his excuses; not before, in one last anticipation of a Kate to come, s/he has vowed to Sly—'I am your wife in all obedience' (107). Then the players—the next lot of players—enter, and Sly and Bartholomew settle down to watch what is rather curiously promised as 'a kind of history' (141—never be too sure which genre you are in in a Shakespeare play). The alehouse yard becomes a bedroom, which in turn becomes a theatre—fairly seamlessly. The boundaries hardly seem fixed; nor, perhaps, determinable. Is what we are about to see just a continuation of Sly's dream (wherever that started or stopped)? Or is it as real as a row in an alehouse yard? Or stage-stuff to entertain a lord? It doesn't really matter. One way and another, implies Shakespeare, it is all pretty theatrical—like much of life.

So, from Wincot (thereabouts) to Padua, and we are soon among the would-be wooers of Baptista's two daughters. Most of them are bidding for the hand of the apparently perfect and demure, Bianca. I say 'bidding' advisedly; it cannot be missed to what extent courtship is involved with money (riches, property, dowries, contracts, etc.) in this play. Romance—no, *marriage*—is, it seems, if not indistinguishable, then inseparable from finance. We may check at this a little—Baptista very clearly auctioning off Bianca is not perhaps how we see a father's role. Perhaps this is Shakespeare's version of how merchants—or Italians!—view marriage; or perhaps it was for him the merest realism. Which is not to say that he put a cash value on true love: *that,* indeed, is priceless. Make sure you find it—if you can. But it arrives, or is come by, in strange ways; and, as it transpires, the infatuated Petrarchanism of Lucentio's wooing of Bianca is by no means a certain way of securing it. How about Petruchionism?

Where Lucentio appears to be a conventional lover ('I burn, I pine, I perish' and so on), Petruchio presents himself as an unashamedly mercenary fortune hunter:

> I come to wive it wealthily in Padua;
> If wealthily, then happily in Padua.
>
> (I, ii, 74–5)

as he makes quite explicit—'wealth is burthen of my wooing dance' (I, ii, 67). He is told about Katherine Minola, who as the elder daughter of Baptista will have a very large dowry (he wants her off his hands, anyway—she is very much 'for sale'); but he is also warned that she is 'intolerable curst/And shrewd and froward' and, adds Hortensio, 'I would not wed her for a mine of gold' (I, ii, 91). 'Thou know'st not gold's effect' is Petruchio's cool reply, and he announces his intention to marry her. The other suitors think that he will not be able to abide, and prevail over, her 'scolding tongue', but there are two hints which may alert us to his subsequent course of action. He dismisses the problem of her shrewish tongue:

> Think you a little din can daunt mine ears?
> Have I not in my time heard lions roar?
> Have I not heard the sea, puffed up with winds,
> Rage like an angry boar chafed with sweat?
> Have I not heard great ordnance in the field
> And heaven's artillery thunder in the skies?
> Have I not in a pitchèd battle heard
> Loud 'larums, neighing steeds, and trumpets' clang?
> And do you tell me of a woman's tongue . . .
>
> (I, ii, 199–207)

The discernible figure behind Petruchio here is Hercules—an identification made explicit a moment later when Gremio, referring to Katherine, says 'Yea, leave that labor to great Hercules' (I, ii, 256). Gunnar Sorelius is the only commentator I know who has pointed to the importance of recognizing Petruchio as a Hercules figure, but there can be doubt that it is central. Sorelius points out that in the speech just quoted you can catch glimpsing references to various of Hercules' labours—the Nemean lion, the Erimanthian boar, and perhaps his capture of Troy. And in his ninth labour, Hercules subjugated the Amazonian, Hippolyte. Hercules was, of course, *the* culture hero, the master of monsters, the controller of the barbaric; as such, he was regarded as a primary civilizing force. Petruchio's treatment of Kate must be seen at least partially in that light.

But there was another side to Hercules, best known to the Elizabethans through translations of Seneca's *Hercules Furens* (from the play by Euripides). This shows Hercules gone mad, and killing his wife Megara. This

should also be remembered when considering Petruchio's treatment of
Kate, who indeed, thinks he is 'mad' from the beginning. His violent and
disruptive behaviour at his own wedding, biffing the priest and throwing
wine over the sexton, indeed suggests a Petruchio *furens* ('Such a mad marriage never was before', III, ii, 182). Likewise, the bizarre, ragged, and desperately slovenly clothes he wears for the wedding, make him 'a very monster in apparel' as well as 'an eyesore to our solemn festival' (III, ii, 70, 101).
But, as the shrewd and perceptive Tranio observes: 'He hath some meaning
in his mad attire' (III, ii, 124). Or, more generally, there is, as we say, method
in his 'madness'. Hercules, the human hero raised to the level of a god, was
famous both for his immense powers of control (including self-control),
and for his *anger*. Not for nothing do we see Petruchio apparently controlling and commanding time ('It shall be what o'clock I say it is', IV, iii, 193);
the planets or heavenly bodies ('this gallant will command the sun', IV, ii,
194; 'It shall be sun or star or what I list', IV, v, 7); and even gender (making
Kate address Vincentio as a young girl and then as an old man). But he also
shows signs of violent anger. We first see him beating his (insolent) servant;
and later he throws dishes, food, clothes about, not to mention roughing
up the clergy (though it should be noted he uses no physical violence with
Kate, and only threatens to hit her after she has struck him—she clearly
believes him!). There is something particularly menacing in absolutely cool
anger—lethal wrath contained within total composure. It is, indeed, god-
like, and this is what marks Petruchio. Kate moves from being furious, to
being bemused and bewildered, to being simply frightened. We hope that
there is a succeeding phase—wifely happiness.

The second early clue as to what to expect from Petruchio, is provided
by his servant Grumio, who clearly knows his master well. 'Scolding' will
have no effect on Petruchio:

> I'll tell you what, sir, and she stand him but a little, he will throw a figure
> in her face and so disfigure her with it that she shall have no more eyes to
> see withal than a cat.
>
> (I, ii, 110–15)

Cats are supposed to have very sharp sight (Kate scratches like a cat, as well
as 'squeaking' like a shrew), so either Grumio has muddled it up, or—Morris suggests—he is referring to the old saying 'Well might the cat wink

when both her eyes were out.' But, whatever his intended meaning, his pre-diction that Petruchio will 'throw a figure in her face' could hardly be more accurate, whether we think of figures of speech or figures as images. It is just how he will proceed. First, by holding up an image of herself to her which is the exact opposite of what she *is,* but a 'figure' of what he wants her to *become:*

> I find you passing gentle.
> 'Twas told me you were rough and coy and sullen,
> And now I find report a very liar,
> For thou art pleasant, gamesome, passing courteous,
> But slow in speech, yet sweet as springtime flowers.
> Thou canst not frown, thou canst not look askance,
> Nor bite the lip as angry wenches will,
> Nor hast thou pleasure to be cross in talk,
> But thou with mildness entertain'st thy wooers,
> With gentle conference, soft and affable.
> Why does the world report that Kate doth limp?
> O sland'rous world!
>   (II, i, 236–47)

It must be particularly galling for Kate, who prides herself on her fast, wounding tongue, to be told that she is 'slow in speech', while as for limp-ing—we have just seen her 'flying' after her sister in violent pursuit. Faced with this unrecognizable image in the mirror of Petruchio's speech, Kate is nonplussed, finding her reality helpless against the fictional being Petru-chio insists upon. It should be noted, here, that Kate is distinctly 'slow in *thought*': she never tries to analyse what this apparent madman might be up to. Like the animals—she is shrew, cat, haggard (untamed hawk)—she re-acts, but does not reflect. Until, perhaps, after her 'conversion'—or capitu-lation—after which she is given all the signs of a thinking being.

The other kind of 'figures' he throws in her face are of a different kind—they are enactments, if she could but see it, of aspects of her own nature and behaviour. When he comes to his wedding in that grotesque tattered mot-ley of hopelessly ill-matched and shoddy garments (described at amazing length—it is like an extended portrait of a person in terms of clothes), it is as if he is saying to her, in visible, material signs—this is about how pre-pared *you* are for marriage, given your dire inner dishevelment. When he makes a messy parody of the wedding, with his loud rudeness, blows, and sop-throwing, he is saying—and *this* is the sort of respect *you* have for the solemn ceremonies of society. And when he throws the food, and pots, and clothes around, and behaves with incomprehensible contrariness, he is offering a representation, for her benefit, of the kind of domestic chaos which sustainedly 'shrewish' behaviour would bring to the household. And so on, with all his other 'counterfeiting' with her. As one of his servants acutely notes: 'he kills her in her own humor' (IV, i, 174). By distortion and exaggeration, he '*dis*figures' her by throwing her own 'figure' back at her in a rather terrifying form. And, just as Grumio had predicted, Kate is, temporarily, blinded. Petruchio is educating and 'taming' Kate in, as he sees it, the only way in which she will learn. (Perhaps inevitably, and not irrelevantly, all this has also been seen—by Ruth Nevo—as a 'therapeutic psychodrama'.)

Importantly, Petruchio reveals these two strategies to the audience in the only two soliloquies of the play. This makes him one of those Shakespearian 'practicers' who, alone of all the characters, knows just what is going on because, to a large extent, he is, as it were, stage-managing it. (It is notable that he has a far larger part than Kate, whose speaking part is, in fact, rather small.) The soliloquies also align us with him through the privilege of shared knowledge—we know exactly what is really happening, while we watch poor Kate flounder in bemused, uncomprehending ignorance. The first soliloquy is early, in Act II. It announces the first strategy—of offering the contradicting, ideal image:

> Say that she rail, why then I'll tell her plain
> She sings as sweetly as a nightingale.
>
> (II, i, 170–71)

and so on. The later soliloquy, in Act IV when the process is well advanced, outlines the other, more rigorous, part of the process:

> Thus have I politicly begun my reign,
> And 'tis my hope to end successfully.
> My falcon now is sharp and passing empty,
> And till she stoop she must not be full gorged,
> For then she never looks upon her lure.
> Another way I have to man my haggard,

> To make her come and know her keeper's call,
> That is, to watch her as we watch those kites
> That bate and beat and will not be obedient.
>
> (IV, i, 182–90)

Falcon, lure, haggard, kite, keeper—this is Petruchio the hunter, the falconer, the tamer. Kate will 'bate and beat' (flap and flutter) for a little while yet; but she will, finally, 'stoop'—which for a bird means swooping back to the lure (a device used in training to entice a hawk to return from flight); for a woman it means to submit—perhaps in time to conquer, but certainly to obey. Petruchio in fact makes clear his intentions and plans to Kate herself almost as soon as he has met her: 'And will you, nill you, I will marry you' (II, i, 264). Her sometimes frantic 'nilling' will prove impotent before his implacable 'will'. He has the real, Herculean power.

> For I am he am born to tame you, Kate,
> And bring you from a wild Kate to a Kate
> Conformable as other household Kates.
>
> (II, i, 269–71)

At this stage, Kate simply thinks him mad. But the inexorable programme and process has been set in motion. Hercules is beginning his 'labour'.

We might want to pause at that line—'a Kate/Conformable as other household Kates'. Does he *really* want a bleached-out conformist, indistinguishable from a crowd of other domestic drudges, or 'household Kates'? Since he 'bought' her from her father sight-unseen, as it were, we cannot say that he fell in love with her at first sight (as Lucentio does with Bianca). It is possible that his interest is aroused by what he is told about her apparently ungovernable tongue (perhaps scenting a challenge worthy of his taming energies and prowess). Certainly, when Hortensio enters with his 'head broke', Kate having beaten him with her lute, Petruchio warms to her in advance of seeing her:

> Now, by the world, it is a lusty wench!
> I love her ten times more than e'er I did.
> O how I long to have some chat with her!
>
> (II, i, 160–62)

One feels that the (apparently) totally-tamed Bianca leaves him cold—she is for romance, he is for hunting. There is no mistaking his enjoyment—as well as his determination—as he sets about the unwincing and unflinching struggle to break Kate's spirit. But is there not a paradox here—is he drawn to a wildness of spirit which he then proceeds to stamp out, or at least bring very much to heel? It is, perhaps, the necessary paradox of all education, and this play is very much about 'education'. It is set in Padua, a famous seat of learning, and in the sub-plot, two of Bianca's suitors (Lucentio and Hortensio) gain access to her father's house by posing as teachers for her— of mathematics and music, and languages and philosophy. A good traditional academic syllabus, you might think. Of course they teach her nothing, though this is hardly the fault of these venerable and estimable subjects. More to the point, Bianca *learns* nothing, nothing at all, and at the end of the play shows signs of shortly needing the sort of 'education' to which Kate has been subjected.

For Petruchio is a teacher, as well as a hunter—he is specifically called 'the master' of 'the taming school' (IV, ii, 55–6). In good education, the aim is to encourage the exfoliation of a pupil's best potentialities, to 'lead' him or her 'out' (e-ducare) of ignorance and uninstructed helplessness. But this also involves a necessary curbing of all kinds of instinctual waywardness, a disciplining of all sorts of temperamental unruliness—otherwise people would be unbearable (perhaps I should say *more* unbearable) and society impossible. To the extent that it hopes to produce citizens, education *could* be said to aim at turning out 'conformists'—though of course there is a positive, productive way of obeying laws and recognizing conventions, as well as more negative, mindless adherence and automatism. Perhaps enough of that. When Kate finally gives up and gives in, conceding Petruchio the Adamic privilege of 'naming' all things ('What you will have it named, even that it is', IV, v, 21), Horatio tells him 'the field is won'. Petruchio answers:

> Well, forward, forward. Thus the bowl should run,
> And not unluckily against the bias.
>   (IV, v, 24–6)

This is the first time that Shakespeare uses this image from bowls (in which the bowl has a weight on one side so that its natural movement is a curve in

one direction). It was to be a very important one and he uses it in subsequent plays, from *Twelfth Night* and *King John* to *Hamlet* and *King Lear*. Its
possibilities are obvious: here, Petruchio is maintaining that he has, in effect, *trained* Kate to move in the proper manner, to stop fighting against the
way she was meant, and made, to go. Now, it is certainly possible to see a
certain amount of what I think is called sexist essentialism in this (it is *natural* for women to be subservient and obedient); and you could say—people
have—that what Petruchio gives Kate is a lesson in old-fashioned patriarchy and unreconstructed male dominance. Certainly, such lines as

> I will be master of what is mine own.
> She is my goods, my chattels; she is my house,
> My household stuff, my field, my barn,
> My horse, my ox, my ass, my anything . . .
> (III, ii, 229–32)

may be thought offensive (though the element of exaggeration is unmistakable—my *barn?* my *anything?*); and making Kate trample her own cap un-
derfoot at the end can be seen as the last stage of enforced abjection and
self-abasement. If you don't like the play, you don't—and you will not be in
bad company. I don't just mean some (by no means all) feminists: George
Bernard Shaw found it 'altogether disgusting to the modern sensibility',
and Quiller-Couch thought it 'brutal stuff and tiresome . . . positively offensive to any modern civilized man or modern woman'. (Finding this play
sexist would go along with finding *Othello* racist, and *The Merchant of Venice* anti-semitic. Quite wrong-headed in my view—but a line which has been
argued.) But it *is* possible to see Petruchio as curbing, rather than crushing,
Kate; making her into a worthy companion instead of an all-over-the-place
wild-cat, beating her head against every convention in sight (the possibility
that her father has contributed to this by his manifest favouritism towards
Bianca is clearly hinted). Seen this way, he is liberating her from a pointless,
self-lashing, 'beastliness'—the Herculean labour. There is certainly no
getting round her final long speech in favour of female 'obedience'. It effectively concludes the play and cannot be heard as irony: nor is it contextu-
ally undermined by any sort of, as it were, Falstaffian sub-commentary. But
the act of *dis*obedience with which the, supposedly, so docile and biddable
Bianca starts her marriage (in the final wager), bodes ill for that couple's

future felicity—Shakespeare may well have thought it was better to start from financial realism and move towards mutual affection, than to begin with intoxicated romanticism and run into disillusion and discord. And when, at the end, Petruchio says 'Come, Kate, we'll to bed', one cannot but feel that, not to put too fine a point upon it, they will have a better time there than Lucentio and Bianca. Her essential vitality ('a lusty wench') is, we feel, still there, if now reined in and directed. In this, she is a forerunner of Shakespeare's later wonderfully spirited heroines. Bianca leads no-where.

The main point in all this—apart from the sense of ubiquitous struggle and contest, between sexes, sisters, suitors, generations—is 'change'. The sub-plot is full of changing—of clothes, names, roles; indeed, emphasizing the prevailing note, disguised Lucentio adopts the name Cambio—which is simply the Italian for change, exchange. But none of the changes are radical, or other than momentary improvisations and opportunistic simulations. The transformation of Kate is clearly another, deeper, matter. For, by the end, changed she certainly is. At her final demonstration of tractability and wifely obedience, Lucentio says 'Here is a wonder, if you talk of a wonder', while her father, more interestingly, more ambiguously, says 'For she is changed as she had never been' (V, ii, 106, 115). Changed as *if* she had never been a shrew? Changed as if she had never existed? Changed as she has never been changed before? William Carroll has noted these ambiguities, and sees them as reflecting an indeterminacy and uncertainty about the finality of Kate's transformation—on the grounds, roughly, that if she has changed once, she can change again. I take the point, but I don't think it quite fits with the spirit of the conclusion—though I suppose one can hear a residual, lingering doubt or scepticism in the very last line of the play—''Tis a wonder, by your leave, she will be tamed so'. I think the multiple possibilities in her father's remark suggest the mysteriousness of a radical transformation of personality, that element of the unfathomable in an apparent identity change. The remark does justice to the *strangeness* of the phenomenon. At one point in her 'treatment', Kate is described as sitting 'as one new-risen from a dream' (IV, i, 180). There is a lot of waking from dreams—literal and metaphoric—in Shakespeare's comedies, and at one extreme it can involve waking to a new self, a new life. The father's remark in _A Shrew_ is—'Oh wonderfull metamorphosis', which, whether or not it is by Shakespeare, points directly (perhaps too directly) to the central action or drama of the play. It is an Ovidian metamorphosis, but with Shakespeare's radical change of that process (metamorphosis metamorphosed). For this is an upward metamorphosis, ending, not like Io, Daphne, and Adonis, in blood, tears, and death, but with a woman woken from shrewishness and turned into a good wife (much better than the other two new wives, one is led to believe). And it is a metamorphosis which, finally, she positively accepts and adopts; thus, says William Carroll, being 'among the first of Shakespeare's characters to embody the necessity of self-willed transformation'.

If the completing of the frame action which is there in *A Shrew* was originally part of Shakespeare's play, then we would see Sly carried on, asleep/drunk, and left in front of the alehouse where the Lord and his men had found him. He is awakened by a Tapster who tells him that he had better get home, where his wife will give him what-for. But Sly, too, has learnt something:

> Will she? I know now how to tame a shrew,
> I dreamt upon it all this night till now,
> And thou hast wakt me out of the best dream
> That ever I had in my life, but Ile to my
> Wife presently and tame her too
> And if she anger me.

Perhaps he will, and perhaps he won't, but as he wakes from his dream, so we must 'wake' from the play. Perhaps we've learned something—and perhaps we haven't, though there is much more to it than the crude apology for patriarchy and phallocentrism which some have discerned. It is, that is to say, a better 'dream' than that. We will encounter, in a later comedy, another simple, uneducated lower-class figure who wakes up from the best dream he ever had in his life—though, as here, *we* can, wakefully, watch the dream. That will be on midsummer night—when, traditionally, anything can happen. And, more importantly, the 'dreamer' will not be a tinker, but—a weaver.

✒ THE TWO GENTLEMEN OF VERONA (1590–4)

It is the lesser blot, modesty finds,
Women to change their shapes than men their minds.
(V, iv, 108–9)

In *The Two Gentlemen of Verona* (in whichever order it was written—some editors think that *this* is Shakespeare's first comedy), we move away from the predominantly bourgeois, mercantile atmosphere of the previous two plays, and enter a world of royal courts, 'tilts and tournaments', emperors, kings, princes, and noblemen. It is still Italy, though a rather geographically indeterminate Italy. It opens with the two young gentlemen moving from Verona to Milan, but, as Dr Johnson observed, keeping a very straight face, 'the author conveys his heroes by sea from one inland town to another in the same country'. Speed says 'welcome to Padua', while the Duke of Milan seems to think he is in Verona. It doesn't matter of course, for this is a generic 'Italy' of story and romance, more Boccaccio than atlas. I mention Boccaccio advisedly, since one of his stories almost certainly lies behind what became the most notorious incident in Shakespeare's play. The eighth story of the Tenth Day of *The Decameron* concerns two inseparable male friends—Gisippus and Titus. Gisippus falls in love with a beautiful woman —Sophronia—and they become engaged. Titus, following the principle described by René Girard as 'mimetic desire' (whereby, roughly speaking, people tend to desire what someone else, particularly a close acquaintance, already desires) promptly falls in love with Sophronia as well. At first, he reproaches himself, invoking 'the duty of a true friend'. 'Will you allow yourself to be carried away by the delusions of love, the specious visions of desire? Open your eyes, you fool, and come to your senses' he says to himself. But other internal arguments prevail. 'But then he remembered Sophronia's beauty, and took the opposite viewpoint, rejecting all his previous arguments. And he said to himself: "The laws of Love are more powerful than any others; they even supplant divine laws, let alone those of friendship . . . Besides, I am young, and youth is entirely subject to the power of Love. So that wherever Love decides to lead me, I am bound to follow."' This sort of sophism, by which the power of Love is used to justify the betrayal of friendship, recurs in Shakespeare's play. But it is Gisippus' reaction, when Titus confesses his disloyal love, that has—translated into Shakespeare's play—caused the trouble: 'he *instantly* decided that his friend's life meant more to him than Sophronia', and simply hands Sophronia over, as it were, to Titus, saying 'you may rest assured that she shall enter the bridal chamber, not as my wife, but as yours' (my italics). Boccaccio's tale has its own ensuing complications and resolutions, which are not germane to Shakespeare's play. But Shakespeare has kept that 'instantaneousness' of the renunciation of beloved woman and bestowal of her on a treacherous friend, and it has proved hard to swallow.

Briefly: at the start, in Verona, Valentine mocks his friend Proteus for his single-minded, stay-at-home love for Julia (he calls it 'sluggardizing'!), saying that he is fancy-free and off to see the world. When he gets to Milan, however, he is enchanted by Silvia, and duly becomes a true 'Valentine' lover: while when Proteus follows his friend to Milan, he turns 'protean'. For he 'instantly' falls in love with Silvia, and forgets Julia. How he treacherously betrays Valentine, who is duly banished by Silvia's father, the Duke (always the prohibiting, obstructing father—as usual, no mothers to be seen), and attempts to seduce Silvia, forms the central action of the play. It all converges on the forest, where Valentine, improbably enough, has become the captain of a band of outlaws, and where Silvia has gone in search of him—followed, for one reason and another, by everybody else. There, Proteus finds Silvia and, failing once again (as he always has) to move her to anything more than contemptuous rejection, resolves to complete his infamy by raping her: 'I'll . . . love you 'gainst the nature of love . . . I'll force thee yield to my desire' (V, iv, 58–9). Valentine, a spectator throughout, steps forward and arrests the attempt, denouncing his 'treacherous friend': 'I am sorry I must never trust thee more', adding 'the private wound is deepest' (V, iv, 69–71)—not a word about the intent to 'wound' Silvia. What follows, follows very quickly. Proteus apologizes, repents, and asks forgiveness (five lines). Valentine accepts, forgives—and 'instantly' offers to hand over, as it were, Silvia to Proteus:

> Then I am paid;
> And once again I do receive thee honest.
> Who by repentance is not satisfied
> Is nor of heaven nor earth, for these are pleased.
> By penitence th' Eternal's wrath's appeased;

> And, that my love may appear plain and free,
> All that was mine in Silvia I give thee.
>
> (V, iv, 77–83)

Silvia is offered by her lover to the man who, *twenty-four* lines previously (three minutes? two?), tried to rape her. Silvia herself doesn't say another word for the remainder of the play—not surprisingly, you may think. But George Eliot described this moment as 'disgusting'; and Quiller-Couch, who, you feel, knows a cad when he sees one, harrumphed that 'there are by this time *no* gentlemen in Verona'. By and large, readers have been able, despite its psychological implausibility, to just about accept the immediate forgiveness—for forgiveness counts as a generosity and a grace, and is god-like. But there's no doing anything about those last two lines. Either they have to be explained away (young Shakespeare in thrall to conventions he had not yet mastered); or allowed to stand as a scandal and disgrace—either as a sign of the playwright's callowness, or as a whiff of a more barbaric age. Clearly, Valentine's offer to Proteus is, by any standard and from any point of view, entirely unacceptable. But, before we retreat to the Club House with Quiller-Couch, we might ask, what was Shakespeare—what might he have been—doing?

Commentators often—and rightly—remind us of the importance of friendship literature, from the Middle Ages to the seventeenth century. Bullough gives a relevant example from Lyly's *Endimion* in which Geron says:

> for all things (friendship excepted) are subject to fortune: love is but an eye-worme, which only tickleth the head with hopes, and wishes; friendship the image of eternitie, in which there is nothing movable, nothing mischievous.

Proteus, who proves to be totally 'movable' and in whom there is a very great deal that is 'mischievous', thus becomes a dark example of the false friend, while Valentine is a perfect embodiment of the true friend. M. C. Bradbrook insisted that we should see this play as illustrating the importance and strength of the Friendship Cult (so that Valentine's offer of Silvia to Proteus shows the true 'courtly virtue of magnanimity'—not quite the

George Eliot reaction). Clearly, Valentine and Proteus are to be seen as closely linked by a strong friendship. Thus Valentine on Proteus:

> I knew him as myself; for from our infancy
> We have conversed and spent our hours together
> . . .
> And, in a word, for far behind his worth
> Comes all the praises that I now bestow,
> He is complete in feature and in mind
> With all good grace to grace a gentleman.
>   (II, iv, 61–2, 70–73)

'I knew him as myself' (in Boccaccio's story Gisippus calls Titus 'my second self')—clearly the bonding is very close. Indeed, you can see Proteus as, effectively, trying to *become* Valentine—take over his other self. Valentine goes to Milan, Proteus follows; Valentine is welcomed into the Duke's family, Proteus ingratiates himself with the father and treacherously ensures that his friend is sent away; Valentine falls in love with Silvia, Proteus (instantly) starts making love to her in his friend's absence. Valentine is, thus, seemingly, almost totally displaced, replaced. It is not surprising that at one point he feels he has become 'nothing'—stripped and deprived of everything that gave him substance, made him him. Now, this may certainly be seen as an exploration of 'friendship', but, despite the incredible magnanimity of Valentine's selfless (self-effacing) offer, hardly an unequivocal celebration of it.

What we have, and arguably more interestingly, is the beginnings of a study of dishonourable conduct deliberately chosen, wrong-doing knowingly pursued. After Proteus come, with all their differences, Richard III, Don John (*Much Ado*), Bertram (*All's Well*), then Iago, finally Macbeth—Shakespeare's greatest exploration of *conscious* evil. Compared to Macbeth, Proteus is a rank amateur; but he is perfidious enough, and points the way. We can follow this in the three important soliloquies by Proteus (the soliloquy always being the privilege of the plotters and 'practicers'—both wicked and benign). In the first (II, iv, 190–213), he examines his instant desire for Silvia and forgetting of Julia:

> Even as one heat another heat expels,
> Or as one nail by strength drives out another,
> So the remembrance of my former love
> Is by a newer object quite forgotten.

The second soliloquy follows almost immediately, and constitutes a whole scene in itself (II, vi, 1–43). We hear him finding arguments to justify his imminent betrayal of Valentine and infidelity to Julia, invoking the irresistible power of Love—'Love bade me swear, and Love bids me forswear'. He knows what he owes to Julia and Valentine, but—as he sees it—'If I keep them, I needs must lose myself'. That this particular 'self' might be better lost, he no longer allows himself to consider. He is resolved:

> I will forget that Julia is alive,
> Rememb'ring that my love to her is dead;
> And Valentine I'll hold an enemy,
> Aiming at Silvia as a sweeter friend.
> I cannot now prove constant to myself,
> Without some treachery used to Valentine.

What *real* constancy is, and might involve, is an important concern of the play. But to maintain that constancy requires 'treachery' is to engage in very special pleading indeed. It is of a piece with the twisted casuistry with which Proteus tries to put a gloss on an indifferent-to-all-other-considerations lust. But he is determined to prove a villain, and immediately sets to work to 'plot this drift'. The third soliloquy (IV, ii, 1–17) shows him continuing in his resolve—'Already have I been false to Valentine,/And now I must be as unjust to Thurio.' While not exactly wading in blood like Macbeth, he is getting deeper into infamy, beginning to discover the inexorable law whereby one bad deed invariably requires another, and so on *ad infinitum*. He is also beginning to realize that his plotting and wickedness will have been all to no purpose, since the truly constant Silvia will not be moved. Like Henry James' Madame Merle, he is about to discover that he has been 'vile for nothing'. But by now he cannot stop himself.

As the play is concerned with friendship, so it is very much about love: commitment and disloyalty, pursuit and rejection, love and betrayal, constancy and change—the play resolves around these issues and tensions. A word with which we are becoming familiar, is used here—and only here—twice. Proteus claims to have been 'metamorphized' by Julia (I, i, 66), while quick-thinking Speed tells his slow-witted master, Valentine, that he is 'metamorphized' by Silvia (II, i, 30). Another word which occurs twice in the play is 'chameleon'—subsequently to be used only by Hamlet, and the future Richard III, who manages to call himself 'chameleon' and 'Proteus' in the same sentence (3 *Henry VI*, III, ii, 191–2); which is apt enough since both words refer to versions of the same phenomenon—sudden, self-activated change. 'Metamorphosis' of one kind and another infects the two inter-involved young couples in various ways. Valentine shifts overnight from being a roaming sceptic to being a committed, Petrarchan lover—which may be counted as a positive transformation. Proteus (and remember that the name of the mythic shape-shifting sea-god was used in the Renaissance as a figure of both good transformation—improvement, and bad—degeneration), manifests the worst kind of unstable volatility and disposition to change. Julia could use the *words* of Proteus, and say that she has to 'lose myself' in order to be 'constant to myself'—she changes her clothes, her gender, and her status to be true to her love (dressing up as a page to become Proteus' servant); but their meaning would point all the other way. In her own words, she may change her 'shape' but she never changes her 'mind'—the latter, in this play, is an exclusively male activity. Silvia, once she has committed herself to Valentine, does not change her shape or her mind: she remains an absolutely fixed point of 'constancy' throughout all the various changings and messing about that go on around her. Her father, the Duke, confident that her affections can easily be weaned from the now disgraced Valentine, asserts:

> This weak impress of love is as a figure
> Trenched in ice, which with an hour's heat
> Dissolves to water, and doth lose his form.
> A little time will melt her frozen thoughts,
> And worthless Valentine shall be forgot.
>   (III, ii, 6–10)

He could not be more wrong. The image is hopelessly misapplied and belongs squarely with Proteus, who has already confessed out loud (concerning his love for Julia):

> for now my love is thawed,
> Which, like a waxen image 'gainst a fire,
> Bears no impression of the thing it was.
>
> (II, iv, 199–201)

In this play, it is the watery men who are the dissolvers, the thawers, the melters. The women, once the fires of love have been ignited within them, burn with a steady, constant flame—melting waxen men, perhaps, but themselves as firm and fixed as, following the images, ice. Hot ice.

Proteus, on the other hand, is as changeable as the English weather, as he unwittingly predicts in one of the most beautiful images in the play (the devil often has the best lines):

> O, how this spring of love resembleth
> The uncertain glory of an April day,
> Which now shows all the beauty of the sun,
> And by and by a cloud takes all away!
>
> (I, iii, 84–7)

This is unmistakably an English, rather than an Italian April. Proteus thinks he is complaining about being separated from Julia by his father's orders that he must go to Milan; but, in fact, he is issuing a weather-forecast about his own coming behaviour in all matters concerning affairs of the heart. His subsequent multiple betrayals provoke this stinging rebuke from faithful Silvia:

> Thou hast no faith left now, unless thou'dst two,
> And that's far worse than none; better have none
> Than plural faith, which is too much by one.
> Thou counterfeit to thy true friend!
>
> (V, iv, 50–53)

Proteus is a counterfeiter all right, and, in matters of love, a manifest 'pluralist'. But there, Silvia insists, two is 'too much by one'. Julia makes a similar point in a poignant little scene when, disguised as a male visitor, she has to listen to the music with which Proteus is serenading Silvia. She is standing with the Host of the inn where she is lodging. He likes the music, but Julia uses the occasion to deliver herself of some heartfelt ironies— which of course only s/he can fully appreciate. Thus, she gives her opinion that Proteus 'plays false', his music 'jars', and 'grieves my very heartstrings'. The Host admires the modulations in the music, which allows Julia to utter perhaps the most important line in the play:

> *Host.* Hark, what fine change is in the music!
> *Julia.* Ay, that change is the spite.
> *Host.* You would have them always play but one thing?
> *Julia.* I would always have one play but one thing.
>   (IV, ii, 66–9)

More arithmetic—and, of course, *we* can follow Julia's point. Music may change, but lovers should not. In matters of love, men ought not to modulate. But, of course, there is an irony here which Shakespeare, so far from wishing to avoid, wants to exploit—and wishes us to enjoy. He is having fun, serious fun if you like, with the comparatively recent phenomenon of professional actors in a full-time theatre. Every actor in his play (whether playing Silvia or Proteus) has already, simply by being in the play, taken on a second part ('too much by one'). In that play, for different reasons, they may then go on to 'play' more than 'one thing'—the actor who played Proteus arguably three or four (Proteus as friend and lover, as scheming betrayer, as penitent, as rueful returned lover), and the Julia actor, in one amazing moment (to which I will return), at least five. They are all, necessarily, 'pluralists'. Of course, one can 'play' the constant lover, and another may change as fitfully and quickly as a chameleon or the weather of an April day. That is understood, and we have no trouble in attending seriously to the spectacle of an actor denouncing histrionic tendencies in another character. But it does raise more far-reaching questions. Can any of us in our, supposedly, non-theatrical waking lives, 'always play but one thing'? More to the point perhaps, *should* we? Repetition is fixity, is rigidity, is stagnation, is—potentially—death. Everything in organic life enjoins the recognition and acceptance of flexibility, adaptability, change. But where then is continuity, fidelity, trust—identity itself? We are back with the problem of distinguishing good and bad metamorphosis, and Shakespeare is clearly deeply interested in the ethical and emotional problems in managing the appropriate, the best, relationship and adjustment between desired constancy and necessary change.

Related matters are raised by the frequent use of the word 'shadow'—which, for the Elizabethans, was one of the synonyms for 'actor'. Let me draw attention to three moments. When Valentine is banished from Milan and Silvia, he feels it as a kind of death—'To die is to be banished from myself;/And Silvia is myself. Banished from her/Is self from self'. As far as he is concerned:

> She is my essence, and I leave [cease] to be,
> If I be not by her fair influence
> Fostered, illumined, cherished, kept alive.
>   (III, i, 171–3, 182–4)

All he will be able to do, separated from Silvia, is *think* about her 'And feed upon the shadow of perfection'. When Proteus begs the unresponsive Silvia, at least to give him a picture of herself, he adds:

> For since the substance of your perfect self
> Is else devoted, I am but a shadow,
> And to your shadow will I make true love.
>   (IV, ii, 121–3)

Poor Julia, who hears this, says in an aside:

> If 'twere a substance, you would, sure, deceive it,
> And make it but a shadow, as I am.
>   (IV, ii, 124–5)

It is Julia, as Sebastian, who has to carry Silvia's picture to her 'master' Proteus, and, taking hold of it, she says, in soliloquy:

> Come, shadow, come, and take this shadow up,
> For 'tis thy rival. O thou senseless form,
> Thou shalt be worshiped, kissed, loved, and adored!

And, were there sense in his idolatry,
My substance should be statue in thy stead.
> (IV, iv, 197–201)

I will come back to 'idolatry', but here let us just consider the play on
shadow (and form) and substance (and essence)—and 'perfection' (this
word, or its cognates, occurs interestingly often in Shakespeare; but nowhere as often as it does in this play). An actor is both a 'shadow' (also a
counterfeit image) and, in as much as he is a corporeal being, 'substance'.
Proteus is, indeed, a double shadow—an actor counterfeiting a counterfeiter. Valentine and Julia feel that they are 'shadows' having, as they think,
lost their lovers, thus feeling dispossessed of themselves. In the Platonic
perspective, all we mortals living in a material world can ever see is shadows of the Real, the Ideal, the truly Substantial, the Essential (and thus
all mimetic art—pictures, statues, plays—offers only secondary copies of
things—shadows of shadows—at one more remove from the Real). Shakespeare plays with this proposition, and turns it round—or perhaps, rather,
scrambles it. Thus, the 'shadows' Julia and Valentine feel, as it were, ontologically emptied out by being bereft of their loves—Valentine has a very
powerful image for the feeling:

O thou that dost inhabit in my breast,
Leave not the mansion so long tenantless,
Lest, growing ruinous, the building fall,
And leave no memory of what it was!
> (V, iv, 7–10)

But these shadows turn out to have true 'substance'. While Silvia is conceived of as being, not a shadow or reflection of the Real (Plato), but an 'essence' in herself (Plato hyperbolically set on his head); so that thinking
about *her* becomes the Platonic exercise whereby a human can intuit an essence, a perfect form. I don't think we should feel we are involved in some
dizzying epistemological regression here—shadows playing shadows who
also carry around other shadows (pictures). Rather, I think Shakespeare
likes the idea of showing substantial shadows discussing who is shadow and
who substance; in the process, certainly, shaking up our ideas of where the

one realm ends and the other begins—indeed, perhaps making us wonder to what extent they are, finally, separable.

'Perfection' points in a Christian as well as a Platonic direction—'Be ye therefore perfect' is the biblical injunction. This age had seen the idea of the 'parfit', gentle knight (there's supposed to be one in this play—Sir Eglamour), the perfect courtier (such as the gentlemen aspire to be), the perfect prince (which the Duke should be), which, in a sense, all reflect, perhaps derive from, the Christian notion of 'perfection'. Julia thinks that Proteus has this star-like, heavenly perfection:

> But truer stars did govern Proteus' birth.
> His words are bonds, his oaths are oracles;
> His love sincere, his thoughts immaculate;
> His tears pure messengers sent from his heart;
> His heart as far from fraud as heaven from earth.
>   (II, vii, 74–8)

—exactly wrong in every particular, of course (the idea that love is either blind or has too many eyes runs through the play). And note the word 'immaculate'—literally, without spot. 'Perfection' comes from 'per-facere', done or made throughout—thus entire, whole; and thus, without blemish. But Shakespeare knew very well that to be human is to be maculate—no 'im' about it. At the moment of his sudden repentance, Proteus remorsefully declares:

> O heaven, were man
> But constant, he were perfect! That one error
> Fills him with faults, makes him run through all th' sins;
> Inconstancy falls off ere it begins.
>   (V, iv, 110–13)

(There is no comment here on the theological doctrine of '*original* sin': these 'sins' are acquired, or 'run through'.) No one with more personal experience of 'inconstancy' than Proteus, and he is shamed by the bravely constant Julia. But the truth holds. We live in change—which need not be, in itself, 'sinful': to some extent, life *is* change and mutability. Perfection, if it exists, belongs, indeed, in 'heaven' with the stars. When Julia excuses her male disguise by saying 'it is the lesser blot . . . Women to change their shapes than men their minds', she is acknowledging that we are all, to some extent, blemished, while making the equally important point that some blots are a good deal worse than others. It is an important part of the play that Proteus turns out to be the spottiest of the lot—maculate through and through—while the 'blots' on Julia, such as they are, seem eminently forgivable.

Julia is the most interesting, we might say the most promising (together with Launce), of the characters in the play. She alone gives the impression of experiencing and knowing what she nicely calls 'the inly touch of love' (II, vii, 18), breaking free from stereotype while the others seem to be operating and speaking mainly from conventions (more of that in a moment). She is the first of Shakespeare's women to dress up as a man and, for honourable reasons, venture out into the world thus disguised. In her own way, she is 'losing' her self, or her identity or 'shape', in order to find, or preserve, it—being 'false' to be true. She thus anticipates the vital, brilliant, and determined heroines of the later comedies—such as Portia, Rosalind, Viola. As Proteus' page Sebastian, she is given the painful task of being sent to plead on his behalf to her rival. Shakespeare makes much more of this situation in *Twelfth Night,* but here it does occasion an amazing moment. Silvia knows that Proteus is committed to a woman named Julia, though of course she has no idea that Sebastian is in fact the woman in question. Virtuous and compassionate gentlewoman as she is, she feels sorry for this Julia, and asks Sebastian for details about her—such as, how tall is she? Julia then gives what has to be called an extraordinary performance:

> About my stature: for, at Pentecost,
> When all our pageants of delight were played,
> Our youth got me to play the woman's part,
> And I was trimmed in Madam Julia's gown,
> Which servèd me as fit, by all men's judgments,
> As if the garment had been made for me.
> Therefore I know she is about my height.
> And that time I made her weep agood,
> For I did play a lamentable part.
> Madam, 'twas Ariadne passioning

> For Theseus' perjury and unjust flight,
>
> Which I so lively acted with my tears
>
> That my poor mistress, movèd therewithal,
>
> Wept bitterly; and would I might be dead
>
> If I in thought felt not her very sorrow!
>
>   (IV, iv, 158–72)

This is sending all kinds of signals, not so much to Silvia who of course cannot pick them up, but to the audience, and to herself. And think about it. A boy actor is playing a woman (Julia), who is playing a boy (Sebastian), who describes being dressed up as a woman who is in fact herself, who then plays the part of the mythical female, Ariadne. Curiously enough, it is at this moment of five-levelled artifice, that she comes across to us most convincingly as 'real', the most substantial of shadows—a grieving, abandoned woman who has lost her love.

Pentecost and Ariadne—the Christian and pagan world again in the same sphere. Pentecost is the festival which comes fifty days after Easter and celebrates the descent of the Holy Ghost, which is a reminder, or re-enactment, of God's willing descent into the lower form of a man in order to achieve salvation for humans. Paula Berggren suggests that this glancingly refers to what Julia herself is doing—taking on the inferior status of a male servant to work for the salvation of 'sinful' Proteus. (She relevantly points out that whereas Rosalind, when she puts on male disguise, chooses the rather sexy name Ganymede—the boy loved by Zeus—and enjoys androgynously charming both Phebe and Orlando, Julia chooses the name Sebastian, a Christian martyr, and 'ultimately it is not the sexual but the social ingredient of Julia's disguise that counts'. Also, where Viola–Cesario and Orsino have a complicated, sexually ambiguous relationship when s/he is acting as his servant, the relationship between Proteus and Julia—Sebastian is perfunctory and undeveloped—some forty lines.) 'Ariadne' reinforces this idea of salvation from a pagan perspective. Ariadne, too, is descended from a god (her father was Minos, a son of Zeus by legend), and she sacrifices herself to help Theseus out of the labyrinth, saving him from the Minotaur and securing his liberation. Theseus then, of course, abandoned her for her pains. Slightly differently, Julia is an abandoned woman who nevertheless enters the labyrinth to save Proteus from the bull of lust, rescuing him from damnation, redeeming his 'sins' (?), and liberating his better self. These Christian–pagan allusions are not elaborated, but they are undoubtedly there.

By comparison, the other main characters seem to remain within the romances and conventions which engendered them. The traces, and bits and pieces, of romance are very clear. Sir Eglamour, as described is, indeed, a veritable anthology of the chivalric virtues of knight errantry and courtly love. We have a princess kept in a tower; a planned escape by ladder; a serenading lover; a forlorn and despairing woman pursuing her lost man; a wicked villain and a trusting friend; reluctant partings, happy reunions, generous forgiving. We also have noble, Robin Hood style, outlaws in the forest: this episode is also rather perfunctory and undeveloped, but it is important since it allows Shakespeare a shift from the court into the country (what Northrop Frye called 'the green world'), which anticipates far more important shifts—to places like the Forest of Arden and Prospero's island. Shakespeare is experimenting with all kinds of 'devices' which he will use in later plays.

The lovers themselves—I am excepting Julia—love according to convention. Valentine, in particular, once he falls in love, not only becomes a walking anthology of Petrarchanism, but also a parody of it, particularly as seen by the mordant eye of his servant, Speed ('these follies are within you, and shine through you like the water in an urinal'—see II, i, 17–40). Even Proteus is moved to protest against his 'idolatry' and 'braggardism' (when Silvia says to Proteus 'I am very loath to be your idol, sir', IV, iii, 126, she not only speaks for the two women, but for women in general against that male cult of 'idolizing' women, which is the very reverse of real love, and is more akin to a form of narcissism).

These figures, particularly the 'gentlemen', love by the book. A 'love-book' is mentioned in the first scene, and the love is, in general, a pretty papery matter—it does not strike one as very 'inly', to use Julia's word. There are constant letters, not to mention sonnets and songs, and we have many orders or observations and requests, such as—writers say, bear this letter, peruse this paper, write some lines. Two early scenes underline this involvement with paper and writing. Julia receives a letter from Proteus, and (playing the cruel mistress) ostentatiously tears it up in front of her maid—'Dare you presume to harbor wanton lines?' Once the maid has left, she scrabbles around on the floor, trying to put some bits together again. Then she starts making love to the reassembled scraps—'I'll kiss each several paper for amends' (I, ii, 108). Finally, she finds a piece with her name on it, and another piece with his name on it, and, effectively, puts them in bed together to 'couple':

> Thus will I fold them one upon another.
> Now, kiss, embrace, contend, do what you will.
>   (I, ii, 128–9)

It is an interesting, perhaps rather charming, displacement or substitution. But it has to be said, it is part of the prevailing indirectness of the 'love' in this play. Indeed, the lovers scarcely make love to each other in any unmediated way; instead, we usually hear them talking about their 'love' to someone else, or to themselves (most of the play is duologue or soliloquy). In a scene which follows shortly after, we see Valentine bring Silvia a letter which she has asked him to write on her behalf to a 'secret nameless friend'. She pushes the letter back at him—'take it for your labor', but Valentine, obtusely, cannot see that the letter is meant for *him*. Speed sees the 'device' immediately:

> Was there ever heard a better,
> That my master, being scribe, to himself should write the letter?
>   (II, i, 136–7)

He tries to get it into Valentine's head that 'she hath made you write to yourself'. Speed spells it out. Silvia is perhaps too 'modest' to reply directly to Valentine's letters to her:

> Or fearing else some messenger that might her mind discover,
> Herself hath taught her love himself to write unto her lover.
> All this I speak in print, for in print I found it.
>   (II, i, 163–5)

Valentine still seems not to understand—he really is an extraordinarily slow fellow. But Speed's last cryptic line should resonate throughout the play, and indeed beyond. Written plays, of course, literally 'speak in print'. Speed may simply mean that he is quoting, but his words point also to the fact that the lovers in the play have a tendency to, effectively, 'speak in print'; for, when it comes to words expressing love, 'in print they found them'. To some extent, this must be true for all of us. One of the concerns of the comedies might then be to explore to what extent—and with what effects—'love' can be *generated* by pre-existing words, books, conventions, forms; and to what extent—and how—a genuine, individual love can discover itself, and express its authenticity, breaking out of, or shining through, the words and conventions which are everywhere in place waiting for it—to shape, deform, distort, deflect, arrest, inflame, perhaps enable, it.

The one character who most conspicuously does *not* 'speak in print', and whom I have deliberately not discussed until now, is of course Proteus' servant, Launce—particularly when he is speaking (soliloquizing) to his dog, Crab. There were comic or 'clownish' servants in Classical comedy, and in Shakespeare's two plays already discussed. Speed is just such another figure, but Launce is something else, something more—and he looks forward to such notable figures as Touchstone and Feste. We first hear him, about to leave for Milan, talking about their leave-takings to (or at) Crab.

> I think Crab my dog be the sourest-natured dog that lives. My mother weeping, my father wailing, my sister crying, our maid howling, our cat wringing her hands, and all our house in a great perplexity, yet did not this cruel-hearted cur shed one tear. He is a stone, a very pebble stone, and has no more pity in him than a dog . . . Nay, I'll show you the manner of it. This shoe is my father; no, this left shoe is my father. No, no, this left shoe is my mother; nay, that cannot be so neither. Yes, it is so, it is so, it hath the worser sole. This shoe, with the hole in it, is my mother, and this my father; a vengeance on't! There 'tis. Now, sir, this staff is my sister, for, look you, she is as white as a lily, and as small as a wand. This hat is Nan, our maid. I am the dog. No, the dog is himself, and I am the dog. Oh! the dog is me, and I am myself; ay, so, so . . . Now the dog all this while sheds not a tear, nor speaks a word; but see how I lay the dust with my tears.
>
> (II, iii, 5–34)

We have, just immediately before this, witnessed a tearless, finally 'dumb' and wordless, parting between Julia and Proteus, and this scene between Launce and Crab marks the start of an increasingly telling parody of (and critical commentary on) that relationship. Proteus will duly turn out to be 'a stone' with 'no more pity in him than a dog'. We shouldn't be too heavy about this, but as we watch Launce's uncertainty about which is the dog and which himself, we can respond to larger, comic implications. You can just never be sure which and who the real 'dogs' are—nor, indeed, when the cats might start wringing their hands! And his confusion over shoes and hats, and which shall play whom, has another resonance—apart from the obvious jokes about holes and soles/souls. I quote a comment by Leonard Barkan:

> Shakespeare also defines theater as the transformation of one thing into another . . . of a whole set of accoutrements into a family romance (Launce and co.) . . . Shakespeare has [here] brought metamorphosis down from Olympus (and its courtly equivalent in contemporary theater) to the level of the Globe groundlings. But it is not merely democracy at work. In the process he has recognized that transformation is a universal feature of his own art, restricting itself neither to monarchs nor to clowns, neither to amateur theatricals nor to kings who see themselves as players—though it is likely to be the clowns who keep us aware that the illusion of metamorphosis is an illusion.

Behind Launce there is Shakespeare saying—give me a shoe and a hat and I'll give you a play.

In a subsequent soliloquy (again, with Crab), Launce laments the recent 'foul' behaviour of his 'cur'—stealing a capon, stinking up the dining room, 'pissing' on 'a gentlewoman's farthingale'. More apt, indirect comment on Proteus' increasingly 'foul' behaviour, of course. But Launce reveals that he has taken the blame for all Crab's mess, and duly, as he has often done before, drawn upon himself all the punishment intended for the miscreant hound (a whipping). 'How many masters would do this for his servant?' (IV, iv, 30). Not, perhaps, *exactly* a Christ-like cry—but very similar to one we hear immediately afterwards from Julia–Sebastian, 'unhappy messenger', ordered to go and woo Silvia on behalf of her beloved Proteus—'How many women would do such a message?' (IV, iv, 90). We are seeing very clearly who are the *true* selfless, self-sacrificing, servants—and who are the dogs.

Canny, 'clownish', Launce also sees clearly enough what is going on, even if he does express himself mainly to, and through, Crab. 'I am but a fool, look you, and yet I have the wit to think my master is a kind of knave. But that's all one, if he be but one knave' (III, i, 262–4). More arithmetic, but Proteus is not a 'one part' man: just as he is engaging in 'plural faith', so he is sinking into plural knavery. But Launce is in love (he tells us), and, once again unconsciously (perhaps) parodying his betters, he '*pulls out a paper*', which carries a 'cate-log of her condition' (III, i, 273). He keeps it 'in print', we may say. There follows a long, comic exchange with Speed: Speed reads out the 'items' concerning the nameless wench (her, distinctly non-Petrarchan, virtues and vices), allowing Launce to comment on each one. I want to single out one item and response:

> *Speed.* 'Item: She hath more hair than wit, and more fault than hairs, and
>   more wealth than faults.'
> *Launce.* Stop there; I'll have her. She was mine, and not mine, twice or
>   thrice in that last article.
>
> (II, i, 348–51)

In *A Midsummer Night's Dream,* Helena will say: 'And I have found Demetrius like a jewel, / Mine own, and not mine own' (IV, i, 194–5). Mine, and not mine: mine own, and not mine own. Shakespeare is here looking at, and acknowledging, the unavoidable, ineradicable, residual uncertainty at the heart of *all* love relationships—whether Launce and his wench (or his dog), or Helena and her jewel. There is *no* complete possessing of another person: 'mine, and not mine' is as far and as close as you can get. But that is right, too. If you do aim, obsessively, at *complete* possession of a loved one, you are in danger of ending up (in one way or another) like 'Porphyria's Lover', in Robert Browning's monologue of that name. He, you may remember, wants to make sure that the lovely Porphyria is 'mine, mine'—entirely, unchangingly. And he is, insanely, sure that he has found the way to ensure this. He has strangled her.

Launce reminds us that this is a romantic *comedy*. Certainly, Shakespeare is, as Bullough suggests, beginning to look at the possibilities offered by the Renaissance world of romance and story for the lyrical treatment, and the ethical exploration, of love and friendship. But the comic perspective is crucial, and not just because the play ends with the usual marriages and festive reconciliations—'One feast, one house, one mutual happiness' is the last line—which conventionally conclude comedy. Consider what Shakespeare does to some of the conventions he deploys. Take Sir Eglamour, that supposed paragon from the world of medieval romance, whom Silvia chooses to be her protector when she ventures into the forest in search of Valentine. At the first sight of the outlaws, he runs away with, apparently, impressive speed—and goodbye knightly chivalry. The outlaws themselves are ludicrous—pantomime pirates. Valentine demonstrates some of the absurd excesses in Petrarchan love (Silvia is an honourable lady from within the convention, while Julia moves off into a new seriousness). The Duke of Milan, having shown exemplary courtesy to his guests, collapses into crude rudeness when he discovers Valentine's love for his daughter—'Go, base intruder! Overweening slave!' There is even something ridiculous in Proteus' wickedness (when Silvia reproaches him for his dastardly advances, she asks—what about your love, Julia? She's dead, says Proteus promptly. And what about your friend Valentine?—er, as a matter of fact, he's dead too. This is lame stuff indeed. Richard III, his near contemporary, could do much better than that, and Iago would have been appalled at the resourceless ineptitude of his feeble precursor). His attempted rape does reveal the latent brutality in conventions of romance, and Launce—the better man—unwittingly (?) shows him up for the dog he is. Perhaps more seriously, Launce shows up the comparative unreality of most of those around him (Julia excepted). I think H. B. Charlton is almost exactly right in his comment on the play—'Clearly, Shakespeare's first attempt to make romantic comedy had only succeeded so far that it had unexpectedly and inadvertently made romance comic.' Almost—because I am not persuaded of the need for the words 'unexpectedly and inadvertently'. Which brings me back to the opening question concerning Valentine's incredible, or unacceptable, offer of Silvia to the man who has just tried to rape her. I think this is part of Shakespeare's discovering of instabilities, absurdities, unrealities in the conventions he was experimenting with. I should, perhaps, make my general position clear. I hold it as axiomatic that, if we find something (or somone) cruel, unconscionable, intolerable (not to mention admirable, lovable, or laughable), in Shakespeare's plays, then so did Shakespeare. I think the same goes for anything which we find implausible or unacceptable. I have little time for the line that begins—you have to bear in mind that, back then, they felt differently about . . . I have no wish to sound like Jan Kott in *Shakespeare Our Contemporary* (though I am not out of sympathy with the implications of the title). I believe we should do all we can to discover the beliefs, values, expectations and so on, of the age Shakespeare lived in. Historicism, old and new, is to be, selectively, welcomed. But if Shakespeare does not appeal to universal feelings, then nothing does. The idea of 'making allowances' for Shakespeare, seems to me some kind of ultimate in benighted presumptuousness. I assume that if we feel something, he felt it too. Shakespeare was certainly learning as he went along, and learning very quickly. But I believe, and thus assume, that he always knew what he was doing. Even if he did not realize quite how extraordinary it all was.

LOVE'S LABOR'S LOST (1588–97)

> *Moth.* They have been at a great feast of languages, and stol'n the scraps.
> *Costard.* O, they have lived long on the alms-basket of words. I marvel thy
>   master hath not eaten thee for a word.
> (V, i, 39–43)

One way to approach this play is to bear in mind the phenomenon alluded to in the title of Richard F. Jones' deservedly famous book—*The Triumph of the English Language.* Even up to the 1580s, in learned circles, where Latin gave dignity and conferred prestige, it was a matter for debate whether English was suitable for anything but low, everyday matters. Then quite suddenly, towards the end of the 1580s, apologies for the barbarousness of the vulgar tongue gave way to a new (nationalistic) triumphalism concerning the English language (a triumph finally sealed with the translation of the bible). English took over everywhere, in all subjects, and spread, and developed, and proliferated in a way that makes one want to refer to a veritable explosion. Barber says of *Love's Labor's Lost* that it catches something of 'the excitement of the historical moment when English, in the hands of its greatest master, suddenly could do anything'. You also feel, in this play, that Shakespeare is beginning to realize that he can do anything, too.

The Elizabethans, it may be said, were, or became, mad about language. Books about rhetoric (usually drawing on Quintilian) were popular and much studied. Two of the most important were Henry Peacham's *The Garden of Eloquence* (1577), and George Puttenham's *The Arte of English Poesie* (1589), which you may be sure Shakespeare knew. When Holofernes modestly boasts of his 'foolish extravagant spirit, full of forms, figures, shapes, objects, ideas, apprehensions, motions, revolutions' (IV, ii, 66–8), he not only reveals that he has been a good student of Puttenham—he is also a representative voice of the age, even if in comical form. When, in the third line of the play, the King of Navarre expresses the hope that fame will 'grace us in the disgrace of death', we are aware that he is playing on a word (and 'grace', in all its senses, will be an important word, occurring more often here than in any other of Shakespeare's plays). We would be less likely to know that this was called *Polyptoton* ('employment of the same word in various cases'—for the explanation of this, and all other rhetorical terms, see *A Handlist of Rhetorical Terms* by Richard A. Lanham: see also *Shakespeare's Use of the Arts of Language* by Sister Miriam Joseph). When Armado explains that the King would like him to arrange 'some delightful ostentation, or show, or pageant, or antic, or fire-work' (V, i, 112–13); or when he holds forth a paper adding 'which here thou viewest, beholdest, surveyest, or seest' (I, i, 242)—why use one word when you can think of four or five?—we know what's going on, but perhaps don't recognize it for *Pleonasmus* or *Macrologia* ('too full speech . . . needless repetition'). When Nathaniel asks Holofernes to 'abrogate scurrility', meaning 'no dirty talk', we probably detect *Euphemismus* ('circumlocution to palliate something unpleasant'); but when Holofernes describes Armado as 'too picked, too spruce, too affected, too odd, as it were, too peregrinate, as I may call it' (V, i, 14–15), could we identify it as *Periergia* ('superfluous elaboration of a point')? And when Armado is amused and says 'thou enforcest laughter . . . the heaving of my lungs provokes me to ridiculous smiling' (III, i, 76–8), I think that none of us, alas, could reach for *Bomphiologia* ('when trifling matters be set out with semblaunt and blazing wordes'—Peacham: as Ruth Nevo lamented, why did we ever lose such a useful word!). Shakespeare, and his audience (almost certainly, initially, an educated one—it was perhaps a court entertainment) would have known these rhetorical terms and many more, even if we no longer do.

   Not that it matters. We can still recognize pedantry and affectation when we hear it (even if less when we speak it?). Shakespeare's play can be seen as offering a satire, parody, burlesque on all the uses and abuses of rhetoric so painstakingly classified and anatomized in the rhetoric handbooks of the day. But it is also a *celebration* of the energy, and pleasure in language, which generated those uses and abuses—and the books which so compendiously analysed them. When Berowne vows to renounce:

> Taffeta phrases, silken terms precise,
> Three-piled hyperboles, spruce affectation,
> Figures pedantical—these summer flies
> Have blown me full of maggot ostentation:
> I do forswear them . . .
>
> (V, ii, 407–11)

his disavowal gives itself the lie by the manifest relish with which the words are chosen and uttered. Nothing like a few taffeta phrases, and some silken terms precise, eh Berowne? Even his vow to aim at plain-speaking comes dashingly dressed in metaphor:

> Henceforth my wooing mind shall be expressed
> In russet yeas and honest kersey noes.
>
> (V, ii, 413–14)

—nice glowing red-brown affirmatives, and good stout woollen negatives. It's rather as if Henry James was trying to promise he would write like Ernest Hemingway! It is all part of the fun, for this *is* a 'great feast of languages', and, as is appropriate at feasts, everyone is, for the most part, having a thoroughly good time—not least, as one feels, Shakespeare himself. If the Princess asks Boyet to open a letter, it is 'you can carve—/Break up this capon' (IV, i, 56–7). Dull is not just illiterate—'he hath never fed of the dainties that are bred in a book./He hath not eat paper, as it were, he hath not drunk ink' (IV, ii, 24–5). At times, it actually does seem surprising that someone has *not* eaten the tasty, morsel-sized Moth 'for a word'! (He is called a 'flapdragon'—a raisin in brandy; and a 'pigeon-egg'—a delicacy.)

And this is a feast to which everyone is invited—'Sir, I do invite you too: you shall not say me nay' (IV, ii, 166–7) as Holofernes kindly says to Dull. Indeed, apart from a bout of disgraceful upper-class boorishness (a timeless enough phenomenon—as Henry James said, there is nothing like the bad manners of good society), the people in this play are extremely generous and nice and polite to each other, and some of the courtesy (for instance that of the Princess) is exquisite. There is nothing like the *good* manners of good society, as well. Nobody is left out, excluded, isolated, or alienated; there are no malcontents, killjoys, or spoil-sports—and certainly no villains, plotters, or practicers. For, as it is a feast, so it is a game—and any number can play. 'Away! the gentles are at their game, and we will to our recreation' says

Holofernes (IV, ii, 167–8). Like his betters, Costard can think of four words for one, when he explains that he was caught with a wench, damsel, virgin, maid. Even Dull has a go at a joke, and is resolved to join in—'I'll make one in a dance, or so', he says, and Holofernes cries encouragingly 'To our sport, away!' (V, i, 154–6). And as this is a feast and a game, so it is a dance, a masque, a sport, a play, a pageant—Armado is right; you need at least five words to describe it.

One thing it is not is a drama—at least in any conventional sense. It not only has no plotters, it effectively has no plot. Significantly, it is the only play by Shakespeare for which there is no written source (all the others avail themselves to some extent of documentary origins). He made it all up— partly, one feels, as he went along. No plotters, only players—literally, people at play. For what, in sum, happens? A king and three lords take a vow to devote themselves to three years of study and chastity. *Immediately,* a princess and three ladies arrive on a diplomatic mission, and have to be received. *Immediately,* the men 'fall in love' with the women, and, sophistically arguing themselves out of their oaths, commence a series of wooing games, involving members of the lower orders in one of their court entertainments. It is all 'pass-time', pastimes. The games are interrupted by a messenger bringing news of the death of the Princess's father, and the play ends in abrupt dispersal, separation, and deferral—instead of the conventional comic resolution of union, consummation, and gathering-in. In fact, it has turned out not be a 'play', as Berowne recognizes in his last words. And yet of course it is—even if we have to see it as a play *about* play.

Shakespeare has moved from ancient Greece and Renaissance Italy to contemporary Reformist France. There was a Henry of Navarre with whom the Elizabethans had some links after the Massacre of St Bartholomew (severed when he reconverted to Catholicism in 1593). He was a patron of learning, and in 1583 an ambassador wrote to Walsingham that Navarre 'has furnished his Court with principal gentlemen of the Religion, and reformed his house'. The play contains echoes of a contemporary pamphlet war between Gabriel Harvey and Thomas Nashe, and the phrase 'school of night' (IV, iii, 254) has led to speculation about a political background involving the two factions of Essex and Southampton, and Ralegh and Northumberland. I think that all we need to bear in mind (and even this is not necessary for an enjoyment of the play), is the balanced summing-up of the Arden editor, R. W. David—'all the evidence goes to show that

Love's Labor's Lost was a battle in a private war between court factions' (and thus almost certainly first written for private performance in court circles). Shakespeare also draws on figures from the *Commedia dell'Arte*—for instance the Spanish fantastic Armado (and the name would, of course, have contemporary resonance) is closely related to the stock Braggart, always called Capitano Spavento del Vall'Inferno; and Holofernes, Nathaniel, and Costard have comparable relations. Though, of course, Shakespeare makes the figures all his own. They enable him to extend the range of the play from the initial court setting, out into the middle-class world of schoolmasters and curates, and down to the simpler world of constables, swains, and country wenches. Each social level is at play in its own way; at the same time, we feel they are a community. Though somewhat scattered at the end.

But, first and foremost, the action is in the language. Armado is said to speak in 'high-born words' of Spanish knights 'lost in the world's debate' (I, i, 171–2). Here, 'debate' carries the meaning of literal warfare (it derives from the same root as 'battle'—*battuere,* to beat); but, of course, it also sounds the meaning it has for us (philosophical debating societies based on the example of Plato were founded in Italy during the Renaissance, and spread to other parts of Europe). The meanings are nicely elided when the Princess refers to 'this civil war of wits' (II, i, 226)—for 'debating' can, indeed, amount to civil (also 'polite') war carried on by other means. Here, the characters 'tilt', joust, spar, fence, and otherwise compete—with words. And this of course, and pre-eminently, includes sexual 'tilting' as well. 'Well bandied both! a set of wit well played' (V, ii, 29), cries the Princess appreciatively. And here is Armado, delighted as ever by another pert sally from the quicksilver Moth: 'Now, by the salt wave of the Mediterranean, a sweet touch, a quick venew of wit! Snip, snap, quick and home! It rejoiceth my intellect. True wit!' (V, i, 59–61). We might stay with that word 'wit' for a moment. It occurs more often in this play than in any other by Shakespeare—and that by some considerable margin (forty-two times). It was a capacious word in the Renaissance, and could refer specifically to poetry, or more generally to felicities of eloquence. It bespeaks a particular zest in words, and points to that wonderful exhilaration experienced when language seems almost autonomously to release ever new potentialities, to take over and start to make happy discoveries off its own bat. In Barber's nice formulation—wit 'gives us something for nothing . . . When wit flows happily, it is as though the resistance of the objective world had suddenly given way.' Wit is the champagne of language—for language can be champagne, as well as small beer. In good champagne, the bubbles keep on rising and rising, as if from nothing, to break at the surface. That is 'true wit'. And *Love's Labor's Lost* is mainly champagne. Which can, of course, become too 'heady', and people have sometimes found, perhaps justifiably, that there is here a superfluity of 'wit', a something too compulsive in the tireless straining after it. What is undeniable is that the play also shows how wit can be abused—that it has a strong anti-social potential, and may have a corrosive rather than generative effect on developing relationships.

I will return to that, but let us stay with the very real pleasures afforded by word-play—language on the loose—in the play. Armado is a representative figure. He is a man of 'fire-new words, fashion's own knight' (I, i, 177) who:

> hath a mint of phrases in his brain;
> One who the music of his own vain tongue
> Doth ravish like enchanting harmony
> (I, i, 164–6)

—in this, though, he is only the lords writ large, or hilariously caricatured. When his letter arrives at court in the first scene, Berowne says: 'be it as the style shall give us cause to climb in the merriness' (I, i, 198–9), while near the end we gather the King has told Armado that he is 'good at'—perhaps he meant 'good *for*'—'eruptions and sudden breaking out of mirth' (V, i, 115). This very exactly describes the play, and its effect on the audience. Personal anecdotes are invariably rather pointless in this matter—but I did once see a perfect performance of this play, and I have never been so conscious of growing communal pleasure. The audience 'climbed in the merriness', and went on climbing and climbing. And, in large part, it was indeed 'the style' that 'gave us cause'—Granville Barker fastened on that word as characterizing the work's very essence, and it is, in every sense, the most 'stylish' of plays.

And not only are the spectators having a merry time, the characters are enjoying themselves, too, relishing every sally, each sparkling bubble. 'Pretty and apt,' says Armado to Moth appreciatively, 'A most fine figure . . . sweet invocation of a child' (I, ii, 18, 55, 96). Costard listens with growing enjoyment to the bantering between the ladies and their attendant lord, Boyet. 'By my troth, most pleasant: how both did fit it.' The sexual *double entendres* grow increasingly broad (and wit is intimately involved with our sexual drives and interests), until Maria cries enough—'Come, come, you talk greasily; your lips grow foul' (IV, i, 138). Costard loves it; and, wittingly or not, chooses just the right word: 'O' my troth, most sweet jests . . . When it comes so smoothly off, so obscenely as it were, so fit!' (IV, i, 143–4). Holofernes intends generosity in his comment on one of Costard's rural efforts—'a good luster of conceit in a turf of earth, fire enough for a flint, pearl enough for a swine. 'Tis pretty; it is well' (IV, ii, 88–90). But he shows the respectful admiration of the connoisseur when Armado refers to 'the posteriors of this day, which the rude multitude call the afternoon'.

> The posterior of the day, most generous sir, is liable, congruent, and measurable for the afternoon. The word is well culled, chose, sweet and apt, I do assure you, sir, I do assure.
>
> (V, i, 91–4)

So far from mocking the man's provincial pedantry, the audience is by this time usually helpless with laughter—and grateful.

The play starts solemnly enough, with the King announcing his intention to make his court into a 'little academe' to which he and his fellow lords will retire for a period of ascetic, celibate contemplation and study: turning their backs on the body, as it were, and making 'war' against 'the huge army of the world's desires' (I, i, 10). The first lines of the play give his reasons:

> Let fame, that all hunt after in their lives,
> Live regist'red upon our brazen tombs
> And then grace us in the disgrace of death

He is seeking honour and eternal 'fame' through this renunciation of the flesh. This way of pursuing 'fame' turns out to be drastically (comically) misdirected (not graceful, and not the way to gain 'grace'). The play makes two basic points about this aspiration. During the hunting scene, the Princess makes a generalization which is, retrospectively, very telling:

Glory grows guilty of detested crimes,

When, for fame's sake, for praise, an outward part,

We bend to that the working of the heart

(IV, i, 31–3)

She is not talking about the King (at least, not directly), but he *has* tried to 'bend . . . the working of the heart' (what he called 'our affections') 'for fame's sake'. He is not exactly guilty of 'detested crimes', but in ordering that 'no woman shall come within a mile of my court . . . on pain of losing her tongue' (I, i, 119–21), he is revealing a streak of patriarchal cruelty (only men talk here), as well as trying to 'bend' himself against the ways of nature. And when, at indeed 'the latest minute of the hour', he asks the Princess for her 'love', she demurs—his turn-around has been all too quick, 'A time, methinks, too short / To make a world-without-end bargain in' (V, ii, 789–90). 'World-without-end' (Amen) has, of course, a religious resonance; here suggesting, certainly, the till-death-do-us-part 'bargain' of marriage; and, perhaps, the 'bargain' we hope we have struck with God for eternal life. Either way, love and marriage point to the true lastingness, not any empty 'fame' won by perverse renunciations.

The King's plan is, of course, doomed to failure. When the imminent arrival of the Princess is announced (who, of course, must be afforded hospitality), Berowne, who goes along with the plan while commenting ironically on its impossibility, immediately points out:

Necessity will make us all forsworn

Three thousand times within this three years' space:

For every man with his affects is born,

Not by might mast'red, but by special grace.

(I, i, 148–51)

Later, he advances the same opinion:

Young blood doth not obey an old decree.

We cannot cross the cause why we were born

(IV, iii, 216–17)

This conviction seems to be quite central to the comedies. It is expressed most succinctly in *All's Well That Ends Well:* 'Our blood to us, this to our blood is born' (I, iii, 133)—'this' being simply sexual desire. It is both risky and wrong—not to say hubristic—for a healthy young man to think he can 'bend' himself *completely* against 'this'. The King, if he could but hear it, receives an even prompter admonition when, immediately after he and his lords have sworn their oaths and taken their vows, Dull comes in with Costard, asking for the King, saying specifically: 'I would see his own person in flesh and blood' (I, i, 184)—which the King has that very minute been resolutely denying. Costard has been 'taken' with Jaquenetta, but, living in a more grounded and realistic world than the court, has no shame in admitting the forbidden deed. 'Such is the simplicity of man to hearken after the flesh', he says with a sort of rural resignation, adding 'Sir, I confess the wench' (I, i, 216, 278). The King and lords will shortly 'hearken after the flesh' themselves, and duly have to confess their wenches. Though of course, it will all be a much more elaborate, elaborated affair than anything offered by the forthright and literal-minded Costard. The simplest confrontation of all occurs between Armado and Jaquenetta, when he (of all people), embarrassed by his emotion, is reduced to the monosyllabic greeting—'Maid!' To which she replies—'Man?' (I, ii, 131–2). This is the basic exchange underlying all other exchanges between the sexes. All the rest is elaboration of one kind or another. Of course, it is those elaborations which provide occasions for grace and civility, not to mention fun and delight, and nobody would wish a two-word play. But that is where all love's labours start, and in a wondrous variety of ways is always being said. 'Maid!' 'Man?'

To read Berowne's seventy-five line paean in Act IV is to realize just what amazing elaborations 'love' can inspire, or permit. The occasion is the climax of the scene of multiple eavesdropping, when Berowne steps forward to 'whip hypocrisy', in the shape of the King, Longaville, and Dumaine, who have, in turn, caught and denounced each other for having love-letters and sonnets for the visiting ladies. Berowne triumphs in his 'over-view'— 'O what a scene of fool'ry I have seen' (IV, iii, 162)—and enjoys scorning 'men like you, men of inconstancy' (IV, iii, 179). At the peak of his derision, Jaquenetta comes in, bringing what turns out to be Berowne's love-letter to Rosaline to be read. Berowne collapses and confesses—'you three fools lacked me fool to make up the mess' (IV, iii, 206). ('Mess' is one of those interesting words which seems to look both ways. Coming from a serving of food, or mixed food for an animal, it came to refer to any confused or shapeless mass—as now. But, in the Elizabethan period, it was also used to mean a small group or party of precisely four people—for meals, dances, games, whatever. Confusion *and* order; shapeless *and* exact. Strange.) Now that they are all discovered to have broken their vows, and fallen for women, they need to find 'some flattery for this evil . . . Some tricks, some quillets [subtleties], how to cheat the devil' (IV, iii, 285–7)—in other words, some casuistry to somehow justify their perjury. Berowne is just the man for the task. Their real 'folly', he declares, is not their present state of being 'forsworn', but their original belief that they could and should 'forswear' women. Using a Christian argument with which we are now familiar in the comedies, he argues:

> Let us once lose our oaths to find ourselves,
> Or else we lose ourselves to keep our oaths.
>   (IV, iii, 361–3)

There is a lot of sophistry, or 'glozing' (superficial word-play used to 'gloss', palliate, extenuate, etc.) in his speech; but, as Holofernes would say, 'the Gentles are at their game'. Berowne finally demonstrates to their group satisfaction that 'It is religion to be thus forsworn' (IV, iii, 362), and, happily bundling up his Christianity with his paganism, the relieved King cries out 'Saint Cupid then! And soldiers to the field!' (IV, iii, 365—an invocation, incidentally, which echoes one by Armado at the end of Act I. In the matter of susceptibility to a woman, there is not much to tell between them).

Berowne is the most surprised at his susceptibility, as the long soliloquy starting—'O, and I, forsooth, in love!'—which ends Act III, reveals (III, i, 175–207). He, too, reluctantly acknowledges the power of 'This wimpled, whining, purblind, wayward boy', but, initially at least, he has small thanks for 'this senior-junior, giant-dwarf, Dan Cupid' (III, i, 181–2). This love, or sudden infatuation, he feels is:

> a plague
> That Cupid will impose for my neglect
> Of his almighty dreadful little might.
>   (III, i, 203–5)

That 'plague' metaphor is by no means all a joke. He returns to it at the end to describe the condition of his companions:

> Write 'Lord have mercy on us' on those three.
> They are infected, in their hearts it lies;
> They have the plague, and caught it of your eyes.
> These lords are visited . . .
> (V, ii, 420–23)

A sign reading 'Lord have mercy on us' was hung on the door of a house which had been infected by the plague, which was also known as a 'visitation'. This play was written very close to, if not in, the year of 1592–3, which was one of the worst 'visitations'. This probably tells us something about how tough-minded the Elizabethans could be in their humour; but it reminds us that they also thought that love could be a sort of sickness, sometimes mortal. In a sudden dark moment (which anticipates the ending), while the ladies are joking about Cupid, there is this exchange:

> *Katharine.* Ay, and a shrowd unhappy gallows too.
> *Rosaline.* You'll ne'er be friends with him: a' killed your sister.
> *Katharine.* He made her melancholy, sad, and heavy;
>   And so she died. Had she been light, like you,
>   Of such a merry, nimble, stirring spirit,
>   She might ha' been a grandam ere she died.
>   And so may you, for a light heart lives long.
> (V, ii, 12–18)

'Gallows' here means someone fit for the gallows (in *Much Ado* Cupid is called a 'hangman', III, ii, 11). This play is almost exclusively for, by, and about 'merry, nimble, stirring spirits' playing with, and at, love. But here is a sudden chill reminder. Like the plague, Cupid can kill.

But in his long paean, it is the positive aspects of love which Berowne wants (has) to emphasize. He evokes its Orphic power—'as sweet and musical / As bright Apollo's lute' (IV, iii, 341–2), and stresses its superior educative potency. His argument—or nimble sophistry, if you will—is, roughly, that we will learn much more from looking at our women, than from hanging over the books in our rotten old academy.

> For where is any author in the world
> Teaches such beauty as a woman's eye?
>   . . .

From women's eyes this doctrine I derive.
They sparkle still the right Promethean fire;
They are the books, the arts, the academes,
That show, contain, and nourish all the world
                        (IV, iii, 311–12, 349–52)

'Eye(s)' occurs over fifty times in this play—more times than in any other
by Shakespeare except *A Midsummer Night's Dream,* and most of the relationships and exchanges between the lords and ladies take place between
sparkling, dancing, 'dazzling' eyes. We still speak of falling in love 'at first
sight' (what the morose Puritan Richardson deprecated as 'the tindery fit'—
no 'right Promethean fire' for him), and whatever it is the lords fall into, it
is almost exclusively concerned with the eyes. Berowne's central contention
is that 'love, first learned in a lady's eye', then

    adds a precious seeing to the eye:
  A lover's eyes will gaze an eagle blind
                        (IV, iii, 332–3)

It would be pointless to go through and examine occasions—eyes are looking and flashing everywhere. But there is one extraordinary description of
that moment when an eye lights up at the sight of a beautiful person (someone who, as we say, catches the eye), which is like nothing else in the whole
of Shakespeare. Boyet is describing to the Princess how he infers that the
King has been 'infected' (again) by seeing her. He is going on what he nicely
calls 'the heart's still rhetoric disclosed with eyes':

    all his behaviors did make their retire
  To the court of his eye, peeping thorough desire.
  His heart, like an agate with your print impressed,
  Proud with his form, in his eye pride expressed.
  His tongue, all impatient to speak and not see,
  Did stumble with haste in his eyesight to be;
  All senses to that sense did make their repair,
  To feel only looking on fairest of fair.
  Methought all his senses were locked in his eye,
  As jewels in crystal for some prince to buy;

Who, tend'ring their own worth from where they were glassed,

Did point you to buy them, along as you passed.

His face's own margent did quote such amazes

That all eyes saw his eyes enchanted with gazes.

(II, i, 234–48)

The mysterious moment of sudden attraction has surely never been more amazingly elaborated than in these 'conceited' couplets. The tongue tripping up in its haste to join the other courtiers already crowded into the eye, peeping through desire . . . (I note in passing that the imperturbably poised, endlessly amused, teasingly gallant, provocatively suggestive Boyet, is called by Berowne—he means to be rude—'Monsieur the Nice' and 'honey-tongued Boyet', V, ii, 326, 335. One of the earliest, contemporary pieces of praise for Shakespeare—by Meres—contains the phrase 'mellifluous and honey-tongued Shakespeare'. Shakespeare could have been aware of this, and we may well have here an amiable, self-referential joke. Certainly, only Shakespeare could have pulled off Boyet's amazing 'eye' conceit.)

But, is this *love?* One cannot help but feel that these young men most enjoy talking about it; trying to find clever ways of expressing how *they* feel, competing in hyperbolic praises of their adored ones. They seem to be caught up in—enjoyable—post-Petrarchan posturings. That the mere sight of the ladies has put paid to their absurd monkish resolves, is certain enough. They have been 'struck'—or indeed, 'infected'. But they don't seem to have moved beyond that to any consideration of the ladies as other individuals, nor given much thought to love as a *relationship* between two people (and none at all to the prospect of sexual consummation—possibly a chivalric touch). Barber rightly pointed out that Berowne's speeches on love tend to become 'autonomous rhapsodies' that 'almost forget the beloved'. When they discover that the ladies deceived them by wearing masks and changing favours—while they thought they were 'disguised' as Muscovites! —Berowne is the first to see the trick:

The ladies did change favors, and then we,

Following the signs, wooed but the sign of she.

(V, ii, 469–70)

He speaks more truly than he knows; for they have, indeed, been wooing 'the sign of she'—i.e. not individuals, but the conventionalized, generic idea of the female. They never, we might say in today's parlance, moved beyond the sign to what, truly, it signified. Even when Berowne thinks he is trying to break out of artificiality, he shows himself to be still inextricably involved in it:

> *Berowne.* My love to thee is sound, sans crack or flaw.
> *Rosaline.* Sans 'sans', I pray you.
>   (V, ii, 416–7)

Sincerity is an elusive thing—hard to detect in others, hard to be sure of even in oneself. Berowne, certainly, has not yet got the knack of it. Rosaline's wry response is definitive, and says it all.

None of what I have said about the young lords as would-be 'lovers' extends to the ladies. They are much more associated with 'grace'; not so much Christian redemptive grace, as the grace of genuinely good, humane, manners. To some extent, they have joined in the game—and with some pleasure, for they are, themselves, attracted to the men. But always in a controlled, realistic, non-deceptive (and non-deceiving) way. The Princess sums up how they took the lords' 'love-making':

> At courtship, pleasant jest, and courtesy,
> As bombast and as lining to the time.
> But more devout than this in our respects
> Have we not been, and therefore met your loves
> In their own fashion, like a merriment.
>   (V, ii, 781–5)

And, we feel, they did absolutely right. *How* right has just been graphically demonstrated at the play, or entertainment (or show, or pageant, or antic, or . . .) put on for the court by the non-aristocratic locals. At the start, when the ladies were discussing the lords, they singled out a characteristic or attribute they all shared—a dangerously compulsive wit which could be 'ravishing', but also sharp to the point of cruelty—they are 'merry *mocking*' lords. Longaville's 'soil' is:

a sharp wit matched with too blunt a will,
Whose edge hath power to cut, whose will still wills
It should none spare that come within his power.

(II, i, 49–51)

Dumaine 'hath wit to make an ill shape good' (59), and Berowne turns everything 'to a mirth-moving jest' (71). When the locals put on their performance of the Nine Worthies—a performance as endearing as it is amusing—the King is worried that 'they will shame us' (V, ii, 510). In the event,
the shame is all the lords'. The Princess is gracious and, as we have seen in
the hunting scene, compassionate: 'Great thanks, great Pompey'—'Alas!
poor Maccabaeus, how he hath been baited!' (V, ii, 555, 632). (In rehearsal,
Moth had spoken of 'the way to make an offense gracious, though few have
the grace to do it', V, i, 141. The Princess has that 'grace'; the lords emphatically lack it.) The players are patient, well-mannered, deferential: 'Sweet
Lord Longaville, rein thy tongue' (V, ii, 658). But the lords display the
higher yobbery throughout, boorishly baiting and mocking the poor players without pause. There really *is* nothing like the bad manners of good society! We may learn from the Arden editor that it was customary for the
courtiers to engage in what he rightly calls 'brutal' mockery at such entertainments. But, here again, I invoke my conviction that if we react to something as cruel, so did Shakespeare. As the crude, rude, mockery continues,
we feel that if *this* is so-called wit, then it is wit at its most despicable, turned
to bad ends. When poor, gentle Holofernes is catcalled completely 'out of
countenance' and is jeered off the stage by Berowne as a Jude-ass, he is
moved to make the reproach which should shame them all—'This is not
generous, not gentle, not humble' (V, ii, 630). This, too, is definitive. Berowne claimed that 'love' would teach them all they needed to know. These
clever, selfish, self-regarding young aristocrats have learned nothing. The
ladies are something more than justified in refusing to commit themselves
to them in their unreconstructed state.

So—no weddings. As Berowne ruefully points out:

Our wooing doth not end like an old play;
Jack hath not Jill. These ladies' courtesy
Might well have made our sport a comedy.

(V, ii, 875–7)

This is the whole point. It is a 'sport' and *not* a 'comedy'. If it had been a comedy, Jack *would* have had Jill; if it had been a history, Jack would have been crowned; if it had been a tragedy, Jack and Jill would probably have both been dead. Here, Jack and Jill just go their separate ways. A play, in the sense of a drama, was, as Shakespeare constructed it, a representation, in some mode and form, of an arc of a significantly completed action—inasmuch as life knows of any completions. It might end, for example, in a marriage, a coronation, a funeral. If we are to regard *Love's Labor's Lost* as a drama, then we should see it as dramatizing how a 'sport' *fails* to become a 'comedy'. It is 'interrupted', or 'dashed', as real life will always interrupt mere 'pastime'; just as 'holiday' cannot go on forever, yet does not have any significant completion. It simply has to, at some time or another, give way to the exigencies of 'workday'. This 'interruption' has been adumbrated and prepared for. When the lords come dressed as Russians, Rosaline is about to start the dance, then stops it.

> Play, music, then. Nay, you must do it soon.
> Not yet! No dance! Thus change I like the moon.
> (V, ii, 211–12)

The episode ends with the 'frozen Muscovites' quite routed, and hopelessly 'out of count'nance' (V, ii, 273). Berowne can see what has happened:

> I see the trick on 't. Here was a consent,
> Knowing aforehand of our merriment,
> To dash it like a Christmas comedy.
> (V, ii, 461–3)

He is alluding to that custom of disrupting with mockery a seasonal entertainment put on by the local other-classes, which I mentioned. And, of course, the lords proceed to do exactly the same thing (only more cruelly) to the performance offered by the poor Worthies, 'dashing' it indeed, and putting the inexperienced players, exactly, quite 'out of countenance' (V, ii, 621). (These men, it should be noted, are all like Nathaniel, who is a 'marvellous good neighbour' but, in Costard's memorable formulation, 'a little o'erparted', 581–2. The lords trying to play at lovers are 'a little o'erparted', too.)

It is worth examining the point at which Shakespeare 'dashes' his own 'merriment'. The entertainment of the Worthies has collapsed, and threatens to end in a fight between Costard and Armado over Jaquenetta. They are supposed to strip to their shirts for combat, but Armado refuses:

> The naked truth of it is, I have no shirt.
>
> (V, ii, 710)

A man without a shirt is a speech without a metaphor. Immediately, the messenger Marcade enters with the naked, unadorned news of the death of the Princess's father. The 'merriment' is not only 'interrupted' (718)—it is definitively dashed. The Princess and her ladies retire to a 'mourning house' (809). The King is dispatched to 'some forlorn and *naked* hermitage' (796—my italics). Berowne is sent to a hospital to try to 'move wild laughter in the throat of death', in the hope that that will 'choke a gibing spirit' (856, 859). Jaquenetta is two months' pregnant, and Armado promises to give up playing and take up 'ploughing' for her sake. The 'sport' is over, and it is back to the naked, unadorned realities of birth, work, sickness, and death. After Carnival, Lent. The play ends with pageant seasonal songs of Spring, *followed* by Winter. The festive interlude is over, and for the moment, it is more a matter of endings than renewals. The songs sing of the year-round, seasonal pleasures and labours of simple, communal rural life. The last line leaves us with the most homely and humble of pictures— 'While greasy Joan doth keel the pot'. Suddenly, we are a long way from princesses and court games. The very last sentence of the play is in larger type in the Quarto and may represent a non-Shakespearian addition. But it may be still Shakespeare—and the somewhat cryptic, enigmatic words are both ominous and fitting. The line is given to Armado; but ideally, I think, it should seem to come from nowhere, or some mysterious source, like the pronouncement of an oracle.

> The words of Mercury are harsh after the songs of Apollo.

'Marcade', messenger of death, is a form of 'Mercury', messenger of the gods. Berowne invoked 'bright Apollo's lute', and tried to emulate his music. But Death always has the last word.

Thus Shakespeare soberly and sombrely ends his lightest, most 'play-ful' play. It is a bracing conclusion to a sufficiency of 'sport'. But I think we most remember the mounting pleasure which preceded it. I am reminded of a statement by Emerson concerning what it is we go to great artists for. 'We came this time for condiments, not for corn. We want the great genius only for joy . . .' Perhaps not *only* for joy, but I feel that the emphasis is right—that art should be, not primarily utilitarian and serviceable, but an addition, an excess, something over and above; not our daily bread, but an added spice, zest, relish. And this, surely, is true of *Love's Labor's Lost*. It gives great joy. I could say, simply, that it makes me laugh a lot. But, on this occasion, I prefer to put it that the heaving of my lungs provokes me to ridiculous smiling. It rejoiceth my intellect.

Come for the condiments.

 ROMEO AND JULIET (1594–6)

> All things that we ordainèd festival
> Turn from their office to black funeral
> (IV, v, 84–5)

> Now art thou sociable, now art thou Romeo; now art
> thou what thou art, by art as well as by nature.
> (II, iv, 93–5)

Romeo and Juliet fails of being a 'comedy' by something under a minute (Juliet wakes up from her pseudo-death twenty-seven lines after Romeo has committed suicide). As a reason for including the play in a volume of Shakespeare's Comedies, this may seem, at best, a rather perverse piece of special pleading. The first good Quarto announced it clearly enough as 'THE MOST EXCELLENT AND LAMENTABLE TRAGEDY OF ROMEO AND JULIET', and by the end the five main protagonists are dead. Of course it is a tragedy. But it contains within it all the lineaments of a Classical comedy. Consider. Two young lovers set about circumventing the obstructiveness of intransigent parents, with the help of servants. When the Chorus announces at the beginning of Act II:

> Now old desire doth in his deathbed lie,
> And young affection gapes to be his heir

it is offering a precise definition of one of the most basic situations of all comedy. In addition, we have a standard Malcontent (or kill-joy, or spoil-sport) in Tybalt, who is a Malvolio at the feast, and, despite familial exhortations, will *not* be festive. Mercutio, full of bawdy jests, provocative, punning, playful, always buzzing in Romeo's ear, is a superb Clown. And we have a comic, garrulous Nurse, whose main interest is helping to get the young into bed together. There is a splendid dance and banquet (from which the churlish Tybalt is banished, and where the young lovers meet); and there is, indeed, a marriage whereby Romeo and Juliet are made 'incorporate two in one' (II, vi, 37)—which, as I have indicated elsewhere, is the ideal conclusion to a Shakespearian comedy. Only here, it happens at the end of Act II. Thereafter, 'ordained festival' does, indeed, turn to 'black funeral'. What (let us ask speculatively) was Shakespeare doing?

There has never been a way of deciding in which order Shakespeare wrote *Romeo and Juliet* and *A Midsummer Night's Dream,* and it seems at least likely that he was writing both plays *at the same time.* Both plays explore similar themes and subjects in, of course, a very different manner. Famously, the play of 'Pyramus and Thisby' put on by Bottom and the 'mechanicals' is a farcical redaction of the whole drama of *Romeo and Juliet* (Mercutio calls Romeo's loved one a 'Thisby'—if we needed a clue); and when Hippolyta pronounces it 'the silliest stuff that ever I heard' (V, i, 211), we can only guess at the fine, ironic pleasure Shakespeare must have had in writing the line. Mercutio's long, almost delirious, invocation of Queen Mab (I, iv, 53–94) seems to point directly to *A Midsummer Night's Dream* (some commentators think it really belongs there); while the cruelly prohibiting Egeus (trying to block and deflect his daughter, Hermia's, true love) is just such a father as the violent, tyrannical old Capulet becomes, when he threatens to turn Juliet out of house and home if she will not obey his orders. And so on—I won't pursue the similarities and echoes. In the one play, Shakespeare explores how 'comedy' can suddenly change, and veer precipitately into tragedy. He shows how everything can go terribly wrong. In the other play he demonstrates how things can all go, magically, right. The two plays were clearly conceived together; and, while I can hardly maintain that separating them is as risky as separating Siamese twins, from the point of view of a literary appreciation of what Shakespeare was doing, I think it is something of that order.

Let me give one example of the inter-involvement, the strange mutual reflectingness, of the two plays. Lysander, confronting the (usual) paternal blockage of his love for Hermia, complains, at length, that 'the course of true love never did run smooth' (a line which has become a truism because it is the simplest possible expression of a simple truth). He takes a perverse pleasure in elaborating on the number of ways in which true love can be variously impeded, frustrated, and otherwise derailed. Including this:

> Or, if there were a sympathy in choice,
> War, death, or sickness did lay siege to it,
> Making it momentary as a sound,
> Swift as a shadow, short as any dream,
> Brief as the lightning in the collied night,
> That, in a spleen, unfolds both heaven and earth,
> And, ere a man hath power to say 'Behold!'
> The jaws of darkness do devour it up:
> So quick bright things come to confusion.
>
> (*MSND*, I, i, 141–9)

That last line is one of the most haunting in the whole of Shakespeare—it is hard to imagine poetry doing more than this in seven simple words, six darting monosyllables brought to a halt in the relative tangle of a trisyllable. But let us just linger, with appropriate brevity, on 'lightning'. When Romeo is trying to swear his love to Juliet in the so-called balcony scene (II, ii), she holds, briefly, back:

> Well, do not swear. Although I joy in thee,
> I have no joy of this contract tonight.
> It is too rash, too unadvised, too sudden;
> Too like the lightning, which doth cease to be
> Ere one can say it lightens.
>
> (II, ii, 116–20)

Benvolio, describing the crucial 'bloody fray' to the Prince, tells how Romeo came looking for Tybalt, to revenge Mercutio, 'and to't they go like lightning' (III, i, 174)—anger can work like love: violent and (for whatever reasons), often shortlived, expiring in the performance. In his last speech,

Romeo, imaginatively transforming Juliet's tomb into a festive chamber, says:

> How oft when men are at the point of death
> Have they been merry! Which their keepers call
> A lightning before death. O, how may I
> Call this a lightning?
>
>   (V, iii, 88–91)

Shakespeare shows how—but I will return to that. Here, I just want to suggest that both plays are concerned, imaginatively, with the 'lightning' of young love. And its possible ramifications. So quick bright things come to confusion—in this play, the confusion leads, tragically, to death; in the other, the confusion is, comically, resolved.

The basic story of Romeo and Juliet can be traced back to folklore, but it was first developed into a popular narrative by a number of Italian *novelle* in the fifteenth and sixteenth centuries. Shakespeare's primary source was unquestionably a translation of the story into English by Arthur Brooke, in a long poem entitled *The Tragicall History of Romeus and Juliet* (published in 1562). Brooke was a Protestant moralist, and he gave as the intention and justification of his poem—'to describe unto thee a couple of unfortunate lovers, thralling themselves to unhonest desire, neglecting the authoritie and advise of parents and frendes, conferring their principall counsels with dronken gossypes, and superstitious friers, attempting all adventures of peryll, for thattaynyng of their wished lust . . . abusing the honorable name of lawefull marriage, to cloke the shame of stolne contractes, finallye, by all means of unhonest lyfe, hastyng to most unhappye deathe'. A cautionary tale, indeed! To be fair, his actual poem is a good deal more sympathetic to the young lovers than this stiffnecked sententiousness suggests will be the case. But Shakespeare clearly had something very different in mind than a demonstration of the folly of aroused youth ignoring parental advice.

Shakespeare took a lot of matter from Brooke's poem (the lyric brilliance of his transformation of Brooke's rather turgid, lugubrious verse is a marvel in itself); but, as always, it is particularly instructive to notice what he changed. He drastically foreshortens the time-scale of the action (as he will

do in the one other tragedy he based on an Italian story of love and intrigue—*Othello*). Where Brooke has weeks between the ball and the lovers'
meeting by moonlight, and months between their marriage and the death
of Tybalt, Shakespeare makes these events occur on the same night and the
same day, respectively. In Brooke, Juliet wakes up an hour after Romeo's
suicide; in Shakespeare, it is less than a minute. In all, he collapses about
seven months into, at most, four days. In Brooke, Romeo kills Tybalt in
self-defence and Mercutio is not involved. In Shakespeare, Mercutio is first
killed, mainly as a result of Romeo's attempt at pacifying interference (good
intentions can have bad outcomes), and Romeo is obliged to adhere to the
revenge code. Juliet is, in some versions, an eighteen-year-old; Brooke
makes her sixteen; Shakespeare brings her down to just *fourteen.* Brooke
leaves the entirely honourable Paris alive at the end; Shakespeare kills him
off. Brooke describes the night after the wedding, when the young lovers
legitimately consummate their love; Shakespeare shows only the dawn
parting. I will, in due course, suggest reasons for all these changes. (One
little change intrigues me, though I have no theories about it. Every other
version of the story, including Brooke's, stresses that Mercutio has very cold
hands—quite a nice touch, given his hot, lecherous banter. But Shakespeare
deletes the manual chill!) Brooke—the Protestant moralist—stresses the
malignancy of Fortune and Fate, on at least fifteen occasions. This was his
gloomy addition to the Italian tale. In the words of H. B. Charlton, 'Brooke
drenched the story in fatality.' Charlton thinks that Shakespeare took over
this sense of Fate, and fatality, from Brooke, which is partly why, in his
opinion, as a tragedy the play is a 'failure'. Thus: 'though *Romeo and Juliet*
is set in a modern Christian country, with church and priest and full ecclesiastical institution, the whole universe of God's justice, vengeance, and providence is discarded and rejected from the directing forces of the play's dramatic movement. In its place, there is a theatrical resuscitation of the
half-barbarian, half-Roman deities of Fate and Fortune.' And: 'Fate was no
longer a deity strong enough to carry the responsibility of a tragic universe . . . It fails to provide the indispensable inevitability.' One can see the
point, but unhappily for Charlton's case, the word 'fortune' appears here
less often than in any other play ('Fortune' is apostrophized twice); while
'fate', with a single appearance, is also a rarer visitor than is the case everywhere else. If anything, Shakespeare *drained* the story of 'fatality'.

I think Charlton is perhaps addressing the difficulty of locating the blame for what happens, of identifying the cause which makes the tragedy 'inevitable'. The point is an important one. In comedy, things are, precisely, 'evitable' (Susan Snyder has developed this point). If this doesn't work, we'll try that; let's hide in the forest, let's dress up as men; so-and-so will help us; we can get round this old man; I know a trick whereby . . . Iron laws can be made to melt; irrevocable prohibitions are rescinded; obstacles are made to be removed or circumvented—it *will* be, somehow, all right in the end. *Romeo and Juliet* starts with something of that atmosphere—come on, let's gatecrash the Capulet ball, we can get away with it. The Friar and the Nurse continue to believe in 'evitability', the possible other way (try this drug, why not marry the other man?), but they become increasingly irrelevant figures. Somehow, the tragic imperatives close in and take over. Things do turn '*in*evitable'. Only just; but, nevertheless, unmistakably. Why? Whence? How? This, of course, is *the* tragic question; and, at the end of the worst and longest day, we might do well to recall Cordelia's piercingly gentle words—'No cause, no cause'.

Who or what is to 'blame' for what happens in *Romeo and Juliet?* There is the futile feud, but no explanation or origin of that is given—it is just one of those irrational things that *are*. (Charlton thought that feuds belong to the 'border country of civilization', and that it is impossible, or anachronistic, for Shakespeare to locate something so tribal and clan-based as a feud in such a civilized city as Verona. Civilized it certainly is, and was, but my sense of the matter is that 'feuding', in one form or another, can hardly be said to go out of date. And wasn't there something about the Guelphs and the Ghibellines, not to mention Yorkists and Lancastrians? The feud in Verona is a 'hurt' to the community, and, as such, it is like Mercutio's fatal wound—''tis not so deep as a well, nor so wide as a church door, but 'tis enough, 'twill serve', III, i, 97–8. As continued by the feeble old men, who need crutches more than swords, it has become ridiculous; but, as perpetuated by Tybalt, it is lethal enough.) It is the plague which is responsible for the temporary incarceration of the monk, who is thus prevented from delivering the Friar's all-explaining letter to Romeo—and the plague is another irrational thing which simply *is*. 'Prince of cats' Tybalt's violence certainly sets a train of events in motion. But, threatening and unpleasant as he is, Tybalt is hardly a proper villain. He appears, rather, as an obsessive psychopath who is only interested in killing Montagues. He is not a 'plotter', not a Richard III; not, certainly, a Iago (though explain why Iago is Iago if you can). An 'earthquake' is mentioned; and, in the case of this dangerously eruptive play, you might say that whatever it is that is really responsible for what happens, may be compared to whatever it is that causes earthquakes. But Fate and Fortune are not serious players—or not serious *as* players. Shakespeare's opening choric sonnet announces that the lovers are 'star-crossed' and their love 'death-marked'; but, although the play is full of premonitions and a growing sense of menace, we never experience it as a demonstration of astrological determinism. It is a very starlit play, even while the 'mark' of death is clearly on it: it is bright to the point of brilliance—and as dark as oblivion itself. The play itself is somewhat like a flash of lightning in the night. In a way, the young lovers *are* crossed with stars, are themselves crossing stars—but I will come to that.

Fate and Fortune figure minimally, and 'Providence' not once (it is, in any case, a rare word in Shakespeare's plays—six occurences have been counted. The Friar finally acknowledges 'A greater power than we can contradict/Hath thwarted our intents', V, iii, 153–4—this is pious, but vague to the point of pointlessness. 'A greater power'—God? An earthquake? Who knows?). The Prince refers to 'heaven' (V, iii, 293)—but this is the habitation of the blind stars, as well as the residence of whatever gods there might be. But, the word 'haste' occurs *more* frequently than in any other Shakespeare play—except *Hamlet.* In the case of *Hamlet,* this is something of a contributory irony, since it is at once the longest and the slowest of Shakespeare's tragedies. But in *Romeo and Juliet,* speed is, indeed, of the essence. It is among the fastest of the plays; as fast, perhaps, even as *Macbeth,* that black arrow of a play. But Macbeth wants to outrun his own mind, and he can never, *could* never, run fast enough. Whereas Romeo is always just too quick, too sudden, too soon. Finally, only by seconds—but it is enough to ensure catastrophe. Coleridge thought this play was particularly marked by 'precipitation', both in language and action, and that is just the right word. The falling in love, the marrying, the brawling, the killing, the plotting, the judgments and decrees, the suicides—all, all too precipitate. Paris says that Juliet is weeping for her cousin's death 'immoderately' (IV, i, 6). In his decent ignorance, he cannot realize that she is weeping for everything, including Juliet—but the word is tellingly apposite. Immoderation rules. Precipitate immoderation.

In this connection, Juliet's invocation to Phoebus *and Phaeton,* as she waits for Romeo on her bridal night, is understandable, apt—and ominous.

Gallop apace, you fiery-footed steeds,
Towards Phoebus' lodging! Such a wagoner
As Phaeton would whip you to the west
And bring in cloudy night immediately.
Spread thy close curtain, love-performing night,
That runaways' eyes may wink, and Romeo
Leap to these arms untalked of and unseen.

(III, ii, 1–7)

She wants the sun to sink and night to fall as quickly as possible—of course she does. And, as we have seen Romeo 'leap' the orchard wall, we may be confident that he will manage this longed-for leap as well. But 'such a wagoner/As Phaeton' (son of Phoebus) was too reckless and inexperienced; when he took over the horses of the sun, he could not control them—they ran unstoppably wild, and he fell, fatally, to earth. (It amuses me slightly that 'runaway's'—wherever the apostrophe belongs—remains a 'famous crux'. This is runaway speech in a runaway play full of runaways—it is a perfect word.) As Jonathan Bate, tracing the Ovidian reference, says—'to put Phaeton in charge is to precipitate catastrophe'. The Phaeton-Romeo connection (or echo) is clinched when, at the end, the Prince, announcing the 'glooming peace' which follows the death of the too-dazzling lovers, predicts that, on this day—'The sun for sorrow will not show his head' (V, iii, 306). This is a direct allusion to Golding's translation of Ovid, in which, after the fall of Phaeton, 'A day did pass without the Sunne.' Phaeton was another quick bright thing that came to confusion. The play is marked by sudden-ness—explosive outbursts of eruptive energies. Violent fighting in the street; urgent passion in the orchard. When Romeo doesn't need a sword, he needs a ladder, or a crowbar. It's all difficult—but, with sufficient determined energy, doable. Penetrating an enemy, a new wife, a tomb—Romeo's youthful vigour is up to it all.

Shakespeare's play starts with lead and ends in gold: in between it is mainly silver, silvery, and iron (daggers are 'iron', while there are 'silver sounds', silver among the musicians, silver-tipped trees at night, and a prevalent silver moonlight). I have no doubt that Shakespeare was alluding to the classical idea of the four Ages of Mankind—as outlined in the first book of Ovid's *Metamorphoses,* for example—with the brass age here elided. But, this being Shakespeare, the Ages are here reversed—so that we are presented with, not the downward declensions of history, but the soaring ascensions of poetry. Romeo is all lead to start with, pure inertia. No dancing for him:

> I have a soul of lead
> So stakes me to the ground I cannot move.
> . . .
> I cannot bound a pitch above dull woe.
> Under love's heavy burden do I sink.
>   (I, iv, 15–16, 21–2)

We will see him 'bounding' soon enough ('He ran this way and leapt this orchard wall', II, i, 5), but he has as yet to be sparked into lightness and leaping, soaring motion. In this, unawakened youth is like age. Juliet, thinking the Nurse much too slow, complains:

> But old folks, many feign as they were dead—
> Unwieldy, slow, heavy and pale as lead.
>   (II, v, 16–17)

It is, of course, primarily Juliet herself who will 'feign as she were dead'— the play is a tissue of unconscious and conscious premonitions, but here, her 'warm youthful blood . . . would be as swift in motion as a ball' (II, v, 13–14).

Romeo, aroused, is now the reverse of leaden. 'O, let us hence! I stand on sudden haste', he says impatiently to the Friar; who replies, with a sagacity which no longer has any purchase—'Wisely and slow. They stumble that run fast' (II, iii, 93–4). Nothing now can stop Romeo in his running—and his stumbling. Contemplating the moment of his imminent marriage, Romeo declares:

> But come what sorrow can,
> It cannot countervail the exchange of joy
> That one short minute gives me in her sight.
>   (II, vi, 3–5)

Another omen—the joy *will* be 'countervailed' by exactly 'one short minute' in the tomb. Here, it is the Friar who gives voice to apprehensions:

> These violent delights have violent ends
> And in their triumph die, like fire and powder,
> Which, as they kiss, consume. The sweetest honey
> Is loathsome in his own deliciousness
> And in the taste confounds the appetite.
> Therefore love moderately: long love doth so;
> Too swift arrives as tardy as too slow.
>
> (II, vi, 9–15)

In many ways, these lines sum up the play. Apart from the honey turning loathsome in its own deliciousness—that belongs squarely in *Troilus and Cressida,* another of the only three plays entitled by a couple's names (the third is *Antony and Cleopatra*—of which, more in due course). Romeo and Juliet's love is too quick and short to have time to curdle. It *is* violent and explosive, and they kiss and 'consume'—and are consumed—at the same moment. In their 'triumph'—i.e. the flash-point of an explosion—they do, indeed, die. But also—they die in triumph, in the wider sense of the word; or, their death *is* their triumph. A triumph was probably originally a *thriambos,* a hymn to Bacchus; and, as Juliet and then Romeo toast each other in festal poison prior to death, that will do nicely for the occasion. 'Moderation' is, of course, out of the question; and 'long love' never on the cards. And they *are* too swift in their tardiness (or too tardy in their swiftness), arriving, and acting, somehow both too late and too soon. (When old Capulet says 'it is so very late / That we may call it early by and by', III, iv, 34–5, he is in the spirit of the play—it is, invariably, both very late, and yet too early.) The precipitately planned marriage of Paris to Juliet 'should be slowed', as the Friar well knows (IV, i, 16). But some things won't be 'slowed' when they should be, just as other things refuse to be accelerated when they need to be. Explaining his failure to deliver the crucial letter to Romeo, Friar John describes how he was forcibly detained in a house of 'infectious pestilence . . . So that my speed to Mantua there was stayed' (V, ii, 10, 12). Things are too fast, or, more rarely, too slow. Nothing seems to go at the right speed. The 'speed' of the young lovers is only 'stayed' in, and by, death. Thereafter, they are transformed into 'pure gold' statues. Permanently slowed—definitively stayed. Art forever.

They are, in a sense, simply too young—love hits them prematurely, as we may say (hence, I think the deliberate juvenalization of Juliet to fourteen; an age at which, even in those days and among high-born families, it was, apparently, very rare for a girl to marry). As John Lawlor puts it—'in both we meet youth on the hither side of experience'. But, if it finds them pre—or im-mature, they are something very different by the end. In a sense (which we will have to explore), they have moved beyond considerations of maturity—as it feels, out of time altogether. But, in the world of the play, in hot, feasting, feuding, fighting, joking, courting, drudging, playing, Verona—where people are 'soon moody to be moved' (III, i, 14)—time is, as it were, everywhere. Characters think back over the years—wasn't that wedding twenty-five years ago, come Pentecost? The Nurse can tell Juliet's age 'to the hour'. In this play, you are never far from a clock, or a time check. Romeo's first words are 'Is the day so young?' 'But new struck nine', answers Benvolio (I, i, 163). Thereafter, Shakespeare 'sustains the emphasis on the continuous counterpoint between extended periods and an exactly stipulated day, hour, moment' in Brian Gibbons' felicitous formulation.

There is recurrent emphasis on the time of dawn—Romeo is described as walking in a sycamore grove at dawn, before we see him: he leaves the Capulet orchard at dawn: he leaves Juliet at dawn after their wedding night: Juliet's supposedly 'dead' body is found at dawn by the Nurse: and it is dawn when the Prince surveys the dead bodies and predicts that the sun will not rise that day. Dawn is, or should be, usually accompanied by a sense of new beginnings, a refreshing and renewing light dispelling the last of the darkness. But in this play, it is more characteristically associated with separation, departure and death. But, for Romeo and Juliet, might death not *be* a new kind of dawn? I think we should feel something like that. Certainly, everyday time is everywhere against them, down to that last single minute when Romeo, ever precipitate, kills himself far too quickly, just too soon. In the inner universe of love they have created for themselves, it is as if they, somehow, recede from the world's time into a private, ecstatic, timelessness. But these worlds collide, and clock time, calendar time, will not let them be. In other plays, time, 'ripe time', is often a restorative, regenerative force, helping to expose evil, bring justice, effect reconciliation. But not in this play. The ever-resourceful, benevolently plotting Friar, still thinks, or hopes, that he is living in a 'comic' world in which everything is still possible. So, after the sentence of exile has been passed, he packs Romeo off to Mantua:

> Where thou shall live till we can find a time
> To blaze your marriage, reconcile your friends,

> Beg pardon of the Prince, and call thee back
> With twenty hundred thousand times more joy
> Than thou went'st forth in lamentation.
>
> (III, iii, 150–54)

In a comedy, this is just what would happen, one way or another. But it is too late, or too early—or too *something*—for that here. The Friar is always optimistic that he will 'find a time'—time for this, for that, for the other. But, here, there is no time to be found; and, as we say, no time to be lost, either. For Romeo and Juliet, there is just no time.

The Friar uses 'blaze' to mean 'make public'; but he could hardly have fastened on a more appropriate verb (it comes from older words meaning both 'blow' *and* 'shine'). The hot afternoon sun blazes down on the square in Verona, heating 'mad blood' to fighting point. In the great houses at night, the torches and fires are blazing as the feasting and dancing go forward. 'More torches here . . . More light, more light!' is the host's cry. Romeo is a torch-bearer first and last—self-effacingly at the ball; brave and determined at the tomb. If his marriage to Juliet is as short as a flash of lightning, it is, for its duration, an incandescent blaze. Fires go out, or are quenched, as surely as lightning disappears. 'Come, we burn daylight . . . We waste our lights in vain, like lights by day' (I, iv, 43–5), says Mercutio, impatient to get to the ball. There *is* something strange about, say, a candle flame in bright sunshine, and 'burning daylight' is a graphic way of evoking that rather curious light-devouring-light phenomenon. The question becomes—is the 'blaze' ignited by Romeo and Juliet's love a wasted light? Or something else? 'What light through yonder window breaks?' (II, ii, 1) becomes, by the end, an almost metaphysical question.

But there is another source of light in the play, which is the reverse of transient—the stars. Before his feast, Capulet in a gracious invitation, declares:

> At my poor house look to behold this night
> Earth-treading stars that make dark heaven light.
>
> (I, ii, 24–5)

There are a number of references to 'earth'. Juliet is, for her father, 'the hopeful lady of my earth' (I, ii, 15), while Romeo addresses himself as 'dull earth' before he leaps the orchard wall, and starts to 'soar'. Beautiful young ladies are 'earth-treading stars'—so much is gallantry, a courteous conceit. But, in a much more powerful and dramatic way, Romeo and Juliet begin to emerge as 'earth-treading stars' in earnest, and it is the earth that they would be glad to leave behind, below. This is adumbrated by Romeo's reaction to his first sight of Juliet:

> O, she doth teach the torches to burn bright!
> It seems she hangs upon the cheek of night
> As a rich jewel in an Ethiop's ear—
> Beauty too rich for use, for earth too dear!
>   (I, v, 46–9)

Not, finally, too expensive for the earth to purchase, since the tomb claims her at the end. But, as M. Mahood suggests, she *will* prove 'too rare a creature for mortal life'. Romeo, who at the start is a young posing, Petrarchan 'lover' who could have walked out of *Love's Labor's Lost,* is still indulging himself in self-congratulatory conceits—hence the 'Ethiop's ear' business. But, once inflamed, he soon 'blazes' into authentic, coruscating poetry. Juliet at the window, not only serves to 'kill the envious moon' (the planet of periodicity and cyclical time), but outshines the stars as well:

> Two of the fairest stars in all the heaven,
> Having some business, do entreat her eyes
> To twinkle in their spheres till they return.
> What if her eyes were there, they in her head?
> The brightness of her cheek would shame those stars
> As daylight doth a lamp [that phenomenon again!];
>   her eyes in heaven
> Would through the airy region stream so bright
> That birds would sing and think it were not night.
>   (II, ii, 15–22)

Reciprocally, Juliet on her wedding night, addresses the darkness:

> Come, gentle night; come, loving, black-browed night;
> Give me my Romeo; and, when I shall die,
> Take him and cut him out in little stars,
> And he will make the face of heaven so fine

> That all the world will be in love with night
> And pay no worship to the garish sun.
>
> (III, ii, 20–25)

As Professor Mahood very accurately puts it, Romeo and Juliet 'stellify each other'. And the reminder of how recently Juliet must have been cutting out stars in some child's nursery game, is not only exquisite. It reminds us that she has been, precipitately, launched into the seas of adult passion, with only a little girl's experience to draw on.

When he enters the tomb where Juliet is lying, sleeping-thought-dead, Romeo transforms this 'bed of death' into a version of a strange celebration. He denies that he is in a 'triumphant grave':

> A grave? O, no, a lanthorn [lantern], slaught'red youth,
> For here lies Juliet, and her beauty makes
> This vault a feasting presence full of light.
> Death, lie thou there, by a dead man interred.
>
> (V, iii, 84–7)

He is laying down the corpse of the unfortunate Paris whom he has killed, and makes it into a burying of Death itself, turning the 'vault' into a 'feasting presence full of light'. This is the 'lightning'—lightening—'before death'. In this strange festal mood, he raises the poison and toasts his Juliet—'Here's to my love!' (V, iii, 119), just as Juliet raised her drugged glass to him—'Romeo, Romeo, Romeo, I drink to thee' (IV, iii, 58). They make their deaths into their own, private banquet. In the outside, public world, all things that were 'ordained festival' have been turned to 'black funeral'. The would-be 'comic' world is truly dead—that, I think, is why Shakespeare kills off the blameless Paris. It means that *all* the young protagonists are dead by the end. There is no 'young affection' gaping to be the heir to 'old desire'—a whole generation has been wiped out, and generational renewal is, here, out of the question. At the end, the scene is peopled entirely by old (or not young) people, standing reconciled but hopeless in the gloom of a sunless dawn. But, in his private world of poetry, Romeo has turned everything that was 'black funeral' into his own form of 'ordained festival', 'celebrating' on, and in, his own terms. The 'comedy', albeit in a rare form, is consummated in the dazzling Juliet-light inside the tomb.

As he dies, Romeo cries out 'O true apothecary!/Thy drugs are quick' (V, iii, 119–20). 'Quick' is 'fast', but it is also 'life'—as in the biblical 'the quick and the dead'. So in one of the many puns in this play (M. Mahood pointed out that they are more prevalent here than in any other play), Romeo is saying, at once, that the drug works very quickly, and that it is life-giving. Similarly Juliet, kissing his dead but still warm lips, hopes to imbibe some 'poison' there 'to make me die with a restorative' (V, iii, 166). The poison that can also be a medicine is a very ancient paradox, and it is very apt for the purposes of the young lovers. In this play, we have the Friar, who is an expert on herbal potions, and an apothecary who specializes in poisons. Shakespeare has extended his treatment of these aspects of the story (and, unlike Brooke, he does *not* have the apothecary hanged at the end), and we might have a word about the role of drugs etc. in this play. In his long disquisition on the properties of herbs, the Friar foregrounds their doubleness, or root ambiguity if you will—'Within the infant rind of this weak flower/Poison hath residence and medicine power' (II, iii, 23–4). He tends to stress the beneficent side of nature:

> O, mickle is the powerful grace that lies
> In plants, herbs, stones, and their true qualities
> (II, iii, 15–16)

and he extrapolates from the opposite powers of different herbs, to the divided nature of man himself:

> Two such opposèd kings encamp them still
> In man as well as herbs—grace and rude will
> (II, iii, 27–8)

But things are not so separate, separable. The Friar is a healthy, benevolent man, and he tries to use his herbs for their 'powerful grace'; but, in the event, indirectly they help to destroy Juliet. By contrast, the Apothecary in his shop (the shop is Shakespeare's invention), looks like Death in a charnel house:

> Meager were his looks,
> Sharp misery had worn him to the bones;

And in his needy shop a tortoise hung,
An alligator stuffed, and other skins
Of ill-shaped fishes; and about his shelves
A beggarly account of empty boxes,
Green earthen pots, bladders, and musty seeds,
Remnants of packthread, and old cakes of roses
Were thinly scatterèd, to make up a show.
                    (V, i, 40–48)

—a wasteland, all sterility, used-up-ness, and desolation. But this is all 'a show'. He has, hidden, something supremely valuable, as far as Romeo is concerned—a pricelesss concoction which will cure all. Romeo pays for it in 'gold'—which, as money, is a 'worse poison to men's souls' (as monument, it will have another value entirely)—and goes away happy with the Apothecary's secret mixture which is now 'not poison' but 'cordial' (V, i, 80, 85)—or 'restorative', as Juliet will shortly call it. Nature's 'grace' comes in strange forms, and from strange places. And works in unpredictable ways —as these herbalist-artists show.

Dr Johnson said of Addison's prose that 'it never blazes into unexpected splendour'. Addison's prose is, in this context, neither here nor there. But we will hardly find a happier phrase than 'blazing into splendour' for what happens to Romeo and Juliet's love—and their poetry. In this, the play is closest in spirit and concluding feeling, to *Antony and Cleopatra* (the other couple-titled play that *is* relevant). There are interesting structural similarities. The feuding Montagues and Capulets may be matched, on a cosmic scale, by the oppugnant Rome and Egypt. In both cases, the putative death of the woman (Juliet by drugs, Cleopatra by false report), leads to the suicide of the man, followed by the real suicides of the women. The lovers in the first play are, at the outset, innocent children; while the later lovers are relatively old, and sexually experienced—we are confronted with springtime, and then autumnal, love. All the lovers die, but in both cases we are made to feel that, in some way, the power of love has 'triumphed' over death. By the end, it is as 'paltry' to be a Montague or a Capulet as it is to be Caesar. In both cases, the poetry of the lovers achieves an *incandescent* quality (= glowing with both heat and brightness), unequalled, I feel, elsewhere in Shakespeare. And the poetry of both plays is marked by the same two crucial qualities. Here is Juliet, expressing her love:

> My bounty is as boundless as the sea,
>
> My love as deep: the more I give to thee,
>
> The more I have, for both are infinite.
>
> (II, ii, 133–5)

'Bounty' is the special mark of Antony, and 'boundlessness' is what distinguishes Antony and Cleopatra's love from severely bounded, banded, bonded, Rome. Cleopatra is known for her 'infinite variety': indeed, all four lovers have their eyes on the 'infinite'. And—as a result—their poetry really does 'blaze into unexpected splendour'.

Other forms of 'love' are intimated early in the play—empty Petrarchan idolatry, and coarse, bawdy cynicism, are first on the scene. Some of the sexual joking is very broad, particularly that coming from Mercutio. One of his lines might have a claim to be the bawdiest in Shakespeare. He says to Romeo that he wishes that Rosaline—Romeo's earlier Petrarchan 'love' object—was 'an open *et cetera,* thou a pop'rin pear' (II, i, 38). That '*et cetera*' was a subsequent delicacy, and the original line was almost certainly 'an open-arse and thou a poperin pear'—the replaced term being a dialect term for a medlar, a fruit often used to refer to female genitalia. In this form, the line could hardly be less unambiguous. But all this encircling vulgarity has an important dramatic role. Just as Romeo will quickly free himself from his residual Petrarchanism, so he must soar above this encroaching obscenity. He will have to find another language altogether. And he does.

The Friar tells Romeo that 'Thy love did read by rote, that could not spell' (II, iii, 88). And when he first kisses Juliet, she says 'You kiss by th' book' (I, v, 112). (The entirely conventional Paris is actually described as a book by Juliet's mother—at length: see I, iii, 80–94). The implication is clear: Romeo's love with Juliet will move beyond all the prescribed, prescripted forms. It will be something new. In one of his first speeches, concerning love and hate, Romeo indulges in some rather book-ish, modish, oxymorons:

> O heavy lightness, serious vanity,
>
> Misshapen chaos of well-seeming forms,
>
> Feather of lead, bright smoke, cold fire, sick health
>
> (I, i, 181–3)

and so on—clever young man! But, in his love, he will discover and live through, live out, *die* out, such seemingly impossible merged opposites. He will meet his end drinking poison as a cordial. And loving will become indistinguishable from, identical with, dying.

Their love is, indeed, from the start 'death-marked'—marked by, and marked (heading) *for* (towards) death. After their first anonymous encounter at the ball, Juliet asks the Nurse who the young man was.

> Go ask his name.—If he is marrièd,
> My grave is like to be my wedding bed.
>> (I, v, 136–7)

And indeed, the one will follow so quickly upon the other as almost to merge with it (because, precisely, of his *name*). There is a lot of play with the idea of Death as bridegroom. When she hears that Romeo has been banished, Juliet says to the Nurse—'I'll to my wedding bed;/And death, not Romeo, take my maidenhead!' (III, ii, 136–7). When told she must marry Paris, Juliet asks her mother, instead, to 'make the bridal bed/In that dim monument where Tybalt lies' (III, v, 202–3)—that, too, shall come to pass. (Later, while Capulet is preparing the guest-list for the wedding of his daughter and Paris, and the cooks are busy with preparations in the kitchens, Juliet is upstairs fantasizing the nightmare of waking up in the tomb 'Where bloody Tybalt, yet but green in earth,/Lies fest'ring in his shroud', IV, iv, 42–3—another lived-out oxymoron.) With desperate ambiguity, Juliet, on hearing of Tybalt's death, vows to her mother:

> Indeed I never shall be satisfied
> With Romeo till I behold him—dead—

which seems clear enough; but she continues

> Is my poor heart . . .
>> (III, v, 94–6)

which is another kind of statement altogether. (Impossibly enough, though, *both* lovers will have the experience of beholding the loved one 'dead'. Juliet's vow will be kept for her.) On hearing of Juliet's 'death', her father explicitly says to Paris:

> O son, the night before thy wedding day
> Hath Death lain with thy wife. There she lies,
> Flower as she was, deflowerèd by him.
> (IV, v, 35–8)

Not true yet. But all in due course—and very soon. 'Beholding' Juliet's 'corpse', Romeo exclaims:

> Why art thou yet so fair? Shall I believe
> That unsubstantial Death is amorous,
> And that the lean abhorrèd monster keeps
> Thee here in dark to be his paramour?
> (V, iii, 102–5)

Death as 'amorous paramour', as *Romeo,* is almost literally enacted within a few minutes, when Juliet, beholding Romeo's corpse, says:

> . . . I'll be brief. O happy dagger! [*Snatches Romeo's dagger.*]
> This is thy sheath; there rust, and let me die.
> [*She stabs herself and falls.*]
> (V, iii, 169–70)

Since 'die' was also used for sexual orgasm, the conflation could hardly be more complete. This is not to suggest that the young lovers have a 'death wish'. This is absolutely not Wagner. The feeling, rather, is that such a 'blaze' *can* only lead quickly to confusion, to extinction. 'Lightning' is indeed the word.

For the Montagues and Capulets, and people like them, marriage is a family business. According to their family, suitors are suitable, or unsuitable, for their children. Here, of course, the family name is everything. Everybody is born into a family name; it is *ineluctable* (literally—cannot be struggled out from). And, of course, for entirely irrational but entirely inescapable reasons, Montagues are *not* 'suitable' for Capulets. This is the point of Juliet's famous lament; uttered, notice, when Romeo, standing below in darkness, is both there and not there, invisible though within earshot, an absent presence. As Juliet asks, when he speaks—'What *man* art thou . . . thus bescreened in night . . . ?' (my italics). In the penumbra of the moment, he is simply a generic 'man' without a social identity. Would that he could stay in that ontological pre-baptismal limbo! I want to examine Juliet's crucial speech, and before doing so I just want to point out the two 'o's in the name. This is Shakespeare's nomination—in Brooke, he is Rome*us*. He will do the same with *Othello,* and I have speculated elsewhere on the significance of this—'O' being, at once, a wordless sigh or cry of despair; the circle of perfection; the nought of nothingness. All this is very relevant to Othello, and I think it applies in the case of Romeo, too. So to Juliet's speech, which starts with a line containing nine 'o's!

> O Romeo, Romeo! Wherefore art thou Romeo?
> Deny thy father and refuse thy name;
> Or, if thou wilt not, be but sworn my love,
> And I'll no longer be a Capulet.
> . . .
> 'Tis but thy name that is my enemy.
> Thou art thyself, though not a Montague.
> What's Montague? It is nor hand, nor foot,
> Nor arm, nor face. O, be some other name
> Belonging to a man.
> What's in a name? That which we call a rose
> By any other word would smell as sweet.
> So Romeo would, were he not Romeo called,
> Retain that dear perfection which he owes
> Without that title. Romeo, doff thy name;
> And for thy name, which is no part of thee,
> Take all myself.
>   (II, ii, 33–6, 38–48)

(Strictly speaking, it is the name 'Montague' which is the 'enemy'—Romeo is a Christian name, not the family name. But I see no point in pursuing this. He is Romeo-the-known-Montague, and it is precisely the individual-inextricable-from-the-family that is being focused on.) Juliet goes to the very heart of the matter. Deny, refuse, doff—father, name, title. But it cannot be done.

Of course the *name* is *not* the *man,* nor is it like a physical *part* of the man. But it is an inseparable, constitutive part of what Henry James calls 'the impress which constitutes an identity'. Once born, a man cannot elude what Jacques Derrida calls 'the law of the name'.* Romeo simply cannot *be* Romeo without the name 'Romeo'. It is *not* the same for a rose. 'Rose', as Juliet correctly differentiates (even if the proverbial version does not) is a 'word' and *not* a 'name'; and, yes, you could call it—what? a weed?—and it *would* smell as sweet. But the analogy does not hold when it comes to the human, familial, social realm. Wherefore is he Romeo? By virtue of having been born of whom, when, and where, he was. Truly speaking, a man's 'name' never can be denied or refused; it is not a hat to be doffed, nor, indeed, a hand to be cut off (this, whatever superficial substitutes are allowed, or 'aliases' had recourse to). Romeo would like to do it, of course:

> I take thee at thy word.
> Call me but love, and I'll be new baptized;
> Henceforth I never will be Romeo.
> (II, ii, 49–51)

There sometimes *are* 'new baptisms' in comedies of renewal and regeneration; but here, it is not an available option. Romeo would even like to get violent with his own name. What 'man' is he?

> By a name
> I know not how to tell thee who I am.
> My name, dear saint, is hateful to myself
> Because it is an enemy to thee.
> Had I it written, I would tear the word.
> (II, ii, 54–7)

---

* I know that too much Derrida is the sort of thing that makes the British think twice about taking their holidays in France, but he has a remarkable meditation on the balcony scene, translated as 'Aphorism Countertime', which may be found in *Acts of Literature* (1992).

Not possible, either. Names are not detachable and eradicable; but, rather, somehow deeply implanted, at once everywhere and nowhere within us. When, later, Romeo hears how Juliet has fallen down, weeping and calling his name, he would like to be even more violent:

> As if that name,
> Shot from the deadly level of a gun,
> Did murder her; as that name's cursèd hand
> Murdered her kinsman. O, tell me, friar, tell me,
> In what vile part of this anatomy
> Doth my name lodge? Tell me, that I may sack
> The hateful mansion.
>
> (III, iii, 102–8)

and he actually tries to stab himself. But, of course, something as non-corporeal, immaterial, as a name is quite beyond any amputation. You can't kill *that* 'lodger' without killing the mansion. On the other hand, in the social arena, a name can be as lethal as a gun. And that is the point. The young lovers would somehow like to get out (back? up? beyond?), to a non-social realm where names no longer (or don't yet) matter, or even obtain. But, as they quickly discover, the only way there is by killing the mansion. Which, shortly, they do. Among other things, this play may be seen as exploring the tragedy latent in the naming process itself.

When Romeo snaps out of his callow 'driveling love' for Rosaline, Mercutio congratulates him.

> Now art thou sociable, now art thou Romeo; now art thou what thou art,
> by art as well as by nature.
>
> (II, iv, 93–5)

He means, simply enough, that Romeo is now 'sociable' because, in addition to groaning away on the reproductive side of his being, as nature prompts, he is also, now, composed, clever, and witty, as culture promotes. As it happens, Romeo would dearly like to be de-socialized altogether, as we have seen. But Mercutio's words have a greater pregnancy for the play—for Shakespeare—as a whole. Art, art, art, art, *by art,* 'as well as by nature'—in the last great comic-romances, Shakespeare will show art and nature working together so that characters can more truly become what they really are, or 'art'. Here, we may say that Romeo is rendered most truly and fully *Romeo* by, in, and through Shakespeare's transforming and perpetuating art, in addition to whatever, by nature, he 'sociably' was in Verona. Of course, from the point of view of the inhabitants of Verona, left stunned and bereft in the gloomy after-vacancy which follows the deaths of the young lovers, it is all unmitigated tragedy. Earth-bound critics may duly, dutifully join them there. But Verona is just exactly where Romeo and Juliet no longer wanted to be, and they have made a 'triumphant' and lightning/enlightening escape. From the stellar perspective, it *is* a form of 'comedy'.

 A MIDSUMMER NIGHT'S DREAM (1595)

> Through the house give *glimmering* light,
> By the dead and drowsy fire
>   (V, i, 393–4)

> These things seem small and *undistinguishable,*
> Like far-off mountains turned into clouds.
>   (IV, i, 190–91)

The two words which I have italicized occur more than once in *A Midsummer Night's Dream*—and *in no other play by Shakespeare*. I want them to, as it were, hover over the following discussion.

When Romeo mentions to Mercutio 'I dreamt a dream tonight', his sceptical, down-to-earth friend is dismissive—'dreamers often lie'. Romeo prefers to keep a more open mind about the possible veracity of dreams—'In bed asleep, while [= sometimes] they do dream things true.' This sets Mercutio careering off on what is certainly the most surprising speech of the play.

> O, then I see Queen Mab hath been with you.
> She is the fairies' midwife, and she comes
> In shape no bigger than an agate stone
> On the forefinger of an alderman,

Drawn with a team of little atomies
Over men's noses as they lie asleep;
Her wagon spokes made of long spinners' legs,
The cover, of the wings of grasshoppers;
Her traces, of the smallest spider web;
Her collars, of the moonshine's wat'ry beams;
Her whip, of cricket's bone; the lash of film;
Her wagoner, a small gray-coated gnat,

. . .

Her chariot is an empty hazelnut,
Made by the joiner squirrel or old grub,
Time out o' mind the fairies' coachmakers.
And in this state she gallops night by night
Through lovers' brains, and then they dream of love . . .

(*Romeo and Juliet,* I, iv, 49–71)

and so on for another twenty-plus lines, all on the magical, and often mischievous, effects of Queen Mab and her entourage on human sleepers. Romeo cannot make head or tail of what he is saying—'Thou talk'st of nothing'; and Mercutio, dismissive once more, agrees—'True, I talk of dreams',
as though he has made his point (I, v, 95–6). Romeo's bewilderment is entirely understandable. 'Mab' is Cymric (or Welsh) for 'small child', and
Mercutio's 'little atomies', in their insect tiny-ness, their filminess, their
domiciliation in the gossamer of spider webs and the 'watery beams' of
moonshine, are undoubtedly British, primarily Celtic, fairies. They certainly have no place in Renaissance Verona. But what, then, are they—what
is an English wood—doing, in *A Midsummer Night's Dream,* just outside
ancient Athens?

The simplest, most general answer would be to suggest that Shakespeare
wants to effect an accommodation, an assimilation of the ancient world of
pagan, classical legend into the local, domestic world of folklore and popular, vernacular superstition (combining an extensive literary heritage with
age-old English customs)—thus, perhaps, forging a new mythology, at least
for the occasion (which was probably a noble wedding in a great house).
Certainly, the occasion—the wedding(s) towards the consummation of
which ('Lovers, to bed') the play moves—is more important than the plot,
which is rudimentary, or, we might more appropriately say, as light as gos-

samer, as transparent as film, as solid as moonbeam. C. L. Barber is at his
festive best on this play, and he shows how Shakespeare 'in developing a
May game at length to express the will in nature that is consummated in
marriage, brings out underlying magical meanings of the ritual'. The May
game—the bringing in of summer—traditionally involved the whole community, and moved from the town, out to the woods or grove, and back
again (as this play moves from palace to forest and back to palace). During
these May games, the young men and maids 'ran gadding over night to the
woods . . . where they spend the whole night in pleasant pastimes', said Puritan Stubbes (as happens in the play, even if the pastimes are not unequivocally 'pleasant'). They might be presided over by a May king (Satan, as far
as Stubbes was concerned), and there was also a Summer Lady, celebrating
the most fertile time of the year. These popular games could be worked up
into more sophisticated pageants to be presented at aristocratic entertainments. Midsummer Night itself was thought to be a magic time when spirits might be abroad, and young minds could be touched with madness
('midsummer madness', as Olivia expressly calls it in *Twelfth Night*). Maying and Midsummer could be easily conflated since, as Barber shows, people went Maying at various times. 'This Maying can be thought of as happening on a midsummer night, even on Midsummer Eve itself, so that its
accidents are complicated by the delusions of a magic time . . . The Maying
is completed when Oberon and Titania with their trains come into the great
chamber to bring the blessings of fertility. They are at once common and
special, a May king and queen making their good luck visit to the manor
house, and a pair of country gods, half-English and half-Ovid, come to
bring their powers in tribute to great lords and ladies.'

Ovid. Jonathan Bate calls this play 'Shakespeare's most luminous *imitatio*
of Ovid . . . a displaced dramatization of Ovid'. Ovid, and the world of
Metamorphoses, are everywhere in this play: in the gods, the characters, the
animals; in the flowers and the woods; in the light and the water; in the
turmoils of love, the experience of transformation, the unavoidability of
change; in the language, the allusions, the symbols; in the very air they
all breathe—*everywhere*. But it is Ovid refracted through Shakespeare, and
so made new, made different, redirected or 'turned' (I'll come back to this
important word). The most engagingly obvious signal of alteration is given
by Helena, as, in a most unmaidenly way, she desperately pursues Demetrius:

Run when you will, the story shall be changed:
Apollo flies, and Daphne holds the chase
(II, i, 230–31)

The most obvious substantial incorporation of Ovid is, of course, the play put on by Bottom and the 'mechanicals'—'Pyramus and Thisby'. As performed by these worthy lads, it is Ovid with a difference indeed. A possible reason for this reversion of Ovid in Shakespeare's play, may become clear later. But here, I want to say something about the setting of the story in Ovid's own work. It is one of the stories told by Minyas' daughters while they are spinning. But this is not wholly innocent spinning. A feast day for the god Bacchus has been decreed, and all the Theban women have been ordered to leave their usual housework to celebrate rites in his honour. But Alcithoe, a daughter of Minyas, denies the divinity of Bacchus—'rash girl' —and she and her sisters blaspheme against the god: they 'remain indoors and mar the festival / By their untimely spinning . . .' Since a crucial figure in Shakespeare's play is a weaver, this is important: perhaps his 'weaving' will be more timely.

The girls tell three stories—including 'Pyramus and Thisbe'—to pass away the time while spinning, but their blasphemy is duly punished. This is what happens, in 'The Daughters of Minyas Transformed' (Book IV, 398–418), as translated by A. D. Melville:

The tale was done, but still the girls worked on,
Scorning the god, dishonouring his feast,
When suddenly the crash of unseen drums
Clamoured, and fifes and jingling brass
Resounded, and the air was sweet with scents
Of myrrh and saffron, and—beyond belief!—
The weaving all turned green, the hanging cloth
Grew leaves of ivy, part became a vine,
What had been threads formed tendrils, from the warp
Broad leaves unfurled, bunches of grapes were seen,
Matching the purple with their coloured sheen.
    And now the day was spent, the hour stole on
When one would doubt if it were light or dark,
Some lingering light at night's vague borderlands.

Suddenly the whole house began to shake,
The lamps flared up, and all the rooms were bright
With flashing crimson fires, and phantom forms
Of savage beasts of prey howled all around.

In Shakespeare's play, Theseus says to his Amazon bride-to-be:

Hippolyta, I wooed thee with my sword,
And won thy love, doing thee injuries;
But I will wed thee in another key,
With pomp, with triumph, and with reveling.
(I, i, 16–19)

The passage from Ovid is one of his great transformation scenes, and, like all his metamorphoses, it is injurious and marked by violence (like Theseus' early wooing). Shakespeare will give us this quintessential Ovid, but *in another key.* The clamouring drums and jingling brass will be quietened into lullabies and soft, sweet music; the purple grapes will be exchanged for a love-flower; the flaring lamps will be dimmed to 'glimmering'; and the savage beasts will be miniaturized into harmlessness (hedgehogs, spiders, beetles, worms, snails). The time of day will, however, remain the same—'at night's vague borderlands' (*dubiae confinia noctis*'), when things are 'undistinguishable'. As usual, where Ovid's transformations are invariably downward and lethal, Shakespeare's are, ultimately, upward and benign. His play concludes with blessings and purifications, while Ovid's tale ends in squeakings and hauntings. Minyas' daughters were transformed into *bats;* and it is perhaps worth noting that, while there are any number of small nocturnal animals in Shakespeare's wood, 'haunting . . . squeaking' bats (Ovid's words) have been banished, or 'turned forth'. As when Theseus gives the order:

Awake the pert and nimble spirit of mirth,
Turn melancholy forth to funerals
(I, i, 13–14)

That is the first 'turn' of the play. The first of many—as it turns out.
    (It is perhaps interesting to note that, in Ovid, 'The Daughters of Minyas'

follows immediately on from the concluding story of Book III, which is
'Pentheus and Bacchus'. Pentheus was another who defied the god, and he
is punished by being torn to pieces by the Theban women—including his
mother—thus being violently transformed into scattered scraps, or nothing
at all. This story also contains one of the other great transformation scenes
in Ovid, when the sailors who are supposed to be taking the child Bacchus
to Naxos, change course, thinking they can sell the pretty child into slavery.
The ship is becalmed, and is slowly thronged with ivy and vines, and pan-
thers and savage beasts—just like the house of Minyas. Golding's translation of this scene inspired Ezra Pound to one of his greatest passages of poetry, in Canto II—'void air taking pelt . . . lynx-purr amid sea', marvellous
line after marvellous line. What both stories address, and dramatize, is the
potentially terrifying—as well as the savagely beautiful—power there is in
the Dionysiac forces, and how foolish and dangerous it is to think they can
be ignored, defied, or denied. How, in the broadest sense, we deal with Dionysus, the Dionysiac in all its guises, seems to me to be a generative concern close to the centre of all art. Be that as it may, I am sure that Shakespeare is very much aware of these Dionysiac monitory fables hovering just
outside the edges of his own play, and I think that the implicit answer of
his play is that the wisest way to recognize and accommodate Dionysus–
Bacchus, is through, by, in—marriage.)

The main 'spinner' in Ovid's work is another god- or goddess-defying
girl—Arachne. Challenging Pallas to a tapestry-weaving competition, she
is duly transformed into a spider—an *animal* weaver—as punishment for
her presumption. The different tapestries the two women weave in the
competition are instructive. Pallas depicts the 'twelve great gods', impos-
ing punishing metamorphoses on hapless humans. By way of response,
Arachne depicts what Melville calls 'a hectic anthology of divine delin-
quency at the expense of deluded women' (some twenty of them)—gods
using metamorphosis to abuse mortals. Angry Pallas tears up the tapestry
(showing those 'crimes of heaven'), and turns Arachne into a spider; yet, at
the end, Arachne 'as a spider, still/Weaving her web, pursues her former
skill'. In her reduced form, she still keeps her web-spinning skills alive; in
this, she is a key image or embodiment of the human spider-artist. And, in
case you are wondering about the possible relevance of all this, I shall be
suggesting that we think of Bottom the weaver as a version of Arachne the
spinner—*in another key*. I quote now from Leonard Barkan's indispensable

book, *The Gods Made Flesh.* 'It requires no great leap of the imagination to see in Arachne's tapestry all the elements of Ovid's own poetic form in the *Metamorphoses,* which is, after all, a poem that eschews a clear narrative structure and rather creates a finely woven fabric of stories related via transformation.' This, as it happens, is just what Shakespeare does in *A Midsummer Night's Dream* (and, as Arachne to Ovid, so Bottom to Shakespeare—but more of that later).

A Midsummer Night's Dream is like *Love's Labor's Lost* in having no one particular primary source—it makes them unique among Shakespeare's plays. But whereas *Love's Labor's Lost* has virtually no sources at all—a hint here, an echo there—*A Midsummer Night's Dream* draws *quite clearly* on perhaps as many as a dozen different works from the far and near of previous literature. It is Shakespeare's contribution—his genius—to select, arrange, combine, fuse, sew seamlessly together; these elements, fragments, patches, strains, skeins; extracted, snipped, cut, siphoned, and unwound from other works. As the admirable Arden editor, Harold Brooks, says, 'Shakespeare *weaves* together material from a whole series of sources' (my italics). He is not alone among editors in using that metaphor, and I confess I find it striking that they seem not provoked to pursue the possibly extrapertinent implications it might have in connection with a play in which one of the main players—take him however you will—*is* a weaver.

A proper study of these multifarious sources would take half a book. Bullough, as usual, lays them out impeccably—I must briefly summarize (must—because an important part of the play is in the weaving). From Chaucer's *Knightes Tale* Shakespeare takes Theseus, the triumphant conqueror, happily married to Hippolyta (he also takes a pair of unhappy young lovers fighting in a wood). From Pluto's *Life of Theseus* he takes Theseus the law-giver and bringer of social order; but he deleted (almost entirely, though not quite) Theseus the notorious rapist and ravisher, and substituted for this a monogamous Theseus based on the parallel *Life of Romulus.* The fairies come, in part, from Lyly's *Endimion,* where they both pinch and kiss; and in part, of course, from the rural air he had breathed (and, possibly, Welsh lore he knew about). Puck looks back to a Cornish earth demon, 'pukka' or 'pixy'; and is identified by Shakespeare with Robin Goodfellow, who was something between a house-fairy and 'the national practical joker'. 'Titania' comes straight from bathing in a pool in Ovid, where it is another name for Diana ('Titania' does not appear in Golding's translation, a fact frequently adduced to show that Shakespeare read Ovid in the original). Oberon comes from a romance entitled *Huon of Bordeaux,* translated by Lord Berners before 1533. He is, as in Shakespeare, an Eastern fairy from the farthest steep of India. He is king of a wood and has 'marvelous' power over nature, though in the end 'all is but fantasie and enchauntments'. Oberon and Titania together owe something to the figures of Pluto and Proserpina in Chaucer's *Merchant's Tale,* where they sit in a garden and discuss the wayward sexual behaviour of the mortals they are watching. Shakespeare removes their divine detachment, and makes them pretty wayward themselves, but they are still fairy gods.

In this fairy-connection, a book by Reginald Scot entitled *The Discoverie of Witchcraft* (1584) should be mentioned. Scot ferociously attacks all belief in fairies, witches, and magic transformations in general. 'Whosoever beleeveth, that anie creature can be made or changed into better or woorsse, or transformed into anie other shape, or into anie other similitude, by anie other than by God hiself the creator of all things, without all doubt is an infidell, and woorsse than a pagan . . . heretofore Robin Goodfellow, and Hob gobblin were as terrible, and also as credible to the people, as hags and witches be now: and inn time to come, a witch will be as much derided and contemned, and as plainlie perceived, as the illusion and knaverie of Robin goodfellow.' But, as is often the case with would-be castigators and casters-out, he provides a great deal of fascinating information, with vivid examples, of just what he is seeking to deride and discredit—in this case, fairies, elves, imps, changelings, dwarfs, spirits, witches, and magical (demonic) transformations. The less censorious, and rurally derived, Shakespeare must have loved it. Curiously, Scot gives details of a trick for setting 'an asses head upon a mans shoulders'; but the 'translation' of Bottom certainly owes more to *The Golden Ass* of Apuleius, which had been translated by Aldington in 1566. His amorous adventures—while an ass—with a princess, prefigure Bottom's amazing experience with Titania (I think there is also an echo of Pasiphae and her beloved bull). Elsewhere, Brooks finds traces of Spenser's *Shepheardes Calender,* and an overlooked debt to Seneca, particularly his *Hippolytus* (the hunting scene; Phaedra's self-abasement in love—like Helena's; and the nurse's invocation to three-formed Hecate— who also presides in Shakespeare's play). And the 'entertainment' which concludes the play, when all the various strands have been deftly woven together, is Ovid's 'Pyramus and Thisbe'—in, of course, another key. We are, inevitably, back with Ovid.

One of the alternative entertainments offered by Philostrate to Theseus is

'The battle with the Centaurs, to be sung/By an Athenian eunuch to the
harp' (V, i, 44–5). 'We'll none of that' says Theseus quickly—and very understandably. Theseus took part in that battle which broke out at the marriage of Pirithous and Hippodame (Ovid, Book XII), and it must be the
most disastrous and violent wedding on record, as some three hundred particularly bloody lines describe. Theseus acquitted himself honourably, as
befits a hero; but it would hardly be an auspicious event to rehearse on *this*
wedding day, just while they are waiting to consummate their marriages.
(The figure of a eunuch would be no more auspicious on such an occasion!)
But we noticed that there was the sign of the Centaur displayed at the first
inn in Shakespeare's works, and, here again, the figure of the half-animal,
half-man (as opposed to the eunuch who is half-man, half nothing at all)
has a general, if oblique, relevance to this play as well. Specifically, it refers us back to Bottom who, but recently, was half-ass, half-man. But it
might remind us of another 'monstrous hybrid beast' in Ovid—the Minotaur (Book VIII). Minotaur, at the centre of his labyrinth or maze, was finally killed by Theseus, with the aid of Ariadne (whom he then abandoned,
but whom Bacchus subsequently comforted and 'stellified'!). Bottom, also
referred to as a 'monster', is somewhere at the centre of *this* play, which is
also a 'maze', full of 'amazed' people. The difference is that, here, Theseus
does no slaying; and Bottom, unmonstered, ends, in his own way, triumphant. Ovid in another key.

   In Ovid's account of the story of Pyramus and Thisbe, the lovers agree to
meet beneath a tree 'laden with snow-white fruit, a mulberry'. When Pyramus, thinking Thisbe has been devoured by a lion, fatally stabs himself, this
is what happens:

> And as he lay outstretched his blood leaped high,
> As when a pipe bursts where the lead is flawed
> And water through the narrow hissing hole
> Shoots forth long leaping jets that cut the air.
> The berries of the tree, spattered with blood,
> Assumed a sable hue; the blood-soaked roots
> Tinged with purple dye the hanging fruits.

And, as a result, 'the mulberry retains its purple hue'. Quince and company, perhaps knowing their limitations, wisely do not attempt to re-enact

this part of the story. But Shakespeare has a use for it, suitably changed, in *his* play. When Titania refuses to part with the changeling child, Oberon plans his revenge, and summons Puck for an errand. He recalls a magic moment involving mermaids, dolphins, civil seas, mad stars, and a maid's music:

> That very time I saw, but thou couldst not,
> Flying between the cold moon and the earth,
> Cupid all armed. [Puck couldn't see him, perhaps because he
> *was* Cupid—certainly Puck is as much Cupid as he is Robin
> Goodfellow.] A certain aim he took
> At a fair vestal thronèd by the west,
> And loosed his love shaft smartly from his bow,
> As it should pierce a hundred thousand hearts.
> But I might see young Cupid's fiery shaft
> Quenched in the chaste beams of the wat'ry moon,
> And the imperial vot'ress passèd on,
> In maiden meditation, fancy-free.
> Yet marked I where the bolt of Cupid fell.
> It fell upon a little western flower,
> Before milk-white, now purple with love's wound,
> And maidens call it love-in-idleness.
> Fetch me that flow'r; the herb I showed thee once:
> The juice of it on sleeping eyelids laid
> Will make or man or woman madly dote
> Upon the next live creature that it sees.
>   (II, i, 155–72)

This play is much concerned with 'doting' (more or less mad as the case may be—'dote' occurs more often than in any other play), to be seen against the background of the sane and steady love of the mature figures, Theseus and Hippolyta. The play ends with the marriages about to be consummated, when, presumably, the bed sheets which were 'before milk-white', like the flower, will soon also be 'purple with love's wound'. And the laying on sleeping eyes of this love juice, is seen to play a crucial, instrumental role in all the doting madness (interestingly, Shakespeare uses a variety of different verbs for the application of the juice to the eyes—from the religious 'anoint' and the artistic 'streak', to the more downright 'sink' and 'crush'). Puck is guilty of putting the love juice in the wrong eyes, but that is appropriate too, since Cupid is blind, and love (sudden overwhelming attraction) strikes randomly. That is the point to Shakespeare's 'metamorphosed' etiology. The white mulberry empurpled by the blood of Pyramus in Ovid, has become the white pansy hit by 'young Cupid's fiery shaft' which missed its intended virginal target. William Carroll makes the very nice point that the pansy thus becomes 'a deflowered flower'. He points to the wonderful aptness of the malapropism uttered by Bottom—Pyramus when, lamenting what he takes to be the death of Thisby, he says—'lion vile hath here deflow'red my dear' (V, i, 293—presumably he intends 'devoured'); for, as Carroll says, given the impending marriages, defloration is necessarily one of the play's main subjects, however understated or obliquely approached. Another lyric justification for having the love juice come from 'Cupid's *flower*'. It is worth noting that there is a flower which has the power to counter Cupid's, restoring the blind besotted to clear-eyed chastity. It is called 'Dian's bud' and this, too, is to hand for Oberon, king of the wood. As when he administers a curing restorative to Titania:

> Be as thou wast wont to be;
> See as thou wast wont to see.
> Dian's bud o'er Cupid's flower
> Hath such force and blessed power.
>   (IV, i, 74–7)

(We might recall the importance of good and bad herbs—medicine, poison, ambiguous 'restoratives'—in *Romeo and Juliet*.) These magically propertied flowers represent—figure forth—the uncomprehended force and untraceable power which causes love (we had perhaps better talk of desire and infatuation) to suddenly 'flare' up, and as suddenly to 'melt' away. When Demetrius is trying to explain the abrupt shifts and swerves in his passional attractions, he casts around:

> But, my good lord, I wot not by what power—
> But by some power it is . . .
>   (IV, i, 168–9)

—that is actually, by way of explanation, about as far as he—perhaps as any of us—will ever get.

The juice is applied to the eyes because that is where all the 'dotings' start; this kind of sudden infatuation appearing as caused by (or intimately related to) an impairment, a disorder, indeed a disease, of the eye. The involvement of the 'eye' in young love was prominent enough in *Love's Labor's Lost,* where the word occurred fifty-two times. But in this play it occurs fifty-six times (top score in Shakespeare's plays), and everything seems to come down to how we look, and how we see. Among the young courtly lovers, it is the men whose eyes malfunction as their affections go awry (as usual in Shakespeare, the young women hold firm); while among the fairies, it is Queen Titania whose seeing is so sorely and humiliatingly afflicted. (We are to infer that Theseus and Hippolyta are beyond such ocular madness and have achieved the Arnoldian vision, seeing life steadily and seeing it whole.) Helena effectively announces a major theme of the play in the first scene:

> Things base and vile, holding no quantity,
> Love can transpose to form and dignity.
> Love looks not with the eyes, but with the mind,
> And therefore is winged Cupid painted blind.
> Nor hath Love's mind of any judgment taste;
> Wings, and no eyes, figure unheedy haste:
> And therefore is Love said to be a child,
> Because in choice he is so oft beguiled.
>
> (I, i, 232–9)

It is the 'transposing' power of Cupidian love, along with its 'unheedy haste', which will be demonstrated in this play. We should note the number of verbs in the play carrying the prefix 'trans-': transpose, translate, transform, transfigure, and (perhaps most important), transport. For '**trans-**', the OED gives 'across, beyond, on or to the other side, into a different state or place'—which will do for now. When Oberon goes around near the end, setting things and people in their proper states and places, he applies his 'liquor' whose 'virtuous property' can make 'eyeballs roll with wonted sight' (III, ii, 369)—presumably, before the Cupidian glaze and slant came over them. Of Titania he says 'I will undo / This hateful imperfection of her eyes' (IV, i, 65–6), and promises:

> And then I will her charmèd eye release
> From monster's view, and all things shall be peace.
> (III, ii, 376–7)

As Puck says over the sleeping lovers, when their eyes have been duly corrected:

> And the country proverb known,
> That every man should take his own,
> In your waking will be shown.
>   Jack shall have Jill;
>   Nought shall go ill;
> That man shall have his mare again, and all shall be well.
> (III, ii, 457–63)

That is the conclusion towards which the play moves. Bemused eyes are 'released' from all deformities and 'monstrosities' of vision (or vision of 'monsters'); all shall go well, and all things shall be at peace; and, unlike the stalled inconclusiveness which ends the 'dashed' wooing games of *Love's Labor's Lost,* here there is the certainty that Jack *shall* have his Jill. In this sense, at least, *A Midsummer Night's Dream* does 'end like an old play'.

But not before we have witnessed the confusions and 'transpositions' precipitated by doting infatuations touched with midsummer madness. The effect on the discrete but converging worlds of the courtiers, the fairies, and the mechanicals, is rather as Theseus describes 'a tangled chain'—there is 'nothing impaired, but all disordered' (V, i, 126). The 'disordering' is not exclusively due to the operations of the love juice. The blocking, or deflecting power of the paternal prohibition (familiar in comedy since comedy began—it is the negative which provokes the play, driving young love to stratagems of circumvention), comes into operation immediately, and effectively sends all the young lovers away from the palace and into the fairy-haunted wood. Egeus, father of Hermia, bursts into the first scene 'full of vexation'. He has promised Hermia to Demetrius, and accuses Lysander of having 'bewitched' her and 'stol'n the impression of her fantasy' (I, i, 32). It is an arresting charge, implying that he has, with all sorts of tricks and magics, corrupted (dis-figured, trans-figured?) her 'fantasy'; and, as Frank Kermode noted, one way and another, 'the disorders of fantasy (imagination) are the main topic of the play'. Egeus continues:

> With cunning hast thou filched my daughter's heart,
> Turned her obedience, which is due to me,
> To stubborn harshness.
>   (I, i, 36–8)

He then proceeds to set a fair example of 'stubborn harshness' himself, by begging 'the ancient privilege of Athens' by which he can 'dispose' of his daughter as he wishes—which here means, her obedience, or her death 'according to our law'. Theseus, the responsible ruler, reluctantly backs him up, telling Hermia that she must obey her father:

> Or else the law of Athens yields you up—
> Which by no means we may extenuate—
> To death, or to a vow of single life.
>   (I, i, 119–21)

Near the end, when Egeus again cries 'I beg the law, the law', Theseus simply brushes him (and 'the law') aside—'Egeus, I will overbear your will' (IV, i, 182). As usual, the 'unextenuatable' inflexibilities of 'the law' in Act I have, by some other 'law' of comedy, mysteriously melted away by the end of play. We are, somehow, in a different place. Transported.

Egeus maintains that Lysander has worked on Hermia, and 'turned her obedience'. 'Turn'—comes from ancient words implying 'rotation' or 'deviation from a course'. If you just think of some of the compounds—turncoat, turnover (kind of tart, amount of business), turnstile, turn-up (on a garment, for the books, what a bad penny always does)—you can begin to get a sense of what an indispensable word it is concerning human doings and dealings and makings; and how wide-ranging are its ramifications and applications. And, of course, it is a simple word for 'metamorphosis'—when someone turns into someone, or something, else. It is such an unobtrusive, familiar word, that it can easily slip past unnoticed. And yet, this play 'turns' on it. There are, as I see it, three major deployments of the word, but when you start to look, you find that the play is full of turns and turnings. Hermia complains that love 'hath turned a heaven unto a hell' (I, i, 207), so she and Lysander resolve to 'from Athens turn away our eyes' (I, i, 218). Puck promises to pursue the frightened mechanicals through the woods, 'Like horse, hound, hog, bear, fire, at every turn' (III, i, 112). Dear, imperturbable, self-sufficient Bottom invariably has 'enough to serve mine own turn' (III, i, 152). To the drugged eyes of Demetrius, 'snow . . . turns to a crow' set next to the whiteness of Helena's hand (III, ii, 142); while poor Helena simply thinks they are all laughing at her 'when I turn my back' (III, ii, 238). Oberon (whose name may be related to that of Auberon, god of the red light of dawn, in old French) sometimes makes 'sport' with 'Morning's love' as the first beam of the sun plays on Neptune's domain, and 'Turns into yellow gold his salt green streams' (III, ii, 392—part of the everywhere ongoing alchemy of nature). When it comes to judgments—say, as between players—'A mote will turn the balance, which Pyramus, which Thisby, is the better' (V, i, 320). And, if things can turn, so they can re-turn —as when the sobered and clarified Demetrius says of his heart 'to Helen is it home returned' (III, ii, 172).

More notably, when Oberon realizes that Puck has put the love juice in the wrong eyes, he says:

> Of thy misprision must perforce ensue
> Some true love turned, and not a false turned true.
>
> (III, ii, 91–2)

The 'misprisions' of love itself, when true, turns inexplicably to false, and false turns magically to true, are a central and animating concern of the play. When the young lovers wake up out of their night's madness, and find themselves, like Oberon and Titania, 'new in amity' (IV, i, 90), they cannot, looking back, quite believe that it was all real. Even now, they don't know if they are truly awake, or still asleep. One imagines them rubbing their eyes.

> *Demetrius.* These things seem small and undistinguishable,
>   Like far-off mountains turned into clouds.

Helena. Methinks I see these things with parted eye,
    When everything seems double.

                    (IV, i, 190–93)

Mountains and clouds are both equally *real*—we can see them in the same
landscape. But, where mountains are the very image of the solid, the immovable, the adamantine, clouds are definitively non-substantial; of ever
drifting, shifting outline; self-dissipatingly vaporous—they seem like brief
compressions of air, as opposed to the great compactions of the earth. What
can 'turn' mountains into clouds? Distance? A trick of the eye? A poet's
metaphor? Any of these can effect the metamorphosis. You can see mountains; and then you can see them as clouds. The human eye is like that—it
can be 'parted' and 'see double'. Mountains–clouds: so, likewise, humans–
animals, humans–fairies, humans–legends, humans–gods. There is a state
of vision—it may only be brief—in which all these become 'undistinguishable'; in which the world, even at its heaviest, becomes nebulous, diaphanous, swimmingly dreamlike. In this play—which takes place in silvery,
watery moonlight, and glimmering starlight which turns dew to 'liquid
pearl', and in which things can merge and melt, dissolve and change—
Shakespeare brings about this state of vision in the spectators, who are kept,
at once, rapt and awake.

One last turn—apt enough phrase for a performing art. In a famous
speech at the start of the last Act, Theseus expresses his scepticism concerning the young lovers' 'strange' experiences during the midsummer night in
the forest. In the process, he generalizes his reservations about the activities
of the human imagination.

        I never may believe
    These antique fables, nor these fairy toys.
    Lovers and madmen have such seething brains,
    Such shaping fantasies, that apprehend
    More than cool reason ever comprehends.
    The lunatic, the lover and the poet
    Are of imagination all compact.
    One sees more devils than vast hell can hold,
    That is the madman. The lover, all as frantic,
    Sees Helen's beauty in a brow of Egypt.

> The poet's eye, in a fine frenzy rolling,
> Doth glance from heaven to earth, from earth to heaven;
> And as imagination bodies forth
> The forms of things unknown, the poet's pen
> *Turns them to shapes,* and gives to airy nothing
> A local habitation and a name.
>
> (V, i, 2–17, my italics)

Commentators have noted that the speech begins with Theseus saying, effectively—to start with, I don't believe in *me;* since of course *he* is pre-eminently a figure of 'antique fable', and a creation of that human imagination he goes on to deprecate and dismiss. Shakespeare is certainly having his fun here. But there is a serious issue. Shakespeare knew very well that the world of 'antique fable', or classical myth, was the Elizabethans' indispensable heritage—as it is ours. Christianity had, of course, intervened, and there were plenty of Christian apologists who were ready to dismiss all those 'antique fables' as childish nonsense or pagan iniquity—and a good deal more vehemently than Theseus. Shakespeare knew, of course, that when it came to products of the human imagination, questions of 'belief' were a good deal more complex and subtle than mere orthodoxy could comprehend. The poet may have the same sort of high-temperature imagination as the lunatic and the lover, but they simply 'see' (devils and beauties), whereas the poet intuits 'the forms of things unknown' and *then* 'turns them to shapes'. So *we* can see them, and share the vision. There is a hint here of the workman at his lathe; and, if we make *that* a metaphor, we can say that art is, indeed, just such a 'turning'. Another artist who clearly saw that art was a sort of 'turning' was Henry James. *The Turn of the Screw*—one of his most enigmatic works—is narrated, mainly, by a governess who is herself a (frustrated) lover, something of an (uncertified) lunatic, and (perhaps more than she knows) a poet, or creative artist. The word 'turn' features constantly in her narration, in all sorts of contexts; and, transcribing the moment when, to her mind, she first saw one of the figures haunting the house, she writes—'What arrested me on the spot . . . was the sense that my imagination had, in a flash, turned real.' She proceeds to turn the 'things unknown' to written shapes, which have driven critics to distraction ever since. But, the imagination 'turned real' is what all great art gives us, and, as Shakespeare clearly saw, we can 'believe' in these 'turnings' in a way quite differently from what is demanded by religion or science. For certainly, there are more things in heaven and earth than the 'cool reason' invoked by Theseus can ever fully 'comprehend'. And, in her response to Theseus, Hippolyta has the better of it.

> But all the story of the night told over,
> And all their minds transfigured so together,
> More witnesseth than fancy's images,
> And grows to something of great constancy;
> But, howsoever, strange and admirable.
>
> (V, i, 23–7)

'Constancy' is an important notion for Shakespeare (and the Elizabethans), and the question of whether there was, or could somehow be inculcated, any 'persistive constancy in men' (*Troilus and Cressida*), was one which, one way and another, he addressed throughout his plays (and, looking at the hapless oscillations of Lysander and Demetrius, not to mention sundry other males in Shakespeare, and the invariable 'constancy' of the women, the emphasis does have to be on *men*). Spenser's 'Mutabilitie Cantos' (at the end of *The Faerie Queene,* and certainly written in the same decade as Shakespeare's play, even though they did not appear until 1609), are written 'UNDER THE LEGEND OF CONSTANCIE', and they tell how the goddess Mutability (and *Change*) tries to lay claim to the whole realm of Nature, since every thing and every creature in it is 'tost, and *turned,* with continuall change' (my italics). *Nature* acknowledges the power of the claim, but has an answer:

> I well consider all that ye have sayd,
> And find that all things stedfastness doe hate
> And changed be: yet being rightly wayd
> They are not changed from their first estate;
> But by their change their being doe dilate:
> And *turning* to themselves at length againe,
> Doe worke their owne perfection so by fate:
> Then over them Change doth not rule and raigne;
> But they raigne over change, and doe their states maintaine.
>
> (Canto VII, 58, my italics)

That, we might say, is the hope or dream of the mutability-obsessed Elizabethans; that there would be a

> time when no more *Change* shall be,
> But stedfast rest of all things firmly stayd
> Upon the pillours of Eternity
>   (Canto VIII—'unperfite'!)

I am not suggesting that Hippolyta had anything so metaphysical in mind;
indeed, it is not very clear what she *does* mean by the 'something of great
constancy' which might grow from all the 'transfigurations' which have
made up 'the story of the night' (pregnant phrase). Perhaps a 'strange and
admirable' exemplary narrative of young love righted, which may have perennial relevance (and Shakespeare's play has proved to be 'something of
great constancy'). Or perhaps she is referring to the 'great constancy' which
is both symbolized and enacted in the marriages they have all just entered
into after all the confused wooing; (solemnized marriage vows are perhaps
the only earthly way of overcoming mutability and change in Shakespeare).
Whatever, she sees more value in the 'story' than the anti-imaginative Theseus.

The spectacle of an order (a 'constancy'?) coming out of a confusion, is
part of the larger frame and setting of the play. Since Oberon and Titania
are, in some sort, gods of the elements, it is not surprising that their quarrel is reflected in larger natural turbulences and disasters—contagious fogs,
overflowing rivers, drowned fields, rotting corn, starved flocks. Titania
evokes at length a veritable wasteland of nature gone wrong:

> The nine men's morris is filled up with mud;
> And the quaint *mazes* in the wanton green,
> For lack of tread, are *undistinguishable*.
> . . .
> The seasons alter: hoary-headed frosts
> Fall in the fresh lap of the crimson rose,
> And on old Hiems' thin and icy crown
> An odorous chaplet of sweet summer buds
> Is, as in mockery, set. The spring, the summer,
> The childing autumn, angry winter, change
> Their wonted liveries; and the *mazed* world,

By their increase, now knows not which is which.
And this same progeny of evil comes
From our debate, from our dissension;
We are their parents and original.

(II, i, 98–117, my italics)

It is the only time in the play when the word 'evil' is used. None of the active *agents*—gods, heroes, mortals, fairies—is 'evil' (though Egeus is, necessarily, a bit of a stick). Traditional fairies could be malign; but, as Oberon
expressly says, 'we are spirits of another sort'.

But Titania reminds us of the possibility of 'evil' in nature itself. She
graphically depicts a vision of chaos, inversion, and confusion, in which
things have become 'undistinguishable' (this is *bad* undistinguishability),
and there is no traceable way out of the 'maze', or labyrinth (remembering
the presence of Theseus, and ass-headed Bottom in the depths of the forest).
It is, indeed, a 'mazed world'. But, with the help of the magic in the story of
the night, the lovers find their way out, and 'dissension' gives way to 'amity'—dawn brings intimations of new harmonies. These are announced, or
evoked, by Theseus and Hippolyta, leading a hunting party into the forest.
Theseus first remarks on 'the music of my hounds' ('matched in mouth like
bells'—a beautiful image), and says to Hippolyta:

We will, fair Queen, up to the mountain's top,
And mark the musical confusion
Of hounds and echo in conjunction.

(IV, i, 112–14)

This reminds Hippolyta of a time she went hunting with Hercules and
Cadmus, and the famous 'hounds of Sparta':

Never did I hear
Such gallant chiding; for, besides the groves,
The skies, the fountains, every region near
Seemed all one mutual cry. I never heard
So musical a discord, such sweet thunder.

(IV, i, 117–21)

This signifies the achievement of a *concordia discors* on all levels. When discord starts to sound like music, and thunder yields a sweetness, (and salt sea

turns to fresh)—when the dogs start barking as sweetly as bells; you may be sure that what Walt Whitman called 'the primal sanities of earth' have begun to reassert themselves, and nature has mysteriously started putting itself to rights. It is a perfectly appropriate end to a comedy. But there is one more act, in which Quince and his men will put on *their* play.

Before that, Bottom has had *his* dream. Bottom is the only person in Shakespeare to undergo a 'literal' metamorphosis; not that he seems to notice any difference, apart from feeling 'marvellous hairy about the face'. He is also the only human in the play who 'literally' sees the fairies; though he talks to Peaseblossom, Cobweb, and Mustardseed as they 'do him courtesies', as easily as he does to Quince, Snug, and Francis Flute—even if he does find himself asking for 'a bottle of hay'. And, when it comes to acting, Bottom reveals himself to be an extreme 'literalist', albeit willing and eager to play every part. When the distractedly doting Titania swears how much she loves him, he seems not to be greatly surprised, though it can hardly be said to go to his head—human or asinine.

> Methinks, mistress, you should have little reason for that. And yet, to say
> the truth, reason and love keep little company together nowadays; the
> more the pity, that some honest neighbors will not make them friends.
>   (III, i, 143–7)

You will hardly find more wisdom in the wood than that.

His encounter with the inexplicably doting Titania must, perforce, be an amazing one, for all his imperturbability. Though, of course, we can hardly follow them when Titania gives the order to her fairies—'Tie up my lover's tongue, bring him silently' (III, i, 201)—and disappears with Bottom into the impenetrable silence of the darkened forest. In this connection, it is both instructive and amusing to see how critics have responded to the temptation to speculate on what happened next. Representing the 'no sex please' British school, Brooks, with honourable *pudeur,* was sure that nothing happened at all—dammit, a fellow wouldn't *deliberately* plan for his wife to go off and have sexual intercourse with someone else. Speaking from the 'a man's a man' American point of view, Carroll has no doubts: 'Titania is tired of Bottom's voice and wants him to perform'. In, boy. Looking with his darkened East European eye, Jan Kott can only imagine bestiality and nightmare—'the monstrous ass is being raped by the poetic Titania, while she still keeps chattering about flowers . . .' I suppose it depends where you are born. But this, more and less, prurient speculation seems to me most extraordinarily to miss the point. What 'happened' belongs, crucially and precisely, in the realm of what Henry James called 'the unspecified' (by implication, the unspecifiable). It is a gap, a silence, an unrecuperable missingness—a mystery. It is a vital blank which we never can fill in—and nor should we try. If anything, the preliminary intimations are more Platonic than sexual:

> And I will purge thy mortal grossness so,
> That thou shalt like an airy spirit go.
> (III, i, 161–2)

But, as to what *happened*—why, even Bottom cannot tell us that. As he makes clear in his quite amazing (and amazed) speech upon waking:

> I have had a most rare vision. I have had a dream, past the wit of man to say what dream it was. Man is but an ass, if he go about to expound this dream. Methought I was—there is no man can tell what. Methought I was—and methought I had—but man is but a patched fool if he will offer to say what methought I had. The eye of man hath not heard, the ear of man hath not seen, man's hand is not able to taste, his tongue to conceive, nor his heart to report, what my dream was. I will get Peter Quince to write a ballet of this dream. It shall be called 'Bottom's Dream,' because it hath no bottom; and I will sing it in the latter end of a play, before the Duke. Peradventure to make it the more gracious, I shall sing it at her death.
> (IV, i, 207–22)

He has been, of a truth, 'transported'. Long before Rimbaud, Bottom has clearly experienced a *'déréglement du sens'*. Though, as many commentators have noted, the relevant voice behind this comes from I Corinthians:

> But we speak the wisdom of God in a mystery, even the hidden wisdom, which God ordained before the world unto our glory: Which none of the princes of this world knew. . . . But as it is written, Eye hath not seen, nor

ear heard, neither have entered into the heart of man, the things which
God hath prepared for them that love him.

(2:7–9)

If Shakespeare can mutate Ovid, Bottom can scramble St Paul. But this is
not simply more fun and parody. Bottom has had a *vision*. In *The Golden
Ass,* Apuleius is finally reprieved from his ass's shape by Isis; he has a vision
of the goddess, and is initiated into her mysteries—which entails never
speaking about them. St Paul also had a visionary initiation into the mysteries of the very religion he had persecuted. Both these men were transformed after being vouchsafed an experience of divine love; and we may
assume that Bottom's vision is something comparable. It is certainly no ordinary dream; such as, we may say, the young lovers feel they have been
through. It is, rather, in Frank Kermode's words, '*oneiros* or *somnium*'; ambiguous, enigmatic, of high import'. Bottom is very distinctly *not* a 'prince
of the world'; that designation more properly fits Theseus who, as we have
seen, believes only in reason, and speaks disparagingly of all mysteries.
Bottom is more like a holy fool—perhaps only the lowest (a man–ass) and
the most literal, can see the highest and most sublime ('a most rare vision').
His ecstatic garbling of St Paul merely intimates that such a vision is beyond speaking of; he speaks, only to say he can't tell. ('Masters, I am to discourse wonders: but ask me not what; for if I tell you, I am not true Athenian', IV, ii, 29–30—'true Athenian' may be a quiet smile to Plato, who also
recognized and respected the ineffable.) This is one occasion for which
the over-used aphorism which concludes Wittgenstein's *Tractatus Logico-
Philosophicus* is absolutely pertinent: 'What we cannot speak about we must
pass over in silence.' Or we might like to recall that marvellous moment
in Dostoevsky's *The Brothers Karamazov,* when Dmitri wakes up in prison
and says—'Gentlemen, I have had a good dream . . .'

Bottom is a weaver, *and* an actor (= a 'patched fool') who feels sure he can
play every role (male, female, animal); just as Arachne would represent all
the Ovidian stories in her tapestry. In this, he is surely like Shakespeare
himself. Peter Quince is the carpenter/stage manager who tries to hammer
and nail the play into a structured shape; Snug, the joiner, does what he can
to join rather incompatible identities together; but it is Bottom who weaves
it all into a seamless fabric. (The Elizabethan theatre was closer to the
workshop than to the court.) Bottom is, indeed, a literalist; but, in being so,

he makes basic discoveries about the art, or 'devices', of theatrical representation. At the first rehearsal, Bottom runs over what he believes to be the problems of audience reaction. Pyramus commits suicide, and you can't have *that* on stage. But Bottom has a saving 'device': he will 'tell them that I Pyramus am not Pyramus, but Bottom the weaver' (III, i, 20–21). Just so: an actor both is and is not himself. Playing the lion is even trickier, since 'to bring in . . . a lion among ladies, is a most dreadful thing'. Bottom sees the way:

> Nay, you must name his name, and half his face must be seen through the lion's neck, and he himself must speak through, saying thus, or to the same defect—'Ladies'—or, 'Fair ladies—I would wish you'—or, 'I would request you'—or, 'I would entreat you—not to fear, not to tremble: my life for yours. If you think I come hither as a lion, it were pity of my life. No, I am no such thing. I am a man as other men are.' And there indeed let him name his name, and tell them plainly, he is Snug the joiner.
>
>   (III, i, 36–46)

Barkan makes the nice observation that this image of Snug showing himself as half-man and half-lion, is reminiscent of familiar book illustrations to the *Metamorphoses* of characters 'in the midst of Ovidian transformation'. Certainly, Bottom is here 'laying bare', in the simplest terms, a basic truth about the curious relation between an *actor* and his role, and a *character* and his metamorphosis. The others see comparable problems in the matter of the requisite moonlight, and the dividing wall. 'Two hard things', they say—'to bring the moonlight into a chamber', and 'you can never bring in a wall'. (Joking allusions, here, to the orchard wall leapt by Romeo in the almost entirely moonlit other play—Shakespeare can, of course, accomplish these 'effects' effortlessly.) Quince and Bottom realize that they must use someone 'to disfigure, or to present, the person of Moonshine . . . [and] to signify Wall' (III, i, 61, 70). First steps in symbolism—something or someone can stand for, present, signify, *dis*-figure (that happens, too) something or someone else; Shakespeare shows Theatre itself beginning to learn its own essential 'devices'. Of course, honest, literal Bottom–Bottom, feeling his way, is ensuring that any chance of achieving convincing 'illusion' in their performance is hilariously destroyed. But that is all right, since Bottom–Shakespeare can effortlessly contain it all within the larger illusion with which he is holding us entranced. 'Pyramus and Thisby' in *A Midsum-*

mer Night's Dream is a play-within-a-play with a difference. *Romeo and Ju-liet*—in another key!

But why *this* play for a wedding night entertainment? Here we need to think of 'exorcism', as first suggested, I think, by Barber. The play is an-nounced in (unintentional) Romeo-ish oxymorons which prompt Theseus to comment:

> Merry and tragical? Tedious and brief?
> That is, hot ice and wondrous strange snow.
> How shall we find the concord of this discord?
>   (V, i, 58–60)

The 'discord' of the performance only serves to emphasize and enhance the 'concord' achieved in the main play. And a self-destroyingly bad play about self-destructive young lovers may be no bad thing to enact on a wedding night—one 'botch' laughingly driving out another, as it were. And, just in case anyone present is lingeringly disturbed even by this minimally con-vincing (indeed, maximally *un*convincing) representation of the ill-fated young lovers, Bottom ('dead' Pyramus) leaps up and, in a last, triumphant, speech, announces that no one is dead—'No, I assure you; the wall is down that parted their fathers' (V, i, 353–4). This is the final 'turn' that Shake-speare gives to his re-vision, re-version, of *Romeo and Juliet*.

The main image in this bridal-night play is not of death, but, fittingly, of fertility. Titania gives us one of the loveliest descriptions of pregnancy in Shakespeare (indeed, I cannot think of another). It concerns the 'little changeling boy' Oberon is demanding:

> His mother was a vot'ress of my order,
> And, in the spicèd Indian air, by night,
> Full often hath she gossiped by my side,
> And sat with me on Neptune's yellow sands,
> Marking th' embarkèd traders on the flood;
> When we have laughed to see the sails conceive
> And grow big-bellied with the wanton wind;
> Which she, with pretty and with swimming gait
> Following—her womb then rich with my young squire—
> Would imitate, and sail upon the land,
> To fetch me trifles, and return again,

As from a voyage, rich with merchandise.
But she, being mortal, of that boy did die;
And for her sake do I rear up her boy,
And for her sake I will not part with him.

(II, i, 123–37)

The smudge of mortality again; even this play has to carry it. But, notwith-
standing, this is a glorious celebration of joyous, female fecundity. The
'changeling boy', who is the unwitting cause of the most seriously disruptive contentions, is a strange, enigmatic figure. He is the obscure, small, absent object of desire, at the heart of the play. And not really a 'changeling',
since that was the name given to a (usually deformed) fairy child, substituted, so superstition had it, for a sound human baby. But this child *is* human ('she, being mortal . . .'). My guess—it can only be that—is that, in a
play so concerned with turns and transformations of all kinds, Shakespeare
wanted that word ringing mysteriously somewhere in the woody depths of
the play—change, changing, changeling. Changelings all, perhaps. But, 'to
a great constancy' too.

   At the end, the forest fairies enter the palace (as, earlier, the palace had
entered the forest). Puck comes on with a broom, to sweep away all possible
present and future ills: Robin–Cupid as good house-fairy (in due course, he
will be transformed into Ariel—but that is another play).

Not a mouse
Shall disturb this hallowed house

(V, i, 389–90)

Titania bestows blessings and 'fairy grace' upon the whole place. Oberon
performs a lustration 'with this field-dew consecrate' ('dew' is another word
which occurs more often in this play than elsewhere), and wards off all possible defects from the children to come:

And the blots of Nature's hand
Shall not in their issue stand.
Never mole, harelip, nor scar,
Nor mark prodigious, such as are
Despisèd in nativity,
Shall upon their children be.

(V, i, 411–16)

Some commentators have seen the whole play as operating as an exorcism of the anxieties and fears associated with leaving the virginal security of childhood, and entering the unknown territory of active sexuality (hence the assorted, though temporary and harmless, terrors and 'monsters' in the woods—the 'spotted snakes' near the sleeping Titania; Hermia's dream of a serpent eating her heart; the threatened 'vile thing' which turns out, however, to be Bottom). Certainly, by the end, all fears and worries have been purged, blessed, washed, wished away. And the sleeping palace is bathed in the distinctive light of the play:

> Through the house give glimmering light,
>   By the dead and drowsy fire
>   (V, i, 393–4)

Glow, gleam, glint, glisten, glitter, glim, glimpse, glimmer (d*im gl*eam), *glimmering*—all from old Saxon and German 'gl-' words describing a light, a something, which shines brightly, shines faintly, shines briefly. This is the almost indescribable light in which we see the play. 'If we shadows have offended' says Puck, coming forward at the end—well, just tell yourselves you fell asleep and had a silly dream. But supposing they haven't 'offended', but, rather, ravished us—what kind of experience shall we say we had then? Everyone will find their own words—but certainly, there is no experience quite like it. Critics often say that *A Midsummer Night's Dream* is Shakespeare's most lyrical play; and that is no less than the truth. Indeed, I cannot see that a more magical play has ever been written.

 THE MERCHANT OF VENICE (1596)

> Which is the merchant here? And which the Jew?
>   (IV, i, 173)

> . . . see how yond justice rails upon yond simple thief. Hark, in thine ear:
> change places, and, handy-dandy, which is the justice, which is the thief?
>   (*King Lear,* IV, vi, 153–6)

When Portia, disguised as Balthasar, 'a young and learned doctor', enters the Court of Justice in Venice, her first business-like question is 'Which is the merchant here? And which the Jew?' It is an astonishing question. We know that Shylock would have been dressed in a 'gaberdine', because, we are told, Antonio habitually spits on it. This was a long garment of hard cloth customarily worn by Jews who, since 1412, had been obliged to wear a distinctive robe extending down to the feet. Shylock would have been literally a 'marked' man (in a previous century he would have had to wear a yellow hat). Antonio, a rich merchant who invariably comes 'so smug upon the mart' (where 'smug' means sleek and well-groomed, as well as our sense of complacently self-satisfied), is more likely to have been dressed in some of the 'silk' in which he trades (look at the sumptuously dressed Venetian merchants in Carpaccio's paintings to get some idea). It would have been unmissably obvious which was the merchant and which was the Jew. So, is that opening question just disingenuousness on Portia–Balthasar's part— or what?

The first Act is composed of three scenes set in the three (relatively) discrete places, or areas, each of which has its distinct voices, values, and concerns. Together, they make up the world of the play. I will call these—Rialto Venice; Belmont (Portia's house, some indeterminate distance from Venice, probably best thought of as being like one of those lovely Renaissance palaces still to be seen in the Veneto); and Ghetto Venice (Shylock's realm). The word 'ghetto' never appears in the play, and, as John Gross has pointed out, Shakespeare makes no mention of it. But the name Ghetto Nuevo (meaning New Foundry) was the name of the island in Venice on which the Jews were effectively sequestered (and from which the generic use of 'ghetto' derives); and clearly Shylock lives in a very different Venice from the Venice enjoyed by the confident Christian merchants. Hence my metaphoric use of the name for what, in Shakespeare, is simply designated as a 'public place'. The opening lines of the three scenes are, in sequence:

> In sooth I know not why I am so sad.
> It wearies me, you say it wearies you . . .

> By my troth, Nerissa, my little body is aweary of this great world.

> Three thousand ducats—well.

Sadness and weariness on the Rialto and in Belmont; money matters in the Ghetto. Is there any inter-connection? Can anything be done?

Antonio speaks first, which is quite appropriate since *he* is the 'Merchant' of the title—not, as some think, Shylock. Had Shakespeare wanted Shylock signalled in his title, he could well have called his play *The Jew of Venice,* in appropriate emulation of Marlowe's *The Jew of Malta* (1589), which was playing in London in 1596 when Shakespeare (almost certainly) started his own play, and which he (most certainly) knew and, indeed, deliberately echoed at certain key points (of which, more by and by). But Shylock is a very different figure from Barabas, who degenerates into a grotesque Machiavellian monster. In fact, Shylock only appears in five of the twenty scenes of the play; though he is overwhelmingly the figure who leaves the deepest mark—'incision' perhaps (see later)—on the memory. He shuffles off, broken, beaten, and ill—sadder and wearier than anyone else in Venice or Belmont—at the end of Act IV, never to return. But, while the triumph and victory belong unequivocally to Portia, it is the Jew's play.

However, Antonio is our merchant, and very Hamletish he is, too. He sounds an opening note of inexplicable melancholy:

> But how I caught it, found it, or came by it,
> What stuff 'tis made of, whereof it is born,
> I am to learn . . .
>   (I, i, 3–5)

We might later have a guess at at least some of the 'stuff' it is made of, but for now Salerio and Solanio (another of those effectively indistinguishable Rosencrantz-and-Guildenstern couples Shakespeare delights in—it offers another 'which-is-which?' puzzle in a lighter key) try to commiserate with him and cheer him up. And in their two speeches, Shakespeare—breathtakingly—manages to convey a whole sense of mercantile Renaissance Venice. Of course, they say, you are understandably worried—'your mind is tossing on the ocean'—about your 'argosies' (a very recent English word for large merchant ships, coming from the Venetian Adriatic port of Ragusa—and also used in Marlowe's play). Salerio, packing all the pride and confident arrogance of imperial, incomparable Venice into his lines, imagines those ship as 'rich burghers on the flood', or 'pageants [magnificent floats in festival and carnival parades] of the sea', which

> Do overpeer the petty traffickers
> That cursy [curtsy] to them, do them reverence,
> As they fly by them with their woven wings.
>   (I, i, 12–14)

Other seafaring traders are 'petty traffickers': Venetian merchants, attracting and exacting worldwide admiration and deference, are something quite
superbly else. Solanio chimes in, evoking a merchant's necessary anxieties
about winds, maps, ports, piers, and everything that, he says, 'might make
me fear/Misfortune to my ventures'—'ventures' is a word to watch. Salerio develops the theme, imagining how everything he saw on land would
somehow remind him of shipwrecks.

> Should I go to church
> And see the holy edifice of stone
> And not bethink me straight of dangerous rocks,
> Which touching but my gentle vessel's side
> Would scatter all her spices on the stream,
> Enrobe the roaring waters with my silks—
> And in a word, but even now worth this,
> And now worth nothing?
>
> (I, i, 29–36)

'But now a king, now thus,' says Salisbury when he watches King John die,
pondering the awesome mortality of kings (*King John* V, vii, 60). In this
Venice there is much the same feeling about the loss of one of their argosies,
monarchs (or burghers—it was a republic) of the sea as they were. And
what a sense of riches is compacted into the lines imagining spices scattered
on the stream, and waves robed in silk—an image of spilt magnificence if
ever there was one.

It is important to note Salerio's reference to 'church . . . the holy edifice of
stone'. In one of those contrasts dear to artists, the stillness and fixity of the
holy edifice of stone is to be seen behind the flying ships on the tossing
oceans and flowing streams—the eternal values of the church conjoined
with, and in some way legitimizing, the worldly wealth-gathering of the
sea-venturing, transient merchants; the spiritual ideals sustaining the material practices. For Venice was a holy city (the Crusades left from there), as
well as the centre of a glorious worldly empire. It was an object of awe and
fascination to the Elizabethans. Indeed, as Philip Brockbank suggested,
Venice was for Renaissance writers what Tyre was for the prophet Isaiah—
'the crowning city, whose merchants are princes, whose traffickers are the
honourable of the earth' (Isaiah 23:8). But Tyre was also a 'harlot' who made
'sweet melody', and Isaiah prophesies that it 'shall commit fornication with

all the kingdoms of the world' (Venice was also famed, or notorious, for its alleged sensualities—in Elizabethan London there was a brothel simply named 'Venice'). But, also this about Tyre:

> And her merchandise and her hire shall be holiness to the Lord: it shall
> not be treasured nor laid up; for her merchandise shall be for them that
> dwell before the Lord, to eat sufficiently, and for durable clothing.
>
> (Isaiah 23:18)

Traditionally, religion is ascetic and preaches a rejection of worldly goods. But here we see religion and the 'use of riches' creatively reconciled—and by spending, not hoarding. As Tyre, so Venice. But there is, in Isaiah, an apocalyptic warning—that God will turn the whole city 'upside down' and 'scatter' the inhabitants:

> And it shall be, as with the people, so with the priest . . . as with the buyer,
> so with the seller; as with the lender, so with the borrower; as with the
> taker of usury, so with the giver of usury to him. The land shall be utterly
> emptied, and utterly spoiled: for the Lord hath spoken this word.
>
> (24:2, 3)

Ruskin would say that this was effectively what *did* happen to Venice. But that is another story. The point for us here is that the Venetian setting of his play allowed Shakespeare to pursue his exploratory interest in (I quote Brockbank):

> the relationship between the values of empire and those of the aspiring
> affections, human and divine; those of the City of Man and those of the
> City of God . . . between the values we are encouraged to cultivate in a
> mercantile, moneyed and martial society, and those which are looked for
> in Christian community and fellowship; between those who believe in the
> gospel teachings of poverty, humility and passivity, and those who (as the
> creative hypocrisy requires) pretend to.

Returning to the play, Solanio says that if Antonio is not sad on account of his 'merchandise', then he must be in love. Antonio turns away the suggestion with a 'Fie, fie!' As it happens, I think this is close to the mark, but

we will come to that. Here Solanio gives up on trying to find a reason for
Antonio's gloom—

> Then let us say you are sad
> Because you are not merry; and 'twere as easy
> For you to laugh and leap, and say you are merry.
> (I, i, 47–9)

And he leaves with Salerio, who says to Antonio—'I would have stayed till
I had made you merry.' 'Merry' is a lovely word from old English, suggesting pleasing, amusing, agreeable, full of lively enjoyment. 'To be merry best
becomes you,' says Don Pedro to the vivacious Beatrice, 'for out o' question,
you were born in a merry hour' (*Much Ado* II, i, 327–9)—and we feel he has
chosen just the right word. The princely merchants of Venice favour the
word, for, in their aristocratic way, they believe in 'merriment'. It is an unequivocally positive word; it has no dark side, and carries no shadow. Yet in
this play, Shakespeare makes it become ominous. When Shylock suggests
to Antonio that he pledges a pound of his flesh as surety for the three thousand ducat loan, he refers to it as a 'merry bond', signed in a spirit of 'merry
sport' (I, iii, 170, 142). The word has lost its innocence and is becoming sinister. The last time we hear it is from Shylock's daughter Jessica in Belmont
—'I am never merry when I hear sweet music' (V, i, 69). After her private
duet with Lorenzo, nobody speaks to Jessica in Belmont and these are, indeed, her last words in the play. It is hard to feel that she will be happily
asssimilated into the Belmont world. Something has happened to 'merry-
ness', and although Belmont is, distinctly, an abode of 'sweet music', a note
of un-merry sadness lingers in the air.

When Bassanio enters with Gratiano, he says to the departing Salerio and
Solanio, as if reproachfully, 'You grow exceeding strange; must it be so?' (I,
i, 67). It is a word which recurs in a variety of contexts, and it reminds us
that there is 'strangeness' in Venice, centring on Shylock, whose 'strange
apparent cruelty' (IV, i, 21) is some sort of reflection of, response to, the fact
that he is treated like 'a stranger cur' (I, iii, 115) in Venice. And he is, by law,
an alien in the city—the stranger within. Gratiano then has a go at Antonio—'You look not well, Signior Antonio' ('I am not well' says Shylock, as
he leaves the play—IV, i, 395: now the merchant, now the Jew. Sickness
circulates in Venice, along with all the other 'trafficking').

> You have too much respect upon the world;
> They lose it that do buy it with much care.
> Believe me, you are marvelously changed.
>
> (I, i, 74–6)

His scripture is a little awry here: what people lose who gain the whole world is the *soul,* not the world. A *mondain* Venetian's slip, perhaps. But we are more likely to be alerted by the phrase 'marvelously changed'. As we have seen, Shakespearian comedy is full of marvellous changes, and we may be considering what transformations, marvellous or otherwise, occur in this play. In the event, the 'changes' turn out to be far from unambiguous 'conversions'. Somewhere behind all these conversions is the absolutely basic phenomenon whereby material is converted into 'merchandise' which is then converted into money—which, as Marx said, can then convert, or 'transform' just about anything into just about anything else. It is perhaps worth remembering that Marx praised Shakespeare, in particular, for showing that money had the power of a god, while it behaved like a whore. Shakespeare, he said, demonstrates that money 'is the visible divinity—the transformation of all human and natural properties into their contraries, the universal confounding and distorting of things: impossibilities are soldered together by it'.

Jessica willingly converts to Christianity, hoping for salvation, at least from her father's house, but it hardly seems to bring, or promise, any notable felicity or grace. Shylock is forced to convert—which, however construed by the Christians (he would thereby be 'saved'), is registered as a final humiliation and the stripping away of the last shred of his identity. When Portia gives herself to Bassanio, she says:

> Myself, and what is mine, to you and yours
> Is now converted.
>
> (III, ii, 166–7)

and this is to be felt as a willing conversion, a positive transformation—just as she will, like a number of other heroines, 'change' herself into a man to effect some genuine salvation. Sad Antonio, it has to be said, is not much changed at all at the end—though his life has been saved, and his ships have come sailing in. Venice itself, as represented, is hardly changed; not, that is, renewed or redeemed—though it is a good deal more at ease with itself for having got rid of Shylock—if that is what it *has* done. One hardly feels that the realm has been purged, and that the malcontent threatening the joy of the festive conclusion has been happily exorcized. The play does not really end quite so 'well' as that. It is not a 'metamorphic' celebration.

It is Bassanio's plea for financial help from Antonio that concludes the first scene, and the way in which he does so is crucial to an appreciation of what follows. He admits that he has 'disabled mine estate' by showing 'a more swelling port' than he could afford. 'Swelling port' is 'impressively lavish lifestyle', but I think we will remember the 'portly sail' of the Venetian argosies just referred to, 'swollen' by the winds (cf. the 'big-bellied sails' in *A Midsummer Night's Dream*). The Venetian princely way of life is both pregnant and distended—fecund and excessive. However inadvertently, Bassanio is recognizing a key word by using it. He is worried about his 'great debts':

> Wherein my time, something too prodigal,
> Hath left me gaged.
>
> (I, i, 129–30)

Shylock calls Antonio a 'prodigal Christian', and it was always a fine point to decide to what extent 'prodigality' was compatible with Christianity (think of the parables of the Prodigal Son, and the Unjust Steward), and to what extent it contravened Christian doctrine. It is one of those words which looks two ways, pointing in one direction to the magnanimous bounty of an Antony, and in the other to the ruinous squandering of a Timon. Clearly, the munificent prodigality of Antonio is in every way preferable to the obsessive meanness and parsimony of Shylock. But there is a crucial speech on this subject, tucked away, as was sometimes Shakespeare's wont, where you might least expect it. Salerio and Gratiano are whiling away the time in front of Shylock's house, waiting to help Lorenzo in the abduction of Jessica. Salerio is saying that lovers are much more eager to consummate the marriage than they are to remain faithful ('keep obliged faith') subsequently. 'That ever holds' says Gratiano:

> All things that are
> Are with more spirit chasèd than enjoyed.
> How like a younger or a prodigal
> The scarfèd bark puts from her native bay,

> Hugged and embracèd by the strumpet wind!
> How like the prodigal doth she return,
> With over-weathered ribs and ragged sails,
> Lean, rent, and beggared by the strumpet wind!
>
> (II, vi, 12–19)

An apt enough extended metaphor in a mercantile society, and the Venetians must have seen many a ship sail out 'scarfed' (decorated with flags and streamers) and limp back 'rent'. It may be added that Gratiano is something of a cynical young blade. But the speech stands as a vivid reminder of one possible fate of 'prodigality', *and* of marriage. Ultimately of Venice too, perhaps.

Bassanio, whatever else he is (scholar, courtier) is a 'prodigal', and he wants to clear his 'debts'. Antonio immediately says that 'my purse, my person' (a nice near pun, given the close inter-involvement of money and body in this play) 'lie all unlocked to your occasions' (I, i, 139). This open liberality might be remembered when we later hear the frantically retentive and self-protective Shy*lock* (a name not found outside this play) repeatedly warning Jessica to 'look to my house . . . lock up my doors . . . shut doors after you' (II, v, 16, 29, 52). The difference is clear enough, and need not be laboured. Antonio also positively invites Bassanio to 'make waste of all I have' (I, i, 157)—insouciantly negligent aristocrats like to practise what Yeats called 'the wasteful virtues'. The contrast with 'thrifty' Shylock, again, does not need underlining.

But Bassanio has another possible solution to his money problems; one which depends on 'adventuring' and 'hazard'.

> In Belmont is a lady richly left;
> And she is fair and, fairer than that word,
> Of wondrous virtues . . .
> Nor is the wide world ignorant of her worth,
> For the four winds blow in from every coast
> Renownèd suitors, and her sunny locks
> Hang on her temples like a golden fleece,
> Which makes her seat of Belmont Colchos' strond,
> And many Jasons come in quest of her.
> O my Antonio, had I but the means

> To hold a rival place with one of them,
> I have a mind presages me such thrift
> That I should questionless be fortunate!
>
> (I, i, 161–3, 167–76)

Antonio, all his wealth at sea, at the moment has neither 'money, nor commodity'; but he will use his 'credit' to get 'the means'. He will borrow the *money* from Shylock to finance Bassanio's quest of a second *golden* fleece. So it is that the seemingly discrete worlds of the Ghetto, the Rialto, and Belmont are, from the beginning, inter-involved.

Rich—fair—virtuous; 'worth' indeed, and well figured by mythologizing Portia's 'sunny locks' into a 'golden fleece'. Perhaps unsurprisingly, we are back into Ovid. Helle, the daughter of Athamas and Nephele, tried to escape from her stepmother Ino on a golden-fleeced ram. Unfortunately, she fell off into the sea then named after her—the Hellespont. Her brother, however, did escape, and sacrificed the ram in gratitude. The ram became the constellation Aries, and Jason was sent on a mission to recover the fleece. This probably tells you more than you want to know, or be reminded of. The more relevant point is that Jason won the golden fleece with the help of the dark magic of Medea, whom he married. So he returned with two prizes from 'Colchos' strond' (Colchis, on the Black Sea, was Medea's homeland). We will encounter another echo of Medea; but the further point to remember here is that Jason was the least heroic of heroes, and that he deserted Medea just as he had previously deserted Hypsipyle. Jonathan Bate says that Jason was 'an archetype of male deceit and infidelity', and, albeit in very different circumstances, we do see Bassanio being 'unfaithful' to Portia almost immediately after their marriage. Portia wants to see Bassanio as a 'Hercules', the *most* heroic of heroes; but the question must remain to what extent he is, in fact, a Jason in Hercules' clothing (since we're talking about sheep and fleeces). And one more point. Jason won the fleece *and* a wife. For Bassanio the fleece *is* the wife. Fittingly, when he opens the right casket, he finds a 'golden mesh'—a painting of Portia's 'sunny locks'. This, it has to be said, was the 'gold' he came for. To keep the analogy alive in our minds, after Bassanio has won Portia, Gratiano exults 'We are the Jasons, we have won the Fleece' (III, ii, 241); and Salerio, keeping the mercantile line of thought going, replies—'I would you had won the fleece that he Antonio hath lost!' (III, ii, 242). 'Fleece' equals 'fleets'? Perhaps. Certainly there is some connection (not necessarily an identification) between Portia, her hair, her gold, Rialto wealth, and—somewhere—Ghetto ducats. Bassanio could not be/play Jason–Hercules winning the Portia–fleece, without the help of Shylock mediated through Antonio.

Venice, as we have seen it and will see it, is overwhelmingly a man's world of public life; it is conservative, dominated by law, bound together by contracts, underpinned by money—and closed. Belmont is run by women living the private life; it is liberal, animated by love, harmonized by music and poetry ('fancy'), sustained by gold—and open. However cynical one wants to be, it will not do to see Belmont as 'only Venice come into a windfall' (Ruth Nevo). It is better to see it as in a line of civilized, gracious retreats, stretching from Horace's Sabine farm, through Sidney's Penshurst, Jane Austen's Mansfield Park, up to Yeats's Coole Park. As Brockbank said, such places ideally offered 'the prospect of a protected life reconciling plenitude, exuberance, simplicity and order'. It was Sidney who said that 'our world is brazen, the poets only deliver a golden', and you might see Belmont as a kind of 'golden' world which has been 'delivered' from the 'brazen' world of trade and money. (The art-gold which builds the statues at the end of *Romeo and Juliet* is not the same as the money-gold with which Romeo buys his poison.) Yes, somewhere back along the line, it is grounded in ducats; but you must think of the churches, palaces, art works and monuments of the Renaissance, made possible by varying forms of patronage, and appreciate that the 'courtiers, merchants and bankers of the Renaissance found ways of transmuting worldly goods into spiritual treasure' (Brockbank). Belmont is a privileged retreat from Venice; but, as Portia will show, it can also fruitfully engage with it.

In scene two we are in Belmont, and Portia is weary. Partly, surely, because she must be bored stiff with the suitors who have come hopefully buzzing round the honey-pot—the silent Englishman, the mean Scotsman, the vain Frenchman, the drunken German, and so on, as she and Nerissa amuse themselves discussing their different intolerabilities. But, more importantly, because she is under the heavy restraint of a paternal interdiction (familiar enough in comedy, though this one comes from beyond the grave). She has been deprived of *choice*—and she wants a mate.

> The brain may devise laws for the blood, but a hot temper leaps o'er a
> cold decree; such a hare is madness the youth to skip o'er the meshes of

good counsel the cripple. But this reasoning is not in the fashion to choose
me a husband. O me, the word 'choose'! I may neither choose who I
would nor refuse who I dislike, so is the will of a living daughter curbed
by the will of a dead father. Is it not hard, Nerissa, that I cannot choose
one, nor refuse none?

(I, ii, 17–26)

Then we learn from Nerissa about the lottery of the caskets, which she
thinks was the 'good inspiration' of a 'virtuous' and 'holy' man. We shall
see. But we note that, in this, Belmont (in the form of Portia) is as much
under the rule of (male) law as Venice. There are 'laws for the blood' in
both places, and they may by no means be 'leaped' or 'skipped' over. In
other comedies we have seen inflexible, intractable, unmitigatable law
magically, mysteriously melt away or be annulled. Not in this play. Here
the law is followed, or pushed, to the limit—and beyond. Indeed, you might
say that Belmont has to come to Venice to help discover this 'beyond' of
the law.

And now, in scene three, we are in Shylock's Venice; and we hear for the
first time what will become an unmistakable voice—addressing, as it were,
the bottom line in Venice: 'three thousand ducats—well'. Shylock speaks
in—unforgettable—prose, and this marks something of a crucial departure
for Shakespeare. Hitherto, he had effectively reserved prose for exclusively
comic (usually 'low') characters. With Shylock, this all changes (with Falstaff too, who emerges shortly after Shylock—though arguably he is, at inception, still something of a comic character). For Shylock is not a comic
character. He has a power, a pain, a passion, a dignity—and, yes, a savagery,
and a suffering—which, whatever they are, are not comic. And here I
would like, if possible, to discredit and disqualify two damagingly irrelevant attitudes to the play. The first is the one which accuses it of anti-
Semitism. This really is, with the best will in the world, completely beside
the point. There *were* Jews in Renaissance European cities; they *were* often
the main money-lenders; no doubt some of them *were* extortionate. Christians who borrowed from them no doubt *did* develop strong antagonistic,
resentful feelings towards them (as people invariably do towards those to
whom they are in any way 'indebted'—'Why do you hate me so much;
what have I done for you recently?' is, here, a pertinent Jewish joke). And,
equally assumable, some Jews came to harbour very understandable feel-

ings of anger and revenge against the people who, at once, used and reviled them. So much is history: so much—I risk—is fact. And Shakespeare knew his facts. Interested in every aspect of human behaviour, for him an archaically vengeful Jew was as plausible a figure as an evil monarch, a betraying friend, a cowardly soldier, an ungrateful daughter.

A more insidious view is that which maintains that Shylock is intended to be 'a purely repellent or comic figure' because 'conventionality' would have it so. These are the words of E. E. Stoll, from a regrettably influential essay written in 1911. Like it or not, he said, that is how Jews were regarded by the Elizabethans, and Shakespeare, 'more than any other poet, reflected the settled prejudices and passions of his race'. 'How can we,' he concluded, 'for a moment sympathize with Shylock unless at the same time we indignantly turn, not only against Gratiano, but against Portia, the Duke, and all Venice as well?' The baneful insensitivity and crass unintelligence of these remarks merit no response, and I would not have resurrected them were it not for the fact that, in our understandably squeamish post-Holocaust time, reasons (justifications, *excuses*) for even performing the play sometimes run along those lines. As I have said before, if something hurts or worries us, you may be very sure that it hurt and worried Shakespeare, and the idea of happily laughing the broken Shylock off stage is simply unthinkable. Now. And then. And some of that 'indignant turning' on Venice, which Stoll found so inconceivable, may well not be out of place. We have here, certainly a 'comedy' as conventionally constituted—group solidarity reconfirmed, a threat disarmed and extruded; but there is something sour, sad, even sick in the air—at the end as at the beginning. As we regard the contented figures at Belmont, we may well agree with Ruth Nevo that 'we do not feel that they are wiser than they were. Only that they have what they wanted.' In pursuit of his vengeance, Shylock becomes a monstrous figure, as does anyone who takes resentment, hatred, and revenge, to extremes. But the play is not a melodrama or morality play, and that is certainly not all there is to him.

On his first appearance, Shylock establishes his 'Jewishness' by, among other things, revealing his adherence to Jewish dietary rules—'I will not eat with you, drink with you, nor pray with you' (I, iii, 345). (But why, then, does he later agree to go to supper with the 'prodigal Christian', which in any case he would not have been allowed to do, since the Jews were locked up in their island at night? On this, and all matters concerning Jews in contemporary Venice, and London, see John Gross's comprehensive *Shylock*. I suppose Shakespeare wants to get him out of the way so Jessica can rob him and flee.) When Antonio appears, Shylock reveals a darker side of his nature in an 'aside' (as we have often seen, potential villains tend to reveal themselves and their intentions in soliloquies or asides—to us).

> I hate him for he is a Christian;
> But more, for that in low simplicity
> He lends out money gratis, and brings down
> The rate of usance here with us in Venice.
> . . .
> He hates our sacred nation, and he rails,
> Even there where merchants most do congregate,
> On me, my bargains, and my well-won thrift,
> Which he calls interest. Cursèd be my tribe
> If I forgive him.
>
> (I, iii, 39–42, 45–9)

Shylock gives three good reasons for his hating of Antonio—insofar as one can have good reasons for hatred: personal, professional, tribal. This is interesting in view of his response during the trial scene, when he is asked why he would not prefer to have ducats rather than Antonio's flesh:

> So can I give no reason, nor I will not,
> More than a lodged hate and a certain loathing
> I bear Antonio . . .
>
> (IV, i, 59–61)

In his two comedies which follow shortly, Shakespeare includes two, relatively minor, characters who cannot find, or offer, any explanation for the irrational hatreds they feel (Oliver in *As You Like It*, and Don John in *Much Ado*). Shylock is a much larger and more complex figure; and, like Iago—Shakespeare's greatest study of 'motiveless malignity'—he can find motives (more plausible than Iago's), but ultimately reveals that he is acting under the compulsion of a drive which defeats and outruns explanation. The phenomenon was clearly starting to engage Shakespeare's serious attention.

His crucial opening exchange with Antonio really defines the central concern of the play. He has already mentioned 'usance' ('a more clenly name for usury' in contemporary terms), 'thrift' (which means both prosperity and frugality—'thrift, Horatio, thrift') and 'interest'. And 'usury', of course, is the heart of the matter. Any edition of the play will tell you that the law against lending money at interest was lifted in 1571, and a rate of ten percent was made legal. Queen Elizabeth depended on money borrowed at interest, so did most agriculture, industry, and foreign trade by the end of the sixteenth century (according to R. H. Tawney). So, indeed, did Shakespeare's own Globe Theatre. Plenty of Christians lent money at interest (including Shakespeare's own father); and Bacon, writing 'Of Usury' in 1625, said 'to speak of the abolishing of usury is idle'. Antonio, scattering his interest-free loans around Venice, is certainly an 'idealized' picture of the merchant, just as Shylock sharpening his knife to claim his debt, is a 'demonized' one. This is John Gross's point, and it could be seen as a version of what psychoanalysts call 'splitting', as a way of dealing with confused feelings: Melanie Klein's good mother—figure of our hopes and desires, that would be Antonio; and bad mother—object of our fears and aggressions, Shylock. But Aristotle and Christianity had spoken against usury, and there was undoubtedly a good deal of residual unease and ambivalence about it. Ruthless usurers were thus especially hated and abused, and since Jews were identified as quintessential usurious money-lenders (and, of course, had killed Christ), they were available for instant and constant execration. This must certainly be viewed as a collective hypocrisy— one of those 'projections' by which society tries to deal with a bad conscience (not that Shakespeare would have seen many Jews in London; it is estimated that there were fewer than two hundred at the time). Shakespeare was not addressing a contemporary problem;* rather, he was exploring some of the ambivalences and hypocrisies, the value clashes and requisite doublenesses, which inhere in, and attend upon, all commerce.

The play is full of commercial and financial terms: 'moneys', 'usances', 'bargains', 'credit', 'excess' and 'advantage' (both used of usury and profit), 'trust', 'bond' (which occurs vastly more often than in any other play: curi-

---

* Though there had been an outbreak of anti-Semitism in 1594, after the execution of Roderigo Lopez, a Portuguese Jew accused by Essex of trying to poison Queen Elizabeth.

ously 'contract' is *not* used—Shakespeare wants us to focus on 'bond'), 'commodity' (you may recall the 'smooth-faced gentleman, tickling commodity . . . this commodity, this bawd, this broker, this all-changing word' from *King John*), and 'thrift'. Launcelot Gobbo is 'an unthrifty knave', while Jessica flees from her father's house with 'an unthrift love'. This last serves as a reminder that both here and elsewhere in Shakespeare the language of finance and usury could be used as a paradoxical image of love (happiness accrues and passion grows by a form of *natural* interest). You will hear it in Belmont as well as on the Rialto. When Portia gives herself to Bassanio, she, as it were, breaks the bank:

> I would be trebled twenty times myself,
> A thousand times more fair, ten thousand times more rich,
> That only to stand high in your account,
> I might in virtues, beauties, livings, friends,
> Exceed account.
>
> (III, ii, 153–7)

Rich place, Belmont; generous lover, Portia!

The absolutely central exchange occurs when Antonio and Shylock discuss 'interest', or 'borrowing upon advantage'. 'I do never use it' declares Antonio (what is the relationship between 'use' and 'usury'? Another consideration.) Shylock replies, seemingly rather inconsequentially: 'When Jacob grazed his uncle Laban's sheep . . .' Antonio brings him to the point. 'And what of him? Did he take interest?' Shylock seems to prevaricate: 'No, not take interest—not as you would say / Directly int'rest', and then recounts the story from Genesis. This tells how Jacob tricked—but is that the right word?—his exploitative uncle, Laban: they agreed that, for his hire, Jacob should be entitled to any lambs in the flocks he was tending, that were born 'streaked and pied'. Following the primitive belief that what a mother sees during conception has an effect on the offspring, Jacob stripped some 'wands' (twigs or branches), so that some were light while others were dark, and 'stuck them up before the fulsome ewes' as the rams were impregnating them. In the subsequent event, a large number of 'parti-colored lambs' were born, which of course went to Jacob. Nice work; but was it also sharp practice? Or was it both, and so much the better? Or, does it matter? Not as far as Shylock is concerned:

> This was a way to thrive, and he was blest;
> And thrift is blessing if men steal it not.
>   (I, iii, 86–7)

'Ewes' may be a pun on 'use'; and for Shylock, it is as legitimate to use ewes in the field as it is to use usury on the 'mart'. Not so for Antonio:

> This was a venture, sir, that Jacob served for,
> A thing not in his power to bring to pass,
> But swayed and fashioned by the hand of heaven.
> Was this inserted to make interest good?
> Or is your gold and silver ewes and rams?

And Shylock:

> I cannot tell; I make it breed as fast.
>   (I, iii, 88–93)

Antonio's last line effectively poses *the* question of the play. It was a line often quoted (or more often, slightly misquoted) by Ezra Pound in his increasingly unbalanced vituperations against usury and Jews. The root feeling behind it is that it is somehow *unnatural* for inorganic matter (gold, silver, money) to reproduce itself in a way at least analogous to the natural reproductions in the organic realm. 'They say it is against nature for *Money* to beget *Money*,' says Bacon, quoting Aristotle, and Pope catches some of the disgust the notion could arouse, in a simple couplet:

> While with the silent growth of ten per cent
> In dirt and darkness hundreds stink content.

This enables Antonio to reject Shylock's self-justifying analogy: Jacob's story does *not* 'make interest good', because he was having, or making, a 'venture', and the result was, inevitably, 'swayed and fashioned' by—heaven? nature? some power not his own. This, revealingly, was how Christian commentators of the time justified Jacob's slightly devious behaviour (as Frank Kermode pointed out)—he was making a *venture*. Antonio's ships are 'ventures', and Bassanio is on a venture when he 'adventures forth' to Belmont. It seems that the element of 'risk' (= to run into danger) and 'hazard', purifies or justifies the act. As 'hazard' was originally an Arabian word for a gaming die, this would seem to enable gambling to pass moral muster as well. Perhaps it does. Whatever, there is seemingly *no* risk, as well as no nature, in usury. Shylock's answer, that he makes his money 'breed as fast', is thought to tell totally against him; and Antonio's subsequent remark, 'for when did friendship take / A breed for barren metal of his friend?' (I, iii, 130–31), is taken to orient our sympathies, and values, correctly. But this won't quite do.

Because, like it or not, money most certainly *does* 'breed'. It may not literally copulate, but there is no way round the metaphor. Sigurd Burckhardt is the only commentator I have read who has seen this clearly, and he wrote: 'metal ["converted" into money] is not barren, it does breed, is pregnant with consequences, and capable of transformation into life and art'. For a start, it gets Bassanio to Belmont, and the obtaining of Portia and the Golden Fleece (or Portia *as* a golden fleece). And—as if to signal his awareness of the proximity, even similitude, of the two types of 'breeding', with the lightest of touches—when Gratiano announces he is to marry Nerissa at the same time as Bassanio marries Portia, Shakespeare has him add, 'we'll play with them the first boy for a thousand ducats' (III, ii, 214). You 'play' for babies, and you 'play' for ducats. Which also means that when Shylock runs through the streets crying 'O my ducats! O my daughter!' (echoing Marlowe's Barabas who cries out 'oh, my girl, my gold', but when his daughter *restores* his wealth to him), we should not be quite so quick to mock him as the little Venetian urchins. He may not use his money to such life-enhancing and generous ends as some of the more princely Venetians; but he *has* been doubly bereaved (which literally means—robbed, *reaved,* on all sides).

Having mentioned that robbery, I will just make one point about the Jessica and Lorenzo sub-plot. However sorry we may feel for Jessica, living in a 'hell' of a house with her father, the behaviour of the two lovers is only to be deprecated. Burckhardt is absolutely right again: 'their love is lawless, financed by theft and engineered by a gross breach of trust'. Jessica 'gilds' herself with ducats, and throws a casket of her father's wealth down to Lorenzo ('Here, catch this casket; it is worth the pains', II, vi, 33—another echo-with-a-difference of Marlowe's play, in which Abigail throws down her father's wealth from a window, to her *father*). This is an anticipatory parody, travesty rather, of Portia, the Golden (not 'gilded') Fleece, waiting to see if Bassanio will pass the test of *her* father's caskets (containing wisdom, rather than simple ducats). He 'hazards' all; this couple risk nothing. They squander eighty ducats in a night—folly, not bounty. Jessica exchanges the ring her mother gave her father as a love-pledge, for—a monkey! They really do make a monkey out of marriage—I will come to their famous love duet in due course. Theirs is the reverse, or inverse, of a true love match. It must be intended to contrast with the marriage made by Bassanio and Portia. Admittedly, this marriage also involves wealth—as it does paternal caskets; but, and the difference is vital, wealth *not gained or used in the same way.*

Those caskets.* Shakespeare took nearly everything that he wanted for his plot (including settings, characters, even the ring business in Act V) from a tale in *Il Pecorone (The Dunce)*, a collection of stories assembled by Giovanni Fiorentino, published in Italy in 1558—everything except the trial of the caskets. In the Italian story, to win the lady, the hero has to demonstrate to her certain powers of sexual performance and endurance. Clearly, this was not quite the thing for a Shakespearian heroine. So Shakespeare took the trial-by-caskets from a tale in the thirteenth-century *Gesta Romanorum,* which had been translated into English. Here, a young woman has to choose between three vessels—gold, silver, lead—to discover whether she is worthy to be the wife of the Emperor's son. All we need note about it is one significant change that Shakespeare made in the inscriptions on the vessels/caskets. Those on the gold and silver ones are effectively the same in each case—roughly, 'Who chooseth me shall gain/get what he desires/deserves'. But in the medieval tale, the lead casket bears the inscription '*Thei that chese me, shulle fynde in me that God hath disposid*'. Now, since the young woman is a good Christian, she could hardly have been told more clearly

---

* My editor does not like footnotes, but I would briefly like to draw attention to an interesting paper on 'The Theme of the Three Caskets' by Freud (Collected Papers IV), not mentioned by commentators on this play whom I have read. He points out how often the theme of having to choose between three women recurs through myth and folk tale (Paris with the three goddesses, the Prince with Cinderella and her two sisters—not to mention Lear and his three daughters); and how, invariably, the 'right' choice is the seemingly least likely one—Cinderella, Cordelia, the lead casket (caskets, of course, represent women). Freud wonders whether, in some refracted way, they figure 'the three forms taken on by the figure of the mother as life proceeds: the mother herself, the beloved who is chosen after her pattern, and finally the Mother Earth who receives him again'. No direct relevance, I think, to the play. But interesting.

that this was the one to go for. It is, we may say, no test at all. Shakespeare
changes the inscription to 'Who chooseth me must give and hazard all he
hath' (II, vii, 9). This is a very different matter. Instead of being promised a
placid and predictable demonstration of piety rewarded, we are in that
dangerous world of risk and hazard which, at various levels, constitutes the
mercantile world of the play. And to the prevailing lexicon of 'get' and
'gain', has been added the even more important word—'give'. One of the
concerns of the play is the conjoining *of giving* and *gaining* in the most appropriate way, so that they may 'frutify' together (if I may borrow Launcelot Gobbo's inspired malapropism). 'I come by note, *to give and to receive*,'
Bassanio announces to Portia (III, ii, 140—my italics). Which is no less than
honesty.

　　While she is anxiously waiting as Bassanio inspects the caskets, Portia
says:

>　　　Now he goes,
> With no less presence, but with much more love,
> Than young Alcides [Hercules], when he did redeem
> The virgin tribute paid by howling Troy
> To the sea monster. I stand for sacrifice;
> The rest aloof are the Dardanian wives,
> With blearèd visages come forth to view
> The issue of th' exploit. Go, Hercules!
>　　　　　　　　(III, ii, 53–60)

The 'virgin tribute' was Hesione, and her rescue by Hercules is described in
Book XI of Ovid's *Metamorphoses* (where it is preceded by stories concerning Orpheus, who turned everything to music, and Midas, who turned everything to gold—they are both referred to in the play, and are hovering
mythic presences behind it). Portia's arresting claim—'I stand for sacrifice'
—resonates through the play; to be darkly echoed by Shylock in court—'I
stand for judgment . . . I stand here for law' (IV, i, 103, 142). When she says
'stand for', does she mean 'represent' or 'embody'; or does she imply that
she is in danger of being 'sacrificed' to the law of her father unless rescued
by right-choosing Hercules–Bassanio? Or is it just that women are always,
in effect, 'sacrificed' to men in marriage, hence the 'bleared visages' of those
'Dardanian wives'? Something of all of these, perhaps. In the event, it is

Portia herself who effectively rescues or—her word—'redeems', not Troy, but Venice. Bassanio (courtier, scholar, and fortune-seeker) is, as we have seen, if not more, then as much Jason as Hercules. The point is, I think, that he has to be *both* as cunning as the one *and* as bold as the other. The 'both-ness' is important.

This is how Bassanio thinks his way to the choice of the correct casket:

> So may the outward shows be least themselves;
> The world is still deceived with ornament.
> In law, what plea so tainted and corrupt,
> But being seasoned with a gracious voice,
> Obscures the show of evil?
>   (III, ii, 73–7)

One of his examples of the deceptiveness of 'outward shows' is:

> How many cowards whose hearts are all as false
> As stairs of sand, wear yet upon their chins
> The beards of Hercules and frowning Mars,
> Who inward searched, have livers white as milk!
>   (III, ii, 83–6)

A Hercules concealing the false heart and milk-white liver for which, as it happens, Jason was renowned—who can Bassanio have in mind? He even says that 'snaky golden locks' on a woman often turn out to be wigs taken from corpses—so perhaps we would even do well to blink at Portia, while Bassanio praises the 'golden mesh' of her hair, though of course she proves true and real enough. I am sure Shakespeare wants us to notice how analogies can sometimes circle round on the characters who offer them. Bassanio, moralizing hard, returns to his theme of 'ornament':

> Thus ornament is but the guilèd shore
> To a most dangerous sea, the beauteous scarf
> Veiling an Indian beauty; in a word,
> The seeming truth which cunning times put on
> To entrap the wisest.
>   (III, ii, 97–101)

This, *mutatis mutandis,* is a theme in Shakespeare from first to last—'all that glisters is not gold', and so on (II, vii, 65). Bassanio is on very sure ground in rejecting the gold and silver and opting for lead, *in the context of the test.* But—ornament: from *ornare*—to equip, to adorn. Now, if ever there was an equipped and adorned city, it was Venice. It is aware of dangerous seas and treacherous shores, of course; but it is also a city of beauteous scarves, and silks and spices—and what are they but 'ornaments' for the body and for food? Bassanio is an inhabitant and creation of an ornamented world, and is himself, as we say, an 'ornament' to it. So why does he win by going through a show of rejecting it? He wins, because he realizes that he has to subscribe to the unadorned modesty of lead, *even while* going for the ravishing glory of gold. *That* was the sort of complex intelligence Portia's father had in mind for his daughter. Is it hypocrisy? Then we must follow Brockbank and call it 'creative hypocrisy'. It recognizes the compromising, and willing-to-compromise, doubleness of values on which a worldly society (a society in the world) necessarily rests, and by which it is sustained. The leaden virtues, and the golden pleasures. Bothness.

Such is the reconciling potency of Belmont; and Portia seals the happy marriage with a ring. But, meanwhile, Shylock is waiting back in Venice for his pound of flesh, and he *must* be satisfied. Must—because he has the law on his side, and Venice lives by law; its wealth and reputation depend on honouring contracts and bonds—as Shylock is the first to point out. 'If you deny my bond, let the danger light/Upon your charter and your city's freedom!' Portia, as lawyer Balthasar, agrees: 'There is no power in Venice/Can alter a decree established' (IV, i, 38–9, 217–18). 'I stay here on my bond' (IV, i, 241)—if Shylock says the word 'bond' once, he says it a dozen times (it occurs over thirty times in this play—never more than six times in other plays). We are in a world of law where 'bonds' are absolutely binding. Portia's beautiful speech exhorting to 'mercy' is justly famous; but, as Burckhardt remarked, it is impotent and useless in this 'court of justice', a realm which is under the rule of the unalterable letter of the law. Her sweet and humane lyricism founders against harsh legal literalism. The tedious, tolling reiteration of the word 'bond' has an effect which musicians know as 'devaluation through repetition'. The word becomes emptier and emptier of meaning, though still having its deadening effect. It is as if they are all in the grip of a mindless mechanism, which brings them to a helpless, dumb impasse, with Shylock's dagger quite legally poised to strike. Shylock, it is said, is adhering to the old Hebraic notion of the law—an eye for an eye. He has not been influenced by the Christian saying of St Paul: 'The letter killeth but the spirit giveth life.' For Shylock, the spirit *is* the letter; and Antonio can only be saved *by* the letter. It is as though Portia will have to find resources in literalism which the law didn't know it had.

And so, the famous moment of reversal.

> Tarry a little; there is something else.
> This bond doth give thee here no jot of blood;
> The words *expressly* are 'a pound of flesh.'
> Take then thy bond . . .
> Shed thou no blood, nor cut thou less nor more
> But just a pound of flesh.
>
> (IV, i, 304–7, 324–5—my italics)

(Compare Cordelia's 'I love your Majesty / According to my bond, no more nor less', *King Lear* I, i, 94–5; scrupulous exactness in honouring a bond turns out to be the most reliable way of recognizing it, in both cases.) Express: to press out. Portia squeezes new life and salvation out of the dead and deadly law—and not by extenuation or circumvention or equivocation. 'How every fool can play upon the word!' says Lorenzo, in response to Launcelot's quibbles. But you can't 'play' your way out of the Venetian law courts. Any solution must be found within the precincts of stern, rigorous law. 'The Jew shall have all justice . . . He shall have merely justice and his bond' (IV, i, 320, 338). And, to Shylock: 'Thou shalt have justice more than thou desir'st' (315). Portia makes literalism yield a life-saving further reach. Truly, the beyond of law.

Life-saving for Antonio—and for Venice itself, we may say. But not, of course, for Shylock. He simply crumples; broken by his own bond, destroyed by the law he 'craved'. But prior to this, his speeches have an undeniable power, and a strangely compelling sincerity. Necessarily un-aristocratic, and closer to the streets (and the Ghetto life back there somewhere), his speech in general has a force, and at times a passionate directness, which makes the more 'ornamented' speech of some of the more genteel Christians sound positively effete. Though his defeat is both necessary and gratifying—the cruel hunter caught with his own device—there is something terrible in the spectacle of his breaking. 'I pray you give me leave to go from hence. I am not well' (IV, i, 394–5). And Gratiano's cruel, jeering ridicule, with which he taunts and lacerates Shylock through the successive blows of his defeat, does Christianity, does humanity, no credit. I think we can 'indignantly turn' on him—for a start. Like the malcontent or kill-joy in any comedy, Shylock has to be extruded by the regrouping, revitalized community, and he is duly chastised, humiliated, stripped, and despatched—presumably back to the Ghetto. He is never seen again; but it is possible to feel him as a dark, suffering absence throughout the final Act in Belmont. And in fact, he does make one last, indirect 'appearance'. When Portia brings the news that Shylock has been forced to leave all his wealth to Jessica and Lorenzo, the response is—'Fair ladies, you drop manna in the way/Of starved people' (V, i, 294–5). 'Manna' was, of course, what fell from heaven and fed the children of Israel in the wilderness. This is the only time Shakespeare uses the word; and, just for a second, its deployment here—at the height of the joy in Christian Belmont—reminds us of the long archaic biblical past stretching back behind Shylock, who also, just for a second, briefly figures, no matter how unwillingly, as a version of the Old Testament God, providing miraculous sustenance for *his* 'children' (a point made by John Gross).

But why did not Shakespeare end his play with the climactic defeat of Shylock—why a whole extra Act with that ring business? Had he done so, it would have left Venice unequivocally triumphant, which perhaps he didn't quite want. This is the last aspect of the play I wish to address, and I must do so somewhat circuitously. Perhaps Shylock's most memorable claim is:

> I am a Jew. Hath not a Jew eyes? Hath not a Jew hands, organs, dimensions, senses, affections, passions?—fed with the same food, hurt with the same weapons, subject to the same diseases, healed by the same means, warmed and cooled by the same winter and summer as a Christian is? If you prick us, do we not bleed?
>
> (III, i, 55–61)

That last question, seemingly rhetorical (of course you do), but eventually crucial (Shylock seems to have overlooked the fact that if he pricks Antonio, *he* will bleed too), is prepared for, in an admittedly small way, by the first suitor to attempt the challenge of the caskets. The Prince of Morocco starts by defending the 'shadowed livery' of his 'complexion', as against 'the fairest creature northward born':

> And let us make incision for your love
> To prove whose blood is reddest, his or mine.
>   (II, i, 6–7)

So, a black and a Jew claiming an equality with white Venetian gentles/ gentiles (another word exposed to examination in the course of the play), which I have not the slightest doubt Shakespeare fully accorded them (the princely Morocco, in fact, comes off rather better than the silvery French aristocrat who follows him). And Morocco's hypothetical 'incision' anticipates the literal incision which Shylock seeks to make in Antonio. When Bassanio realizes that Portia is going to ask to see her ring, which he has given away, he says in an aside:

> Why, I were best to cut my left hand off
> And swear I lost the ring defending it.
>   (V, 1, 177–8)

So, there may be 'incisions' made 'for love', from hate, and out of guilt. Portia describes the wedding ring as:

> A thing stuck on with oaths upon your finger,
> And so riveted with faith unto your flesh.
>   (V, i, 168–9)

Riveting on is, I suppose, the opposite of Shylock's intended cutting out; but, taken together, there is a recurrent linking of law (oaths, bonds, rings) —and flesh. The play could be said to hinge on *two* contracts or bonds, in which, or by which, the law envisions, permits, requires, ordains, the exposing of a part of the body of one party to the legitimate penetration (incision) by the other party to the bond. If that party is Shylock, the penetration/incision would be done out of hate—and would prove mortal; if that other party is Bassanio it should be done out of love—and give new life. Shylock swears by his 'bond'; Portia works through her 'ring'.

It should be noted that, in the last Act, when Bassanio is caught out with having given Portia's ring away to Balthasar, he stands before Portia as guilty and helpless as Antonio stood before Shylock. And, like Shylock, she insists on the letter of the pledge, and will hear no excuses and is not interested in mercy. Like Shylock too, she promises her own form of 'fleshly' punishment (absence from Bassanio's bed, and promiscuous infidelity with others). As with the word 'bond' in the court scene, so with the word 'ring' in this last scene. It occurs twenty-one times, and at times is repeated so often that it risks suffering the semantic depletion which seemed to numb 'bond' into emptiness. *Both* the word 'bond' and the word 'ring'—and all they represent in terms of binding and bonding—are endangered in this play. But the law stands and continues to stand. Bonds must be honoured or society collapses; there is nothing Bassanio can do. Then, just as Portia-as-Balthasar found a way through the Venetian impasse, so Portia-as-Portia has the life-giving power to enable Bassanio to *renew* his bond—she gives him, mysteriously and to him inexplicably, the same ring, for a second time. (She has mysterious, inexplicable good news for Antonio, too, about the sudden safe arrival of his ships.) A touch of woman's magic. For Portia is one of what Brockbank called Shakespeare's 'creative manipulators' (of whom Prospero is the last). Like Vincentio (in *Measure for Measure*), she uses 'craft against vice'. She can be a skilful man in Venice (a veritable Jacob), and a tricky, resourceful, ultimately loving and healing woman in Belmont (a good Medea with something of the art of Orpheus—both figures invoked in the scene). She can gracefully operate in, and move between, both worlds. Because she is, as it were, a man–woman, as good a lawyer as she is a wife (more 'both-ness'), she figures a way in which law and love, law and blood, need not be mutually exclusive and opposed forces. She shows how they, too, can 'frutify' together.

The person who both persuades Bassanio to give away his ring, and intercedes for him with Portia ('I dare be bound again') is Antonio. He is solitary and sad at the beginning, and is left alone at the end. He expresses his love for Bassanio in an extravagant, at times tearful way. It is a love which seems to be reciprocated. In the court scene, Bassanio protests to Antonio that:

> life itself, my wife, and all the world
> Are not with me esteemed above thy life.
> I would lose all, ay sacrifice them all
> Here to this devil, to deliver you.

Portia (she certainly does 'stand for sacrifice'!), permits herself an understandably dry comment:

> Your wife would give you little thanks for that
> If she were by to hear you make the offer.
>   (IV, i, 283–8)

Perhaps this is why she decides to put Bassanio to the test with the ring. I
have already had occasion to recognize the honourable tradition of strong
male friendship, operative at the time. I also know that 'homosexuality', as
such, was not invented until the late nineteenth century. I am also totally
disinclined to seek out imagined sexualities which are nothing to the point.
But Antonio is so moistly, mooningly in love with Bassanio (and so conspicuously uninvolved with, and unattracted to, any woman), that I think
that his nameless sadness, and seemingly foredoomed solitariness, may
fairly be attributed to a homosexual passion, which must now be frustrated
since Bassanio is set on marriage. (Antonio's message to Bassanio's wife is
'bid her be judge / Whether Bassanio had not once a love', which implies
'lover' as much as 'friend'; revealingly, Antonio's one remaining desire is
that Bassanio should witness the fatal sacrifice he is to make for him.) Even
then, we might say that that is neither here nor there. Except for one fact.
Buggery and usury were *very* closely associated or connected in the contemporary mind as unnatural acts. Shylock is undoubtedly a usurer, who becomes unwell; but if Antonio is, not to put too fine a point on it, a bugger,
who is also unwell . . .

Perhaps some will find the suggestion offensively irrelevant; and perhaps
it is. But the atmosphere in Venice–Belmont is not unalloyedly pure. The
famous love duet between Lorenzo and Jessica which starts Act V, inau-
gurating the happy post-Shylock era—'In such a night . . .'—is hardly an
auspicious one, invoking as it does a faithless woman (Cressid), one who
committed suicide (Thisbe), an abandoned woman (Dido), and a sorceress
(Medea whose spells involved physical mutilation), before moving on to a
contemporary female thief—Jessica herself. I hardly think that she and
Lorenzo will bear any mythological 'ornamenting'. And that theft has become part of the texture of the Belmont world. It is a place of beautiful
music and poetry—and love; but with perhaps just a residual something-
not-quite-right lingering from the transactions and 'usages' of Ghetto–

Rialto Venice. (The very last word of the play is a punningly obscene use of 'ring' by Gratiano, the most scabrous and cynical voice in Venice—again, a slightly off-key note.) There is moonlight and candlelight for the nocturnal conclusion of the play, but it doesn't 'glimmer' as beautifully as it did at the end of *A Midsummer Night's Dream*. Portia says:

> This night methinks is but the daylight sick;
> It looks a little paler. 'Tis a day
> Such as the day is when the sun is hid.
>
> (V, i, 124–6)

A little of the circulating sickness has reached Belmont. The play *is* a comedy; but Shakespeare has here touched on deeper and more potentially complex and troubling matters than he had hitherto explored, and the result is a comedy with a difference. And, of course, it is primarily Shylock who *makes* that difference.

Now, let's go back to the beginning. 'Which is the merchant here? And which the Jew?' It turns out to be a good question.

THE MERRY WIVES OF WINDSOR (1597)

> What tempest, I trow, threw this whale, with so many tuns of oil in his belly, ashore at Windsor?
>
> (II, i, 62–4)

The whale is Falstaff; the speaker is merry wife Mrs Ford; and the question is a good one. What *is* Falstaff doing in Windsor? Ephesus, Padua, Verona, Navarre, Athens, Messina, Arden, Illyria, Rousillon—Shakespeare habitually set his romantic comedies in exotic-sounding placeless places, as often as not in somewhat timeless times as well. But in this play we are in a completely recognizable contemporary Windsor. This comedy, like T. S. Eliot's history, is 'now and England'. There are identifiable inns, chapels, rivers and parks. The characters sup on good Elizabethan fare—hot venison pasty, possets, Banbury cheese, stewed prunes. They climb stiles, and keep dogs. The women 'wash, wring, brew, bake, scour, dress meat and drink, make the beds' (I, iv, 94–5)—though I suppose that they have been doing that for time out of mind. Still, it all contributes to the feeling that we are amid the familiar domestic routines of a small Elizabethan country town. Since we last encountered Falstaff—not to mention Bardolph, Pistol, Nym, Shallow, Mistress Quickly—in the reign of Henry IV, i.e. some two centuries earlier (though, if we had been Elizabethan playgoers, it would have been an extremely recent encounter), it is necessarily something of a surprise (though hardly an unwelcome one for us, whatever it might be for the good wives of the town) to see the debauched old rogue trying to wing it and make out in Elizabethan Windsor. The question is—is it the *same* Falstaff?

When Falstaff says: 'If it should come to the ear of the court how I have been transformed, and how my transformation hath been washed and cudgeled, they would melt me out of my fat drop by drop, and liquor fishermen's boots with me' (IV, v, 93–8), it suggests that he is the same man we saw bantering with the 'wild Prince' (also referred to in this play). On the other hand, he does not seem to know Mistress Quickly, who is herself recognizably the same, yet manifestly different. One school of thought holds that this Falstaff is 'a new character with an old name'. Another, exemplified by Ruth Nevo, confidently asserts that 'the character of Falstaff has not changed—the craft, the shrewdness, the brass, the zest are all there'. Against that, set H. B. Charlton: 'His wits have lost all their nimbleness.' It has to be said that Charlton's reading is strange to the point of derangement. He sees the play as a 'cynical revenge which Shakespeare took on the hitherto unsuspecting gaiety of his own creative exuberance'. He maintains it was a sense of 'bitter disillusionment' that allowed Shakespeare 'to call the contemptible caricature of *The Merry Wives of Windsor* by the name of Sir John Falstaff'. He speaks of 'malicious laceration', and 'a crime worse than parricide'. You rub your eyes in disbelief.

This is the sort of disagreement which can get literary criticism a bad name. Have these critics read the same play? An attempt to adjudicate between such contradictory views is hardly called for. The point, surely, is that Shakespeare has taken a recently created and very successful character, retained a number of his most distinguishing characteristics (verbal inventiveness, resilience, and so on), but placed him in an entirely different setting and situation. On his own turf, in the easy-going inns of London, Falstaff is more or less the boss; in the respectable bourgeois world of a quiet

country town, he is a fish out of water—or better, a beached whale, as the
good lady has it. So that in some ways he is bound to look rather different.
It has been suggested that one reason for the reappearance of Falstaff in an
unlikely setting was the request of the Queen. This tradition, or legend,
was started in the eighteenth century by Dennis and Rowe. 'She was so well
pleas'd with that admirable Character of *Falstaff* in the two Parts of *Henry
IV,* that she commanded him to continue it for one Play more, and to shew
him in Love. This is said to be the Occasion of his Writing *The Merry Wives
of Windsor.*' The Arden editor, H. J. Oliver, pertinently comments that it is
unlikely that the Queen would have asked to see Falstaff 'in love' if she had
seen him with Doll Tearsheet in *2 Henry IV*—a consideration which adds
to the evidence that the play was written in 1597, immediately after the first
part of *Henry IV.* Dr Johnson was sceptical about the legend, and in his
comment offers a powerful account of what makes Falstaff Falstaff. 'Shakespeare knew what the Queen, if the story be true, seems not to have known,
that by any real passion of tenderness, the selfish craft, the careless jollity,
and the lazy luxury, must have suffered so much abatement, that little of
his former cast would have remained. Falstaff could not love, but by ceasing to be Falstaff. He could only counterfeit love, and his professions could
be prompted, not by the hope of pleasure, but of money.' Dr Johnson is, of
course, absolutely right. Falstaff in Windsor does need money—but I will
come back to him.

There *is* a love plot in the play, involving the sweet English maid, Anne
Page, and the young gentleman, Fenton, who 'dances', 'has eyes of youth',
'writes verses', 'speaks holiday', and 'smells April and May' (III, ii, 63–5). A
perfectly matched couple. Together, they conspire to circumvent her obstructive parents. There is no more basic plot to comedy than this, but as a
whole the play is not a romantic comedy. Nor is it a satire, as, say, in the
manner of Jonson. No one is savaged, no one is relentlessly ridiculed, no
one is deflated beyond restoration. Falstaff has his discomforts, but as he
dusts himself down at the end, he is effectively unscathed—and off to supper with everyone. Jealous Ford has to be made to look *and* feel ridiculous,
if only for the easing of his good wife. But, on the whole, no grievances are
laceratingly felt, no grudges are unforgivingly borne (with perhaps one tiny
exception). People are mocked, but the mocking is merry: there is quarrelling, but it is dissolved in laughter and hospitality. Inviting everyone in for
dinner near the beginning, Page says 'Come, gentlemen, I hope we shall

drink down all unkindness' (I, i, 189–90). At the end, his wife repeats the invitation—'let us every one go home,/And laugh this sport o'er by a country fire' (V, v, 243–4). This is the prevailing benign atmosphere of the play.

If anything, it is almost a kind of farce, centring on the blundering mishaps of Falstaff, and the foiled misprisions of Ford. It has been called a 'citizen comedy', and compared to, among others, Dekker's *Shoemaker's Holiday* (1599). Bullough points out that a number of realistic comedies of town life (i.e. not the court or the palace or the manor) were written in the last few years of the sixteenth century. It *is* extremely funny, sometimes in a slapstick, or Box-and-Cox sort of way, and gives unfailing pleasure (though not to poor Professor Charlton); but it remains something of an anomaly among Shakespeare's comedies. Written almost entirely in prose, it seems strange that it follows the iridescent magic of *A Midsummer Night's Dream;* and with its elements of knock-about farce, it feels odd that it precedes the sophisticated courtly brilliance of *Much Ado About Nothing.* And why Windsor between Athens and Messina; why so unmistakably contemporary England? It is a play which unarguably shows signs of hurried composition. There are lots of loose ends; situations are set up but not resolved; incomplete episodes are left unintegrated into the play (whatever happened to the German horse-thieves?); several unemployed characters seem to have no real role, though we are happy enough to see them enter and speak their bits, however inconsequential they may seem. (Who would be without Slender, in whom, said F. S. Boas, 'not only do we see intellect flickering with its last feeble glimmer, but the will attenuated almost to vanishing point. Palpitating on the brink of nonentity, he clings for support to the majestic figure of Shallow.' With just a few strokes, Shakespeare has created an unforgettable figure. And, as H. J. Oliver says, Slender's proposal to Anne—III, iv—is perhaps the funniest proposal in English literature, matching anything in Jane Austen.)

A possible answer to all these questions about a play which somehow does not seem to 'fit' in the line of Shakespeare's development, was first suggested by J. L. Hotson, who said that the play could have been written specifically, and hastily, for the Garter festivities in April/May 1597. William Green developed this idea in his *Shakespeare's Merry Wives of Windsor,* and I shall simply summarize briefly some of his work. In Act V, scene v, there is a reference to 'our radiant Queen'; and Mistress Quickly as Queen of the Fairies sends the boys dressed as fairies to 'Windsor Castle' with orders to 'strew good luck . . . on every sacred room'. She tells them to scour 'the several chairs of Order', mentions the 'loyal blazon', refers to 'the Garter's compass', and instructs them to write *Honi soit qui mal y pense* in flowers (this, of course, is the motto of the Order of the Garter). Earlier in the play, Mistress Quickly notes that the town is filling with courtiers, while Dr Caius says he is hurrying to court for a 'grand affair'. Clearly, an installation of Knights-Elect to the Order of the Garter is about to take place in Windsor. And in the real Windsor too. William Green: 'Now the Windsor setting makes sense, for if Shakespeare chose to allude to a Garter installation, what more appropriate place to locate the play than in Windsor, home of the Order of the Garter since the fourteenth century? Moreover, what need to state that the preparation of castle and chapel is for this ceremonial? The Elizabethans knew that the only Garter rite celebrated in Windsor was an installation—this by decree of Elizabeth in 1567. And the Elizabethans —at least those in courtly circles during the late 1590s—further knew what Garter installation Shakespeare was referring to—that of May, 1597.' One of the individuals to be named to the Order on this occasion was George Carey, the second Lord Hunsdon. Hunsdon was patron of Shakespeare's company at this time. He was also a favourite cousin of Queen Elizabeth, and the not unreasonable speculation is that the Queen's request for another Falstaff play was conveyed through Hunsdon. Tradition further has it that he had to write it in fourteen days, perhaps to be ready for presentation at the April 1597 St George's Day festivities. This last bit cannot be verified, of course; but, on this occasion, the whole line of conjecture makes a lot of sense in that it explains much that is otherwise inexplicable about this anomalous play.

The main incidents are all to be found in earlier European and English stories and farces. The themes of the presumptuous suitor punished; and the jealous husband fooled; and, indeed, the forbidding parents foiled, are all old and familiar. Shakespeare, of course, infuses new life into them, and weaves them together brilliantly, even if there are some bits left hanging out. The play opens with some comical talk of coats of arms, old family lines, prerogatives and titles—suitable enough for a Garter entertainment, quickly moving on to talk of 'pretty virginity' and family inheritances, and soon settling into its central bourgeois concerns—marriage, money, and class. A speech by Fenton (a Gentleman, and thus out of his class with the Pages and Fords) brings these matters together. He is explaining to Anne Page why her father disapproves of him:

> He doth object I am too great of birth,
> And that my state being galled with my expense,
> I seek to heal it only by his wealth.
> Besides these, other bars he lays before me:
> My riots past, my wild societies;
> And tells me 'tis a thing impossible
> I should love thee but as a property.
> (III, iv, 4–10)

Here is a defining bourgeois wariness—suspicion of the upper classes as dissolute and wasteful; belief that they are after middle-class daughters to get at their money. The defining word is 'property'. Anne, refreshingly, replies by saying 'May be he tells you true'. Good for her! Though with a very small part, Anne is one of those independent young women who very definitely refuse to behave like property when men—or parents—try to treat them as such. (Anne's reaction to the proposal that she marry Caius shows commendable spirit and that gay inventiveness which is the hallmark of the Shakespearian comic heroine: 'I had rather be set quick i' th' earth,/And bowled to death with turnips', III, iv, 86–7.) But the possession of property is what the bourgeois live by, and live for, and by this reckoning wives and daughters *are* a form of property. Being robbed, being cuckolded, and being duped are all forms of that great bourgeois dread—theft. And there is a great deal of stealing and cheating going on, or being attempted, in this play, both by the visitors and among the locals. Marilyn French pointed out that 'everyone in the play cozens, is cozened, or both' (except Page's son, William—too young for it). Certainly, the words 'cozen', 'cozened', 'cozenage' are heard more frequently in this play than in any other. 'I would all the world might be cozened, for I have been cozened and beaten too' (IV, v, 92–3) is a late cry from Falstaff. Shakespeare has found his integrating master-theme.

Once settled in his room at the Garter Inn, where he doubtless feels most at home, Falstaff is soon talking about 'filching' and theft with his ruffianly followers. As he later admits to Pistol (whom he nicely addresses as 'thou unconfinable baseness'—given his size, a perfect self-description)—'I, I, I myself sometimes, leaving the fear of God on the left hand and hiding mine honor in my necessity, am fain to shuffle, to hedge, and to lurch' (II, ii, 23–6)—three words for cheating and pilfering. He soon makes clear his intentions concerning two local wives, candidly revealing his venal, commercial motives.

> I am about thrift. Briefly, I do mean to make love to Ford's wife. I spy entertainment in her: she discourses, she carves, she gives the leer of invitation . . . the report goes she has all the rule of her husband's purse . . . I have writ me here a letter to her; and here another to Page's wife, who even now gave me good eyes too . . . She bears the purse too. She is a region in Guiana, all gold and bounty. I will be cheater to them both, and they shall be exchequers to me. They shall be my East and West Indies, and I will trade to them both.
>
> (I, iii, 42–71)

He has lost none of his expansive opulence of language, his gift for the fecund phrase ('the leer of invitation' is marvellous). The images of trading, banking, and exotic foreign lands to be explored and exploited for their riches have, of course, a contemporary aptness. By one of those tricks whereby language has it both ways, 'cheater' denominates both an escheator, an official who looked after lapsed estates which were forfeit to the crown; and someone who defrauds. Momentarily, looking after becomes indistinguishable from taking away—and indeed, you can't always tell guardianship from theft, or protection from subtraction. Falstaff aims to be every way a 'cheater'. For this, and for the shameless fatuity of his vain assumption that the two respectable wives are consumed with lust for his grotesque body, he must and will be punished.

The details of the plots or schemes whereby—out of fear of the madly jealous Ford—Falstaff is inveigled, first, into a laundry basket full of filthy clothes which is then emptied in a muddy ditch near the Thames, and secondly, into wearing the gown of the fat woman of Brainford, to be cudgelled from the house by an irate Ford ('Out of my door, you witch, you rag, you baggage, you polecat, you runnion!', IV, ii, 180–82, this is Punch and Judy stuff)—these details require no comment. They are part of the unambiguous, depthless fun of the play. His third punishment, however, merits a little consideration. Mrs Page draws on a folk figure called Herne the Hunter, said to roam at midnight in Windsor Forest with 'great ragg'd horns' upon his head, blasting trees and taking cattle. The plan is to persuade Falstaff to dress up in some horns and, disguised as Herne the Hunter, keep an assignation with the two wives in the forest at midnight. He will then be exposed and lightly tormented—pinches and little taper burns—by children dressed as fairies. Amazingly enough, fresh from a dousing and a beating, Falstaff agrees to keep the tryst in the recommended horn disguise. This is sometimes seen as showing his limitless gullibility, or the degrading unquenchability of his lust and desperation. But such responses quite miss the tone. If anything, you have to admire the old boy for returning *yet again* to a manifestly and disastrously lost cause.

But something more than that. This is his soliloquy as he stands in his preposterous disguise next to the oak tree at midnight, waiting for his women:

> The Windsor bell hath struck twelve; the minute draws on. Now, that hot-blooded gods assist me! Remember, Jove, thou wast a bull for thy Europa; love set on thy horns. O powerful love, that in some respects makes a beast a man; in some other, a man a beast. You were also, Jupiter, a swan for the love of Leda. O omnipotent love, how near the god drew to the complexion of a goose! A fault done first in the form of a beast. O Jove, a beastly fault! And then another fault in the semblance of a fowl; think on't, Jove; a foul fault! When gods have hot backs, what shall poor men do? For me, I am here a Windsor stag; and the fattest, I think, i' th' forest. Send me a cool rut-time, Jove, or who can blame me to piss my tallow? Who comes here? My doe?
>
> (V, v, 1–16)

This is the only time that this play reaches back to the great pagan world of Ovid. The speech has a depth of perspective, a richness of reference, a wealth of suggestion, not found elsewhere in the play. Of course, the figure of fat old Falstaff in his horns invoking the Greek gods is comic—mock-epic. But, as he stands there, opening up the myths of divine promiscuity, he becomes a reminder of more awesome things and figures. At a simple level, horned Falstaff evokes both a satyr waiting to couple with his nymphs, and a cuckold, the generically emasculated male. But he is also effectively a reincarnation of the figure of Actaeon, habitually represented as having a stag's head, a human body, and wearing hunter's clothes. Actaeon is the huntsman who accidentally caught sight of the goddess Diana naked while bathing. As punishment for this profane act, Diana turns him into a stag, in which form he is hunted down and torn to pieces by his own dogs.* Shakespeare (along with other Renaissance writers) uses the myth as a figure of self-destructive sexual desire. As in *Twelfth Night:*

> O when mine eyes did see Olivia first
> Methought she purged the air of pestilence;
> That instant was I turned into a hart,
> And my desires, like fell and cruel hounds,
> E'er since pursue me.
>
>   (I, i, 18–22)

Pistol, telling Ford that Falstaff is in pursuit of his wife, describes him as 'Like Sir Actaeon he, with Ringwood at thy heels' (II, i, 117). (Because of his horns, Actaeon was an Elizabethan name for a cuckold, and Ford thinks, quite wrongly, that he will expose his trusting friend Page as being 'a secure and willful Actaeon', III, ii, 39. After this play, the name never appears again in Shakespeare.) Actaeon was punished for his sexual transgression or presumption, and so it will be with this contemporary version of Actaeon, preying in Windsor Forest. But instead of real dogs—pretend fairies.

Actaeon is very brutally torn to pieces by his own dogs:

> Now they are all around him, tearing deep
> Their master's flesh, the stag that is no stag.

By contrast, Falstaff is pinched by children dressed as fairies. As the sound of real hunting approaches, he can discard his horns in a way unavailable to luckless Actaeon. Thus the stage direction: *And a noise of hunting is made*

---

* Thirty-five of them: Shakespeare delighted in dogs' names, and he must have relished in this list—Blackfoot, Tracker, Glance, Glutton, Ranger, Rover, Stalker, Storm, Hunter, Woodman, Dingle, Snatch, Catch, Shepherd, Spot, Gnasher, Tigress, Courser, Lightfoot, Strong, Sooty, Branch, Woolf, Cyprian, Spartan, Tempest, Clinch, Blackie, Shag, Furie, Whitetooth, Barker, Blackhair, Killer, Climber.
   Good. But it's not Tray, Blanche and Sweetheart.

within, and all the Fairies run away. Falstaff pulls off his buck's head and rises.
Falstaff, we may note, always rises, rises again, after every fall. He always
has done. This (characteristic) draining of the actual violence from Ovid's
story may be seen in different ways—as a 'demetaphorization' of Ovid's
terrible image; as a domestication of the wilder pagan story; as a comic reminder, as Falstaff pulls his stage-prop buck's head off, that we no longer
live in a mythic age—this is theatre within theatre. François Laroque adds
a slightly more sombre note:

> In this final scene, Falstaff plays the role of a 'scape-deer', abandoned to
> the mercies of the fairies and elves by whom he is cornered. Beneath the
> farce, there clearly lie primitive myths associated with the notions of sac-
> rifice, courage and metamorphosis. The dynamic of the images is in-
> tended to reveal the 'accursed side of festivity' in which what Jeanne Rob-
> erts calls 'the "innocent" revenge of its night-wandering spirits' in truth
> masks a scene of ritual sacrifice or sacred lynching.

Perhaps, though that sounds a shade heavy to me. Bearing in mind the fairies, we might do better to think of the only other visibly metamorphosed
comic figure Bottom among his elves. He had his moment of visionary
glory; and the figure of Falstaff as a Windsor stag, invoking as precedent the
polymorphous amorous exploits of Jove, has a certain overreaching splendour which momentarily eclipses both past and imminent humiliations.

   Despite those humiliations, Falstaff remains throughout a figure of real
comic stature; not just because of the size of his body, but through his relationship *to* that body.

> Sayest thou so, old Jack? Go thy ways; I'll make more of thy old body
> than I have done. Will they yet look after thee? Wilt thou, after the ex-
> pense of so much money, be now a gainer? Good body, I thank thee.
>
>   (II, ii, 138–42)

The accounts he gives of his misadventures—'you may know by my size
that I have a kind of alacrity in sinking', 'Think of that, a man of my kid-
ney—think of that—that am as subject to heat as butter; a man of continual
dissolution and thaw' (see the speeches in III, v, 1–18 and 94–121)—are
not the words of a broken man. He can be funnier about his own body

than anybody else. With his rich elaborations, he transforms what was pure knock-about farce into something of grander proportions and resonances —mock epic perhaps, but the epic note is there. Even when he discovers that the fairies were only children, his rhetoric lends a kind of dignity to the delusion:

> And these are not fairies? I was three or four times in the thought they were not fairies; and yet the guiltiness of my mind, the sudden surprise of my powers, drove the grossness of the foppery into a received belief, in despite of all the teeth of rhyme and reason, that they were fairies.
>
> (V, v, 124–9)

This is to make simple, scared error into a complex moral and psychological experience. Perhaps it always is—again these are not the words of a terminally humiliated man. He says, soberly enough, 'I do begin to perceive that I am made an ass' (V, v, 122)—an ass, rather than the bull and swan he was hoping to emulate. It is a clear enough piece of self-recognition. Thus it is that, after the assembled group submit him to a sustained bout of insults —'hodge-pudding', 'bag of flax', 'old, cold, withered, and of intolerable entrails', 'slanderous as Satan', 'given to fornications, and to taverns, and sack and wine and metheglins' and so on—he seems notably unbruised by the onslaught. His reply is hardly a flinching one: 'Well, I am your theme. You have the start of me; I am dejected . . . Use me as you will' (V, v, 165–8). 'Well, I am your theme' . . . hardly a cry from the cross. They will 'use' him by inviting him to supper. And he has the next-to-last laugh, when it is disclosed that Anne and Fenton have foiled the Pages and are now married. 'When night dogs run, all sorts of deer are chased' (V, v, 240) comments Falstaff with the wisdom of experience. He knows he is not the only ass in the forest. The man is intact.

The other figure who needs punishing, or humiliating back into his senses, is the jealous husband, Ford. He is subject to what Evans calls 'fery fantastical humors and jealousies' (III, iii, 168), and Evans warns him 'you must . . . not follow the imaginations of your own heart' (IV, ii, 153). All of Windsor knows that he is off his head in this matter, and his wife clearly has some grim times with him. He has one monologue, after posing as Mr Brooke to persuade Falstaff to seduce his wife, only to gather that, as Falstaff thinks, the matter is already well in hand, which reveals him to be pathological. This is at II, ii, 286–312, the key part running from 'See the hell of having a false woman! My bed shall be abused, my coffers ransacked, my reputation gnawn at'—the bourgeois triple nightmare—to the deranged cry 'God be praised for my jealousy'. The Arden editor, along with others, thinks that in Ford, jealousy 'is depicted "in the round"', and that Ford's suffering is 'acute'. The alternative view sees Ford, with his obsessive, repetitive, knee-jerk suspicions, as a 'humour' figure (such figures, in whom, to simplify, a single characteristic or temperamental trait completely predominates, were becoming popular in drama towards the end of the sixteenth century). If his jealousy is 'in the round', then he is anticipating Othello and we suffer with him and sympathize. If he is a 'humour' figure, he could easily appear in a Ben Jonson satire and we should laugh at him and condemn. I suppose you take your pick. It is very hard for Shakespeare not to humanize what he touches, and he does not offer the skeletally thinned-down humour-figures of a Ben Jonson. On the other hand, given the manifest virtue and probity of his wife, and the attitude of his fellow citizens—'the lunatic is at it again'—I think he is more of an amplified humour than an inchoate Othello. Still, jealousy is a phenomenon which can always generate tragedy, and in this comedy, it has to be very thoroughly defused. Shakespeare has just the verb for it; they have to '*scrape* the figures out of [his] brains' (IV, ii, 212—my italics). By the end, we are to take it that they have succeeded.

There are other characters who are something between humours and humans, types and individuals—Mistress Quickly, Welsh parson–schoolmaster Evans, the French doctor Caius, the jovial benign Host, Pistol, Bardolph, Nym, Slender, Shallow. Whatever they contribute to the movement of the main plots—and here and there they do—as a group they contribute hugely to the rippling laughter of the play as a whole. This is mainly a matter of language. When Henry James returned to America after a long absence, he was taken aback by the variety of accents, the weird immigrant manglings of English, he heard in the cafés on New York's East Side—'torture-rooms of the living idiom' he called them. The world of Shakespeare's Windsor is more a funhouse than a torture-room, but English certainly gets put through the wringer. When Mistress Quickly accuses Caius of the 'abusing of God's patience and the King's English' (I, iv, 5–6), she hits the mood of the play; as does Page when he says of Nym 'Here's a fellow frights English out of his wits' (II, i, 135–6). When Evans hears Bardolph say 'the gentleman had drunk himself out of his five sentences', he pedantically comments

'It is his "five senses." Fie, what the ignorance is!' (I, i, 169–71). He is hardly one to talk. More than the pinching and burning in the final scene, what causes Falstaff most pain is the way Evans speaks to him. 'Have I lived to stand at the taunt of one that makes fritters of English?' (V, v, 146–7). We hardly need to know that 'fritters' were bits of fried batter: it is the perfect word. Mistress Quickly contributes her inspired malapropisms—a 'fartuous . . . civil modest wife' (II, ii, 97–8); or, trying to cheer up the half-drowned Falstaff and reassure him of Mrs Page's honest intentions, 'She does so take on with her men; they mistook their erection.' 'So did I mine' replies Falstaff somewhat grimly—what else could he possibly say? (III, v, 39–41). The admirable Host, tricking Evans and Caius out of their intended duel, says 'Disarm them, and let them question. Let them keep their limbs whole and hack our English' (III, i, 72–3). That is the mood of the play. The only wounding is of the English language (it is possible that Caius storms off angrily at the end after he discovers he has 'married' a boy—'Be-gar, I'll raise all Windsor', V, v, 211—but I think it is quite wrong to see him as a Malvolio figure). The Host proves a perfect reconciler between the doctor and the priest. 'Shall I lose my doctor? No; he gives me the potions and the motions. Shall I lose my parson, my priest, my Sir Hugh? No; he gives me the proverbs and the no-verbs. Give me thy hand, terrestrial; so. Give me thy hand, celestial; so. Boys of art, I have deceived you both; I have directed you to wrong places. Your hearts are mighty, your skins are whole, and let burnt sack be the issue. Come, lay their swords to pawn. Follow me, lad of peace . . .' (III, i, 97–105). It is as amiable a little speech as you will find in Shakespeare. In general we can say that Shakespeare has not had so much fun with the English language—whether indulging its over-spilling plenitude with Falstaff (and triplets are everywhere—'accoutrement, complement, and ceremony', 'a knot, a ging, a pack', 'speak, breathe, discuss', etc.), or letting it run wildly off the leash with Mistress Quickly, Evans, Caius, and others—since *Love's Labor's Lost*. Take the play as a whole and Evans is right—'It is admirable pleasures and fery honest knaveries' (IV, iv, 80–81).

But we must not forget the 'merry wives' of the title. Mrs Page and Mrs Ford are distinctly *not* 'humours' or types, and they admirably demonstrate that 'Wives may be merry, and yet honest too' (IV, ii, 100) And they, after all, are the ones who initiate the plots—this is where the real, inventive power is in Windsor. Together, they are the master-minder. They have the comic initiative—not the men. So adroit in London, in Windsor Falstaff is nowhere (he is even humiliated in female clothes—the only time a *man* cross-dresses in Shakespeare). Ruth Nevo sees this as part of a central development in the role of Shakespeare's comic heroines. 'The transmission to the women of a masculine comic energy, of racy wit and high spirits, of irony and improvisation, of the uninhibited zest for mockery which were the prerogatives of maverick and adventurous males, was a gradual process'—Beatrice, Rosalind, Viola to follow. Nevo suggests that the transfer of comic energies to the women required the emasculation of Falstaff. This may well be true, and in an important sense this play belongs to the women. But Falstaff has that one moment of commanding presence as he stands there like a stag (at bay, as it turns out) and proclaims—'When gods have hot backs, what shall poor men do?'

It is another good question.

MUCH ADO ABOUT NOTHING (1598)

> There is some strange misprision in the princes.
>   (IV, i, 184)

>   Of this matter
> Is little Cupid's crafty arrow made,
> That only wounds by hearsay.
>   (III, i, 21–3)

This is a comedy built around, generated by, 'misprision' (to be heard again in *Twelfth Night* and *All's Well*) and 'hearsay' (Shakespeare's only use of the word). It is also perhaps Shakespeare's most perfectly constructed play, every part in its place, and working so smoothly and easily as to make the whole work seem like a piece of effortless, seamless spontaneity. You can't see the joins, or hear the engine—from this point of view, it is a Rolls-Royce of a play. Swinburne was justified in his claim that 'for absolute power of composition, for faultless balance and blameless rectitude of design, there is unquestionably no creation of his hand that will bear comparison with *Much Ado About Nothing*'. He built on previous work (understandably enough—he was writing at an astonishing rate; averaging two plays a year throughout this decade). He had experimented with contrasting heroines in *The Taming of the Shrew*: one, docile and submissive; the other, sharp-tongued and wilful. They were wooed by equally contrasting suitors: one, conventionally romantic; the other, resolutely unsentimental. Bianca and Kate will blossom into Hero and Beatrice, while Lucentio and Petruchio will mutate into Claudio and Benedick. Wooing could be this, wooing could be that—worth exploring further for comic, dramatic possibilities. And the combative relationship between Kate and Petruchio proved capable of a rich turn in the debonair duelling and sparring between Berowne and Rosaline in *Love's Labor's Lost*—good basis here for the 'merry war' between Beatrice and Benedick. That play had shown that there was a lot of potential for amusing badinage and banter in concentrating on a courtly circle—particularly if the characters are engaged in wooing games. 'Cupid' is invoked some ten times in both *Love's Labor's Lost* and *Much Ado About Nothing* (much more often than elsewhere), and they could be well called Shakespeare's Cupid plays. 'Wit' and 'woo' are words which—again—occur far more often in these two plays than in any others (except for 'woo' in *The Taming of the Shrew*); and, if I may be allowed to press a noun into service as a verb, we might say that 'to wit' and 'to woo', 'witting' and 'wooing', go together, flow together, as interrelated activities and drives. As the anonymous contemporary commentator said, they are both 'borne in the sea that brought forth Venus'.

But, while *Love's Labor's Lost* was an incomparable entertainment, it was hardly a play; for the simple reason that, when all was said and done, it lacked a plot. Couldn't really do that again. And a good way to make sure of a plot, as Shakespeare was learning, was to have a plotter *in* the play. So he invented, or imported (the figure of the saturnine, melancholic, Machiavellian malcontent was becoming a familiar one on the Elizabethan stage), Don John. When Hero's maid, Ursula, announces near the end—'Don John is the author of all' (V, ii, 97), she speaks more truly than she knows; for without his malign, contriving mischief there would not be a play. And Shakespeare, the other 'author', had a plot to draw on—a story he knew in at least three versions (by Ariosto, Bandello, Belleforest). There are variations and differing elaborations in each version, but the basic plot involves a jealous lover engaged to be married to a pure heroine; a wicked intriguer who contrives a 'demonstration' (for the lover) of the heroine's sexual impurity by persuading a maid to impersonate her and let one of his accomplices in through her bedroom window; the shared belief in the heroine's guilt, and her public condemnation followed by her apparent death; her concealment and the subsequent exposure of the villainy against her; her re-emergence and return, leading to the appropriate happy conclusion. Shakespeare took, as usual, many details from these sources, including names and the setting in Messina, though of course making his own distinctive modifications and changes. The theme of the supposed death of the heroine prompted him to redeploy the way he had handled it in *Romeo and Juliet;* to give the figure of the Friar a different kind of wisdom and authority; and to begin to explore the regenerative possibilities in the feigned death motif (which would come to full fruition in the last plays). Since the romance story in his sources was entirely devoid of any comedy, he invented Dogberry and Verges and the Watch as a—literally—indispensable plebeian adjunct to the rather closed and rarefied world of the court. They amplify the sense of a varied and interrelated society in Messina. With all these elements to hand, all Shakespeare had to do was to interweave them, and then fill in the words. Which, of course, is when it all starts to become quite unique.

A word about the title. It can certainly mean just what it seems to mean—to 'make great ado about small matters' is another contemporary formulation. In addition, a Victorian editor (Richard Grant White) maintained that, in Elizabethan pronunciation 'nothing' and 'noting' sounded much the same, and that the plot of the play depends on 'noting'—watching, judging, noting, often incorrectly. This is certainly central to the play, and there is an odd bit of banter between Balthasar and Don Pedro, just before Balthasar sings his famous song 'Sigh no more, ladies'.

> *Balthasar.* Note this before my notes:
> There's not a note of mine that's worth the noting.
> *Don Pedro.* Why, these are very crotchets that he speaks!
> Note notes, forsooth, and nothing!
> (II, iii, 54–7)

(The song itself is full of dire warnings to the ladies: 'Men were deceivers ever . . . To one thing constant never . . . The fraud of men was ever so . . .' —apt enough, in view of what is to transpire.) I am actually a little dubious about 'nothing' and 'noting' having been homophonic, though this has become part of the standard reading of the play.

But there were other associations around 'nothing' for the Elizabethans, which, indeed, a Victorian critic would have gone out of his way not to 'note'. To my knowledge, Roger Sales was the first person to spell these out. A 'thing' was common slang for the phallus, so 'no thing' could be used—mockingly, even insultingly—of the female genitalia. Remember Hamlet and Ophelia:

> *Hamlet.* Do you think I meant country matters?
> *Ophelia.* I think nothing, my lord.
> *Hamlet.* That's a fair thought to lie between maids' legs.
> *Ophelia.* What is, my lord?
> *Hamlet.* Nothing.
>   (*Hamlet,* III, ii 119–24)

And thus Benedick and Beatrice, as they finally reveal their attraction for each other:

> *Benedick.* I do love nothing in the world so well as you. Is not that strange?
> *Beatrice.* As strange as the thing I know not.
>   (IV, i, 266–8)

Sales suggests that 'the title probably offered both a sexual statement and, more importantly, the promise of more sexual jokes to come. Benedick and Beatrice fulfil such expectations, even during the play's potentially sombre moments.' It is perhaps worth remembering that the main males in the play are just back from a victory in some unspecified war which is now over. The Elizabethans used to say that armies in peacetime were like chimneys in summer (and the phallic aspect of a chimney is appropriate). It is now *après la guerre,* and it will take something, it will take 'nothing'—it will take *women*—to get these unemployed soldier–chimneys smoking again. As Claudio says:

> But now I am returned and that war-thoughts
> Have left their places vacant, in their rooms
> Come thronging soft and delicate desires . . .
>   (I, i, 291–3)

Just so.

The court of Messina is a new kind of world in Shakespeare's comedies. It is as though he has decided to shed most of the usual romantic trappings

—of landscapes, disguisings, dialogues. There is no Belmont adjacent to this Messina. The play is mostly in prose, with few opportunites for self-inflaming lyricism. It has been called (by David Stevenson) 'the most realistic of Shakespeare's love comedies'; and, while Rossiter did not diagnose a lack of feeling in the play, he felt he detected a certain '*hard*' quality—'a bright hardness runs through the play'. Bright it is: it glitters and sparkles and flashes. These people are so quick and inventive; yet so nonchalant and casual, withal. There is so much happy, self-delighting intelligence and mental alertness in the air—what Rossiter called 'impetuous exuberance' and 'competitive vitality'. Wit abounds; and it is not the cerebral wit of a Voltaire, but something altogether more expansive, unexpected, joyous. Coleridge compared it to 'the flourishing of a man's stick while he is walking, in the full flow of animal spirits, a sort of exuberance of hilarity which . . . resembles a conductor, to distribute a portion of gladness to the surrounding air' (quoted by A. R. Humphreys in his Arden edition).

Though this atmosphere is a function of the whole group, with Dogberry and Verges making a distinctive, illiterate contribution, the leading generators are, of course, Beatrice and Benedick (for a while, the play became known as *Benedick and Beatrice*). Beatrice in particular, though she is said to be 'too curst' and 'shrewd of tongue', is a far cry from the earlier 'shrew', and is Shakespeare's most complex and attractive heroine to date. 'I was born to speak all mirth and no matter' she says gaily, though of course there is matter in her mirth. On Don Pedro's appreciative reply, 'out o' question you were born in a merry hour', she is quick with another turn of the conversation:

> No, sure, my lord, my mother cried; but then there was a star danced, and under that was I born. Cousins, God give you joy!
>
> (II, i, 326–32)

Out of question, she has a dancing mind, and it gives *us* joy. One is happy to believe the ensuing description of her by her uncle, Leonato:

> There's little of the melancholy element in her, my lord. She is never sad but when she sleeps, and not ever sad then; for I have heard my daughter say she hath often dreamt of unhappiness and waked herself with laughing.
>
> (II, i, 338–42)

'You will never run mad, niece,' he says elsewhere (I, i, 89), and—out of question—hers is a mind of the most felicitous sanity.

But to Benedick she is Lady Disdain, Lady Tongue, a chatterer, a parrot-teacher, 'infernal Ate [goddess of discord] in good apparel' (II, i, 253–4)—'she speaks poniards, and every word stabs' (II, i, 245–6). She 'turns . . . every man the wrong side out' (III, i, 68), and she can take a simple word and so play with it and torment it that Benedick, invariably beaten, has to concede, somewhat complainingly: 'Thou hast frighted the word out of his right sense, so forcible is thy wit' (V, ii, 55–6). To Beatrice, Benedick is a stuffed man, a braggart, caught like a disease, the Prince's jester, a dull fool, and so on. They are both resolutely unsentimental, positively misogamous in their resistance to the idea, ideal, of marriage. How much of his misogyny, and how much of her shrewishness is the expression of genuine feeling, and how much is—playfully or defensively—assumed, can hardly be ascertained; probably even by themselves. (At one point, Beatrice speaks of 'taming my wild heart to thy loving hand', III, i, 112. If this, far more self-controlled, 'shrew' is to be 'tamed', she will tame *herself*.) Even before they are tricked into love and partly (only partly) let their defences down, they are clearly obsessed with each other. From the first moment, they cannot let each other alone. 'I wonder that you will still be talking, Signior Benedick; nobody marks you' says Beatrice, clearly revealing that she has been 'marking' him for all of the approximately thirty seconds he has been in the room in the first scene. 'What, my dear Lady Disdain! Are you yet living?' counters Benedick, and they are off—for the rest of the play. What they engage in is 'flouting'—another word which occurs more often here than in any other play. The word comes from *fluiten,* an old Dutch verb meaning to whistle, play the flute, and hiss—thence to the Elizabethan sense of 'to treat mockingly, with derision'. Given the sort of hissing, whistling music this pair make together, it is a very suitable word for them.

And it is clear that they have a history. Beatrice's first backward reference may be somewhat cryptic. 'He set up his bills here in Messina and challenged Cupid at the flight; and my uncle's fool, reading the challenge, subscribed for Cupid and challenged him at the burbolt' (I, i, 37–40). But later, when laughingly accused of having lost the heart of Benedick with her scolding mockery, her answer is quite unambiguous. 'Indeed, my lord, he lent it me awhile, and I gave him use for it, a double heart for his single one. Marry, once before he won it of me with false dice; therefore your Grace my well say I have lost it' (II, i, 275–9). She once thought he loved her, and returned his love with interest ('use'): but he was playing—and playing with false dice. Having been once bitten, perhaps it is not surprising—attack being the best form of defence—that she is so self-protectively aggressive towards him. For his part, there seems to be some fear of women underlying his virile scorn for 'love'. 'Prove that ever I lose more blood with love than I will get again with drinking, pick out mine eyes with a ballad maker's pen and hang me up at the door of a brothel house for the sign of blind Cupid' (I, i, 241–5). Without wishing to get psychoanalytical, this does sound like castration anxiety. There is no significant metamorphosis in this comedy, but there is a joke about it. When Benedick is wondering whether he will ever be so foolish as to fall in love like Claudio, he muses: 'May I be so converted and see with these eyes? I cannot tell; I think not. I will not be sworn but love may transform me to an oyster' (II, iii, 22–4). In the event, this is just what happens. After he has succumbed to love and rejoins his friends, Benedick glumly announces 'Gallants, I am not as I have been' (III, ii, 15). His friends proceed to tease and rag him, and like any good oyster, he most uncharacteristically says not a word. He has, as we say, clammed up. Even at the end, his capitulation bears all the marks of apprehensive reluctance—'I cannot woo in festival terms . . . I love thee against my will . . . Thou and I are too wise to woo peaceably' (V, ii, 41, 67, 72). And the 'merry war' is hardly over by the end, which smacks more of truce than victory. Their last words to each other are:

> *Benedick.* Come, I will have thee; but, by this light, I take thee for pity.
> *Beatrice.* I would not deny you; but, by this good day, I yield upon great
>   persuasion, and partly to save your life, for I was told you were in a con-
>   sumption.
> *Benedick.* Peace! I will stop your mouth. [*Kisses her.*]
>   (V, iv, 92–7)

Long before this, we can see that they were made for each other.

Benedick's penultimate words are 'Prince, thou art sad; get thee a wife, get thee a wife! There is no staff more reverend than one tipped with horn' (V, iv, 122–4). It is fitting that almost his last word should be 'horn'. The play is full of jokes about cuckoldry, which are also jokes about sexual appetite, since the 'horn' symbolized both; so that, for a man to be 'horn-mad' means he could be wild with jealousy, or sexually insatiable—or both. There is, throughout, a great deal of bawdy word-play, by the women as well as the men. This takes place exclusively at court, and is perhaps a function of idleness and luxury. The unluxuried, uneducated figures certainly have cleaner, if less nimble, tongues; perhaps they do not have much time to think about such things. (Incidentally, George Bernard Shaw was very huffy about Benedick, asserting that he 'is not a wit but a blackguard', thus showing that, like many promiscuous men, Shaw was also a prig.)

Beatrice sees the relations between the sexes in terms of dance. She says to her cousin: 'hear me, Hero: wooing, wedding, and repenting is as a Scotch jig, a measure, and a cinquepace. The first suit is hot and hasty like a Scotch jig (and full as fantastical); the wedding, mannerly modest, as a measure, full of state and ancientry; and then comes Repentance and with his bad legs falls into the cinquepace faster and faster, till he sink into his grave' (II, i, 71–9). The play indeed has wooing, wedding, and repentance—danced at different paces and with different steps. Immediately after this speech, the 'revelers' enter, masked, and there is an actual dance. In a way, it is a version of the play in little. Couples pair off, and engage in deceitful words behind false faces. It occasions the one explicit Ovidian reference in an exchange between Don Pedro and Hero:

> *Don Pedro.* My visor is Philemon's roof; within the house is Jove.
> *Hero.* Why then, your visor should be thatched.
> (II, i, 95–7)

The humble peasants Baucis and Philemon hospitably entertained the disguised Jove in their simple thatched cottage—the moral playfully drawn here is that you can never be sure what may be inside a misleadingly simple container. 'Seeming' and 'being' will, not for the first time in Shakespeare, turn out to be a serious theme of the play. Another couple have a related exchange. Ursula identifies her masked partner, correctly, as Antonio.

> *Antonio.* To tell you true, I counterfeit him.
> *Ursula.* . . . You are he, you are he!
> *Antonio.* At a word I am not.
> *Ursula.* Come, come, do you think I do not know you by your excellent
>   wit? Can virtue hide itself? Go to, mum, you are he. Graces will appear,
>   and there's an end.
> (II, i, 115–23)

Serious matters, lightly touched upon. Can a person 'counterfeit' himself, herself? Does virtue sometimes hide itself; may graces be sometimes *un*apparent? Matters to be more seriously explored. This leads easily to a third exchange, between the masked Beatrice and Benedick. Beatrice quotes something said by 'Signior Benedick':

> *Benedick.* What's he?
> *Beatrice.* I am sure you know him well enough.
> *Benedick.* Not I, believe me.
>   (II, i, 131–3)

Do they know each other behind their masks? Indeed, do they know each other, or even themselves, *without* their masks? *Are* they ever, truly and fully, *un*masked? Benedick may very well be speaking simple truth when he protests that he does not know him(self) 'well enough'. Is the truth in the mask, or behind it? Describing this encounter, Benedick says: 'she misused me past the endurance of a block! . . . my very visor [mask] began to assume life and scold with her' (II, i, 237–40). Is the *real* life in the 'assumed' life of the mask? Perhaps. Perhaps not. This masked ball is only a game of seeming and deceit; but deceiving words, false names, and misleading dress will produce the play-acted defamation of Hero—with the most unseeming, unseemly, results. But, in general, life in this Messina is much like a varying dance in which you can never be *absolutely* sure when or whether the masks are finally off. It is not unusual for a comedy to end with weddings and then a dance. But, here again, they do things in Messina a bit differently. 'Let's have a dance *ere* we are married, that we may lighten our own hearts and our wives' heels' (V, iv, 117–19—my italics). It is the concluding desire of the play, and Benedick gets his way. Meanwhile, above Messina, the dancing stars look down.

You may be sure that a dancing society takes care about how it is dressed, so it is hardly surprising that the word 'fashion' occurs far more often in this play than elsewhere (fifteen times). It comes from *facere,* and it has the straightforward, honest meaning of 'to make, to shape', as in what a craftsman does. But it soon acquired a potentially somewhat more sinister usage to indicate a more manipulative activity—to *re*-shape or *mis*-shape. As when Brutus says of a possible recruit to his conspiracy—'Send him but hither, and I'll fashion him' (*Julius Caesar,* II, i, 220). The Friar in this play uses it in this sense, but positively—'doubt not but success/Will fashion the event in better shape' (IV, i, 233–4). And planning the—benign—deception of Benedick and Beatrice to bring them 'into a mountain of affection th' one with th' other', Don Pedro says 'I would fain have it a match, and I doubt not but to fashion it' (II, i, 362–3). The malign plotter, Borachio, promises—'I will so fashion the matter that Hero shall be absent' (II, ii, 48–9). Given the right, and the wrong, motive, anyone can 'fashion' any appearance they choose. Craftsmanship gone wild.

As a noun, 'fashion' soon came to refer to custom or mode, including in matters of manners and clothing, which is, I suppose, its dominant meaning today. 'He wears his faith but as the fashion of his hat; it ever changes with the next block [mould for the latest shape of hat]' (I, i, 71–3)—is one of Beatrice's earliest tart, pejorative comments on Benedick. Beatrice herself perhaps goes to the other extreme:

> No, not to be so odd, and from all fashions,
> As Beatrice is, cannot be commendable.
>   (III, i, 72–3)

That is Hero's opinion, who, we infer, does not deviate from fashion one inch either way. A good girl. But even when Benedick sees Beatrice as goddess of discord, Ate, he adds—'in good apparel' (II, i, 253). They must all have been beautifully dressed. But the most interesting use of the word comes when Borachio is recounting to Conrade the villainy he has just perpetrated on Don John's behalf. Instead of simply describing what he did (pretend to enter Hero's bedroom with the somewhat unwitting aid of Margaret), Borachio—to Conrade's understandable bemusement—embarks on a disquisition on fashion. The exchange is seldom commented on, but I think it is a key to an appreciation of the play.

> *Borachio.* Thou knowest that the fashion of a doublet, or a hat, or a cloak, is
>   nothing to a man.
> *Conrade.* Yes, it is apparel.
> *Borachio.* I mean the fashion.
> *Conrade.* Yes, the fashion is the fashion.
> *Borachio.* Tush! I may as well say the fool's the fool. But seest thou not what
>   a deformed thief this fashion is?

(At this point, the listening Watch pick up on what they take to be a thief named 'Deformed'. Mr Deformed takes on a life of his own, and by the end has acquired a lock *and key* in his ear. But the admirable Watch are not all wrong; there are quite a lot of 'Deformed's about.)

> *Borachio.* Seest thou not, I say, what a deformed thief this fashion is? How
> giddily 'a turns about all the hotbloods between fourteen and five-and-
> thirty? . . .
> *Conrade.* All this I see; and I see that the fashion wears out more apparel
> than the man. But art not thou thyself giddy with the fashion too, that
> thou hast shifted out of thy tale into telling me of the fashion?
> *Borachio.* Not so neither. But know that I have tonight wooed Margaret,
> the Lady Hero's gentlewoman, by the name of Hero.
>   (III, iii, 117–47)

At the end of the play, Benedick sums up—'for man is a giddy thing, and this is my conclusion' (V, iv, 107–8). If you dance too fast, or for too long, you are likely to become 'giddy' (coming from a word meaning 'possessed by a god'!); something of this seems to be happening in Messina. The point forcefully made here is that this is a society governed, for good and bad, by fashion. This is underlined by the very next scene, in which Hero and Margaret discuss dresses, ruffs, sleeves, skirts, pearls, silver lace, cloth of gold, and so on, in connection with Hero's wedding dress—'your gown's a most rare fashion, i' faith' (III, iv, 14–15). A concern for fashion is good in that it makes people care about beautiful appearances and elegant manners—'style', in short. But it can be bad or dangerous in that the 'apparel' may be more regarded than what may, or may not, lie beneath it; as the rogue himself says, with the usual insight of the wicked, fashion, apparel—doublets, hats, cloaks—'is nothing to a man' i.e. reveals nothing of the real person. Messina tends to live by fashion (perhaps this gives the slightly hard and glittering feel which Rossiter sensed), and this makes it vulnerable to 'fashioned' appearances—both benign and malign. 'De-formation' either way. (This is why Borachio precedes his description of deception with a discussion of fashion—he knows very well that they are intimately related; if not, indeed, at bottom, the same phenomenon.) Which brings us to 'misprision' and 'hearsay'.

To begin to understand why this play proceeds so purringly, one must ap-

preciate how elegantly Shakespeare has plotted the plottings 'authored' by
his characters. Both the malign plot to deceive Claudio into poisonous jealousy, and the benign plot to trick Benedick and Beatrice into 'a mountain of
affection th' one with th' other' (II, i, 362), depend upon staged hoaxes, and
eavesdropping by the deluded, concealed victims. Taken in by, and relying
upon, varied forms of 'hearsay', they fall into the 'trap' of 'misprision' (literally, mistaking), and 'misprizing' (estimating value wrongly); leading to
misunderstandings, misinterpretations, misapprehensions—things going
amiss. It is a world in which appearances cannot be trusted—men are not
what they seem; words are not what they say. When the Watch ask Dogberry what they should do to recalcitrant drunks, he says 'you may say they
are not the men you took them for' (III, iii, 49). In Messina, you may say
that again. The two 'plotters' follow hard on each other's heels. Don Pedro
exits, promising to 'practice on Benedick', and claiming 'we are the only
love-gods' (II, i, 382), to be replaced by Borachio, explaining to Don John
how he will 'practice' on Claudio. He will, says Borachio, 'hear me call
Margaret Hero, hear Margaret term me Claudio' ('hearsay' indeed), and:

> I will so fashion the matter that Hero shall be absent; and there shall ap-
> pear such seeming truth of Hero's disloyalty that jealousy shall be called
> assurance and all the preparation overthrown.
> (II, ii, 48–52)

Here we have, in embryonic form, what will be the whole plot of *Othello;*
and, to the extent that Don Pedro plays a 'love-god', we may say that Borachio takes the role of an Iago–devil, manipulating appearances for diabolical ends. And problems concerning '*seeming* truth' pervade Shakespeare
from first to last.

But if, in some ways, the plots run in parallel, in other ways they are antithetical, as Bullough pointed out. Hero and Claudio, following romantic
conventions almost mindlessly, are effortlessly brought together with the
help of experienced mediators. They are then jarringly separated by 'hearsay' and false report. It is exactly the other way round with Beatrice and
Benedick. Resisting all conventions of courtship, they seem entirely at their
ease in unwedded singleness. It would seem an almost impossible task to
bring them into union—though, here again, deft mediators and a judicious
use of 'hearsay' and false report accomplish what Don Pedro specifically

likens to 'one of Hercules' labors' (II, i, 360—shades of the Ur-Tamer, Petruchio!). The two plots become inter-involved, thus providing dramatic
momentum (coming to a peak, perhaps, with Beatrice's arresting, and testing, order to her new-found lover—'kill Claudio', IV, i, 287). One can profitably take the point made by Carol Neely:

> Together the two plots maintain an equilibrium between male control
> and female initiative, between male reform and female submission, which
> is characteristic of the romantic comedies. In this play, wit clarifies the
> vulnerability of romantic idealization while romance alters the static, self-
> defensive gestures of wit.

The very different wooings, and eventual matings, of these two interlocking couples, enable Shakespeare to probe and explore myriad aspects of
possible relations between the sexes—in the real world—more brilliantly
and searchingly than in any previous play.

   The play effectively starts with a 'hearing', Claudio announcing his love
for Hero ('If my passion change not shortly,' he adds, ominously as it turns
out)—followed by an 'over hearing'. 'The Prince and Count Claudio, walking in a thick-pleached alley in mine orchard, were thus much overheard
by a man of mine' (I, ii, 7–10). The 'man' gets it wrong, of course, as will all
the other differing overhearers to follow (with widely varying results)—
overhearing is invariably *mis*hearing. The man thinks that the Prince is
avowing his love for Hero, whereas, in fact, he is promising to woo her on
Claudio's behalf. The error is quick to circulate, as errors are; and, during
the masked dance, Don John, pretending that he thinks he is talking to
Benedick, is happy to stab Claudio with the information that Don Pedro is
'enamored on Hero'. The main point here is that Claudio *instantly* takes
this as ascertained truth. ''Tis certain so. The Prince woos for himself' (II, i,
172). People are not to be trusted. 'Let every eye negotiate for itself / And
trust no agent' (II, i, 176–7). This is just a preliminary version of the main
plot. Don John promises to demonstrate Hero's infidelity on the eve of the
wedding. Don't trust me, intimates Don John, trust what you will see. 'If
you dare not trust that you see, confess not that you know. If you will follow
me, I will show you enough' (III, ii, 115–17). If you will 'follow' him (and
his slanders and faked 'evidence'), he certainly will show you enough. It
doesn't take much—just a few clothes, and a misleading dialogue. Iago,

who also leads while pretending only to 'show', can do it with a single hand-kerchief. What Claudio is too culpably gullible to realize is that, while he thinks his eye is 'negotiating' for itself, he is in fact 'trusting' another 'agent'—but this time, not one who helps to make his marriage, but one who seeks to work his ruin. We, the audience, do not see the 'scene' put on for Claudio's benefit—a shrewd decision on Shakespeare's part since it keeps us, too, in a world of 'hearsay' and report—but we gather that Claudio was, again, instantly convinced of Hero's infamy by what he saw and heard. And even Don Pedro, who accompanied him, was taken in—later insisting that Hero was 'charged with nothing / But what was true, and very full of proof' (V, i, 104–5). This is what Othello will call 'ocular proof and to 'trust' and 'follow' it can have disastrous, tragic results. This is part of Shakespeare's growing concern about what sort of evidence can be relied on; indeed, what 'evidence' really was. In the realm of human feeling and action, can you ever, finally, *prove* anything?

The benign deception of Benedick and Beatrice is a different sort of af-fair, although we notice that the credulousness of the 'overhearers' is once more immediate. Plato recognizes different forms of deceit—the mani-festly wicked kind; the legitimate deceits of warfare (ambushes); and the good, or useful, or 'medicinal' lie, which you might tell a friend for his own good (when he is about to do himself some harm). We should place 'the false sweet bait' and 'honest slanders' (III, i, 33, 84) with which Benedick and Beatrice are baited, hooked and landed (hunting and angling images dominate these scenes), in this last category of Plato's. If there can be such a thing as 'the lie beneficent' (and Plato's authority is hardly negligible), then this is what the 'plotters' use on Benedick and Beatrice. And, of course, there is another possible twist. Without knowing or intending it, they may *actually* be telling the (hidden) truth about Beatrice's and Benedick's feel-ing—in which case, their inventions serve the honourable role of revela-tions.

The apparent paradox of 'honest slanders' may serve as a reminder that the word 'slander' (and 'slanderous', 'slandered') occurs far more often in this play than elsewhere. And while we may say that Beatrice and Benedick are 'slandered' into love, Hero is, officially at least, 'slandered to death by villains', 'Done to death by slanderous tongues' (V, i, 88; V, iii, 3). Shake-speare had an acute sense of (and revulsion for) the gratuitous, irreparable damage than can be done by malicious slander (what Spenser, with a com-

parable loathing, allegorized as the Blatant Beast). There is an enormous
delight in word-play throughout, but there is a concurrent suspicion of the
wayward power of tongues, and of the man who is, as it were, all tongue.
'But manhood is melted into cursies, valor into compliment, and men are
only turned into tongue, and trim ones too' (IV, i, 317–19). The tongue set
free may 'transshape' virtues into vices, evil into good, and anything into
anything. The word 'transshape' only appears in this play (V, i, 169), like
'hearsay', and it is clearly all part of Shakespeare's particular interest here in
'misprision' (that Shakespeare himself 'transshapes' life into art, is only another aspect of this endlessly complex matter). When Constable Dogberry
brings Conrade and Borachio before the Prince, for once, in his muddled
way, he puts his wobbling lexical finger on the central matter—his rambling redundancies are spot on.

> Marry, sir, they have committed false report; moreover, they have spoken
> untruths; secondarily, they are slanders; sixth and lastly, they have belied
> a lady; thirdly, they have verified unjust things; and to conclude, they are
> lying knaves.
>
> (V, i, 214–18)

I don't see how Solomon himself could have said it much better than that!
And it is because so many people in this Messina are given to 'committing
false report' (of very varying degrees of seriousness), that when Beatrice
comes forward, after 'overhearing' accounts of Benedick's love for her, and
says—to herself and us—'and I believe it *better than reportingly*' (III, i, 115–
16—my italics), we thrill to feel that she has stepped beyond the tangled
world of hearsay and misprision, into the more serious, more risky world of
'trust' (it doesn't matter if we think she is—the more, or less—deceived).
Shakespeare uses the word 'report' hundreds of times, but the curious ad-
verb 'reportingly' just this once. It is, perhaps, that people in this Messina
tend to live *too* reportingly (which is why 'slander' thrives), and Shakespeare is intimating that there must be a better way than that.

   The drama of *The Merchant of Venice* gathers to a head and finally breaks
in Act IV in the courtroom. Something very similar happens in the fourth
Act of *Much Ado* though this time the scene is a chapel. In both cases, a key
civic ritual is interrupted, disrupted, turned askew—first a trial; now a
wedding. And in both scenes, there is an identical moment which turns out

to be the turning point of the play. I will come to this. The outburst which profanes and violates the holy orderliness of the chapel ceremony is precipitated by 'mis*prision*' leading to 'mis*prizing*'—the two errors being often, of course, closely inter-involved. That second word is, in fact, only used of Beatrice in this play:

> Disdain and Scorn ride sparkling in her eyes,
> Misprizing what they look on.
> >   (III, i, 51–2)

But Beatrice's disvaluing, or devaluing, remarks are a form of non-lethal mockery; at bottom, a sometimes astringent merriment. A 'sparkling'. But there is nothing merry or sparkling about Claudio's public 'misprizing' of Hero in church. He has already promised to 'shame her . . . in the congregation' if Don John 'proves' her infidelity, which leads to these comments:

> *Don Pedro.* O day untowardly turned!
> *Claudio.* O mischief strangely thwarting!
> >   (III, ii, 127–8)

Don John is the embodiment of the will to 'thwart'. It is one of his favoured words, and, seemingly, 'thwarting' is the only activity which gives him a perverse sort of pleasure. (As a word, it draws together crooked, crossed, transverse; to twist, oppose, frustrate—the quintessential drive to block and spoil.) Don John thus 'turns' the play away from its planned felicitous route to marriage and happiness—he derails the comedy. It will take another 'turn' to regain that route, set things to rights, and repair the damage.

And shame Hero 'in the congregation', Claudio duly does—with words of extraordinary virulence and loathing:

> There, Leonato, take her back again.
> Give not this rotten orange to your friend.
> She's but the sign and semblance of her honor.
> . . .
> >   Would you not swear,
> All you that see her, that she were a maid,
> By these exterior shows? But she is none.

> She knows the heat of a luxurious bed;
> Her blush is guiltiness, not modesty.
>
> > (IV, i, 30–32, 37–41)

And to Hero directly:

> Out on thee, seeming! I will write against it.
> . . .
>
> But you are more intemperate in your blood
> Than Venus, or those pamp'red animals
> That rage in savage sensuality.
>
> > (IV, i, 55, 58–60)

'Seeming' is, indeed, one of Shakespeare's great themes, and *he* wrote against or about it continually. The irony here, of course, is precisely that Claudio has been taken in by signs, semblances, and seeming. But, hearing Claudio's amazingly immoderate, intemperate language, one feels that something else is going on as well. Benedick's comment, 'This looks not like a nuptial' (IV, i, 67), must rank as the understatement of the play.

But what *does* it look like? Let's start with that orange, since, oddly, it is the only orange in Shakespeare (there is an 'orange-tawny beard' in *A Midsummer Night's Dream,* and an 'orange-wife' in *Coriolanus*). To refer to a woman as a 'rotten orange' is to allude disgustedly to her private parts, suggesting not only promiscuity but venereal disease (the relatively recent rampant spread of syphilis was a major worry in Shakespeare's London). Shakespeare has prepared for this startlingly unpleasant image, by having Beatrice, earlier, describe Claudio as 'civil as an orange, and something of that jealous complexion' (II, i, 291–2). The pun is on civil/Seville (Seville oranges, as far as I can find out, were the only oranges known in Shakespeare's London—presumably for jam-making). Hero, it need hardly be said, is nothing of a 'rotten orange'—no woman less so. The oranges are in Claudio's head—the very colour and contents of his sexually unbalanced (immature? prurient? lubricious? frightened?), distinctly male, imagination. I make that stress because, in his nauseated, nauseous outburst against female sexuality, Claudio is only the first of a number of men in Shakespeare who indulge in similar inflamed and disgusted tirades—they include Angelo, Troilus, Hamlet, Othello, Posthumus, Leontes. Whether these speeches reveal something about Shakespeare's own ambivalent feelings

and fears concerning female sexuality may be left to the individual to decide, since it is a manifestly imponderable question. I would only point out
that, in every case, the fears and suspicions are groundless, the accusations
utterly wild, the revulsion totally unjustified by anything that is discover-
ably the case—*all* misprision and misprizing. (I have left out Lear's famous
denunciation since, considering the antics of Goneril and Regan, it might
be felt that he has a point.) For what it is worth, I think Shakespeare is saying, showing, something about the nature of male sexual imaginings.

None of this is of any help to Hero who, confronted with such incomprehensible and insane accusations, can only respond by swooning. Her shame,
defamation, and rejection reach apparent completeness when her own father cries out—'Let her die' (IV, i, 153). At which point, the Friar steps forward—'Hear me a little'. He then advances the defining wisdom of the
play: 'There is some strange misprision in the princes' (IV, i, 184), a consideration which seems to occur to no one else except Beatrice (followed,
quickly enough, by Benedick). When all seems lost, irremediable, unre-
deemable, the Friar stops all the hopelessness with—'Pause awhile' (IV, i,
199). This echoes Portia's 'Tarry a little', and has exactly the same effect and
function. Here the play begins to 'turn' again; turn back, this time, to the
right track, though it will involve quite a detour. I have written elsewhere
of the importance of the 'pause' (during which things may be 'scanned'),
and 'the pauser, reason', in the tragedies. 'Tarry a little' and 'Pause awhile'
are adumbrations of this crucial moment (Hamlet tarries and pauses, arguably for too long; Macbeth doesn't want to tarry and pause at all). The
'pause' is what arrests an apparently headlong and unstoppable rush of
the dramatic action to disaster. The interposed gap of reflection opens up
the possibility of another way. In the two comedies under discussion, it allows the action to be pulled back from veering off into tragedy. And here,
the Friar is crucial.

This Friar has a more important, more creative, role than the well-
wishing, would-be helper of Romeo and Juliet. The latter suggested the
'feigned death' of Juliet stratagem as simply a trick, a tactic, for gaining
time. This Friar sees the same device as having far greater potential:

> And publish it that she is dead indeed;
> . . .
>
> Marry, this well carried shall on her behalf
> Change slander to remorse; that is some good.

> But not for that dream I on this strange course,
> But on this travail look for greater birth.
>   (IV, i, 203, 209–12)

Greater birth—he has in mind a process involving remorse, repentance, and regeneration. This theme of (apparent) death, followed by (greater) rebirth, will be most fully worked out in the last plays. Success, says the Friar, 'Will fashion the event in better shape' (IV, i, 234)—this is the most positive use of 'fashion' in the play, suggesting an almost god-like activity or magic. Thus, his last advice to Hero sounds the note—a note of 'strangeness'—which will dominate the rest of the play; and which will be heard again hereafter.

> For to strange sores strangely they strain the cure.
> Come, lady, die to live. This wedding day
> Perhaps is but prolonged. Have patience and endure.
>   (IV, i, 251–3)

With the indispensable help of the Watch—'What your wisdoms could not discover, these shallow fools have brought to light', as Borachio says (V, i, 231–3), a very Shakespearian note—the plot to defame Hero is revealed, and it remains for Claudio to perform rites of mourning and repentance. Hence the scene at Hero's monument, before the final reconciliation scene when Claudio agrees to marry, as he thinks, 'another Hero'; who, of course, turns out to be the same Hero, to the bewilderment of the onlookers. 'She died, my lord, but whiles her slander lived' (V, iv, 66), explains her father. And the Friar, who has become, in effect, the director of the play, issues a last promise and instruction:

> All this amazement can I qualify,
> When, after that the holy rites are ended,
> I'll tell you largely of fair Hero's death.
> Meantime let wonder seem familiar,
> And to the chapel let us presently.
>   (V, iv, 67–71)

One can see the intention. This is a very important development in Shakespeare's comedies and the slightly mysterious, benignly inventive and ministering Friar is something of an embryonic Prospero. But, arguably, the figures of Claudio and Hero (and Don John) are insufficiently developed for this part of the play to generate the sort of 'wonder' which will so richly and rarely suffuse the last plays. For a lot of people, the play *is,* primarily, *Beatrice and Benedick.*

I have noted that Shakespeare sometimes marks the distinctive light in which his comedies conclude—the 'glooming' morning at the end of *Romeo and Juliet;* followed by the wonderful 'glimmering' which illuminates the finale of *A Midsummer Night's Dream;* then, the more equivocal 'daylight sick' in which *The Merchant of Venice* is concluded. Here the light, as you might expect, is, finally, good enough.

> Good morrow, masters; put your torches out.
> The wolves have preyed, and look, the gentle day,
> Before the wheels of Phoebus, round about
> Dapples the drowsy east with spots of gray.
> Thanks to you all, and leave us. Fare you well.
> (V, iii, 24–8)

The wolves *have* preyed; but in Messina, clearly, the sun also rises.

 AS YOU LIKE IT (1599)

> happy is your Grace
> That can translate the stubbornness of fortune
> Into so quiet and so sweet a style.
> (II, i, 18–20)

> Your If is the only peacemaker. Much virtue in If.
> (V, iv, 102–3)

> My way is to conjure you.
> (Epilogue, 10–11)

This is, unambiguously, the happiest of Shakespeare's comedies. Happiest, in this sense—there is certainly evil (or a kind of folk-tale figuring of evil) in the first Act: a cruel elder brother dispossessing a younger brother; a tyrannical younger brother usurping the rightful dukedom of an elder brother; the unjust banishment of the manifestly good characters. But by the end, not a trace of that initial, initiating evil remains. And there are no ritual expulsions, exclusions, expurgations; no defeats, no punishments, no disappointments even; no one is hunted down, hunted out. The evil characters are simply, perhaps miraculously, 'converted' (key word). Old Adam, who foresees a time

> When service should in my old limbs lie lame
> And unregarded age in corners thrown.
> (II, iii, 41–2)

—graphic lines, which perfectly describe the old servant, Freers, at the end of *The Cherry Orchard,* when he is left, lying down, abandoned and forgotten in the empty house—is spared that indignity, and simply fades out of the play when he has served his loyal turn. (In Shakespeare's source, Adam is made 'Captain of the Kings Gard . . . that Fortune might everie way seeme frolicke', and I will return to Fortune's frolics.) Importantly, Adam is not there at the close to remind us of the distinctly uncomic seventh age of man, which, in Jaques' mordant words, is:

> second childishness and mere oblivion,
> Sans teeth, sans eyes, sans taste, sans everything.
> (II, vii, 165–6)

The play ends with a completely clean sheet, as it were. To be sure, the sour and melancholy Jaques refuses to join in the final harmonizing dance of multiple weddings (four—more than in any other Shakespearian comedy), and blissful reconciliations and restorations. But, as he leaves, he is no scapegoat, no spoil-sport kill-joy to be chased from the feast. Nobody wants him to go. 'Stay, Jaques, stay,' implores the Duke. You do not hear people saying 'Stay, Shylock, stay', or 'Stay, Malvolio, stay'. By voluntarily absenting himself from the concluding celebrations, he, wittingly or not, indicates or demonstrates that there are people, things, which remain inconvertible, unaccommodatable, inassimilable to the great comic resolutions on offer.

He, and he alone, cannot, or will not, be 'converted'. 'Will you, won't you, will you, won't you, won't you join the dance?' says the whiting to the snail, in the Mock Turtle's song (*Alice in Wonderland*). Well, Jaques *won't*. 'I am for other than for dancing measures,' he says in a tone of disdainful refusal, as the concluding celebrations commence (V, iv, 193). Jaques is He Who Will Not Be Included. He consciously and deliberately withdraws from what Rosalind nicely calls 'the full stream of the world' (III, ii, 410). The stream which the others, we may take it, will happily rejoin. But I will come back to Jaques.

After the opening outburst of evil in Act I, during which the holy bonds of family are brutally broken as brother turns unnaturally on brother, and the good are banished from manor and court, effectively all the rest of the play takes place in the Forest of Arden, where the banished take refuge. The woods of the Ardennes, somewhere between Bordeaux and Lyons, were well established as a pastoral region; and the Forest of Arden (not, of course, on any map) was the setting for the pastoral romance on which Shakespeare based his play (Thomas Lodge's *Rosalynde*—of which more later). 'Pastoral' literally means pertaining to shepherds (from *pascere*—to graze), and pastoral poetry habitually describes the loves and sorrows of (very poetical and musical) shepherds and shepherdesses, living a rustic, idle and innocent life in some imagined Golden Age or idealized Arcadia (the founding, generative texts are the Idylls of Theocritus and the Eclogues of Virgil). It is, of course, a distinctly urban (or courtly) and sophisticated genre, convention-driven and highly artificial—and most successful when it never pretends to be anything else. Pastoral romances tend to show heroes and heroines from the outside ('real') world (often the court), becoming, out of whatever exigency, temporary sojourners of this Arcadian 'world elsewhere', and then returning to their own world, usually in better shape. At the time Shakespeare wrote this play, there was something of a vogue for pastoral and woodland (Robin Hood) plays, and Shakespeare's contribution is an unparalleled exploration of the genre of pastoral. He leads his characters into the curiously suspended, time-out-of-time, pastoral moment or interlude, and then sets about exposing, testing, mocking, celebrating, elaborating pastoral's conventions, assumptions, and pretensions—in the process, not only laying bare its manifest limitations, but also revealing new possibilities in its artifice—its obvious artificiality.

Shakespeare gives the clearest possible indication of the world we are heading for in the first scene when Charles the wrestler gives Oliver news of the whereabouts of the banished Duke Senior.

> They say he is already in the Forest of Arden, and a many merry men with him; and there they live like the old Robin Hood of England. They say many young gentlemen flock to him every day, and fleet the time carelessly as they did in the golden world.
>
> (I, i, 111–15)

That 'golden world' is the Golden Age, the first age of man, in the first book of Ovid's *Metamorphoses*.

> The world untroubled lived in leisured ease.
> Earth willingly, untouched, unwounded yet
> By hoe or plough, gave all her bounteous store;
> Men were content with nature's food unforced,
> And gathered strawberries on the mountainside
> And cherries and the clutching bramble's fruit,
> And acorns fallen from Jove's spreading tree.
> Springtime it was, always, for ever spring . . .
>
> (I, 101–8)

A vegetarian diet; and permanent spring. But in the Forest of Arden, the Duke and his men are terrific eaters of meat and keen killers of deer; and the winters, by all accounts, are dreadful. (According to the classical myth, retold by Ovid, seasonal variations entered the world after the fall of Saturn, and the declension of mankind into the Silver Age. There *is* a slight feeling of permanent springtime in Shakespeare's Arden, but Duke Senior and his merry men inhabit the fallen world and experience 'The seasons' difference, as the icy fang / And churlish chiding of the winter's wind', II, i, 6–7.) There is also, in Shakespeare's play, a fallen acorn, but it turns out to be the hero, Orlando.

> *Celia.* I found him under a tree, like a dropped acorn.
> *Rosalind.* It may well be called Jove's tree when it drops forth fruit.
>
> (III, ii, 233–5)

Shakespeare is having his fun. But somewhat more serious matters are being engaged as well. Shakespeare is not simply offering some wry, undermining comments on the myth of a Golden Age which never was, and
never could have been. It is that in part of course, but his aim is not simply demolition. He knew, if only from his own early life, what country life
was actually like, and he here allows some rural realities to enter and im-
pinge on—if you like, contest, and even contaminate (but *not* destroy)—the
unactual, pastoral Arden. In addition to bad weather and bloody hunting, there are some distinctly unpastoral, even unpleasant, characters in
this Arden. Corin reminds us of the realities of the helpless bondage of vil-
leinage:

> But I am shepherd to another man
> And do not shear the fleeces that I graze.
> My master is of churlish disposition
> And little recks to find the way to heaven
> By doing deeds of hospitality.
> Besides, his cote, his flocks, and bounds of feed
> Are now on sale, and at our sheepcote now,
> By reason of his absence, there is nothing
> That you will feed on . . .
>   (II, iv, 78–86)

There *is* 'hospitality' in this forest (it is the crucial, originary, cultural value);
but, fleetingly, there is the chill shadow of its absence as well. Audrey, William, even Sir Oliver Martext (all Shakespeare's additions to his source),
come from a different world from that of Silvius and Phebe, with whom
they nevertheless rub shoulders, as it were. Or, rather, they seem to come
from the 'real' world (say, round Stratford), while the others emerge, fully-
formed, from pastoral convention—and very unreal, and sometimes silly,
they seem. I might add that, in addition to the direct references to the
Golden Age, there are also glancing allusions to the Garden of Eden, and
the 'fall' that ended *that* idyll. The first character to be addressed in the play
is 'Adam', while Duke Senior refers to 'the penalty of Adam' (II, i, 5)—
seasonal variation followed that 'fall' as well. Shakespeare also introduces a
snake into his Arden/Eden which was not there in his source. And there is
some interesting play to do with the matter of 'ribs', as there is in Genesis,

to which I will return. Not for the first time, Shakespeare is conflating pagan (or classical) and Hebraic-Christian myths, and bringing his own questioning eye to bear on them.

Certainly, the play starts with expulsion—not from, but *to* a radically reconstituted and re-imagined Eden/Arden. The expellers—the cruel Oliver who plans to burn his younger brother, Orlando, in his lodging, and the tyrant Frederick who, having usurped his elder brother's kingdom, now suddenly banishes that brother's daughter, Rosalind—seem more like figures from Ovid's fourth, last age of man—the Age of Iron, a time of terminal degeneration.

> In that hard age
> Of baser vein all evil straight broke out,
> And honour fled and truth and loyalty,
> Replaced by fraud, deceit and treachery
> And violence and wicked greed for gain.
> . . .
> Friend was not safe from friend, nor father safe
> From son-in-law, *and kindness rare between*
> *Brother and brother . . .*
> > (I, 128–32, 48–50—my italics)

That's the Age they come from; that's where they belong. There is also a distinct hint at the sort of unmotivated malignity we have seen occupying Shakespeare's interest a number of times already: 'I hope I shall see an end of him; for my soul, yet I know not why, hates nothing more than he,' Oliver confesses right at the start (I, i, 157–9). The sudden eruptiveness of evil is manifested in Frederick—'his malice 'gainst the lady / Will suddenly break forth' (I, ii, 272–3) warns Le Beau, and it promptly does in the next scene. Villains, right enough. Yet they bear some of the lineaments of the menacing figures in folk tale (from which, indeed, the story ultimately derives), or the threatening ogre/giant types in fairy tales. They are even imaginable in pantomime. The evils which are sketched out or, as it were, succinctly anthologized in them, seem real enough. But they, somehow, are not, quite. After the initial flurry of compacted nastiness, we *know* things are going to be all right. As Celia and Rosalind set out for the forest at the end of Act I, Celia says:

> Now go in we content
> To liberty, and not to banishment.
>
> (I, iii, 135–6)

By an affirmative inversion, 'banishment' is turned into 'liberty'. It is the first in a series of vital 'conversions' which runs through the play.

Once Shakespeare has got his good characters out of harm's way and safely into the Forest of Arden, what does he do with them to generate a play? It is a pertinent question since the play has almost no plot (in this, and in some of its atmosphere and effects it has some resemblance to *Love's Labor's Lost*)—no plotters, no schemers, no intrigue; nothing and no one to circumvent, outmanoeuvre, or supplant (though, of course, a couple to flee from at the start). There are none of the usual obstacles to provoke a devised and pursued line of action. There is, mainly, just love, and talk of love. Very pastoral. Except, this being Shakespeare, it is pastoral with a difference. In this connection, it is instructive to note where Shakespeare deviates from his source—what he deletes, changes, and adds. In addition to the realistic 'country copulatives' I have mentioned, he adds the sophisticated, melancholic, cynical Jaques who brings a crucial tartness and bitterness to the 'sweet especial scene' of this green and pleasant pastoral interlude. And, perhaps even more importantly, he adds Touchstone, the first of his professional court jesters, or 'allowed fools'. He has, of course, brought on fools, buffoons, and 'clowns' (from an old word for clod) before. But they were, more or less, sublimely unaware of their folly, daftness, or general incompetence. To be sure, there are distinct glimpses of a self-aware shrewdness and ironic questioningness in Launce (*The Two Gentlemen of Verona*) and Launcelot Gobbo (*The Merchant of Venice*), but Touchstone is something else again; a major innovation who inaugurates a line which will run through Feste, Lavatch, Lear's Fool, and Trinculo. Touchstone problematizes every aspect of court and country he meanderingly encounters.

What Shakespeare dropped from Thomas Lodge's *Rosalynde* is also illuminating. He kept the plot line, along with incidents and names, *almost* intact. But he cuts out almost all the violence. In Lodge, the younger brother Rosader suffers from his elder brother Saladyne's malevolent plan —'though he be a Gentleman by nature, yet forme him anew, and make him a peasant by nourture'—just as Orlando is deliberately brought-*down,* rather than being properly brought-up, by Oliver. 'He lets me feed with his hinds, bars me the place of a brother, and, as much as in him lies, mines my gentility with my education' (I, i, 18–20). Shakespeare is greatly interested in the respective influences of nature and nurture in our lives, and the relation between innate 'gentility' and the refining furtherances of 'education'. Indeed, the opening scene is a debate concerning 'breeding', 'gentility', 'education', 'blood', 'gentlemanlike qualities', 'the courtesy of nations', 'nature', and 'fortune'. But, to stay with the matter of violence. Rosader is driven 'halfe mad' by his treatment, and when he finally rebels he erupts into such murderous anger that he kills many people and devastates and empties his elder brother's house. Orlando, driven beyond endurance by Oliver—'You have trained me like a peasant, obscuring and hiding from me all gentlemanlike qualities' (I, i, 66–7)—merely 'seizes' Oliver, after Oliver has added insolence to injury by striking him. Orlando is a good wrestler, and he once draws his sword when he is desperate to get food for the starving Adam. But he is distinctly not a violent man.

Now I think Shakespeare is engaging in some sort of a deep joke here which I am not sure I fully understand. Shakespeare keeps a lot of Lodge's names—notably, Adam, Rosalind, Aliena, and Ganymede—but he changes Rosader to Orlando. The most famous Orlando was of course Ariosto's *Orlando Furioso* (1532), which was translated, and indeed performed (in a play by Greene), in 1591. In Ariosto, Orlando is a man of mighty angers, and when he *finds* poems on trees concerning his beloved Angelica and her love for another, he gets very *furioso* indeed, tearing up forests and destroying towns as he raves across the continents. Very different from our English Orlando, who is, if anything, given to great mildness—not to mention the fact that he puts the poems on the trees himself. Perhaps Shakespeare said to himself—let's see what we can do with an Orlando *Un*furioso.

That he effectively wanted to drain all the violence from his source is made very clear by a change to the ending. In Lodge, the wicked, usurping King of France brings an army to the Forest of Arden in an attempt to slaughter his banished brother and his men. Battle is duly joined, and the bad figures are defeated or slain. Shakespeare has it otherwise. The bad Duke Frederick (nothing so specific as 'France' for the strange placeless geography of this play):

> Addressed a mighty power, which were on foot
> In his own conduct, purposely to take
> His brother here and put him to the sword;

> And to the skirts of this wild wood he came,
> Where, meeting with an old religious man,
> After some question with him, was converted
> Both from his enterprise and from the world . . .
>
> (V, iv, 156–62)

Similarly, Oliver, Orlando's 'unnatural' elder brother, undergoes a change
—metamorphosis again—as his motiveless malignity drops from him once
he enters the forest:

> *Celia.* Was't you that did so oft contrive to kill him?
> *Oliver.* 'Twas I. But 'tis not I. I do not shame
>   To tell you what I was, since my conversion
>   So sweetly tastes, being the thing I am.
>
> (IV, iii, 135–8)

'Twas I. But 'tis not I. How many characters in Shakespeare's comedies
have occasion to say that, in one form or another! Shakespeare wants his
Forest of Arden to be a place of slightly magical 'conversions', as well as unchanging country copulatives. Conversion at all levels. Duke Senior's opening speech in Arden celebrates life in the woods as being 'more sweet' than
the 'painted pomp' of the 'envious court' and 'public haunt'. 'Sweet are the
uses of adversity,' he claims, which enables them to:

> Finds tongues in trees, books in the running brooks,
> Sermons in stones, and good in everything.
>
> (II, i, 12, 16–17)

This provokes Amiens to exclaim:

>   happy is your Grace
> That can translate the stubbornness of fortune
> Into so quiet and so sweet a style.
>
> (II, i, 18–20)

This is a good description of what Shakespeare himself does—translate the
stubbornness of fortune into so sweet a style. We begin to notice the recurrence of the word 'sweet'. Oliver tells of Orlando pacing through the forest

'Chewing the food of sweet and bitter fancy' (IV, iii, 103), and we can appreciate how necessary is the sourness of Jaques, not to mention the saltiness of Touchstone, to prevent this pastoral from becoming *too* 'sweet'. But sweet it is, and is meant to be. Shakespeare does away with the decisive effects of violence to explore and draw attention to the possibilities of 'conversion' and 'translation'. Con-vert—to turn completely: trans-late—to carry across, into another place, another language. Life *is* 'stubborn'; it does not easily or readily turn and carry in the ways we would like it to. The sweet magic of this play is really Shakespeare's demonstration of the converting, translating powers of the imagination. Not as fortune has it, but as *we* like it.

There is one other change to the source—a small addition—which invariably goes unnoticed. There is of course the wrestling tournament in Lodge, at which Rosader/Orlando is successful, and catches Rosalind's eye and heart. Characteristically, the wrestling is a degree more lethal in Lodge, but I am more interested in something which Lodge does not mention and Shakespeare does. In Lodge, details of the wrestling include references to broken necks, limbs, sinews, and chests—but not ribs. Shakespeare mentions *only* broken ribs. To explain what I think is going on, I must bring together a few quotations, noting the words 'sport' and 'fall'. When we first see Rosalind and Celia they are trying to 'devise sports', and Rosalind says—'Let me see, what think you of falling in love?' (I, ii, 24). When Le Beau brings them news of the wrestling immediately after this conversation, he starts by declaring 'Fair princess, you have lost much good sport' (I, ii, 95). He describes how Charles, the Duke's wrestler, has despatched three brothers, breaking their 'ribs'. Touchstone is quick off the mark:

> But what is the sport, monsieur, that the ladies have lost?
> *Le Beau.* Why, this that I speak of.
> *Touchstone.* Thus men may grow wiser every day. It is the first time that ever I heard breaking of ribs was sport for ladies.

To which Rosalind adds:

> But is there any else longs to see this broken music in his sides? Is there yet another dotes upon rib-breaking?
>   (I, ii, 125–34)

Shortly after Orlando has tried 'one fall' with Charles, 'throwing' him, and, in another sense 'throwing' Rosalind as well, Celia admonishes Rosalind:

> *Celia.* Come, come, wrestle with thy affections.
> *Rosalind.* O, they take the part of a better wrestler than myself!
> *Celia.* O, a good wish upon you! You will try in time, in despite of
>   a fall.
>
>   (I, iii, 21–5)

('Try' is sometimes amended to 'cry', meaning you will cry when your time comes, in the throes of labour. But 'try' is in the Folio and as the Duke has just said to Orlando 'You shall try but one fall', it makes perfectly good sense as it is—you will risk a (sexual) bout in due course.) The concluding quotation I need is, of course, from Genesis:

> And the Lord God caused a deep sleep to fall upon Adam, and he slept:
> and he took one of his ribs, and closed up the flesh instead thereof;
> And the rib which the Lord God had taken from man, made he a woman,
> and brought her unto the man.
> And Adam said, This is now bone of my bones, and flesh of my flesh: she
> shall be called Woman, because she was taken out of Man.
>
>   (2:21–3)

Arden is not Eden—what with the inclement weather, the blood sports, and feudal servitude; but the emphasis on ribs, the punning play on 'fall', not to mention Adam, and the added snake, make it clear that Shakespeare intends us to hear refracted echoes of the first book of the Bible. To what end, it may be asked? Eve tempted Adam, and Adam fell—we all fell. To what extent was it a 'fortunate fall'? Redemption is not on Shakespeare's mind here; he is more concerned with love, love between the two sexes so mysteriously engineered in Eden and thus, unavoidably, sexual love. He is taking a laughing look back to that mythical time when the whole man —woman business began. Physical lovemaking can be indistinguishable from wrestling—the combative and the erotic seem to merge into each other, and wrestling with emotions is only one metaphorical step away ('I'll wrestle with you in my strength of love,' says Antony to Caesar, *Antony and Cleopatra* III, ii, 62, while Orlando, for his part, is 'overthrown', not by

Charles, but by Rosalind). Sexual congress usually involves a literal fall—down to the horizontal—but it also re-enacts the primal fall when Adam succumbed to the seduction of Eve. Rosalind is not Eve, though she certainly has more knowingness, quicker wits, arguably more guile and certainly more attractiveness, than anyone else in the Forest of Arden. She is Eve-ish at least in her irresistibility; and she has certainly eaten well of the Tree of Knowledge—to beneficent, and what used to be called life-enhancing, effect. So perhaps yes, a *fortunate* fall.

Rosalind certainly wants a literal, legalized, fall with Orlando; but, or perhaps and, with her lightness of touch she does turn love and loving into a kind of 'sport'. We tend to restrict 'sport' to those activities invariably covered in the last section of the newspaper, but the word was much more capacious for Shakespeare and he uses it from first play to last. It can cover any kind of amusement, pastime, frolic, diversion, distraction. Those last two words come from verbs meaning, literally, turn away, and drag away. 'Sport' comes from disport—literally, carry away. Once again, we seem to have a positive turning, carrying activity. In Nathaniel Hawthorne's tale, 'Endicott and the Red Cross', he describes a young woman in Puritan Salem who has been forced to wear the letter A on her gown. 'And even her own children knew what that initial signified. Sporting with her infamy, the lost and desperate creature had embroidered the fatal token in scarlet cloth, with golden thread, and the nicest art of needlework; so that the capital A might have been thought to mean Admirable, or any thing rather than Adultress.' She is clearly a forerunner of Hester Prynne in *The Scarlet Letter*—though in that novel, for his own reasons Hawthorne never uses the word 'adultress', and the A is even more possibly polysemous, suggesting Art, America, Almost Anything you care to read off it. But it is that fine phrase 'sporting with her infamy' that I want. Here is a playing which transforms stigma into adornment, punishment into play, guilt into grace. This is sport as art—something, indeed, to outwit the stubbornness of fortune, and hard, unbending Puritans, alike. Rosalind lives in a happier land and a more hospitable climate—no stigma for her to cope with, no infamy to transform (unless you include the initial banishment, which the two girls instantly change into 'liberty'). But she does turn love into a sport of the highest kind. We start with the rather primitive sport of wrestling (which perhaps also suggests the primitiveness of carnal embraces); but by the end,

the sport of love is 'converted' into an art—and Rosalind is the artist. Indeed, such a fine artist that some critics have been prompted to call this
play, *her* play, Mozartian.

In their opening scene, Celia deflects Rosalind's suggestion of sporting
with love.

> *Rosalind.* What shall be our sport then?
> *Celia.* Let us sit and mock the good housewife Fortune from her wheel,
>   that her gifts may henceforth be bestowed equally.
> > (I, ii, 29–32)

And they begin to banter about how Fortune's 'benefits' are often 'mightily
misplaced'. But when Celia points out that honesty and beauty rarely go
together, Rosalind insists on a distinction:

> Nay, now thou goest from Fortune's office to Nature's. Fortune reigns in
> gifts of the world, not in the lineaments of Nature.
> > (I, ii, 39–41)

Nature is what you are born with; Fortune is what you get thereafter. It is
of course an unstable opposition or differentiation, and the matter can be
argued in different ways—Orlando is a gentleman by Nature, but he had
the good Fortune to be born of a noble father, as well as the bad Fortune to
have such a rotten elder brother, while the workings of Nature make Rosalind fall Fortunately in love with him, and so on. It is rather like contemporary debates about Nature/Culture (or Nurture). If you inquire deeply
enough, the distinction starts to disappear or become meaningless—particularly down among the genes. Emerson has it sufficiently succinctly—
'Nature, that made the carpenter, made the house.' But we still know what
we mean when we say that a man is born a male = nature, while the culture he is born into will decree how he will manifest his masculinity. These
distinctions are meaningful, if, finally, provably ungrounded. They are useful in discussions considering *why* we are *what* we are. Similarly, the Elizabethans loved debates concerning the relative powers, and spheres of influence, of Nature and Fortune, more or less apotheosized as the case may be.
Celia, in this particular bantering bout, makes the important point that

'Nature hath given us wit to flout at Fortune' (I, ii, 44). 'Mind is life's self-criticism,' said George Bernard Shaw; and the simple, though very important point, is that—like Pascal's thinking reed which can protest even as the boulder crushes it—we *can* 'take issue' with whatever particular sea of troubles rolls our way, and, not indeed 'end them', but 'flout' them. Listen to Rosalind.

References to, and invocations of, Fortune are seeded throughout Lodge's *Rosalynde*—indeed, I gave up counting after the word had already occurred twenty times. Among many rather sobering pronouncements, there is this doleful contention: 'when Fortune hath done her worst, then Love comes in to begin a new tragedie'. From one point of view and in another genre, the mighty misplacements of Fortune's 'benefits' might well be the prelude to tragedy. But—as far as Shakespeare is concerned in this play—not here, not now. There is also this in Lodge, from 'Alinda's [= Shakespeare's Celia] Comfort to Perplexed Rosalynde': 'If then Fortune aimest at the fairest, be patient Rosalynde: for first by thine exile thou goest to thy father: nature is higher prised than wealth, & the love of ones parents ought to bee more precious than all dignities.' Shakespeare refers to 'the natural bond of sisters' (I, ii, 266), and there is a deep feeling throughout his plays that it is more 'natural' to honour familial bonds than it is to break them; more 'natural' to be Cordelia than to be Goneril and Regan, though they all came, by the way of 'nature', from the same womb. Thus the initial actions of Oliver and Frederick, prizing wealth higher than love of family, have made the court (which should be 'cultivated') an 'unnatural' realm. True court-esy has fled to the forest, and, by a pastoral inversion–conversion which Shakespeare enjoys, genuine culture can only be found in the realm of nature.

In this play, all true civility, hospitality (courtly, and rustic), refinement, and respect for the bondings of love and family, is to be found in Arden. This is nicely brought out when Orlando, desperate to find food for the starving Adam, approaches Duke Senior and his men with drawn sword. There follows this central exchange:

> *Duke.* Art thou thus boldened, man, by thy distress,
>   Or else a rude despiser of good manners,
>   That in civility thou seem'st so empty?
> *Orlando.* You touched my vein at first. The thorny point
>   Of bare distress hath ta'en from me the show

> Of smooth civility; yet am I inland bred
> And know some nurture
>   . . .
> *Duke.* What would you have? Your gentleness shall force
> More than your force move us to gentleness.
>   (II, vii, 91–7, 101–3)

'Show of smooth civility' makes it sound as if civility is only a veneer which can be (hypocritically) assumed—as it undoubtedly can (and is still preferable to coarse candour). It is all part of the big question—how deep does 'civility' go, reach, come from? Being 'inland bred' is, precisely, not being 'outlandish'—doubtless unfair to many of the inhabitants of our 'outlands', but meaning well brought up. But that, as we have seen, is just what Orlando has not been—it is his prime complaint—and he has been allowed all too little of the 'nurture' he should have enjoyed. To the extent that he is a 'gentleman', it is by 'nature'. And 'gentle' is the word. He replies to the Duke:

> Speak you so gently? Pardon me, I pray you.
> I thought that all things had been savage here
>   . . .
> Let gentleness my strong enforcement be;
> In the which hope I blush, and hide my sword.
>   (II, vii, 106–7, 118–19)

We are told that only human beings can blush—it is one of our distinguishing traits—and then, only those sufficiently principled to be capable of shame are, presumably, liable to the revealing suffusion. In this play, all shameless savagery is to be found in the court. Only the forest is 'gentle' (though, we are reminded, not always and in all parts)—and has a gentling influence. As soon as Oliver and Frederick reach it, they are 'converted'.

Jaques is, perhaps, hardly to be described as 'gentle'. He has been seen as Shakespeare's mockery of the growing cult of the Melancholic Man, the Malcontent; or a wearied, debauched and now disillusioned *fin se siècle* figure (his famous speech on 'all the world's a stage' is, among other things, a self-conscious allusion to the Globe Theatre—where the play was performed—having just opened in 1599, when the play was almost certainly written). Commentators differ as to the effect his bitter presence has on the Arcadian atmosphere of Arden. The editor of the Arden edition thinks that Jaques has no specific sense of personal injury; that 'in Arden, his cynicism looks ridiculous'; and that he is 'a satirist in a milieu proof against satire'. A. D. Nuttall, by contrast, maintains that 'because he is radically wretched he is a walking affront to the felicity of Arden', and that, while he does not endanger the pastoral idyll, he is a threat to Duke Senior and 'marks the mendacity of the situation'. The case Nuttall makes is an interesting one. He compares Jaques to Caliban, maintaining that 'Caliban is that of which Jaques is the social sophistication'. As outsiders, they are both opposed, in their different ways, to the preferred harmony of society. Nuttall bases his case on the fact that they are both characterized as being less than human by their respective masters (Duke Senior says of Jaques 'I think he be transformed into a beast,/For I can nowhere find him like a man', II, vii, 1–2; while Prospero calls Caliban 'a thing most brutish', 'not honored with a human shape', *The Tempest* I, ii, 357; I, ii, 283–4). Awareness of the possibility of downward or degenerative metamorphosis is in Shakespeare from the start, though it might be thought that the Duke is joking while Prospero manifestly is not. But it turns out to be a rather pointed joke since, as Nuttall shows, shortly afterwards the Duke rounds on Jaques with a kind of lashing, disgusted anger, otherwise unheard in Arden, but certainly heard when Prospero castigates Caliban.

> For thou thyself hast been a libertine,
> As sensual as the brutish sting itself;
> And all th' embossed sores and headed evils
> That thou with license of free foot hast caught,
> Wouldst thou disgorge into the general world.
>   (II, vii, 65–9)

Jaques is notably unmoved by the attack, and, losing no cool, defends himself suavely and effortlessly. And perhaps that's it—the Duke is angry because Jaques will not join in his Robin Hood game, thus effectively giving it the lie. He remains out of the reach of the Duke's power and influence— as of course he does at the end. Both Caliban and Jaques are recalcitrant to their governors; and while Caliban is, supposedly, finally domesticated, Jaques enacts a possibly deeper unassimilability—*un*convertibility. Nuttall suggests that 'it is not a waste of the imagination to consider Jaques as a Caliban who has been civilized'—or, we might add, over-civilized; there are reminders in the play of how, as 'we ripe' we also 'rot', and Jaques may be a case of an over-ripeness giving way to a premature rottenness. Or perhaps he was never truly civilized at all. Or perhaps he is something else again—a cold voice from the outlands commenting acidly on inland cultural presumptions. Whatever, he is a provoking figure; and he certainly provokes the otherwise always equable Duke.

We first hear of him weeping over a dying stag, wounded by the Duke's hunters. Noting that the stag is ignored by a 'careless herd / Full of the pasture', Jaques, so a lord reports, broke out into what amounted to a condemnation of the world's heartlessness.

> 'Sweep on, you fat and greasy citizens,
> 'Tis just the fashion; wherefore do you look
> Upon that poor and broken bankrupt there?'
> Thus most invectively he pierceth through
> The body of the country, city, court,
> Yea, and of this our life, swearing that we
> Are mere usurpers, tyrants, and what's worse,
> To fright the animals and to kill them up
> In their assigned and native dwelling place.
>
> (II, i, 55–63)

There is no plausible case to be made out for Jaques as a potential Animal Rights sympathizer. He enjoys wrong-footing people, making them uneasy in their assumed positions and aims, so it pleases him to take the negative line—most inventively—and see the usurped Duke as himself a kind of usurper of the forest animals. The Duke seems unmoved, and purports to enjoy Jaques in his 'sullen fits', but he cannot exactly relish having his forest lifestyle cast in that light. There is a touch of self-deception in his rather self-contratulatory Sherwood Forestry, and it is better that it should be audibly pointed out. For his part, Jaques prefers to 'avoid' the Duke as being 'too disputable' (II, v, 30). He doesn't care for the company of 'Signior Love', Orlando, either—'let's meet as little as we can', and Orlando has as little liking for 'Monsieur Melancholy'—'I do desire we may be better strangers' (III, ii, 255–6). He doesn't get on much better with Ganymede–Rosalind, to whom he boasts of his unique, *sui generis,* 'melancholy of mine own' and his 'humorous sadness' (IV, i, 15–19). Rosalind declares that she prefers merriness to sadness, and he quickly leaves. He certainly sees himself as a serious satirist, 'anatomizing' folly, trying to 'cleanse the foul body of th' infected world' (II, vii, 60); but perhaps he might best be regarded as, more generally, a requisite principle of dissonance. Early on, when the Duke is told that Jaques has been caught in an uncharacteristically 'merry' mood 'hearing of a song' (there are, incidentally, more songs in this play than in any other—the forest is full of music, as is Prospero's Isle), the Duke exclaims:

> If he, compact of jars, grow musical,
> We shall have shortly discord in the spheres.
> (II, vii, 5–6)

If *Jaques* starts becoming harmonious, the very music of the spheres will go out of tune, because he lives by disagreement and by being contrary, and he can only be what the other isn't. He is 'compact of jars'—*composed* of discord, not just occasionally discordant: we have lost much of the force of the old word 'jar', but for Shakespeare it carried a powerful harshness (civil wars were civil jars). Jaques lives by and for 'jars': he *is* the jarring sound which makes you appreciate what true harmony is, and as such he is, in this play, indispensable. It would be an immeasurably weaker, more flaccid affair without him. It is oddly fitting that he is given what is effectively the final 'bequeathing' speech, which lays out all their futures. He delivers it with strange dignity and authority, before taking his 'jars' away from a scene of what must be by now, for him, altogether too much harmony.

The person in the forest whom Jaques finds most congenial, or enjoyable, or even estimable, is, of course, Touchstone, whom he extols in his first actual speech. 'A fool, a fool! I met a fool i' th' forest,/ A motley fool!' (II, vii, 12–13). As Jaques describes him, Touchstone 'hath been a courtier', and his somewhat scrambled brain is 'crammed' with all sorts of unusual observations 'the which he vents/ In mangled forms'. A mangling man is bound to appeal to a jarring man. And Jaques concludes his eulogy—'O that I were a fool!/ I am ambitious for a motley coat.' He has met his welcome contrary —and equal (II, vii, 40–43). Touchstone is (as I have mentioned) a new kind of fool in Shakespeare, and the decision to bring him into the pastoral was as inspired as the introduction of Jaques. He is called, variously, 'Nature's natural' (I, ii, 47) and 'clownish fool' (I, iii, 128), yet, silly as he sometimes seems, he is really, as we say, nobody's fool. He has his wits about him, but uses them in unusual, unpredictable ways. Those critics—there are some—who think he simply spouts nonsense, are themselves the more deceived—fooled, we might say. Duke Senior is closer to the mark when he says—'He uses his folly like a stalking horse, and under the presentation of that he shoots his wit' (V, iv, 106–7).

That he is going to be an antithetical presence in the Arden pastoral, he makes clear with his first words in the forest. 'Ay, now am I in Arden, the more fool I. When I was at home, I was in a better place, but travelers must be content' (II, iv, 15–17). (Perhaps pertinently, Jaques also sees himself as 'a traveler', IV, i, 20—these two are rootless, they drift anywhere.) Touchstone has a mocking, or undermining, or teasing—or simply rude—word for everyone, Duke or peasant, court lady or goat-girl. And only he can reduce aloof Jaques to helpless laughter. He is sophisticated enough to cite Ovid—the last time the Roman poet appears by name in Shakespeare. In his wooing of Audrey, which serves as a tolerably rank burlesque of the courtly and poetic courtship which elsewhere prevails in Arden, Touchstone strikes an ironic pose:

> I am here with thee and thy goats, as the most capricious poet, honest Ovid, was among the Goths.
>
> (III, iii, 6–8)

The joke is multiple. Goths were pronounced 'Goats' in Elizabethan England; Latin goats were '*capers*', and not-so-honest Ovid was exiled among the Gothic Getae for writing some distinctly *caper*icious poetry (*Ars Amatoria*); while Touchstone is intending some strictly goatish business with goat-girl Audrey. Not the usual pastoral tone. Jaques (listening and speaking aside) responds with a by now familiar allusion to Ovid's *Metamorphoses*:

> O knowledge ill-inhabited, worse than Jove in a thatched house!
>
> (III, iii, 9–10)

In *Much Ado* the story was invoked in connection with misleading appearances: here Jaques refers to finding things in incongruous places—for the impoverished Baucis and Philemon were surprisingly courteous and generous to the disguised Jove. In a pastoral play where harshness and rejection reign at court and love and hospitality have removed to the forest, the allusion is especially apt (as Lodge says in his pastoral—'crownes have crosses when mirth is in cottages').

Touchstone's attitude to love is unequivocally carnal, sexual, without romantic sentiment or rhetoric. Introducing himself to Duke Senior at the end he says: 'I press in here, sir, amongst the rest of the country copulatives, to swear and to forswear, according as marriage binds and blood breaks' (V, iv, 56–8). 'Copulatives' was the Latinate term for couples about to get married (those who would couple); but of course it cannot but bring to mind the fact that an important part of love between young men and women involves copulation. Copulate is what the animals do, as Touchstone reminds the honest shepherd, Corin—'That is another simple sin in you: to bring the ewes and the rams together and to offer to get your living by the copulation of cattle' (III, ii, 78–80). It is what humans do, too, but the high, idealizing romantic love of conventional pastoral does not care to look that way (though Rosalind glances at it a couple of times). Touchstone *only* looks that way, lining himself up with the animals. 'As the ox hath his bow, sir, the horse his curb, and the falcon her bells, so a man hath his desires; and as pigeons bill, so wedlock would be nibbling' (III, iii, 76–9). Shakespeare never ever suggests that love can be reduced to sexual gratification, and Touchstone's view of the matter is hardly endorsed in a play dominated by Rosalind. But a full love importantly includes it, and to ignore or occlude the fact is to risk vaporizing away into the simpering silliness of a Silvius. Silvius is true to the pastoral convention which produced him; but Shakespeare, of course, is true to life. So he sends Touchstone to press in, not just among the country copulatives, but among the courtly and Arcadian romantic lovers as well. He also reminds them—and us—that 'We that are true lovers run into strange capers; but as all is mortal in nature, so is all nature in love mortal in folly' (II, iv, 51–4). In Barber's words, Touchstone 'forestalls potential audience cynicism'—we will hardly find a more deflationary, unromantic voice than his. It is because of Touchstone wandering around the forest—with Jaques on the loose as well—that we have pastoral with a difference; which includes a much more comprehensive consideration of what might be held in that 'captious and inteemable sieve' of a word (I steal from *All's Well That Ends Well*)—love. (He is once called a 'whetstone', and he *is* a sort of 'touchstone'—he does serve to sharpen things up, and, indirectly, test their real qualities. There are also some sparks.)

One of the most important encounters he has is with Corin. Like their betters, they discuss manners, breeding, art and nature, with the good Corin —he has an honest rustic dignity which is proof against mockery and not reducible to pastoral convention—giving at least as good as he gets. Arguably better. 'Those that are good manners at the court are as ridiculous in the country as the behavior of the country is most mockable at the court' (III, ii, 45–8). True. And there is truth, too, in what seems like Touchstone's equivocating answer to Corin's question—'how like you this shepherd's life?'

> Truly, shepherd, in respect of itself, it is a good life; but in respect that it is a shepherd's life, it is naught. In respect that it is solitary, I like it very well; but in respect that it is private, it is a very vile life. Now in respect it is in the fields, it pleaseth me well; but in respect it is not in the court, it is tedious. As it is a spare life, look you, it fits my humor well; but as there is no more plenty in it, it goes much against my stomach.
>
> (III, ii, 13–21)

I have seen this described as a piece of double-talking nonsense to bamboozle the simple Corin, but of course it is nothing of the kind. You can look at the same thing in different ways, from different perspectives. One description need not cancel out another. Indeed, if it is an equally plausible description, it supplements the first and we are the richer. Of course you can look at the same life with courtly eyes, and with country eyes. That is what Shakespeare himself is doing, with the implicit exhortation—be flexible, be plural, be inclusive. Monocularity is impoverishing.

Touchstone's proposed rough-and-ready country marriage with Audrey (a rural reality, called a hedge-wedding), serves as a contrast, perhaps a travesty, in advance, of the mock marriage played out by Rosalind–Ganymede and Orlando just two scenes later. (Not so mock either. Harold Brooks pointed out that an espousal, called in legal terms *sponsalia per verba de praesenti,* takes place if the couple declare that they take each other as husband and wife right now, at this very moment. Marriage by this means was, apparently, still valid in the sixteenth century. This gives an extra piquancy to the scene. No wonder Rosalind is so particularly high-spirited and playful afterwards. It's not every day that a girl gets married, even if the husband doesn't realize it has happened!) Touchstone, regretting that his Ovidian wit cannot be appreciated by the simple Audrey ('I am not a slut, though I thank the gods I am foul', III, iii, 36), says to her 'Truly, I would the gods had made thee poetical', and the following exchange is vital to the whole play:

> *Audrey.* I do not know what poetical is. Is it honest in deed and word? Is it a true thing?
> *Touchstone.* No, truly; for the truest poetry is the most feigning, and lovers are given to poetry, and what they swear in poetry may be said as lovers they do feign.
>   (III, iii, 16–21)

Is it a true thing? No one better to ask than, indirectly, Shakespeare, whose whole play may be seen as an extended pondering and answering of this deepest of questions. Touchstone's response is both cynical-sounding and arrestingly to the point. The question as to whether poets were liars was a commonly debated one, and Touchstone's succinct formulation—'the truest poetry is the most feigning'—goes to the heart of the matter. It depends on hearing 'fain' behind, or within 'feign'—etymologically unrelated but exact homophones (a moment later Jaques says 'I would fain see this meeting', III, iii, 44, as they prepare for the wedding). 'Feign' comes from *fingere*—to form, conceive, contrive, subsequently to pretend. 'Fain'—gladly, willingly—comes from an old word for joy, and indicates desire. We can fashion a pretend-form of what it is we want. Poetry—art—thus becomes a glad contrivance through which we project and dramatize our desires. Seen this way, the truest poetry *is* the most feigning–faining—the highest artifice satisfying our deepest needs. Life re-presented just as we would like it.

Curiously enough, Jaques interrupts the hedge-wedding—perhaps not liking to see a court man (even a court fool) go rustic; perhaps because he is turning ascetic and religious, and is disgusted by such country 'copulatives' (at the end, he leaves to seek out the company of a 'convertite').

> And will you, being a man of your breeding, be married under a bush like a beggar? Get you to church, and have a good priest that can tell you what marriage is.
>   (III, iii, 80–83)

Touchstone and Audrey duly join all the other couples in honourable wedlock at the end, though Jaques himself foresees that Touchstone will 'break'
his 'bond' within two months—a courtier/animal (Ovid/goat) to the end.
But Touchstone makes one more crucial contribution to the play. Just before the end, concerning the matter of lying and quarrelling, he gives a brilliant account of 'the degrees of the lie'. His two long speeches here (V, iv,
69–82, 90–103) are often seen as a mockery, a parody, of the minutely dis-
criminated niceties of court etiquette. Possibly (although avoiding the brutality of duelling through adroit formulaic politeness is not a trivial matter);
but they make a point on which the—peaceful—conclusion of the play depends. Again, as so often in the play, there is a concern with manners—and
the taming of incipient violence. At issue is how you may avoid coming to
blows over an accusation of lying. 'O sir, we quarrel in print, by the book, as
you have books for good manners. I will name you the degrees.' And so he
does—Retort Courteous, Quip Modest, Reply Churlish, Reproof Valiant,
Countercheck Quarrelsome, Lie with Circumstance, Lie Direct.

> All these you may avoid but the Lie Direct, and you may avoid that too,
> with an If. I knew when seven justices could not take up [settle] a quarrel,
> but when the parties were met themselves, one of them thought but of an
> If: as, 'If you said so, then I said so'; and they shook hands and swore
> brothers. Your If is the only peacemaker. Much virtue in If.
>
> (V, iv, 96–103)

Almost immediately, the figure of Hymen enters to soft music, and the play
resolves itself in the doubly manifest artifice of a Masque.

If—such a small, but such a potent conjunction (from the old Norse
ef, but ultimately, and fittingly—when did humans start thinking alterna-
tively?—'of unknown origin'). It opens up a whole new space of condition-
ality and supposition—the world of might be, could be, should be; the
boundless realm of *may*-be. This tiny little sound significantly reveals that
the human mind, while it is eager to establish actualities, also wants to entertain possibilities. Theatre drama itself depends on a massive 'If', being
conditional on what Coleridge called 'the willing suspension of disbelief'
(cf. Dr Johnson—in connection with Shakespeare's plays—'delusion, *once
delusion be admitted,* knows no certain limit'—my italics). The title of one
of Pirandello's most famous plays is *Cosi e, se vi pare!*—translated as *It Is*

So! (*If You Think So*). In this case, the satire is against malign gossips, who insist that what they speculatively like to imagine about a family is the actual truth concerning that family. This is the dark downside of the willingness to believe in one's own ill-founded fabrications and projections. But in art, consciously deployed, it can bring great benefits. Hans Vaihinger wrote a work entitled *The Philosophy of 'As if'*, and what it had to say about the rich role that possible, plausible, provisional fictions may play in our life and thinking had an influence on Wallace Stevens—a poet of 'If' if ever there was one ('The final belief is to believe in a fiction, which you know to be a fiction, there being nothing else'). I will stray no further afield into the theory of fictions. But in his theatre, Shakespeare can give Pirandello's title a happy turn, and say—*if* you are willing to believe, make-believe, in Rosalind and the others, as *they* believe, make-believe in Hymen and the Masque orchestrating the peaceful, harmonious conclusion, if you can just think so; then, for a time anyway, it is so. Much virtue in If.

Much virtue in Rosalind, too—'the mannish Rosalind' as Henry James interestingly called her; Lodge's 'amorous Girle–boye'. Like 'If', she is, in this play, 'your only peacemaker': she arranges, directs, and stages the gathering harmonizations and couplings with which the action concludes. (For the *dénouement* she plans, she has an 'if'—five of them—for all the unsatisfied lovers as she promises them, variously, contentment: 'I will content you if what pleases you contents you, and you shall be married tomorrow' and so on, V, ii, 108–119. If you follow my commands, it will all be as you would like it.) She is also the leading actor–actress in her own play. We have seen, once before, a boy actor playing a girl playing a boy who describes playing a girl (Julia in *The Two Gentlemen of Verona*); here, we have a further refinement, since here the heroine plays a boy who then proceeds to play at being—herself! One may well feel that this disorienting recesssional device can hardly be taken further. When Rosalind–Ganymede—teasing, provocative—says to Orlando (who is, we may note, a rather simple, straightforward lad, with none of the sparkling wit of a Berowne or a Benedict):

> Come, woo me, woo me; for now I am in a holiday humor and like enough to consent. What would you say to me now, an I were your very very Rosalind?
>
> (IV, i, 64–7)

she is at play in the wide world of the conditional ('an' = 'if'), and having tremendous fun. It is a game with an agreeable sexual piquancy and ambiguity, for both of them perhaps. At the same time, she *is* his 'very very Rosalind'; here the 'most feigning' ('I would cure you, if you would but call me Rosalind', III, ii, 416; let's pretend) is also the simple truth. Just so, when she entices Orlando into the mock marriage, it is, did he but know it, also a real one. Touchstone's definition of the 'truest poetry' is perceptibly justified.

Once she assumes men's clothes, it is as if boundless performing energies are released in her. She becomes positively Protean, a virtuoso of transformations. Seemingly, she can do anything, play anyone, every kind of woman and, man (except a physically tough one: she faints at the sight of Orlando's blood, though she tries to pretend it is a 'counterfeit' swoon. But, for once, this is *not* 'feigning'; there are limits even to her creative simulations. Involuntarily, she is very very true to her woman's tenderness.) Being no longer confined to a woman's restricted role, Rosalind is free to enter more deeply into masculine proclivities and potencies than any of the other Shakespearian heroines who assume male disguise. Like Portia, she becomes the master–mistress of the whole situation. She is the central consciousness in the forest, where she takes control. Ultimately, she runs things. Her disguise affords her detachment, even while her engaged feelings ensure her involvement; so that she can comment ironically, wisely, angrily (to Phebe), wryly, sadly, happily on all the lovers, including herself. She can look at love from every angle, so that her vision and comprehension is much wider and more inclusive than the partial attitudes displayed by goatish Touchstone and soppy Silvius. Yeats once said of John Donne that he could be as metaphysical as he pleased because he could be as physical as he pleased. Adapting this, we may say that Rosalind can be as romantic as she pleases because she can be as realistic as she pleases—and knows to be necessary. Orlando, a conventional hero–romantic lover all the way down, maintains that he will love 'for ever and a day'.

> *Rosalind.* Say 'a day,' without the 'ever.' No, no, Orlando. Men are April
>   when they woo, December when they wed. Maids are May when they
>   are maids, but the sky changes when they are wives.
>
>   (IV, i, 139–42)

By her own account, Rosalind is 'many fathom deep' in love; but her enlarged forest consciousness knows that love, too, has its seasons.

What Rosalind will not tolerate is affectation, humourless pretensions, and self-deception. Hence her rebuke to the coquettish Phebe:

> But mistress, know yourself. Down on your knees,
> And thank heaven, fasting, for a good man's love.
>
> (III, v, 57–8)

Know thyself. Bullough pointed out that it is really with this play that self-knowledge starts to become an important theme for Shakespeare, and he added that this state is easier to achieve in the green world than in the court—Rosalind's forest, Lear's heath, Prospero's island. It is as if the green world was a place of unavoidable honesties, irrefutable exposures. Touchstone, wonderfully cryptic, at one point says to Rosalind: 'You have said; but whether wisely or no, let the forest judge' (III, ii, 121–2). As who should say—the forest will always find you out. The difficulties of achieving self-knowledge (and the resistances to, and avoidances of it) are central to the great tragedies. Lear, tragically in the event, 'hath ever but slenderly known himself (I, i, 295–6). While Macbeth, who knows himself only too well, moves tragedy into a new key when he realizes 'To know my deed, 'twere best not know myself' (II, ii, 72). But, in this play, self-knowledge is arrived at through, and in, comedy. And it is the 'amorous Girle–boye' Rosalind, by common consent the most delightful of all Shakespeare's heroines, who is the principal enabler, just as it is she who arranges the concluding multiple marriages. Though, to do this, she has to have recourse to a little 'conjuring'.

At the end, Ganymede reverts to being very Rosalind who, having made 'all this matter even' (V, iv, 18), then, in the Epilogue, reverts to being a, by this time very hermaphroditic, boy actor. This final step back into the *he*ness of the actor from the *she*ness of the character ensures that gender distinctions remain provocatively problematical to the end—as David Carroll nicely says about this final appearance of the amorous girl–boy character/boy–girl actor—'we had forgotten she was not a woman'. In that Epilogue, he/she says 'My way is to conjure you'. *Con-jurare* is to band together with an oath, thence to conspire, to plot, to exorcize: also (OED) 'to constrain to appear by invocation ... effect, bring out, by juggling ... produce magical effects by natural means, perform marvels, cause to appear to the fancy'. Thus, a 'conjurer' can be one who (seriously) conjures up spirits, and one who (admittedly) uses legerdemain to 'produce magical effects'. Clever tricks or solemn summonings. Conjuring can be a kind of feigning, and vice-versa. You could hardly find better words for what Shakespeare does in the theatre, and how he does it. And it all depends on a kind, on many kinds, of 'magic'. A 'Magus' was a member of an ancient Persian priestly caste (the *magi* were the wise men from the East who came to worship the child Jesus); anglicized as 'mage' it can mean a wise man or a magician. Perhaps, also, a Shakespeare. Certainly, a Rosalind. Promising Orlando a happy resolution to his longings, she tells him:

> Believe then, if you please, that I can do strange things. I have, since I was three year old, conversed with a magician, most profound in his art and yet not damnable . . . it is not impossible to me, if it appear not inconvenient to you, to set her [Rosalind] before your eyes tomorrow, human as she is, and without any danger.
>
> (V, ii, 58–68)

Of course it is 'not impossible' since she *is* Rosalind; and anything less than 'inconvenient' to Orlando than seeing Rosalind, it is hard to imagine. By his own account, he is by now close to bursting. So why the mystification; why this circuitous route to happiness? Why the ensuing artifice; the staging of Hymen? Shakespeare wants us to see the magic, and also see it for what it is. It is a conjuring trick; it is also a serious invocation working to wondrous effect. Note that it is good magic, white magic—'not damnable'. This is the first time that Shakespeare brings benign magic into his drama (Richard III was execrated as a 'black magician'—fair enough). And of course, that drama will culminate in the awesome magic of Prospero. And what more fitting words for Shakespeare himself than 'a magician, most profound in his art and yet not damnable'. Rosalind is acting as his deputy.

Hymen is the spirit of concord:

> Then is there mirth in heaven
> When earthly things made even
>   Atone together
>   . . .

> Peace ho! I bar confusion:
> 'Tis I must make conclusion
>   Of these most strange events.
>   (V, iv, 108–10, 125–7)

So should the best comedies end; with bad things 'atoned' for, and people at one with each other. In this play, Shakespeare shows—to perfection—how to bring it off. A final point. The last song of the play is to Hymen.

> Wedding is great Juno's crown,
>   O blessed bond of board and bed!
> 'Tis Hymen peoples every town;
>   High wedlock then be honored.
> Honor, high honor, and renown
> To Hymen, god of every town!
>   (V, iv, 141–6)

The last song in Lodge's *Rosalynde* is a true eclogue, about a shepherd and his lass who finally marry 'And fore God Pan did plight their troth'. Pan was an essentially rural god; Shakespeare, realist and now Londoner, wants the final stress of his play to look back to the town. Though only after the testing, healing forest has judged. And the magic has worked.

 TWELFTH NIGHT (1601)

> *Viola.* I am not that I play. Are you the lady of the house?
> *Olivia.* If I do not usurp myself, I am.
>   (I, v, 182–4)

> *Olivia.* I prithee tell me what thou think'st of me.
> *Viola.* That you do think you are not what you are.
> *Olivia.* If I think so, I think the same of you.
> *Viola.* Then think you right. I am not what I am.

> *Olivia.* I would you were as I would have you be.
> *Viola.* Would it be better, madam, than I am?
>
> (III, i, 140–45)

Julia dressed as a page-boy in order to follow and serve her faithless lover, Proteus (*The Two Gentlemen of Verona*); Portia dressed as a man to enter the male world of the law and rescue her husband's friend; Rosalind adopted 'a swashing and a martial outside' to reduce the dangers to two helpless women fleeing into the forest from the court (*As You Like It*). But Viola, in what is sometimes called the last of Shakespeare's 'happy comedies', gives no clear reason for assuming male disguise. After being rescued from the shipwreck, she finds herself without role and direction in a strange land. 'And what should I do in Illyria?' (I, ii, 3) she rhetorically asks the good captain who has saved her. She asks who governs in Illyria and learns about Orsino and his love for the lady Olivia. After being told that Olivia has 'abjured the sight / And company of men', Viola responds:

> O that I served that lady,
> And might not be delivered to the world,
> Till I had made mine own occasion mellow,
> What my estate is.
>
> (I, ii, 41–4)

The Captain points out apparently insuperable difficulties, and Viola switches to the Duke.

> I prithee (and I'll pay thee bounteously)
> Conceal me what I am, and be my aid
> For such disguise as haply will become
> The form of my intent. I'll serve this duke.
> Thou shalt present me as an eunuch to him;
> It may be worth thy pains.
>
> (I, ii, 52–7)

The Arden editors comment that this indicates 'neither a deep-laid scheme nor an irresponsible caprice' and add in a footnote: '"Till I had made mine own occasion mellow" will pass in the theatre. There is, and can be, no sound reason given for her taking service with either Olivia or Orsino: this is simply required by the plot, from which Shakespeare has dropped the original motivation of the heroine's disguise (to serve the man she secretly loves).' Certainly, Shakespeare can set his plot in motion in any way he wants, and he is under no obligation to provide motivated reasons for opening actions. But, since the theme of a woman dressing up as a page or servant to gain proximity to a man is a very familiar one from a number of sixteenth-century plays and narratives (mainly Italian), and since her motive is *always* the fact that she *already* loves that man, Shakespeare's decision to drop that traditional reason, indeed to obscure if not erase motive altogether, is perhaps worth a little more consideration than a parenthesis in a footnote.

Considering her speech to the Captain, Barber admires 'the aristocratic, free and easy way she [Viola] settles what she will do'; and later, 'Viola's spritely language conveys the fun she is having in playing a man's part, with a hidden womanly perspective about it. One cannot quite say that she is playing in a masquerade, because disguising *just* for the fun of it is a different thing. But the same sort of festive pleasure in transvestism is expressed.' Twelfth Night concluded the twelve days of Christmas festivities which traditionally was a period of 'misrule', when the world could, temporarily, be turned upside down, or inside out (like Feste's glove), and clothes, genders and identities swapped around. (See François Laroque on this.) So 'festive pleasure in transvestism' seems to point in the right direction. But I am intrigued that Viola should resolve to go as a 'eunuch'. Some editions will tell you that Shakespeare dropped this idea, or simply forgot all about it. But I wonder if he did. For instance, when the letter from 'THE FORTUNATE UNHAPPY' reminds Malvolio that 'Some are born great, some achieve greatness, and some have greatness thrust upon 'em' (II, v, 144–5), it is engaging in a barely submerged parody of the biblical verse:

> For there are some eunuchs, which were so born from their mother's womb: and there are some eunuchs, which were made eunuchs of men: and there be eunuchs, which have made themselves eunuchs for the kingdom of heaven's sake. He that is able to receive it, let him receive it.
>
> (Matthew 19:12)

Something is going on in this play about what it is to be, and to fail to be, properly gendered; what it is for nature to draw to her 'bias', or swerve from it. I think Viola's resolve to enter Illyria as a eunuch will stand a little more pondering. Ruth Nevo can see that it matters, and she interprets it in her own way. Noting Viola's 'ambivalence' about whom to serve, she writes:

> But she does not fly to the Countess Olivia for succour, woman to woman, despite her sympathy for a fellow-mourner. Instead she chooses to be *adventurously epicene* in the Duke's entourage. Viola escapes her feminine state but at the cost of a (symbolic) castration: it is as a eunuch (to account for her voice) that she will 'sing,/And speak to him in many sorts of music'
>
> (I, ii, 57).

(my italics). William Carroll also raises the question—'But why a eunuch?' —and his answer is instructive:

> Shakespeare's initial choice of the eunuch role may have been for pragmatic reasons. 'Cesario' would not be sexually identified and as a neutral figure could more easily become a confidant of Olivia. But somewhere along the way, Shakespeare changed his mind and dropped the idea, perhaps because Viola is already a eunuch as far as Viola goes; and a *man* playing a eunuch affords comic possibilities, but a woman playing a eunuch—nothing. As the play continues, we see that Cesario must in fact be essentially bisexual, not neuter, as Viola is both firm and flexible, both deliberate and careless, both committed and disengaged.

Suppose we think of this play as centring on a figure who sets out to be 'adventurously epicene' and discovers that s/he is, has to be, 'bisexual, not neuter'—the would-be eunuch who became the inadvertent hermaphrodite. How or why might a great romantic comedy emerge from such a proposition, it might be asked? That is what I will try to explore.

'Epicene' comes from *epi-* (close up) *koinos* (common). Epicene nouns, in Greek and Latin, are words which have only one form for both the masculine and feminine case—for example, *poeta* is morphologically feminine and grammatically masculine, and refers to a poet of either sex. We can say, then, that it elides marks of sexual difference, and brings two into one. This is what Viola, for her own reasons, sets out to do. 'Hermaphrodite' is, of course, Hermes plus Aphrodite, and refers to a being who has all the sexual characteristics (and equipment) of both sexes, and thus transforms one into two. Such a natural anomaly would be something of a monster. Yet it is just such a being that Viola finds herself, impossibly, turning into. As she recognizes, when she refers to herself as 'poor monster':

> What will become of this? As I am man,
> My state is desperate for my master's love.
> As I am woman (now alas the day!),
> What thriftless sighs shall poor Olivia breathe?
>
> (II, ii, 36–9)

At the start, we saw Viola wavering between the Countess and the Duke—this way or that way? At the end she tells her brother what has happened since their separation:

> All the occurrence of my fortune since
> Hath been between this lady and this lord.
>
> (V, i, 257–8)

—which we might also hear as saying, I have spent my time being something between a lady and a lord. When Viola–Cesario first makes her way to Olivia's house, Olivia asks Malvolio 'Of what personage and years is he?' Malvolio has a rather elaborate answer:

> Not yet old enough for a man nor young enough for a boy; as a squash is before 'tis a peascod, or a codling when 'tis almost an apple. 'Tis with him in standing water, between boy and man.
>
> (I, v, 155–8)

This reminds me of the image Antony uses for Octavia:

> the swan's-down feather
> That stands upon the swell at the full of tide,
> And neither way inclines.
>
> (*Antony and Cleopatra*, III, ii, 48–50)

Twelfth Night is one of the most watery of Shakespeare's plays, so Malvolio's image is particularly appropriate. We may feel that young Viola, fresh from the sea, is sexually still labile, not yet fully differentiated; that, for the moment, she 'neither way inclines' (I need hardly point out, by now, how having a boy actor play the girl would add to this effect). But Malvolio's description also points, however unawarely, to another figure who is of central importance in this play—Narcissus. Once again, we are back with Ovid. Here is how he describes Narcissus:

> Narcissus now had reached his sixteenth year
> And seemed both man and boy; and many a youth
> And many a girl desired him . . .

Drinking from a pool, he sees:

> A form, a face, and loved with leaping heart
> A hope unreal and thought the shape was real.
> Spellbound he saw himself . . .

He falls in love with his own 'fleeting image' and Ovid comments:

> You see a phantom of a mirrored shape;
> Nothing itself . . .

In Ovid's account, he simply pines away on the bank, and after his death is turned into a white and yellow flower. But there also grew up a version of the myth which had Narcissus drowning trying to kiss and embrace his own reflection. It is this version which Shakespeare draws on in both of his major poems:

> Narcissus so himself himself forsook,
> And died to kiss his shadow in the brooke.
> > (*Venus and Adonis*)

> That, had Narcissus seen her as she stood,
> Self-love had never drowned him in the flood.
> > (*The Rape of Lucrece*)

'O, you are sick of self-love, Malvolio'—these are the first words Olivia speaks to her steward (I, v, 90), and we learn from Maria that he likes 'practicing behavior to his own shadow' (II, v, 16). He is, indeed, a very obvious study in narcissism in a comically exaggerated form (even his grotesque crossgarters are the Narcissus colour—yellow, as pointed out by Jonathan Bate). But there is subtler and more serious narcissism in the leading figures in Illyria—Olivia and Orsino, both in danger of drowning in various forms of self-love. The indeterminate, could-seemingly-go-either-way, Viola–Cesario will change all that. Prior to her arrival, we feel that a curious stasis, or even stagnation, prevailed in Illyria—the sterile, repetitious, self-directed, self-obsessed emotions of the Duke and Countess going, growing, nowhere. Viola proves to be the crucial catalyst for change, emergence, growth. She herself, despite her 'standing-water' status and appearance, is decidedly *not* a Narcissus. She is more reminiscent of the other key figure in the myth—Echo. Echo was a nymph who used to distract Juno's attention by her talking, while Jove had his way with other nymphs. As a punishment, Juno reduced her powers of speech to the ability to repeat the last words of any voice she hears. Echo falls in love with Narcissus, who rejects her in disgust. Echo takes her shame to the woods, 'yet still her love endures and grows on grief. She wastes away and is finally just a discarnate voice, left to echo the wailing of the water dryads, mourning the death of Narcissus. There is something of all this in two of Viola's key speeches, when she is, as it were, talking indirectly about her own love, since her disguise has reduced her to something of an echo (repeating Orsino's overtures to Olivia, and Olivia's rejections to Orsino). Unlike Echo, she can release herself, anonymously, in lyric flights of poetry. What would she do if *she* loved Olivia?

> Make me a willow cabin at your gate
> And call upon my soul within the house;
> Write loyal cantons of contemnèd love
> And sing them loud even in the dead of night;
> Hallo your name to the reverberate hills
> And make the babbling gossip of the air
> Cry out 'Olivia!'
>
>   (I, v, 269–75)

As Jonathan Bate says, 'babbling gossip of the air' is effectively an explicit reference to Echo; but the beauty of the poetry is all her own. No wonder Olivia reacts with 'You might do much'. After all her proud, house-bound, self-bound, posturing mourning for her brother, this is, perhaps, her first encounter with a genuinely felt and powerfully expressed emotion of love, and, her narcissism cracked open, she finds it irresistible.

Similarly, there is something of the faithful though fading Echo in her account of the hopeless love suffered by her imaginary sister, indirectly, of course, describing her own. 'And what's her history?' asks the Duke, confident that no woman's love could match his own.

> A blank, my lord. She never told her love,
> But let concealment, like a worm i' th' bud,
> Feed on her damask cheek. She pined in thought;
> And, with a green and yellow melancholy,
> She sat like Patience on a monument,
> Smiling at grief. Was not this love indeed?
>
> (II, iv, 111–16)

Her answer has some general force. The history of women is all too often 'a blank'; theirs tend to be the unwritten lives—'hidden from history', as they say. And Viola also feels she is blanked out, having made herself invisible as a woman in front of the man she now loves. But from the deep feeling in her words, we surely agree that this is 'love indeed'. Characteristically, the Duke's only response is to ask if the sister died or not. He cannot hear the cadences of true feeling, preferring his own music-fed moods of languorous sentimentality and affected infatuation. Viola remains something of a hapless Echo to Orsino to the end. His emergence from narcissism is extremely peremptory, if indeed it happens. At the end, learning that Cesario is a woman, he agrees to take her, on account of her expressed devotion to him.

> Give me thy hand,
> And let me see thee in thy woman's weeds.
>
> (V, i, 272–3)

It is notable that we never see Viola back in her 'woman's weeds'—as we do the triumphant Rosalind, and Portia and Julia. It is possible that Orsino actually prefers her as Cesario—the adoring, beautiful boy servant. For the audience, at least, she remains the ambiguous Viola–Cesario composite figure she has become. It is also notable that after this moment when she is accepted by the Duke, she never says another word throughout the remaining one hundred and thirty-five lines of the play—as if faithful Echo has finally, fully, faded away. (Rosalind, of course, had the last word—lots of them—in a masterly, confident epilogue.) Jonathan Bate's suggestion about Viola–Echo is a good one. 'Echo functions in Ovid as an alternative to self-love: had Narcissus responded to her love, neither of them would have been destroyed. Viola's function is to enable characters to respond, to see that love requires echoing instead of narcissism.' Though I suppose since Echo can only give you back your own words—just as mirrors and ponds give you back your own image—she might well contribute to your narcissism. It is only while Viola is Cesario that she finds that enlargement of voice which Shakespeare's heroines characteristically enjoy once they have assumed male disguise. With the mention of 'woman's weeds' to be re-assumed, Viola is, seemingly, silenced. As Jonathan Bate says, you can either read this, happily, as indicating that she has done her work in Illyria (released the lord and lady from their narcissism), and now has her husband–reward; or, rather more darkly, as intimating, as wife, her history will return to being 'a blank'.

I have not mentioned Sebastian, but he of course is Viola's other half; Shakespeare here, once again, having recourse to the 'divisible indivisibility' of identical twins, though this time of opposite sexes. This multiplies and deepens the thematic possibilities of identity and gender confusion when one twin decides to go same-sex. This move in turn allows Viola an experience, a perception, not vouchsafed to the other cross-dressing heroines—the possible dangers of this device.

> Disguise, I see thou art a wickedness
> Wherein the pregnant enemy does much.
>   (II, ii, 27–8)

With identical twins, Shakespeare can put on stage the apparently bewildering phenomenon whereby one is two, and two are one. It is a visible rendering of the more ineffable two-into-one mystery of marriage. In one case literally, in the other metaphorically, therein is number slain (*The Phoenix and the Turtle*).

> How have you made division of yourself?
> An apple cleft in two is not more twin
> Than these two creatures. Which is Sebastian?
>> (V, i, 222–4)

says Sebastian's loyal lover, Antonio (and that, incidentally, is the last we hear from him. Like that other spokesman for homosexual devotion, also named Antonio—in *The Merchant of Venice*—he is just vaguely left out of things at the end as others pair up, or leave.) The Duke's response to the seemingly impossible phenomenon is famous:

> One face, one voice, one habit, and two persons—
> A natural perspective that is and is not.
>> (V, i, 216–17)

Just before Sebastian enters, poor Andrew comes rushing in with his broken head, claiming that seemingly cowardly Cesario has turned out to be 'the very devil incardinate' (V, i, 182–3). He surely means 'incarnate' but 'incardinate' is happier than he knows, since it would mean 'without number' (a point made by William Carroll), which fits someone who is apparently both one and two, and, as a 'eunuch', nought—hence, no 'cardinal' number will serve. With reference to 'incarnate', commentators sometimes make the point that Twelfth Night marked the Eve of Epiphany, which saw the announcement of another yet more mysterious incarnation. This might seem a little far-fetched, were it not for Sebastian's strange response when Viola accuses him of being the spirit of her dead brother.

> A spirit I am indeed,
> But am in that dimension grossly clad
> Which from the womb I did participate.
>> (V, i, 236–8)

It is a strange way of saying, I am still a body; but the somewhat hieratic turn of phrase does indeed invoke a reminder of God putting on flesh—

which is, I suppose, the ultimate two-in-one miracle. Certainly, the last scene of the play, while not in any way explicitly religious, should gradually be bathed in a sense of expanding wonder.

This wonder is connected with the sea—as it will increasingly be in Shakespeare's last plays. The sea is the unstable element of mutability and transformation; people crossing the sea often undergo strange sea-changes. On land, it can surge into people's metaphors. The play starts with Orsino asking for 'excess' of music, so that 'surfeiting,/The appetite may sicken and so die'. Shakespeare is to refer to 'the never-surfeited sea' (*The Tempest* III, iii, 55), and it is not surprising that Orsino's melancholy insatiability turns his thoughts seawards.

> O spirit of love, how quick and fresh art thou,
> That, notwithstanding thy capacity,
> Receiveth as the sea. Nought enters there,
> Of what validity and pitch soe'er,
> But falls into abatement and low price
> Even in a minute.
>
> (I, i, 9–14)

He is both right, and very wrong. The sea drowns, but it can also save and renew. As the very next scene reveals, Viola 'entered' the sea, was wrecked, but has been 'saved'; and, so far from falling into 'abatement and low price', will bring some much-needed quickness and freshness to stagnating Illyria. She thinks her brother drowned, though the Captain last saw him holding 'acquaintance with the waves', riding them 'like Arion on the dolphin's back' (I, ii, 15). The dolphin, famously, shows his back above the element he lives in (see *Antony and Cleopatra* V, ii, 89–90). Feste, making a contemporary joke of it, says to Viola–Cesario 'Who you are and what you would are out of my welkin; I might say "element," but the word is overworn' (III, i, 58–60). But he is right; fresh-from-the-sea Viola effectively comes from another element (as does her brother, Sebastian, who, we will learn, was 'redeemed' from 'the rude sea's enraged and foamy mouth', V, i, 78. The sister 'saved', the brother 'redeemed'—the words are, surely, not idly chosen.) ('I am not of your element' says Malvolio to, really, everyone, III, iv, 130, and that's true, too—he is in a bleak, unpeopled, self-incarcerating element of his own making—imaged by the darkened room in which he is imprisoned to cure his 'madness'.) Sea-going touches everyone's speech:

'she is the list of my voyage' (III, i, 77–8); 'you are now sailed into the North of my lady's opinion' (III, ii, 26–7); 'board her, woo her, assail her' (I, iii, 56); 'Will you hoist sail, sir? . . . No . . . I am to hull here a little longer' (I, v, 201–3). There are also Olivia's copious tears, which we hear about before we see her—'she will veiled walk,/And water once a day her chamber round/With eye-offending brine' (I, i, 29–31), 'brine' serving to bring the sea into the house. Sebastian also weeps for a lost sibling—'She is drowned already, sir, with salt water, though I seem to drown her remembrance again with more' (II, i, 30–32). Even landlocked Sir Toby is like a 'drowned' man when he is 'in the third degree of drink' (I, v, 134–5). The play is, as it were, awash with liquidity. Viola, we recall, started out as 'standing water'. And it is her words on learning of the possible salvation of her brother which, above all, determine the atmosphere at the end of the play.

> O, if it prove,
> Tempests are kind, and salt waves fresh in love!
> (III, iv, 395–6)

That is probably the most defining sentence in Shakespearian comedy: salt becomes fresh; wreckage generates love; the world turns kind. Briney blessings.

Something of this prevailing liquidity reflects a certain incipient uncertainty and instability in the identities and emotions of some of the characters. The Duke is, by all accounts including his own, very labile. Feste, with the clown's licence, tells him as much to his face. He minces his words, ironically, with what sounds like elaborate nonsense; but the truth is all there.

> Now the melancholy god protect thee, and the tailor make thy doublet of changeable taffeta, for thy mind is a very opal. I would have men of such constancy put to sea, that their business might be everything, and their intent everywhere; for that's it that always makes a good voyage of nothing.
> (II, iv, 73–8)

Shot-silk and the opal both change colour endlessly according to light and movement—the Duke is, to all intents and purposes, permanently tossing about on the waves, or, as Shakespeare will later, breathtakingly, put it, 'lackeying the varying tide' (*Antony and Cleopatra,* I, iv, 46). Feste has his man. Up to a point, the Duke concedes as much. He generalizes to Cesario:

> Our fancies are more giddy and unfirm,
> More longing, wavering, sooner lost and worn,
> Than women's are.
>
> (II, iv, 33–5)

Of himself he claims:

> For such as I am all true lovers are,
> Unstaid and skittish in all motions else
> Save in the constant image of the creature
> That is beloved.
>
> (II, iv, 17–20)

To define true constancy turns out to be one of the concerns of the play. Claiming that his passion is greater than any woman could feel—because their hearts 'lack retention'—he again, revealingly and inappropriately, invokes the sea:

> But mine is all as hungry as the sea
> And can digest as much. Make no compare
> Between that love a woman can bear me
> And that I owe Olivia.
>
> (II, iv, 101–4)

The sea is his image for unsatisfiability; it is also the world's image for inconstancy. As is now familiar from Shakespeare's comedies, it is the woman who will show 'retention'.

Ironically, Orsino exhorts Cesario to an immovable constancy—on his behalf:

> Be not denied access, stand at her doors,
> And tell them there thy fixèd foot shall grow
> Till thou have audience.
>
> (I, iv, 16–18)

Viola obeys him—pretty literally, according to Malvolio:

> he says he'll stand at your door like a sheriff's post, and be the supporter
> to a bench, but he'll speak with you.
>
> (I, v, 146–8)

To be as fixed as a post and as stiff as a bench-leg is, certainly, one kind of constancy, and we may say of Viola that she holds her ground (except when it comes to duelling). But, clearly, there is constancy and constancy. There is this little exchange in the last Act before things have started to sort themselves out.

> *Duke.*   Still so cruel?
> *Olivia.* Still so constant, lord.
> *Duke.* What, to perverseness?
>
> (V, i, 110–12)

There is such a thing as bad constancy—as, for instance, in the extreme case of Malvolio. Now *there's* someone who really is as stiff as a post. He manifests just that inflexibility and intractability, that refusal to change, which always shows itself as a negative feature in Shakespeare's comedies. But then, opal-headed fickleness and shot-silk variability are not exactly, in and of themselves, positive virtues. Here again, we see Shakespeare interested in trying to identify the best combination of openness to change and aptness for commitment, adaptation and 'retention', yielding and holding fast, flexibility and stability. Orsino and Olivia, initially at least, certainly don't have it; they are both constant to their chosen 'perverseness'. It is Viola who best shows it—the nimblest of shape-shifters, not to say gender-crossers, who yet remains absolutely steadfast and loyal.

In this connection, another piece of advice, or rather another order, which Orsino gives his nuncio, Cesario, points to larger issues—'Be clamorous and leap all civil bounds' (I, iv, 21). In the immediately preceding scene, we have just heard Maria advise Sir Toby 'Ay, but you must confine yourself within the modest limits of order' (I, iii, 8–9), and we have seen Sir Andrew literally dancing and leaping his way out at the end of the scene, at Sir Toby's incitement: 'Let me see thee caper. Ha, higher; ha, ha, excellent!' (I, iii, 137–8). As often happens in Shakespearian comedy, the characters messing around below stairs offer, unintentionally of course, a crude and literal parody of things going on metaphorically at the higher, courtly level. Viola has already made a great leap across the gender gap; she thereby certainly does *not* keep 'within the modest limits of order' as far as the prescribed behaviour for women was concerned; and, speaking as a humble, abject messenger to a great lady, her sometimes tart and independent (though always courteous) remarks to Olivia could sometimes be said to 'leap all civil bounds', at least to the eye of convention.

In this connection, it is worth considering something said by Sebastian in *his* first scene on the sea-coast. Whither are you 'bound', asks the life-saving and already devoted Antonio? Sebastian has no plans, directions, or aims. 'My determinate voyage is mere extravagancy' (II, i, 11–12). 'Extravagancy' means 'wandering', but there is more in the word than that. As, much later, the American writer Thoreau realized: 'I fear chiefly lest my expression may not be *extra-vagant* enough—may not wander far enough beyond the narrow limits of my daily experience, so as to be adequate to the truth of which I have been convinced. *Extra vagance!* it depends on how you are yarded. The migrating buffalo, which seeks new pastures in another latitude, is not extravagant like the cow which kicks over the pail, leaps the cow-yard fence, and runs after her calf, in milking time. I desire to speak somewhere *without* bounds . . .' (*Walden*—Conclusion). Characters in Illyria strike one as being very 'yarded' indeed—house-bound in innutrient, self-devouring emotional states. The place is certainly in need of some extra-vagance. And Viola starts the play by, if I may so put it without offence, leaping over 'the cow-yard fence'. With the advent of the shipwrecked twins, 'extravagancy' has entered the country. Pails are duly kicked over, 'civil bounds' will be broken and transgressed. In her very first audience with Olivia, Viola–Cesario soon departs from the 'poetical' encomium which she has prepared. Instinctively, she starts speaking frankly to Olivia, then realizes 'But this is from my commission' (I, v, 187). When, perhaps on a woman's impulse, Viola asks to see her face, Olivia gently chides 'You are now out of your text' (I, v, 231–2), but complies anyway. Viola's refreshing sincerity is irresistible in the elegant but self-stultifying airlessness of Illyria. Viola must depart from her commission to bring about some requisite rein-vigoration. She is certainly 'out of her text' in Illyria—indeed, she is out of her sex. She must, indeed, 'leap all civil bounds'—and textual ones. She will break free from conventional prescriptions. 'Yarding' fences need to be jumped in Illyria: Sir Toby's and Sir Andrew's drunken caperings are amusing, but no good for the purpose. Viola will find the way. Sebastian has the way made for him.

When Olivia first sees Sebastian and, of course, thinks he is Cesario, she begs him into her house with endearing familiarity. Though quite uncomprehending, Sebastian—it is a point in his favour—accepts the invitation. We may say that he trustingly embraces his good fortune.

> What relish is in this? How runs the stream?
> Or I am mad, or else this is a dream.
> Let fancy still my sense in Lethe steep;
> If it be thus to dream, still let me sleep!
>
> (IV, i, 60–63)

'Relish' is nice: this, whatever it is, tastes good to Sebastian, and he is man enough to trust his senses. The 'stream' quickly turns into a 'flood' as Olivia showers gifts on him and hastens to hustle him to the altar. Given the prevailing watery imagery, we can justifiably say that Sebastian goes with the flow.

> And though 'tis wonder that enwraps me thus,
> Yet 'tis not madness.
> . . .
> For though my soul disputes well with my sense
> That this may be some error, but no madness,
> Yet doth this accident and flood of fortune
> So far exceed all instance, all discourse,
> That I am ready to distrust mine eyes
> And wrangle with my reason that persuades me
> To any other trust but that I am mad,
> Or else the lady's mad. Yet, if 'twere so,
> She could not sway her house, command her followers,
> Take and give back affairs and their dispatch
> With such a smooth, discreet, and stable bearing
> As I perceive she does. There's something in't
> That is deceivable. But here the lady comes.
>
> (IV, iii, 3–4, 9–21)

So she does; and with neither the chance nor the inclination to resist, he is off to church to be married.

There are observations to be made concerning this episode which have relevance for the whole play. In the comparable incident in a work which Shakespeare certainly drew on for some plot details (*Riche his Farewell to Militarie Profession,* 1581), the lady, Julina, persuades the mistaken man, Silvio, not to church but to bed. He, knowing perfectly well that he is the sexual beneficiary of a case of mistaken identity, ungallantly skips town next morning, leaving the lady (a widow) embarrassingly pregnant. This apparently minor change in the direction of decorum makes one realize anew how very little actual sexual reference there is in a play which, when you think about it, offers virtually unlimited opportunity for almost every kind of heterosexual and homosexual allusion or innuendo (for instance, in most of the source narratives using the girl-dressed-as-page theme, the infatuated great lady invariably falls on him–her physically). Call it taste, call it what you like, but Shakespeare leaves the overt sex out—or, rather, he leaves it to take care of itself. The only bawdy, and it is very explicit, occurs in Olivia's putative letter to Malvolio—'These be her very C's, her U's, and her T's, and thus makes she her great P's' (II, v, 87–9). Like our not dissimilar word, 'cut' was familiar slang for the female genitals, and P's speaks for itself. This manifest obscenity is there for a purpose. It is a measure of poor Sir Andrew's simplicity that he doesn't understand ('Her C's, her U's, and her T's? Why that?' You may be sure the audience laughed at that!); just as it is a measure of Malvolio's blind self-infatuation that he does not notice. He is too busy 'crushing' the more enigmatic 'M.O.A.I.' to form his own name. (Incidentally, O.A.I. occur in both Olivia and Viola which are, of course, effectively anagrams of each other; in which connection I like Leonard Barkan's comment that it is as if there is 'a kind of enigma of coalescing identity that hangs over the apparent frivolities of the play'.) No one is more interested in the whole man–woman business, and any ancillary swerving affective intensities, than Shakespeare, and he perfectly well appreciated the comedy (as well as the pathos) latent in misdirected sexual desires. But he eschewed the naming and showing of parts. Besides, he has a lot invested in the sanctity of marriage. (See the priest's speech starting 'A contract of eternal bond of love', V, i, 156–61.)

Sebastian mistaken by Olivia is a replay of Antipholus of Syracuse mistaken by Adriana, and anyone who has a memory of *The Comedy of Errors* will recognize how much *Twelfth Night* reworks situations and themes from that earlier, Plautine play. Like Antipholus, Sebastian doesn't know whether he is awake or dreaming, sane or mad, and, like him, he goes along with his unforeseen and inexplicable good fortune. Here a word might be said about 'madness' (and 'witchcraft', mentioned in both plays). The word 'mad' occurs more often in this play than in any other of Shakespeare's (twenty times). Just about everybody in Illyria is called 'mad' by one character or another, on one occasion or another. 'Are all the people mad?' cries an exasperated and non-comprehending Sebastian at one point (IV, i, 27), and this is the tone of the times. But most (not all) of the supposed 'madness' is simply the confusion caused by the 'extravagant' and unco-ordinated arrival in Illyria of identical twins unaware of each other's presence (it had the same effect in Ephesus in the earlier play, where the word 'mad' occurs seventeen times—second highest rate). True, Olivia says of her uncle Toby, 'He speaks nothing but madman' (I, v, 105–6), but that refers to his drunken burblings: Malvolio is conspiratorially locked up to 'cure' his stage-managed madness; but as he, rightly, claims—'I am as well in my wits as any man in Illyria' (IV, ii, 109–10). How well that is, individual spectators may decide; but this play is decidedly not a study in lunacy and mental derangement. What Shakespeare is interested in here is the dramatic possibilities latent in the obvious comedy of mistaken identity. Profounder themes are touched on. Can we trust what we see, what we hear? Do we know who we are? Come to that, as we watch Viola–Cesario moving between lord and lady, do we know *what* we are? Questions of identity and self-knowledge are often rather tortuously engaged, as in the quotation set at the start of this introduction. When Feste engages with Sebastian, thinking of course that he is Cesario, he is brusquely rebuffed. Feste defends himself with heavy irony: 'No, I do not know you . . . nor your name is not Master Cesario; nor this is not my nose neither. Nothing that is so is so' (IV, i, 5–9). This is still comedy; but take a turn into seriousness, and you could soon arrive at Macbeth's incipient mental malfunctioning in which 'nothing is/But what is not' (I, iii, 141–2). Frank Kermode calls *Twelfth Night* 'a comedy of identity, set on the borders of wonder and madness'. As he invariably does, he has caught the mood of the play. But we might remember Sebastian's judgement—'though 'tis wonder that enwraps me thus/Yet 'tis not madness'. As I said, this is still comedy, and wonder prevails. Real madness must wait for the tragedies (and not wait long; *Hamlet* was, almost certainly,

Shakespeare's next play—'to define true madness,/What is't but to be nothing else but mad?', Polonius tautologously raises the big question, II, ii,
93–4).

Prior to the arrival of Viola and Sebastian, life in Illyria seems to adhere
to a very fixed, repetitive text—Orsino swoons, Olivia weeps, Sir Toby
drinks. Nothing changes. So it goes. The twins bring with them, though
they cannot know it, the germ of a new life—the galvanizing disease of
love. Not for the first time in Shakespeare's comedies, this is exactly the
image used. Thus Olivia's reaction after her first encounter with Viola–
Cesario:

> How now?
> Even so quickly may one catch the plague?
> Methinks I feel this youth's perfections
> With an invisible and subtle stealth
> To creep in at mine eyes. Well, let it be.
>   (I, v, 295–9)

Among other things, this gives a premonitory edge to the first words spoken by Sir Toby, two scenes previously:

> *What a plague* means my niece to take the death of her brother thus? I am
> sure care's an enemy to life.
>   (I, iii, 1–3—my italics)

So it is: though to be completely care-less or care-free will not do either.
Care, as we say, must be responsibly taken. Narcissists, too easily caring
only for their own images, do not manage this. Which is why, paradoxically, the Illyrians need the disease of love—to get them out of their mirrors
and into true relationships. This is the force behind Sebastian's reassuring
words to Olivia who, after all, has impulsively married herself to a completely strange male.

> So comes it, lady, you have been mistook.
> But nature to her bias drew in that.
> You would have been contracted to a maid . . .
>   (V, i, 259–61)

This is a central Shakespearian belief: left to itself, nature goes this way rather than that way. It is *biased*—towards dutiful daughters, faithful wives, heterosexual marriages. But, of course, humans do not leave nature to itself; they buck the bias, and bring into play every kind of perverse swerving—which is why we have Shakespearian drama; because you cannot have five Acts of Desdemona and Cordelia rehearsing the predictable texts of their fidelity. Well, you could; but it wouldn't be drama. Surprised by love, Olivia makes another striking comment:

> Fate, show thy force; ourselves we do not owe [= own].
> What is decreed must be—and be this so!
>
> (I, v, 311–12)

Ourselves we do not know; ourselves we do not own—these could be said to be two of Shakespeare's central concerns as his comedies deepen towards tragedy. It is difficult enough to know yourself—myriad-minded Hamlet doesn't know what *a* self might be; Othello? Lear? they fight self-knowledge until almost the end. Macbeth knows himself all right; but what about 'owning' yourself—knowing what you are going to do, and why you are going to do it; being completely *responsible* for your deeds? Even Macbeth falls down there, as probably we all do. Self-possession is a crucially difficult matter. It is perhaps no wonder that Olivia, thus early, relinquishes matters to the 'force' of 'Fate'; just as, two scenes later, Viola hands things over to Time:

> O Time, thou must untangle this, not I;
> It is too hard a knot for me t' untie.
>
> (II, ii, 40–41)

This spirit of resignation to the solving or resolving forces of larger powers is more familiar from the tragedies. 'Well, let it be' says 'plague'-struck Olivia when Viola–Cesario leaves after their first conversation: 'Let be' says Hamlet, as he is about to submit to the final, poisoned, duel. What can you do? 'The readiness is all'—certainly; what both plays discover is that some people are readier than others. Comedy does not usually put down such deep feelers; and, indeed, Shakespeare is about to abandon the genre—even in this play, he is stretching it towards something else.

So what then, finally, of Shakespeare's Illyria? It is not Verona, or Messina, or Arden—not Windsor either, though one can imagine Sir Toby drinking with Falstaff at the Garter Inn. In Ovid, it is where shipwrecked Cadmus lands, not knowing that his daughter, Io, has been both saved and transformed. Bullough suggests that this vague place on a little-known coast allowed Shakespeare to mix Mediterranean romance plausibly with Northern realism (not that many Elizabethans would have known or cared, Illyria was on the coast of Yugoslavia—at this time of writing, unhappily more renowned for atrocity than romance). There is no alternative realm in this play—no forest, no Belmont; but there is a running contrast between the elegant, rather melancholy-mannered court of Orsino, where people speak verse (there is much rather Italianate talk of manners and courtesy); and the much more easy-going, belching, swigging, knock-about household of Olivia, where prose predominates (except when infatuation drives Olivia into poetry). The atmosphere at court seems dominated by music and melancholy, while over at Olivia's house there seems to be a permanent nocturnal drinking party. Maria is, certainly, 'as witty a piece of Eve's flesh as any in Illyria' (I, v, 27–8), and the joke she plays on Malvolio is perhaps the funniest thing in Shakespeare, no matter how often seen or read (at least, that is my experience). But there is a feeling that the revels have been going on for too long. There is no more revealing moment than when, having had 'sport royal' with Malvolio and fooled him 'black and blue', Sir Toby suddenly says to Maria 'I would we were well rid of this knavery' (IV, ii, 69–70). To use a chilling line of Emily Dickinson's, 'the jest has crawled too far'. Laroque is perhaps too grim when he detects 'the boredom of a world grown old' and says that, here, 'festivity seems doomed to sterile, boring repetition. The veteran champions of festivity have become the pensioners of pleasure. The Puritans may be odious and malicious, but the old merrymakers are plain ridiculous.' This is, arguably, too censorious a view. But you see his point. There is something pathetic about poor, exploited, Sir Andrew ('for many do call me fool', II, v, 82), and I have a good deal of sympathy with Dr Johnson's view that it is unfair to mock his 'natural fatuity'. Sir Toby, seen rather generously by Barber as 'gentlemanly liberty incarnate', is agreeable inasmuch as he is festively anti-Malvolio and pro-cakes and ale; but his unscrupulous abuse of Sir Andrew's mindlessly trusting gullibility is unattractive, and he reveals a brutally unpleasant side in his final exchange with him. They have both been wounded by Sebastian, and Sir Andrew, rather sweetly, says—'I'll help you, Sir Toby, because we'll be dressed together'. Sir Toby's very unsweet response is:

> Will you help—an ass-head and a coxcomb and a knave, a thin-faced knave, a gull?
>
> (V, i, 205–7)

These are his last words to Sir Andrew, who is not heard from again. Not nice.

Assorted Illyrians, then, repeating fixed routines until they are disrupted into new life by the arrival of Viola and Sebastian from the sea. But Feste the clown seems to come from somewhere else again. Barber says 'the fool has been over the garden wall into some such world as the Vienna of *Measure for Measure*', and that feels right. He is not as bitter or cynical as Touchstone. He sings, he fools, he begs; he talks nonsense for tips. But you feel that he has seen a wider, darker world than the predominantly sunny Illyria. 'Anything that's mended is but patched; virtue that transgresses is but patched with sin, and sin that amends is but patched with virtue' (I, v, 45–8). You don't acquire that kind of shrewd, worldly knowingness by tippling with Sir Toby. When Olivia starts by saying 'Take the fool away' (I, v, 37), he nimbly turns the tables on her, saying 'Misprision in the highest degree. Lady, *cucullus non facit monachum*. That's as much to say as, I wear not motley in my brain' (I, v, 54–6). There is no taking away of this fool; he will be there to the very end, when, quite decisively, he has the last words. 'Misprision' is a good defining word for what is going on around him, for people are constantly mis-taking themselves or others. The cowl does not make the monk is his Latin tag; and he is anything but a fool in his brain. The male outfit does not make the man, either, as Viola will both learn and demonstrate. Just what people *do* wear in their brains is, of course, a matter of continuously increasing interest for Shakespeare. There is another glance at Viola–Cesario when Feste is persuaded to put on a gown and beard to play the curate, Sir Topas, and further madden Malvolio. 'Well, I'll put it on, and I will dissemble myself in't, and I would I were the first that ever dissembled in such a gown' (IV, ii, 4–6). Orsino, more correctly than he knows, says approvingly to his new page, Cesario—'all is semblative a woman's part' (I, iv, 34). Viola later admits to Olivia that she is 'out of my part' (I, v, 177). What *is,* or should be, her 'part'—

is she most herself when she is 'sembling', or when she is 'dissembling'? People are often not what they seem, and seldom just what they wear. Among other things, Feste serves to open up doors onto problems of identity.

He opens up words, too; or rather, he shows that they are infinitely malleable, and can be made to do anything. Anyone who can say, as he does to Malvolio concerning the dark room in which he is imprisoned—'it hath bay windows transparent as barricadoes, and the clerestories toward the south north are as lustrous as ebony' (IV, ii, 37–9)—clearly has language completely at his disposal. He calls himself Olivia's 'corrupter of words' (III, i, 37), and inasmuch as he can seduce words into doing anything, break them up this way and that, it is an apt enough self-designation. It is Feste who provides one of the key images of the play when he remarks to Viola: 'To see this age! A sentence is but a chev'ril glove to a good wit. How quickly the wrong side may be turned outward! (III, i, 11–13). Quite a lot of things get turned inside out, or are reversed, in this play; just as there is 'midsummer madness' (III, iv, 58) in the depths of winter. Wandering between court and house, fooling and singing for a living but profoundly unattached, Feste can truly say—in this most liquid of plays—'I am for all waters' (IV, ii, 65).

There is bad blood between him and Malvolio from the beginning, as you would expect between the humourless and vain would-be social climber and the professional anarch. Malvolio starts by sneering at Feste—'Unless you laugh and minister occasion to him, he is gagged' (I, v, 86–7). Malvolio sounds an uncomfortably discordant tone in Illyria, rather as Shylock does in Venice. There are, indeed, similarities between these two figures (I have seen it suggested that, in his depiction of the sober but unpleasantly grasping Jew, Shakespeare was actually aiming at the figure of the contemporary Puritan businessman). Whether or not Malvolio is a Puritan is hardly relevant. As Barber says of him, he is more of a businessman who 'would like to be a rising man, and to rise he *uses* sobriety and morality'. It is curious that Shakespeare allows the releasing of 'THE MADLY USED MALVOLIO' to occupy the last part of the play, while Viola stands silently by. Malvolio, of course, fills the traditional role of the kill-joy spoilsport who is scapegoated out of the final happy ensemble. Though it has to be said that, compared with the flood of marriages which concludes *As You Like It,* this is a rather reduced and muted ending—with half the characters absent and the main hero and heroine completely silent. Feste gets his dig in to the in-

furiated Malvolio—'And thus the whirligig of time brings in his revenges'
(V, i, 378–9). Whether we think he has been 'most notoriously abused', or
whether, with Fabian, we think his punishment—for his 'stubborn and un-
courteous parts'—'may rather pluck on laughter than revenge' (V, i, 368),
will depend on individual weightings. He is certainly not the broken man
that Shylock is, as he storms out crying 'I'll be revenged on the whole pack
of you!' Indeed, we may take Barber's neat point: 'One could moralize the
spectacle by observing that, in the long run, in the 1640s, Malvolio *was* revenged on the whole pack of them' (he is referring to the closure of the
theatres by the Puritans).

For all the spreading wonderment in the last Act, we have a sense that
this is comedy on the turn. There is that shockingly violent outburst from
Orsino, when he thinks his Cesario has secretly married Olivia:

> But this your minion, whom I know you love,
> And whom, by heaven I swear, I tender dearly,
> Him will I tear out of that cruel eye
> Where he sits crownèd in his master's spite.
> Come, boy, with me. My thoughts are ripe in mischief.
> I'll sacrifice the lamb that I do love
> To spite a raven's heart within a dove.
>   (V, i, 125–31)

There is an ugly side to the man, for all the elegance of his court, and the
refinement of his manners. A comparably ugly side is revealed to jolly Sir
Toby, when he turns so unpleasantly on Sir Andrew. There is the strange
silencing of Viola, as well as the unappeased fury of Malvolio. There is even
that surgeon, who, when he is needed, it turns out has been drunk since
eight in the morning—which sounds something more than festive. The
Duke speaks of 'golden time' at the end (V, i, 384), but the glow is fading.
Feste, clearly aware of life's rougher weather, ends the play with his song
about the wind and the rain, with its reiterated reminder that 'the rain it
raineth every day'. As a matter of fact, he leaves one verse out.

> He that has and a little tiny wit,
>   With heigh-ho, the wind and the rain,
> Must make content with his fortunes fit,
>   Though the rain it raineth every day.

But he, or someone very like him, will sing it to the truly mad King Lear, during conditions which are unimaginable in Illyria (*King Lear* III, ii, 74–7).

 ## ALL'S WELL THAT ENDS WELL (1603)

> *Clown.* O madam, yonder's my lord your son with a patch of velvet on's face; whether there be a scar under't or no, the velvet knows, but 'tis a goodly patch of velvet. His left cheek is a cheek of two pile and a half, but his right cheek is worn bare.
>
> *Lafew.* A scar nobly got, or a noble scar, is a good liv'ry of honor; so belike is that.
>
> *Clown.* But it is your carbonadoed face.
>
> (IV, v, 95–102)

The hero is home from the wars—or is he the villain? Half his face is covered in velvet, but what is it concealing—a noble scar, sign of honour; or the marks made by incisions made to drain syphilitic ulcers, a wound of shame? Only the velvet knows. In this, Bertram's face is rather like the play itself. Part of it is plain and simple—a bare cheek; but part of it is covered in a thick pile of velvet language, and it is not always clear what, exactly, is going on. As if only the language knows. There is certainly not much that is comic about the play; Barber excluded it from his work, *Shakespeare's Festive Comedy,* on the well-justified grounds that there is nothing festive in it. There is a clown; but he is 'a shrewd knave and an unhappy' (IV, v, 64)—'shrewd' here meaning 'bitter', an apt word for the mood of much of the play. The Clown suggests that Parolles contributes to 'the world's pleasure and the increase of laughter' (II, iv, 37), and Parolles himself is tricked 'for the love of laughter', said twice (III, vi, 34 and 41). But the words are curiously hollow: while there may be the occasional rictus, sign of incipient mirth, here true laughter dies on the lips. The play as a whole better fits Mark Twain's definition of a German joke—'no laughing matter'. It is fairly obviously from the same hand which (almost certainly) had recently written *Troilus and Cressida* and *Hamlet,* and Shakespeare is opening up strange territories for his own purposes. The play leaves us with residual uncertainties—undecidabilities; as if we never are to learn *exactly* what has been going on under the velvet. But one thing is certain and clear. Shakespeare has taken something very simple and transformed it into something very complicated.

The simple story on which he based his play is in Boccaccio's *Decameron* (Day III, story ix), effectively translated by William Painter in *The Palace of Pleasure* (published in 1566 and 1575)—a work which Shakespeare certainly knew. This tale brings together two themes familiar from folk or fairy tales—these are usually called 'the sick king' (whose apparently incurable ailing affects the whole kingdom); and 'the impossible tasks' (usually set for a woman before she can gain her beloved). The tale also avails itself of the 'bed trick' (or 'substitute coupling') which was curiously popular in Shakespeare's time (apparently, over twenty contemporary plays make use of it). It is a short, direct, unambiguous tale—all situation, complication, and resolution. It is enacted by what Muriel Bradbrook called 'shrewd unsentimental vigorous Italians', without a whiff of psychological probing. Here is Painter's summary of the little 'Novel'.

> Giletta a Phisition's doughter of Narbon, healed the French King of a Fistula, for reward whereof she demaunded Beltramo Counte of Rossiglione to husband. The Counte being married against his will, for despite fled to Florence, and loved another. Giletta his wife, by pollicie founds means to lye with her husbande, in place of his lover, and was begotten with childe of two sonnes: which knowen to her husband, he received her againe, and afterwards he lived in great honour and felicitie.

There it is. A sick king, a reluctant courtier, a clever wife; one, two, three —six pages, and the tale is told. The figures are types; there is no characterization or individuation, never mind complex psychological motivation. Shakespeare changes all that, completely transforming the romance atmosphere and environment, bringing the whole story out of the remote distance of folk tale into all sorts of troubling proximities, and introducing all manner of proliferations, circumlocutions and complications. Indeed, what he did with his simple source is a wonder.

Let us just consider some of the additions and changes he made in substantive matters of character and plot. He gives Bertram a mother, the Countess of Rousillon, a maternal figure of the utmost sweetness and compassionate concern ('the most beautiful old woman's part ever written', according to George Bernard Shaw). He gives her a companion in her palace, Lafew, 'an old lord'. Together, these two wise and good patricians stand for, and embody, the moral standards and high good manners of an older, and nobler, order, which was generous, seemly and fair—almost, one feels, an *ancien régime* of feudal honour, graciousness and courtesy, which is giving way to a cruder, coarser, less principled generation (it is sometimes remarked that all the virtuous characters at court in this play turn out to be elderly). The play starts in an autumnal register, with two noble fathers lately dead, and a king seemingly sickening unto death—and it can hardly be said to move towards a springtime of regeneration.

The best, we feel, is past. The sick king remembers the words of one of his now-dead friends:

> 'Let me not live,' quoth he,
> 'After my flame lacks oil, to be the snuff
> Of younger spirits, whose apprehensive sense
> All but new things disdain; whose judgments are
> Mere fathers of their garments; whose constancies
> Expire before their fashions.'
>
> (I, ii, 58–63)

We have heard much of garments and fashions in the comedies, and of the besetting problems of changeableness and constancy. For this play, Shakespeare brings on a character who is, effectively, composed *entirely* of garments and inconstancies, with speech to match. I will come back to this extraordinary creation—Parolles; suffice it here to say that in his cavalier rejection of court values (*of all* values), he is not to be mistaken for a Falstaff or a Shylock. In their extremely corporeal presence, these two men embody and inhabit a world outside of, if adjacent to, the official citadels of the constituted authorities. Perhaps they *have* to be vanquished, marginalized, or extruded; but they have an undeniable, potentially damaging and threatening, reality. None of this applies to Parolles—he is something new in Shakespeare. There is a story by Edgar Allan Poe called 'The Man Who Was Used Up', concerning a flashy, fashionable socialite. The narrator goes to visit him at his private address, during the daytime. On being admitted to his room, all he can see is a little heap of clothes on the floor. The heap begins to assemble itself, with the aid of all sorts of artificial devices, into the recognizable fashionable figure who haunts the evening salons. But the narrator has seen what there really is to the man. There is something of this about Parolles; though it should be stressed that even when he seems most washed-up, he is never, ever, 'used up'. There is nothing to him—but he is inextinguishable.

If Bertram is representative of the 'younger spirits' poised to take over, then we may well sympathize with the sick king's wish to be 'quickly . . . dissolved from my hive' (I, ii, 66). This Bertram is not going to bring any honey home (syphilis is more likely). It is notable that Shakespeare makes Bertram plunge himself far deeper into ignominy and disgrace than does his original, compounding his dishonesty and treachery in the perversely protracted fifth Act. Shakespeare certainly seems to want to make Bertram blacker than black, with *no* extenuations. (The proposition, sometimes advanced, that the simple young lad is seduced and led astray by the demon, Parolles, won't do. Even if accepted, it would only make Bertram even more stupid and corruptible than he already appears. But Bertram is his own man. It just happens that it is a particularly rotten sort of man to be.) Whether, by the same token, Shakespeare wants to make Helena appear whiter than white, is a more complex and interesting question, here deferred. We may, however, note that Shakespeare increases the social distance between Bertram and Helena—in the original, Helena is independently wealthy and much closer to being Bertram's equal. Whether this goes any way towards helping to explain her adoration or his revulsion, must be left to individual response (for me it doesn't, but I can see that for some it might).

It will come as no surprise to anyone even slightly familiar with Shakespeare's treatment of his sources to learn that he markedly compressed the more leisurely time-scheme of the original. But it is worth drawing attention to one particular result of this contraction. In the original, Giletta (the Helena figure), having arranged the 'bed trick' with her husband, repeats it 'manye other times so secretly, as it was never knowen'. She not only conceives, but is delivered of, 'two goodly sonnes' which 'were very like unto their father'. When she produces the two sons at the final revelatory feast, Beltramo (Bertram) accepts the children as his—'they were so like hym'—and 'abjected his obstinate rigour'. In Shakespeare's play, the contrived illicit/licit bedding is a one-night-only affair; and when Helena *fi-*

nally confronts Bertram with 'evidence' of his paternity of her child in the final scene, she is—pregnant. Without pushing the matter too pointlessly far, there is surely a signal difference between confronting a man with two bouncing baby boys who are his spitting image, and standing, visibly pregnant, in front of him and asserting that you are carrying his child. Paternity is notoriously difficult to establish incontrovertibly, and this seemingly slight plot change is characteristic of the widespread introduction of uncertainty—or the draining or diffusing away of certainty—which marks this play. All you can feel at the end is that it is, indeed, a conclusion 'pregnant' with possibilities. We cannot possibly see which way things will turn out—what, if you like, is waiting to be born.

I have mentioned that Shakespeare added a clown—given, deliberately as one supposes, the rather unpleasant name of Lavatch. His is a sneering, bawdy, nihilistic voice; and as a figure he is closer to Thersites than to Touchstone and Feste. We are a long way from Arden and Illyria. The other figures to be added by Shakespeare are some French captains and Florentine soldiers. This is more interesting than it perhaps sounds, and pursuing the matter a little further may provide us with an oblique approach to the strangeness of this play. In Boccaccio's little story, the unwilling Beltramo, having been virtually forced into marrying Giletta, pretends to be returning home but immediately takes flight into Italy. This is what we are told. 'And when he was on horseback hee went not thither but took his journey into Tuscane, where understanding that the Florentines and Senois were at warres, he determined to take the Florentines parte, and was willingly received and honourablie entertained, and was made captaine of a certain nomber of men, continuing in their service a long time.' And that is all we hear about the wars, and Beltramo's soldiering. See how Shakespeare elaborates and complicates it.

> *King.* The Florentines and Senoys are by th' ears,
>   Have fought with equal fortune, and continue
>   A braving war.
> *First Lord.*   So 'tis reported, sir.
> *King.* Nay, 'tis most credible. We here receive it
>   A certainty, vouched from our cousin Austria,
>   With caution, that the Florentine will move us
>   For speedy aid; wherein our dearest friend

> Prejudicates the business, and would seem
> To have us make denial.
>
> *First Lord.*   His love and wisdom,
> Approved so to your Majesty, may plead
> For amplest credence.
>
> *King.*   He hath armed our answer,
> And Florence is denied before he comes;
> Yet, for our gentlemen that mean to see
> The Tuscan service, freely have they leave
> To stand on either part.
>
> (I, ii, 1–14)

The Florentines were fighting the Sienese (Senoys) in Boccaccio, but what is Austria doing here, which was, anyway, in no sense France's 'dearest friend'? Be that as it may—Austria *'prejudicates* the business', a word Shakespeare uses nowhere else (this is not mere pedantry on my part—he forces a number of rather awkward and unusual words into service in *All's Well That Ends Well* which he does not use elsewhere; this is part of the thick velvet side of the play). But 'judicating' all round seems rather precarious and insecure in this play: though Austria apparently deserves 'amplest *credence*' (another rather formal 'silver' word, used only in this play and in *Troilus and Cressida*), and though the King vows he will deny Florence help—he then says he will let his men take whichever side they like. So much for the 'amplest credence' of 'our dearest friend'. A quite unnecessary scene; unless Shakespeare wants to show that, despite the high-sounding, sonorous language, loyalties and friendship are fading all round.

There is a comparably supererogatory-seeming scene somewhat later, in the Duke's palace in Florence.

> *Duke.* So that from point to point now have you heard
> The fundamental reasons of this war,
> Whose great decision hath much blood let forth,
> And more thirsts after.
>
> *First Lord.*   Holy seems the quarrel
> Upon your Grace's part; black and fearful
> On the opposer.
>
> *Duke.* Therefore we marvel much our cousin France

Would in so just a business shut his bosom
Against our borrowing prayers.
Second Lord.   Good my lord,
The reasons of our state I cannot yield,
But like a common and an outward man
That the great figure of a council frames
By *self-unable* motion; therefore dare not
Say what I think of it, since I have found
Myself in my incertain grounds to fail
As often as I guessed.

(III, i, 1–16—my italics)

The quarrel between the holy and the black might certainly be said to be engaged by the confrontation of Helena and Bertram, but we are given no insight into the apparently elemental issues at stake in the war. In this, we are somewhat in the position of the Second Lord. It's easy enough to get the hang of what he says—I can't really tell you anything about our reasons of state because I am always outside the council chamber. I just have to make guesses and here I'm as wrong as often as I'm right. But he 'frames' his guesses by '*self-unable* motion'. Not only is this another word (or compound-word) that Shakespeare never uses elsewhere; my guess is that this is its only appearance in the whole of English literature. Obviously it refers to some kind, or degree, of incompetence or disability or just inability. But it is an unusual mouthful for a second lord. However we can readily respond to his feeling that he is in 'incertain grounds'. In this play, so are we.

In the event, Bertram and the other young French blades decide to fight for Florence; but not, we understand, from any feelings of siding with an honourable (or even holy) cause. Boredom seems to be one motive (they 'surfeit on their ease', III, i, 18); while Bertram has his own determinants.

This very day,
Great Mars, I put myself into thy file!
Make me but like my thoughts and I shall prove
A lover of thy drum, hater of love.

(III, iii, 8–11)

The word 'drum' does not appear in the translation of Boccaccio's tale; it occurs more often in this play than in any other by Shakespeare. Such a foregrounding of the 'drum' might seem to suggest that Shakespeare wants to invoke the martial and heroic values—perhaps to set up a tension between the masculine claims and appeal of Mars against the feminine enticements and allure of Venus. This could make for a perfectly good drama (there is something of it in *Antony and Cleopatra*), but it is not the case in this curiously skewed play. The next voiced concern about the drum comes from Parolles, as the Florentine army re-enters the city, presumably returning from battle. 'Lose our drum! Well' (III, v, 87). It is his only line in the scene. Now, it was well known that for a regiment to lose its drum (which bore the regimental colours) was some form of ultimate military disgrace. But here, it appears that *only* Parolles cares about the loss. The general attitude of the soldiers is expressed by that Second Lord, speaking, as it were, without velvet. 'A pox on't, let it go, 'tis but a drum' (III, vi, 46). As though only he feels the dishonour, Parolles grandiloquently vows to recover the lost drum. But if empty, say-anything-noisy, Parolles is the only voice speaking up for traditional notions of honour, then one has to feel that the old values are in a parlous state. In the event, his vainglorious boast that he will go and reclaim the drum is used by the other drum-indifferent officers to trick Parolles and catch him out in all his hypocrisies, mendacities, treacheries, betrayals, cowardices, and whatever else of abject baseness a man is capable of. Parolles is caught out all right; but whatever military dignity and honour may have been associated with the drum is entirely sullied and degraded by its being the central point in this farcical exposure of the least brave and heroic of men. But truly, no one here gives a damn about 'the drum' and whatever traditions of valour and honour it may symbolize.

Parolles, the manifestly pseudo courtier and soldier, a 'counterfeit module' (IV, iii, 104), a creature of 'scarves' (military sashes) and 'bannerets' is, variously and then comprehensively, seen through, 'smoked' (III, vi, 106), and 'found' out (III, vi, 95; V, ii, 46). This, it should be noted, is exactly what happens to the one man willing to believe in him and accept him as a companion, if not a guide—Bertram. Where Parolles is literally blindfolded and bamboozled and frightened into revealing the extent of his utter cowardice, Bertram is more subtly, and elaborately hoodwinked before his final, devastating, unmasking. Not for the first time in Shakespeare, the sub-plot parodies the main one, with worrying, undermining consequences. It becomes something of a question to what extent Parolles and Bertram (for all his true blue blood) might not be two of a kind. But where Bertram, for the most part, seems to alternate between sullen aphasia and a crude or cloddish manner of speaking (Helena is 'my clog'—II, v, 55), Parolles, as his name suggests, has any number of words at his disposal. And as we listen to his facile, improvising, opportunistic, unprincipled loquaciousness, we realize that this is a new voice in Shakespeare.

Nadia Fusini has suggested that Parolles is related to the *picaro* (= rogue, scoundrel) figure who was emerging in Spanish fiction (and probably in European cities) in the second half of the sixteenth century (the first 'picaresque' novel is usually taken to be the anonymous *Lazarillo de Tormes,* 1554). The *picaro* is a deracinated, lower-class figure (an orphan, a discharged servant, some piece of social flotsam), with no family, belonging nowhere, owning nothing, who moves on, takes whatever is going, and lives by his wits. He has no aims, ambitions, or goals—or rather, he has one: survival. In the form of Parolles—I think Nadia Fusini is right—he has found his way onto the Shakespearian stage. Wise old Lafew sees him for what he is from the start—not deserving the title of 'man'. 'Yet art thou good for nothing but taking up, and that thou'rt scarce worth' (II, iii, 208–9). For Lafew, Parolles is totally transparent: 'thy casement I need not open, for I look through thee. Give me thy hand' (II, iii, 215–16). (I would just note that this sort of quite unanticipated shift of tone—you're obviously a total fraud; shake hands—occurs quite often. Having promised to deny Florence any help, the King immediately says his men can fight for whom they like; similarly, in the last scene, when Bertram offers an incredibly contorted and implausible explanation of his conduct, the King says 'Well excused' and then goes on to describe the excuse as totally inadequate—V, iii, 55–72. That somewhat unnerving, unpredictable discontinuity of response is another characteristic of this strange play.)

But Parolles really reveals himself in the episode of his supposed attempt heroically to recapture the lost drum. He quickly realizes he has made a boast he cannot possibly carry out, and he turns on—his own tongue. 'I find my tongue is too foolhardy . . . Tongue, I must put you into a butter-woman's mouth, and buy myself another of Bajazet's mule if you prattle me into these perils' (IV, i, 29–30, 42–4). Iago calculates every cutting, killing word—Parolles will simply say anything if he thinks it might please or impress on a particular occasion. We have the expression—his tongue ran away with him; Parolles is a cautionary example of the vagabond tongue which will stray, roam, run, rush anywhere—because his utterance is not rooted in, or motivated by, anything except an instinct to smooth, mollify, and get by. It duly 'prattles him into perils'. And when he thinks he has been captured by foreign enemies (it is apt that he is completely taken in by figures gabbling actual nonsensical gibberish—in a play in which quite a lot of the speech moves towards the edges of comprehensibility), Parolles reveals, as it were, his true colours: 'Let me live, sir, in a dungon, i' th' stocks, or anywhere, so I may live' (IV, iii, 256–8). It is the eternal cry of the *picaro*. It is not surprising that he adds, in an aside: 'I'll no more drumming. A plague of all drums!' (IV, iii, 312–13).

But he attains his zenith, or nadir—hard to say which—when, after his stream of betrayal and calumny of everything and everyone, his fellow officers 'unmuffle' him, and he stands exposed in what you might think was the last degree of ignominy. His reaction? 'Who cannot be crushed with a plot?' (IV, iii, 340). There is no other line quite like this in the whole of Shakespeare. To be sure, Falstaff dusts himself off fairly breezily after he realizes he has been made 'an ass' in *Merry Wives*. But his attitude is more resigned—you win some, you lose some, and as you get older you lose more. But Parolles is another creature entirely. It is not that he is beyond shame. He has clearly never known what shame is—or guilt, or morality, or principle, or loyalty, or anything else by which society has tried to bind, and bond, and dignify itself. He is not, certainly not, *evil*. He is nothing at all. But there he breathingly is, demanding to live. His soliloquy, after his fellow officers leave him alone with his disgrace, is uttered, one feels, with a certain placidity and peace of mind, and is in some way definitive:

> Yet am I thankful. If my heart were great
> 'Twould burst at this. Captain I'll be no more,
> But I will eat and drink and sleep as soft
> As captain shall. Simply the thing I am
> Shall make me live. Who knows himself a braggart,
> Let him fear this; for it will come to pass
> That every braggart shall be found an ass.
> Rust, sword; cool, blushes; and Parolles live

Safest in shame! Being fooled, by fool'ry thrive!
There's place and means for every man alive.
I'll after them.

(IV, iii, 345–55)

If my heart were great—but it isn't, and that's that. 'Simply the thing I am shall make me live'—it is a far cry from Richard's 'I am myself alone'. It is the difference between heroic, overreaching Renaissance individualism, and an impoverished cluster of the most basic appetites. With Parolles, we could join the mean streets of the twentieth-century city. But he won't die, and you won't shake him off—'I'll after them.' This is the point of his final exchange with Lafew (who can't resist teasing him—'How does your drum?'). Parolles is a suppliant: 'It lies in you, my lord, to bring me in some grace, for you did bring me out' (V, ii, 49–50). (Bertram will also, shortly, need someone to bring him in some grace.) Lafew at first responds chidingly: 'Out upon thee, knave! Dost thou put upon me at once both the office of God and the devil? One brings thee in grace and the other brings thee out.' (Again, a larger theme is glanced at—do, can, humans take on the office of God, and the devil?) But he concludes compassionately: 'Sirrah, inquire further after me. I had talk of you last night; though you are a fool and a knave you shall eat. Go to, follow' (V, ii, 51–7). This is part of the final muted mood of this curious 'comedy'; not, certainly, festive—but nobody, not even the fools and knaves, will starve.

The most succinct comment on Parolles comes from a lord who overhears some of his shameless self-communings (if nothing else, Parolles knows himself clearly and unself-deludingly enough)—'Is it possible he should know what he is, and be that he is?' (IV, i, 45–6). That is the wonder of the man. Not that he is a rogue (nothing new there); but that he seems oblivious to notions of roguery (no wallowing in villainy here, no determined embrace of evil)—he just doesn't care. It is a little frightening—ethical discourse would be meaningless to him; he is completely unreachable on such matters. Yet there he stands like the rest of us—a hungry human being. But meanwhile, during the Florentine military scenes, Bertram is acquitting himself even more dishonourably. The timing is nice—his fellow captains have set the trap for Parolles and promise Bertram some 'sport': 'When his disguise and he is parted, tell me what a sprat you shall find him'

(III, vi, 107–8). (It will, of course, be only a matter of time before Bertram's 'disguise and he is parted' as well.) But Bertram first wants to pursue some other sport, with a local lass (Diana).

> *Second Lord.* But you say she's honest.
> *Bertram.* That's all the fault.
>
> (III, vi, 115–16)

Fault indeed, when a lass should be tiresomely 'honest': but whatever happened to the chivalric code, the courtier's code, the gentleman's code, all the codes? And the other captains see Bertram, what he is, as clearly as they see through Parolles.

> *Second Lord.* He hath perverted a young gentlewoman here in Florence, of a most chaste renown, and this night *he fleshes his will in the spoil of her honor*; he hath given her his monumental ring, and thinks himself made in the unchaste composition.
> *First Lord.* Now, God delay our rebellion! As we are ourselves, what things are we!
>
> (IV, iii, 15–21—my italics)

The italicized words express a powerful, vehement disgust. This man is a disgrace—he is sunk in spoilt honour. And there is a curious half-echo of the recent comment on Parolles—'Is it possible he should know what he is, and be that he is?': 'As we are ourselves, what things are we!' There is a scent here of a sort of weary incredulousness at just how awful humans can be, which lingers in the louring air of the play.

Bertram thinks he is buying Diana's body by giving her his 'monumental ring'. There is such a ring in the original tale; it is one of the wife's 'impossible' tasks to get it off her husband's finger. Shakespeare adds a second ring, which, among other things, allows for further complications and attenuations in the last scene (and, not incidentally, allows Bertram to double his ignominy). Rings (female) and drums (male) should symbolize some kind of honour, and Shakespeare brings both into the foreground of his play; not just to point up the always possible struggle between the ring and the drum (and all they stand for), but also to show them both sullied, devalued, de-

graded. The drum is simply a farcical factor in Parolles' disgrace. The
'monumental ring' should fare better: in Bertram's own words to Diana
when, following instructions, she requests it:

> It is an honor 'longing to our house,
> Bequeathèd down from many ancestors,
> Which were the greatest obloquy i' th' world
> In me to lose.

To which Diana has an unanswerable reply:

> Mine honor's such a ring;
> My chastity's the jewel of our house,
> Bequeathèd down from many ancestors,
> Which were the greatest obloquy i' th' world
> In me to lose.
>
> (IV, ii, 42–9)

So Bertram makes the 'unchaste composition' (bargain, arrangement):
'Here, take my ring./My house, mine honor, yea, my life be thine' (IV, ii,
51–2). As Helena predicted he would:

> a ring the County wears,
> That downward hath succeeded in his house
> From son to son some four or five descents
> Since the first father wore it. This ring he holds
> In most rich choice; yet, in his idle fire,
> To buy his will it would not seem too dear,
> Howe'er repented after.
>
> (III, vii, 22–8)

There is something rather awesomely biblical about 'the first father': cu-
mulatively, it feels as if there were some ancient, even primal, virtue, as well
as dynastic honour and paternal potency, mystically lodged in the ring. The
more profane and sacrilegious, then, Bertram's easy surrendering it as part
of a dirty deal—'to buy his will' (lust). So much for the regimental drum; so
much for the family ring. 'Obloquy' indeed ('obloquy'—to be everywhere

spoken against: there is, indeed, nothing to be said *for* Bertram by the time
Shakespeare has finished with him).

Helena also has something handed down to her by her father which she,
by contrast, respects, preserves, and puts to beneficial use.

> You know my father left me some prescriptions
> Of rare and proved effects, such as his reading
> And manifest experience had collected
> For general sovereignty.
>
> (I, iii, 223–6)

'General sovereignty' is a rather vague phrase which could mean 'universal supremacy' as well as, more specifically, master medicines which cure
all. From the first scene, this now dead father is credited with having had
strange, mysterious, almost miraculous powers; his 'skill was almost as
great as his honesty; had it stretched so far, would have made nature immortal, and death should have play for lack of work' (I, i, 20–23). These
mysterious powers—they become increasingly important in Shakespeare—
seem to be in some sort religious, or more than mundane, though with no
suggestions of any orthodox theology. Ruskin once said that Shakespeare's
religion is 'occult behind his magnificent equity', and we will hardly find a
better formulation. There are certainly suggestions of 'occult' (concealed,
hidden, secret) powers in this, as in later plays; and, in the material form of
his almost magical prescriptions, Helena has inherited something of her father's power which, we come to feel, is spiritual as well.

Trying to persuade the sceptical sick King to let her try to cure him, she
says that her father gave her one very special 'receipt' which 'He bade me
store up as a triple eye,/Safer than mine own two' (II, i, 110–11). Wilson
Knight, who was much drawn to such things, happily asserted that this was
the ' "triple eye" of occult doctrine and practice—located on the forehead,
and used in spirit-healing as a source of powerful rays'. Something of that,
perhaps: but, as Philip Brockbank pointed out, the 'triple' or third eye was
most traditionally an attribute of the goddess Prudentia; it was also a bawdy
way (common in Jacobean drama) of referring to virginity. This is more to
the point. Impoverished and orphaned Helena will have to be nothing if
not prudent if she is to make her way in this increasingly ruthless society;
and her virginity—traditionally associated with magic power—is indeed

her most valuable 'receipt' which she will have to deploy with the utmost care (and, in the event, deviousness).

The King, having experienced many failed attempts to ameliorate his condition, is no longer 'credulous of cure', adding that the 'most learnèd doctors . . . have concluded':

> That laboring art can never ransom nature
> From her inaidable estate.
>
> (II, i, 120–21)

That one sentence covers a major part of the thrust of Shakespeare's dramatic explorations—particularly the later ones. To what extent *is* nature 'inaidable' (another strong, angular word used solely this once by Shakespeare); and how might 'laboring art' (medicine–drama) in some way 'ransom' it? In the event, the King submits to Helena, and proves to be 'aidable' through her, paternally-derived, 'laboring art'. He is cured, and the reactions to this apparent miracle are notable (Bertram, typically, has no significant reaction at all and stays sullen-dumb). For Lafew, it justifies the faith of an older world:

> They say miracles are past, and we have our philosophical persons, to
> make modern and familiar, things supernatural and causeless. Hence it is
> that we make trifles of terrors, ensconcing ourselves into seeming knowl-
> edge, when we should submit ourselves to an unknown fear.
>
> (II, iii, 1–6)

When Ruskin compared his contemporary, faithless, complacent Victorians, with the pious Venetians of the Middle Ages, he saw a vast difference between 'the calculating, smiling, self-governed man, and the believing, weeping, wondering, struggling, Heaven-governed man'. Lafew feels something of this about the difference between his generation and Bertram's, and it is a deep concern of the play to what extent life, lives, might be said to be, in some way, 'Heaven-governed'. Lafew also reads from what must be a broadsheet ballad (such as would have been quickly produced to welcome the recovery of the King): 'A showing of a heavenly effect in an earthly actor' (II, iii, 24). One feels that it is somehow characteristic of Shakespeare to have ascribed what is, in effect, the most succinct description possible of the central action of the play, to an anonymous pamphlet.

For we, as audience, are invited to watch seemingly 'heavenly effects' brought about by, or through 'earthly actors' (agents—but play-actors as well)—provoking us, perhaps, into peripheral ponderings about the larger relations between heaven and earth. But it is important always to bear in mind—in view of frequent attempts to sanctify and spiritualize her—that Helena is, unambiguously, an *earthly* actor.

But perhaps the most enthusiastic response to the miraculous cure comes from—Parolles. 'Why, 'tis the rarest argument of wonder that hath shot out in our latter times' (II, iii, 7–8). 'Shot out' is rather odd; one hardly knows whether he is thinking of comets or guns. But 'arguments of wonder' feature increasingly in Shakespeare's later comedies, and Parolles' comment is entirely fitting. But then he piles on the words, trying to match Lafew's more gravely measured expressions of awe. The 'very hand of heaven,' says Lafew; Parolles seeks to go one better—'great power, great transcendence' (II, iii, 32–6). We must pause on that last word. Not only is it yet another word which Shakespeare uses only in this play; the OED gives it as the first example of its use in English! Wilson Knight wrote that 'what is remarkable in this play is the more near-distance, immediate and detailed, treatment of transcendence'. Now, clearly there are intimations of transcendence hovering intermittently around Helena. But Parolles is a man who devalues everything he embraces, sullies everything he speaks. It was Parolles, remember, who seemed to make the strongest plea on behalf of the honour of the regimental drum. So when he speaks up so positively for the recognition of 'transcendence' (I like to think of him as the first man in England to do so!), we are bound to wonder just how much weight and authentic content the word carries—or is meant to carry.

Nevertheless, Helena has attracted something more than admiration from the commentators. For Coleridge, she was 'Shakespeare's loveliest character'; Bullough finds her 'entirely good' (though not witty after the first scene); Wilson Knight, never one to modify his raptures, found her 'almost beyond the human . . . almost a divine or poetic principle'—certainly a 'miracle worker', and 'a channel, or medium, of the divine, or cosmic powers'. She is, he says, 'the supreme development of Shakespeare's conception of feminine love'. Most find her 'a ministering angel' (healing the King); though some have regarded her use of the bed trick as rather odiously manipulative. Clearly she is the central character (though Charles I apparently found Parolles the chief attraction!), and the whole play revolves and evolves around her. And she is various. Angelic she may be; but she certainly wants to go to bed with Bertram. As the anonymous ballad unambiguously reminds us, she is an *'earthly* actor'. And the first Act reveals that she certainly commands a number of different styles and voices —at least three—and we will start there.

Her first words are something of a quibble—'I do affect a sorrow indeed, but I have it too' (I, i, 57)—suggesting that she is aware that the emotions you show are not always in synchrony with the emotions you feel. Her first soliloquy starts, rather strikingly, with the admission that paternal veneration has been somewhat dislodged—'I think not on my father':

> I have forgot him; my imagination
> Carries no favor in't but Bertram's.
>   (I, i, 85–9)

But, she realizes, doting on him is like loving a 'star' (there are lots of stars in this play), 'he is so above me', she is 'not in his sphere' (I, i, 92–5). Since he has left for Paris, all she can do, she rather extravagantly says, is 'my idolatrous fancy / Must sanctify his relics', as if to turn desire into hagiolatry. Then Bertram's friend Parolles enters, and Helena reacts:

> I love him for his sake,
> And yet I know him a notorious liar,
> Think him a great way fool, solely a coward . . .
>   (I, i, 105–7)

—another example of the discontinuous—not to say contradictory— response I have already mentioned as being strangely characteristic of this play. Her tone then changes radically as she and Parolles engage in some extended, and fairly earthy, banter about 'virginity'—how to keep it; when best to lose it. At this point, seemingly irrelevant matters—yet they are to be central concerns of the play. Here, Helena speaks a tolerably tough sort of prose. 'Bless our poor virginity from underminers and blowers-up! Is there no military policy how virgins might blow up men?' (I, i, 126–8). 'Pollicie' was what Giletta employed to regain her husband, and it would be only a slight exaggeration to say that Helena rather satisfactorily 'blows up' Bertram by the end of the play. Parolles' response comes in the form of one of dozens of paradoxes and seeming oxymorons which bestrew the play. 'Virginity by being once lost may be ten times found; by being ever kept it is ever lost' (I, i, 136–8). More oxymorons follow when Helena imagines Bertram at court:

> His humble ambition, proud humility;
> His jarring, concord, and his discord, dulcet;
> His faith, his sweet disaster; with a world
> Of pretty, fond, *adoptious* Christendoms
> That blinking Cupid gossips. Now shall he—
> I know not what he shall.
>   (I, i, 178–83—my italics)

She can't keep it up; and small wonder, since it is not at all clear what on earth she is talking about (I have italicized another word which only occurs in this play). Not for the last time, one has a sense of an over-ornate language taking over from the speakers and covering parts of the play in a thick, semi-incomprehensible, velvet.

When Parolles leaves, Helena, with an utterly different voice, shifts into rhymed couplets for a soliloquy full of that incantatory, apodictic confidence which is often generated by couplets in Shakespeare (it is with just such incantatory couplets that Helena will, effectively, mesmerize the initially sceptical King into trying her 'remedy' for him).

> Our remedies oft in ourselves do lie,
> Which we ascribe to heaven; the fated sky
> Gives us free scope; only doth backward pull
> Our slow designs when we ourselves are dull.
> What power is it which mounts my love so high,
> That makes me see, and cannot feed mine eye?
> The mightiest space in fortune nature brings
> To join like likes, and kiss like native things.
>   (I, i, 223–30)

Helena here sees and speaks with what we might indeed call almost occult clarity. We *do* have some 'free scope', though living under a 'fated sky'— Helena is recognizing the reality and force of free will in a world of everywhere more powerful influences. Whatever power it is that makes her yearn for Bertram—call it what you like; spiritual, carnal—its strength cannot be denied, even if it unacceptably transgresses an all but sacrosanct class barrier. And, yes—nature can join what fortune seems to have placed far apart (the debate about their respective powers is joined again). Helena is clearing her ground for action—already thinking about going to Paris to cure the King:

> my project may deceive me,
> But my intents are fixed, and will not leave me.
>   (I, i, 235–6)

It is the first scene, and Helena has already started to plot.

There follows an interview with Bertram's mother, the Countess, and Helena reverts to blank verse for a mode of speaking marked by ellipsis, ambiguity and cirumlocution. Before the interview, there is an exchange— preparatory as one comes to feel—between the Countess and the Clown, in which the Countess asks the Clown why he wants to get married. 'My poor body, madam, requires it' and 'I have other holy reasons, such as they are' (I, iii, 28, 32). It is generally thought that, this Clown being as he is, 'holy' is probably a bawdy pun, perhaps 'reasons' (raisings), too. It is tolerably clear that Helena's body 'requires' Bertram; the question will be—how unob- scenely 'holy' are her other reasons? The Steward then tells the Countess that he has heard Helena soliloquizing about her love for Bertram. The re- action of the Countess—to herself—is one of profound understanding:

> Even so it was with me, when I was young;
> If ever we are nature's, these are ours; this thorn
> Doth to our rose of youth rightly belong;
> Our blood to us, this to our blood is born.
> It is the show and seal of nature's truth.
>   (I, iii, 130–34)

I find it almost touching that the Arden editor thinks that 'these' (line two above) refers to 'situations'. They are, surely, importunate sexual desires, so thorningly and prickingly born in us. As Shakespeare here recognizes, with his own matchless directness, they come with our blood. Certainly we are 'nature's'; the question, here and always, is what we do about that inelucta- ble fact.

Confronted by the Countess, in a kindly enough manner, with the dis- covered fact of loving her son, Helena prevaricates and prevaricates, until

the Countess is provoked to say—'Go not about' (I, iii, 190). It is an injunction or imperative which could be issued to many other figures in this play,
in which the dominant (though not exclusive) mode is, indeed, to 'go about'
and about—to the point of provoking an irritated impatience in other characters and audience alike. It is a play in which, for the most part, directness
is drowned, or relentlessly abjured; (in the interests of tolerance, we might,
perhaps, remember John Donne's lines to the effect that 'he who truth
would seek, about must and about must go'). Admitting the fact in her own
baroque, or indeed Mannerist, way, Helena says:

> I know I love in vain, strive against hope;
> Yet, in this *captious and inteemable* sieve,
> I still pour in the waters of my love,
> And lack not to lose still. Thus, Indian-like,
> Religious in mine error, I adore
> The sun that looks upon his worshipper
> But knows of him no more.
> (I, iii, 203–9—my italics)

'Love' as a 'sieve' which will take as much as you pour into it, but which
doesn't pour anything back, is a recognizable image for the relationship
between the selfless/selfish love of Helena/Bertram. But, 'captious and inteemable' (italicized because, again, unique to this play)? This is amazingly wrought utterance. (We might compare, from the previous scene, the
King's phrase 'On the catastrophe and heel of pastime', I, ii, 57: it recognizably means simply 'towards the end of his pleasure or recreation', but what
an extraordinarily rich, redundant way of saying it! Such formulations,
both dazzling and perverse, are the hallmark of this play.) Helena ends her
confessional speech in riddles. She is one who can only:

> But lend and give where she is sure to lose;
> That seeks not to find that her search implies,
> But, riddle-like, lives sweetly where she dies.
> (I, iii, 217–19)

In fact, the whole play tends towards riddle.

When Helena claims her reward for successfully curing the King, and
moves to choose a man for her husband, she says:

Now, Dian, from thy altar do I fly,
And to imperial Love, that god most high,
Do my sighs stream.
                        (II, iii, 75–7)

The real 'Diana' in the play is the chaste Florentine girl so-named, whom
Bertram seeks to debauch, and who helps Helena in her plot to gain access to Bertram's bed. Helena (whose namesake's sexual attractiveness was
the 'cause . . . the Grecians sacked Troy', as the Clown reminds us—I, iii,
72) has to enter the arena of sexual love—*use* her virginity—to achieve her
ends, physical or spiritual as they may be. Bertram, of course, rejects 'a poor
physician's daughter' with deep 'disdain', thus exciting the King's anger:

'Tis only title thou disdain'st in her, the which
I can build up. Strange is it that our bloods,
Of color, weight, and heat, poured all together,
Would quite confound distinction, yet stands off
In differences so mighty.
. . .
          Good alone
Is good, without a name; vileness is so:
The property by what it is should go,
Not by the title. She is young, wise, fair;
In these to nature she's immediate heir;
And these breed honor.
                        (II, iii, 118–22, 129–34)

There is much undeniable wisdom here, and we should recognize that,
though it comes from a king, it represents a potential threat to all distinctions, differences, titles, names—with only 'nature' left to 'breed honor'.
Though, of course, at the beginning and at the end of the day we *are* nature's. Certainly, Helena is good; and, make no mistake, Bertram is 'vile'.
Nature certainly humbles class hierarchy here. The matter has been in
question from the beginning. Helena profits from both culture and nature;
from what 'her *education* promises' and the 'disposition she *inherits*'—'she
derives her honesty and *achieves* her goodness' (I, i, 42–7—my italics). Bertram, by starkly emphasized contrast, inherits his father's 'shape' and 'title'

(name), but none of his 'manners'; and his ineducable wilfulness takes him from bad to worse. It is all part of that ongoing debate in Shakespeare concerning the relationship between, precisely, what we 'derive' and what we 'achieve'. In rejecting Helena, Bertram sufficiently reveals himself in all his amoral obtuseness:

> Proud, scornful boy, unworthy this good gift,
> That dost in vile misprision shackle up
> My love and her desert ...
>
> (II, iii, 152–4)

says the furious King (to be soon after echoed by the Countess condemning her son's 'misprizing of a maid too virtuous'). We have encountered 'misprision' among princes before. Shakespeare was very attuned to all the arrogance and 'prejudicating' blindness that can come with name and title.

When Helena receives Bertram's 'dreadful' letter ('Till I have no wife, I have nothing in France', III, ii, 76), with its apparently impossible conditions, her first reaction seems to be to blame herself and retreat:

> I will be gone;
> My being here it is that holds thee hence.
> Shall I stay here to do't? No, no, although
> The air of paradise did fan the house
> And angels officed all. I will be gone.
>
> (III, ii, 127–31)

When Helena speaks such, indeed, 'angelic' poetry, one can understand Wilson Knight's enthusiasm. She suddenly seems to come from somwhere else. In the next scene, the aura of holiness around Helena increases as the Countess reads the letter from her in which she announces:

> I am Saint Jaques' pilgrim, thither gone.
> Ambitious love hath so in me offended
> That barefoot plod I the cold ground upon,
> With sainted vow my faults to have amended.
>
> (III, iv, 4–7)

—as if her love was a sin to be expiated. To the Countess, this makes her son appear, by contrast, even worse.

> What angel shall
> Bless this unworthy husband? He cannot thrive,
> Unless her prayers, whom heaven delights to hear
> And loves to grant, reprieve him from the wrath
> Of greatest justice.
>
> (III, iv, 25–9)

Helena certainly seems a good deal closer to God than Bertram, and in most readings of the play she does indeed become the 'angel' who forgives, blesses, and thus redeems her *very* 'unworthy husband'. And perhaps that is right—it is certainly an interpretation the play permits. But there is a point worth noting. In Boccaccio, Giletta, on receiving the rejection letter from her husband, immediately sets about planning to perform the impossible conditions. Her announcement that she is departing on a perpetual pilgrimage is simply a concealing ruse—she heads straight for Florence and Beltramo. Most readers of Shakespeare's play think that Helena's penitential religious feelings are sincere, and her intention to be a pilgrim, genuine. Perhaps they are. But why then did Shakespeare have her say she is 'Saint Jaques' pilgrim' (not mentioned in the source)? To any Elizabethan audience this would mean that she was going to the shrine of Saint James at Compostella. Now, as Dr Johnson remarked, drily as one feels, Florence is 'somewhat out of the road from Rousillon to Compostella'. So it is; but Florence is where Helena turns up in the next scene. By accident; by chance; is she just going a *very* long way round? Inconceivable, surely. The Arden editor thinks that 'Saint Jaques' is simply Shakespeare's mistake; but I doubt that, too. It looks more like false bait to me. And in Florence she soon has her plot arranged, along with some semi-specious-sounding justifications and rationalizations for it.

> Why then tonight
> Let us assay our plot, which, if it speed,
> Is wicked meaning in a lawful deed,
> And lawful meaning in a lawful act,

Where both not sin, and yet a sinful fact.
But let's about it.

(III, vii, 43–8)

Since they are, in fact, arranging for a wife to go to bed with her husband, it is lawful enough. As for the deception—well, 'craft against vice', as the Duke will say in *Measure for Measure*. Nevertheless, Helena has to find her way to the deed through paradox and ambiguity. But, in the world of this play, that is too often what you need.

The last scene, in which everything is finally, *finally*, made clear, is marked by prolix protractions, elaborate mendacities, futile denials, and maddening evasions. There is also a lot about 'haggish age', forgetting, oblivion, and 'th' inaudible and noiseless foot of Time' (V, iii, 41). In one extraordinary contorted and mannered speech, (fantastically different from his usual semi-literate thuggish mode, V, iii, 44–55), Bertram attempts to convince the court that he has always actually, really, loved Lafew's daughter, Maudlin—the unlikeliest of unlikely stories. When pressed about the second ring (which Helena put on Bertram's hand during the dark night of their consummation), Diana prevaricates—no, she didn't buy it; no, she didn't find it; no, she wasn't given it; no, she wasn't lent it. At which point, the exasperated King sends her off to prison—and one can sympathize; the obfuscations seem almost to be getting out of hand. (Of course, Diana simply never *had* the ring—but, when once we practise to deceive . . .) Helena finally appears, clearing everything up, and in a dozen, businesslike lines, claims Bertram as 'doubly won' (V, iii, 314), and effects needed clarifications and reconciliations. Even more brusquely, in a couple of peremptory lines Bertram asks pardon and promises love (by this time he seems pretty crushed). There is no sense of great happiness; certainly no feeling of either ecstatic personal reunion, or welcome social regeneration. More a feeling of somewhat weary relief that the rather wretched business has finally been tidied up and is at last all over. 'All's well that ends well' says Helena, optimistically, twice (V, iv, 35; V, i, 25); but the King's concluding comment sounds more appropriate—'All yet *seems* well . . .' (V, iii, 333—my italics).

This is not intended to be reductive about Helena and her role as saviour (of Bertram, as well as the King); it is possible to see her as an instrument of the Divine, or more than human, Will, without failing to discern that she is

a woman who very much wants her man. The final completion of the marriage can be seen as the climax to a mysterious, providential design, as well
as clever Helena's personal triumph. Like other heroines before her, she
is resourceful enough to take over the play, thus appearing as some sort of
superior power in control; but, for all that, she is an earthly actor. Perhaps
it is best to see the advantage she takes of her 'free scope' implementing,
complementing, working in conjunction with the 'fated sky'. She may say,
modestly and piously, to the King:

> But most it is presumption in us when
> The help of heaven we count the act of men . . .
>   (II, i, 153–4)

but this is her incantatory couplet mode, when she takes on the role of a
sort of priestess. Elsewhere, she stakes everything on the acts of women—
starting with herself; 'the help of heaven' may operate in its own way, but it
is hardly to be passively counted on. That her acts involve deception (including a feigned death—another one!) is more a comment on the world
in which she has to act and find her way, than on her personal morality. It
remains something of a puzzle why she should want the despicable Bertram so much; Shakespeare has clearly gone out of his way to make sure he
has *no* redeeming feature (though I suppose we are to assume he has patrician good looks). Some think that Shakespeare does this to make Helena's
love, mercy and forgiveness seem almost divinely beneficent, and that may
well be right; for love and forgiveness *are* miracles—earthly miracles. But
there remains a sense of residual mystery to the play—as I suggested, it is as
if half of it were concealed by the strange velvet of its language, like Bertram's handsome but probably pox-scarred face. The play opens with a riddle—'In delivering my son from me I bury a second husband' (I, i, 1–2),
thus the Countess bids farewell to her son, playing on 'delivering' as 'giving
birth' and 'letting go'; and it goes on riddling to the end—thus Diana:

> Dead though she be, she feels her young one kick.
> So there's my riddle: one that's dead is quick.
> And now behold the meaning.
> *Enter Helena*
>   (V, iii, 302–4)

Helena is the answer to the riddle; but she is herself a riddle. And the riddles are deep. Burials yielding deliveries; the dead strangely transformed to the quick—though the great tragedies are still to come, we are already well on the way to the last plays.

MEASURE FOR MEASURE (1604)

> Which is the wiser here, Justice or Iniquity?
>
> (II, i, 172)

> What's this? What's this? Is this her fault or mine?
> The tempter or the tempted, who sins most?
>
> (II, ii, 162–3)

This is a worryingly claustrophobic play. It opens in some unspecified room, perhaps in the Duke's palace, only to show the Duke making rather furtive arrangements to leave ('I'll privily away', I, i, 67); we are next in a street, peopled mainly by characters who bring the fetid reek of the brothel with them; thence to a Friar's cell in a monastery, and thence to the coolness of a nunnery. The important scenes in Act II take place in a courtroom and then a smaller ante-room, where the atmosphere grows more intense and stifling. For all of Act III and most of Act IV we are in a prison, with one excursion to a moated grange. Act V does, at last, bring all the characters into a 'public space near the city gate'; but although this is, as it should be, a site for clarifications, uncoverings, revelations, solvings—people and events finally appearing in their true light, as it were—the longing for fresh, refreshing air and expansive breathing space, which grows throughout the play, is hardly satisfied.

There is nothing romantic about this Vienna, in which the play is set—no nearby Belmont, no reachable Forest of Arden. No 'green world' at all, really; only a 'moated grange' and a reference to Angelo's garden. One would hardly look for release and revivification in a garden belonging to Angelo. Interestingly, it is a 'garden circummured with brick' (IV, i, 28). Shakespeare invents the word 'circummured' for this play, and never uses it again. It means—obviously enough—walled around, or walled in. Not surprisingly, it is the perfect word for the world of this play, for these are 'circummured' people. Literally, of course—if not in the courtroom or the brothel, then in the secular prison or the holier confinement of monastery or nunnery. (There are no domestic spaces or scenes in what Mary Lascelles rightly called 'this strangely *unfamilied* world'.) But a lot of the main characters are walled up mentally and emotionally—say 'humanly'—as well. In this respect, the three main characters are oddly similar. The Duke likes to avoid his people and 'assemblies', and prefers to withdraw—'I have ever loved the life removed' (I, iii, 8). Angelo, in the Duke's own terms, is 'precise . . . scarce confesses / That his blood flows, or that his appetite / Is more to bread than stone' (I, iii, 50–53); he is 'a man of stricture and firm abstinence' who has blunted his 'natural edge / With profits of the mind, study and fast' (I, iii, 12 and I, iv, 60–61); he is the very type of the repressed, self-immuring Puritan—except, as we might say, when his blood is up. We first see Isabella in a nunnery 'wishing a more strict restraint / Upon the sisterhood'—this, in the famously strict order of Saint Clare (I, iv, 4–5). She, too, seems dedicated to a cloistral sequestering, and a chaste coldness—except when *her* blood is up, when she displays, in Walter Pater's words, 'a dangerous and tigerlike changefulness of feeling'. In their very different ways, all three find that they cannot live 'the life removed'. The Duke's apparent abdication is the prelude to his disguised descent into the lives of his people; thrust into high office and rendered effectively omnipotent, the apparently bloodless Angelo finds himself swamped with lust and driven to (attempted) murder; Isabella is drawn out of the nunnery, never to return—unavoidably involved in the plots and snares of the distinctly 'fallen' world of Vienna. But these emergings from the various retreats of withdrawal and withholding—both actual and temperamental 'murings'—are hardly liberations into a new-found freedom. For Vienna, like Hamlet's Denmark, is itself a prison.

As portrayed here, there are two worlds in this Vienna—the realm of the palace, the monastery, the lawcourt, the nunnery; but something has gone wrong with authority and things go variously, and sometimes dreadfully, amiss, until they are rather desperately righted at the end: then the brothel world, with its atmosphere of compulsive yet joyless lust, listless lawlessness, disease, degeneration and decay, where things, unchecked, go from bad to worse (or just from bad to bad). Lucio, something of a Mercutio, something of a Parolles, and something all himself, buzzes between the two worlds—and all realms come together in the prison, which becomes, through its occupants, at once brothel, lawcourt, nunnery—and, did but the others know it, the palace is there as well. Normality—if we may so designate reciprocal love and reproductive sexuality—is represented solely by Claudio and Juliet, the only genuine 'couple' in the play. Their sexual intercourse is described as 'our most mutual entertainment' (I, ii, 157), and the act was, both agree, 'mutually committed' (II, iii, 27). These are the only times the word appears in the play: apart from this couple, there is no 'mutuality' in this world—and he is in prison under sentence of death, while she is allowed barely sixty words, hardly there at all. There just doesn't seem to be any ordinary, straightforward love around. This hapless couple apart, we are confronted with, on the one hand, a merciless and tyrannous legalism, a ferocious and rancid chastity, and whatever it is the Duke thinks he's up to; on the other, 'mere anarchy' and '*concupiscible* intemperate lust' (V, i, 98). This is the only time Shakespeare uses the italicized word (or any of its derivatives); it comes ultimately from *cupere,* to desire, which can be innocent enough; but the word, just by its sound, irresistibly suggests extreme lubricity and uncontrolled sexual desire. Admittedly, these are Isabella's words about Angelo, but one feels that Shakespeare came to share some of her nausea at the idea of unbridled sexuality. And the fact that Angelo succumbs to a more terrifying and deranging lust than is manifested by any of the brothel regulars, tells us something about Puritans, certainly, but more generally enforces the recognition that the realms of authority and anarchy are not so firmly and stably separate and discrete as society, perhaps, likes to imagine. Of course, sex is always *potentially* a great leveller. What the law—any law—can do about sex, is one of the problems explored by the play. And it has got to do something—unless you regard Isabella's hysterical chastity, and Mistress Overdone's punks and stewed prunes, as viable options.

Interestingly and perhaps understandably—the prospect of a few drinks at Mistress Overdone's is surely more appealing than the idea of arguing forensics with Angelo—some major critics have shown themselves disinclined to be censorious about scenes involving the denizens of the brothel world. Dr Johnson found them 'very natural and pleasing', which could make you wonder how he spent his evenings in London, if we didn't know better. Walter Pater is even more enthusiastic. 'It brings before us a group of persons, attractive, full of desire, vessels of the genial, seed-bearing powers of nature, a gaudy existence flowering out over the old court and city of Vienna, a spectacle of the fullness and pride of life which to some may seem to touch the verge of wantonness.' *Touch the verge!* One applauds the tolerance, but perhaps has to deprecate the idealizing—some of the figures are amiable enough, and they certainly provide the only *comedy* in the play; but they are meant, surely, to be seen as emissaries from a pretty foul and degraded world. These critics, and many others, are in part responding to the telling poetry Lucio uses to plead the case of Claudio and Juliet to ice-maiden Isabella:

> Your brother and his lover have embraced;
> As those that feed grow full, as blossoming time
> That from the seedness the bare fallow brings
> To teeming foison, even so her plenteous womb
> Expresseth his full tilth and husbandry.
>
> (I, iv, 40–44)

Put like *that* (no coarse brothel squalor in these lines—we are out in the fields we never see, and I doubt Lucio's competence in husbandry) it seems like the most natural thing in the world. Which of course it is—one more example of the ongoing miracle of nature's bounty. And the death sentence passed on Claudio *is* an absurdity as well as an atrocity. Pompey lives by being a bawd:

> *Escalus.* Is it a lawful trade?
> *Pompey.* If the law would allow it, sir.
> *Escalus.* But the law will not allow it, Pompey; nor it shall not be allowed in Vienna.
> *Pompey.* Does your worship mean to geld and splay all the youth of the city?
> *Escalus.* No, Pompey.
> *Pompey.* Truly, sir, in my poor opinion, they will to't, then.
>
> (II, i, 226–33)

Of course they will. We scarcely need a play by Shakespeare to remind us that you—they—cannot stamp out legally unsanctioned sexual behaviour, nor decree it away. Pompey makes a sharper point. It *would* be legal if the legitimating authorities legalized it—the law is, at bottom, as tautologous as that. It certainly cannot invoke the authority of nature, since nature not only allows unrestricted sexuality, it seems positively to demand it. The law can either invoke the will of God; or point to the requirements of civic order and decency; or simply rule by fiat, fear, and force. These are complex and perennial matters: how and to what extent a society controls the sexuality of its members is perhaps its most abiding problem and concern (even today, different societies have different ideas about what to do about the world's oldest profession—legalize it? tolerate it? wink at it? ghetto-ize it? try to eradicate it? But whatever they decide, you may be sure people 'will to't'.)

As he does so often, Shakespeare, in this play, has taken familiar tales and themes and synthesized them in a completely original way, giving them a twist in the process. There are three such discernible in this play, usually referred to (following Arden editor J. W. Lever) as the story of the Corrupt Magistrate (also called 'The Monstrous Ransom' by Mary Lascelles); the legend of the Disguised Ruler; and the tale of the Substituted Bedmate. The first story turns on the abuse of authority and power and must be as old as Authority itself. A generic version would have a woman pleading to a local authority for the life of her husband, under sentence of death for murder. The authority promises to release the husband if the wife will sleep with him. She does; but he executes the husband anyway. The wife appeals to the great ruler of the land, and the Corrupt authority is ordered to marry the wronged wife (to make her respectable) and is then executed. An eye for an eye—very satisfying. In his *Hecatommithi* (1565), Cinthio, offering a more romantic version, made certain changes to the plot, which were adopted by Shakespeare. The husband and wife become brother and sister; the brother's original crime was not murder but seduction of a virgin; the brother is not executed after all; and the sister pleads for and obtains mercy for the corrupt magistrate who is now her husband. Much happier all round. According to Lever, 'The end of the story was explicitly designed to show the courtesy, magnanimity, and justice of the Emperor Maximian.' This has particular contemporary relevance for Shakespeare's play, written as it was the year after James I came to the throne (1603)—of which, more later. A more recent source for Shakespeare was George Whetstone's two-part play, *Promos and Cassandra* (1578). These two leading figures, greatly altered, mutate into Angelo and Isabella. Their two great interviews occur at about the same stages in both plays, and for two Acts, Shakespeare follows Whetstone's structure and scene sequence quite closely. He also takes over some minor characters, characteristically altered and individualized —though he added Elbow and Froth, Abhorson and the crucial Barnardine, Lucio and Mariana, and effectively reinvents the great ruler, since, as Bullough pointed out, 'in no other version of the tale is the overlord given the same prominent part'. Of course, Shakespeare's masterstroke, which changes everything, is to make the heroine a novitiate nun, and to have her *refuse* to sacrifice her chastity to save the life of her brother.

The stories of monarchs moving among their people in disguise are likewise numerous and ancient. The Roman Emperor Alexander Severus was famous for it: here is Sir Thomas Elyot writing about Severus in *The Image of Governance* (1541)—a title with obvious relevance for Shakespeare's play.

> [he] used many tymes to disguise hym selfe in dyvers straunge facions.
> . . . and woulde one day haunte one parte of the citee, an other day an
> other parte . . . to see the state of the people, with the industrie or negligence of theym that were officers.

The figure of the Disguised Ruler had become popular on the contemporary stage: in Shakespeare's play he becomes the crucial mediating, moderating and *manipulating* figure. The Substituted Bedmate—the bed trick—was an even more familiar and popular motif which Shakespeare has, of course, used before, not least in the immediately preceding *All's Well That Ends Well*. But by bringing in Mariana, who is sort of Angelo's fiancée, to be the substitute; and by having Isabella, who is almost a nun, agree to the trick, Shakespeare opens up all sorts of legal, moral and spiritual issues. As, of course, does the whole play.

One general point should be made about the genre of this strange play. Just at this time, the emergent genre of 'Mongrell tragicomedy' (as Sidney called it), was being 'theorized' by one Guarini in his *Compendio della Poesia Tragicomica* (1601). I quote Lever's summary of Guarini's defence of the 'mongrel'. 'The form was defined as a close blend or fusion of seeming disparates; taking from tragedy "its great characters, but not its great action; a likely story, but not a true one . . . delight, not sadness; danger, not death"; and from comedy "laughter that was not dissolute, modest attractions, a well-tied knot, a happy reversal, and, above all, the comic order of things."' Shakespeare's play hardly meets all these requirements, even though it does end with the marriages, pardons and reconciliations, and apparent harmonizations of 'the comic order of things'—even Lucio, who looks set to act as the usual requisite scapegoat excluded from the final ensemble, is forgiven. So all *seems* well. But what laughter there is is resolutely 'dissolute'; the arranged marriages have not been sought and pursued by the couples involved—there is no genuine *love* (as opposed to lust) in this play—but are imposed by the Duke (we get no sense of Claudio and Juliet as a happy couple); the knots don't come across as very 'well-tied' (Isabella doesn't even get to answer the Duke's unprecedentedly peremptory proposal of marriage); there is certainly danger rather than death, but not much of a sense of delight or happiness comes off the resolving reversals. The questions raised by the play remain unanswered—are perhaps unanswerable. A. P. Rossiter's redefinition of Tragicomedy comes nearer the mark. 'Tragicomedy is an art of inversion, deflation and paradox. Its subject is tragicomic man; and my repetition is not tautology, because genuine tragicomedy is marked by telling generalizations about the subject, *man,* of a seriousness which is unexpected in comedy and may seem incongruous with it.' He takes up a term first used by F. S. Boas in 1896, when he described *Troilus and Cressida, All's Well That Ends Well, Measure for Measure* and *Hamlet* as 'Problem Plays'. Rossiter says that in these 'problem plays', 'we are *made to feel the pain*—of the distressing, disintegrating possibilities of human meanness (ignobility and treachery, craft and selfishness)'. Such plays, he suggests, are marked by *'shiftingness.* All the firm points of view or *points d'appui* fail one', and human experience 'seems only describable in terms of *paradox'.*

The play opens with a ruler announcing his imminent 'absence'. It is all rather stealthy—he wants to slip away silently and secretly; unnoticed and unaccompanied. He gives absolutely no reason or explanation for this unducal move. It is not how rulers were expected to behave—it is as if he is abdicating from the responsibilities of his regal role, which for Elizabethans would serve as a dire presage of civil disorder to come in his 'absence', an opening to be taken up again in *King Lear* which can be seen as another experiment in civil disorder ensuant on the self-removal of the keystone of the state. The Duke will return in a very public way with full pomp and ceremony—we hear him ordering trumpets at the city gates. The experiment—or whatever it was—is over, and he will appear as a true Duke again.

His opening speech is also strange. The first line has a fine, royal ring to it:

> Of government the properties to unfold . . .
>
> (I, i, 3)

—and we feel we are in for another eloquent speech like the one given by Ulysses on 'degree' (*Troilus and Cressida*), this time on the 'properties of government', an always urgent concern for the Elizabethans. But no—that won't be necessary, he says to Escalus, *you* know all about that already. He seems to promise one thing, then fails to deliver, or goes off in another direction. This is how he is going to behave, apparently. Near the end, an increasingly bewildered Escalus complains: 'Every letter he hath writ hath *disvouched* other' (IV, iv, i). It is an ungainly negative—rather as if one should say dis-confirm, dis-call, un-speak—and Shakespeare has invented it for this play. Again we can see the rightness of the word—this is to be a disvouching Duke; it is one of the seemingly ungainly ways in which he works. But to return to that opening line: the coming play *will* 'unfold' the properties of government—the properties; and the difficulties, the obligations, the temptations, the abuses, the failures—all the *un*-properties too. 'Unfold' is a crucial word in the play, and has become very important for Shakespeare. Near the end, when Isabella thinks her appeal to the Duke has been incredulously denied, she cries out:

> Then, O you blessèd ministers above,
> Keep me in patience, and with ripened time
> Unfold the evil which is here wrapped up
> In countenance.
>
> (V, i, 115–18)

She is anticipating Cordelia in *King Lear;* and, indeed, how wrapped-up evil does, finally, get 'unfolded', may be said to be the main concern of Shakespeare's tragedies. It is certainly the theme of the second half of this play—and a tricky and messy business it turns out to be. Not for the first time, Shakespeare has given us a clear pointer into his play in the first line.

The Duke's next speech is to Angelo, and the word recurs:

> Angelo
> There is a kind of character in thy life,
> That to th' observer doth thy history
> Fully unfold.
>
> (I, i, 26–9)

'Character' is to be another crucial word in the play. It was coming to have something of our meaning—the qualities that make up a person, say. But the stronger meaning was of a distinctive mark, an inscription, a graphic symbol (hence handwriting), an engraving (coming, indeed, from the Greek word for the instrument used for marking, scratching). You can read Angelo from the outside—the marks reveal the man. Dramatic irony of course—it will take a great deal to 'fully unfold' Angelo. Some writing *is* reliably legible. In the very next scene Claudio tells Lucio:

> The stealth of our most mutual entertainment
> With character too gross is writ on Juliet.
>
> (I, ii, 157–8)

She is manifestly pregnant, which is a true indication of our sexual coupling. When the disguised Duke wants to persuade the uncertain Provost to follow his plan, he shows him 'the hand and seal of the Duke', adding 'You know the character' (IV, ii, 195–6). The Provost hesitates no longer. However, when the returning Duke greets Angelo thus:

> O, your desert speaks loud, and I should wrong it
> To lock it in the wards of covert bosom,
> When it deserves, with characters of brass,
> A forted residence 'gainst the tooth of time
> And razure of oblivion . . .
>
> (V, i, 9–13)

he is engaging in deliberate, penetrative irony. Isabella is of course right to denounce the misleading appearance of Angelo:

> even so may Angelo,
> In all his dressings, caracts [characters, distinctive badges], titles,
> forms,
> Be an arch-villain.
>
> (V, i, 55–7)

As in other plays, but here with unusually excoriating power, Shakespeare is engaging that central problem of 'seeming'—what signs, which 'characters', can you trust? The Duke's last line before disappearing is:

> Hence shall we see,
> If power change purpose, what our *seemers* be.
>
> (I, iii, 53–4—my italics)

It is the only time Shakespeare used that particular cognate of the word.

To return to the Duke's first speech to Angelo. He continues with an important exhortation.

> Thyself and thy belongings
> Are not thine own so proper as to waste
> Thyself upon thy virtues, they on thee.
> Heaven doth with us as we with torches do,
> Not light them for themselves; for if our virtues
> Did not go forth of us, 'twere all alike
> As if we had them not.
>
> (I, i, 29–35)

He is drawing on the Bible, of course:

> No man, when he hath lighted a candle, covereth it with a vessel, or putteth it under a bed; but setteth it on a candlestick, that they which enter in may see the light . . .
>
> (Luke 8:16)

and the episode with the woman who has an 'issue' of blood:

And Jesus said, Somebody hath touched me: for I perceive that *virtue is*
gone out of me.

(Luke 8:46—my italics)

The injunction is, effectively, for Angelo to give up all that isolated study
and fasting and put his private virtues to public use. But the words could be
self-admonitory—'it's about time *I* emerged from "the life removed" and
did something' (as he is, rather rumly, about to) and they could be addressed
proleptically to the nunnery-seeking Isabella, who elevates her own chastity
over her brother's life. 'I cannot praise a fugitive and cloistered virtue, un-
exercised and unbreathed, that never sallies out and sees her adversary'—
Milton's words could almost have Isabella in mind (I think Jocelyn Powell
first noted this). In Isabella's case, we might add the line from Langland—
'Chastity without charity is chained in hell.' As I suggested, there are odd
psychic similarities in the three main players. In their different ways, they
do step out from 'the life removed'; and we see what, variously, goes forth
from them.

Two scenes later the Duke is in a monastery . . . explaining to Friar
Thomas why he is disappearing, and handing over his 'absolute power' to
Angelo. Presumably because of his preference for 'the life removed', he has
allowed the 'strict statutes and most biting laws' of the city to slip, so that
now:

> Liberty plucks Justice by the nose;
> The baby beats the nurse, and quite athwart
> Goes all decorum . . .
>
> (I, iii, 29–31)

—the world upside down. Whatever else this means, it indicates that he has
been responsible for some sort of dereliction of duty and neglect of good
'government'. The play shows what he tries to do about it. Here is his plan.
Install Angelo in his, the Duke's, office:

> And to behold his sway,
> I will, as 'twere a brother of your order,
> Visit both prince and people. Therefore, I prithee,
> Supply me with the habit and instruct me

How I may formally in person bear
Like a true friar.

(I, iii, 43–8)

At a stroke, Shakespeare opens another dimension to his play. As Duke, Vincentio represents the acme of temporal power; then, 'in disguising the Duke as Friar Shakespeare intends to raise questions of spiritual responsibility inherent in the course of temporal power' (Powell). The King was, of course, head of the Church in England, so this image of the composite, dual nature of authority—the Duke–Friar—would, again, have carried a contemporary relevance. But this dual figure also allows Shakespeare to address Renaissance theories of the law and government (the appropriate administering of Vienna), *and* to draw on the teaching of the Church and the sayings of the Bible (matters concerning repentance, forgiveness, charity, mercy)—crimes, and sins; the control of man as body; the salvation of man as soul. And what is it for a mere, mortal *man* to have 'authority' over *other* men? Shakespeare has hardly gone as deep as this before now.

When the cat's away . . . and when the *Duke's* away (or living the 'life removed'), the rats seem to take over the city.

Our natures do pursue,
Like rats that ravin down their proper bane,
A thirsty evil, and when we drink, we die.

(I, ii, 131–3)

Thus Claudio, on his way to prison, sentenced to death, under Angelo's new dispensation, for fornication. It is a powerful image. Whether the 'thirsty evil' is 'too much liberty' or simply lechery, the transposition of the epithet makes it seem as if the evil is drinking the rats. 'Bane' is poison, and is presumably the arsenic put down to kill rats—it induces thirst and when the rats drink to slake that thirst, they die. The greedy attempt to satisfy our insatiable appetites inevitably proves mortal. And the appetite in this play is sexual—lust is everywhere on the loose. Immediately after the Duke's initial departure, the brothel people—customers and providers— are on the scene. Whenever these people are present they bring with them a certain air of rank vitality, which certainly seems preferable to the stunning hypocrisy of Angelo. But it should not be romanticized. Sex is degraded into crude lechery ('groping for trouts in a peculiar river', I, ii, 92; 'filling a bottle with a tundish funnel', III, ii, 173), and is everywhere associated with disease, disfigurement, treatment for syphilis—rotting, stinking. We can all respond to the foul, bawdy talk since we all have a component of animal sexuality, while fewer of us are pathological puritans. But the vitality is verminous, and points to beastliness and the disorder of a completely non-moral world. Sex can, of course, lead to 'blossoming' and 'teeming foison', as invoked in Lucio's entirely out of character and—in this play—dissonant bit of pastoralizing to Isabella (even he won't talk dirty to 'a thing enskied and sainted', I, iv, 34); but hardened vice is something else—a thirsty evil—and the harvest is death. It is with a characteristically deft touch that Shakespeare has Pompey invited to become an executioner's assistant in prison. Abhorson, the resident professional executioner, finds the idea insulting to his trade: 'A bawd, sir? Fie upon him! He will discredit our mystery.' But the Provost's reply is definitive: 'Go to, sir; you weigh equally; a feather will turn the scale' (IV, ii, 28–31). There's nothing to choose between them—in their different ways they both dispense death.

The first two scenes of Act II show the result of the Duke's 'absence' (in a sense, he has absented himself from office for years). The subtle balancings, adjustments, temperings, reparations and restitutions of the law as it should be administered, have collapsed into the stark alternatives of chaos and tyranny. In the first scene, the under-deputy Escalus, who clearly shares what we are to believe was the Duke's habitually lax tolerance, tries to make some sense out of constable Elbow's malapropisms (he is bringing in the denizens of a 'naughty house' whom he refers to as 'notorious benefactors', II, i, 50), and Pompey Bum's weirdly inconsequential ramblings (Angelo won't hear him out—'This will last out a night in Russia / When nights are longest there', II, i, 133–4—and leaves Escalus to pass sentence). It becomes a parody of what should be the properly conducted arguments for the prosecution and defence in a decent court of law. Ethics are dissolved—logic and relevance nowhere to be found. It is comical enough; but if this is 'law' in Vienna, then the law is indeed an ass, or as Angelo would say, 'a scarecrow' (II, i, 1). Escalus simply gets lost—'Which is wiser here, Justice or Iniquity?' (II, i, 172), and ends muddle-headedly ordering Pompey to go on just as he is—'Thou art to continue now, thou varlet; thou art to continue' (II, i, 191). Tolerance is invariably preferable to harshness; but you really can't run a city this way. *Not* good 'government'.

Then, in the next scene, we see Angelo, newly invested with 'absolute power', in action when Isabella comes to intercede for her brother. 'Absolute' is a word which attaches itself to Angelo; and he certainly merits the criticism addressed by Volumnia to Coriolanus—another fanatic—'You are too absolute' (*Coriolanus* II, ii, 39). 'Precise' is another word which sticks to him; this is appropriate since Puritans (and this was a time of Puritan reform agitation in England) *were* self-confessedly and boastingly 'precise'— meaning strict in observance. But it is curiously appropriate that 'precise' comes from *prae-caedere* meaning to cut short, abridge, since this is just what Angelo wants to do to lusty young men, if not to sexuality itself. (In an excellent essay, Paul Hammond makes the neat point that 'precise' Angelo 'needs to be tackled by imprecise means, by approximate, devious, and even lying methods'—as we shall see.) The 'removing' Duke instructs Angelo as he leaves:

> In our remove be thou at full ourself;
> Mortality and mercy in Vienna
> Live in thy tongue and heart.
>   (I, i, 43–5)

He has, he says, 'lent him [Angelo] our terror, dressed him with our love' (I, i, 19). Angelo, we quickly see, has gone for terror and mortality, and dropped the mercy and love. This scene (Act II, scene ii) is the first of two interviews with Isabella, and I might just say here that these two scenes are like nothing else in the whole of Shakespeare for white-hot, scorching psychological power, and intensity mounting to exploding point. Before looking at these incandescent exchanges, I want to insert a quotation from Henry James: 'Great were the obscurity and ambiguity in which some impulses lived and moved—the rich gloom of their combinations, contradictions, inconsistencies, surprises.' ('The Papers')—different era; same phenomenon. As we are about to see dramatically enacted.

Isabella and Angelo are both absolutists—in this, they are two of a kind. Isabella almost gives up before she has started, as one intransigent idealist conceding to another:

> O just but severe law!
> I had a brother, then. Heaven keep your honor.
>   (II, ii, 41–2)

Indeed, whatever else we might think of the *louche* Lucio, we must recognize that it is only his prompting of Isabella ('You are too cold') that finally saves Claudio's life. As the legalistic Angelo coldly reiterates:

> Your brother is a forfeit of the law,
> And you but waste your words.
>
> (II, ii, 71–2)

Isabella's temper begins to rise, and with it her eloquence:

> Why, all the souls that were were forfeit once;
> And He that might the vantage best have took
> Found out the remedy. How would you be,
> If He, which is the top of judgment, should
> But judge you as you are?
>
> (II, ii, 73–7)

'Remedy' is a key word in the play (occurring more often than in any other); ranging from Pompey's 'remedy' as described by Elbow—'Nay, if there be no remedy for it, but that you will needs buy and sell men and women like beasts' (III, ii, 1–3), to God's remedy, through Christ, for the sins of men. But we are neither beasts nor gods, and some other 'remedy' for our ills and confusions must be found. Angelo's implacable 'no remedy' (II, ii, 48) means a reign of terror—the Duke will have to find a better way.

The first interview is a terrible collision between insistent Christianity and intractable law; and since we are not in the nunnery but rather in the realm of the social law where Angelo owns the discourse, as we used to say, Angelo is bound to win. But Isabella's passionate rhetoric continues to gain in heat and power, until Angelo seems to flinch a little—'Why do you put these sayings on me?'; and Isabella thrusts home:

> Because authority, though it err like others,
> Hath yet a kind of medicine in itself,
> That skins the vice o' th' top; go to your bosom,
> Knock there, and ask your heart what it doth know
> That's like my brother's fault; if it confess
> A natural guiltiness such as is his,

> Let it not sound a thought upon your tongue
> Against my brother's life.
>
>   (II, ii, 134–41)

Angelo turns aside to murmur: 'She speaks, and 'tis/Such sense, that my sense breeds with it' (II, ii, 141–2). She's got him! But not quite in the way she intended. When Isabella has left, Angelo *does* knock on his bosom to ask what's there—and to his horror, he finds foulness.

> What's this? What's this? Is this her fault or mine?
> The tempter or the tempted, who sins most?
> Ha, not she. Nor doth she tempt; but it is I
> That, lying by the violet in the sun,
> Do as the carrion does, not as the flow'r,
> Corrupt with virtuous season. Can it be
> That modesty may more betray our sense
> Than woman's lightness? Having waste ground enough,
> Shall we desire to raze the sanctuary,
> And pitch our evils there? O fie, fie, fie!
> What dost thou, or what art thou, Angelo?
> Dost thou desire her foully for those things
> That make her good?
>
>   (II, ii, 162–74)

There is no more electrifying speech in Shakespeare. And note the aptness, as well as the power, of his images. The same sun which brings the flowers to bloom (as in Lucio's blossoming fields), makes dead flesh even more putrid. And 'evils' was a word for privies—thus, why should I want to devastate the temple-pure Isabella by using her as a place of excrement? The sewer-like, stinking lust of old Vienna—it is the world, after all, of Pompey *Bum,* an unusual, but surely deliberately designated, surname— has erupted in Angelo himself.

Isabella's sound 'sense' has started his 'sense' (sensuality) 'breeding', and we shortly hear the results in a long soliloquy, uttered in the feverish anticipation of Isabella's imminent second visit. His religion is in tatters and is now no help to him:

> When I would pray and think, I think and pray
> To several subjects: heaven hath my empty words,
> Whilst my invention, hearing not my tongue,
> Anchors on Isabel: heaven in my mouth,
> As if I did but only chew his name,
> And in my heart the strong and swelling evil
> Of my conception.
>   (II, iv, 1–7)

This, of course, is like Claudius trying to pray in *Hamlet:* 'My words fly up, my thoughts remain below:/ Words without thoughts never to heaven go' (III, iii, 97–8), and there is something anticipatory of Macbeth's 'swelling act' (I, ii, 128) as well. The other 'swelling' in the play is Juliet's pregnancy. As so often in Shakespeare, it becomes a dramatic question of increasing urgency whether the 'swelling evil' will outgrow and obliterate the good signs of new life. Angelo's tormented state is one which increasingly attracts Shakespeare's scrutiny (compare Macbeth's 'pestered' senses). Here it makes Angelo realize the utter falseness of his position of authority:

> O place, O form,
> How often dost thou with thy case [outside], thy habit [dress],
> Wrench awe from fools, and tie the wiser souls
> To thy false seeming! Blood, thou art blood.
>   (II, iv, 12–15)

It is a King Lear-like moment of sudden devastating realization ('a dog's obeyed in office', IV, vi, 161); and this almost torrential uprushing of blood in its undeniable, unstaunchable reality, will also afflict Othello. We are already in Shakespeare's tragic world.

The second interview with Isabella is even more powerful than the first —a sustained crescendo to a heart-stopping climax. Angelo, deploying his legal skills to serve his lust, uses specious arguments and a deformed (not to say depraved) logic to manoeuvre Isabella into an impossible position. When he advances the apparently hypothetical case that she might save her brother if she would 'lay down the treasures of your body' (II, iv, 96), she responds with a revealing passion:

Th' impression of keen whips I'd wear as rubies,
And strip myself to death as to a bed
That longing have been sick for, ere I'd yield
My body up to shame.
                                    (II, iv, 101–4)

It is hard not to hear the distorted (masochistic?) sexuality which goes into these overheated words in favour of cold chastity. Better her brother die than she lose that priceless treasure. This enables Angelo to pin her on the contradiction in her stance and arguments. 'Were not you, then, as cruel as the sentence/That you have slandered so?' (II, iv, 109–10). There would be no point here in tracing all the twists and turns in this desperate, gripping disputation. Isabella believes—or purports to believe—that Angelo is engaging in somewhat perverse casuistry; as it were, trying to fend off the real import in, or behind, his words as long as possible. Angelo begins to lose patience: 'Nay, but hear me./Your sense pursues not mine; either you are ignorant,/Or seem so, crafty; and that's not good' (II, iv, 73–5). So—'I'll speak more gross'. No more sophistry, no more forensics—'Plainly conceive, I love you ... My words express my purpose' (II, iv, 141, 148). Isabella can no longer deflect or evade his intention, and cries out in outrage—'Seeming, seeming!/I will proclaim thee, Angelo' (II, iv, 150–51). But 'absolute' Angelo now gives himself over absolutely to lust and corrupt abuse of authority:

Who will believe thee, Isabel?
My unsoiled name, th' austereness of my life,
My vouch against you, and my place i' th' state,
Will so your accusation overweigh,
That you shall stifle in your own report,
And smell of calumny. I have begun,
And now I give my sensual race the rein.
Fit thy consent to my sharp appetite,
Lay by all nicety and prolixious blushes,
That banish what they sue for; redeem thy brother
By yielding up thy body to my will ...
                                    (II, iv, 154–64)

or I will have him *tortured* to death. Angelo makes his exit with the chillingly triumphant line—'Say what you can, my false o'erweighs your true' (II, iv, 170). It is a terrifying speech, laying bare the awesome potential for evil there is in 'absolute power'. As for Isabella—what can she do? 'To whom should I complain? Did I tell this,/Who would believe me?' (II, iv, 171–2). But, whatever happens, she is absolutely firm about one resolve— 'More than our brother is our chastity' (II, iv, 185). Thus ends this extraordinary Act—in a state of total impasse, a sort of throbbing paralysis, with incredibly urgent matters of life and death hanging in the air. Isabella has, after all, only twenty-four hours.

This is only the end of Act II: no play could continue at this level of intensity for long. It carries over to the next scene, in the prison, in which the Duke disguised as a friar seeks to reconcile Claudio to dying—'Be absolute for death' and so on (III, i, 5–41). It is a long speech and a curious one for a friar, containing not a trace or hint of Christian hope, redemption, the soul, the after-life, immortality, whatever. It is, in fact, much more in the tradition of the ancient Stoics, the overall drift being that, when it comes to life, you are better off without it. This is certainly a tenable position; but, for a man of God, an odd one to advance. It denies man any dignity and honour, and human existence any point or value. It could have been spoken by Hamlet, and is in keeping with the bleak mood which often prevails in these 'problem plays', but it is hard to see what the Duke–Friar is up to. However, that turns out to be true of a lot of what he does. This is followed by the mountingly intense scene between Isabella and her brother which comes to a head when Claudio learns that there *is,* in fact, a 'remedy' (III, i, 61—i.e. Isabella's going to bed with Angelo) and after an initial brave attempt to respond to her appeal to his nobility and sense of honour, he understandably breaks down—'Ay, but to die, and go we know not where' (III, i, 118–32). It is an incredibly powerful speech (justly famous), and you can feel the dread of death whipping through it like an icy wind. It is a fear which must surely touch all mortals at one time or another, whatever they believe. 'Sweet sister, let me live' (III, i, 133)—anyone can understand the appeal. Her answer reveals the hysterical nature of her abhorrence of unchastity.

> Die, perish! Might but my bending down
> Reprieve thee from thy fate, it should proceed.

I'll pray a thousand prayers for thy death,
No word to save thee.

(III, i, 144–7)

Here is a flaring up of that 'vindictive anger' Pater noted in the young novitiate. The impasse is now complete: Claudio, surely, dies tomorrow.

Then the Duke–Friar steps forward and says 'Vouchsafe a word, young
sister, but one word' (III, i, 152)—and the play suddenly changes. For one
thing, it shifts into prose. Up till now, all the main characters have spoken
in verse; the low life, as usual, alone speaking prose (and even Lucio speaks
verse to Isabella). From now on, nearly all the exchanges are conducted in
prose until the last Act, which returns to verse, but verse of a rather flat,
formal kind—more geared to making pronouncements than discoveries.
Claudio's fear-of-death speech is the last of the searing, intensely dramatic,
image-packed verse which brings the second Act of the play to its almost
unbearably intense pitch. After the Duke–Friar moves into prose, everything seems to get quieter and slow down: the mode changes, the mood
changes, the atmosphere changes, the pace changes—instead of dramatic
confrontations and agonistic struggles, we have a more narrative mode of
intrigue and arrangement. It is quite a shock. As Brockbank says, 'we pass
from Shakespeare's poetry at its most urgent and exploratory to the easy lies
and evasions of the Duke's "crafty" talk'. We also move from 'consummate
psychological insight' (Wilson Knight) to something much more like Romance, and as we approach this strange second part of the play, we would
do well to bear in mind Brockbank's reminder that Shakespeare is 'the romantic playwright, using Romance tricks to recover order from human
disarray'. And so, in his way, is the Duke.

One result of this shift is that everything now centres on the disguised
Duke, and Isabella—the Isabella we have seen in verbal combat with Angelo—disappears. Unlike most of Shakespeare's other comic heroines, she
fades away into obedient submission and docile compliance. 'Fasten your
ear on my advisings . . . be directed . . . be ruled' is the Duke's line to her;
and advised, directed and ruled she duly is. She becomes almost dumbly
passive, and remains silent for the last eighty-five lines of the play. Marcia
Poulsen describes her as 'speechless, a baffled actress who has run out of
lines', and sees her as a 'victim of bad playwriting'—the Duke's, that is; but

also perhaps Shakespeare's. She diagnoses an 'unusual sense of female pow-
erlessness' in this play, and thinks the play as a whole 'explores the incompatibility of patriarchal and comic structures'. This may be a rather too contemporary way of looking at it; but it is true that while Isabella starts with
something of the independence and spirit of a Beatrice, a Rosalind (without, of course, the humour), all the life and vitality drain out of her. Shakespeare invented another woman, Mariana, who is just as bidden and obedient as Isabella. When, at the Duke–Friar's urging, the two women join
hands as 'vaporous night approaches' in the sad, suggestive moated grange
(impossible to forget Tennyson's poem), he 'seems almost to merge them
together into a single being' (Jocelyn Powell). Strong female identity seems
to be waning in the dusk—generic 'Woman' is as wax in the Duke's hands.
Certainly, it becomes entirely the Duke's play, the Duke's world.

Many critics have noticed a gradual loss of autonomy and spontaneity in
the characters, as the Duke moves them around (Lucio and Barnardine excepted—I'll come to them). William Empson said the Duke manipulates
his subjects 'as puppets for the fun of seeing them twitch'. Manipulate them
he certainly does, but is it just 'for fun'? Was Hazlitt correct in saying that
the Duke is 'more absorbed in his own plots and gravity than anxious for
the welfare of the state'? How we answer these questions and charges will
determine how we view and value the second part of the play; for many
people have become understandably impatient at the excruciating attenuations and prolongations involved in the Duke's complicated and often inept
plottings and stagings. Why so devious when the power and authority is his
to reclaim at any second he chooses? That, it must be said, would hardly be
the 'remedy' he seeks for the people and condition of Vienna. Nobody and
nothing would be changed—Claudio's execution could be stayed, and Angelo's hypocrisy exposed, but the previous civic disarray would not be radically healed. You *could* see the Duke engaged in an uncertain experiment to
see how—or even if—justice and mercy can be combined in a moderate, mediating, measured way—*not* by the 'measure for measure' of the Old Law.
When the Duke—as Duke—urges the fittingness of the execution of Angelo to Isabella, he says:

> The very mercy of the law cries out
> Most audible, even from his proper tongue,

'An Angelo for Claudio, death for death!'
Haste still pays haste, and leisure answers leisure;
Like doth quit like, and Measure still for Measure.
                         (V, i, 410–14)

He is, of course, alluding to a saying in Matthew, but, as with so many of
the arguments he uses, he is twisting it somewhat, so what he misleadingly
calls 'the *mercy* of the law' turns out to be old-style vengeance—an eye for
an eye. One can only surmise that, as with the seemingly perverse and cruel,
prolonged pretence that Claudio is really dead, he is testing Isabella; educating her out of *her* absolutism—her first instinct certainly was for violent
revenge on Angelo ('I will to him and pluck out his eyes', IV, iii, 121)—into
true mercy and forgiveness, bringing her to the point when she will actually
plead for Angelo's life, albeit in stiltedly legalistic terms. Perhaps, as Lever
suggests, he is re-educating her 'cloistered virtue' into a virtue which can
serve as an active force in the real world. Similarly, the seemingly perverse
way he prolongs his apparent faith in Angelo, and the consequent public
humiliation of Isabella (and Mariana) can be appreciated if, as Jocelyn Powell suggests, we see him as showing Isabella what she would have been up
against if he really *had* been absent. Of *course* trusted Angelo would have
got away with it, with no redress for the women. This in turn shows all of
us just how fragile and vulnerable justice is.

Perhaps it does seem like 'a mad fantastical trick of him to steal from the
state' (III, ii, 94) as Lucio says, but he should be seen as engaged in a difficult and circuitous quest—to see for himself the condition he has allowed
his state to fall into, and to try what shifts and stratagems might put things
to rights. When he says

        My business in this state
     Made me a looker-on here in Vienna,
     Where I have seen corruption boil and bubble
     Till it o'errun the stew . . .
                         (V, i, 317–20)

he is speaking as the Friar, but also as the Duke. The idea of absconding
from his manifest role, but still surveying his realm, has some sort of a pre-

cedent in the notion of a *deus absconditus,* an idea which goes back to the Old
Testament ('Verily thou *art* a god that hidest thyself, O God of Israel, the
Saviour', Isaiah 45:15). But we should certainly not be tempted to regard
the Duke as an incarnate figure of God. Some nourishment for this idea is
provided by the lines of Angelo, when the Duke is revealed in Act V:

> O my dread lord,
> I should be guiltier than my guiltiness,
> To think I can be undiscernible,
> When I perceive your Grace, like pow'r divine,
> Hath looked upon my passes.
>   (V, i, 369–73)

From this, some critics (notably Wilson Knight) have gone on to treat the
whole play as an orthodox Christian allegory based on the gospel teaching.
This is very wide of the mark. The Duke—like the English kings—rules
by divine right; but he is, himself, a 'deputy elected by the Lord'—just as he
appoints Angelo to be *his* 'Deputy'. When Angelo comes before the Duke
to be judged, it is an image of the position the Duke himself (like everyone
else) will be in before the truly divine God. On earth, he is only *'like* pow'r
divine'. That he seeks to act as a sort of secular providence, sometimes co-
ercively, sometimes fumblingly, is a better description. Centrally, he is a
seventeenth-century ruler, trying to work out the best way to rule—getting
the balance of justice and mercy right.

But he is also, as is often noted, a sort of playwright and theatre director,
and not always a very good one—certainly, he does not have Prospero's serene power. He makes mistakes, stratagems don't work as he intends, some
things (and people) he just cannot control, and he loses his temper in a
rather un-ducal way. That is part of the point of the somehow admirable
brute obstinacy and total intransigence of Barnardine (no 'seemer', he),
whose execution is part of one of the Duke's more desperate plots. The following scene is illustrative of the limits to the Duke's power. The Duke tells
Barnardine he is to die:

> *Barnardine.* I swear I will not die today for any man's persuasion.
> *Duke.* But hear you—

> *Barnardine.* Not a word. If you have anything to say to me, come to my
> ward, for thence will not I today. *Exit.*
>
> (IV, iii, 60–64)

'Not a word' is a marvel of insolence, and the Duke is left spluttering with
impotent rage. There is a similar point in the Duke's inability to shake Lucio off, or make him shut up. Lucio's talk is scabrous and obscene, and he
often appears in an unamiable light; but some of the few comic moments
occur (or so I find) when the disguised Duke, hearing himself traduced and
mocked ('the old fantastical Duke of dark corners', IV, iii, 160), simply can't
get rid of him—'Nay, friar, I am a kind of burr; I shall stick' (IV, iv, 181)
and again when the Duke, increasingly irritated, simply can't get Lucio to
stay silent in the last, big juridical scene. Unlike Isabella, these two will *not*
be directed or advised. An allegorical reading of the play has nothing to say
regarding the Duke's helplessness with burrs that insist on sticking.

In the strange couplets, gnomic rather than theophanic, in which the
Duke soliloquizes at the end of Act III, he tells us something of his strategies and intentions, concluding:

> Craft against vice I must apply:
> With Angelo tonight shall lie
> His old betrothèd but despisèd;
> So disguise shall, by th' disguisèd,
> Pay with falsehood false exacting,
> And perform an old contracting.
>
> (III, ii, 280–85)

This is the sort of questionable ethical casuistry we heard in *All's Well That
Ends Well;* I will out-disguise disguise, beat falsehood with more falsehood
—exactly, use 'craft against vice'. It has been called 'redemptive deceit' and
'creative deception', and it certainly requires some such paradoxical gloss.
'Craft' might be taken to include stagecraft, and the Duke certainly uses
quite a few tricks of the trade, not always successfully or convincingly.
(Brockbank made the nice point that he seems to invent the moated grange,
Mariana, and Angelo's previous engagement—which exactly mirrors that
between Claudio and Juliet, down to the blocked dowry which prevents
both marriages—as a sort of desperate remedy, 'finding a theatrical solu-

tion to an otherwise insoluble human problem'.) Everything seems to come right in the end—just about, more or less—but without any of the feeling of joyful regeneration and renewal, a world transformed, that a truly successful comedy should arouse.

If the Duke is, in truth, not a very good playwright, the unanswerable question is to what extent his failings are Shakespeare's failings as well. Some critics think that the dramaturgical ineptness is Shakespeare's, and no one can deny that after the thrilling drama of Act II, the play seems to slacken and lose force. But, arguably, no play could continue at that level of intensity, and perhaps we should see the Duke—with an awakened concern for 'good government'—as trying, with rather hastily devised tricks and ruses (time is short), to steer things into calmer, quieter waters, patching up a solution to the impasse which has so quickly developed. Perhaps Shakespeare is, in fact, exposing the often rather crude and necessarily mendacious ways in which any playwright somehow stitches things together for a tolerably harmonious conclusion. Perhaps he is also showing how easily and rapidly evil can burst out and take over—in a man, in a city (the first two Acts); and how difficult and awkward it is to achieve some sort of restitution and bring about a balanced, precarious, justice (the last three Acts).

One thing is certainly true and is often remarked on—while attempting to minister to all his subjects in both worldly and spiritual matters, the Duke does not learn anything about himself. Indeed, he is in danger of becoming something of a cipher—the *type* of good governor. It is possible that this might be related to the recent accession of James I. It has long been suggested that the Duke was intentionally modelled on the King, who was also the patron of Shakespeare and his company. If he was meant to be so viewed, then the Duke could hardly have been given the sort of turbulent and developing inwardness we associate with Shakespeare's main characters—that would have been *lèse majesté*. James I's *Basilicon Doron* had been published in 1603, and was, we may say, required reading. Shakespeare certainly knew it, and, as has been noted by scholars, many of the concerns and exhortations articulated in that book could equally well have come from the Duke. I give two examples:

> even in your most vertuous actions, make ever moderation to be the chief ruler. For although holinesse be the first and most requisite qualitie of a

> Christian, yet . . . moderate all your outwarde actions flowing there-fra.
> The like say I nowe of Justice . . . For lawes are ordained as rules of vertu-
> ous and sociall living, and not to be snares to trap your good subjectes:
> and therefore the lawe must be interpreted according to the meaning, and
> not to the literall sense . . . And as I said of Justice, so I say of Clemencie
> . . . *Nam in medio stat virtus.*

And (this for Angelo, say):

> he cannot be thought worthie to rule and command others, that cannot
> rule and dantone his own proper affections and unreasonable appetites
> . . . be precise in effect, but sociall in shew . . .

It is perhaps relevant that James issued a proclamation 'for the reformation of great abuses in Measures' (again, 1603). The King also insisted that
certain laws that had fallen into disuse or abeyance should be tightened up.
He showed irritation if his proclamations were not obeyed (the Duke and
Barnardine), was apparently over-sensitive in his reactions to calumny (the
Duke and Lucio), and wanted to visit the Exchange in secret to observe
the behaviour of his subjects, though it proved impossible to maintain the
secrecy. In short, many similarities between the Duke and James I are discernible and there is extensive work on this topic; I have listed helpful items
in the bibliography. However, I think it would be wrong to see the figure
of the Duke as simply a flattering idealized version of James I. The Duke
is far from faultless and infallible; and one of the forceful demonstrations
of the play is that you cannot simply translate abstract precepts concerning
conduct and justice (such as are to be found in *Basilicon Doron*) into the
actual human flesh-and-blood realm of mixed motives, contradictory passions, and endless ambiguities of word and deed. If James I *did* see himself
in Duke Vincentio, he should have found it a cautionary experience.

How do you legislate for a carnal world; how can justice keep up with
human wickedness; what kind of 'government'—in the individual, in the
state—is both possible and desirable? These are some of the urgent questions the play dramatically explores. Pater catches well the prevailing ethical concerns of the play:

> Here the very intricacy and subtlety of the moral world itself, the diffi-
> culty of seizing the true relations of so complex a material, the difficulty

of just judgment, of judgment that shall not be unjust, are the lessons conveyed . . . we notice the tendency to dwell on mixed motives, the contending issues of action, the presence of virtues and vices alike in unexpected places, on 'the hard choice of two evils', on the 'imprisoning' of men's 'real intents'.

This Vienna is a very long way from the Forest of Arden—but very close to Elsinore and Venice.

HISTORIES

When Richard, then Duke of Gloucester, and the Duke of Buckingham are 'persuading' the young Prince Edward to 'sojourn' in the Tower of London, whence he will never emerge, prior to his 'coronation', which of course will never take place, there occurs this rather strange exchange:

> *Prince.* I do not like the Tower, of any place.
>   Did Julius Caesar build that place, my lord?
> *Buck.* He did, my gracious lord, begin that place,
>   Which since succeeding ages have re-edified.
> *Prince.* It is upon record, or else reported
>   Successively from age to age, he built it?
> *Buck.* Upon record, my gracious lord.
> *Prince.* But say, my lord, it were not regist'red,
>   Methinks the truth should live from age to age,
>   As 'twere retailed to all posterity,
>   Even to the general all-ending day.
>   (*Richard III*, III, i, 68–78)

This moment is entirely Shakespeare's invention; there is nothing remotely like it in his sources. It might strain credulity to think that Prince Edward, rightly very apprehensive on being unrefusably urged into the Tower, should pause for a brief discussion concerning matters of historical authentication and verifiability. But, at this moment, that is exactly what Shakespeare chooses to foreground. Julius Caesar was indeed in London in 55 and 54 BC, and fortified buildings were erected there in Roman times. But the Tower of London was built during the reign of William the Conqueror (possibly over a Roman bastion), and extended by Henry III. Buckingham —'the deep-revolving, witty Buckingham'—is certainly no historian, but presumably he will say anything to mollify the young prince at this point, since his only objective is to bed him down—terminally—in the Tower. But the prince has good and pertinent questions: recorded or reported; registered or retailed? Not just—what happened? But—how do we *know* what happened? Did you *hear* it: or did you *read* it? Julius Caesar, the prince goes on, was 'a famous man':

> With what his valor did enrich his wit,
>
> His wit set down to make his valor live.
>
> Death makes no conquest of this conqueror,
>
> For now he lives in fame, though not in life.
>
> (III, i, 85–8)

Caesar was not only a valorous *doer,* he was also a 'witty' *writer;* and so—'now he lives in fame, though not in life'. At a climactic point in his Histories—the lawful king of England, though not yet crowned, is being led away to be murdered—Shakespeare, as it were, turns his play to face the audience and asks the spectators to consider how things—facts, names, deeds, events—are handed on, handed down; how do they come through to us? How, *when* they do, do they leave life only to enter 'fame'? All the etymologies of 'fame' (Latin *fama,* Greek *pheme*) refer to speaking and speech—a saying, report, rumour, hence reputation and renown. That would certainly cover 'reporting' and 'retailing', but—the prince has a point, though it is a singularly strange time to make it—they are not quite the same as 'recording' and 'registering'. This is the reverse of a trivial matter. The Elizabethans were becoming very interested in matters of historiography; and Shakespeare, as this crucial little exchange indicates, was clearly aware of the rich problems (or ambiguities, or what you will) inhering in his own position of a *reader* of chronicles and a *listener* to legends, *writing plays* which, though he could hardly have expected this, will almost certainly be both *read* and *spoken* 'even to the general all-ending day'. *History* is 'knowing', and how did *Shakespeare* know what he knew—or thought he knew?—when he came to write his Histories?

Here is Sir Philip Sidney in his *Apologie for Poetrie* (1580, about ten years before Shakespeare started writing history plays):

> The historian, loden with old mouse-eaten records; authorising himself
> for the most part upon other histories, whose greatest authorities are built
> upon the notable foundation of hear-say; having much ado to accord dif-
> fering writers and to pick truth out of partiality ...

Sidney is mocking historians in order to promote the superior merits of poetry. But even as he intends an irony he is making an important point—history *is* ultimately 'built upon the notable foundation of hear-say'. If you go far enough back, *hear-say* (an engagingly accurate compound phrase) al-

ways and inevitably precedes *read-write* (if I may be permitted the complementary nonce term). History may end in registers and records, but it
starts in 'tails' and tales (tells), retailings and reportings. We perhaps tend
to forget how comparatively recent printing, indeed literacy, was for the
Elizabethans. The first official English printed Bible (the Miles Coverdale
translation) dates from 1535—thirty years before the birth of Shakespeare.
The earlier shift, from memorizing things to writing them down, can be
marked by the date of 1199 when chancery clerks began to keep copies, on
parchment, of the main letters sent out under the great seal. From then on
it meant that the whole population was, in Kenneth Morgan's phrase, 'par-
ticipating in literacy' (*The Oxford History of Britain,* pp. 124–5). By the beginning of the sixteenth century, it is estimated that more than fifty per cent
of Englishmen were literate (and that meant *English* English—French was
in marked decline before the end of the fourteenth century). To illustrate
the significance of the shift, historians compare the two popular uprisings
of the later Middle Ages—the Peasants' Revolt (1381) and John Cade's rebellion (1450). 'In 1381 the complaints of the peasantry from Kent and Essex were (as far as we know) presented to Richard II orally, and all commu-
nications with the king during the revolt appear to have been by word of
mouth. Compare this with 1450, when the demands of Cade's followers,
also drawn from Kent and the south-east, were submitted at the outset in
written form, of which several versions were produced and circulated.'
(Morgan, p. 246). (Cade's revolt features in *Henry VI* Part 2, though Shakespeare curiously makes it seem more like Wat Tyler's rising of 1381. But
more of this in due course.) The Elizabethans, of course, had writings; but
they also still had 'tellings'—myths, apocrypha, legends, and a very active
oral tradition.

When Shakespeare began writing, then, 'history' was hear-say *and* read-
write. Higden (a fourteenth-century monk) ends his *Polychronicon* with the
reign of Edward III, but starts with the Creation: Holinshed comes up to
Henry VIII, but starts with Noah. They both include entirely legendary
material from Geoffrey of Monmouth's *Historia Regum Britanniæ* (first half
of the twelfth century), which purports to give an account of 'the kings who
dwelt in England before the incarnation of Christ' and especially of 'Arthur and the many others who succeeded him after the incarnation'. This
included the story of Gorboduc, stemming from the legend of the Trojan
Brute, descended from Aeneas, who founded Troynovant, or London, the
first of a long line of glorious British kings (which included Lear). In gen-

eral, the Elizabethans, and this included many of their historians, had no
very clear idea where the myths ended and what we would think of as the
facts began.

Shakespeare wrote ten English history plays. Leaving aside *King John* and
Henry VIII, the remaining eight plays cover the period from 1399 (the deposition of Richard II) to 1485 (the death of Richard III at the battle of Bosworth and the accession of Henry VII). They fall into two tetralogies—in
terms of historical chronology they run *Richard II, Henry IV,* Parts 1 and 2,
Henry V; and *Henry VI,* Parts 1, 2, and 3, and *Richard III.* Oddly, Shakespeare wrote the second tetralogy first (1590), and the first one second
(1595–9). But perhaps not so oddly. Out of the chaos of the Wars of the
Roses between the Lancastrians and Yorkists had emerged the Tudor dynasty, bringing much-needed peace and stability (relatively speaking) to
England. By the 1590s the Elizabethans were becoming increasingly worried about who would succeed their childless queen—and how the succession would come about. The troubles had all started when Richard II died,
also leaving no son and heir, thereby triggering nearly a century of contesting usurpations and the nightmare of prolonged civil war. It is perhaps
not surprising that Shakespeare should first choose to make a dramatic exploration of how that nightmare came about, and how it ended with the
establishment of Tudor order. These were comparatively recent events for
Shakespeare and his contemporaries, and questions of succession were matters of real urgency. Shakespeare's first tetralogy could be seen as dramatizing a warning and concluding with a hope. In the event, the accession of
James VI of Scotland to Elizabeth's throne was peaceful enough—though
of course the nightmare duly returned with the Civil War of 1642–9. But
that is another story.

   Before considering how and where Shakespeare found his 'history', and
what sort of historiography was available to him, I intend to set down some
basic historical details for those who, like myself, have some difficulty in
getting, and keeping, straight some of the whos and whens and whys involved in the historical period he is dramatizing. More securely grounded
historians may safely skip the next few paragraphs. It is worth remembering that, after Roman Britain, the country fell into a number of kingdoms
with many 'kings'. (It is possible that in AD 600 English kings could be
counted in dozens.) Alfred the Great (871–99) was more truly 'king of the

English' than any ruler before him. (He was the first writer known to use the word 'Angelcynn'—land of the English folk. 'Englaland' does not appear for another century.) From the time of the Norman Conquest there was a line of legitimate and legitimated kings until the deposition of Richard II. Richard II, it is important to remember, was the last king ruling by undisputed hereditary right, in direct line from William the Conqueror— 'the last king of the old medieval order', Tillyard calls him. (In 1327 Edward II was deposed, thus breaking the inviolability of anointed kingship; but his son was crowned in his place, thus maintaining the hereditary principle.) Of course, what 'legitimated' William was primarily successful conquest. If you follow 'legitimation' far enough back, you will invariably come upon some originating or foundational act of appropriating violence which, once in position and in possession, seeks means (call them mystifications if you will) of retrospective self-legitimation. But that is too large a matter for consideration here. Suffice it say that, for the Elizabethans, Richard II was the last truly legitimate king, to be followed by over a century of more and less successful usurpers who ruled *de facto* rather than *de jure*.

Not surprisingly, then, the fifteenth century was a particularly turbulent time. War and murder were seldom far away. 'Towards the end of the fifteenth century, French statesmen were noting with disapproval Englishmen's habit of deposing and murdering their kings and the children of kings (as happened in 1327, 1399, 1461, 1471, 1483, and 1485) with a regularity unmatched anywhere else in Western Europe' (Morgan, p. 192). There was a growing emphasis on the king's sovereign authority which was reinforced by the principle (from 1216) that the crown should pass to the eldest son of the dead monarch. The centralization of power with the king was at the expense of the feudal, regional power of the great landowners—those barons and magnates who are forever jostling around the throne in Shakespeare's history plays. If there was intermittent uneasiness and struggle in the court, there was more serious trouble further afield for, under Edward I (1272–1307), England entered an era of perpetual war. 'From Edward I's reign onwards, there was no decade when Englishmen were not at war, whether overseas or in the British Isles. Every generation of Englishmen in the later Middle Ages knew the demands, strains, and consequences of war—and more intensely than their forbears' (Morgan, p. 194). With France alone there was what has been called the Hundred Years War (1337–1453), never mind problems with the Welsh, Scots, and

Irish. Following on from that was the period of dynastic struggle known as the Wars of the Roses. And here we need a bit of detail.

Richard II finally alienated too many powerful people by his behaviour and that of his discredited favourites, and in 1399 he was dethroned. As he was childless, the question was who should now be king? Who had the strongest claim—who had the most power? 'Custom since 1216 had vested the succession in the senior male line, even though that might mean a child-king (as in the case of Henry III and Richard II himself). But there was as yet no acknowledged rule of succession should the senior male line fail. In 1399 the choice by blood lay between the seven-year-old Earl of March, descended through his grandmother from Edward III's second son, Lionel, and Henry Bolingbroke, the thirty-three-year-old son of King Edward's third son, John. Bolingbroke seized the crown after being assured of support from the Percy family whom Richard had alienated. But in the extraordinary circumstances created by Richard II's dethronement and imprisonment, neither March nor Bolingbroke had obviously the stronger claim. No amount of distortion, concealment, and argument on Bolingbroke's part could disguise what was a *coup d'état*. Hence, as in the twelfth century, an element of dynastic instability was injected into English politics which contributed to domestic turmoil and encouraged foreign intrigue and intervention in the following century' (ibid, p. 221). For Bolingbroke read 'Lancastrian'; for March read 'Yorkist'; and for 'dynastic instability' read—finally—'the Wars of the Roses'. It should also be remembered that, though 'the Tudor myth' would have it otherwise, in fact Henry VII had no stronger claim to the throne than Bolingbroke. The Tudors were simply the third of the three usurping dynasties of the fifteenth century who seized the crown by force.

The Lancastrians ruled from 1399 to 1461 and in many ways enjoyed considerable success both at home and in France. Under Henry V, and with famous victories at Agincourt (1415), Cravant (1423), and Verneuil (1424), the English acquired a considerable portion of France. But under Henry VI, who reigned from 1422 to 1461 (he briefly reigned again from 1470 to 1471, in which year he was, almost certainly, murdered in the Tower), the Lancastrian rule disintegrated; nearly all the land in France was lost; and, what with viciously squabbling magnates, and a popular uprising in 1450, everything was going wrong. The Yorkists took over in 1461, and throughout the 1470s, under Edward IV, England enjoyed a period of relative stability and peace. But, when Edward IV died in 1483, his son and heir, also Edward, was only twelve. After nearly a century in which the most ruthless dynastic ambition had manifested itself in the bloodiest of ways, the time was ripe for the emergence of the most unprincipled schemer of them all, Richard of Gloucester, who made no bones about having his nephew murdered and seizing his crown—to become, of course, Richard III. His brutal reign lasted only two years before he was killed at Bosworth Field on 22 August 1485—by Henry Tudor, from Wales by way of France. Henry VII, as he was to become, had two signal advantages. He was the only one of the fifteenth-century usurpers to kill his childless predecessor in battle. And, most importantly, he was supported by the Yorkists who had become disillusioned with the increasingly impossible Richard. But we should heed the historian's point. 'The Wars of the Roses came close to destroying the hereditary basis of the English monarchy, and Henry Tudor's seizure of the crown hardly strengthened it. Henry posed as the representative and inheritor of both Lancaster and York, but in reality he became king, and determined to remain king, by his own efforts' (Morgan, p. 236).

Having said which, we may also note the historian's opinion that 'there is much to be said for the view that England was economically healthier, more expansive, and more optimistic under the Tudors than at any time since the Roman occupation of Britain'. When Henry VIII died in 1547, there was another of those dreaded power vacuums at the centre, and for the next two years there was rioting nearly everywhere, and there were many disturbances during the short reigns of Edward VI and Mary. It is perhaps not surprising that when Elizabeth was crowned in 1558 her coronation slogan was 'concord'. And perhaps not surprising, too, that, in the 1590s, with her death just around the corner, so to speak (she was born in 1533), many people fearfully wondered whether they might not be in for another packet of upheaval and dissension—like the Wars of the Roses. When Shakespeare was writing his history plays, 'Englaland' was very far from being a complacent country. Stability, peace, and 'concord' could by no means be taken for granted. If anything, just the reverse was true.

In this connection, one other momentous historical event should be mentioned here. Between 1533 and 1536, by a series of Acts (including the Act of Supremacy and the First Act of Succession—1534; and, finally, the Act against the Pope's Authority—1536), Henry VIII and his parliament broke free of Rome, so that all English jurisdiction, both secular and religious, henceforward came from the king, and the last traces of Papal power were eliminated. England became a Protestant nation (soon to produce its own schism in the fiery post-Reformation form of the disaffected 'Puritans'). But Catholics and Catholicism did not disappear overnight. Far from it. It is worth remembering that Catholicism still predominated at the time of Elizabeth's accession, and throughout her reign there were constant fears of Catholic intrigue and an awareness of the real dangers of a Catholic coalition (which could bring in the Papacy, Spain, and France) against England. Mary Stuart was finally executed in 1587, a year before the defeat of the Spanish Armada. But the possibility of other Catholic plots was felt to be a constant one. *That* was where the next Wars of the Roses might come from. And it is just around this time—two years after the Armada—that Shakespeare began to write his history plays.

Such are the bare historic facts, as near as it is possible to ascertain, set down as neutrally and untendentiously as possible—uninterpreted, unarranged, with a minimum of narrative consequentiality. But Shakespeare did not acquire his history in this way or this form, and we must briefly consider how history was written in the Tudor period. The Tudors themselves initiated a new historiography, which can be said to begin in 1501 when Henry VII commissioned an Italian scholar, Polydore Vergil, to write a history of England—a history which would establish the right of the Tudors to the throne. So, according to Vergil, the Tudor dynasty emerged *of necessity,* with God punishing the various crimes of the Lancastrians and Yorkists, and guiding Henry through exile to the crown. This was history as (Tudor) propaganda, and it would influence history writing for the rest of the century. But not only propaganda. Tillyard calls Vergil 'the first chronicler of English history to be seriously concerned with cause and effect' and, as one of the authors of the later *A Mirror for Magistrates* (published 1559 and also very important for Shakespeare) would write:

> But seeing causes are the chiefest things
> That should be noted of the story writers,
> That men may learn what ends all causes brings,
> They be unworthy the name of chroniclers

> That leave them clean out of the registers
> Or doubtfully report them . . .

The difference between history as memorial—an iterated commemoration of events and deeds—and history which explores causes, is also the difference between ritual and drama, and it is in Shakespeare that we see history finally emerge from ritual into drama (there are, of course, antecedent attempts which I will mention later). Vergil starts his *Anglica Historia* (not published until 1534) with fabled, misty beginnings. Where he does discern (impose?—hard to separate the two cognitive activities) a specific pattern in English history is, precisely, the period from Richard II to Henry VII.

Much more influential was the work of Edward Hall who, in 1548, published *The Union of the two Noble and Illustre Famelies of Lancastre and Yorke,* a work which was to have a direct influence on the sense of history in Shakespeare's plays. Hall was a convinced Protestant who firmly believed in the autocracy of the Tudors as recently established by Henry VIII. He built on the work of Vergil, complete with its propaganda, and made an evolving moral drama out of the dissensions between 'the two noble and illustre famelies of Lancastre and Yorke' and the final triumphant resolution of that strife in 'the reign of the high and prudent prince King Henry the Eighth, the indubitable flower and very heir of the said lineages'. Hall imposed a secular, rather than a sacred, pattern on his material: as Tillyard says, 'Hall's chief importance is that he is the first English chronicle-writer to show in all its completeness that new moralizing of history which came in with the waning of the Middle Ages, the weakening of the Church, and the rise of nationalism.' And I must take one more point from Tillyard. Hall's work is divided into eight chapters, one for each king from Henry IV to Henry VIII. Each chapter title characterizes the nature of that king's reign—'The unquiet time of', 'The troublous season of', 'The prosperous reign of', 'The pitiful life of' and so on. But two titles stand out. 'The victorious *acts* of King Henry the Fifth' and 'The tragical *doings* of King Richard the Third' (my italics). Tillyard is surely right to point to the deliberately dramatic implications of these titles, and indeed Hall presents these reigns in an unusually dramatic way. Shakespeare would certainly have noticed this, and 'acts' and 'doings', victorious and tragical, are the very stuff of his history plays (and, of course, his tragedies).

The other major source for Shakespeare, and arguably the most influen-

tial, was the *Chronicles of England, Scotlande and Irelande* by Raphael Holinshed, first published in 1577 but appearing in an altered second edition in
1587, the edition Shakespeare drew on. Holinshed was, by common consent, less of an artist and more of a compiler than Hall; but he used the
work of Hall and covered more history than the earlier writer. His history
was less 'providential' than Hall's—though it should be noted that in the
1587 edition of Holinshed (prepared by Abraham Fleming after Holinshed's death) the sense of history as being a working out of God's scheme
was *more* strongly stressed than in the earlier Holinshed or in Hall. But
Elizabethan historiography was not exclusively 'providential'. Irving Ribner explains that 'we can isolate two distinct trends which exerted an influence upon Elizabethan historiography: a humanist trend essentially classical in origin, and a medieval trend based upon the premises of Christian
belief. We cannot suppose, however, that in the minds of the Elizabethans
there was any clear distinction between these two lines of influence. The
English Renaissance, in most intellectual areas, shows an easy merging of
the medieval and humanist' (*The English History Play in the Age of Shakespeare,* pp. 21–2). Humanist history, as written by Leonardo Bruni, Fran-
cesco Guicciardini, and above all Niccolo Machiavelli, was didactic, instruc-
tional, and nationalistic—more secularized, rationalistic, and 'political'
than Christian history, which tended to be providential, apocalyptic, and
universal. Is history made by man, or decreed by God? The Elizabethans
seemed to have felt that it was something of both.

    The subject matter of Renaissance historiography was the life of the state
—in Fulke Greville's words 'the growth, state and declination of princes,
change of government, and laws, vicissitudes of sedition, faction, succession, confederacies, plantations, with all other errors or alterations in public
affairs'. The purposes for which these matters were treated by writers of
history are usefully summarized by Irving Ribner under two headings.
'Those stemming from classical and humanist philosophies include (1) a
nationalistic glorification of England; (2) an analysis of contemporary affairs, both national and foreign so as to make clear the virtues and the failings of contemporary statesmen; (3) a use of past events as a guide to political behaviour in the present; (4) a use of history as documentation for
political theory; and (5) a study of past political disaster as an aid to Stoical
fortitude in the present. Those stemming from medieval Christian philoso-

phy include: (6) illustration of the providence of God as the ruling force in human—and primarily political—affairs, and (7) exposition of a rational plan in human events which must affirm the wisdom and justice of God' (op. cit., p. 24). All of these uses of history may be found in Shakespeare's plays—whether just glanced at, provisionally entertained, seriously questioned, or hopefully embraced. But there is one purpose which has not been mentioned so far.

Between the end of Roman Britain and the Norman Conquest, there had evolved (in the eleventh century) and decayed (in the fourteenth and fifteenth centuries) a unique form of society—feudalism, which had its own economic system, social hierarchy, codes of value and conventions of behaviour. To what *extent* Shakespeare knew about the details of this society we cannot know; but we can be sure that he was aware of historical *discontinuity* and social *change* in Britain's past. It is sometimes maintained that Shakespeare's history plays are indirectly (or directly) addressed to matters concerning contemporary Tudor Britain, either as loyal propaganda or adversarial critique according to the reading. But to the extent that this is true, it is certainly only partly true. Shakespeare is manifestly interested in the past *as* past—as *different* from the present. Graham Holderness has written well about this, and I will simply quote his main contention.

> Shakespeare's plays of English history are chronicles of feudalism: they offer empirical reconstruction and theoretical analysis of a social formation firmly located in the past, and distinctly severed from the contemporary world. In this historiographical reconstruction, which focuses on the decline of feudalism in the fourteenth and fifteenth centuries, society is seen as a historical formation built on certain fundamental contradictions, and incapable of resolving or overcoming them within the framework of political and ideological determinants provided by the historical basis itself. As the vision of feudal society is historically specific, the disclosure of contradictions cannot be defined as reversion to medieval pessimism or a compliance with Machiavellian pragmatism: if a conception of the past admits the possibility of fundamental social change, the contradictions of a particular historical formation cannot be identified with 'the human condition' . . .
>
> (*Shakespeare Recycled,* p. 19)

There is no suggestion that this was a merely antiquarian exercise for Shakespeare, and of course 'universals' can be (perhaps may best be) discovered by studying an 'historically specific' society, event, place, person. By exploring how we lived *then,* we may—this is perhaps the tacit hope in all historiography—the better understand the way we live *now.* And—who knows?—perhaps improve it.

The earliest English drama—the Miracle plays, the Christian 'cycles' (probably a twelfth-century development)—emerged out of the static liturgy of the Church. Literally emerged as well, leaving the church for the streets. Towards the end of the fourteenth century a new kind of play can be found—the Morality play; a kind of play still being performed in the time of Elizabeth. The Miracle play necessarily dealt with 'universals'— the universal truths of the Catholic Church (when Henry VIII assumed the role of head of the Church, the cycles were suppressed—too Roman). The Morality play also dealt in universals, allegorically presenting the conflict of opposing powers (as it might be, Mischief and Mercy) for the soul of Man— as in *Mankynd* and *Everyman.* But this genre had an important potentiality—as A. P. Rossiter puts it, 'a potential frame for a life-story: not of mankind as *Humanum Genus,* but the human-kind as revealed in One Man' (*English Drama,* p. 99). More than that. 'The Morality not only got at the dramatic essential of protracted conflict in a world of jarring wills, but also arrived at one of the simple formulae for play-making.' Simply, the 'moral' had to have a point towards which the action moved, and that meant—*plot.* In the sixteenth century and with the coming of the Renaissance, there is a narrowing of focus and a growing interest in more political matters concerning rule and policy, princecraft and governorship. In Skelton's *Magnyfycence* (1516), for instance, the hero is a prince. He is confused and led astray by such incomparably named figures as Counterfeit Countenance, Crafty Conveyance, Cloaked Collusion, and Courtly Abusion. We will meet such figures in the Histories, except that there they will be called Buckingham—or Richard. (The prince, I may say, is tempted to suicide by Despair, but is saved by Good Hope who administers the Rhubarb of Repentance!) From the prince generic to the king specific is but a step, and with the assertion of Tudor autocracy the figure of the king takes on a special interest since he is now the absolute power.

Sure enough, by 1536 we have *Kynge Johan* (altered in 1539, surviving only in a revision of 1561). In this play, John is a Christian hero who stood up against the Pope. The play is not very concerned with historical accuracy, but it was just what the Tudors wanted, or perhaps ordered (the Act of Supremacy, remember, was 1534). The important thing about this play is that it shows a way of using history for a predetermined purpose. (We will see what Shakespeare made of King John.) In Rossiter's words, 'the point of *Kynge Johan* is that it suggests a method by which any not-wildly-unsuitable "chronicle" stuff can be made into a history-play: by beginning with "what you want to prove" and patternizing history in accordance with set dogmas' (ibid., p. 122). With this sense that history can be patterned for a purpose (which, of course, need not necessarily be didactic or propagandist), we are close to the history play proper. But it is important to bear in mind that, even when we move to drama that is historically specific (*Richard II,* not *Mankynd*), we will find traces, or after-glimpses, of the Morality pattern, as the plays still present struggles between opposed abstractable qualities, albeit now locked together *inside* human consciousness. Rossiter quotes the contemporary Thomas Lodge who, in his 'A Defense of Plays' of 1580, says that the dramatists 'dilucidate and well explain many darke obscure histories, imprinting them in men's minds in such indelible characters that they can hardly be obliterated'. Rossiter comments: 'the suggestion of an allegoric shadow-show behind the historic characters, on another plane than the clash of transient personalities, was an essential part of that "dilucidation"' (ibid., p. 155).

Gorboduc (1561) is regarded as the first English history-tragedy, but the subject was taken from the legendary chronicles of early Britain, and the play was something of a neoclassical Senecan exercise. This was not to be Shakespeare's way. But by the time Shakespeare started writing his history plays, Marlowe's *Tamburlaine the Great* had been published. This not only marked a revolutionary step in the use of blank verse; it brought a new Renaissance type of amoral hero to the English stage. Marlowe's plays manifest that fear of man's potentialities which seems to increase towards the end of the Elizabethan period when writers, Shakespeare supremely, began to contemplate what kind of figure man might become 'given freedom from all the Christian and medieval restraints' (ibid.). But while Tudor drama is very much a phenomenon and product of the English Renaissance, it is still very involved, as I have tried to stress, in what we call the

Middle Ages. As we turn to Shakespeare, we might bear in mind Rossiter's simple but suggestive generalization that much of Elizabethan drama consists of 'the adventures of Renaissance Man in a Medieval World-Order'.

HENRY VI, PART ONE (1589–92)

> Henry the Sixth, in infant bands crown'd King
> Of France and England, did this king succeed;
> Whose state so many had the managing,
> That they lost France and made this England bleed:
> Which oft our stage hath shown . . .
> (*Henry V,* V, ii, 9–13)

At the end of this second tetralogy, Shakespeare looks back to where he began the first. He started with the funeral of Henry V, accompanied by dark forebodings and ominous portents, and went on to dramatize the losses and bleedings which England suffered during the reign of Henry VI —'which oft our stage hath shown'. Henry V was the last great heroic warrior-knight king; thereafter came 'declension'—disagreement, dissention, disorder—'jars'; then, disintegration and degeneration until, in Part 3, England has collapsed into a 'slaughter house'. Henry Tudor arrives to tidy up the shambles. But the *Henry VI* trilogy is really about—as far as England is concerned—diminution, dissolution, loss. Joan of Arc's words are both lyrically fitting and historically accurate:

> Glory is like a circle in the water,
> Which never ceaseth to enlarge itself
> Till by broad spreading it disperse to nought.
> With Henry's death the English circle ends;
> Dispersèd are the glories it included.
> (I, ii, 133–7)

The *Henry VI* plays survey (and inquire) how England's glories—after the death of Henry V—'disperse to nought'.

That this did happen, and the trajectory of its happening, is of course inscribed in the Chronicles. Hall announced, clearly enough, that his theme was 'what mischief hath insurged in realms by intestine division . . . what calamitee hath ensued in famous regions by domestical discord & unnatural controversy'; while Holinshed states, succinctly enough, 'through dissention at home, all lost abroad'. The first, if not the prime, cause of the trouble, was that king 'in infant bands'—'woe to the nation whose king is a child' was a familiar adage for the Elizabethans. But that alone could not account for England's collapse into ungloried chaos. The Chronicles record that this did happen. Shakespeare sets out imaginatively to recreate the occasions—the causes—of its happening. And to transform 'chronicle' into 'drama', he had to set about 'patterning' his material. This he did so freely, and to such effect, that Bullough—the great master of Shakespeare's sources—gives his opinion that what Shakespeare finally produced is 'not so much a Chronicle Play as a fantasia on historical themes'.

In no other history play does Shakespeare so freely disrupt and alter the time sequence of his Chronicle material. He brings events together that were years apart; he inverts the order of their happening; he makes sudden what was slow; he makes simultaneous what was separate. He expands and contracts; he omits—and invents. As Andrew Cairncross well puts it in his introduction to the Arden edition of the play, Shakespeare throws 'the events of thirty years into the melting-pot' and, just because he makes so free with chronology, he has to 'avoid precise indications of time' (there are no dates)—'events must happen, as it were, in a great sea of time with no fixed points of reference but the death of Henry V behind and the Wars of the Roses before'. Just to give a few examples of the liberties Shakespeare took with his material: the episodes in the play cover more than thirty years, from the start of Henry's reign (1422) to the death of the heroic Talbot (at Bordeaux in 1453); but, from the start, disparate events are yoked together—thus, the siege of Orleans (1428–9) is depicted as taking place during the funeral of Henry V (seven years earlier). Joan was burned in 1431, while Talbot was buried in 1453—yet in the play, she lives to see him dead. Joan was captured in 1430, though not by York as in the play. In the play, this is *immediately* followed by the (completely fictitious) capture and wooing of Margaret by Suffolk. In fact, negotiations for Henry's marriage did not take place until 1444. Burgundy's defection from the English takes place over twenty years in Hall. In the play, it is effected on the instant as a result of a patriotic appeal by Joan (quite unhistorical—she had been burned some years previously). And so on. Shakespeare is tightening his pattern—pointing up the conflict between the once heroic English and the devious, effeminate French; the undermining of chivalric ideals, the decay of feudal loyalties, and loss of old values; the fading of the old, noble heroic ethos, and the rise of a generation driven by ruthlessness, expediency, and cunning; and (this is not so commonly noted) the capitulation—on certain fronts—of the masculine to the feminine. Everywhere, ceremony is, if not drowned, then disrupted, spoiled, profaned. The sense of growing disaster and impending dissolution is relentless. Chaos is not quite come again; but it is surely not far away.

We might start by considering interrupted ceremony, since that is how the play starts. A history play dealing with kingly matters is bound to contain a lot of pageantry—processions, flourishes, drums, flags. This is the very panoply of the feudal courtly world—its binding ritual: everyone in their place; hierarchy and degree visibly enacted; order celebrated and power and authority manifested. So this play opens with the great solemn Dead March at Henry V's funeral. But the dignified exequies and formal lamentations are almost immediately disrupted by a most unseemly squabble between Gloucester and Winchester, signs of a bitter rivalry which will dominate the first part of the play. Bedford seeks to turn their attention away from private rancour and back to the public ritual—'cease these jars . . . Let's to the altar' (I, i, 44–5). ('Jars' is a recurrent word in this long study of discord.) Bedford tries to invoke and prolong the spirit of the dead king:

> Henry the Fifth, thy ghost I invocate:
> Prosper this realm, keep it from civil broils,
> Combat with adverse planets in the heavens!
> A far more glorious star thy soul will make
> Than Julius Caesar or bright—
>
> (I, i, 52–6)

But just there, with the name of Julius Caesar on his lips, he is interrupted by a messenger with tidings 'Of loss, of slaughter, and discomfiture'—more specifically, with news of the loss of seven towns in France. 'What treachery was used?' asks incredulous Exeter. 'No treachery, but want of men and money' (I, i, 69). This is important. Throughout, it is made clear that, for all the talk of the diabolical French and witchcraft, for every setback and loss, England has only itself to blame. 'Through dissention at home, all lost abroad.' A second messenger brings 'letters full of bad mischance' (the Dauphin has been crowned king). Then a *third* messenger brings the 'dismal' news of Talbot's capture. I stress 'three' because the play is full of triads (observed by Lawrence V. Ryan and others). I will come back to this. The scene ends, interestingly, exactly as it began—that is, it starts with speeches from Bedford, Gloucester, Exeter, Winchester, and it ends with speeches from them in the same order, as they variously exit. The king being an infant, they are responsible for managing the realm. They leave to take up their duties—except for Winchester. He remains behind to give the first soliloquy in the history plays:

> Each hath his place and function to attend;
> I am left out; for me nothing remains.
> But long I will not be Jack out of office.
> The king from Eltham I intend to send
> And sit at chiefest stern of public weal.
>   (I, i, 173–7)

The repetition witnessed in the entrances and exits suggests order, an ordering; things and people in their proper sequences. But the amoral candour, the revealed personal ambition of the voice alone, offers a violation and threat to that order. As disorder and disarray increase, so do the soliloquies and asides; while ritual, processional confidences and enactments wane.

The play has sometimes been described as the tragedy of Talbot, the honest old English hero whose destruction is engineered by the wily French witch, Joan. So much is there but to see it that way makes, I think, for an uncomfortably coarse, not to say jingoistic, play. And it ignores the fact that Talbot dies at the end of Act IV and clearly, quite deliberately, Shakespeare concludes his play, not just with the death of Joan, but also—and instantly ensuant on that death—the (unhistorical) wooing of Margaret by Suffolk, and his persuading Henry to break a previous contract of marriage and instead take Margaret (a critical act of 'oath-breaking' which anticipates many more). Joan, the 'scourge of the English', is dead. Long live Margaret, who will be a scourge of the English for years to come (she is the only character to appear in every play of the tetralogy).

But let me turn to the matter of threes and triads. There are, most obviously from the start, three heroic English generals—Salisbury, Bedford,

Talbot; grey-haired and ageing, they seem like increasingly isolated survivors from another, simpler, nobler age. They meet their deaths in battle at the three French towns which figure in the play—respectively, Orléans, Rouen, Bordeaux. (Talbot, I might mention, has 'three attendants,/Lean Famine, quartering Steel, and climbing Fire': IV, ii, 11.) Correspondingly, three ruthlessly ambitious and distinctly *ig*noble nobles emerge in the course of the play—Winchester, York, and Somerset—representing a new breed of men who know the chivalric gestures, and postures, and words, but have none of the old chivalric sense of duty, obligation, and loyalty. Between them, they are preparing the wars and discords of the morrow. There are three interrupted ceremonies. The funeral, already mentioned: the parliament-house where the young king makes his first appearance in the play (III, i), only to have the occasion violently disrupted by Gloucester's and Winchester's fighting serving-men: and the king's coronation in Paris (IV, i), which is marred, first by Talbot's stripping of the Garter from cowardly Falstaff (no relation)—Talbot accompanies this act with what amounts to an elegy for the old heroic knightly virtues; secondly, by the news of Burgundy's treacherous defection; and thirdly by the request by Vernon and Basset—'presumptuous vassals'—to be allowed the right to combat. They are serving-men belonging to York and Somerset, who do nothing to contain and curb this grossly unseemly behaviour on the part of their servants. The stains of discord are seeping down through the ranks of society.

But, perhaps most importantly, there are three women, all French, and the only women in the play. There are three scenes in which each of them exercises her seductive wiles on a man in a superior position of power— twice with complete success, but once, most instructively, to no avail. The first encounter is between Joan and the Dauphin in the second scene in the play. She appears here as 'a holy maid' with 'the spirit of deep prophecy'. The encounter is recorded in the Chronicles. What Shakespeare adds is their engaging in a round of single combat, which opens itself to sexual *double entendre*—'thou shalt buckle with me', etc. The Dauphin's abject capitulation to her—'Let me thy servant and not sovereign be . . . thy prostrate thrall' (I, ii, 111, 117)—represents a dramatic inversion—male king craving the domination of a peasant girl—which the Elizabethans would find shocking, or perhaps amusing (that's the French for you!). Very different is the strange little incident involving the Countess of Auvergne and her attempt to trap Talbot in her castle (II, iii). This scene is completely

Shakespeare's invention. Tillyard dismissed it as an 'irrelevant anecdote'
introduced as fun for the audience. It is rather more interesting than that.
The countess has asked to entertain Talbot, who has graciously—he *is* a
knight—accepted. Upon seeing him, the countess evinces surprise that he is
so small and un-heroic looking—'What! Is this the man?'

> I see report is fabulous and false.
> I thought I should have seen some Hercules . . .
> Alas, this is a child, a silly dwarf!
>   (II, iii, 18–22)

After this piece of opening politeness, the countess announces that he is her
prisoner (such is her plot). She adds that, in a way, he has been her 'prisoner' for a long time.

> Long time thy shadow hath been thrall to me,
> For in my gallery thy picture hangs.
> But now the substance shall endure the like,
> And I will chain these legs and arms of thine . . .
>   (II, iii, 36–9)

Talbot simply laughs, as well as he might since half his army is waiting outside the door. But he goes on to say that she never had more than his shadow
anyway.

> *Countess.* Why, art not thou the man?
> *Talbot.* I am indeed.
> *Countess.* Then have I substance too.
> *Talbot.* No, no, I am but shadow of myself:
>   You are deceived, my substance is not here,
>   For what you see is but the smallest part
>   And least proportion of humanity.
>   (II, iii, 48–53)

And the countess finds this a riddle:

> He will be here, and yet he is not here.
>   (II, iii, 58)

The countess's mistake is to identify bodily presence—which in this case is relatively puny—with true 'substance'. But Talbot's real—male—'substance' is in his name, his fame, and the power at his disposal. Just as he is, there alone in the countess's room, temporarily reduced to his body, he is effectively, like his painted image, a 'shadow' (doubly so, since 'shadow' was also a word for an actor—Shakespeare is already beginning to exploit the available ironic analogies between history and theatre). The countess recognizes her mistake:

> Victorious Talbot, pardon my abuse;
> I find thou art no less than fame hath bruited
> And more than may be gathered by thy shape.
>
> (II, iii, 67–9)

This episode represents a complete defeat of the feminine. The virile old English knight is immune to the effeminizations of France. But he is a dying breed.

The third male encounter with a French female—again, Shakespeare's invention—takes place in the last Act between Suffolk and Margaret. Suffolk enters holding Margaret's hand and gazing at her, even as the other captured French female, Joan, is led off. It is immediately clear that he has been entirely captivated by her beauty and charm. And she uses no (obvious) seductive arts: in this play she is passive and decorous throughout her appearances. Suffolk, desperate somehow to keep Margaret close to him, conceives the plan of persuading Henry to take her as his bride. In this, he is successful, and the last lines of the play see him happily setting off for France again, to bring Margaret to England. The lines could hardly be more ominous.

> Thus Suffolk hath prevailed, and thus he goes,
> As did the youthful Paris once to Greece,
> With hope to find the like event in love,
> But prosper better than the Trojan did.
> Margaret shall now be queen, and rule the king;
> But I will rule both her, the king, and realm . . .
>
> (V, v, 103–8)

Since Britain was, mythically, descended from Troy, the proposed importation of a second Helen into the realm presages an interminable period of disaster.

Can anything legitimately be made of these recurrent triads? Not, certainly, anything to do with whatever mystic properties might be thought to be associated with the number three. I think it has to do with that 'patterning' which the dramatist has to impose on his material. Historically, things happen just once. But if, in a representation of it, things seem to come in threes, you get the sense that perhaps there are echoes, recurrencies, repetitions, symmetries which, while you live through the actual day, you never notice. As Philip Brockbank well says, Shakespeare's Histories 'give us the sense of being close to the event together with a sense of knowing its consequences . . . The rhythm between pattern and process is maintained; the play like the history must be both reflected upon and lived through, its moral shape apprehended but its clamor and hurly-burly wracking the nerves' (*On Shakespeare,* p. 83). This is why we are afforded long backward —and forward-looking vistas, from Mortimer's long genealogical speech tracing the succession from Edward III, to the many speeches of foreboding and prophecy which Shakespeare inserts, often at the end of a scene. One example: the Temple Garden scene—again, completely Shakespeare's invention—serves in an almost heraldic way to give a sharp and highlighted beginning to the Wars of the Roses proper (this is nothing like so clear in the Chronicles). Warwick declares:

> And here I prophesy: this brawl today,
> Grown to this faction in the Temple garden,
> Shall send, between the red rose and the white,
> A thousand souls to death and deadly night.
>
> (II, iv, 124–8)

Shakespeare uses prophecies, and later curses and dreams, not just to relate and bind together the three parts of the trilogy, but to suggest that English history does *have* a perceptible pattern. Albeit, for a while it is a pattern of accelerating disaster.

Much of the play does concentrate on the struggle between Talbot and Joan. Talbot is certainly the noble old heroic soldier from another age—English, virile, unquestioningly loyal, implacably ferocious in battle. Just there we might pause, for there is in fact something barbaric, atavistic, about his fury. 'Your hearts I'll stamp out with my horse's heels,/And make a quagmire of your mingled brains' (I, iv, 108–9). This doesn't, to me, have the smack of chivalry about it. Similarly, he reveals that, when a prisoner of the French, 'I with my nails digged stones out of the ground' to hurl at his captors. Brave, perhaps. But this is just how the mob which interrupts parliament behaves: they

> Have filled their pockets full of pebble stones
> And banding themselves in contrary parts
> Do pelt so fast at one another's pate
> That many have their giddy brains knocked out.
>   (III, i, 80–83)

Talbot, one feels, would be a good man in a mob action—on either side. He is one of those archaic warrior figures, seemingly dominated by a disposition of unrelenting ferocity, who recur throughout Shakespeare (Coriolanus is, of course, the last). He has much to say about the French 'fiends'; but to the French, *Talbot* is the 'fiend'. 'I think this Talbot be a fiend of hell' (II, i, 46). Who is 'saviour' and who is 'fiend' clearly depends on what side you are on. And, for all the talk of witchcraft and diabolical assistance of the French, the death of Talbot is shown to be, four-squarely, the fault of England. York and Somerset won't send him the help they were pledged to provide, because they are jealous of each other. As Lucy—another Shakespearian invention—says to them:

> Thus, while the vulture of sedition
> Feeds in the bosom of such great commanders,
> Sleeping neglection doth betray to loss . . .
>   Whiles they each other cross,
> Lives, honors, lands, and all hurry to loss
> . . .
> The fraud of England, not the force of France,
> Hath now entrapped the noble-minded Talbot;
> Never to England shall he bear his life,
> But dies betrayed to fortune by your strife.
>   (IV, iii, 47–53: IV, iv, 36–9)

Talbot is, in fact, very much at sea in this new world which fights by rules, or guiles and stratagems, that he does not understand. Lost and bewildered in one battle, he says despairingly:

> My thoughts are whirlèd like a potter's wheel;
> I know not where I am, nor what I do.
>
> (I, v, 19–20)

There is no way such a figure could survive.

But he survived a good deal longer than Shakespeare allows him to, so that—quite anachronistically—Joan is in at his death. This is a crucial scene; but, before looking at it, we must briefly consider Shakespeare's Joan. In the early part of the play, she is allowed some speeches of (from the French point of view) impeccable patriotism, which Shakespeare could only have approved. But he is soon allowing an equivocation on 'Pucelle or pussel' (virgin or whore). He allows her a scorching indictment of English hypocrisy (V, iv, 36 ff.), but also portrays her in converse with evil spirits. She—damnably—denies her peasant father, and finally loses all credibility and dignity as she casts around, admitting to any sexual liaison, to avoid the stake. There are, of course, English and French versions of Joan, and Shakespeare finally endorses an English one. But the English are in no point exempted from the chaos they have caused, the deteriorations they have permitted. Concerning a final judgment of Joan, I prefer the humane exhortation of Holinshed—'cast your opinions as ye have cause'.

At the death of Talbot, Lucy gives a long commemorative speech which spells out all his titles:

> Valiant Lord Talbot, Earl of Shrewsbury,
> Created, for his rare success in arms,
> Great Earl of Washford, Waterford, and Valence,
> Lord Talbot of Goodrig and Urchinfield,
> Lord Strange of Blackmere, Lord Verdun of Alton,
> Lord Cromwell of Wingfield, Lord Furnival of Sheffield,
> The thrice victorious Lord of Falconbridge,
> Knight of the noble order of Saint George,
> Worthy Saint Michael, and the Golden Fleece,

Great Marshal to Henry the Sixth
Of all his wars within the realm of France.

(IV, vii, 61–71)

To which Joan comments:

Here's a silly stately style indeed!
The Turk, that two and fifty kingdoms hath,
Writes not so tedious a style as this.
Him that you magnifi'st with all these titles
Stinking and fly-blown lies here at our feet.

(IV, vii, 72–6)

Interestingly, it has been established that Lucy's words are taken from an actual historical monument, Talbot's tomb at Rouen. A lapidary speech indeed—words of stone, words in stone. The true identity—'substance'— of the man is asserted to exist and persist in his name and fame. Look for the man in the monument. Joan, the woman, concentrates on the rotting physical body (rotting rather quickly, as has been pointed out: Shakespeare wants the stark contrast of the male/female attitudes). Joan is defeated, and Talbot's name lives on. But her mockery of the male 'silly stately style' leaves its mark, sows its doubt. Leaving monuments to the English heroes who die in France is very important in this play. And one result of the disastrous marriage between Henry and Margaret is that all historical records and monuments may well be lost. As Gloucester says to his fellow nobles at the beginning of the next play:

Fatal this marriage, canceling your fame,
Blotting your names from books of memory,
Razing the characters of your renown,
Defacing monuments of conquered France,
Undoing all, as all had never been.

(Part 2, I, i, 99–103)

The whole record and celebration of heroic England is under threat of erasure. That would be Joan's revenge indeed. History is just corpses.

Henry is the man of peace and piety, preferring meditation to action, and prayer to policy. He has too much 'lenity' to control and govern the warring factions springing up around him. He is something of a saint, and he certainly becomes a martyr. But he is a disastrously ineffectual king, and some of his innocence may be held to be culpable. His last speeches in the play, in which he allows himself to be swayed by Suffolk's descriptions of Margaret, portend disaster:

> So am I driven by breath of her renown
> Either to suffer shipwreck or arrive
> Where I may have fruition of her love.
>   (V, v, 7–9)

The pilot of the ship of state should not even countenance 'shipwreck'.

> I feel such sharp dissension in my breast,
> Such fierce alarums both of hope and fear,
> As I am sick with working of my thoughts.
>   (V, v, 84–6)

If there is 'sharp dissension' *within* the oscillating, unstable king, what hope that he can control the 'sharp dissensions' that are beginning to spread through the land?

In one of his late soliloquies, the besotted Suffolk thinks how much he wants Margaret, but pulls himself up, realizing he must try to persuade Henry to take her for his wife:

> O wert thou for myself! But, Suffolk, stay;
> Thou mayst not wander in that labyrinth;
> There Minotaurs and ugly treasons lurk.
> Solicit Henry with her wondrous praise . . .
>   (V, iii, 187–90)

He does enter that labyrinth, and for most of the next three plays, it seems that England does, too. And the real Minotaur, lurking to emerge, will prove to be the monstrous, misshapen Machiavel—Richard.

HENRY VI, PART TWO (1589–92)

Given that he was so hopelessly inadequate and ineffectual as a king, Henry VI's reign was a surprisingly long one—about fifty years if we include his short, second reign. During that time, all manner of political events occurred, but, as it might be felt, in a random and disconnected way. It was all very rambling and scattered. Shakespeare simply had to take hold of a chunk of that time and make it appear as a self-explanatory sequence, all contributing to a single dramatic line. He fixed on the period from 1444, when Henry welcomes his French queen Margaret to England, to 1455, the battle of St Albans, and the final, unambiguous emergence of York as an intending usurper. To achieve the concentration and focus he wanted, Shakespeare omitted a large amount of Chronicle material which would not have served his purpose; he tightens and emphasizes causes by linking what was historically unlinked (thus, both the Armourer scenes, and the Cade rebellion, are directly related to York's treason); he conflates with ruthless economy (the subversion of Salisbury and Warwick dragged on for twenty years—it is here reduced to a single scene—II, ii); he reaches into other periods for what he wants (Eleanor, Duchess of Gloucester, in fact fell four years *before* Margaret landed from France; Shakespeare clearly wants them contemporary). More remarkably, when it comes to the Jack Cade rebellion, Shakespeare ignores most of his Chronicle material, and goes back to sources concerning Wat Tyler and the Peasants' Revolt of 1381. This play will show the tragic fall of Gloucester, and the irresistible rise of York.

In the first part of the trilogy, England lost its old heroes. In this second part, it loses (in the symbolic form of one man) its law-givers. The fall of Gloucester effectively occupies the play until his murder in the middle of Act III. Gloucester is a strong and active man (he is not a feeble relic like John of Gaunt). The play opens with high ceremony as Henry's French queen is welcomed to the English court. It must be stressed that this marriage is seen as the triggering disaster behind the events of the play. Gloucester, it should be remembered, had proposed an eminently sensible, diplomatic marriage to which the young king had at first agreed. Then he succumbed to Suffolk's guile—'which fact,' says Hall, 'engendered such a flame, that it never went out, till both the parties with many other were

consumed and slain, to the great unquietness of the king and his realm'.
This is the marriage which Gloucester says will wipe out England's old heroic history. His first task in the scene—he is Protector—is to read out the
contracted articles pertaining to the marriage. When he comes to the quite
shameful surrender of Anjou and Maine, he lets the paper fall from his
hand and can read no more. Power and authority have begun—literally—
to slip from his hands, as other plots—out of his cognizance and control—
begin to seethe around him. Almost as soon as he leaves, a small group is
planning to 'quickly hoise Duke Humphrey from his seat' (I, i, 169). And
when they have gone we are left with York—alone. He speaks the first of
a series of long—dangerously long—soliloquies. Dangerous because the
more time and space are, as it were, arrogated by the private voice going
over its own intentions and devices, the less time and space seem to be committed to publicly performed, orderly, communal life. This voice is not remotely interested in 'common-wealth'.

> Then, York, be still awhile, till time do serve:
> Watch thou and wake, when others be asleep,
> To pry into the secrets of the state;
> Till Henry surfeit in the joys of love
> . . .
> And, force perforce, I'll make him yield the crown,
> Whose bookish rule hath pulled fair England down.
>   (I, i, 248–51, 258–9)

We have already seen man plotted-against (Gloucester); and man-plotting
(York). The die is cast. And we are heading for a period during which England as a whole will fall under the sway of—'force perforce'.

For two Acts we see Gloucester administering law with robust confidence and justice (which is perhaps a little severe). The business of Simpcox
and the false miracle, and the fighting armourers, presumably shows him
looking after the law of the land. While he is there, there is still some social
order. But the plot to set up his ambitious wife, and bring her to disgrace on
account of her trafficking in black magic (here arranged by Suffolk for
the queen), effectively brings him down as well. This is presumably why
Shakespeare wanted both events brought together. When Eleanor is arraigned, he is bowed down by the 'dishonour', and, in tears, asks the king's

permission to leave. Surrendering his staff of office, he shuffles off—suddenly an old man. (He is not old in the Chronicles. It is as if, while in the first part Shakespeare saw heroes to be a dying breed, so in this part he sees 'honour' fading out of England.)

But Gloucester is still confident that he remains outside of the reach of the law ('I must offend before I be attainted': II, iv, 59—already a touchingly old-fashioned trust). When Gloucester arrives at the abbey in Bury, and Suffolk arrests him 'of high treason', he is unmoved:

> Well, Suffolk, thou shalt not see me blush,
> Nor change my countenance for this arrest:
> A heart unspotted is not easily daunted.
> The purest spring is not so free from mud
> As I am clear from treason to my sovereign.
>   (III, i, 98–102)

But then the false accusations mount up against him, and he realizes the case is lost.

This occasions two of the most important speeches of the play, concerning the positive values which, the play suggests, are certainly under threat, if not in the process of being dismantled. Gloucester turns to the king:

> Ah, gracious lord, these days are dangerous:
> Virtue is *choked* with foul ambition,
> And charity chased hence by rancor's hand;
> Foul subornation is predominant,
> And equity exiled your Highness' land.
> I know their complot is to have my life,
> And if my death might make this island happy,
> And prove the period of their tyranny,
> I would expend it with all willingness.
> But mine is made the prologue to their play:
> For thousands more, that yet suspect no peril,
> Will not conclude their plotted tragedy.
>   (III, i, 142–53—my italics)

He tells the king he has thrown away his 'crutch':

> Thus is the shepherd beaten from thy side,
> And wolves are gnarling who shall gnaw thee first.
>
>   (III, i, 191–2)

At first, Henry seems to touch the bottom of his abject, concessionary hope-lessness—'My lords . . . do or undo' . . . Do what you like. But then, in a speech of high passion, of which there is not a trace in the Chronicles, Henry laments Gloucester and turns on his queen. It is his most sustained piece of oratory, and as one must feel, one of his most heart-felt, in the trilogy. As Gloucester recedes, it is as if Henry sees more clearly all the values he embodied.

> Ah, uncle Humphrey, in thy face I see
> The map of honor, truth, and loyalty;
> And yet, good Humphrey, is the hour to come
> That e'er I proved thee false or feared thy faith?
> What louring star now envies thy estate,
> That these great lords, and Margaret our Queen
> Do seek subversion of thy harmless life?
> Thou never didst them wrong, nor no man wrong:
> And as the butcher takes away the calf,
> And binds the wretch, and beats it when it strays,
> Bearing it to the bloody slaughter-house,
> Even so remorseless they have borne him hence;
> And as the dam runs lowing up and down,
> Looking the way her harmless young one went,
> And can do nought but wail her darling's loss,
> Even so myself bewails good Gloucester's case
> With sad unhelpful tears, and with dimmed eyes
> Look after him and cannot do him good,
> So mighty are his vowèd enemies.
> His fortunes I will weep, and 'twixt each groan
> Say "Who's a traitor? Gloucester he is none."
>
>   (III, i, 202–22)

He leaves. It is a final flaring, a last attempt to express his sense of what is happening around him. Henceforward he is effectively extinct, politically impotent. But he is absolutely right, of course. England *is* headed for the 'slaughter-house'. Meanwhile Suffolk articulates the complete lack of interest in ceremony or law, or anything else which constrains and guides conduct:

> And do not stand on quillets how to slay him:
> Be it by gins, by snares, by subtlety,
> Sleeping or waking, 'tis no matter how,
> So he be dead.
>
> (III, i, 261–4)

Just *kill* him—any way at all. Force perforce.

We do not see the murder—that is night-time, secret work. The butcher's shop, or slaughter-house, is now open for a new sort of business. But, in a gruesome scene—which feels like something in a medieval Morality— Gloucester's corpse is exposed on stage. For a second time, the audience is invited to consider the dead body of an old Englishman, whose world is being supplanted by one dominated by people who are immeasurably littler, and inexpressibly meaner. The spectacle is macabre—grotesque—and a minute description follows. This is the real close-up of Death in the play. From the black face and starting eyes, it is clear he has been strangled. Gloucester's earlier Morality abstraction has been terribly literalized. 'Virtue' really *has* been '*choked* with foul ambition'.

After the death of Gloucester, Shakespeare allows things to happen very quickly; or rather, things seem to tumble pell-mell towards disintegration. Holinshed emphasizes that Gloucester's murder brought about the end of the rule of law: 'while the one partie sought to destroie the other, all care of the common-wealth was set aside, and justice and equitie clearlie exiled'. Hall makes clear what an unmitigated disaster the death was—not least, indeed, for the queen herself. She 'procured and consented to the death of this noble man, whose only death brought to pass that thing, which she fain would have eschewed . . . if this Duke had lived, the Duke of York durst not have made title to the crown: if this Duke had lived, the nobles had not conspired against the king, nor yet the commons had not rebelled: if this Duke had lived, the house of Lancastre had not been defaced and destroyed.' If this Duke had lived—perhaps, no War of the Roses. But this Duke died—look at the stage—and the roads to chaos are open.

Eruption is the word. The dangerously buzzing commons threaten to erupt against Suffolk, who is summarily exiled for Gloucester's murder (no more trials now). This is immediately followed by the completely unexpected death of Cardinal Beaufort, raving mad in his bed, as if the pent-up guilt of a lifetime of ruthless greed and ambition has finally burst within him. ('So bad a death argues a monstrous life.') Then, the people erupt in the streets, and at sea. Pirates and mobs completely dominate the whole of Act IV. The pirates who capture Suffolk are pure anarchy. Perhaps rather bravely, Suffolk maintains his contemptuous and haughty 'obscure and lousy swain' tone with the pirates throughout—or perhaps he just realizes that nothing he says can help him now. But the 'lieutenant' of the pirates is not your average marauder of the high seas. Before sending Suffolk off to be killed, he addresses a long speech to him:

> Ay, kennel, puddle, sink, whose filth and dirt
> Troubles the silver spring where England drinks.
> Now will I dam up this thy yawning mouth
> For swallowing the treasure of the realm;
> Thy lips, that kissed the Queen, shall sweep the ground;
> And thou that smil'dst at good Duke Humphrey's death
> Against the senseless winds shalt grin in vain,
> Who in contempt shall hiss at thee again.
> And wedded be thou to the hags of hell,
> For daring to affy a mighty lord
> Unto the daughter of a worthless king,
> Having neither subject, wealth, nor diadem.
>   (IV, i, 71–82)

Twenty lines follow, showing a remarkable knowledge of what has been going on in England since Henry's marriage, concluding:

> The commons here in Kent are up in arms;
> And, to conclude, reproach and beggary
> Is crept into the palace of our King,
> And all by thee. Away! Convey him hence.
>   (IV, i, 100–104)

It is as if he is aware of himself as an agent in a scheme of ruthless retributive morality (the Christian cult of *Vindicta Dei*). It is as if *some* sort of law, however archaic, has caught up with Suffolk. He has much to answer for, and we recognize a certain kind of justice as he is hauled off to be beheaded. But as the attendant gentleman comments, the murder is also a 'barbarous and bloody spectacle'. In the world into which we are moving, acts of 'retribution', like the crimes which provoke them, take place in a sickening miasma of evil.

And Jack Cade. Shakespeare's Cade hardly resembles the 'young man of goodly stature and pregnant wit', 'the subtle captain' portrayed by Hall. And, whereas Hall's Cade appreciated 'teachers' and 'privy schoolmasters', Shakespeare's Cade is violently against *all* forms of literacy. Similarly in Holinshed, Cade is 'of goodlie stature and right pregnant wit', and his 'fair promises of reformation' and his (written) 'Complaint of the Commons of Kent' are responsible and sensible. There is none of this in Shakespeare. Shakespeare's Cade and his merry men are a very, very crude lot. Some think this is more evidence of Shakespeare's personal antipathy—he loathed mobs. Perhaps that is not so very hard to understand. But there must be a little more to it than that. *At this point in his pattern,* having shown all English law and order gone to the grave with Humphrey, Shakespeare hardly wants the sudden appearance of a reasonable, civilized, and literate mobleader, with a manifest respect for law and letters. As Brockbank says, this rebellion must appear as a direct evil consequence of misrule, specifically the misrule of Suffolk (we see this starting when he cruelly tears up the petitions of the conscientious citizens, in I, iii) and the forces of negation which that helped to release. So Shakespeare turned back to the Wat Tyler rebellion of 1381, and took just what he needed for his plan—the killing of the lawyers, the destruction of the Savoy and the Inns of Court, and the burning of the records of the realm. The death of Cade in Iden's all-tooperfect pastoral retreat is not very interesting. Iden is a little mannikin of Tudor order and degree, and hardly credible. But the way Cade's followers turn against him is more interesting. Confronting the mob, Clifford invokes Henry V, with obscure relevance. The mob immediately cries to follow Clifford. Cade is justified in his appraisal. 'Was ever feather so lightly blown to and fro, as this multitude? The name of Henry the Fifth hales them to an hundred mischiefs and makes them leave me desolate' (IV, viii, 56–9). Clifford has not dealt with the problem of mob violence. He has sim-

ply found a way to divert it in another direction. Brockbank is surely right
to see distant promise in this early scenario:

> It is assimilated into a firm comprehensive structure, a version of political
> and historical tragedy that will serve later as the ground of *Julius Caesar*
> —another play which moves through the plotting and execution of an as-
> sassination, through the generation of lynch law in the streets, to the de-
> flection of that violence into civil war.
>
> (op. cit., p. 95)

Pirates, mobs, and York and his sons—these are the phenomena which
emerge in the post-Humphrey lawless wasteland of England. As far as
Henry is concerned, some 'pirate' is trying to board his ship of state (IV, ix,
33)—Cade or York, it hardly matters. Since York started Cade on, it might
be felt he will serve as the representative figure. York, we must feel (historically this is very unjust), is an adequate progenitor of that entirely new animal in English history and politics—Richard. Young Clifford has an eye
for the Yorks. 'Why, what a brood of traitors have we here!'—and specifically for Richard:

> Hence, heap of wrath, foul indigested lump,
> As crooked in thy manners as thy shape!
>
> (V, i, 157–8)

Clifford will become an arguably insane figure of violence in the next Part.
But it is Clifford who speaks some of Shakespeare's most awesome lines
about war, starting with an utterance about the general chaos of war, and
moving on to a long lament for his father whose corpse he has just found
(V, ii, 31–65).

> Shame and confusion! All is on the rout;
> Fear frames disorder, and disorder wounds
> Where it should guard.
>
> (V, ii, 31–3)

These famous lines are not clear to me. The idea of 'fear' 'framing'—
arranging, putting in order—anything, hardly sits easily, though when you

take into account the fact that the verb could more generally mean simply 'shapes', then it presents no problems. And what should 'disorder' 'guard'? Does it mean that those forces which should be protecting are wounding those in their care? Perhaps. Things are becoming unsettled in the mists of war. And what about the king, whose play this is—what has he been doing? As you might expect, very little. We last see him hopelessly trying to keep up with events until the queen says with pardonable exasperation —'What are you made of? You'll nor fight nor fly' (V, ii, 74). Clifford helps to pack him off. But he will have to endure a whole further play, during which uncertainties come inseparable from atrocities. It will be the worst.

HENRY VI, PART THREE (1589–92)

The most vivid image of *Henry VI* Part 3 is of a figure of mad energy fighting to escape from a wild wood:

> And I—like one lost in a thorny wood,
> That rends the thorns and is rent with the thorns,
> Seeking a way and straying from the way,
> Not knowing how to find the open air,
> But toiling desperately to find it out—
> Torment myself to catch the English crown:
> And from that torment I will free myself,
> Or hew my way out with a bloody ax.
>
> (III, ii, 174–81)

The old chivalric heroes have gone; the great law-givers have been removed; anarchy is the 'order' of the day. England is ready for the emergence of its most monstrous creation—Richard.

   The first two Acts concern the battles of 1460–61, when Henry was still king, in name. Acts III and IV concern the manoeuvring of the various parties of nobles with their rival kings; while the last Act presents the campaigns of 1471—all war. Shakespeare had a morass of more or less shapeless material in front of him, suggesting no one particular dramatic or moral plan—just victories and defeats, victories and defeats. (One or two events *did* have an inherent dramatic significance—the breach of faith of Edward's marriage to Lady Grey; the perfidiousness of side-changing Clarence; and these Shakespeare duly exploited.) He compressed, streamlined, amalgamated, telescoped, until the play became a sharpened study of anarchy—in state, family, and individual—and disorder itself. The characters appear to have no inner life; they move like masks through this disintegrating world, and hardly seem responsible for what they do. They are driven by primary passions—fury, hate, ambition, lust—and see nothing outside their own dominant passion and its aims. They resemble Morality types—vengeful Clifford, holy Henry, lustful Edward, perjured Clarence, ambitious Richard, she-wolf Margaret—and seem to be as unchanging. They whirl around, as if oblivious of the chaos that is their world—custom, trust, duty, self-control, all forgot. I must here cite an important point made by Brockbank concerning this dehumanizing 'characterisation':

> So long as the characterisation is neutral the first tetralogy displays a barbarous providence ruling murderous automatons whose reactions are predictable in terms of certain quasi-Hobbesian assumptions about human nature: when argument fails men resort to force; when an oath is inconvenient they break it; their power challenged, they retort with violence; their power subdued they resort to lies, murder or suicide; their honor impugned, they look for revenge; their enemies at their mercy, they torture and kill them; and if a clash of loyalties occurs they resolve it in the interest of their own survival. Such might be the vision of the play's pantomime, but its dimensions are not confined to its pantomime and to its shallower rhetoric. The anarchic, egocentric impulses are not presented as the inescapable laws of human nature; they are at most manifestations of forces that automatically take over when the constraints of government are withheld. Law and order cease to prevail when men cease to believe in them, and the process by which this comes about is explored in the play's dominant characters.
>
> (op. cit., p. 98)

The play opens with York and his gang strolling into the parliament house and simply taking possession. Richard throws the head of the Duke of Somerset on the floor, and there is much showing of bloody swords. Indeed, they decide to call it 'the bloody parliament' and resolve to stay there, still in their armour. There is no longer any pretence at, or interest in, public ritual. Henry enters, and his followers immediately want to fall on the

Yorkists; but, peace-loving and shrinking from action as always, Henry will not let them 'make a shambles of the Parliament House'. After another of those unresolvable arguments as to who has the stronger title or better claim, Henry suddenly capitulates and offers a shameful deal, saying to York: 'Let me for this my lifetime reign as king . . . Enjoy the kingdom after my decease' (I, i, 171, 175). The dismayed reactions of his followers cover the implications of what he has done:

> What wrong is this unto the Prince your son?
> What good is this to England and himself!
> Base, fearful, and despairing Henry!
> How hast thou injured both thyself and us!
>
> (I, i, 176–9)

Henry will remain a curiously isolated figure—in or out of captivity—throughout the play until his death. But while he stands as a permanent protest against the horrors of civil war, and there is a permanent pathos in his continuously disappointed faith in the political efficacy of mercy, pity, and peace, his indisputable 'virtue' ('I'll leave my son my virtuous deeds behind': II, ii, 49) is catastrophic for England at large. It is this betrayal and the craven disinheritance of his son, Edward, that goads the mother, Queen Margaret, to show herself for the Fury she is, as she effectively banishes Henry ('get thee gone': I, i, 258) and, with her son, takes over control of his forces and allies.

Richard soon persuades his father to abandon his promise to allow Henry to see out his life as king:

> And, father, do but think
> How sweet a thing it is to wear a crown,
> Within whose circuit is Elysium
> And all that poets feign of bliss and joy.
>
> (I, ii, 28–31)

Clearly, the actual crown—easy to fetishize—had a disturbing magic and allure all of its own. York says: 'Richard enough; I will be King or die' (I, ii, 35). But what is another act of perjury in a world in which allegiances, loyalties, and the keeping of words, have gone out of fashion?

But Margaret is on the move, along with the mad nihilist Clifford, and we soon see what sort of war we are in for. Clifford finds York's youngest son, Rutland, with his chaplain. He bundles the chaplain out of the way, and turns to little Rutland:

> The sight of any of the house of York
> Is as a Fury to torment my soul;
> And till I root out their accursèd line
> And leave not one alive, I live in hell.
> Therefore—
>
> (I, iii, 30–34)

Therefore, he stabs him to death. This is immediately followed by the capture, and the prolonged baiting and mockery, of York. He is made to stand on a molehill in a vaguely crucifixion pose; he is crowned with a paper crown; and offered a napkin stained with the blood of his freshly murdered son, Rutland. It is an outrageous profanation and mutilation of the ideals (and idols) of kingship, knighthood, fatherhood, womanhood—everything concerning family and state. Margaret evinces a powerful sadistic pleasure in her prolonged mental torturing of York, who is nevertheless allowed a long, powerful speech of recrimination ('She-wolf of France, but worse than wolves of France') of nearly sixty lines, before Margaret and Clifford stab him to death. Shakespeare is just following his sources in showing this whole atrocity as a prolonged, blasphemous inverted ritual. But he clearly wants it to carry more general implications concerning the brutal, anti-chivalric nature of this civil war.

A similar scene is almost re-enacted when, later, Clifford falls in battle. The York boys gather round, as they 'devise fell tortures' for their number one enemy. Fortunately for Clifford, he is already dead though the Yorks, thwarted of their anticipated ghoulish pleasures, can hardly accept the fact. Richard:

> 'Tis but his policy to counterfeit,
> Because he would avoid such bitter taunts
> Which in the time of death he gave our father.
>
> (II, vi, 65–7)

Ideally, Clifford and Richard would like to go on taunting each other, and fighting each other, forever. As psychopaths, they are evenly matched. But

Clifford has dropped from the field. And there will be no one else who can take on Richard for a long time.

Henry has been kept entirely apart from the action, so when he appears, he speaks as a solitary, melancholy observer, able to subsume the surgings of the war into the great struggles of nature:

> This battle fares like to the morning's war,
> When dying clouds contend with growing light,
> What time the shepherd, blowing of his nails,
> Can neither call it perfect day nor night.
> Now sways it this way, like a mighty sea
> Forced by the tide to combat with the wind.
> Now sways it that way, like the selfsame sea
> Forced to retire by fury of the wind.
> Sometime the flood prevails, and then the wind;
> Now one the better, then another best;
> Both tugging to be victors, breast to breast,
> Yet neither conqueror nor conquerèd:
> So is the equal poise of this fell war.
> Here on this molehill will I sit me down.
> To whom God will, there be the victory!
>   (II, v, 1–15)

This is, at least theatrically, the same molehill on which York was mocked, so it is a good site for kingly meditation. And there, Henry draws out his pastoral fantasy:

> O God! methinks it were a happy life,
> To be no better than a homely swain;
> To sit upon a hill, as I do now,
> To carve out dials quaintly, point by point,
> Thereby to see the minutes how they run—
> How many makes the hour full complete,
> How many hours brings about the day,
> How many days will finish up the year,
> How many years a mortal man may live;
> When this is known, then to divide the times—
> So many hours must I tend my flock,

> So many hours must I take my rest,
> So many hours must I contemplate,
> So many hours must I sport myself,
> So many days my ewes have been with young,
> So many weeks ere the poor fools will ean,
> So many years ere I shall shear the fleece.
> So minutes, hours, days, months, and years,
> Passed over to the end they were created,
> Would bring white hairs unto a quiet grave.
> Ah, what a life were this! how sweet! how lovely!
>   (II, v, 21–41)

It is a dream of a world slowed down to its lowest pulse-rate; a life reduced to seasons and cycles and their repetitions and recurrencies. A life and a world which history does not penetrate and violate. But then, as if in a tableau, two figures carrying corpses enter from different directions. Only now do they realize that one is a father who has just killed his own son; the other a son who has killed his own father. The grief is very stylized and antiphonal, and the theme was a common one, showing up:

> What stratagems, how fell, how butcherly,
> Erroneous, mutinous and unnatural,
> This deadly quarrel daily doth beget!
>   (II, v, 89–91)

It allows Henry to lament over the whole war:

> Woe above woe! grief more than common grief!
> O that my death would stay these ruthful deeds!
> O, pity, pity, gentle heaven, pity!
> The red rose and the white are on his face,
> The fatal colors of our striving houses:
> The one his purple blood right well resembles;
> The other his pale cheeks, methinks, presenteth:
> Wither one rose, and let the other flourish!
> If you contend, a thousand lives must wither.
>   (II, v, 94–102)

Henry's recipe for peace—'wither one rose'—has no future, though his desire for peace is manifestly heart-felt. But this rather dream-like little heraldic, or emblematic, tableau-interlude is soon over, and we are back among
the real fighting.

In this play that means pre-eminently with Richard. His father, York,
had already started to develop the potentialities, and exploit the privileges,
of the soliloquy—getting the audience on your side, tapping into its willingness to take a low view of human nature and a completely cynical attitude to politics. In an astonishing speech, Richard shows that he has appro-
priated the soliloquy prerogative, and is capable of developing it in entirely
new ways for his own ends. Nothing would have prepared the audience for
this speech, and they would have heard nothing like it in the theatre before.
King Edward (as he now is—though the crown shifts between Edward
and Henry for the rest of the play) has just announced his determination to
marry Lady Grey—he must have his will, and that's that. He exits, looking
like a figure for whom kingship means primarily the chance to pursue sexual pleasure. Henry, we are told, has just been taken to the Tower. Richard
stands back and begins to reveal himself:

> Ay, Edward will use women honorably.
> Would he were wasted, marrow, bones and all,
> That from his loins no hopeful branch may spring,
> To cross me from the golden time I look for!
> And yet, between my soul's desire and me—
> The lustful Edward's title burièd—
> Is Clarence, Henry, and his son young Edward,
> And all the unlooked-for issue of their bodies,
> To take their rooms, ere I can place myself:
> A cold premeditation for my purpose!
> Why then, I do but dream on sovereignty;
> Like one that stands upon a promontory,
> And spies a far-off shore where he would tread,
> Wishing his foot were equal with his eye,
> And chides the sea that sunders him from thence,
> Saying, he'll lade it dry to have his way:
> So do I wish the crown, being so far off;
> And so I chide the means that keeps me from it;

And so (I say) I'll cut the causes off,

Flattering me with impossibilities

. . .

I'll make my heaven to dream upon the crown,

And, whiles I live, t' account this world but hell,

Until my misshaped trunk that bears this head

Be round impalèd with a glorious crown.

And yet I know not how to get the crown,

For many lives stand between me and home . . .

     (III, ii, 124–143, 168–173)

Then follow the lines I quoted at the start of this section, about fighting his way out of a wild wood with a bloody axe, hinting at some monstrous, un-natural birth. But it is the final lines that are the most astonishing:

Why, I can smile, and murder while I smile,

And cry "Content" to that which grieves my heart,

And wet my cheeks with artificial tears,

And frame my face to all occasions.

I'll drown more sailors than the mermaid shall;

I'll slay more gazers than the basilisk;

I'll play the orator as well as Nestor,

Deceive more slily than Ulysses could,

And, like a Sinon, take another Troy.

I can add colors to the chameleon,

Change shapes with Proteus for advantages,

And set the murderous Machiavel to school.

Can I do this, and cannot get a crown?

Tut, were it farther off, I'll pluck it down.

     (III, ii, 182–95)

Richard reveals that he has at his disposal the energies and proclivities of all the other characters—York's steely ambition and crown-hunger; Clif-ford's dedication to pure violence and killing; Edward's soft, indulgent pru-riences; Margaret's soaring ruthlessness, and so on. And those last lines are addressed to the audience. He will outplay all the famous dissemblers and shape-changers of legend and epic. Indeed, he promises them a performance the like of which has never been seen before. He will treat history as his theatre, which he will dominate because he is capable of playing any and every role. The ground is here laid for the mood and atmosphere of the first three Acts of *Richard III*.

Almost the last atrocity we have to witness is the death of brave young Prince Edward (Henry's son), who is systematically stabbed by King Edward, then Richard, then Clarence. It is brutal butchery, but not, it has to be admitted, so very different from the stabbing of Rutland at the beginning. The play is *all* one long butchery. Queen Margaret is so distraught at the killing of her child that she asks to be killed as well. Richard, of course, is instantly willing to oblige, but Edward stays his hand, prompting Richard to say: 'Why should she live, to fill the world with words?' (V, v, 44). It is a line we may well have occasion to remember in the next play.

The ultimate confrontation of the play, of the whole trilogy, is between Henry and Richard. These are the two extreme products of the terrible years covered by the plays—the Martyr and the Machiavel, as Brockbank designates them. Richard has gone to Henry in the Tower, to murder him as Henry well divines. And, speaking with great moral force and authority, Henry utters his indictment of Richard:

> And thus I prophesy, that many a thousand,
> Which now mistrust no parcel of my fear,
> And many an old man's sigh and many a widow's,
> And many an orphan's water-standing eye—
> Men for their sons, wives for their husbands,
> Orphans for their parents' timeless death—
> Shall rue the hour that ever thou wast born.
> The owl shrieked at thy birth—an evil sign;
> The night-crow cried, aboding luckless time;
> Dogs howled and hideous tempest shook down trees;
> The raven rooked her on the chimney's top,
> And chatt'ring pies in dismal discords sung.
> Thy mother felt more than a mother's pain,
> And yet brought forth less than a mother's hope,
> To wit, an undigested and deformèd lump,
> Not like the fruit of such a goodly tree.

> Teeth hadst thou in thy head when thou wast born,
> To signify thou cam'st to bite the world.
> And, if the rest be true which I have heard,
> Thou cam'st—
>
> (V, vi, 37–56)

This is quite enough for Richard. 'I'll hear no more. Die, prophet, in thy speech.' And stabs him. One feels that it is the only way this kind of uncompromising moral force can be stopped—pure principle silenced by pure power. This is the final issue of these wars. The prophet dying in his speech may not be quite a tragic death, but it has a dignity not accorded to any of the other victims of the play.

Richard—it is his last soliloquy in this play—accepts the birth, identity, and destiny outlined for him by Henry. He remembers being told he was born with teeth:

> which plainly signified
> That I should snarl and bite and play the dog.
> Then, since the heavens have shaped my body so,
> Let hell make crook'd my mind to answer it.
> I have no brother, I am like no brother;
> And this word 'love', which graybeards call divine,
> Be resident in men like one another
> And not in me: I am myself alone.
>
> (V, vi, 76–83)

I am myself alone. This is the first time but far from the last, that these words are heard in Shakespeare. A certain kind of hard, Renaissance individualism is beginning to speak out, and it can take frightening forms.

The very last scene shows King Edward comfortably enthroned—'Now am I seated as my soul delights'—talking of autumn and harvests and 'lasting joy'. He points to his young baby who will reap the gain of their labours. Richard has his own ideas about that, as expressed in an aside to the audience:

> I'll blast his harvest, if your head were laid,
> For yet I am not looked on in the world.

> This shoulder was ordained so thick to heave,
> And heave it shall some weight, or break my back.
> Work thou the way, and that shalt execute.
>   (V, vii, 21–5)

And when he is invited to kiss the baby, he is ready—with the Judas kiss.

> And, that I love the tree from whence thou sprang'st,
> Witness the loving kiss I give the fruit.
> [*Aside*] To say the truth, so Judas kissed his master,
> And cried, "All hail!" whenas he meant all harm.
>   (V, vii, 31–4)

Richard, unashamedly intending 'all harm', can, by this time, hardly wait to take over the whole historic show. And, by this time, the audience, perhaps, can hardly wait to watch him do it.

RICHARD III (1592–4)

Edward IV reigned for quite a long time—some twenty years in all. When Henry VI finally died (was murdered), in 1471, Edward was at last secure and undistracted on the throne; and for the dozen years until his death he was quite a popular king reigning over a stable and recovering England. I mentioned that Hall had a different epithet for the reigns of each of the kings he deals with, and it is worth noting that 'The troublesome season of King Henry the Sixth' is followed by 'The prosperous reign of King Edward the Fourth'. There is *nothing* of this in Shakespeare, and he lets all Edward's good kingly years quietly drop away. Shakespeare's Edward performs effectively only two significant acts—he capitulates shamelessly to his lust for Lady Grey and marries her, and, near the start of *Richard III,* he dies. And that is all. This is seldom commented on, and, indeed, it is hard, *now,* to imagine an *Edward IV* coming between *Henry VI,* and *Richard III.* Yet it is worth a moment's speculation. Perhaps Shakespeare found Edward dramatically uninteresting. But we can be certain that he wanted nothing—for example, a tolerably successful pragmatist—to get in the way of the dramatic contrast between the two extreme types engendered by the wars—meek martyr Henry, and monster Machiavel Richard. At the start of *Richard III,* Henry VI is finally dead and, *as if immediately following this* (in fact it was ten years later), Richard takes over centre-stage, and starts to run literally everything. And there is one more consideration. If Richard was just a singularly nasty historical interruption (to a decade of peace and recovery under Edward), rather than the culmination and final flower of a long-gathering evil (as Shakespeare wants us to feel), then Richmond is less the agent of God, finally bringing peace and reconciliation, and, frankly, more just another Machiavellian, moving in to take over a land in a mess. For all sorts of reasons, Shakespeare does not want his tetralogy to conclude on such a note. His Richmond *is* part of a larger pattern. But, as we contemplate the triumphalist end, it might be worth remembering that the other, less providential, account was probably nearer to the truth of the matter.

Richard III is Shakespeare's longest history play. Indeed, it is longer than any of his plays except *Hamlet,* and it is entirely dominated by Richard, rising and falling. He appears in fourteen out of twenty-five scenes, and even when he is not actually present, his shadow hangs over everything. He speaks nearly a third of the lines—i.e. about one thousand out of some three thousand, six hundred. This is completely Richard's play. Shakespeare actually devises more villainies for him than the sources offered. Apart from that, the only scenes which Shakespeare invented are—the wooing of Anne, Clarence's dream, the wailing queens, and the second wooing scene. But it should be noted from the outset that, although the play covers two years of multiplying and accelerating horrors, we see none of them—nothing which might give rise to direct pathos or horror—on stage. Indeed, the only person who actually dies on stage is Richard himself; and that takes place in a flash of dumb-show at the start of the last scene—no death speech for Richard—so that one would be justified in wondering if one had actually seen it. Richard is a very violent man; and yet the play resolutely refuses to allow any of that violence to leak on to the stage. Whatever else, Shakespeare clearly wanted to forestall and prevent any simple 'oh my God, whatever next?' sort of response on the part of the audience. There is nothing to blur and shake us out of sustained, intelligent appreciation.

Early in the third Act, Richard openly acknowledges his theatrical-historical legacy from the Morality play: 'Thus, like the formal Vice, Iniquity, I moralize two meanings in one word' (III, i, 82–3). The Vice was

the self-avowed mischief-maker, if not chaos-bringer, and we should remember that one of his satanic privileges was to inveigle the audience into
laughing at evil. The figure of the Vice was clearly invaluable to Shakespeare when it came to depicting inexplicable evil, evil which seems gratuitous, unmotivated, simply for its own sake. From any point of view, Richard's behaviour is profoundly irrational, and is finally both horrifying and
incomprehensible even to his closest accomplices (in fact, no one is close to
him at all; simply, some accompany him further into his evils than others).
Richard is, as he has told us, an expert Machiavel; he is also a Senecan tyrant
and a Marlovian villain (closest to Barabas in *The Jew of Malta*). But he is
primarily a Vice. However—and this is crucial—he is a Vice who acquires
(no matter how foully) the legitimate robes of a king. 'On the face of it, he
is the demon-Prince, the cacodemon born of hell, the misshapen toad, etc.
(all things ugly and ill). But through his prowess as actor and his embodi-
ments of the comic Vice and impish-to-fiendish humour, he offers the false
as more attractive than the true (the actor's function), and the ugly and evil
as admirable and amusing (the clown's game of value reversals)' (A. P. Rossiter, *Angel with Horns,* p. 20).

Shakespeare emphasizes Richard the actor. When Richard and Buckingham 'dress up' in 'rotten armor, marvellous ill-favored', as if having prepared in desperate haste to defend themselves against an armed plot, Richard briefs Buckingham:

> Come, cousin, canst thou quake and change thy color,
> Murder thy breath in middle of a word,
> And then again begin, and stop again,
> As if thou wert distraught and mad with terror?

Buckingham knows the game:

> Tut, I can counterfeit the deep tragedian,
> Speak and look back, and pry on every side,
> Tremble and start at wagging of a straw,
> Intending deep suspicion. Ghastly looks
> Are at my service, like enforcèd smiles;
> And both are ready in their offices
> At any time to grace my stratagems.
>   (III, v, 1–11)

Buckingham is, of all the nobles, most fitted to be Richard's henchman and accomplice in crime. Though, of course, Richard finally has his head cut off as well.

We might just stay with the death of Buckingham, since in some ways it is exemplary of an important part of the atmosphere of the play. Asked by the dying King Edward to swear devotion to Queen Elizabeth and the children, Buckingham formulates a rather elaborate oath. He turns to the queen:

> Whenever Buckingham doth turn his hate
> Upon your Grace . . .
>   God punish me
> With hate in those where I expect most love!
> When I have most need to employ a friend,
> And most assurèd that he is a friend,
> Deep, hollow, treacherous, and full of guile
> Be he unto me! This do I beg of God,
> When I am cold in zeal to you or yours.
>   (II, i, 32–40)

This is *exactly* what happens, when Richard, to whom his dedication has been complete, murderously turns on him. Buckingham recognizes this terrible irony:

> That high All-seer which I dallied with
> Hath turned my feignèd prayer upon my head
> And given in earnest what I begged in jest.
>   (V, i, 20–22)

Something very similar happens to Anne. Confronted by Richard's preposterous proposal of marriage, she makes a mighty curse of misery for any future wife of Richard's. She becomes that wife and discovers she has 'proved the subject of mine own soul's curse' (IV, i, 80). She is finally whisked off to death so quietly, you could be forgiven for not noticing it had happened. Such dire reversals of intention are characteristic. They are, suggests Rossiter, 'on precisely the pattern of the repeated reversals of human expectation, the reversals of events, the anticipated reversals (foreseen only by the audience), which makes "dramatic irony"'. Rossiter mentions

Buckingham, whose words 'have been reversed into actuality', and goes on:
'The same irony plays all over *Richard III.* It lurks like a shadow behind
the naively self-confident Hastings; it hovers a moment over Buckingham
when Margaret warns him against "yonder dog" (Richard), and, on Richard's asking what she said, he replies, "Nothing that I respect, my gracious
lord" (I, iii, 295)—and this at a time when Buckingham is under no threat
whatever. Its cumulative effect is to present the personages as existing in a
state of total and terrible uncertainty.' It *is* a terrible state, spreading out like
a toxic fog to affect the ordinary citizens, one of whom says:

> Truly, the hearts of men are full of fear.
> You cannot reason, almost, with a man
> That looks not heavily and full of dread.
>   (II, iii, 38–40)

Mostly, the people stand silently—waiting for the worst.

Richard starts the play with forty lines on his own, and he has a number
of important soliloquies in the first three scenes. The stage is his. His first
speech affords us an important insight into the man. Everything is fine,
now, in Edward's court, and everyone is happy:

> But I, that am not shaped for sportive tricks
> Nor made to court an amorous looking glass;
> I, that am rudely stamped, and want love's majesty
> To strut before a wanton ambling nymph;
> I, that am curtailed of this proportion,
> Cheated of feature by dissembling Nature,
> Deformed, unfinished, sent before my time
> Into this breathing world scarce half made up,
> And that so lamely and unfashionable
> That dogs bark at me as I halt by them;
> Why, I, in this weak piping time of peace,
> Have no delight to pass away the time
> Unless to spy my shadow in the sun
> And descant on mine own deformity.
> And therefore, since I cannot prove a lover

To entertain these fair well-spoken days,

I am determinèd to prove a villain

And hate the idle pleasures of these days.

(I, i, 14–31)

These are not the words of a man seething with anger, or boiling with resentment. He is as cool as could be. He is *bored*. He is capable of changes of mood of lightning-like suddenness and unpredictability—always disturbing. But—until he becomes king—he is always icily in control. He is elegant, mannered, even fastidious—you will never find a drop of blood on *his* hands. He just wants something fully to engage his intelligence and energies. He wants his fun, and it's going to be dark fun.

As I am subtle, false, and treacherous,

This day should Clarence closely be mewed up . . .

(I, i, 3–8)

Sit back and watch. Richard's play is about to begin.

His first 'scene' is almost too easy. Clarence is on his way to the Tower, and Richard sympathizes deeply, though he faked the 'evidence' and contrived the arrest. Clarence has no idea what is going on, and as, all-bemused, he is led away, Richard permits himself a joke:

Simple plain Clarence, I do love thee so

That I will shortly send thy soul to heaven,

If heaven will take the present at our hands.

(I, i, 118–20)

Clarence, alas, is a knock-over. But what follows offers a supreme, histrionic challenge. He determines to woo and win the hand of Anne, whose husband and father-in-law he personally murdered. As a project, it sounds not only deeply distasteful, but utterly impossible. Richard rises to the challenge. (Anne, incidentally, is depicted as taking the body of Henry VI from St Paul's to the abbey at Chertsey. Although Henry has been long dead, Shakespeare wants, as I have suggested, to give us the sense of passing almost immediately from Henry dead to Richard rampant. Anne's sense of outrage certainly seem very fresh.) How Richard wins over Anne, who only has reasons to loathe and execrate him, involves a dazzling, bravura performance on Richard's part (and on Shakespeare's—it is all his invention). You've never seen anything quite like that. Breathtaking. Richard is even rather impressed at himself.

> Was ever woman in this humor wooed?
> Was ever woman in this humor won?
> I'll have her, but I will not keep her long.
> What! I that killed her husband and his father
> To take her in her heart's extremest hate,
> With curses in her mouth, tears in her eyes,
> The bleeding witness of my hatred by,
> Having God, her conscience, and these bars against me,
> And I no friends to back my suit at all
> But the plain devil and dissembling looks,
> And yet to win her, all the world to nothing!
> Ha!
>
>   (I, ii, 227–38)

There's the satisfaction—that of the supreme gambler. The odds against his success must have been thousands to one—no, everything to nothing. Yet he pulled it off! Ha!

Richard shows himself in yet another role—the injured innocent—in the next scene. Queen Elizabeth and some nobles are wondering gloomily what will happen if Edward dies and Richard takes over as Protector, when Richard bursts in, almost beside himself, as it seems, with aggrieved fury.

> They do me wrong, and I will not endure it!
> Who is it that complains unto the King
> That I, forsooth, am stern, and love them not?
> By holy Paul, they love his Grace but lightly
> That fill his ears with such dissentious rumors.
> Because I cannot flatter and look fair,
> Smile in men's faces, smooth, deceive, and cog,
> Duck with French nods and apish courtesy,
> I must be held a rancorous enemy.
> Cannot a plain man live and think no harm

> But thus his simple truth must be abused
> With silken, sly, insinuating Jacks?
> . . .
> When have I injured thee? When done thee wrong?
> Or thee? Or thee? Or any of your faction?
> A plague upon you all!
>
> (I, iii, 42–58)

And he scatters accusations and imputations all over them. It is all shameless, outrageous stuff, of course—a farrago of nonsense from out of nowhere. But the ferocity of the performance leaves his listeners helpless, and quite unable to answer in any adequate way. And indeed, subjected to such a mad torrent of simulated suspicions and fantasized outrage, it is hard to think where they would begin. Frightening, really. Out of nothing this man can do anything. (I will note here that it is in this scene that old Queen Margaret starts to speak out against Richard. Hers is the voice Richard can never silence, and she haunts him throughout the play. This is quite anachronistic, since she died in 1482 and in fact never returned to England after being ransomed years before. But I will return to the importance of Queen Margaret.) Richard is sufficiently pleased at how things went, as he soliloquizes:

> I do the wrong, and first begin to brawl.
> The secret mischiefs that I set abroach
> I lay unto the grievous charge of others
> . . .
> But then I sigh, and with a piece of Scripture
> Tell them that God bids us do good for evil;
> And thus I clothe my naked villainy
> With odd old ends stol'n forth of holy writ,
> And seem a saint when most I play the devil.
>
> (I, iii, 323–5, 333–7)

This man turns evil into an art.

For the first time in the play Richard is absent, for the last scene of the first Act. This is entirely as it should be, since, for the first and only time, we see one of his murderous orders being executed. Usually, all we see is the almost ritual marching off of people to what will be called in *Henry VIII* 'the long divorce of steel'. Here we see some of Richard's nasty business being done for him, as the two murderers enter the Tower to deal with Clarence. Clarence's dream, which he describes to his keeper before the arrival of the murderers, is another of Shakespeare's extraordinary inventions. In dreaming that Richard actually pushed him overboard to drown on a turbulent Channel crossing, Clarence reveals the accuracy of his unconscious fears. He describes the horror of drowning, and the greater horrors that awaited him in the realm after death as the reproachful ghosts gathered:

> "Clarence is come, false, fleeting, perjured Clarence,
> That stabbed me in the field by Tewkesbury.
> Seize on him, Furies, take him into torment!"
>   (I, iv, 55–7)

It is like a massive explosion of conscience as the denied guilt of an evil life comes flooding into the helpless mind. I take it that Shakespeare thought the case of Clarence would serve as exemplary of what must have been the hidden state of mind of many of those around Richard.

Clarence sleeps, and the murderers enter. The Second Murderer seems disinclined to go through with the job—he feels 'a kind of remorse' and is resolved to let Clarence live. He *wants* to go ahead, but is impeded by 'some certain dregs of conscience . . . yet within me' (I, iv, 122). Then the First Murderer reminds him of the promised reward, and the Second Murderer immediately regains his resolve. The exchange that follows is very important:

> *First M.* Where's thy conscience now?
> *Second M.* O, in the Duke of Gloucester's purse.
> *First M.* When he opens his purse to give us our reward, thy conscience flies
>   out.
> *Second M.* 'Tis no matter, let it go. There's few or none will entertain it.
> *First M.* What if it come to thee again?
> *Second M.* I'll not meddle with it; it makes a man a coward. A man cannot
>   steal, but it accuseth him; a man cannot swear, but it checks him; a man
>   cannot lie with his neighbor's wife, but it detects him. 'Tis a blushing
>   shamefaced spirit that mutinies in a man's bosom. It fills a man full of

> obstacles. It made me once restore a purse of gold that, by chance, I
> found. It beggars any man that keeps it. It is turned out of towns and cit-
> ies for a dangerous thing, and every man that means to live well endeav-
> ors to trust himself and live without it.
>
> (I, iv, 129–46)

What *has* happened to conscience in this world? Has it been turned out of towns and banished the land? There seems precious little of it around, though there are vestigial flashes and 'dregs' of it, as in the Second Mur- derer, and these become increasingly important. The light of conscience never quite goes out entirely. The Murderers finally manage to stab Clar- ence (the only stabbing we see on stage in this play—contrast the *Henry VI* trilogy), though he presumably expires off-stage in his famous butt of malmsey. But the Second Murderer does not stab, and deplores 'this most grievous murder'. To the First Murderer he says: 'Take thou the fee. . . For I repent me that the Duke is slain' (I, iv, 280–81). He may not wish to 'med- dle' with conscience, but he cannot prevent conscience from meddling with him.

Shakespeare was clearly fascinated by the question of whether there could be a man *completely* devoid of conscience (i.e. not conscience totally repressed, but just nothing there at all). Iago appears to be his only conces- sion that such a monstrous aberration might occur. Richard seems another candidate, and he certainly shows no trace or hint of conscience throughout the play. But on the eve of the battle of Bosworth (when he will die), in a dream-troubled night of which Clarence's nightmare seems an early adum- bration, the avenging ghosts of Richard's victims return to accuse him and he finds his conscience tormentingly awake:

> O coward conscience, how dost thou afflict me!
> . . .
> My conscience hath a thousand several tongues,
> And every tongue brings in a several tale,
> And every tale condemns me for a villain.
>
> (V, iii, 180, 194–6)

There was a Richard who would have been quite unmoved by any inward voice telling him he was a villain. Indeed, it was his chosen ambition. But this Richard is a broken man, and he cannot cope with a sudden outburst of something he had never looked to have.

How and why does Richard collapse? It is certainly something *in* Richard, since there is not a figure in the play, up to his gaining of the crown, who is capable of mounting anything remotely like significant opposition to him. Richard carries on with his plottings and ordered beheadings—ever the dark play-master—until he is finally crowned in Act IV. But it should be noticed that at every step, some accomplice seems to hold back. The defection of the Second Murderer is the first sign; then Hastings refuses to see him crowned; Buckingham baulks at murdering the princes. They are finally murdered by Tyrrel who, in a long speech, expresses his horror at 'the tyrannous and bloody act . . . [this] deed of piteous massacre' (IV, iii, 1–2). Such compunction is completely alien to the pitiless Richard, who is unmoved by the deed. He has become very frightening. But, as he climbs, he empties his world. In *A Kingdom for a Stage* Robert Ornstein puts it well: 'each of Richard's triumphs is purchased with a diminishing Machiavellian capital, and though his political debts are self-liquidating, so too are his political assets. When he gains the pinnacle of power, he stands alone, isolated from other men by his criminality, and hated by those whose allegiance he nominally commands.' As a matter of fact, Richard begins to crack up the very minute he ascends to the throne, but just prior to that we have had two unmistakable signs that he has hit his limit.

In a very short scene, a Scrivener comes on stage with a paper in hand. It is the entirely false 'indictment of the good Lord Hastings', whom Richard has had beheaded. The Scrivener is revolted by his task:

> Who is so gross
> That cannot see this palpable device?
> Yet who so bold but says he sees it not?
> Bad is the world, and all will come to nought
> When such ill dealing must be seen in thought.
>   (III, vi, 10–14)

The moral outrage of anonymous servants at the cruel and shameless doing of their 'superiors' is very important in Shakespeare (absolutely crucial in *King Lear*), and at this moment we realize that the whole world is beginning to see through Richard. In the next scene, Buckingham reports back to Richard concerning the response of the London citizens to the proclamation that Richard will be king. 'The citizens are mum, say not a word . . . they spake not a word,/But like dumb statues or breathing stones/Stared each on other and looked deadly pale' (III, vii, 3, 24–6). This bodes very badly for Richard, since without the 'acclaim' of the people of London, no man could truly be king of England, whatever his claim. Richard will never *really* be king.

As Buckingham hands Richard to the throne, Richard's very first words are:

> But shall we wear these glories for a day?
> Or shall they last, and we rejoice in them?
>   (IV, ii, 5–6)

This is something new, and potentially fatal, in Richard—anxiety, loss of nerve. He immediately, and utterly pointlessly, decides to test Buckingham, the one man above all others who helped him to the throne. He asks him to murder the princes. 'Shall I be plain? I wish the bastards dead' (IV, ii, 18). Even Buckingham draws back at this—'Give me some little breath, some pause, dear lord' (IV, ii, 24)—and Richard immediately, insanely, catastrophically, sets down Buckingham in his mind as an enemy. He has gratuitously alienated his most loyal accomplice. And he is letting his uncertain emotions show: 'The King is angry. See he gnaws his lip' (IV, ii, 27). He becomes permanently irritable, something quite different from the earlier cool, controlled master of his moods. He responds indecisively to news of invasions, and, disastrous for an actor-director, seems to be forgetting his lines:

> *Ratcliffe.* What, may I please you, shall I do at Salisbury?
> *Rich.* Why, what wouldst thou do there before I go?
> *Rat.* Your Highness told me I should post before.
> *Rich.* My mind is changed.
>   (IV, iv, 453–6)

He no longer knows his own mind: his usually deft plotting hand is faltering. He tries one more wooing, but it entirely lacks the old panache (he thinks he has succeeded, but there is every reason to think that Elizabeth is simply playing for time). He begins to rely on wine:

> Give me a bowl of wine.
> I have not that alacrity of spirit
> Nor cheer of mind that I was wont to have.
>   (V, iii, 72–4)

He used to be *all* 'alacrity of spirit', and for such a figure to be reduced to relying on stimulants is a terrible falling-off. His desperate attempts to cheer himself up with false jocular bravado—'Norfolk, we must have knocks; ha, must we not?' (V, iii, 5)—are simply embarrassing. Where is the imperturbable satanic wit of yester-year? He is finally reduced to the supreme indignity of spying on his own troops, to see if any are disloyal:

> Under our tents I'll play the easedropper
> To see if any mean to shrink from me.
>   (V, iii, 222–3)

This hopeless creature is not even a shadow of his former self. (There are just one or two Macbeth-like hints—'But I am in / So far in blood that sin will pluck on sin' (IV, ii, 62–3); and his anger at the messengers who bring him bad news—'Out on ye, owls! Nothing but songs of death?' (IV, iv, 507). But Richard, while he has also been a bad man and a king, has nothing of Macbeth's extraordinary, searching subjectivity.)

When he wakes up from his dreadful dream, the night before the battle of Bosworth, he reveals a state of almost total mental disintegration:

> What do I fear? Myself? There's none else by.
> Richard loves Richard: that is, I am I.
> Is there a murderer here? No. Yes, I am.
> Then fly. What, from myself? Great reason why!
> Lest I revenge. What, myself upon myself?
> Alack, I love myself. Wherefore? For any good
> That I myself have done unto myself?
> O no! Alas, I rather hate myself
> For hateful deeds committed by myself.

> I am a villain. Yet I lie, I am not.
> Fool, of thyself speak well. Fool, do not flatter.
>
> (V, iii, 183–93)

'I am myself alone.' Whatever happened? Is this where such proud, supreme individualism, or impossible egoism, ends? Call it schizophrenia, call it what you like, but this is the self in complete tatters and fragments. Richard, himself alone, the supreme impresario of evil, is ending in gibberish.

Richard was at his best, his most brilliantly adroitly active, in reaching out for a seemingly impossibly remote crown. But he is a completely hopeless king. The minute he takes on that role, he suffers a vertiginous loss of control. Clearly, all his genius is for plotting: he has none at all for ruling. John Danby once made the point that 'in Richard . . . the corruption of his time is made aware of itself. This is the ambiguity of his role: to be the logical outcome of his society, and yet a pariah rejected by his society; a hypocrite, yet more sincere in his self-awareness than those he ruins and deceives.' There is an important point here, though it is overstated. In no way is Richard *representative* of his society—he is an aberration, a monster, a permanent outsider. He seems not even to understand what society might be for. But it is true that everyone in the play (except, of course, the princes —and Richmond) is in some way guilty, tainted by the times. It is certainly significant that the word 'guilty' occurs more times in this play than in any other by Shakespeare. Richard manipulates an already fairly rotten world.

As well as Richard's darting, flashing, seemingly improvised way of talking, there is another kind of rhetoric which runs continuously throughout the play, against which Richard's individual voice is heard. This is a formal, incantatory, marmorealizing, ritualized, choric rhetoric of lamentation and mourning, most closely associated with the wailing queens. Dominant here is Queen Margaret, a Senecan Fury, a hideous archaic figure howling for revenge, who is in some ways the voice of the past—of all the treachery and pitiless cruelty and bloody butchery of the long years of civil war. She haunts Richard, who can ignore, but not silence, her. Every word she speaks drips with blood, and she merely hates Richard as a dog rather than condemning him for being a villain. Some quite other voice is needed if England is to break through into a different future.

That voice, of course, is Richmond's. He has been untouched, uncontaminated by the civil wars—this was an important part of the Tudor myth—and can enter as a clean figure, with unbloodied hands. Shakespeare had prepared his audience for the important role Richmond would play, in *Henry VI,* in which King Henry singles out the young Earl of Richmond:

> Come hither, England's hope. (*Lays his hand on his head.*)
>   If secret powers
> Suggest but truth to my divining thoughts,
> This pretty lad will prove our country's bliss.
> His looks are full of peaceful majesty,
> His head by nature framed to wear a crown,
> His hand to wield a scepter, and himself
> Likely in time to bless a regal throne.
> Make much of him, my lords, for this is he
> Must help you more than you are hurt by me.
>   (*Henry VI,* Part 3, IV, vi, 68–76)

And Somerset immediately resolves to send Richmond away from the gathering anarchy of England:

> Forthwith we'll send him hence to Brittany,
> Till storms be past of civil enmity.
>   (IV, vi, 97–8)

He is thus the appropriate person to come back to England, finish off Richard, clear up his mess, and restore peace and concord to the land. Marrying Elizabeth, he is the pious reconciler. As he makes clear in the last speech of the play:

> And then, as we have ta'en the sacrament,
> We will unite the White Rose and the Red.
> Smile heaven upon this fair conjunction,
> That long have frowned upon their enmity!
> What traitor hears me and says not amen?
> England hath long been mad and scarred herself;
> The brother blindly shed the brother's blood,

> The father rashly slaughtered his own son,
> The son, compelled, been butcher to the sire.
> All this divided York and Lancaster,
> Divided in their dire division,
> O, now let Richmond and Elizabeth,
> The true succeeders of each royal house,
> By God's fair ordinance conjoin together!
> . . .
> Now civil wounds are stopped, peace lives again;
> That she may long live here, God say amen!
>   (V, v, 18–31, 40–41)

So ends the play, and so begins the Tudor peace. So much was orthodox Elizabethan history, and Shakespeare is happy enough to bring his tetralogy to a conclusion in this way. But it is worth saying one or two things about Shakespeare's Richmond. Although he notionally overcomes Richard, we see no battle (only Richard, famously crying for a horse), and Richmond can hardly be said to 'defeat' Richard who, indeed, rises and falls all by himself. We see nothing of Richmond as a soldier or general, and, indeed, he is hardly individuated at all. He is a curiously transparent figure—more like a principle of Good than a man of action. It is important that he justifies himself as *God's* soldier, fighting against 'God's enemy', 'a bloody tyrant and a homicide'—if a king was a 'tyrant', there was justification for insurrection against him. Richmond must represent his campaign as a crusade and not a coup. He does not offer any genealogical claims to the throne (he had none), and his (doubtful) legitimacy rests on his moral and religious authority. He is not a chivalric hero of the old school—no need to be back to *that*. Something new and post-feudal is called for. He seems to come more from a spiritual realm than a political one. Most importantly, he is just what England needs—someone untouched by the dynastic feuds which have ruined the country. He promises the indispensable fresh start.

I do not want to suggest that Shakespeare is undermining or mocking the Tudor myth (he is perhaps attenuating it), and its insistence that there was a providential pattern running through English history which had to culminate in the blessed arrival of the Tudors. He respects and accepts the frame of that orthodoxy—it is hard to see how he could not have—and Richmond duly takes over. But as we watch the play, we hardly feel we are seeing

God's long plan working itself out through English history (the feeling of the whole tetralogy is much more Aeschylean than biblical). As an individual, Richard is too irruptive, disruptive, to participate in, or confirm, any pattern. With his demonic humour and uncontainable energies, he threatens to make a nonsense of the wished-for processional solemnities of history. He challenges all framings and certainties, and with his effortless inversion of any accepted moral order, he brings in ironies and ambiguities everywhere. He has brought Shakespeare to write a new form of what Rossiter calls 'comic history', and, in time, he will develop into Iago, and then Macbeth—as Shakespeare seems to discover that the real truth of history is tragedy.

KING JOHN (1594–6)

If *Richard III* and the three parts of *Henry VI* lead up to the Tudor triumph, *King John* foreshadows it in complex ways. It is not surprising that Shakespeare took the reign of King John (1199–1216) as the subject for a history play. As far as the Tudors were concerned, John was the one British king before Henry VIII who had defied the Pope, and the Protestant chroniclers had made a pre-Reformation hero out of him. (Catholic writers stressed John's subsequent re-surrender of his crown to the Pope, which meant that Henry VIII was only a vassal and his Reformation a civil and ecclesiastical rebellion.) John Bale's *Kynge Johan,* first written in 1536 (two years after Henry VIII's Act of Supremacy), is arguably the first time the history play begins to emerge from the Morality play, as it concentrates on an actual king in a specific historical moment (that Bale's King John bears little resemblance to what we know of the actual John is not, here, relevant). It was a violently anti-Catholic play which praised John for his opposition to the Pope, and his attack on the abuses of the Church. *The Troublesome Raigne of King John of England* was published anonymously in 1591, and it supports Bale's picture of John as a victim of papal and French plots and ambition. But it also, following Holinshed's more critical account of John, shows him to be a weak and violent man, who could alternate between a resourceful alacrity of response and a fatal inertia. After John expediently submits to the Pope's legate, Pandulph, everything goes wrong for him, until he is poisoned by a monk (for Protestant apologists, this made him a martyr to the Catholics). Most scholars have regarded this as Shakespeare's source-play, which he studied and re-wrote.

There were also perceived similarities between the reigns of John and Elizabeth which gave the play a topical bite. Like John, Elizabeth defied the Pope and was excommunicated, with the Pope promising her murderer canonization; and, like John, she was attacked by a Catholic monarch (Philip II of Spain) who tried to invade England, but whose armada was destroyed at sea (as is the armada of Philip of France in the play). In addition, neither John nor Elizabeth were entirely secure in their claims to the throne, and both had rivals supported by Catholics. John's rival claimant was Arthur, son of his elder brother Geoffrey, who was supported by King Philip of France and the Papacy. Elizabeth's rival was Mary Stuart, Queen of Scots, supported by the Spanish King and Papacy (and many English Catholics). Both claimants or pretenders were barred from the crown by a royal will. John's desire for Arthur's death, and subsequent remorse for it, could be seen as comparable to Elizabeth's handling of the problem of Mary Stuart—by execution—and subsequent troubled feelings (Irving Ribner says that 'adherents of the cause of Mary . . . had traditionally used John's treatment of Arthur as an example of usurpation parallel to Elizabeth's treatment of Mary Stuart'). There were further similarities—between the position of Hubert, ordered by John to murder Arthur and then violently blamed by the King for having (as he thinks) done it; and Secretary Davidson, who was rumoured to have been persuaded by Elizabeth to have Mary murdered, but who was subsequently made a scapegoat, fined and imprisoned. Bullough thinks that some of these allusions, or similarities, were too dangerous for Shakespeare to have intended them; but, for the informed eye, they were—and are—undoubtedly there to see.

King John has been called Shakespeare's most unhistorical play. It certainly plays fast and loose with facts and time. It is incredibly compressed. One scene, for instance (Act IV, ii), brings together events which cover just about John's whole reign: the seeing of the five moons (1200); the death of Constance (1201); the (rumoured) death of Arthur and the second coronation of John (1202); the death of John's mother, Elinor (1204); the Peter of Pomfret episode (1213); and the landing of the French (1216). In the last century, one P. A. Daniel pointed out that the whole reign is made to seem a matter of a few months, and that the action actually requires only seven separate days, with intervals. Shakespeare sometimes liked to collapse and foreshorten historic time in this dramatic way (most notoriously in *Othello*), and here it serves to jam cause and effect very tightly together.

To what end? John emerges as a very defective king. At times, he fulfills his traditional, dignified monarchical role and issues ringing defiance to his enemies. But for the most part he is shown as weak and treacherous—mean, manipulative, and opportunistic—before his final collapse into utter impotence, and poisoned madness. He does defy the Pope—but for purely political and financial reasons; and he is quick to hand his crown back to Pandulph, the papal legate, when expediency demands. The increasingly discontented barons duly defect from John and go over to the French, and England is consequently, and shamefully, invaded. (It is notable that Shakespeare never mentions Magna Carta (1215), forced on John by the nobles to retain their ancient rights.) England is finally saved by the timely sinking of the French supply ships, the adroit political manoeuvring of Pandulph, and the revelation of the French lord Melun which sends the rebellious English barons hurrying back to the English side. No great victories: no outstanding heroes.

John Masefield thought the play to be primarily a study in treachery, and, indeed, it is full of traitors and turncoats; changing sides, yielding to shifting solicitations and pressures, breaking oaths as soon as they have made them, abandoning sworn loyalties as the wind changes. Some examples of completely hollow rituals of allegiance would include: Arthur willingly embracing Austria (who killed his father); the cynical marriage of Lewis and Blanche; Philip's oath to Constance ('In her right we came,/Which we, God knows, have turned another way,/To our own vantage': II, i, 548–50); John forcing new oaths of allegiance out of his nobles at his second coronation; John's show of renewed allegiance to the Pope as he hands his crown back to Pandulph; and the revelation of the dying Melun to the English lords which, though a good deed in itself (he confesses that the French intend to kill the defecting English lords once victory has been achieved), does break his oath to the Dauphin, who in turn intended to break his oath to the English nobles, who had already broken their oaths of loyalty to the English king—showing, graphically enough, how one broken oath leads to another!

This aspect of the atmosphere of the play is best exemplified by the exchange between the French king, Philip, and the papal legatee, Pandulph.

Peace between England and France has just been sealed by the marriage
of Blanche and the Dauphin. Pandulph enters, demanding to know why
John has spurned the Pope's choice in the appointing of the new Archbishop of Canterbury. John is peremptorily dismissive—'no Italian priest
/Shall tithe or toll in our dominions' etc. (this was the sort of defiant stuff
the English Protestants loved). Pandulph duly curses and excommunicates
John (though, of course, he will later help him); and he orders the Catholic Philip to turn his forces against the English king. To his credit, Philip
is torn:

> I am perplexed, and know not what to say
> . . .
> This royal hand and mine are newly knit,
> And the conjunction of our inward souls
> Married in league, coupled and linked together
> With all religious strength of sacred vows;
> The latest breath that gave the sound of words
> Was deep-sworn faith, peace, amity, true love
> Between our kingdoms and our royal selves
> . . .
> And shall these hands, so lately purged of blood,
> So newly joined in love, so strong in both,
> Unyoke this seizure and this kind regreet?
> *Play fast and loose with faith?* so jest with heaven,
> *Make such unconstant children of ourselves*
> As now again to snatch our palm from palm,
> *Unswear faith sworn,* and on the marriage bed
> Of smiling peace to march a bloody host,
> And make a riot on the gentle brow
> Of true sincerity?
> 　　　　(III, i, 147, 152–8, 165–74—my italics)

Surely not. It would be intolerable so to turn the back on all the values a
Christian king is supposed to believe in. But Pandulph is adamant. Let go
of England's hand, and prepare to fight. Philip still complains, resists:

> I may disjoin my hand, but not my faith.

To which Pandulph replies with a masterpiece of casuistry which is one of the central speeches of the play.

> So mak'st thou faith an enemy to faith,
> And like a civil war set'st oath to oath,
> Thy tongue against thy tongue . . .
> What since thou swor'st is sworn against thyself
> And may not be performèd by thyself,
> For that which thou has sworn to do amiss
> Is not amiss when it is truly done;
> And being not done, when doing tends to ill,
> The truth is then most done not doing it.
> The better act of purposes mistook
> Is to mistake again; though indirect,
> Yet indirection thereby grows direct,
> *And falsehood falsehood cures,* as fire cools fire
> Within the scorched veins of one new burned.
> It is religion that doth make vows kept,
> But thou hast sworn against religion
> (By what thou swear'st against the thing thou swear'st)
> And mak'st an oath the surety for thy truth
> (Against an oath the truth); thou art unsure
> To swear—swears only not to be forsworn,
> Else what a mockery should it be to swear!
> But thou dost swear only to be forsworn,
> And most forsworn, to keep what thou dost swear . . .
>   (III, i, 189–213—my italics)

and endlessly more of the same. This was the kind of Jesuitical 'equivocation' which drove Elizabethan Protestants mad. Philip duly capitulates— 'England, I will fall from thee'. In an atmosphere in which such a speech can dominate and prevail, it is going to be very hard to work out, or hold onto, what might genuinely constitute 'honour', 'loyalty', 'true duty', not to mention 'majesty' and 'nobility'. It is all very unedifying.

If this is all there was to it, it would be a lowering play indeed; and one might well have asked—what was Shakespeare trying to show—if not, more simply, why did he write the play? But I have yet to mention its most important feature—the invention of the Bastard, Philip Faulconbridge, supposedly the illegitimate son of Richard Coeur de Lion, the previous king. There is simply a brief reference in Holinshed to the effect that 'Philip, bastard sonne to king Richard . . . killed the vicount of Limoges, in revenge of his father's death.' The author of *The Troublesome Raigne* developed this hint into a dynamic character who both brings comic relief, and manifests heroic energy. Shakespeare took this figure and, in turn, developed him into, arguably, his most powerfully original creation to date. Critics and commentators have compared and related him to numerous other Shakespearian characters: these include—Petruchio, Berowne, Mercutio, Falstaff, Touchstone, Jaques, Autolycus, and Henry V (he is contrasted with the bad bastards, Don John and Edmund). Of these, the most relevant as far as I am concerned are—it sounds a curious conjunction—Falstaff and Henry V. But Shakespeare has clearly created a complex, multi-faceted character who is in many ways seminal for his own work.

Before considering the Bastard, I must point to two highly relevant changes Shakespeare made to his sources. In the play, John is a self-acknowledged usurper (he does not object when Chatillion rudely refers to his 'borrowed majesty'—I, i, 4; and his mother reminds him of 'your strong possession much more than your right'—I, i, 40), while Arthur is offered as having much more 'right' to the crown. But historically—the chroniclers agree—John's claim to the throne was quite as strong as Arthur's, and, since Richard I had named him as his heir, possibly stronger. (In medieval times, primogeniture was not the sole justification for succession. The 'designation' by the previous, dying, king of his preferred successor could be equally important.) And, while Arthur is a young warrior in Holinshed, Shakespeare turns him into a feeble, helpless child. Thus, not only do we have 'possession' versus 'right'; we have a *de facto* king who turns out not to have the qualities to make a good ruler, and we have a *de jure* 'king' who would clearly prove hopeless and disastrous were he to be installed on the throne. This leaves the way clear for the appearance of a character who, though having neither 'right' nor 'possession', manifests the desirable, requisite kingly characteristics. And this, indeed, is one of the Bastard's roles. He develops and holds onto a true concept of 'honour'; he renews the proper meaning of 'loyalty' and 'duty' by remaining unflaggingly steadfast in his support of king and country; he doesn't turn his coat or change his side, and he never 'plays fast and loose with faith' or, indeed, anything else. If this were all he was, he would simply be an idealized stereotype of patriotism etc. But he is a good deal more complex and interesting than that.

We first encounter him when he and his legitimate half-brother, Robert, are brought before the king, who is asked to adjudicate in an argument they are having over the inheriting of the Faulconbridge lands. The Bastard's first words—to the king—are 'Your faithful subject' (I, i, 50), and so, importantly, he proves to be. Indeed, when, later, the English nobles defect to the French, it is as if he is the *only* 'faithful subject' remaining loyal to the king. He knows that John is a bad and defective king—indeed, he has to take over from him when the French invade ('Have thou the ordering of this present time,' says the helpless John—V, i, 77)—but he remains faithful to the kingly office (let's say the symbol more than the man), and never permits himself any thoughts of removing or supplanting the king. Even when the present order is weakened and in disarray, he defends it against any insidiously, or treacherously, suggested alternative. In the quarrel with his half-brother, he gives up his claim quite cheerfully, with a characteristic insouciance and unusual indifference to possessions—'Brother, take you my land, I'll take my chance' (I, i, 151). The king immediately knights him —'Arise Sir Richard, and Plantagenet' (I, i, 162)—and the Bastard is happier to have the 'honor' of being the knighted son of Richard Coeur de Lion than to inherit any lands. His developing conception of 'honor'—he is still learning—is crucial to the play, peopled as it is, for the most part, with varyingly dishonourable characters. And he has a touch of that Renaissance sense of the reality and integrity of his own identity—'And I am I, howe'er I was begot' (I, i, 175). Whatever else, he is clearly his own man.

Shortly after, he has his first soliloquy. It starts, understandably enough, with a bit of summarizing musing:

> A foot of honor better than I was,
> But many a many foot of land the worse.
>
> (I, i, 182–3)

But what follows is rather remarkable:

> Well, now can I make any Joan a lady.
> "God den, Sir Richard!"—"God-a-mercy, fellow"—
> And if his name be George, I'll call him Peter,

> For new-made honor doth forget men's names:
> 'Tis too respective and too sociable
> For your conversion. Now your traveler,
> He and his toothpick at my worship's mess,
> And when my knightly stomach is sufficed,
> Why then I suck my teeth and catechize
> My pickèd man of countries: "My dear sir"—
> Thus, leaning on mine elbow, I begin . . .
>   (I, i, 184–94)

and so he goes on, fantasizing a posturing, pretentious encounter. Shakespeare does this elsewhere—has a character on-stage now, in front of us, going through, in imagination, future scenarios in which he exercises and deploys some new-won position and power; but, to my knowledge, this is the first time he attempts it, and the effect is curiously arresting—it adds a dimension to the character. Here it is comic of course; the Bastard is having fun with imagining the possibilities opened up by his new title. More seriously, it suggests he might be preparing for a career of courtly affectation and ambition. This impression is both strengthened and qualified by some important lines which follow:

> But this is worshipful society,
> And fits the mounting spirit like myself;
> For he is but a bastard to the time
> That doth not smack of *observation*.
> And so am I, whether I smack or no:
> And not alone in habit and device,
> Exterior form, outward accoutrement,
> But from the inward motion to deliver
> Sweet, sweet, sweet poison for the age's tooth,
> Which, *though I will not practice to deceive,*
> *Yet, to avoid deceit, I mean to learn;*
> For it shall strew the footsteps of my rising.
>   (I, i, 205–16—my italics)

This certainly seems to suggest that he is preparing for a career of calculated social climbing ('mounting'). The determination to deliver a triply sweet 'poison' to 'the age's tooth', should indicate a commitment to limitless ingratiation and flattery. If he is going to move into a world of deceit, he will out-deceive them all. But although 'observation' can mean obsequiousness, it can also mean straightforward, vigilant, clear-eyed attention. And the lines I have italicized could well mean—though I have no intention to be dishonest myself, I am certainly going to watch out for, and self-protectively learn, all the dishonest tricks going on around me. He could be resolving to lead an honest life in a world in which everything seems to make against such an intention. Although the Bastard will come to embrace what seem like simplicities—king and country; he is not, as I have indicated, a simple character.

For the next two Acts, as the English and French kings and nobles spar for positions in France, the Bastard is something of a loose cannon. He makes ironic, realistic comments (he is, indeed, an 'observer'), in particular mocking and goading the Duke of Austria, to the latter's mounting irritation and discomfiture (Austria would be wearing the famous lion skin of Richard Coeur de Lion whom he had killed, which is provocation enough for Richard's spirited son who will, shortly, kill Austria and retrieve the skin). His caustic comments on the follies of the main players have made some critics deem him a cynic (hence the Touchstone, Jaques comparisons, etc.), but this seems to me wrong. He is more of a potential Falstaff, an ironic realist, contemptuous of the rhetorical hypocrisies and mendacities circulating around him. At the impasse in front of Angiers when, after some pointless but bloody fighting, both kings claim victory and the right of entrance, the Bastard comments:

> Ha, majesty! How high thy glory tow'rs
> When the rich blood of kings is set on fire!
> O now doth death line his dead chaps with steel;
> And now he feasts, *mousing the flesh of men*
> *In undetermined differences of kings.*
>   (II, i, 350–55—my italics)

The compressed power of those last two lines is, I think, something new in Shakespeare, and marks a sudden step closer to his mature style. Certainly, at times the speech of the Bastard represents a qualitatively new burst of linguistic energy. This is nowhere more clear than in the Bastard's reaction to the cynically proposed, politic marriage of Blanche and the Dauphin. Hubert of Angiers, who suggests the marriage, conceals the motivating

cynicism under an excessively cosmetic, hyperbolic rhetoric. This way of
talking is anathema to the Bastard, who is ever a plain speaker:

> Here's a large mouth, indeed,
> That spits forth death and mountains, rocks and seas
> . . .
>
> Zounds! I was never so bethumped with words
> Since I first called my brother's father dad.
>
> (II, i, 457–8, 466–7)

But it is the marriage itself that repels him. First, because the Dauphin,
with his empty, insincere and formulaic love rhetoric, strikes him as horrible ('In such a love so vile a lout as he'—II, i, 509). Secondly, because
Blanche in her honesty—'Further I will not flatter you, my lord' (II, i, 516)
—and her obedience—she will do, she says, 'That she is bound in honor
still to do' (II, i, 522)—reveals to the Bastard a notion of 'honor' which nothing he has so far seen can match. At the end of the scene, he sums up what
he feels about all the manoeuvrings he has been watching. This is the famous 'Commodity' soliloquy (it is the first time Shakespeare used the word)
and it is one of the most important speeches in early Shakespeare—again,
it is a new step. The speech should be studied in its entirety (II, i, 561–98),
but some lines must be singled out. After his opening comprehensive comment—'Mad world! Mad kings! Mad composition!'—the Bastard goes
over what he has seen, and decides on a word for the kind of unprincipled
self-interest which seems to determine almost everyone's actions. It is 'that
sly devil . . . That daily break-vow'—

> That smooth-faced gentleman, tickling commodity,
> Commodity, the bias of the world,
> The world, who of itself is peisèd well,
> Made to run even upon even ground,
> Till this advantage, this vile drawing bias,
> This sway of motion, this commodity,
> Makes it take head from all indifferency,
> From all direction, purpose, course, intent.
> And this same bias, this commodity,
> This bawd, this broker, this all-changing word . . .
>
> (II, i, 573–82)

There is a reference to bowling in *The Taming of the Shrew*, but this is Shakespeare's first extended use of what was to become a favourite metaphor. Since, in bowls, the ball always had a 'bias' or weight in one side, it never went straight. The possibilities of the image are many and obvious. To the Bastard's eye, apart from pawns like Blanche and victims like Arthur, everybody has a built-in 'bias' which he calls 'commodity'—self-servingness, expediency, compliance, casuistry, opportunism, compromise, vow-breaking; it has a hundred names—and nobody maintains a straight course, variously abandoning fixed resolves, and deviating from set intentions. And note—'this all-changing word'. A casuist like Pandulph can, with the 'right', specious words, change 'treachery' into 'loyalty'—and vice versa—in a matter of seconds. The implications are frightening. Anything can be changed into anything. What, then, becomes of stable values, or indeed any of the settled meanings by which we orient ourselves? That way, chaos.

The Bastard has seen—and learned—a lot: his 'observing' has carried him far. But then come some unexpected lines which have confused some critics:

> And why rail I on this commodity?
> But for because he hath not wooed me yet:
> Not that I have the power to clutch my hand,
> When his fair angels would salute my palm,
> But for my hand, as unattempted yet,
> Like a poor beggar, raileth on the rich.
> Well, whiles I am a beggar, I will rail
> And say there is no sin but to be rich;
> And being rich, my virtue then shall be
> To say there is no vice but beggary.
> Since kings break faith upon commodity,
> Gain, be my lord, for I will worship thee!
>   (II, i, 587–98)

This seems plain enough—since Commodity reigns, he will submit to its rule. But this is to miss the tone, which is more like—'I'm probably going on like this because I've never actually been directly tempted; very likely, given the chance, I'd jump at the offer of some corrupt money. Probably, this is all envy and, if I became rich, I might well change my tune. Anyway, seeing what kings do, I'd better prepare for a comparable change in myself.' The Bastard is growing in self-knowledge and self-awareness; and there is a lot of protective, excessive self-honesty in these lines—the kind of honesty that over-accuses itself, damns itself in advance, in order to guard against self-righteous, self-deceiving complacency. We are watching, and hearing, the Bastard learn. This man will never be a hypocrite.

The next episode in which the Bastard plays a major role, shows him to considerable advantage. It follows the sequence in which Hubert goes to put out Arthur's eyes; decides to let Arthur live; and then Arthur, trying to escape, jumps to his death from the castle walls. The English nobles, already disaffected from King John, now pretend to uncontainable horror at what they assume to be the murder of Arthur ordered by the King. As their simulated outrage approaches hysteria, the Bastard counsels calm—and good manners:

> Whate'er you think, good words, I think were best.
> . . . 'twere reason you had manners now.
> (IV, iii, 28, 30)

When they find Arthur's corpse, the nobles leap to the worst conclusions and try to outdo each other in hyperbolic expressions of horror. Only the Bastard keeps balance and sanity:

> It is a damnèd and a bloody work,
> The graceless action of a heavy hand,
> *If that it be the work of any hand.*
> (IV, iii, 57–9—my italics)

He, and he alone, wisely reserves judgement. When Hubert appears, the nobles simply want to 'cut him to pieces'. The Bastard maintains order— 'Keep the peace, I say'; and to the over-inflamed Salisbury—'Your sword is bright, sir; put it up again' (IV, iii, 79—a memorable line anticipating, of course, Othello at his initially most authoritative). The nobles leave with their tails between their legs, heading for the French. It is a very impressive performance on the Bastard's part. This is indeed a mature, stalwart, authoritative figure—as solid as rock.

Left alone with Hubert, he says—*if* in fact you *did* do the murder—

> do but despair,
> And if thou want'st a cord, the smallest thread
> That ever spider twisted from her womb
> Will serve to strangle thee! A rush will be a beam
> To hang thee on.
> . . .
> I do suspect thee very grievously.
>
>   (IV, iii, 126–30, 134)

But he accepts Hubert's protestations of innocence, and tells him to carry away Arthur's body. There follows a moment of bemusement, and another crucial speech.

> I am amazed, methinks, and lose my way
> Among the thorns and dangers of this world.
> . . .
> Now for the bare-picked bone of majesty
> Doth doggèd war bristle his angry crest
> And snarleth in the gentle eyes of peace:
> Now powers from home and discontents at home
> Meet in one line, and vast confusion waits,
> As doth a raven on a sick-fall'n beast,
> The imminent decay of wrested pomp.
> Now happy he whose cloak and center can
> Hold out this tempest. Bear away that child,
> And follow me with speed: I'll to the King.
> A thousand businesses are brief in hand,
> And heaven itself doth frown upon the land.
>
>   (IV, iii, 140–41, 148–59)

He is briefly lost, and is not sure where he stands; then—the images are very powerful—he surveys the imminent chaos and loss of centre as the rebellious English lords join up with the French; then—crucially—he decides upon immediate action (lots to be done), and a resolute direction and commitment—'I'll to the King'. This is a man now capable of making up his mind in the midst of 'vast confusion'. Invaluable.

Throughout the last act, the Bastard, in effect, takes over trying to orga-
nize the defence of England against the French. First he attempts to rouse
the king to kingly behaviour:

> But wherefore do you droop? Why look you sad?
> Be great in act, as you have been in thought;
> Let not the world see fear and sad distrust
> Govern the motion of a kingly eye;
> Be stirring as the time; be fire with fire.
>
> (V, i, 44–8)

To no avail—the king has handed power over to Pandulph to try to arrange an agreed peace. This is 'inglorious' to the Bastard, who does not
think that England should

>   make compromise,
> Insinuation, parley, and base truce
> To arms invasive.
>
> (V, i, 67–9)

He is for direct, honest confrontation—'stirring' and meeting fire with fire
—and he now speaks for the king and with a king's voice. It is notable that
when he goes to speak to the French directly, he says:

> According to the fair-play of the world,
> Let me have audience . . .
>
> (V, ii, 119–20)

There is precious little 'fair-play' in the world we have seen, and it is almost
as if he is appealing to some forgotten ideal—an ideal which, however, he
himself has come to embody. 'Fair-play' is what you respect if you haven't
gone over to 'commodity'. To the French he says:

> Now hear our English king,
> For thus his royalty doth speak in me . . .
>
> (V, ii, 128–9)

and he duly utters a long speech of kingly defiance (this is his Henry V side). By this time, he *is* to all intents and purposes 'king', and we feel him to be such—though historically we know this cannot happen. Shakespeare here takes his play as near to the radical re-writing of history—pushing it off in another direction—as it was possible for him to go.

This is the point of the final scene, in which Prince Henry, John's son and legitimate heir to the throne, suddenly appears. Not only have we not seen him before; no mention has been made of him (nor, indeed, of John's wife, Isabel). It is as if Shakespeare has been deliberately holding him back while we watch the unimpeded growth of the Bastard into the true kingly figure which, in the event, England did not get (or, at least, not until Henry V). To the end, the Bastard sees his job as:

> To push destruction and perpetual shame
> Out of the weak door of our fainting land . . .
>   (V, vii, 77–8)

But, with the appearance of the true heir, he abdicates his leadership, and turns and kneels:

> To whom, with all submission, on my knee,
> I do bequeath my faithful services
> And true subjection everlastingly.
>   (V, vii, 103–5)

He is a figure, now, of truly selfless loyalty. Prince Henry's task, says Salisbury, referring to the mess John has made of England, is

> To set a form upon that indigest
> Which he hath left so shapeless and so rude.
>   (V, vii, 26–7)

The Bastard, we feel, would be a better man for that job. But real history makes its impositions, and marches on. Still, it is given to the Bastard to voice the concluding sentiment of the play—a very important one to the Elizabethans, always afraid of the possibility of civil war:

> Naught shall make us rue
> If England to itself do rest but true!
>
> (V, vii, 117–18)

King John is a new kind of history play for Shakespeare. There is no shadow of the Morality play in the background; nor are there any ritual elements—in the action or in the language (we hear none of the antiphonal exchanges audible in *Richard III*). I have not mentioned some of the elements of the play—the pathos of young Arthur pleading with Hubert not to put out his eyes; the hysterical, though often powerful, complaints and laments of the demented Constance (she dies 'in a frenzy')—in her speeches a descendant of Queen Margaret. But it is clear to me that by far its most important feature is the development of the imaginary character, the Bastard. It *is* worth noting, as E. A. J. Honigman pointed out in his magisterial edition, that certain key words occur more often in this play than in any other Shakespeare play. These include 'blood' (40 times) and 'right' (28 times). The recurrence of 'right' is perhaps hardly surprising since much of the play consists of endless debating about what, in this world where the 'morality' of politics is discussed in terms of games ('Have I not here the best cards for the game / To win this easy match played for a crown?'— V, ii, 105–6) and one good treachery deserves another ('Paying the fine of rated treachery / Even with a treacherous fine of all your lives'—V, iv, 37–8), 'right' actually is, and what *is* 'right'. Perhaps only the Bastard gets and keeps a fast hold on this. 'Blood' lines up with other frequently occurring words referring to parts of the body—'hand' (52), 'eye' (47), 'arm' (27), 'breath' (18), 'mouth' (14), 'foot' (12), 'brow' (11), 'bosom' (10), 'tooth' and 'teeth' (5), 'spleen' (4), 'bowels' (3)—this is a lot in a comparatively short (2,600 lines) play. It certainly indicates that this is an intensely corporeal play: the emphasis is very much on the body and there is very little sense of the transcendent or the spiritual. In a world dominated by 'commodity', the body is, as it were, the central commodity. Again, this is a new feeling in Shakespeare. But I stay and end with the Bastard as the crucial invention and innovation. He represents the introduction of a new (and fictitious) comic-heroic element into the history play, which will enable Shakespeare to progress to his supreme achievements in the genre—*Henry IV, Parts 1 & 2.*

⚡️ RICHARD II (1595–6)

> What must the King do now? Must he submit?
> The King shall do it. Must he be deposed?
> The King shall be contented. Must he lose
> The name of king? a God's name, let it go.
>   (III, iii, 142–5)

On her death-bed, Queen Elizabeth is said to have remarked that 'must' was not a word which may be used to princes. It is a word which comes to be used to Richard II, but only after he has consistently used the word to, and of, himself. In the scene after the one quoted above, there is the following exchange:

> *Richard.* What you will have, I'll give, and willing too,
>   For do we must what force will have us do.
>   Set on towards London, cousin, is it so?
> *Bolingbroke.* Yea, my good Lord.
> *Richard.*   Then I must not say no.
>   (III, iii, 204–7)

Richard seems almost too ready, even eager, to put himself under compulsion—to exchange being absolute ruler for being absolutely ruled. It is not too much to say that Richard starts to abdicate ('From Richard's night to Bolingbroke's fair day', III, ii, 218) some time before Bolingbroke announces his intention to usurp ('In God's name, I'll ascend the regal throne', IV, i, 113)—though Bolingbroke's intentions are something of a mystery, perhaps even to himself. The definitive concession—self-inflicted abnegation, perhaps—occurs one scene later.

> *Bolingbroke.* Are you contented to resign the crown?
> *Richard.* Ay, no; no, ay: for I must nothing be.
>   (IV, i, 199–200)

From one point of view, this is simply a sombre recognition of the inevitable—all men must die; but, in the circumstances, it has the tremendous pathos of the anointed king, God's minister on earth, visibly, audibly confronting what has come to seem the unavoidability of, effectively, self-nihilation.

The pathos and paradox of the king who 'must' was also dramatized by Marlowe in his *Edward II* (1592), in which there is the following exchange:

> *Edward.* And, Leicester, say what shall become of us?
> *Leicester.* Your majesty must go to Killingworth.
> *Edward.* Must! 'tis somewhat hard, when kings must go.

Marlowe's play almost certainly influenced Shakespeare's *Richard II*. Both plays depict weak kings, who are irresponsible, arbitrary, and self-indulgent while they are secure on the throne (both, incidentally, from the same dynasty). They both ignore and alienate their wise counsellors and turn to favourites (perhaps not coincidentally, there are three of these in each play). I quote Geoffrey Bullough: 'In both plays the king is deposed, ill-treated, and then murdered in an interesting manner, leaving the kingdom in the hands of a better ruler. In each the king becomes more likeable in defeat than he was in power, and the play becomes an experiment in counter-pointing the tragedy of a weak and erring central figure against the conflict of opposing groups ("upstarts" and true nobility). This idea was perhaps Shakespeare's biggest debt to Marlowe in *Richard II*.' With this play, Shakespeare goes back to the beginning of the sequence of events which led to the Wars of the Roses, the tyranny of Richard III, and the advent of Henry VII and the Tudors. But this second tetralogy is to be different from the first. It is more complex and subtle and, arguably, reveals a new attitude to politics. Bullough gives a conventional description of the difference. 'Whereas the first tetralogy was mainly concerned with negatives, the evils of dissension, the fratricidal strife of barons, disorder triumphant, the second group is concerned with positive values, the nature of good government, the qualities needed by a strong and wise ruler: prudence, leadership, consideration for popular feeling, ability to choose rightly between good and bad counsel, to put the public weal before private pleasures.' This is not wrong, but perhaps it makes the second tetralogy sound a shade too bland, tending towards the untested complacencies of the instruction manual. As we shall see, it is, and does, a good deal more than this.

In his portrayal of Richard, Shakespeare had two traditional versions to draw on, to be found in Tudor chronicles. One stressed the weak and irresponsible king who deserved to lose his throne: the other saw him as a betrayed martyr. In this play he is both, as if Shakespeare could see how the latter could be latent and dormant in the former, how a king could be a 'degenerate' fool *and* a Christ-like saint. And a 'nothing' too. In the first three scenes, Richard, in his handling of the quarrel between Mowbray and Bolingbroke, can be seen as behaving like a responsible king. It is not, as is sometimes suggested, a foolish and capricious act to stop the combat between the two men by throwing down his 'warder' or truncheon, and he has good reasons for banishing the dangerous and war-like adversaries, since the

> grating shock of wrathful iron arms,
> Might from our quiet confines fright fair Peace,
> And make us wade even in our kindred's blood
> (I, iii, 136–9)

We might pause on 'kindred's blood'. The ceremony, pageantry, formality of these opening scenes are often commented on as bespeaking an older medieval world which the more Machiavellian power-politics of Bolingbroke will, in due course, supplant. But if we listen to the language employed by Mowbray and Bolingbroke—'rites of knighthood', 'chivalrous design of knightly trial', and talk of kinsmen, honour, blood, vengeance—we soon realize that we are hearing the older voice of feudalism. When Richard fails to dissuade the combatants from insisting on entering the lists, we are witnessing the failure of monarchy to assert its authority over the power of feudalism. I take the point from Graham Holderness, and his account of what is going on seems to me right. 'The conflict which ultimately leads to the king's deposition is not a conflict between old and new, between absolute medieval monarchy and new Machiavellian power-politics. It is a conflict between the king's sovereignty and the ancient code of chivalry, which is here firmly located in the older and more primitive tribal and family code of blood-vengeance. Richard initially acquiesces in this code . . . but subsequently attempts to affirm a policy of royal absolutism, which insists on the king's prerogative overriding the procedures of chivalric law. Richard's political response to this constant clamouring for power on the part of the feudal lords, is to impose a policy of *absolutism* . . . [Shakespeare] sees the deposition of Richard II, not as the overturning of a traditional order by new, ruthless political forces, but as the consequence of an attempt by a later medieval monarch to impose on feudal power an absolutist solution. The victorious forces are not new but old: feudal reaction rather than political revolution. The society we see dissolving had been an effective unity and balance of royal prerogative and feudal rights—both parties in the conflict have pushed their interests to the point of inevitable rupture.' 'We were not born to sue, but to command,' asserts Richard, perhaps a little desperately, at the end of the first scene. To the extent that the play is a 'Tragedy' (as it was entitled when first printed), it is in the painful spectacle of the King Who Would Command transformed into the King Who Must.

Richard, then, appears sufficiently, if precariously, kingly in the first three scenes, trying, though only imperfectly succeeding, to control the unruly and quarrelsome barons. But the next, more private, less formal scene, among his favourites, reveals a cynical and callous side to his character as we hear him expressing the hope that John of Gaunt will die ('God . . . help him to his grave immediately!') so that they can raid his 'coffers'. And the next scene (II, i) shows him in much the same vein as John of Gaunt indicts him with his dying breath. Gaunt, at this point, takes on prophetic status:

> Methinks I am a prophet new inspired,
> And thus expiring do foretell of him:
> His rash fierce blaze of riot cannot last,
> For violent fires soon burn out themselves.
>   (II, i, 31–4)

and utters his famous lament over England ('This precious stone set in the silver sea'), because, under Richard, 'this dear dear land'—

> Is now leased out—I die pronouncing it—
> Like to a tenement or pelting farm.
> England . . .
>   is now bound in with shame,
> With inky blots, and rotten parchment bonds.
>   (II, i, 59–60, 63–4)

Blots on parchment, on paper, on books, on 'pride', or just 'blots'—the image occurs more often in this play than in any other by Shakespeare. It refers here, literally, to the deeds and leases by which Richard has 'farmed' out the royal demesnes—substituting economic contracts for earlier bonds of fealty; but also metaphorically to the growing evil which seems to be staining the land (not just from Richard's dissolute mismanagement; Bolingbroke is called a 'pernicious blot' by Aumerle—IV, i, 324). Gaunt repeats his reproach to Richard's face:

> Why, cousin, wert thou regent of the world,
> It were a shame to let this land by lease;
> But for thy world enjoying but this land
> Is it not more than shame to shame it so?
> Landlord of England art thou now, not king.
>   (II, i, 109–13)

He also says something else to Richard which is more prophetic, perhaps, than he realizes:

> O, had thy grandsire with a prophet's eye
> Seen how his son's son should destroy his sons,
> From forth thy reach he would have laid thy shame,
> Deposing thee before thou wert possessed,
> Which art possessed *now to depose thyself.*
>   (II, i, 104–8, my italics)

The second line refers, in particular, to Richard's murder of his uncle, the Duke of Gloucester (Woodstock) which was, indeed, an infamous 'blot' on Richard's reign. This murder is rather glossed over in the play—indeed, Shakespeare makes it uncertain whether Mowbray, Aumerle, or Richard was the murderer. Only the dying Gaunt speaks out unequivocally about it:

> My brother Gloucester, plain well-meaning soul
> . . .
> May be a precedent and witness good
> That thou respect'st not spilling Edward's blood.
>   (II, i, 128–31)

The line I have partially italicized continues that compulsive play on words which marks Gaunt's last speeches. He is saying that though Richard is 'possessed' of the crown, he is now also 'possessed' in the sense of being in the grip of diabolical influences—to the extent that he will lose the throne. But Gaunt could not have foreseen how accurately his words describe what we are about to see—which is, exactly and literally, a king deposing himself.

At the news of Gaunt's death Richard continues to show his callous side —('His time is spent . . . so much for that')—and announces, ruthlessly, his intention to 'seize' all that Gaunt possessed—'for our Irish wars'. In doing this, he is robbing Gaunt's son, the banished Bolingbroke (Hereford), of his legitimate inheritance, his 'rights and royalties'. This provokes another of Richard's wise-counselling uncles, the stalwart and long-suffering York, to protest:

> Take Hereford's rights away, and take from time
> His charters and his customary rights,
> Let not tomorrow then ensue today;
> Be not thyself. For how art thou a king
> But by fair sequence and succession?
>
> (II, i, 195–9)

Matters of 'sequence and succession' were of vital concern to the Elizabethans, not only as they surveyed their turbulent history, but also as they wondered whether the 'succession' to their own Queen would be 'fair' or, in one way or another, foul. Richard was the last king ruling by direct hereditary right in 'succession' from William the Conqueror, and to see him thus ignoring, or rather profaning and violating, 'customary rights', those same sacrosanct rules of inheritance which had made him king, is, indeed, shocking. He is wilfully disrupting those sacred continuities on which all peaceful transactions and transmissions depend—the 'sequence of days' no less than the succession of kings. And he will prove to be the most spectacular victim of his culpable abrogations. But, for now, he is mindlessly indifferent to York's warnings:

> Think what you will, we seize into our hands
> His plate, his goods, his money, and his lands.
>
> (II, i, 209–10)

and it's off to Ireland, to settle those 'rug-headed kernes' (at which, incidentally, he was very successful—though Shakespeare leaves that out as well).

We will not see Richard again until Act III, scene ii, when he will soon seem a changed man as the long ordeal and anguish of his self-deposition begins. In the interim we witness Bolingbroke's return to England, and the nobles', if not the country's, rush to support him. And here we should note one of those interesting departures by Shakespeare from his sources. The Holinshed Chronicles make it absolutely clear that Bolingbroke (Hereford, and now, after the death of Gaunt, Lancaster) was invited back to England by the discontented nobles ('requiring him with all convenient speed to convey himself into England, promising him all their aid, power, and assistance, if he, expelling King Richard, as a man not meet for the office he bare, would take upon him the scepter, rule, and diadem of his native land and region'). Whatever else, this at least exonerates Bolingbroke from having initiated the idea of usurpation. Not a word of this in Shakespeare. Instead, when the nobles collude in exasperation after Richard has left for Ireland, Bolingbroke is already, mysteriously, back in England, and had been waiting in Brittany, with allies and troops, simply for Richard's departure for Ireland. This puts a very different colour on Bolingbroke's possible motives and intentions. Until he suddenly announces that he will 'ascend the regal throne', he continually insists that he has only returned to claim his rightful inheritance—'I come for Lancaster', 'I am come to seek that name in England', 'I lay my claim / To my inheritance of free descent'. But, in the time scheme of the play, he is already in England sixty lines after Richard announces he is going to Ireland, which in turn occurs only some seventy-five lines after the death of Gaunt (all in the same scene). This means that, dramatically, Bolingbroke could hardly have known of his father's death and of Richard's infamous expropriation of the whole Lancaster estate. Or at least, to a spectator it would seem that way. It is another example of the way Shakespeare likes to problematize time, inducing, in this case, a calculated and crucial uncertainty. *Did* Bolingbroke somehow know about his father's death and the regal robbery, and did he *genuinely* come just for his 'rights and royalties'—with subsequent unforeseen circumstances somehow propelling him on to the throne? Or was he already bent on invasion and usurpation? One thing is certain—there was no prior invitation and request from the English nobles. This man came of his own volition.

The matter is of vital importance, since it was this usurpation that set in motion what would become the long train of disasters culminating in Richard III and the subsequent accession—usurpation—of the Tudors. And

Shakespeare makes sure that we have no certain access to the originating moment, the originating motive, of that history-changing usurpation. Is Bolingbroke a Machiavellian who had the whole take-over plotted from day one? Or is he simply borne along on a tide of events, one thing leading to another as things do? He does not seem to exercise any cunning or special skills, and power and support just seem to melt and slide away from the absent Richard 'with the speed of an avalanche' (the felicitous image is Peter Ure's). So perhaps he is simply an angry baron who, effectively, stumbles on the crown. Yet he sometimes gives the impression of only seeming not to have any ulterior motives, while moving shrewdly if warily so that his usurpation will appear, in R. F. Hill's words, 'inevitable but undesigned'. We cannot resolve these uncertainties for the simple reason that Shakespeare gives us no insight into, indeed no glimpses of, Bolingbroke's motives, aims, and intentions. We are never let into his mind. We have seen the growing importance of the soliloquy in the history plays, and it is surely remarkable that, alone among the villains and schemers of the histories (if he is one), Bolingbroke never soliloquizes. He remains shut up, shut off, and we can never know what truly moves him. And the ambiguity is not resolved by him in *2 Henry IV*. At one point he says, actually quoting words spoken by Richard II in the earlier play:

> 'Northumberland, thou ladder by the which
> My cousin Bolingbroke ascends my throne'—
> (Though then, God knows, I had no such intent,
> But that necessity so bowed the state
> That I and greatness were *compelled* to kiss)
>   (III, i, 70–74, my italics)

then, on his death-bed:

>   God knows, my son,
> By what bypaths and indirect crooked ways
> I *met* this crown, and I myself know well
> How troublesome it sat upon my head.
> . . . It seemed in me
> But as an honor *snatched* with boisterous hand
>   (IV, v, 183–6, 190–91, my italics)

'Compelled' is passive; 'met' is neutral; 'snatched' is active. The English language itself recognizes and respects the unfathomable uncertainties and ambiguities of the decision-making process—we can 'come to' a decision (that could be like meeting); we can 'take' a decision (more like snatching); or we can 'make' a decision (perhaps an altogether more responsible, artefactual matter). It is entirely possible that Bolingbroke's impulses remain mysterious to himself. He certainly shows signs of a guilty conscience (though he never reveals, or perhaps confronts, the cause), and he may indeed be—in *Richard II*—a rather unscrupulous, power-hungry, scheming politician who prefers to disavow his own deepest intentions, pretending, instead, to be 'compelled' by circumstances. Or he may genuinely not know exactly *why* he does *what* he does, not be able to disentangle and distinguish seeking from meeting, snatching from being compelled—in a word, his motives from his opportunities. All this makes him at once mysterious and human, and I think this root uncertainty or ambiguity is a masterstroke on Shakespeare's part. Such are the figures who, at once, make and are made by history.

Two short premonitory scenes, which follow one after the other immediately prior to Richard's reappearance, seem almost to prefigure what is to happen. We have seen the support of the nobles fall away from Richard in his absence (even that of loyal York), and then we watch as the Captain of the Welsh army (on which Richard is relying to fight Bolingbroke) announces that his army is dispersing because ''Tis thought the King is dead: we will not stay' (II, iv, 7); and Salisbury reads the gathering omens clearly enough:

> Ah, Richard! With the eyes of heavy mind
> I see thy glory like a shooting star
> Fall to the base earth from the firmament;
> Thy sun sets weeping in the lowly west,
> Witnessing storms to come, woe and unrest
>   (II, iv, 18–22)

It is just this 'falling' and 'setting' we are about to see. But if the King is proleptically 'dead', his rival and antagonist is very much alive, as we see in the next scene in which Bolingbroke's behaviour is almost regally autocratic as he orders the summary execution of Richard's favourites, Bushy and

Green. 'See them delivered over / To execution and the hand of death.' This
is the man now in charge. The king is 'dead': long live the 'king'. But we
should take note of another gesture on Bolingbroke's part. Before despatch-
ing Bushy and Green, he announces: 'yet, to wash your blood / From off my
hands . . . I will unfold some causes of your deaths' (III, i, 5–7). This is the
(would-be self-exculpating) Pilate gesture, and it is arguable that Bolingbroke, in time, plays Pilate to Richard's 'Christ'. This is certainly how Richard will come to see it:

> Though some of you, with Pilate, wash your hands,
> Showing an outward pity: yet you Pilates
> Have here delivered me to my sour cross,
> And water cannot wash away your sin.
>   (IV, i, 238–41)

And after Richard has been murdered, in almost the last lines of the play,
Bolingbroke vows:

> I'll make a voyage to the Holy Land,
> To wash this blood off from my guilty hand.
>   (V, vi, 49–50)

He never makes that voyage to the Holy Land—though he is recorded as
dying in the Jerusalem Chamber of Westminster, a circumstance which it
pleases him to regard as auspicious, but which Shakespeare may have regarded more ironically. Certainly, it is not clear that he can (indeed, that
anyone can) 'wash off' blood from guilty hands, just as it is unclear whether
Richard, approaching the depths of his abjection, can 'wash away my balm'
(i.e. the anointing ointment used at the coronation, IV, i, 206)—balm may
stick to a consecrated head as long as blood to a guilty hand. *May*. There can
be no certainty in such matters.

   Richard is very conscious of being the 'Lord's Anointed', and it is very
easy for him to see himself as a Christ figure, now surrounded by Judases
and Pilates. (The King as God's substitute on earth, and thus a God-like
figure with 'divine right', became crucial to Tudor political theory.) In three
scenes—on the Welsh coast, at Flint Castle, and in Westminster—we see
Richard, effectively, enduring his stations of the cross, as he suffers more

and more humiliation and descends to the depths of abjectness (A. P. Rossiter suggested the possible influence of the 'staged spectacle of a sacrificial king of sorrows', familiar from the Mystery Cycles). Before considering these scenes, I want to quote a remarkable passage from Walter Pater's *Appreciations* concerning these scenes:

> In the Roman Pontifical, of which the order of Coronation is really a part, there is no form for the inverse process, no rite of 'degradation', such as that by which an offending priest or bishop may be deprived, if not of the essential quality of 'orders', yet, one by one, of its outward dignities. It is as if Shakespeare had had in mind some such inverted rite, like those old ecclesiastical or military ones, by which human hardness, or human justice, adds the last touch of unkindness to the execution of its sentences . . .

Richard's grief, Pater asserts, 'becomes nothing less than a central expression of all that in the revolution of Fortune's wheel goes *down* in the world'.

When Richard first lands on the coast of Wales, he touches, and conjures, and puts his confidence in 'my earth' (a much-repeated word in this play, fittingly enough as the down-sinking Richard moves inexorably 'to earthward', if I may borrow an apt phrase from Robert Frost). He starts by enunciating a conventional regal confidence:

> So when this thief, this traitor, Bolingbroke,
> Who all this while hath reveled in the night
> Whilst we were wand'ring with the Antipodes,
> Shall see us rising in our throne, the east,
> His treasons will sit blushing in his face,
> Not able to endure the sight of day,
> But self-affrighted tremble at his sin.
>   (III, ii, 47–53)

Wrong, of course. Richard's sun is already setting, while Bolingbroke is 'rising'—without a tremble.

> Not all the water in the rough rude sea
> Can wash the balm off from an anointed king;

The breath of worldly men cannot depose
The deputy elected by the Lord.
                    (III, ii, 54–7)

Richard had 'breathed' Norfolk into permanent exile (I, iii, 153), and com-
muted Bolingbroke's banishment by four years with 'a word'—prompting
Bolingbroke to comment—'such is the breath of kings'. For one last moment, Richard sees himself as untouchable (out of reach of any sacrilegious
'water' and 'breath'), invincible, asserting that God and his angels will fight
on his side—'for heaven still guards the right'. But he is destined, and that
shortly, to do the impossible unanointing washing and the inconceivable
deposing breathing—himself.

The first piece of bad news (the dispersal of the Welsh army—admittedly
a blow) seems to precipitate instant collapse—'All souls that will be safe fly
from my side.' He briefly rallies (in this scene he experiences those sudden
alterations between extreme moods which often testify to some sort of severe psychic instability):

I had forgot myself: am I not King?
Awake, thou coward majesty! Thou sleepest.
Is not the King's name twenty thousand names?
Arm, arm, my name! a puny subject strikes
At thy great glory. Look not to the ground,
Ye favorites of a king, are we not high?
High be our thoughts.
                    (III, ii, 83–9)

The name 'Richard'; or the name 'King'? Can one sleep while the other
wakes? (Shortly, he will lose all his names: 'I have no name, no title . . . And
know not now what name to call myself', IV, i, 254–8). There is more than
a touch of incipient amnesiac-somnambulism here—he is losing his grip on
his unitary self. And within fifty lines, in total reversal, the cry is—look *to*
the ground, and *low* be our thoughts.

Let's talk of graves, of worms, and epitaphs,
Make dust our paper, and with rainy eyes
Write sorrow on the bosom of the earth.
                    (III, ii, 145–7)

He indulges what must be this pleasurable morbidity for some thirty lines, until he reaches that easeful stage of nihilism when you simply give up *everything*.

> throw away respect,
> Tradition, form, and ceremonious duty;
> For you have mistook me all this while:
> I live with bread like you, feel want,
> Taste grief, need friends—subjected thus,
> How can you say to me, I am a king?
> (III, ii, 172–7)

This is what he, very accurately, calls 'that sweet way I was in to despair'. He is briefly interrupted when he is encouraged to make one more, now totally implausible, gesture of regal confidence—'An easy task it is to win our own' (III, ii, 191)—but more bad news quickly returns him to 'that sweet way'. 'I'll pine away;/A king, woe's slave, shall kingly woe obey' (III, ii, 209–10). His last words of the scene presage all that is to follow:

> Discharge my followers, let them hence away,
> From Richard's night to Bolingbroke's fair day.
> (III, ii, 217–18)

The next scene takes place in front of Flint Castle where the 'sacred king' (III, iii, 9) has found temporary refuge. Bolingbroke arrives, seemingly behaving as an impeccably loyal subject.

> Henry Bolingbroke
> On both his knees doth kiss King Richard's hand,
> And sends allegiance and true faith of heart
> To his most royal person . . .
> (III, iii, 34–7)

Yet in instructing Northumberland to convey this message to the King, he tells him to send it 'Into his ruined ears' (III, iii, 33), thus, it seems, betraying the fact that, while showing the correct courtly decorum for the moment, he can already see the actual ruined man through the fast dissolving sacred king. I use the metaphor deliberately. As Richard Altick noted in an important article: 'In no other history play is the idea of tears and weeping so insistently presented. It is this element which enforces our impression of Richard as a weakling, a monarch essentially feminine in nature, who has no conception of stoic endurance or resignation but a strong predilection for grief. This is why the play seems so strangely devoid of the heroic . . .' In this play, there is, strangely, no fighting—but a lot of crying. It is, indeed, a play about a 'King of Sorrows'.

When Richard first appears, high on the walls, he is still regal—'Yet looks he like a king,' says York—and Bolingbroke, perhaps diplomatically deferring to convention, likens him to the sun *rising*:

> See, see, King Richard doth himself appear,
> As doth the blushing discontented sun
> From out the fiery portal of the East.
> (III, iii, 61–3)

Yet very soon, almost immediately in fact, he is seen 'setting', literally coming 'down'. Northumberland asks him to 'come down' so that he can talk to Bolingbroke in 'the base court' (simply, the *basse cour,* the lower courtyard). Richard takes the literal request and turns it into a metaphor, working it for all it is worth:

> Down, down I come, like glist'ring Phaethon,
> Wanting the manage of unruly jades.
> In the base court! Base court where kings grow base,
> To come at traitors' calls, and do them grace:
> In the base court, come down: down court, down king,
> For night owls shriek where mounting larks should sing.
> (III, iii, 177–82)

This is the scene in which he starts to use, compulsively, the language of 'must' ('Must he be deposed?', etc.). And all this, be it noted, before Bolingbroke has issued any threats or, indeed, shown his hand at all. Perhaps this simply indicates that the prescient king has a very clear view of Bolingbroke's as yet unstated intentions. Nevertheless, it is an incredibly quick capitulation. He appears eager to give (in this case his crown), *before* he has been asked (never mind ordered or coerced). Perhaps this means that he can already see the writing on the wall; but to a certain, quite distinct, extent, he himself is doing the writing. He seems to luxuriate in long, morbid and self-pitying speeches—'And my large kingdom for a little grave,/A little, little grave, an obscure grave', etc. (III, iii, 152–3)—and at times he talks himself into incoherence, sounding less like a king than a 'fool'. 'I talk but idly, and you laugh at me' (III, iii, 170); 'Sorrow and grief of heart/Makes him speak fondly like a frantic man' (III, iii, 183–4). Certainly, to use his own words, he 'plays the wantons with [his] woes' (III, iii, 163). No restraint, no restraint—as Conrad might have said. Indisputably, by the end of this scene, his 'Highness' has become his 'Lowness' and not, certainly not, without his own collusion.

There is one more stage in this 'rite of degradation' to be gone through (or acted out), for the King must experience the passage from 'lowness' to nothingness. This, the third station if you like, takes place in Westminster Hall.

> *Bolingbroke.* Are you contented to resign the crown?
> *Richard.* Ay, no; no, ay: for I *must* nothing be.
> Therefore no, no, for I resign to thee.
> Now, mark me how I will *un*do myself.
> I give this heavy weight from off my head,
> And this unwieldy scepter from my hand,
> The pride of kingly sway from out my heart;
> With mine own tears I wash away my balm,
> With mine own hands I give away my crown,
> With mine own tongue deny my sacred state,
> With mine own breath release all duteous oaths;
> All pomp and majesty I do forswear;
> My manors, rents, revenues, I forgo;
> My acts, decrees, and statutes I deny:
> . . .
> God save King Henry, *un*kinged Richard says.
>   (IV, i, 200–12, 219, my italics)

This is, perhaps, the most crucial speech in the play—and note, first, the verbs: resign, give away, wash away, deny, release, forswear, forgo, deny. This is the lexicon of compulsive, even desperate, repudiation, relinquishment, self-negation, self-erasure. This is an inverted rite, by a king, of self-stripping, denudation, which we will see again, albeit in different circumstances, in *King Lear*. The 'unkinging' king. Scholars have noted the unusual number of negative words with privative prefixes in the play—producing such unusual coinages as 'undeaf', 'unhappied', 'uncurse', 'unkiss' and—above all—'unkinged' (twice). 'Undo' is common enough, but it is certainly not common to watch (and Richard *wants* to be watched—'Now, mark me . . .') a king 'undo' himself, still less to witness a king 'unking' himself—the language itself resists the formulation as if it is trying to refer to something which is, or ought to be, an impossibility.

In the second scene of the play, the widow of the murdered Duke of Gloucester laments, helplessly, to her brother-in-law, Gaunt:

> grief boundeth where it falls,
> Not with empty hollowness, but weight.

She then thinks of asking York to visit her, but, on consideration, changes her mind:

> and what shall good old York there see
> But empty lodgings and *un*furnished walls,
> *Un*peopled offices, *un*trodden stones . . .
>   (I, ii, 58–9, 67–9)

Un– un– un–. Such is the world of deprivation, loss, grief. A world of 'un'—and it is this world which Richard, perhaps the most dazzlingly and richly accoutred of all English kings (see the glorious Wilton Diptych to start with), is going to have to enter. Is this world of grief, of loss, 'empty', 'hollow'—or does it have its own 'weight'? The Duchess of Gloucester does not put in another appearance, but, in fact, this is to become *the* question of the play (so Shakespeare works—five minutes with a dispensable Duchess before, seemingly, the play has got going, and the deepest issue of the play is already adumbrated). Back in Westminster Hall, Richard, now completely deprived of any sense of who, or what, he is, asks for a mirror:

> Let it command a mirror hither straight,
> That it may show me what a face I have,
> Since it is bankrout of his majesty.
>   (IV, i, 264–6)

Of course, it doesn't tell him anything helpful or, in more sombre terms, anything ontologically stabilizing. Simply the perennial message of the incomprehensible difference between 'then' and 'now'.

> Was this face the face
> That every day under his household roof
> Did keep ten thousand men?
> . . .
> Was this the face that faced so many follies,
> And was at last outfaced by Bolingbroke?
>> (IV, i, 280–82, 284–5)

Hard to face that. Richard smashes the mirror.

> Mark, silent king, the moral of this sport:
> How soon my sorrow hath destroyed my face.
>> (IV, i, 289–90)

But the 'destruction' of the living self is not so easy, as the more realistic, less metaphorical Bolingbroke points out:

> The shadow of your sorrow hath destroyed
> The shadow of your face.
>> (IV, i, 291–2)

Bolingbroke lives in the world of power, of steel, of 'iron'; he is not given to 'reflection'—mirrors and images are nothing to him. But Richard is going all the other way—he takes the hint and, crucially, turns it.

> Say that again.
> 'The shadow of my sorrow'? Ha, let's see.
> 'Tis very true, my grief lies all within,
> And these external manners of laments
> Are merely shadows to the unseen grief
> That swells with silence in the tortured soul.
> There lies the substance . . .
>> (IV, i, 292–8)

Where lies the substance? Richard makes this *the* question. Was it in the court that has vanished, the favourites that have gone, the armies that have dispersed, the kingly glory that has melted away? Was that ever-deliquescent world truly 'substantial'—did it have real 'weight'? Or was the 'emptiness', the 'hollowness' exactly there? Richard has already begun to see it that way:

> within the hollow crown
> That rounds the mortal temples of a king
> Keeps Death his court, and there the antic sits,
> Scoffing his state and grinning at his pomp,
> Allowing him a breath, a little scene,
> To monarchize, be feared, and kill with looks,
> Infusing him with self and vain conceit,
> As if this flesh which walls about our life
> Were brass impregnable; and, humored thus,
> Comes at the last, and with a little pin
> Bores through his castle wall, and farewell king!
>   (III, ii, 160–70)

The material world of externalities, seemingly so solid and physical, is not, truly, the 'substance', but, paradoxically, 'hollow', a realm of shadows. Obliterated in an instant with a pin. The *real* 'lies all within', with 'unseen grief' and the silence of the 'tortured soul'. This is how Richard is intent, determined, on seeing things, embarking on his irreversible and uncompromising journey into interiority. This scene—Bolingbroke quietly 'doing' himself, Richard loquaciously 'undoing' himself—brings, and 'jars', two worlds together. Rossiter: 'One is the half-fantasy world of the Court, where Richard's half-dream kingship reigns, with angels at his beck and serpents for his foes; the other is that other dream, of action, will, and curt-worded decision, in which he is nothing, or a passive sufferer, a king of woes (or merely a king of words). In the mirror-episode the two dreams doubly confront each other.' The breaking of the mirror is the final shattering of Richard's kingly identity.

A very interesting way of considering what happens to Richard is provided by Ernst Kantorowicz's important book, *The King's Two Bodies* (1957). The title refers to a legal fiction, promulgated by Tudor jurists to support the notion of the divine right of secular powers. To simplify (though not by much), this 'fiction' asserted that the king has 'two Bodies': one is the 'Body natural'—the creatural, physical body that dies; and the other the 'Body politic', also known as the 'mystical Body', which 'contains his royal Estate and Dignity'—'and in this Name the King never dies'. (Thus, at the time of the Civil War the Puritans could say—'we fight the king to defend the King'.) Kantorowicz: 'The legal concept of the King's Two Bodies cannot . . . be separated from Shakespeare. . . It is he who has eternalized that metaphor. He has made it not only the symbol, but indeed the very substance and essence of one of his greatest plays: *The Tragedy of King Richard II* is the tragedy of the King's Two Bodies.' Kantorowicz traces out how, in Richard, these two bodies (which should, of course, be as one) fall apart, as it were, and engage in self-destructive struggle until, finally, one betrays the other. 'The Universal called "Kingship" begins to disintegrate; its transcendental "Reality", its objective truth and god-like existence, so brilliant shortly before, pales into nothing, a *nomen* . . . Not only does the king's manhood prevail over the godhead of the Crown, and mortality over immortality; but, worse than that, kingship itself seems to have changed its essence. Instead of being unaffected "by Nonage or Old Age and other natural Defects and Imbecilities", kingship itself comes to mean Death, and nothing but Death . . . The king that "never dies" here has been replaced by the king that always dies and suffers death more cruelly than other mortals. Gone is the oneness of the body natural with the immortal body politic, "this double Body, to which no Body is equal". Gone also is the fiction of royal prerogatives of any kind, and all that remains is the feeble human nature of a king.' In Westminster Hall, Richard's tear-filled eyes mistily make out traitors all round him, but then:

> Nay, if I turn mine eyes upon myself,
> I find myself a traitor with the rest;
> For I have given here my soul's consent
> T'undeck the pompous body of a king;
> Made glory base and sovereignty a slave,
> Proud majesty a subject, state a peasant.
>   (IV, i, 246–51)

Richard perceives, says Kantorowicz, that 'he is a traitor to his own immortal body politic and to kingship such as it had been to his day . . . the king body natural becomes a traitor to the king body politic . . . It is as though Richard's self-indictment of treason anticipated the charge of 1649, the charge of high treason committed by the *k*ing against the *K*ing.' After this, there is only the inner world left to him. He is despatched to the Tower (later changed to Pomfret Castle).

On his way there, the people throw 'dust and rubbish' on his 'sacred head',

> Which with such gentle sorrow he shook off,
> His face still combating with tears and smiles,
> The badges of his grief and patience . . .
>
> (V, ii, 31–3)

Having played out his scenes before his Judas and Pilate figures, he is now approaching his Calvary or Golgotha (referred to by Carlisle in his tremendous warning to Bolingbroke, IV, i, 114–49, see line 144), and, once again, he briefly takes on the lineaments and demeanour of a Christ figure. In addition to becoming a genuine figure of pathos, he now takes on a strange beauty, quite missing in his earlier appearances. His Queen, Isabel, shortly before their final parting, describes him as a 'beauteous inn' compared to Bolingbroke, who is a mere 'alehouse' (V, i, 13, 15)—odd but rather powerful metaphors. Isabel plays a very small part in the play. She is a witness in the overtly emblematic Garden Scene (III, iv); and she has an oddly premonitory early scene with Richard's favourites in which she complains of a nameless apprehension and unhappiness—'my inward soul/With nothing trembles . . . makes me with heavy nothing faint and shrink . . . nothing hath begot my something grief' (II, ii), which seems to provide an anticipatory fore-echo of the 'nothing' which Richard is to become, and his dungeon soliloquy:

> But whate'er I be,
> Nor I, nor any man that but man is,
> With nothing shall be pleased, till he be eased
> With being nothing.
>
> (V, v, 38–41)

Her parting from Richard has little true pathos, he seeming to be more intent on narcissistic self-pity:

> Tell thou the lamentable tale of me,
>
> And send the hearers weeping to their beds.
>
> (V, i, 44–5)

Etc. . . . And that is about all we see of the Queen. Isabel was in fact a very young girl at the time, and perhaps Shakespeare had that in mind. Whatever, unlike many regal women in Shakespeare, she is, effectively, kept in the margins of the play.

Richard's long dungeon soliloquy (V, v, 1–66)—the only soliloquy in the play—is not at all serene; being king of the inner world brings no royal satisfactions. He tries to fabricate an alternative world, and fails. Alone, he is everybody and nobody:

> Thus play I in one person many people,
>
> And none contented . . .
>
> . . .
>
> Then am I kinged again and, by and by,
>
> Think that I am unkinged by Bolingbroke,
>
> And straight am nothing.
>
> (V, v, 31–2, 36–8)

The question is often raised as to whether Shakespeare here achieves, or conveys, a sense of deeply felt inwardness, that authentic, anguished self-probing and analysis which we associate with the great tragedies. Or whether there is too much self-pleasing artifice in the language, too much formal antiphony, too many elegant conceits, too much smooth patterning of statement, to convince us we are hearing the urgent flow of true feeling. This is perhaps related to the question of whether or not Richard is a 'poet'. Many have thought him one. According to Walter Raleigh, 'it is difficult to condemn Richard without taking sides against poetry'. Walter Pater found him 'an exquisite poet if he is nothing else, from first to last', exclaiming enthusiastically, 'What a garden of words!' (Some have found him simply a *bad* poet.) Others have denied him the status, suggesting instead that he likes to spin out elaborate speeches because he is too weak to act (it might just be noted that he is active enough when his murderers set on him—he kills two of them, four in Holinshed!). One thing is certain—the idea and activity of 'speech' is given extraordinary emphasis. The word 'tongue' occurs more often than in any other play, and 'breath', 'mouth', 'speech', 'word' are frequent. Richard Altick thinks that this 'draws constant attention to the propensity for verbalizing ... which is Richard's fatal weakness', and, more generally, underlines 'the unsubstantiality of human language'. As I have mentioned, there is, remarkably, no fighting in the play (the knightly combat which is about to occur at the start is arrested and prevented by ceremony—this sets the tone), and Richard does at times give the impression of wishing to arrest the world with words. By contrast, Bolingbroke is almost dumb about his doings and movings. It is perhaps worth remembering that Richard II's court (in the play only slightingly referred to for its interest in foreign fashions and luxury) was known for its splendour, elegance, refinement—including an interest in the arts. Chaucer and Gower wrote during his reign, as Tillyard reminds us. I don't think the question of whether Richard was a good or bad poet (or no poet at all), or the matter of the relative sincerity or 'conceit-edness' of his speech, are particularly central (or decidable). The play is contemporary with *A Midsummer Night's Dream* and *Romeo and Juliet,* and clearly Shakespeare was interested in pushing the lyric potentialities of language in new directions. Richard is plausibly presented as a medieval king of sensibility, who prefers refinement to valour, ceremony to combat, fine words to ferocious wars (perhaps that is why Shakespeare kept silent about his success in fighting the Irish). When his (too luxurious, too irresponsible) world collapses around him, he falls back on what he knows, and does, best. Into what new areas of suffering and deprivation—and 'degradation'—all this would take him, he could hardly have foretold. That is what Shakespeare shows us. The spectacle is of—the king unkinged. And it is awesome.

 HENRY IV, PART ONE (1596–7)

> *Gadshill.* Give me thy hand. Thou shalt have a share in our purchase, as I
>   am a true man.
> *Chamberlain.* Nay, rather let me have it, as you are a false thief.
> *Gadshill.* Go to; 'homo' is a common name to all men.
>   (II, i, 94–8)

Richard II contains no comedy—and no prose. As befits, it might justly be thought, its almost continuously ceremonial, even sacramental (no matter how inverted) character. *Henry IV* very notably, indeed explosively, has both comedy and prose—and this difference allows us to glance at a major problem, or at least a determining factor, for Shakespeare when he wrote his history plays. To put it very simply, as a creative dramatist he is hemmed in by history. When it comes to events—let us unblushingly call them the facts—he is limited by, and pretty strictly adheres to, the chronicles. Of course, within these givens he can be, as we have seen, marvellously adroit and inventive, with his conflations, rearrangings, telescopings, omissions, and—though these are comparatively rare—additions. And it goes without saying that, when it comes to revelation of motive and exhibition of character, Shakespeare has and takes all the liberties he wants. Just occasionally, it seems as if he is on the brink of pushing history off in a non-historical direction (in *King John* for example), but he always comes back to the facts as then known. His Richard III may multiply his murders unconscionably, but will have to turn up to meet his fate at Bosworth. Prince Hal can spend as many, entirely legendary, hours in taverns as Shakespeare decides, but he has a date he must keep at Shrewsbury (albeit Shakespeare takes great liberties with the ages of the leading players). And when Hal speaks as a prince, in princely mode, he speaks poetry. History, it seems, demands the muse.

But bringing in a figure like Falstaff (though, to be sure, there isn't another figure in literature 'like' Falstaff), opened up entirely new areas of possibility for Shakespeare. Falstaff is related to an historical predecessor in only the most tenuous of ways, and the origins of the Falstaff we see are, ultimately, unknowable, untraceable. From one point of view, he is not an historical character at all. Yet there he is, in history (he is at Shrewsbury, too), even while he seems to be making very free with history, indeed threatening 'history', at least in its official, chronicle form. You don't make annals out of Falstaff's anarchic antics. Yet with Falstaff, Shakespeare was able to perfect a genre of 'comic history' which added a whole new dimension to historical drama—arguably to drama *tout court*.

To get some sense of the new kind of historical drama Shakespeare was able to effect with the presence of Falstaff, I want to consider the first three scenes in some detail. We start where we might expect to start—in the King's palace in London. The King's opening speech is grave, and as so often in Shakespeare, the first lines set the tone of the play.

> So shaken as we are, so wan with care,
> Find we a time for frighted peace to pant

And breathe short-winded accents of new broils
To be commenced in stronds afar remote.

The immediate impression is of a strained and insecure monarch, and an
apprehensive nation, seriously out of breath. We are reminded how recently
it was that the 'thirsty' soil was 'daub(ing) her lips with her own children's
blood', and 'trenching war' 'channel(ing)' the fields and 'bruise(ing)' the
flowers. How 'opposed eyes . . . Did lately meet in the intestine shock / And
furious close of civil butchery'. The King's hope is that

The edge of war, like an ill-sheathèd knife,
No more shall cut his master.

But there is a lot of that cutting edge and civil butchery to come. Once more
the King has to defer his promised Crusade (to expiate the murder of Richard II) because of more local 'broils' in Wales, Scotland, and the north of
England (uprisings and rebellions or incursions from these realms were to
trouble most of Henry IV's reign, dubbed, accurately enough, by Hall 'The
Unquiete Time of King Henry the Fourthe'). Westmoreland tells of the
success of 'wild Glendower' and how a thousand Englishmen have been
'butchered':

Upon whose dead corpse there was such misuse,
Such beastly shameless transformation
By those Welshwomen done, as may not be
Without much shame retold or spoken of.
                    (I, i, 43–6)

This probably refers to castration—but in due course we are to see for ourselves some 'misuse' of a 'dead corpse', different but perhaps no less shocking; and there are 'transformations' to come, how 'beastly' or 'shameless'
may be individually decided.

There has also been a 'sad and bloody hour' in Northumberland against
Douglas and the Scots, but here Hotspur has had success and taken some
important prisoners, described by the King as 'honorable spoil', 'a gallant
prize' (I, i, 74–5)—a vocabulary of robbery we are to hear much of. More
to the point, the King makes it clear that he wants, and intends to have,
those prisoners for himself—despoiling the spoiler of his spoils we may say,

glancing ahead at what is to come. The King also reveals his discontent with his son, particularly in comparison with Hotspur—'sweet fortune's minion and her pride' (I, i, 82). Hotspur is 'the theme of honor's tongue', while

> See riot and dishonor stain the brow
> Of my young Harry.
>
> (I, i, 84–5)

The contrast, comparison, and competition between the two 'young' Harrys will be central to the play (Hotspur was, in fact, twenty-three years older than Hal—indeed, he was two years older than the King), as will be the theme of 'honor'. In one short scene, a lot of the play has been prospectively opened up.

The language throughout is grave, compacted, dignified blank verse, and the atmosphere is of serious state business. Posts and messengers arrive; news—'uneven and unwelcome' or 'smooth and welcome'—keeps coming in; questions are of 'power', and matters are mainly military. Speed is of the essence—'this haste was hot in question', 'come yourself with speed to us again'—as we watch a pale and troubled king trying to manage volatile and discontented factions erupting all over the land. I note that the last word of the King's first speech is 'expedience', and with this king, in this court, the politics of expediency are paramount.

The first line of the second scene—actually set in the Prince's 'lodging', presumably in a 'tavern' part of London—introduces us to Falstaff, asking the time. 'Now, Hal, what time of day is it, lad?' This provokes, by way of a response from the Prince of Wales, a most unprincely blast of demotic prose:

> What a devil hast thou to do with the time of day? Unless hours were cups of sack, and minutes capons, and clocks the tongues of bawds, and dials the signs of leaping houses, and the blessed sun himself a fair hot wench in flame-colored taffeta, I see no reason why thou shouldst be so superfluous to demand the time of the day.
>
> (I, ii, 6–12)

Time is for soldiers and statesmen; for utilitarians and fixers; for schedulers and planners. Time is for kings, particularly if, like this king, they have a lot of 'business' (key word). 'Come yourself with speed to us again'—because we'll need all the time we can get. Hal is right. Falstaff has nothing whatever to do with such closely observed clock time. He is exclusively physical and corporeal, and is mainly concerned—still Hal's response—with eating and drinking and 'unbuttoning' after supper. The literal act is apt for metaphorical extrapolations, since Falstaff inhabits, and to some extent presides over, a world of multiple 'unbuttonings'—of trousers, morals, religion, codes, language—ultimately perhaps, the unbuttoning of value itself. We will see. Falstaff's immediate response to the Prince is characteristic—'Indeed you come near me now, Hal.' Not only can he always deflect any criticism; he can invariably turn it to his advantage, even when it seems completely unanswerable. On this occasion he asks Hal—'when thou art king'—to dignify Falstaff and his gang. 'Let us be Diana's foresters, gentlemen of the shade, minions of the moon; and let men say we be men of good government, being governed, as the sea is, by our noble and chaste mistress the moon, under whose countenance we steal' (I, ii, 25–30). And let them say that black is white. But how plausible-sounding, and, anyway, pleasurable, is this brazen casuistry; and he has enough bits of the lexicon of mythology and polity to make his case sound sonorous and dignified—he sounds as if he is talking a compound of heraldry and law. The pun on that last word, 'steal', is perfection—at once, telling a truth and showing a lie. Inasmuch as 'steal' can mean 'creep quietly for protection', this is just what he is doing at this moment, hiding his nefarious activities behind a mystifying mythological panoply of Diana and the moon. Inasmuch as 'steal' means steal, this is exactly what they do—they rob by night. This is pure Falstaff, of course. But by the end of the play, when we have seen and heard the nobles, the princes, the King himself, in action, we might well want to avail ourselves of Falstaff's words and ask—under whose countenance do *they* steal?

'When thou art king'—the words are often in Falstaff's mouth: 'shall there be gallows standing in England when thou art king? And resolution thus fubbed as it is with the rusty curb of old father Antic the law? Do not thou, when thou art king, hang a thief' (I, ii, 61–4). Falstaff is, of course, imagining and anticipating a, to him, Utopian upside-down world of permanent carnival and anarchy—'when thou art king'. He is, of course, to be hopelessly, cruelly?, disappointed, and in the event 'old father Antic the law' will prove to be a good deal less 'Antic' than Falstaff can ever have feared. But as long as the Prince is content to play, or be, a 'madcap', Falstaff feels free to expand, 'unbutton', and luxuriate—which is, of course, our, very considerable, fun.

But the 'fun' is full of potentially serious points and allusions (as perhaps all really good fun is). When he says to the Prince 'I would to God thou and I knew where a commodity of good names were to be bought' (I, ii, 85–6), we can recognize the shameless cynicism, but may pause to ponder where some of the established men of repute—the King, for example—procured their 'good names'. And when, after a farrago of Puritan cant (which he does very well), Falstaff announces 'I must give over this life, and I will give it over! By the Lord, and I do not, I am a villain!', we are alerted to a theme of repentance and 'conversion' (transformation) which will become crucial. The Prince deflects Falstaff 'from praying to purse-taking' (I, ii, 99–101, 107), and they are soon planning the robbery at Gad's Hill. At which point, Poins engages the Prince in his planned 'jest' to allow Falstaff and his gang to rob the travellers they have in mind, and then to 'rob' them of their booty—just what the King was planning to do to Hotspur in the previous scene. When the Prince asks how they can avoid recognition, Poins has disguises of buckram ready—'to immask our noted outward garments' (I, ii, 184). We are still in that lawless night-time world in which robbery and jesting are scarcely distinguishable. But even at this point, as they prepare for 'fun', they are adumbrating the use of disguise and 'counterfeit' by the King at the Battle of Shrewsbury.

At the end of the scene the Prince is left alone, and he has a soliloquy (it is notable that he has just one soliloquy in each of the three *Henry* plays). Men tend to be honest in soliloquies; they are, as we have seen, often rogues who play a deceptive role to the other characters, a role which they drop when they are alone (alone with us). The Prince's speech has been seen as problematical, but we can be sure that he is speaking in his own, princely, voice; that this is the man. Significantly, he reverts to the courtly mode of poetry—buttoning himself up again we might say.

> I know you all, and will awhile uphold
> The unyoked humor of your idleness.
> Yet herein I will imitate the sun,
> Who doth permit the base contagious clouds
> To smother up his beauty from the world,
> That, when he please again to be himself,

> Being wanted, he may be more wond'red at
> By breaking through the foul and ugly mists
> Of vapors that did seem to strangle him.
>
>   (I, ii, 199–207)

He's just playing with them. This is the realization that has shocked some, while others seem to think that he is revealing his true princely quality as one who can handle pitch without being defiled. It is—I think—unarguably unpleasant, and if it is so for us it is simply calumny to think it wasn't for Shakespeare. Nobody likes someone who so coldly uses other people. We don't now, and the presumption must be that they didn't then. And more:

> So when this loose behavior I throw off
> And pay the debt I never promisèd,
> By how much better than my word I am,
> By so much shall I falsify men's hopes;
> And, like the bright metal on a sullen ground,
> My reformation, glitt'ring o'er my fault,
> Shall show more goodly and attract more eyes
> Than that which hath no foil to set it off.
> I'll so offend to make offense a skill,
> Redeeming time when men think least I will.
>
>   (I, ii, 212–21)

First, his patrician disgust at the company he has decided to keep—base contagious clouds, foul and ugly mists. Then, behaviour he can apparently 'throw off'; as, perhaps, he can 'throw on' royalty—this is conduct as costume. Conduct as 'commodity' we might say. Certainly, his talk of 'debt' suggests the market world of 'business', and he treats his 'reformation' as, indeed, a commodity which must be shown to its best advantage 'to attract more eyes'. There is nothing very inward going on here—in a later age, such a 'reformation' might well be termed 'other-directed'. As Ornstein points out, the Prince is talking like a clever shopkeeper who 'knows how to display the merchandise of his behaviour'. From any point of view, it is a speech of extreme and unappealing calculation. He might, he will, turn out

to be a good king. But what sort of a man will he be? Rossiter once suggested that Sonnet 94 might provide a way of reading the Prince:

> They that have pow'r to hurt and will do none,
> That do not do the thing they most do show,
> Who, moving others, are themselves as stone,
> Unmovèd, cold, and to temptation slow;
> They rightly do inherit heaven's graces
> And husband nature's riches from expense;
> They are the lords and owners of their faces,
> Others but stewards of their excellence.

It may not fit in every respect, but it will do to be going on with.

   The next scene opens with a speech from the King which could almost be
a continuation of his son's, which it immediately follows.

> My blood hath been too cold and temperate,
> Unapt to stir at these indignities
> . . .
> I will from henceforth rather be myself,
> Mighty and to be feared, than my condition.
>   (I, iii, 1–2, 5–6)

Myself—as king? My condition—my natural disposition? It is a wise man
who knows the one from the other, if, indeed, they are finally separable.
Whether Prince Hal eventually manages to bring 'self' and 'condition' har-
moniously together will remain a debatable point. For a prince in line for
the throne, where lies the 'self' and when and where is he most 'being' it?
But the importance of this scene lies in the introduction of Hotspur—and
his barely controllable fury at the King's peremptory demand that he hand
over his prisoners. Hotspur is the leading representative of the third important realm of the play, termed by Maynard Mack 'the feudal countryside'.
This is a world away from the court and the tavern; based in the north of
England, it is more in touch with Wales and Scotland than London, though
of course the lines of communication are open, and, indeed, this scene takes
place in the council chamber at Windsor. But this is not Hotspur's natural
habitat, and, as Holinshed rather nicely puts it, he is 'not a little fumed'

at the King's arrogant and even supercilious deportment towards him. Hotspur, with his almost fanatical chivalric code, and his headlong, uncalculating (note!), impetuosities, is an almost anachronistic figure, at times made to sound foolish, even childish (petulant beyond constraining, more interested in his horse than his wife, more concerned with romantic honour than prudent strategy); yet he speaks some of the most powerful, trenchant lines in the play, and we would do well to attend to his opinion of King Henry—or, as he would more forcefully have it, 'this unthankful king,/...this ingrate and cank'red Bolingbroke' (I, iii, 134–5). Anger sometimes arrives at ferociously penetrating perceptions.

Harking back to a chivalric age in which he would have been more at home, Hotspur bitterly regrets that his family and friends did help 'To put down Richard, that sweet lovely rose' (I, iii, 173—they are always good, being gone). Henry IV, he sees, is a 'vile politician ... this king of smiles, this Bolingbroke' (I, iii, 239, 244), and he recalls 'what a candy deal of courtesy/This fawning greyhound then did proffer me' (I, iii, 248–9). Readers of Shakespeare will not need reminding of the nausea associated with candy-courtesy in his plays. Hotspur and his associates plan 'revenge' (the old code). By the end of Act I, Henry is not looking so good or so secure—'wan' indeed. He has grief from his own son whom he takes to be a derelict delinquent (in time, a would-be parricide); and he is threatened by a potentially more serious act of insubordination on the part of his wished-for surrogate 'son' (see I, i, 85–9). All my sons—and they are all against me. Hotspur is certainly after both father and son:

> All studies here I solemnly defy
> Save how to gall and pinch this Bolingbroke;
> And that same sword-and-buckler Prince of Wales
>
> (I, iii, 226–8)

And, to keep vividly alive our sense of the contrast between Prince Hal—so sunk in 'dishonor' as far as his father is concerned—and Hotspur, we have Hotspur's vainglorious address to honour:

> By heaven, methinks it were an easy leap
> To pluck bright honor from the pale-faced moon,
> Or dive into the bottom of the deep,

> Where fathom line could never touch the ground,
> And pluck up drownèd honor by the locks
>   (I, iii, 199–203)

A lot of 'honor' is 'drowned' in this play, and how much is finally 'plucked up' is perhaps a moot point.

The scene ends, as have the previous two, with plotting. Hotspur, being Hotspur, can hardly wait.

> O let the hours be short
> Till fields and blows and groans applaud our sport!
>   (I, iii, 298–9)

Every realm has its sports—Hotspur's are fields and blows and groans; Falstaff's sack and thieving and unbuttoning; the King's are, well, the somewhat subtler sports of expediency, counterfeit-regality, and crown-retention.

In this first Act Shakespeare has laid out the topography—geographical and psychological—of his play, and the main figures from each realm have, variously, 'disported' themselves. Bolingbroke, Falstaff, Hotspur—plus the, apparently, so far disengaged and floating Prince; the main thrust of the play will be to trace out how the Prince manages his relationship with these three men, and these three worlds. It matters; it greatly matters —because he is unavoidably due to become the most famous of all English kings. The King and Falstaff look like opposites—true paternal authority and legitimate rule versus a disreputable corrupter of youth and the spirit of misrule. But the King's 'legitimacy' won't bear much scrutiny, and the disorder abroad and spreading in the land is, arguably, of his own bringing and making; and Falstaff, as an undeniable sort of father-figure, can show to the Prince a spirit of inclusive, tolerant humanity, which his real, 'expedient', father shows no sign of possessing. (William Empson once wrote: 'If you compare Hal to his brother and father, whom the plays describe so unflinchingly, it is surely obvious that to love Falstaff was a liberal education.') Again, Hotspur and Falstaff seem to offer the Prince quintessential examples of opposed codes—chivalry and cynicism. Yet both are rebels against the constituted authority in place; both—it is part of their undoubted appeal—are in some ways childish, retarded (from the sombre standpoint of joyless, unenthusing maturity), and both are marked, or marred, by a disabling excess; for if Falstaff drinks too much sherris-sack to be good for anything much, Hotspur so intoxicates himself with fuzzy notions of 'honor' that he finally unfits himself for efficient soldiery. There is no more apt cameo in the play than the spectacle of Falstaff carrying the dead Hotspur from the battlefield on his back in front of the incredulous Prince Hal. 'I am not a double man', he calls out reassuringly to the Prince (V, iv, 137), but Falstaff–Hotspur do, incongruously enough, make up a composite figure (a 'double' act) that Hal will have to go beyond—'transcend' if you like (some critics do), certainly leave behind. Yet Hal is like Hotspur in being young and brave (which is why Shakespeare suggests, unhistorically, they are of an age). Hal is also like Falstaff, at least for a time, joining him in anarchic mockeries on the uncourtly side of town. Hal is also like the King—his first, calculating soliloquy reveals him to be very much his politic father's son, even if repentance and reconciliation are deferred. That is perhaps the main point. Hal is 'like' everybody, and can beat them all at their own games. He out-policies his bemused father; he outwits Falstaff in his tavern knaveries; and he defeats Hotspur at his own chosen sport—on the killing-field of chivalric combat. He knows them all. Certainly, he is the lord and owner of his face.

We have had ruthless kings and rebellious lords before. The crucial addition in the two *Henry IV* plays is, of course, Falstaff and his milieu. The court and the tavern, or the tavern revellers and the noble rebels, might initially seem worlds apart, but they are brought into all sorts of provocative relationships by what A. R. Humphreys nicely calls 'the fabric of linkage'. The behaviour, and thus the authority and proclaimed values, of the court and the nobles, are too often parodied, or travestied, or comically paralleled by what goes on around Falstaff, for us to regard them as anything but seriously challenged and called into question, if not actively undermined. Nothing and no one remains uncontaminated by the prevailing, often quite corrosive, irony—except, perhaps, our ice-cool Prince. But that might prove to be the biggest irony of them all. The point about the various alternating plots—they come together at Shrewsbury—is that 'the more they are scrutinized, the more connected they appear, the connection being sometimes of parallelism and reinforcement, sometimes of antithesis and contrast, sometimes a reversal by which serious or comic is judged by the other's values' (A. R. Humphreys). And the main point about the differing worlds is that, mutually exclusive though they may seem, they all co-exist in one world. For this is all England; and, the point enforces itself, this is all—*all*—history. Well, as far as Shakespeare is concerned.

Before considering the rest of this play, I think it might be advisable to say something about Falstaff as a character, a figure, an emanation, a whatever-he-is. There was a real Sir John Oldcastle (Falstaff's original name) who lived from 1378 to 1417. He was, apparently, a serious gentleman (though he might have been a wild youth), who became High Sheriff of Hereford-shire and later Lord Cobham. A friend of King Henry, he was, subse-quently, 'banished'. He was a Lollard convicted of the Wycliffite heresy, for which he was condemned, captured, and, finally, hanged and burnt. He next appears, or rather his name does, in a play called 'The Famous Victo-ries of Henry the Fifth', probably written around 1594. This anonymous play is crude and chaotic ('like going through the *Henry IV–Henry V* se-quences in a bad dream' as A. R. Humphreys says), and, apart perhaps from its depiction of the young Prince as an out-and-out delinquent, its main interest lies in the fact that one of the Prince's madcap companions is called Sir John Oldcastle. But he is neither funny nor fat, and it's not even clear that he likes a drink. He only speaks some 250 flat words, the likest of which to any spoken by Shakespeare's Falstaff are: 'We shall never have a merry world till the old King be dead' (iv, 39). From Oldcastle to Falstaff is truly a miraculous metamorphosis. (Maynard Mack pointed out another example of what Shakespeare could do with a hint from this play. Mistress Quickly springs from an offhand reference by the Prince to 'the old tavern in Eastcheap' where 'there is a pretty wench that can talk well'.)

Of course, there are other detectable influences. John Dover Wilson set out some of these clearly enough in his *The Fortunes of Falstaff* (1943). Of first importance is the figure of the Devil, or his Vice, from Miracle and morality plays and interludes. He gives as an example 'Youth' (1520) in which Youth insolently banishes Charity to be joined by Riot who intro-duces him to Pride and Lechery. Youth repents, and is saved by Humil-ity. (Falstaff is specifically referred to as riot and Vice and the Devil—'old white-bearded Satan'—in Shakespeare.) Gluttony was a common tempter of youth in these morality plays and interludes, as was Sensual Appetite, Sloth, Idleness, and World, Devil, and Flesh (see, for example, 'The Castell of Perseverance', 'The Interlude of the Four Elements', 'The Trial of Trea-sure'). You can find traces, and more than traces, of all of them in Falstaff.

And of many other figures too—the Clown, the Jester, the Fool, the Lord of Misrule, and the *miles gloriosus* (boasting of bravery but avoiding battle —the braggart, cowardly soldier). Throw in, too, the parasite, the sponger, the trickster—the list seems almost infinitely extendable—many of them, says Dover Wilson, 'antic figures the origins of which are lost in the dark backward and abysm of folk custom'. With all this, we must never forget that Falstaff is never remotely stupid. He is phenomenally adroit and inventive with words, endlessly resourceful, unflaggingly creative. It is interesting that, according to J. P. Collier, Coleridge said: 'It was in characters of complete moral depravity but of first-rate wit and talents, that Shakespeare delighted', and 'instanced Richard the Third, Falstaff, and Iago'. Richard III and Iago! Falstaff is certainly no Father Christmas but, while Coleridge is justified in according him a comparable mental fertility and agility, I don't believe that Falstaff deserves quite to be grouped with such unmitigated evil (would you like a meal with Richard, a drink with Iago?). Dr Johnson hits perhaps a happier note: 'But Falstaff, unimitated, unimitable Falstaff, how shall I describe thee? Thou compound of sense and vice; of sense which may be admired but not esteemed, of vice which may be despised but hardly detested. Falstaff is a character loaded with faults, and with those faults which naturally produce contempt.' Johnson lists the faults —forcefully enough, as you may imagine—and concludes: 'Yet the man thus corrupt, thus despicable, makes himself necessary to the Prince that despises him, by the most pleasing of all qualitites, perpetual gaiety, by an unfailing power of exciting laughter. . .' The thought of Dr Johnson enjoying Falstaff is one which, I think, we can all savour. But, here again, 'perpetual gaiety' doesn't seem quite right by the end of the two plays, by which time also the Prince signals his decision that Falstaff is distinctly *un*necessary to him now that he is King. So—not *toujours Iago,* but not *toujours gai* either.

'And who, in fact, is "he"? "He", really, is the comic personality given a chance by the dramatist to revel in a comic role.' Thus A. R. Humphreys in his admirable Arden edition. And when Humphreys concludes his comments on Falstaff, he is closer to Dr Johnson than to Coleridge. 'In other words, Falstaff, though immensely "living", is not like any single real man. But he is symbolically like life itself; the large comedy of humanity is embodied in him. He expresses the indispensable spirit of fun.' This is certainly one way of looking at Falstaff, though I think it takes us a step closer to Father Christmas than is appropriate. We should, perhaps, set against this a mordant and extremely negative view of Falstaff and the whole world of the play, articulated by John Danby in *Shakespeare's Doctrine of Nature*. We have presented, says Danby, a nation 'disintegrated into mutually exclusive spheres', which is pervaded by 'pitiless fraud'. Falstaff's code of 'Commodity' is the code by which everyone, high and low, lives.

> Analysis leaves us, then, with symbols of Power and Appetite as the keys to the play's meaning: Power and Appetite, the two sides of Commodity . . . The England depicted in *Henry IV* . . . is neither ideally ordered nor happy. It is an England, on the one side, of bawdy house and thieves' kitchen, of waylaid merchants, badgered and bewildered Justices, and a peasantry wretched, betrayed, and recruited for the wars: an England, on the other side, of the chivalrous wolf-pack . . . Those who see the world of *Henry IV* as some vital, joyous, Renaissance England must go behind the facts that Shakespeare presents. It is a world where to be normal is to be anti-social, and to be social is to be anti-human. Humanity is split in two. One half is banished to an underworld where dignity and decency must inevitably submerge in brutality and riot. The other half is restricted to an over-world where the same dignity and decency succumb to heartlessness and frigidity.

This is eloquent, and certainly reminds us of aspects of the play(s) which we must not forget. But ultimately, this isn't quite right either.

Falstaff is not quite such a nihilistic figure as Danby would seem to imply. It is probably better to see him as, in part, embodying the spirit of carnival, as defined by Mikhail Bakhtin in his seminal work, *Rabelais and His World*. This has been done at some length by Graham Holderness (in *Shakespeare Recycled*), to which more interested readers are referred. For Bakhtin, in the Middle Ages 'a boundless world of humorous forms and manifestations opposed the official and serious tone of medieval ecclesiastical and feudal culture . . . the culture of folk carnival humour'. In carnival, social hierarchy was inverted, authority mocked, conventional values profaned, official ceremonies and rituals grotesquely parodied, the normal power structures dissolved—in a word, Misrule, Riot, the world-upside-down. For Bakhtin—he has a political programme—carnival amounted to 'the second life of the people, who for a time entered into the utopian realm of com-

munity, freedom, equality and abundance'. In particular, carnival emphasized, often grotesquely, the flesh and all bodily appetites and functions—
'all that is bodily becomes grandiose, exaggerated, immeasurable'. Most of
this fits 'fat-guts' Falstaff very well (his gross fleshy size and general immersion in physicality is often emphasized; on the other hand, he shows no
very great interest in 'equality'—he has his own knightly contempt for the
poor wretches beneath him, though he will rob and drink with them). To
this extent, Holderness is justified in his general claim that Falstaff is a figure of carnival (though it should be stressed that Falstaff 'embodies' traces
and vestiges and lineaments of many other figures and types—long before
Walt Whitman, Falstaff 'contains multitudes').

> Falstaff clearly performs the function, in *Henry IV Parts One and Two,* of
> carnival. He constitutes a constant focus of opposition to the official and
> serious tone of authority and power: his discourse confronts and chal-
> lenges those of king and state. His attitude to authority is always parodic
> and satirical: he mocks authority, flouts power, responds to the pressures
> of social duty and civic obligation by retreating into Bacchanalian rev-
> elry.

Of course, carnival was a strictly controlled and temporary period of liberation and inversion—a permitted period of licence which arguably served
to consolidate the social hierarchies and institutions which obtained for the
non-carnivalesque rest of the year. Inasmuch as Falstaff wants carnival to
be the permanent and everyday state of affairs, he represents—Holderness
would argue, I think rightly—a potentially dangerous, subversive, uncontainable force or spirit. And, inasmuch as Falstaff is *not* pinned down and
penned down in the chronicles—he inhabits the unconfined spaces of unwritten history—he allows Shakespeare to introduce something dangerous,
subversive, and perhaps ultimately uncontainable into his history *plays.*

Act II is effectively dominated by Falstaff, though I note that it opens
with carriers and ostlers talking about horses. Horses are often referred to
in the play, understandably enough since it is almost seething with people on the move—messengers, traders, merchants, highwaymen, pilgrims,
whole armies either advancing or scattering in retreat. (We tend to forget
how crucial horses were in those days: when Vernon is trying to dissuade
Hotspur from a premature attack, his reason is that the *horses* are tired—

'not a horse is half the half of himself', IV, iii, 24). Horses are also, of course, essential to chivalric deportment. Falstaff roars 'Give me my horse' after Poins and the Prince have 'removed it' (he may or may not be echoing Richard III's famous line) since it is undignified for a knight to go on foot; later, the Prince extends the, rather cruel, joke by arranging for Falstaff to lead a 'charge of foot' ('I would it had been of horse', says Falstaff, rather plaintively). Quite apart from suffering loss of status, anyone less suited to the ambulant mode of travel than Falstaff would be hard to imagine. When Vernon describes Harry 'vaulting' so perfectly on to his horse, it is as though Hal has transformed himself into a true prince. Vernon's description inflames Hotspur with lust for combat. 'I am on fire', he says, and then:

> Come, let me taste my horse,
> Who is to bear me like a thunderbolt
> Against the bosom of the Prince of Wales.
> Harry to Harry shall, hot horse to horse,
> Meet . . .
>
> (IV, i, 118–22)

Hotspur clearly has more 'taste' for his horse than his wife (see II, iii, 75–105), and one can sense his almost erotic excitement at the prospect of meeting 'hot horse to horse'. This is very much a man's world.

The double robbery at Gad's Hill provides an occasion for plenty of ironies. The well-named Gadshill sets the tone when he boasts that he does not rob with vagabond trash, but with those 'who do the profession some grace'. There is a fair amount of punning fun with that last word: 'I am joined with . . . nobility and tranquillity'—he means Sir John, and that last word is a nice collective noun for the idle and the privileged who live life very easily and unpainstakingly—'they pray continually to their saint, the commonwealth, or rather, not pray to her, but prey on her, for they ride up and down on her and make her their boots' (II, i, 82–5). We have already seen Falstaff shift 'from praying to purse-taking' in a trice; and there is much in the play to suggest that, more generally, there is barely a letter's worth of difference between 'praying' and 'preying' among most of the main players, the tranquil and the untranquil alike, so that, in effect, it doesn't take much rhetorical adroitness to mask or cover the latter with the former. They all ride up and down on the commonwealth—when they can find their horses.

When Falstaff finds his horse has been stolen, he memorably complains 'A plague upon it when thieves cannot be true one to another' (II, ii, 27–8)—thus, not coincidentally one feels, anticipating an outburst by Hotspur not a hundred lines ahead (there were no scene divisions, remember) when he complains (in a rather Falstaffian tirade) about fellow conspirators who have let him down. A plague upon it! After the first robbery (i.e. by Falstaff and his men), the Prince says to his fellow-plotter Poins: 'The thieves have bound the true men. Now could thou and I rob the thieves and go merrily to London.' Which is just what they do, the Prince commenting, 'Got with much ease. Now merrily to horse' (II, ii, 93–4, 105). Merrily, merrily indeed (it is a Falstaffian word—'What, shall we be merry?', II, iv, 280). The Prince finds particularly funny the thought that the horseless Falstaff 'sweats to death and lards the lean earth as he walks along' (II, ii, 109)—there is rather an edge to his 'merriment'. Perhaps more pertinently, we may remember that Hal's father 'got' the crown from the 'true' king Richard 'with much ease' (in the next play, we will see Hal literally removing his father's crown, also 'with much ease', though it is a more complex incident). With thieves robbing thieves at every level, can we be sure that there are any 'true men' left? For Gadshill, as we have heard, when it comes to differentiating 'a true man' from 'a false thief' it is pretty much six of one and half a dozen of the other. 'Go to; "homo" is a common name to all men.'

Act II, scene iv, is Falstaff's 'biggest', longest (550 lines) scene, and is in many ways the pivotal scene of the play. Thereafter, the tavern world recedes (apart from one important scene), and we are in the politico-military worlds of the King and the rebels. All roads lead to war. But before that—Eastcheap. It opens with Hal laughing, still in a 'merry' mood, because he has been 'with three or four loggerheads amongst three or fourscore hogsheads. I have sounded the very bass-string of humility' (II, iv, 4–6). He has been drinking and ingratiating himself with a bunch of poor, illiterate sots (loggerheads and hogsheads), calling them by their Christian names, with the result—he boasts—'I am so good a proficient in one quarter of an hour that I can drink with any tinker in his own language during my life' (II, iv, 17–19): 'when I am King of England I shall command all the good lads in

Eastcheap'. They call him, he says, 'the king of courtesy'. Is this a democratic feeling for the people—or is he 'slumming'? King Henry will shortly
advise him to follow his own example:

> And then I stole all courtesy from heaven,
> And dressed myself in such humility
> That I did pluck allegiance from men's hearts.
>   (III, ii, 50–52)

Like father, like son. Hal has anticipated his father's advice—already 'stealing' courtesy, and 'dressing' in humility (we will later hear of 'the garment
of rebellion'—all attitudes and modes of behaviour seem available ready-
to-wear, so to speak). And 'allegiance', like 'honor' is apparently there for
the plucking. The 'proficient' Prince (son of an 'expedient' father) says to
Poins: 'I tell thee, Ned, thou hast lost much honor that thou wert not with
me in this action.' What kind of 'honor' the Prince can 'pluck' from the
tavern, and just how ironic he is being in the use of the word, is indeterminable. Shortly after this speech, he, notoriously, plays his mocking game with
'my puny drawer' Francis, who is gratuitously bewildered and made to
look and sound a fool. It wouldn't do to get too soft or solemn about a bit of
tavern knock-about, but not much 'honor' accrues to the Prince from this
episode. Is he demonstrating how easy it is to fool the people, if necessary
with 'humility' and 'courtesy'? He says of Francis 'His industry is upstairs
and downstairs, his eloquence the parcel of a reckoning' (II, iv, 100–102).
Curiously—or perhaps not so curiously in this play of endless echoing ironies—the words, taken at a slant, are self-applicable. The Prince's 'industry' is both 'upstairs' (the court) and 'downstairs' (the tavern). 'Parcel of a
reckoning' means adding up bills, and if we gloss that as 'calculation'—
what's the profit, what's the loss?—we can say the same of the Prince's 'eloquence'.

Immediately following this description of Francis, the Prince rather
unexpectedly invokes Hotspur—to mock *his* 'industry' (killing dozens of
Scots at breakfast) and 'eloquence' (horsey, and full of martial bravado). Is
this cold-eyed young Prince measuring himself up against *both* Francis *and*
Hotspur? Perhaps. Certainly he goes on to say: 'I prithee call in Falstaff. I'll
play Percy, and that damned brawn shall play Dame Mortimer his wife' (II,
iv, 109–11). They do shortly 'have a play extempore'—where better than

in a tavern where much Elizabethan drama was originally played?—but in the event they don't play the Percys—they play the Bolingbrokes. (Of course, Hal *will* 'play' Hotspur in due course—indeed *out*-play him, at his own game. But not yet.)

This 'play' comes after Falstaff's truly fabulous account of the Gad's Hill episode, followed by his quite dazzling act of self-extrication when the Prince confronts him with the truth of what happened and his own masked participation ('By the Lord, I knew ye as well as he that made ye' II, iv, 268 et seq.). Comment here is quite superfluous. But the 'play extempore' is another matter. It comes after, and is prompted by, an interruption in the tavern by the court—upstairs reaching downstairs—in the form of a messenger described simply but significantly as 'an old man' and 'gravity'. He is a 'nobleman . . . from your father' (this to the Prince)—a grave, parental surrogate sent to call the errant 'madcap' children (various) to order. 'Villainous news,' says Falstaff to the Prince, 'you must to the court in the morning.' Official history is imperiously beckoning, and will not be denied. All very disagreeable and frightening, and, as Falstaff says to the Prince, his father, the King, will give him a very hard time. 'If thou love me, practice an answer.' And the ensuing play shows us, indeed, a prince at 'practice'.

'Do thou stand for my father' (II, iv, 376). Using to-hand appurtenances which are a travesty of the adjuncts of royalty: 'this dagger my scepter . . . this cushion my crown'—even here one feels a barb, for, at one level, what is kingship if not comfort (cushions) defended by force (daggers)?—Falstaff acts the King and starts arraigning the Prince. He takes the opportunity to insult the Prince's appearance and deplore the company he keeps (defiling pitch) with, of course, the exception of one 'virtuous man' often in his company—'there is virtue in that Falstaff. Him keep with, the rest banish' (II, iv, 429–30). That's enough for the Prince, who now wants to change roles. 'Do thou stand for me, and I'll play my father.' Falstaff playing the King is one sort of a joke—we have already gathered that he is, in *some* unspecifiable sense, a surrogate father, or father-figure, for Hal. But the Prince playing the King—the son playing the father—is a different matter. 'Depose me?' complains King Falstaff, staying with the game; yet it will become at least possible that Hal would like to depose his father in good earnest, just as his father had deposed Richard. And when he *is* the king, as he surely will be, will he still be *playing* the king; how will we ever know if this player-king leaves off 'playing'? We are skirting serious matters. Hal takes his opportunity to subject Falstaff to an unrestrained hail of abuse of such virulence that it begins to sound heart-felt. Not just a 'stuffed cloakbag of guts' (par for the course), but 'reverend vice', 'gray iniquity', 'abominable misleader of youth', 'father ruffian', 'white-bearded Satan', and even, simply, 'devil'. James Winny, fastening on *father* ruffian', has suggested that Hal is 'tacitly denouncing his father's viciousness', and that Falstaff is 'unwittingly standing in for the man whose moral character he shares'. This is possible—it might explain the sudden flow of venom if Hal has indeed found a scapegoat for his putative father-hatred; but it is undemonstrable. You just can't tell with Hal. Prince Falstaff of course puts in a spirited defence of the 'merry' old man who keeps the Prince company, ending, famously:

> No, my good lord: banish Peto, banish Bardolph, banish Poins; but for sweet Jack Falstaff, kind Jack Falstaff, true Jack Falstaff, valiant Jack Falstaff, and therefore more valiant being, as he is, old Jack Falstaff, banish not him thy Harry's company, banish not him thy Harry's company, banish plump Jack, and banish all the world!
>
> (II, iv, 474–80)

To which, the King-Prince, as famously, replies: 'I do, I will.'

At this point a chill comes over the play—over both plays—which is never quite warmed away. Partly because one of the effects of the Prince's response is that feeling you get when someone says something outrageous, or deeply disturbing, to you, at the same time maintaining an absolutely impassive face which tacitly says—I defy you to tell whether I am joking or not. Is the Prince still 'playing' the King; or is this the Prince taking the chance to rehearse ('practice') what he will do and say when he *is* king? Is he still playing at all, or has he stepped out of the game? Perhaps he stopped acting some time before this: indeed, did he ever start? Where did all the 'merriment' go? If this can worry and unsettle us, it must trouble Falstaff a good deal more. He, understandably, would like the play to go on indefinitely—'Play out the play'—but, as if on cue, after the Prince's words, a knocking at the door puts an end to the 'sport', and this time it is the Law, in the shape of the Sheriff and the watch, breaking in on the revels. They are after Falstaff, who characteristically sleeps behind the arras while the Prince, with gracious equivocations, sees off the Law. But that knock on the door was a loud one, for history really is breaking in on the play-world of the tavern. As the Prince declares, with all due finality—'We must all to the wars' (II, iv, 546).

The third Act shows us the three worlds for the last time. In Wales, the rebels are dividing up the map in anticipation, and Hotspur loses his temper with what he calls the 'skimble-skamble stuff' of Glendower, who is out-bragging him. Worcester reproaches Hotspur with 'Defect of manners, want of government', and tells him 'You must needs learn, lord, to amend this fault' (III, i, 183, 179). The next scene in the Palace in London, has another intemperate (or thought to be) youth being reproached by a graver elder, this time the King to his son. Rather in the spirit of the parent who says to the child, 'you have been sent to try me', the King tells Hal that, the way he is behaving, he must be serving as 'the rod of heaven / To punish my mistreadings' (III, ii, 10–11). He does not, nor does he ever, confess or spell out what those 'mistreadings' were, but he is clearly a man carrying some guilt. He alludes to 'heaven', and there are scattered references to 'sin' and the like, but—and this is also something of a departure—there is little religious sense in this play, not much 'celestial superintendence' as Maynard Mack put it, no sense of a divine or providential plan. These people, anachronistically or not, inhabit what the commentators call a Tudor Erastian world. Erastus was a sixteenth-century Swiss theologian, promoted in England by Hooker, who maintained—against the extreme Calvinists—that the civil authorities should exercise jurisdiction both in civil and ecclesiastical matters. Generally speaking, 'Erastianism' indicates the ascendancy of the State over the Church in ecclesiastical matters. The most 'religious' language is in the mouth of Falstaff, drowned in flesh and parody. The King believes in 'necessity' and regards ruling as 'business'—'Our hands are full of business' (III, ii, 179)—a word favoured in Shakespeare, by unprincipled plotters. This is a very secular world. The King compares his 'degenerate' son unfavourably with Hotspur, but Hal promises that he will 'redeem all this on Percy's head' (III, ii, 132). His language is, again, revealing. He says he will force Hotspur to '*exchange* / His glorious deeds for my indignities'; Hal will 'call him to so strict *account* / That he shall *render* every glory up . . . Or I will tear *the reckoning* from his heart' (III, ii, 145–52). This is the language of a merchant: Hal will go shopping for honour.

At the end of the scene, the King says: 'Let's away: / Advantage feeds him fat while men delay' (III, ii, 180)—to be immediately followed by Falstaff, complaining, implausibly, that he is getting thinner. 'Bardolph, am I not fall'n away vilely since this last action? Do I not bate? Do I not dwindle?' (III, iii, 1–2). This is a simple joke, but what follows has deeper resonances. 'Well, I'll repent, and that suddenly, while I am in some liking.' We have just heard the Prince promise sudden (opportunistic?) repentance, and when Falstaff goes on to admit 'And I have not forgotten what the inside of a church is made of, I am a peppercorn, a brewer's horse', we may wonder if the Prince is any more familiar with the interior of religious buildings—or beliefs. Most of the rest of the scene has Falstaff bamboozling the honest Hostess, and refusing to pay her what he owes her. Rather shrewdly she says to him: 'You owe me money, Sir John, and now you pick a quarrel to beguile me of it' (III, iii, 68–9). Falstaff is certainly not alone in using this strategy to avoid an incurred debt; indeed, it pretty exactly describes how the King has treated the rebel nobles who once helped him to the throne ('well we know the King/Knows at what time to promise, when to pay', says Hotspur, drily enough—IV, iii, 52–3). There is a lot of stealing in this play, but not much honest repayment of debt. In the previous Act, when the Sheriff arrived and the Prince tells Falstaff to hide behind the arras, he then says, 'Now, my masters, for a true face and good conscience'; Falstaff's parting line is 'Both which I have had; but their date is out, and therefore I'll hide me' (II, iv, 502–5). Their date is out. So it would seem—and the arras is not the only place to hide.

The rest of the play consists of the convergence of all the parties on war, and the concluding battle at Shrewsbury. The most important event, or phenomenon, is the almost miraculous transformation of Prince Henry. Legends of Henry's wild and dissolute youth, and the sudden change and reformation that came over him when he became king, started in his own life-time (in his youth, says a chronicler of 1516, he 'applied him unto all vyce and insolency, and drewe unto him all ryottours and wylde disposed persones'), though it appears there is no historical basis for these stories. Dover Wilson suggested that fifteenth-century allegorical (morality play) taste needed a Prodigal Prince who would then be miraculously converted into the hero of Agincourt. Perhaps. Shakespeare's cool, detached Prince (himself, not so wild after all) is a world away from the unreconstructed, vandalizing thug of *The Famous Victories;* though, interestingly, as Bullough pointed out, he diminishes the Prince's administrative work and experience (he was, in fact, governor of North Wales and the Marches from 1400). Bullough also suggests that if he did have some wild years, they would most likely have been between 1405 and 1410 (when the King was ill, and Hal was aged eighteen to twenty-three)—i.e. *after* Shrewsbury. As usual, Shakespeare wants to tell it his way.

The transformation is, certainly, 'miraculous'. It is celebrated by, occurs in, Vernon's famous 'I saw young Harry with his beaver on' speech (IV, i, 96–109), which is in answer to Hotspur's inquiry as to where the 'madcap Prince of Wales' is, and which starts:

> All furnished, all in arms;
> All plumed like estridges that with the wind
> Bated like eagles having lately bathed;
> Glittering in golden coats like images;
> As full of spirit as the month of May
> And gorgeous as the sun at midsummer

and so on. It concludes by comparing Henry to Mercury and likening him to an 'angel' dropped from the clouds on to a 'Pegasus' who is about to 'witch the world with noble horsemanship'. The poetry of this description has been rightly praised, but I find that there is something strange about it. It is not just the extreme fulsomeness of the admiration, which, understandably enough, irritates Hotspur. It is as if the words were spoken by someone hypnotized, in a trance, as if Vernon has seen a vision. Something similar happens when Vernon describes the exquisitely princely way in which Henry offered his challenge to single combat (V, ii, 51–69). It sounds like an anthology of the principles of 'courtesy', drawing from Hotspur, again understandably, the comment—'Cousin, I think thou art enamored.' Vernon is dazzled; and so are we. I honestly can't quite work out what I think Shakespeare is doing here. Miraculous transformations are, of course, perennially popular, and not just in folk tale, legend, and myth. And here the audience is given, if not quite frog-into-prince, at least tavern layabout into chivalric hero. Perhaps it is as simple as that. Yet Shakespeare has provided such a subtle, penetrating portrait of this complex prince that I find it hard to think that he intended us to forget all we have seen of the unmoved calculator. Vernon's descriptions are marked by excess; they are 'idealized', too much so for Hotspur and perhaps they should be a bit too much for us. Shakespeare likes having soldiers provoked into wonder and praise—as with Enobarbus on Cleopatra in her barge. But I cannot help thinking that Shakespeare would have us think that, in some way, Vernon has been

'taken in', as we say—'enamored' is no bad word for his almost ecstatic evocations. Hal has 'thrown off' his tavern role, and 'put on' the panoply of
chivalry. The indications are that this capable, controlled manipulator has
an extensive 'wardrobe'. I use the word advisedly, for it is used later in the
play, in very telling circumstances. In this connection it is worth noting that
Hal is compared to Mercury, where we might expect—because of Pegasus
—Perseus. Mercury—god of furtiveness and trickery—is always devious,
and traditionally comes disguised or invisible. Perhaps Shakespeare is giving a sign—this prince is always Mercurial. I owe this observation to Jonathan Bate in *Shakespeare and Ovid*.

   The aforementioned use of the word 'wardrobe' occurs during the Battle of Shrewsbury. Fierce Douglas thinks he has killed the King, only to
be told by Hotspur that, in fact, he has killed Blunt, who is 'semblably
furnished like the King himself' (i.e. disguised as the King—V, iii, 21).
Hotspur explains—'The King hath many marching in his coats' (V, iii, 25),
to which Douglas—angry at the rather cowardly cheating (a true soldier
would hardly stoop to this)—answers:

> Now, by my sword, I will kill all his coats:
> I'll murder all his wardrobe, piece by piece,
> Until I meet the King.
>   (V, iii, 26–8)

When he does meet up with King Henry, he suspects another disguised
substitute—another coat to kill:

> Another king? they grow like Hydra's heads.
> . . .   What art thou
> That counterfeit'st the person of a king?

When the King asserts 'The King himself . . . the very King', Douglas is
understandably sceptical:

> I fear thou art another counterfeit;
> And yet, in faith, thou bearest thee like a king
>   (IV, iv, 24, 26–8, 34–5)

The word 'counterfeit' was first heard in Act II, scene iv, when they are told that the Sheriff has arrived at the tavern, and Falstaff, very cryptically, says to Hal: 'Never call a true piece of gold a counterfeit. Thou art essentially made without seeming so' (II, iv, 492–3). This is a much discussed passage, of uncertain meaning and undecidable application. Who is the 'true piece of gold'? Falstaff? The Prince? And in what sense is Hal 'essentially made' (some editors rather desperately suggest it should be 'mad')? We have already seen both Falstaff *and* the Prince to be notable counterfeiters in their different ways, and it becomes evident that 'counterfeiting', in one form or another, is widespread at every level in the land. The battle scenes quite clearly and centrally present us with a 'counterfeit' king, leaving it quite uncertain how far back the counterfeiting goes; where—on all levels—it started, where it stops. Whether, that is, 'appearance' ever gives way to 'essence'; where, and if, true gold is to be found. By extension, I don't think we can ever be quite confident that we meet the 'true', the 'very', Prince—as opposed, that is, to another part of his—undoubtedly well-stocked and carefully maintained—wardrobe. And yet, in faith, he bears himself like a prince at Shrewsbury? Certainly he does. Whatever else, he is his father's son.

The danger and threat of counterfeiting (a hanging offence until comparatively recently) is that it destroys trust and devalues the currency. Something like this happens to the crucial notion of 'honor'. Hotspur, we might say, is the 'essence' of chivalric honour, albeit of a distinctly feudal kind, at times verging on hyperbolic self-parody. Prince Hal overtly parodies him, but at Shrewsbury it seems as if he is determined to replace him—on the self-equivalizing grounds that there is no room for 'two stars':

> Nor can one England brook a double reign
> Of Harry Percy and the Prince of Wales.
> (V, iv, 65–6)

Specifically, he is determined to take Hotspur's honour:

> And all the budding honors on thy crest
> I'll crop to make a garland for my head.
> (V, iv, 71–2)

A cynic might suggest that he wants the garland for his wardrobe; the line at least implies that honour is a movable, removable commodity—not, that is, of the essence. You can crop it off and put it on.

While Hotspur is being truly killed by Henry (for which, incidentally, there is no proper chronicle evidence. Shakespeare clearly wants them to seem rather like 'doubles', with one finally vanquishing the other; the Renaissance displacing feudalism, perhaps—but I won't push that), Falstaff is pretending to be killed by Douglas. Seeing him lying on the ground, the Prince bids him a fairly fond farewell and passes on. As he 'rises up' once the coast is clear (some have detected a resurrection joke), Falstaff self-justifyingly soliloquizes:

> 'Sblood, 'twas time to counterfeit, or that hot termagant Scot had paid me scot and lot too. Counterfeit? I lie; I am no counterfeit. To die is to be a counterfeit, for he is but the counterfeit of a man who hath not the life of a man; but to counterfeit dying when a man thereby liveth, is to be no counterfeit, but the true and perfect image of life indeed ... Zounds, I am afraid of this gunpowder Percy, though he be dead. How if he should counterfeit too, and rise? By my faith, I am afraid he would prove the better counterfeit.
>
> (V, iv, 112–23)

So he stabs Hotspur's corpse—a kind of ultimate physical profanation and desecration of chivalry. And by the time he has repeated the word 'counterfeit' for the ninth time, he has done even more damage, for he has sent the word mockingly echoing into every corner of the play. This occurs barely eighty lines after the exchange between Douglas and the King just discussed, and it opens up the possibility, or suggests the thought, that perhaps the only pertinent consideration, at every level, is—who proves the better counterfeit?

Falstaff, stabbing dead Hotspur, is 'killing' chivalry, and he has already had a comparable deflating effect on the concept and notion of 'honor'. We have already heard his 'catechism' on honour on the eve of the battle— 'What is honor? A word. What is in that word honor? What is that honor? Air—a trim reckoning! Who hath it? He that died a Wednesday. Doth he feel it? No.' (And so, famously, on—see V, i, 129–41.) He strikes the same note when he comes across the body of Blunt. 'I like not such grinning honor as Sir Walter hath. Give me life; which if I can save, so; if not, honor comes unlooked for, and there's an end' (V, iii, 58–61). At such moments, Falstaff is the honest coward, laying no claim to any of the martial, heroic virtues. (We have just seen that he carries a bottle of sack in his pistol case.) Such words and sentiments have an irresistible appeal to the life-at-all-costs coward who exists in, at least, most of us. We invariably feel a spasm of pleasure and liberation when someone 'blows the gaffe on human nature', as Falstaff so often, consciously and unconsciously, does. By a recognizable convention, a soliloquizing figure is telling the truth to us, and himself, about what he is, what he believes, what he desires, what he intends. At such moments, at least, Falstaff is *not* counterfeit. He may not be gold, but he is, we feel, being true. The effect he has on the play can hardly be calculated. By what he says, by what he *is*, Falstaff calls into question, makes a mockery of, undermines (many verbs are applicable to his effect) the ideals, values, virtues which men cherish and invoke (if not embrace) as giving meaning, dignity, purpose to their lives. He does, indeed, seem to have the effect, intended or not, of devaluing—perhaps *dis*valuing is better—all values: not just, as we have seen, kingship and honour; but honesty, courage, responsibility ('I have misused the King's press damnably', IV, ii, 12), compassion ('food for powder, food for powder, they'll fit a pit as well as better. Tush, man, mortal men, mortal men', IV, ii, 67–8), continence, and so on indefinitely. There is no being serious about any serious things around Falstaff—he can reduce them to absurdity with a word. A great unbuttoner, indeed! Falstaff's effectual destruction of values and, let us call them, the official virtues, wherever he goes, has led some to detect more than a touch of the true Devil (Uncreator, Disvaluer Supreme) about him, and one can see why. Certainly, we can hardly take the King, Hotspur, and, I think, Prince Hal, at face value, or at their own self-estimations, with the proximity of Falstaff. We can never quite get away from the possibility that, simply, they prove the better counterfeits. Just before the Battle of Shrewsbury, the King says—'nothing can seem foul to those that win' (V, i, 8), while after the successful conclusion, in the last words of the play, he says:

> And since this business so fair is done,
> Let us not leave till all our own be won.
>
> (V, v, 43–4)

Simple. If you win, the 'business' is 'fair'. 'Foul-ness' is losing. It is impossible not to call this Machiavellian. If Falstaff makes 'fair' things 'foul'—or simply dissolves the difference between them—he is certainly not alone in so doing.

But because there is widespread 'counterfeiting' it does not mean there is nothing 'true', nor does the shameless displaying of cowardice discount the reality of courage—even if you will find most honesty in a tavern hostess (Mistress Quickly) and true bravery in a poor country conscript, Feeble (Part Two). It may be, as Falstaff laments, 'a bad world', but it is *not* the case, as he all too self-applicably asserts, that 'there is nothing but roguery to be found in villainous man' (II, iv, 132, 125). There are no (or few) absolute conditions. Things come mixed, and in the matter of values and virtues too, it is nearly always a matter of more and less. A usurper king still has to reign, and he may be better at it than his legitimate predecessor. Shakespeare was not a nihilist, though his all-encompassing realism necessarily made him sceptical—and nowhere more far-reachingly so than in the *Henry IV* plays which comprise his finest achievement in the history genre (and in which the poetry is everywhere marked by a particular metaphorical force and pungency, abstractions constantly becoming physical—'Supposition all our lives shall be stuck full of eyes,' says one of the rebels—V, ii, 8; I choose almost at random. There is, in the *Henry IV* plays, poetry of the sort of compact power and metaphorical velocity we associate with *Macbeth*.) What Shakespeare does, in these plays preeminently, is expose the realities of the amoral concern for power behind the pious orthodoxies and beneath the self-protective carapaces of men in high —and not so high—places. These words by A. P. Rossiter get it right, I think:

> Because the Tudor myth system of Order, Degree, etc. was too rigid, too black-and-white, too doctrinaire and narrowly moral for Shakespeare's mind: it falsified his fuller experience of man. Consequently, while employing it as FRAME, he had to undermine it, to qualify it with equivocations: to view its applications with sly or subtle ambiguities: to cast doubts on its ultimate human validity, even in situations where its principles seemed most completely applicable. His intuition told him it was *morally* inadequate.

There is a lot of unfinished business left by the end of the play, and it seems clear that Shakespeare already had the second part in mind.

HENRY IV, PART TWO (1597–8)

> From a God to a bull? A heavy descension! It was Jove's case. From a
> prince to a prentice? A low transformation!
>
> (II, ii, 173–5)

Perhaps rather surprisingly, Shakespeare only used the word 'metamorphosed' in one play, *The Two Gentlemen of Verona* (where he uses it twice); but the words 'transform', 'transformed', 'transformation', recur in his plays from early to late: it was a phenomenon, a process, which continually interested him. And this part of *Henry IV* is primarily a play of 'low transformations' and 'heavy descensions'. The main movement is that of downward degeneration. Royalty is tired; characters are visibly ageing or sick; things are 'dull', 'heavy', 'lead'; one image has men's spirits frozen up 'as fish are in a pond'; a man's tongue tolls bad news like 'a sullen bell'; the recruited militia is Feeble, Moldy, Shadow. The scenes in Gloucestershire bring rustic provincial England into the play, and allow some amiable intimations of rural realities; but the supervising Justices are Shallow—a comic analogue to the Lord Chief Justice in Westminster, who, by a 'low transformation', has 'turned into a justice-like servingman', and whose 'justice' indeed proves to be 'shallow'—and Silence. It is a comic enough world, but it is a world grown senile and sleepy, ripe for falling. Falstaff has become a much coarser, at times rather sinister, figure; the tavern has become a brothel; Pistol's bragging, bar-room violence is a sad travesty of Hotspur's rash, feudal valour; and the ending of the second rebellion, in the Forest of Gaultree, is a much nastier, meaner business than the open fighting on the battlefield at Shrewsbury. There is *no* honour, no chivalry, not even any honest combat in this play. 'What trust is in these times?' asks the Archbishop despairingly (I, iii, 100), and the answer is—virtually none: words are not kept, debts are not paid. The feeling could be called entropic: death and termination are in the air.

When Henry IV finally appears—which is not until Act III—he is in his 'nightgown'; it is hardly a regal entry. If he started 'shaken' and 'wan', he is in visibly worse shape now. In a remarkably powerful, heart-felt soliloquy, he laments his terrible insomnia:

> O sleep, O gentle sleep,
> Nature's soft nurse, how have I frighted thee,
> That thou no more wilt weigh my eyelids down
> And steep my senses in forgetfulness?
>   (III, i, 5–8)

Not quite 'Macbeth hath murdered sleep', perhaps; but not far from it. Certainly, when he concludes—

> Uneasy lies the head that wears a crown
>   (III, i, 31)

—we are convinced that this head is very uneasy indeed (as usual, he never quite says why, though it becomes unmistakably clear that the cause is the 'unkinging' and murder of Richard). He is 'weary' and 'sick' throughout, complaining that 'health . . . is flown/From this bare, withered trunk' (IV, v, 229). (Falstaff, the other 'father-king', is addressed as 'thou dead elm', II, iv, 339: this part of the 'forest' is failing.) Shakespeare's intention is fairly clear here. Holinshed gave Henry a healthy and active ten years between Shrewsbury and his death. Samuel Daniel, in his long poem on the Civil Wars between the Two Houses of Lancaster and York, depicts a sleepless king, beset by 'intricate turmoils, and sorrows deep' some time before his death. Shakespeare makes him continuously sick from the time of Shrewsbury. This, no doubt, because he wished to show, or suggest, a sick nation. The King sees it in these terms:

> you perceive the body of our kingdom
> How foul it is, what rank diseases grow,
> And with what danger, near the heart of it.
>   (III, i, 38–40)

and so do the rebels:

we are all diseased,
And with our surfeiting and wanton hours
Have brought ourselves into a burning fever,
And we must bleed for it. Of which disease
Our late king, Richard, being infected, died.

(IV, i, 54–8)

In a word, each party sees the other as the source of the 'disease', but all agree there is a prevailing sickness. (The King foresees more 'rotten times' to come, when his riotous son succeeds him, though here, of course, Shakespeare, and history, have a surprise in store.) There is much talk of individual sickness—pox, gout, gluttony, apoplexy, and so on—and the need for doctoring, physic, medicines, diet, purging, and other remedies (there are a number of references to 'vomit') is often remarked on. At the very start, Northumberland is 'crafty-sick'. Then Falstaff, notably, makes his entrance asking what the doctor says 'to my water', to be told that the diagnosis is that 'the party that owed it . . . might have moe diseases than he knew for' (I, ii, 5). It is typical of the rather acridly cynical turn his speech has taken, that Falstaff should say: 'A good wit will make use of anything. I will turn diseases to commodity' (I, ii, 258–9). 'That smooth-faced gentleman, tickling commodity . . . this bawd, this broker, this all-changing element', as the Bastard in *King John* put it, shows here with more ravaged features. The prostitute Doll (there were no manifest prostitutes in Part One—the tavern has become more sordid) asks Falstaff when he is going to 'begin to patch up thine old body for heaven?' (II, iv, 237). And it is that 'old body' which is now very much to the fore.

Reminders of age and ageing are everywhere. The Lord Chief Justice has 'some smack of an age in you, some relish of the saltness of time in you' (I, ii, 101–2). Falstaff is not alone in being 'as a candle, the better part burnt out' (I, ii, 161). The one-time merry-making acquaintance of Falstaff and Shallow, Jane Nightwork, is old—'Nay, she must be old. She cannot choose but be old. Certain she's old' (III, ii, 212–13). When Falstaff, preposterously, tries to pass himself as young, he gets this from the Lord Chief Justice:

Do you set down your name in the scroll of youth, that are written down old with all the characters of age? Have you not a moist eye, a dry hand, a yellow cheek, a white beard, a decreasing leg, an increasing belly? Is

not your voice broken, your wind short, your chin double, your wit single, and every part about you blasted with antiquity, and will you yet call
yourself young? Fie, fie, fie, Sir John!

(I, ii, 185–93)

Falstaff has a deflecting, parrying answer—he always does, and his re-
sourcefulness is still intact; but he may have felt, as Hamlet put it, also talking about the condition of old men, 'we hold it not honesty to have it thus
set down!' But Falstaff knows his condition; knows he is an 'old pike' still
snapping up 'young dace' (III, ii, 341). He confesses in a soliloquy, 'Lord,
Lord, how subject we old men are to this vice of lying!' (III, ii, 313). And,
lying in the arms of Doll Tearsheet at the tavern, he says, with an uncharacteristic simplicity which has its own pathos—'I am old, I am old' (II, iv,
278). He adds—''A grows late; we'll to bed. Thou'lt forget me when I am
gone,' and we feel that it is growing late in every sense, that this world is
grown old and is entering a terminal twilight, moving towards its final
sleep and oblivion as a last dusk settles over it. It is a curiously moving moment, in what has become a rather squalid setting. It even sets the tempes-
tuous and rather foul-mouthed Doll 'a-weeping'.

When Doll mentions 'heaven', Falstaff gives a shiver—'Do not speak like
a death's-head. Do not bid me remember mine end' (II, iv, 240). But 'ends'—
conclusions and concludings, outcomes and terminations—are constantly
referred to. 'Let the end try the man,' warns the Prince while still in his
tavern days (II, ii, 46): 'Well, hearken o' th' end,' says Doll, fatalistically (II,
iv, 287): 'Let time shape, and there an end,' says Falstaff, with perspicuous
resignation (III, ii, 343). The sense of time past, time passing, is strong in
this play. 'We see which way the stream of time doth run,' says the Archbishop (IV, i, 70), referring to 'the rough torrent of occasion' which has
forced them into rebellion: the rebels stand in time present, aiming to
change time future. But, the 'rough torrent of occasion' is wearing them all
down, sweeping them all away; and, from the court to the tavern, 'the
stream of time' often runs backwards. The King remembers Richard with a
guilty sadness; Hostess Quickly recalls the twenty-nine years she has known
Falstaff with a forgiving fondness; Shallow casts his mind back fifty-five
years to what he likes to think of as his wild youth at the Inns of Court. 'We
have heard the chimes at midnight, Master Shallow' (III, ii, 220), Falstaff
nods concurringly. A slightly melancholy, 'long-ago' feeling is pervasive.

The 'endless end' is, of course, death, and it tolls throughout the play, from Morton bringing the news of the 'hateful death' of Hotspur—ending with 'Brother, son, and all are dead' (I, i, 81), to Shallow's intimations of mortality, 'shallow' though they may be: 'and to see how many of my old acquaintance are dead! . . . Death, as the Psalmist saith, is certain to all, all shall die' (III, ii, 35–40). From Northumberland's castle, to the Court and taverns of London, to the houses of Gloucestershire—all shall die. It becomes a question whether this sick, weary, ageing, dying world can produce anything regenerative for the future; whether, that is, there is any new world waiting to be born—or, perhaps, waiting to reign.

From the beginning, when Northumberland, with 'strained passion', hysterically cries out: 'Now let not Nature's hand / Keep the wild flood confined! Let order die!' (I, i, 153–4—with a contradictoriness typical of the play, he talks the lion and acts the coward, persuaded by his womenfolk to flee to Scotland); to the King on his death-bed, foreseeing that, under his son, his kingdom 'wilt be a wilderness again' (IV, v, 136), crying despairingly:

> Pluck down my officers, break my decrees,
> For now a time is come to mock at form.
> (IV, v, 117–18)

there is a growing sense of a world about to collapse in ruin and chaos, all form and order mocked or gone. When the King dies, the Lord Chief Justice succinctly sums up the general dread—'I fear all will be overturned' (V, ii, 19). In such a state of affairs, Falstaff would be in his element; indeed, as a kind of Lord of Misrule, he is committed to the overturning (as well as the unbuttoning) of order and form. He thinks the death of the King marks the beginning of *his* reign—'be what thou wilt, I am fortune's steward! . . . the laws of England are at my commandment. Blessed are they that have been my friends, and woe to my Lord Chief Justice' (V, iii, 132, 139–40). Given what we have seen of his 'friends', not to mention his disdain for all laws, this would promise anarchy indeed. But, there is another King and, as he and we are soon to discover, he has other ideas.

In his gross, deteriorating physicality, Falstaff almost literally 'embodies' all the diseases, corruptions, and degenerate appetites of the dying world, which must be somehow rejected, dismissed, purged, or just left behind.

Perhaps, as has been suggested, he does figure the old 'god' who must be slain or banished in a sacrificial rite in order to restore health to the blighted, blasted land. He seems, curiously, at once more threatening and less powerful in this play. He still manifests, for the most part, that 'absolute self-possession and masterly presence of mind' which Hazlitt admired. He still has his adroit way of 'wrenching the true cause the false way' (II, i, 113). But when the Chief Justice says to him, almost contemptuously—'You speak as having power to do wrong' (II, i, 133), we realize he has none in any significant sense (he can still abuse a tavern hostess or a country simpleton). His world is beginning to disintegrate around him—we last see his women being arrested and taken away, charged with complicity in some unspecified murder, and despite his boast he cannot save them. He is not the man he was, and in his ill-founded conviction of personal invulnerability and influence in high places, he is in increasing danger of emerging more clearly as the 'great fool' the Chief Justice thinks him. Crucial here is his changed relationship with the Prince, which is central to the play.

We hear at the start that 'the King hath severed you [Falstaff] and Prince Harry' (I, ii, 211), but there is much to suggest that the Prince has already started to separate himself from Falstaff. When we first see the Prince, he is back with Poins and other taverners asking for 'small beer', and of course we think he has simply regressed to his old low-life habits. (We have already heard of his—legendary—striking of the Lord Chief Justice, dramatized in the *Famous Victories,* but, perhaps discreetly, left off-stage by Shakespeare.) But the tone is different. His opening words—'I am exceeding weary'—suggest he partakes of the general tiredness; then when he goes on to say that he is 'out of love with my greatness' (II, ii, 1, 13), we may begin to wonder how far his feelings of disaffection and alienation extend. Certainly, Poins tells him that everyone thinks he is still 'so lewd and so much engraffed to Falstaff' (II, ii, 62), and even near the end the King is convinced (and informed) that his son is still accompanied by his 'continual followers', indulging his 'headstrong riot' (IV, iv, 62). But, even in that first scene with Poins, it is clear that the Prince no longer knows whether Falstaff frequents his old drinking haunts, and he has never heard of Doll Tearsheet. In the event, he shares only one scene with Falstaff, prior to the climactic rejection scene, and the scene merits some particular comment.

After receiving a rather pompous and patronizing letter from Falstaff, which however touches a nerve when it airily says, 'Repent at idle times as thou mayst' (II, ii, 129)—since he will have to 'repent' a second time—the Prince resolves to go to the tavern with Poins, disguised as drawers, to 'see Falstaff bestow himself tonight in his true colors' (II, ii, 170). The resulting scene is clearly intended as a dark echo of the comparable long tavern scene in Part One, and is situated at exactly the same point in the play— the end of Act II. Almost Falstaff's first words are 'Empty the Jordan!' (i.e. chamber pot) which, like his opening reference to his urine, link him more firmly than ever with the lower bodily functions. He immediately engages in rather abrasive banter about venereal disease with Doll Tearsheet. The Hostess has already addressed Falstaff as 'honeysuckle villain . . . honeyseed rogue' (II, i, 51)—but she means, of course, 'homicidal', and in truth much of the 'sweetness'—the more delectable part—has drained away from this coarser, 'sourer', Falstaff. 'These are very bitter words,' says the Hostess, accurately enough, about the general level of conversation in the tavern which is, by turns, salacious, insulting, and violent. Falstaff engages in some extravagant abuse of the Prince, unaware, of course, that he is listening. When the Prince reveals himself and accuses Falstaff—'You whoreson candle-mine you, how vilely did you speak of me' (II, iv, 308)—Falstaff can only rather lamely insist, 'No abuse Hal. None, Ned, none.' It is a marked falling off from the inspired way he self-exculpatingly extricated himself from his blatant lies about the Gad's Hill fiasco. The Prince has no pleasant or fond, or even friendly, words for Falstaff. The scene is interrupted, as was its counterpart in Part One, by a knocking on the door and a summons from Westminster, and 'Falstaff, good night' are the only polite words the Prince says to his old companion of the revels as he takes up his sword and cloak and leaves. Falstaff follows soon after—they are all off to the wars— and we should note that the sorely-tried Hostess says to him 'an honester and truer-hearted man—well, fare thee well' (II, iv, 394), while Doll 'comes blubbered' (i.e. marked with weeping). The tears of a sentimental whore, perhaps: but perhaps also, the man has still 'honey' enough in him to love.

Watching Falstaff and Doll at dalliance, the Prince comments to Poins— 'Saturn and Venus this year in conjunction!' (II, iv, 270). He has already compared himself to Jove, as he disguised himself as a tavern 'drawer'— 'From a God to a bull? A heavy descension! It was Jove's case' (II, ii, 173–4). At his coronation procession (when he is finally crowned King), Falstaff, still confident of his favour, calls out to him—'My king! My Jove! I speak to thee, my heart!' (V, v, 47)—only to receive what is, I suppose, the most

famous rebuff in literature: 'I know thee not, old man.' Jove–Jupiter–Zeus
(= father of the bright heaven) was the god of the new order who deposed
his 'father', Saturn–Cronos (associated, it might be remembered, with agriculture and fertility, and whose celebrations—saturnalia—were periods of
festivity and licence); and this is the moment when Jove–Henry V displaces,
and terminates the 'reign' of, the old 'god', Saturn–Falstaff. (I think Philip
Williams is justified in suggesting that the real sick, old, father-king who
has to be displaced by the regenerating son is Henry IV, and that the rejection of Falstaff is, among other things, a sacrificial rite, the 'slaying' of the
surrogate 'father', the scapegoat.

Much has been written justifying Hal's spurning of Falstaff at this point.
History, legend, and the chronicles all required the abrupt rejection by the
Prince-now-King of his former reveller-friends. And, clearly, Falstaff is a
most inappropriate leader and guide (a false staff to lean on, indeed) for a
king who will reign over one of the glorious periods of English history. We
have seen the miraculous transformation of the madcap rioter into chivalric warrior at Shrewsbury; and, so the argument goes, we here witness the
transformation of the clearly somewhat disenchanted reveller into committed upholder of justice at his coronation at Westminster—when Hal adopts
the impeccable Lord Chief Justice as his appropriate new father figure:
'You shall be as a father to my youth' (V, ii, 118). Moreover, we have been
well prepared for the rejection. Both Hal's first soliloquy ('I know you all'
etc.), and the 'play' ('Banish plump Jack, and banish all the world'—'I do,
I will'), give clear notice of what is to come. Only recently, Warwick has
sought to reassure the King:

> The Prince but studies his companions
> Like a strange tongue . . .
> The Prince will in the perfectness of time
> Cast off his followers . . .
>   (IV, iv, 68–9, 74–5)

though quite how Warwick knows this when the King and the rest of the
court still think the Prince to be an unreconstructed reprobate, is not clear.
Some critics regard the rejection of Falstaff as a, perhaps regrettable, necessity, but certainly an inevitable one. It is pointed out that he is not *so* harshly
treated, and will, in any case, be provided for. It gave Dr Johnson no prob-

lems, insisting that 'since Falstaff has nothing in him that can be esteemed, no great pain will be suffered from the reflection that he is compelled to live honestly'. All this is true enough, and, from the point of view of the theatrical effect, the rejection has to be both anticipated and, when it comes, a sudden shock. Inevitable, yes; but by any standards it is a cruel public humiliation.

> I know thee not, old man. Fall to thy prayers.
> How ill white hairs becomes a fool and jester!
> I have long dreamt of such a kind of man,
> So surfeit-swelled, so old, and so profane,
> But, being awaked, I do despise my dream.
> Make less thy body hence, and more thy grace.
> . . .
> Presume not that I am the thing I was,
> For God doth know, so shall the world perceive,
> That I have turned away my former self.
>   (V, v, 48–53, 57–9)

He has 'put on' the mantle of majesty ('I will deeply put the fashion on'— this, of mourning for his father—V, ii, 52), as his father used to 'dress' himself in humility; and, perhaps, as he put on a leather jerkin and apron to spy on Falstaff in the tavern, which he has now, presumably, finally 'thrown off'. He is, as always, the lord and owner of his face—and as unmoved as stone. Shakespeare has prepared us for this, too.

'I know you not'—these were Christ's words to the foolish virgins; He uses them again in the parable of the few who shall be saved, and the many who shall be excluded—presumably to be damned. The 'master of the house' says to those knocking on the door—'I know you not whence ye are':

> 26. Then shall ye begin to say, We have eaten and drunk in thy presence, and thou hast taught in our streets.
> 27. But he shall say, I tell you, I know you not whence ye are; depart from me, all ye workers of iniquity.
>   (Luke 13)

The echo of these familiar words from the gospels would not, I surmise, have been lost on much of Shakespeare's audience. Falstaff has certainly eaten and drunk in the princely presence, and qualifies with little trouble as a 'worker of iniquity'. However, I hardly think this makes of the Prince a Christ-figure. In a play (both parts) of such multiple, trenchant, often subversive ironies, I think it is more likely to be sombrely parodic (indeed, I might even suggest that the always straight-faced Prince is permitting himself a slightly blasphemous quotation). For it is quite inconceivable to me that Shakespeare did not feel, and thus intend to portray, the inhumanity, not of the 'severance' itself (it has clearly been coming), but of the mode and manner—this actual moment—of the rejection. Falstaff may deserve what he gets, and be lucky to get off with a pension; and so, very sensibly, we could continue our justifications and extenuations. But the tavern Hostess, arguably the most honest character in the plays (though I suppose I should add the Lord Chief Justice—which makes a happy pairing!), seems to me to have the truth of the matter when she says of her old friend quite simply—'The King has killed his heart' (*Henry V,* II, i, 91). In banishing plump Jack, Hal has not banished the *whole* world, but he *has* banished *a* world which, no matter how disreputable, coarse, and unruly, contains genuine values and important qualities not to be found at court; and, arguably, he has banished a part of his own humanity as well. (Even more seriously, for us, he has banished Falstaff from his next play. But more of that in due course.)

The play, unusually for Shakespeare, starts with a Prologue (or Induction) spoken by 'Rumor, painted full of tongues'.

> Upon my tongues continual slanders ride,
> The which in every language I pronounce,
> Stuffing the ears of men with false reports.
>
>   (6–8)
> ...   The posts come tiring on,
> And not a man of them brings other news
> Than they have learned of me. From Rumor's tongues
> They bring smooth comforts false, worse than true wrongs.
>
>   (37–40)

The play is full of 'tongues' (Falstaff claims to have 'a whole school of tongues in this belly of mine', and he is certainly a fit emissary of Rumor), 'false reports', 'smooth comforts false', unreliable 'news', 'rotten opinion'. The very first scene has Lord Bardolph bringing the 'certain news' to Northumberland that his son, Hotspur, has killed Prince Harry, which quickly proves to be *un*certain news indeed. ('News' also has uncertain, even contradictory effects. 'In poison there is physic,' says Northumberland, finally convinced of the truth of the news of his son's death: 'these news . . . being sick, have in some measure made me well', I, i, 139. It seems there is also poison in physic: 'wherefore should these good news make me sick?' says the King, taken ill even as he is told of the successful defeat of his enemies, IV, iv, 102. Inexplicably, the people are said to be 'sick of happiness', IV, i, 64.) But nearly everyone falls victim, one way or another, to 'false report' and 'smooth comforts false'. The King believes his son has gone to the dogs, while Falstaff is confident of his benevolent patronage—both are proved wrong. Falstaff, a character of 'pure fear and entire cowardice' (II, iv, 333), has gained a reputation for bravery (presumably by having claimed to have killed Hotspur) in which even the Lord Chief Justice seems to believe, and to which the genuine warrior Coleville surrenders, to be promptly executed —a rough reward for his credulity. Shallow believes Falstaff will return the thousand pounds he has borrowed; while, probably an even wilder expectation, Mistress Quickly thinks Falstaff will keep his promise to marry her. Even names can be misleading—Bullcalf is a coward, Feeble is brave, and Fang is pretty toothless. 'Words' are everywhere, but it is uncertain how many of them are to be trusted. What certainty is in these times? After the rebels have worked through a series of architectural images for their planned rebellion ('When we mean to build,/We first survey the plot, then draw the model' and so on—see I, iii, 41–62), the Archbishop says:

> An habitation giddy and unsure
> Hath he that buildeth on the vulgar heart.
>
> (I, iii, 89–90)

They want to make sure they have 'a sure foundation' on which to 'build' their rebellion, but, like so many of the structures of expectation erected by hope, desire, fear, or trust, it turns out to be 'an habitation giddy and unsure'—and not just because of the 'vulgar heart'. The lack of 'sure foundation'—grounds for total trust—is pervasive, ubiquitous. The Prince-now-King, about to effect his sudden transformation into regality, promises 'To mock the expectation of the world' (V, ii, 126). Everywhere, expectation is mocked, and people disillusioned into ruin and death.

Nowhere more graphically and shockingly than at Gaultree, when John of Lancaster (Hal's younger brother) promises the rebels that, if they 'discharge' their armies ('as we will ours'), their 'griefs shall be with speed redressed'. 'I . . . swear here, by the honor of my blood,' he says. The Archbishop accepts the pledge: 'I take your princely word for these redresses.' John says, 'Let's drink together friendly and embrace' to celebrate 'our restored love and amity' (IV, ii, 54–66). They duly drink, and the rebels discharge their men who are soon dispersed. At which point, John, whose army has remained in place, arrests the rebel leaders on charges of 'capital treason' and orders their immediate execution—adding, with supreme pious hypocrisy:

> God, and not we, hath safely fought today.
>
> (IV, ii, 121)

Much the Bolingbrokes have ever cared about 'God'.

Now all this is clearly appalling. Mowbray's complaint, 'Is this proceeding just and honorable?' (IV, ii, 110), seems mild indeed. Some critics commend John for being a good Machiavel; others say he is just playing by the stern laws of 'necessity' which are constantly invoked. ('Construe the times to their necessities'—IV, i, 102—says Westmoreland, in justification of all the King's crimes. Henry himself says, 'Are these things then necessities? / Then let us meet them like necessities'—III, i, 92–3. 'Necessity' rules all; explains all; excuses all. Henry's 'necessitarianism' might argue him a pragmatist; but it can serve as an amoral, self-exculpating creed.) I have even read one who maintains that Shakespeare would probably have approved of John's trick—on the grounds, roughly, that with rebels, anything goes. I find the suggestion utterly extraordinary. I have no doubts that Shakespeare shared the general Elizabethan horror of rebellion and civil war, and that, quite apart from his need to defer to historical fact, he would have thought that Henry, no matter how illegitimately he came by the crown, had to contain the threat of civic disorder. But the manner of the 'defeat'—the deceit, the betrayal, the smooth, unperturbed ruthlessness—is shocking; and if we find it shocking, then we may be sure that Shakespeare found it so too, and wrote it to be so. A Prince foresworn; the 'princely word' broken; the rites of reconciliation and amity profaned; God blasphemed—it is a sorry day's work. What trust is in these times indeed? (One interesting change Shakespeare made to the account of this event in his source—Holinshed has Westmoreland entirely responsible for the whole treacherous trick, whereas Shakespeare makes John of Lancaster the only begetter of the shameless strategy. Why? Perhaps he wants to show another Bolingbroke as a cool, unprincipled operator. Henry's handling of Richard; Hal's treatment of Falstaff; the way 'sober-blooded' John deals with the rebels—by this time, we may begin to think it runs in the family!)

We must conclude by considering the Prince-now-King, since clearly the end of the play celebrates a 'high' transformation—not exactly from a bull to a God; but at least from an apparent (and in Shakespeare, *only* apparent) madcap rioter capable of boffing the Lord Chief Justice, to a perfect King, implacable upholder of the Law. (To make the metamorphosis seem more sudden and miraculous, Shakespeare omits any reference to the fact that Prince Henry was active in national politics from 1410–1413, and, on his accession, was already an experienced administrator. He was also clearly ambitious and something of a schemer, trying to force his father's abdication in 1411—Shakespeare leaves that out, too.) In short, errant Hal must now emerge, as from a chrysalis, as the glorious Henry V. The prince in waiting need kick his heels no longer. For good or bad, good *and* bad perhaps, there can, and will, be no more tavern-house regressions.

Henry IV, weary and seemingly conscience-plagued, has become a brooding pessimist:

> O God, that one might read the book of fate,
> And see the revolution of the times
> Make mountains level, and the continent,
> Weary of solid firmness, melt itself
> Into the sea! And other times to see
> The beachy girdle of the ocean
> Too wide for Neptune's hips. How chances, mocks,
> And changes fill the cup of alteration
> With divers liquors! O, if this were seen,

> The happiest youth, viewing his progress through,
> What perils past, what crosses to ensue,
> Would shut the book, and sit him down and die.
>
> (III, i, 45–56)

There is more than a hint of tragic feelings in these lines—more King Lear than King Henry. At the very least, we can say that Henry IV is losing his taste for history, and the making of history. But the last thing his son can do is 'sit him down and die'. His father is a dying king reigning over a dying world: England needs a new king, a new start, a new 'mood'. And this is promised. On his death-bed, Henry says to Hal:

> And now my death
> Changes the mood, and what in me was purchased
> Falls upon thee in a more fairer sort,
> So thou the garland wear'st successively.
>
> (IV, v, 198–201)

For Henry, the crown has always sat 'troublesome' on his 'uneasy' head. Because it was 'purchased'—i.e. *not* acquired by inheritance, as crowns should be. His hope is that 'succession' is hereby restored, and his son will enjoy 'better quiet,/ Better opinion, better confirmation' (IV, v, 187–8). Of course, legitimate succession has not *really* been restored—and the Wars of the Roses are less than fifty years away. But for now, the death of Henry IV 'changes the mood'. And Hal has converted, apparently, to true kingliness.

As a prince, he shows no very evident desire for the crown, no usurping or parricidal hunger to take his father's place (here again, one suspects that Shakespeare is deliberately keeping his record rather cleaner than a fuller 'history' would allow; grooming him, perhaps, for repentance, conversion, and the great things to come—which will be more plausible if he was never really *that* bad). He insists that he feels genuine sorrow at his father's sickness ('my heart bleeds inwardly'), but explains that he would be thought a hypocrite if he made a display of grief—as well he might. The testing moment is his legendary taking of the crown from the pillow while his father is asleep. This is usually taken as a fairly unequivocal sign of his eagerness to be king. In Holinshed, when the King wakes up and asks the Prince what on earth he thinks he is doing, the Prince—'with a good audacity'

—simply says: I thought you were dead and thus the crown was mine. At which point, the King shruggingly relinquishes it with a remark to the effect that he didn't have much right to it in the first place. Shakespeare makes much more out of the episode. First, the Prince meditates on the ambivalences, the paradoxes of the crown and all it implies—'O polished perturbation! Golden care!':

> O majesty!
> When thou dost pinch thy bearer, thou dost sit
> Like a rich armor worn in heat of day,
> That *scald'st with safety*.
> (IV, v, 27–30, my italics)

Then, thinking his father dead, he takes the crown as his 'due', and shows all his father's tenacity of power in his articulated resolve to hold on to it, come what may:

> And put the world's whole strength
> Into one giant arm, it shall not force
> This lineal honor from me.
> (IV, v, 43–5)

The King, on waking, reads the worst into the Prince's premature and stealthy purloining of the crown (which he himself, you may remember, had 'snatched'), and feels it as a death blow. This, he says:

> helps to end me. See, sons, what things you are!
> How quickly nature falls into revolt
> When gold becomes her object!
> (IV, v, 64–6)

which leads on to a powerful speech on filial ingratitude. This is followed by some forty lines of uninterrupted kingly rebuke to his son, ending with the bitter prophecy that, under him, England will 'be a wilderness again' (IV, v, 92–137). The Prince protests that he sincerely thought his father dead, and that he was actually 'upbraiding' the crown for 'eating up' his father. Then:

> Accusing it, I put it on my head,
> To try with it, as with an enemy
> That had before my face murdered my father,
> The quarrel of a true inheritor.
>   (IV, v, 165–8)

He insists that he felt not a trace of 'pride' when he put on the crown, nor did he give it a hint of 'welcome'. Whether this is all said 'with a good audacity' or with an unfeigning heart, we can scarcely decide—the Prince has always been the master of his words, as well as the owner of his face. He certainly *seemed* glad enough to put it on. But the remarkable thing is that the King instantly believes him (his previous contritions have not been notably reliable), giving the act an amazing gloss.

> O my son,
> God put it in thy mind to take it hence,
> That thou mightst win the more thy father's love,
> Pleading so wisely in excuse of it!
>   (IV, v, 177–80)

'God' again; only invoked by the Bolingbrokes, it seems, when a highly dubious act is to be ascribed to a higher authority. Of course, it is entirely understandable that the dying King should desperately want to believe his son, and the reconciliation is made to seem genuine; just as, I make no doubt, we are intended to believe in the Prince's genuine conversion to just rule and good government—the fruits of which conversion, and his taking on the burdens and responsibilities of office, we duly see in Act V. But Shakespeare has shown up so many of the ambiguities involved in the taking and handling of power (purchased or inherited, eagerly snatched or reluctantly accepted), that I hardly suppose he intends us suddenly to start reading his complex Prince in a monocular way. Whatever else he may have done, the Prince has not converted to an undimensional simplicity. He has decided to put on, or accept, the role of good kingship, and being such a cool and clear-eyed operator, he will do it very well. (In *Henry V*, Shakespeare seems to show that he has *become* a good king—but that is another play.) I don't think Shakespeare's Hal has, really, changed at all; and that, indeed, it is precisely Shakespeare's intention (and wonderful achievement) to show how this might be so, through all the apparent 'transformations' of the Prince, from tavern to battlefield to court. He knows them all—all the time. All this will be good for England; but what might be the cost to the Prince in terms of humanity is much more of an open question—and I think Shakespeare shows that too.

The play ends—again, unusually—with an epilogue (probably a mixture of more than one epilogue). It is 'spoken by a dancer' and is full of play with the idea of 'debtors' and 'creditors', 'debts' paid and unpaid, 'promises' kept and broken. This is clearly the playwright's hope that he has paid his debt, kept his word, to his paying audience; that their expectations have been fulfilled rather than 'mocked'. But then we realize that the whole play has been—at varying levels—about this too. One of the more surprising moments comes right at the end, when the banished Falstaff turns to Shallow and says, with uncharacteristic simple directness: 'Master Shallow, I owe you a thousand pound. . . . I will be as good as my word' (V, 74, 86). Were that to happen, it would be an expectation mocked indeed. But perhaps his knightly word is no better than John's 'princely word'. We can never know. And Shakespeare has one more little tease for us. The speaker of the Epilogue promises that 'our humble author will continue the story, with Sir John in it, and make you merry with fair Katharine of France. Where, for anything I know, Falstaff shall die of a sweat. . .' The expectations raised *here* are, in due course, mocked. Did Shakespeare already know that he would, indeed, continue the story; but that Sir John would *not* be in it, that Falstaff would never get to France, and he would die, not of a sweat, but a broken heart? I wonder.

⚜ HENRY V (1599)

> for Falstaff he is dead,
> And we must earn [grieve] therefore.
> (II, iii, 5)

> Your Majesty came not like yourself . . .
> (IV, viii, 50)

The unimpeded triumph of Henry V seems to have necessitated the death of Falstaff. The usually accepted reason for his exclusion from the play is the continued opposition of the Brooke family who were Oldcastle's (Fal-

staff's original name and, perhaps, remote source) descendants. A further
justification, or explanation, is often offered—to the effect that Shakespeare
couldn't have Falstaff up to his usual deflationary fun and games at Agincourt. Not, that is, if Agincourt was to remain the glorious, indeed almost
miraculous, British victory enshrined in history-chronicle-legend. And if—
if—Henry is to be allowed to appear unequivocally as *the* great saintly warrior English king, he must be entirely protected and insulated from the
caustic, irresistible whiff of parody and burlesque which Falstaff's mere
presence inevitably diffuses. So far, so understandable. But you can also find
a stronger attempt to demonstrate the entire appropriateness of the death of
Falstaff on the grounds that he has been superseded, that Henry has truly
outgrown him and left him definitively behind. Here is the Arden editor,
J. H. Walter: 'The play gains in epic strength and dignity from Falstaff's
death, even as the *Aeneid* gains from Dido's death, not only because both
accounts are written from the heart with a beauty and power that have
moved men's hearts in after time, but because Dido and Falstaff are sacrifices to a larger morality they both ignore.' The account of his death given
by the Hostess of the London tavern (Mistress Quickly as was), is indeed
not only very moving—

> for after I saw him fumble with the sheets, and play with flowers, and
> smile upon his finger's end, I knew there was but one way; for his nose
> was as sharp as a pen, and 'a babbled of green fields (see II, iii, 9–27)

—it is also quite unforgettable. But as for being 'sacrificed to a higher morality'—that is more questionable. And Henry will not be compared to Aeneas, but to Alexander—Alexander the Great, certainly; but more specifically, and very pointedly, Alexander the killer of his best friend. Falstaff's
death is laid squarely at Henry's door. 'The King has killed his heart'—
and:

> *Nym.* The king hath run bad humors on the knight; that's the even of it.
> *Pistol.* Nym, thou hast spoke the right;
> His heart is fracted and corroborate.
> *Nym.* The King is a good king, but it must be as it may: he passes some hu-
>   mors, and careers.
> (II, i, 124–9)

'Run bad humors' is usually glossed as 'vented his ill humour'; and 'humors and careers' as 'wild and freakish behaviour' (as in 'careering')—we should not forget those 'bad humors' and that wildness, no matter how regal a performance Henry contrives. And for all his terminal banishment, Falstaff is evoked once more and to devastating effect, at what I take to be the most critical point in the play—to which I will come in due course. Falstaff does not haunt Henry—Shakespeare's Henry is hardly a hauntable man: but, I maintain, his absence haunts the play.

Henry V—'this star of England' as the concluding choric epilogue calls him—was fixed in, or perhaps we should more properly say *by,* both chronicle history and popular legend as the ideal king; both pious saint *and* patriotic hero—unlike Richard II, with whom he was often compared (or, more accurately, contrasted). For Holinshed, Shakespeare's main source for this play, Henry was 'a paterne in princehood, a lode-starr in honour, and mirrour of magnificence'; while Sir Walter Raleigh, looking back on English kings, asserted that 'None of them went to worke like a Conquerour: save onely King *Henrie* the fift.' Many works had been written seeking, or offering, to describe the ideal king, or perfect 'Christian Prince', and the prescribed virtues, gifts, and characteristics, seem obvious enough—he should be learned, just, and merciful; he should not seek vengeance and should always show self-control (no 'running bad humors', perhaps then); he should allow himself to be counselled by wise men, and be gracious and familiar with humble people (supposedly Henry's *forte,* though, as we shall see, 'a little touch of Harry in the night' is not quite what people think it is); he should be constantly concerned with affairs of state, and should banish flatterers and parasites (out goes Falstaff); he should command obedience, remember his responsibility for his people (particularly in war), live as a Christian, and make an honourable marriage (Henry gets round to this last, and tolerably brusquely). You can go through the play—some have—and find evidence that, checked against a list of such requisites, Henry scores nearly one hundred per cent—at times, indeed, in a rather heavy-handed and even too obvious way. He seems to have lost his habit of irony, and makes speeches of such bombastic patriotism that another age would surely have found them unashamedly jingoistic. Curiously—or, perhaps, not so curiously—Henry V has found something less than full favour in the eyes of some of the most English, 'patriotic', critics. Tillyard seems positively to dislike him, writing disparagingly of his lugubrious, pedestrian thoughtfulness; his orotund, detached eloquence; his pious platitudes. Writing of the histories, John Masefield found Henry 'the one commonplace man in the eight plays'. Dr Johnson, more tellingly, says—'I know not why Shakespeare gives the king nearly such a character as he made him formerly ridicule in *Percy*' What these, and many other critics are saying—among other things—is that, as Tillyard complained, this Henry is 'utterly inconsistent with his old self' and that 'it is not the same man speaking'. As a result, says Tillyard, 'the play constructed round him shows a great falling off in quality'. Is this right? Did Shakespeare somehow unaccountably 'nod' between writing *Henry IV* Part Two and *Julius Caesar* and *Hamlet* (within a year of *Henry V*)? Was the obligatory theme of the *perfect* king too intractable, or ungrateful, a subject for his questioning, heterodox mind? Did it require too tight a reining in of his wonderful, roaming ironies? Was the elimination of Falstaff too high a price to pay? Is the flat poetry, the conventional piety, the strident patriotism Shakespeare's—or is it Henry's? Is *Henry V* really as triumphalist as it sometimes sounds, and is often thought to be? These are real questions—though it is not clear to me that they are susceptible of definitive answers.

Is Henry the same man? Much has to be made, necessarily, of what legend and chronicle alike held to be his almost miraculous conversion—'But after he was admitted to the rule of the lande, anon and sodainely he became a newe man, and turned all that rage and wildenesse into sobernesse and wise sadnesse, and the vice into constant virtue' (Fabyon—*Chronicle,* 1559). The important point—the miraculous touch in the conversion-transformation—is 'anon and sodainely': 'all at once' as Canterbury says.

> Never was such a sudden scholar made;
> Never came reformation in a flood
> With such a heady currance scouring faults
>
> (I, i, 32–4)

Canterbury, Archbishop that he is, sees the conversion in purely religious terms, with talk of 'th' offending Adam', 'celestial spirits', angels, paradise, and so on. And in this opening scene—doubtless to prepare us for a changed Henry—we are given what might be called the official version of Henry's almost miraculous repentance and conversion ('almost' because, for Protestants, true miracles ended with the revelation of Christ); along with a eulogy by Canterbury of the King as the prince of all perfections. The Bishop of Ely turns to nature for an explanation of the sudden change in Henry:

> The strawberry grows underneath the nettle,
> And wholesome berries thrive and ripen best
> Neighbored by fruit of baser quality;
> And so the Prince obscured his contemplation
> Under the veil of wildness, which (no doubt)
> Grew like the summer grass, fastest by night,
> Unseen, yet crescive in his faculty.
>
> (I, i, 60–66)

Hazlitt thought that, incidentally, this was Shakespeare's account of 'the progress of the poet's mind'. It is an interesting, rather Romantic, thought. In any case, the two prelates give a formal description of the conversion as being brought about by the mysterious processes of both religion and nature, strongly implying that, hereafter, the King enjoys the sanction of both. However, I will just note here that the formulation in Holinshed, perhaps quite unintentionally, allows us at least to consider the possibility of regarding the conversion in a slightly different way. Holinshed writes that Henry 'determined to put on him the shape of a new man'. I don't want to make too much of this, but the point about 'metamorphosis'—an important process, or phenomenon, or possibility, or almost-miracle, for Shakespeare as I have indicated—is that, though the shape may change, change utterly, some essential part of the person carries through and remains the same. Proteus may make himself appear as a lion, a serpent, water, or a tree—but he is always Proteus. Henry must still, in some way, be Hal, even though he seems to have changed his shape *completely*. He was, anyway, from the beginning, particularly good and adept at 'putting on' new shapes.

The rest of Act I shows the two Bishops—'we of the spiritualty'— providing genealogical and historical justifications for Henry's claims to France, and indeed urging him 'With blood, and sword and fire, to win your right!' Thus we see the Church giving its authorizing legitimation to a ruthless war of conquest. How much of all this is casuistry and policy is perhaps undecidable—but a good deal, certainly. What is even more undecidable is whether Henry has already resolved to attack France (his dying father advised him to make foreign wars), and merely wants an ever-ready Church to provide a justifying gloss; or whether he is genuinely trying to discover whether his cause is just. For all his protestations of reluctance, pause, and scruple, it is hard (I find) to rule out a sense that the former is, in fact, the case. Whatever, the 'spiritualty' soon gives him all the reassurance he wants, or needs.

> Now we are well resolved, and by God's help
> And yours, the noble sinews of our power,
> France being ours, we'll bend it to our awe,
> *Or break it all to pieces*
>   (I, ii, 222–5, my italics)

And watch out for Henry's 'bad humors', France! It does not require the Dauphin's silly, and ill-advised, 'gift' of tennis balls to provoke Henry to a determination to invade France; any more than he *really* needed the Church to stiffen his resolve in that direction (to give it a veneer of respectability, yes). For all his coolness in his debate with the Bishops, Henry is hot to go. As his long, often furious and bloodthirsty speech to the French Ambassador surely indicates (I, ii, 259–97). Note that, after some twenty-five lines of violent threats, Henry says:

> But all this lies within the will of God,
> To whom I do appeal, and in whose name,
> Tell you the Dauphin, I am coming on
> To venge me as I may, and to put forth
> My rightful hand in a well-hallowed cause.
>   (I, ii, 289–93)

He invokes God, as he will continue to do (a Bolingbroke habit), though it is notable that, after Act I, the Bishops never reappear. From now on, Henry will be his own priest. But, though he talks of a 'well-hallowed cause', he is thinking of 'glory' and revenge. Henry hasn't changed, perhaps, quite as much as we thought—or the official version claims.

With a by now familiar shift, Act II moves us from the court to the tavern, or a street before a tavern (I will discuss the choric introductions to each Act later). Here is the Falstaff gang—Nym, Bardolph, Pistol, the Hostess—

but, of course, without Falstaff. As Hazlitt said—'Falstaff is dead, and without him, Pistol, Nym, and Bardolph are satellites without a sun.' They squabble, and swear, and generally 'cynicize' (if I may be allowed the word); but they present no anarchic threat, nor do they offer any seriously subversive ironic parallel to the doings at court. Though Pistol's departing words to the Hostess, now his wife, are worth noting:

> Trust none;
> For oaths are straws, men's faiths are wafer-cakes,
> And Hold-fast is the only dog, my duck . . .
> Let us to France, like horse-leeches, my boys,
> To suck, to suck, the very blood to suck!
>   (II, iii, 51–7)

Oaths, and their (unspoken) breakability, will loom large at the end of the play, where there will also be a reminder that 'Hold-fast' is exactly what England did *not* do, once it had conquered France. As for the rather ghoulish relish at the prospect of sucking French blood—it is not at all certain that a comparable anticipation is not somewhere lurking in Henry's mind as well.

It might be noted here that the play shows (and thus invites) very little sympathy for Nym, Bardolph, and Pistol. They are the voice of the non-heroic, disaffected, impoverished under-class; but whereas such a voice, elsewhere in Shakespeare, can exercise a strong claim on our sympathies, these three are so coarse and snappish (soldiers are commonly dogs, curs, hounds, in this play), so crassly immoral, cowardly, and self-serving that, rather than attracting us by touching our reserves of anti-heroic laughter (Bardolph's rather ludicrous 'On, on, on, on, on, to the breach' is but a limping bit of mockery of Henry's 'Once more unto the breach, dear friends' which it follows), they seem more calculated to arouse execration and disgust. The Boy (Falstaff's old servant) leaves them with a sort of nauseated contempt ('Their villainy goes against my weak stomach, and therefore I must cast it up,' III, ii, 54–5); and Gower's verdict on Pistol stands uncorrected and unchallenged: 'Why, 'tis a gull, a fool, a rogue, that now and then goes to the wars, to grace himself at his return into London, under the form of a soldier' (III, vi, 69–71). In the event, Bardolph and Nym are hanged; and Pistol, suffering the final humiliation of being forced to eat Fluellen's leek, makes an exit which is at once pathetic, abject, and squalid.

> Doth Fortune play the huswife with me now?
> News have I, that my Doll is dead i' th' spital
>   of malady of France;
> And there my rendezvous is quite cut off.
> Old do I wax, and from my weary limbs
> Honor is cudgeled. Well, bawd I'll turn,
> And something lean to cutpurse of quick hand.
> To England will I steal, and there I'll steal;
> And patches will I get unto these cudgeled scars,
> And swear I got them in the Gallia wars.
>   (V, i, 83–92)

So fades away the last remnant of Falstaff's world. It seems a cruelly de-graded conclusion. Henry (and his rhetoric) deserve to have had a more persuasive, invigorated challenge from below than this.

The containment, indeed, the liquidation, of any potential opposition—the stamping out, or removal (at times, self-eradication), of any possible points of insurrection or resistance—is a notable feature of the play. This is nowhere made more obvious than with the implausibly abject and ingrati-atingly complete submission and repentance of the (easily discovered) trai-tors, Cambridge, Grey, and Scroop. Henry sets them up by staging a kind of theatre of mercy in front of them (they do not know he knows about their plotting), in which he ostentatiously pardons some drunken wretch who has 'railed against our person' (I wonder what he had to say in his cups). He thus provokes them into reproaching him for injudicious leni-ency—'That's mercy, but too much security:/Let him be punished' (II, ii, 45–6). When Henry then instantly produces proof of their treasonable plot, they are, of course, in no position to appeal to a mercy they have just so intransigently censured. There is something of the old cool and cat-like Hal in these manipulated proceedings. A little touch of Harry can be a danger-ous thing. What strains credulity is the abject gratitude which they express at their discovery and consequent sentence:

> But God be thankèd for prevention,
> Which I in sufferance heartily will rejoice. [Cambridge]

Never did faithful subject more rejoice
At the discovery of most dangerous treason
Than I do at this hour joy o'er myself,
Prevented from a damned enterprise. [Grey]
(II, ii, 158–64)

Meeting death with dignity is one thing ('Nothing became his life like the leaving of it')—but this seems excessive. Dollimore and Sinfield are justified in their sceptical observation—'It is of course one of the most authoritative ideological legitimations available to the powerful: to be sincerely validated by former opponents.' Certainly, Shakespeare makes any potential source of opposition to Henry fall away—or assimilate itself—with extraordinary ease. The wily Church disappears at the end of Act I; the fractious part of the ruling class troops happily to execution in Act II. We have seen how the last of the disaffected under-class retreats like a whipped cur before the end of the play. That leaves a few fellow aristocrats, and the loyal soldiers, including Irish, Welsh, and Scottish representatives shown to be (quite unhistorically) cheerfully (and at times rather embarrassingly comically—touches of national caricatures here) subservient to the English king. Compared with previous history plays (for instance, *Richard III*), the British cast of *Henry V* is rather small and circumscribed, giving the impression of a few simplified representatives, rather than a seething and varied population. From this point of view, if from no other, one has to say that, by Shakespeare's standards, this is an impoverished play.

There is another interesting feature of the treatment of the conspirators. Their treachery occasions an impassioned speech from Henry which, occasionally, shows some of the disgust and outrage of Hamlet and even later figures. Calling the conspirators 'dogs' and 'English monsters', he turns to Scroop:

What shall I say to thee, Lord Scroop, thou cruel,
Ingrateful, savage, and inhuman creature?
Thou that didst bear the key of all my counsels,
That knew'st the very bottom of my soul,
That (almost) mightst have coined me into gold,
Wouldst thou have practiced on me for thy use?
(II, ii, 94–9)

(cf. 'do you think I am easier to be played on than a pipe? Call me what in-strument you will, though you fret me, you cannot play upon me,' *Hamlet,* III, ii, 377–80). Such an 'evil' can scarcely be credited, even when discov-ered.

> 'Tis so strange
> That, though the truth of it stands off as gross
> As black and white, my eye will scarcely see it.
> (II, ii, 102–4)

Henry invokes 'fiends', 'devils', 'hell', and we hear that Hamletic, indeed ubiquitously Shakespearian, nausea at 'seeming' and 'glist'ring semblances of piety':

> Show men dutiful?
> Why, so didst thou. Seem they grave and learned?
> Why so didst thou. Come they of noble family?
> Why, so didst thou. Seem they religious?
> Why so didst thou . . .
> Such and so finely bolted didst thou seem;
> And thus thy fall hath left a kind of blot
> To mark the full-fraught man and best indued
> With some suspicion. I will weep for thee;
> For this revolt of thine, methinks, is like
> Another fall of man.
> (II, ii, 127–42)

There is, indeed, no art to find the mind's construction in the face. This can work two ways—the French have been 'too much mistaken' in Henry. As the Constable says to the Dauphin (shortly after Henry's speech) concern-ing Henry:

> And you shall find vanities forespent
> Were but the outside of the Roman Brutus,
> Covering discretion with a coat of folly;
> As gardeners do with ordure hide those roots
> That shall first spring and be most delicate.
> (II, iv, 36–40)

What looks like folly might conceal discretion, just as 'ordure' might be overlaying healthy roots. And thus Henry—before and after his 'transformation'. But that, too, is reversible. What now shows as a truly regal 'discretion' (Henry V *now*), might conceal folly and ordure. Might, might not; but you cannot be sure.

So, the conspirators were purely, inexplicably 'evil'—another fall of man. That was perhaps the ultimate mystery and horror for Shakespeare—the Iago phenomenon. But the actual, historical conspiracy was more a matter of politics than theology. As Henry IV's son, Henry V is far from secure on the throne—as he himself reveals:

> Not today, O Lord,
> O, not today, think not upon the fault
> My father made in compassing the crown!
> (IV, i, 297–9)

he prays on the eve of battle. Cambridge and his allies were involved in a dynastic contestation with the Bolingbrokes—indeed, Cambridge's son was to claim the crown in the reign of Henry VI, and this Yorkist line would eventually take over the throne. By ascribing pure evil to the conspirators (instead of the impure motivations of factional struggle), Henry is, in effect, purifying himself. And in the total absence of any critical, questioning, contesting voices near him, Shakespeare lets him have it his way.

And that, perhaps, is the trouble with the play. That Henry seems to have it all so effortlessly his own way. No shadows fall on him; he is not beset by doubts; he never loses his mental footing, or misses a step, as it were. There is, effectively, only one soliloquy; in general, (that important soliloquy apart), he never breaks off to explore some troubling inner thoughts; never turns away to utter some questioning aside; never loses himself in doubt or inconsequentiality, or breaks out into an unexpected strangeness (nor does anyone else behave in this way). He is always the central character, invariably appearing and behaving as a public figure; and it is as if we only ever see him in one perspective and in single focus, with no glimpses of peripheral alternatives or possible criticisms or hidden privacies. From this point of view, he does seem to be allowed to appear as the unquestioned, unquestioning English patriot hero—a development of Faulconbridge (in *King John*), though without the latter's irony and wit. (Such comic scenes as there are are fragmentary and undeveloped, lacking in any incendiary or

detonative power.) His contemptuous speeches to the French, and his galvanizing exhortations to his troops, are too famous to need citing here.
Though we should, perhaps, remind ourselves of the strong strain of sheer
brutality in many of his words. To the Governor of Harfleur, for instance,
he demands capitulation, or—

> The gates of mercy shall be all shut up,
> And the fleshed soldier, rough and hard of heart,
> In liberty of bloody hand shall range
> With conscience wide as hell, mowing like grass
> Your fresh fair virgins and your flow'ring infants.
> What is it then to me if impious war,
> Arrayed in flames like to the prince of fiends,
> Do with his smirched complexion all fell feats
> Enlinked to waste and desolation? . . .
>   in a moment look to see
> The blind and bloody soldier with foul hand
> Defile the locks of your shrill-shrieking daughters;
> Your fathers taken by the silver beards,
> And their most reverend heads dashed to the walls;
> Your naked infants spitted upon pikes,
> Whiles the mad mothers with their howls confused
> Do break the clouds, as did the wives of Jewry
> At Herod's bloody-hunting slaughtermen.
>   (III, iii, 10–18, 33–41)

and many more bloody lines of the same. I don't wish to be a twentieth-
century sensitive about such matters (though the lines *do* put me in mind of
Picasso's *Guernica*), and no doubt war at that time was conducted in much
such terms. But there is a less than saintly relish in Henry's words—he is
clearly enjoying being/playing Herod, famed slaughterer of Innocents. In
the event, Harfleur surrenders, and Henry instructs his army—'Use mercy
to them all' (III, iii, 54). But according to the chronicles he *did* sack Harfleur: Shakespeare's omission of that piece of bloodshed may, indeed, represent an inclination to protect Henry's image. Though, as we shall see, the
sanitization is not complete.

As traditional enemies, the French were legitimate objects of scorn and ridicule, and, with their bragging and their cowardice, they cut sorry enough figures in the play (the King apart—as father of Katherine who will, in due course, be the mother of the future Henry VII, he is allowed his dignity). But one of the most powerful speeches in the play is an impassioned account by Burgundy of the horrifying ruin and desolation the wars have brought to France—'this best garden of the world'.

> Her vine, the merry cheerer of the heart,
> Unprunèd dies; her hedges even-pleached,
> Like prisoners wildly overgrown with hair,
> Put forth disordered twigs; her fallow leas
> The darnel, hemlock, and rank fumitory
> Doth root upon, while that the coulter rusts
> That should deracinate such savagery
> . . .
> And all our vineyards, fallows, meads, and hedges,
> Defective in their natures, grow to wildness,
> Even so our houses, and ourselves, and children,
> Have lost, or do not learn for want of time,
> The sciences that should become our country;
> But grow like savages—as soldiers will,
> That nothing do but meditate on blood—
> To swearing, and stern looks, diffused attire,
> And everything that seems unnatural.
>   (see the whole speech—V, ii, 23–67)

Such a vision of utter disorder would have brought a chill to any good Elizabethan heart—irrespective of ancient enmities. The horror of war knows no patriotism.

As usual, Shakespeare omitted many things included in the more meandering progress of the chronicles. These include the conflict with the Lollards, and the capture and execution of Sir John Oldcastle (something too much of Oldcastle, perhaps; the Lollard controversy and troubles were also omitted in *The Famous Victories of Henry V,* from which Shakespeare again took many incidents—as usual, completely transforming them). He also leaves out most of the events of 1416–19 (including the murder of Burgundy and the terrible siege of Rouen), presumably so that he can pass almost immediately from Agincourt to Henry's marriage and the acceptance of his claim to France. This sort of contraction and occlusion is understandable enough—in the interests of focusing on select dramatic moments. More strange, to me, is the complete absence of any reference to the particular battle tactics used by Henry at Agincourt. The English were hopelessly outnumbered; yet, through the skilful deployment of archers (the release of their arrows was perhaps the most memorable moment in the Olivier film), and the famous use of stakes, the heavily armoured French were, indeed, utterly confounded. Holinshed gives *lots* of details:

> he caused stakes bound with iron sharpe at both ends, of the length of five or six foot to be pitched before the archers, and at each side the footmen like an hedge, to the intent that if the barded horses ran rashlie upon them, they shortlie be gored and destroied.

> the archers in the forefront, and the archers on that side which stood in the medow, so wounded the footmen, galled the horsses, and combred the men of armes, that the footmen durst not go forward, the horssemen ran togither upon plumps without order, some overthrew such as were next to them, and the horsses overthrew their masters, and so at the first joining, the Frenchmen were foulie discomforted, and the Englishmen highlie encouraged.

There is a lot more. Whatever else you may think about this, it was terrific soldiering. And of all this, in Shakespeare's play—nothing. A glimpse of some of the French in panic and disarray, and then—

> *Herald.* The day is yours.
> *King.* Praised be God, and not our strength for it!
>   (IV, vii, 88–9)

and later:

>   O God, thy arm was here!
>   And not to us, but to thy arm alone,
>   Ascribe we all! When, without stratagem,
>   But in plain shock and even play of battle,
>   Was ever known so great and little loss

On one part and on th' other? Take it, God,
For it is none but thine!

(IV, viii, 108–14)

Without stratagem? What about those stakes and arrows? Bullough ratio-
nalizes the omission thus: 'The complex spirit in which the battle was
fought, is alone important, the mingling of soaring patriotism with comic
gaiety and realism, as English courage brings the French to shame, the victim turning victor and overthrowing the braggart foe.' Perhaps that *is* how
we are intended to respond—though it strikes me as a rather breathlessly
generous over-reading. What is striking is Henry's persistent and repeated
'ascription' of the whole victory to God. He does this over and over again,
culminating in the strangely fierce order:

And *be it death proclaimèd* through our host
To boast of this, or take that praise from God
Which is His only.

(IV, viii, 116–18, my italics)

All commendably pious, no doubt. But we may recall that the steely 'neces-
sitarian' Bolingbrokes have a way of invoking—intoning—'God' at strategic moments when it suits them to stand aside from their own deeds. Remember John, after the basely won 'victory' at Gaultree, solemnly saying
—'God, and not we, hath safely fought today'. (And we may also remember that Falstaff, on his death-bed, 'cried out "God, God, God" three or
four times'—about the same number of times as his old drinking companion calls it out after Agincourt.) Not that there was anything treacherous
about the victory at Agincourt; but war is always a dirty business (and
we know from his Harfleur speech that Henry is willing to abandon all
chivalric rules of war and let his men do their damnedest). Perhaps he prefers to cover the 'ordure' of battle with a carapace of self-exculpating
piety. I did nothing (how modest): God did *all* (how convenient). I allow
myself this somewhat sceptical reading, because there is one piece of 'ordure' which Henry—as aspirant to saintly reputation—might well prefer
to have hidden with a 'coat' of sanctity. And this, Shakespeare, notably, *does*
include.

This is the incident which has come to be known as 'the killing of the
prisoners'. All the chroniclers regard it as an indisputable historical fact

that, at some point in the battle, Henry suddenly ordered the slaughter of all the French prisoners (by any standards of war, then and now, a foul 'stratagem'). It is also agreed that, at some point in the battle, a group of the French attacked the English baggage train, and killed the helpless 'boys' looking after it. Whether there was a (causal) relationship between these two events is the very reverse of a trivial matter. Some chroniclers simply assert that, when Henry heard that the French were regrouping for another attack, he ordered the prisoners killed. Holinshed, however, links the order to Henry's anger at the attack on what Fluellen calls 'the poys and the luggage', as well as his anxiety about the possibility of another attack by the French. Though even Holinshed seems not to like this 'lamentable slaughter' much. Henry, he writes:

> contrarie to his accustomed gentlenes, commanded by sound of trumpet, that everie man (upon paine of death) should incontinentlie slaie his prisoner. When this dolorous decree, and pitifull proclamation was pronounced, pitie it was to see how some Frenchmen were suddenlie sticked with daggers, some were brained with pollaxes, some slaine with malls, others had their throats cut, and some their bellies panched, so that in effect, having respect to the great number, few prisoners were saved.

Some more recent English critics have been far more comfortable with the episode, seemingly finding it not at all 'dolorous', 'pitifull', 'lamentable'. Dover Wilson took the lead in commending Henry for doing exactly what had to be done and no nonsense; and here is the Arden editor—'Gower's remark, "the King most worthily hath caused every soldier to cut his prisoner's throat. O! 'tis a gallant king!", shows wholehearted approval of Henry's promptness in decision and his resolute determination. The rage of the epic hero leading to the slaughter of the enemy within his power is not without Virgilian precedent.' I have to confess that I read that opinion with entire incredulity.

But how does Shakespeare show it? The battle is not yet over, despite initial English success, and Henry hears an 'alarum':

> But hark, what new alarum is this same?
> The French have reinforced their scattered men.

Then every soldier kill his prisoners!
Give the word through.

(IV, vi, 35–8)

Notice that there is no mention of the French killing the boys minding the baggage—this is cool (or coldly furious) military 'necessity'. Now, immediately *after* this, we shift to Fluellen talking to Gower, and Fluellen's first words follow directly on Henry's order:

Kill the poys and the luggage? 'Tis expressly against the law of arms; 'tis as arrant a piece of knavery, mark you now, as can be offert—in your conscience, now, is it not?

(IV, vii, 1–4)

This *does* refer to the French killing of the boys. But, coming immediately after Henry's order to kill the prisoners, the comment ''tis expressly against the law of arms' could equally apply to *that* order, because it was also 'against the law of arms'—in our conscience, now, is it not? In the play, it is certainly not an act justified by the French 'knavery'. And, crucially, there is more. Fluellen rambles on in what seems like his comical Welsh-garrulous way, but what he says could not, in fact, be more pointed. He suddenly starts going on about Alexander, and Macedon and Monmouth:

If you mark Alexander's life well, Harry of Monmouth's life is come after it indifferent well, for there is figures in all things. Alexander, God knows, and you know, in his rages, and his furies, and his wraths, and his cholers, and his moods, and his displeasures, and his indignations, and also being a little intoxicated in his prains, did, in his ales and his angers, look you, kill his best friend, Cleitus . . . I speak but in the figures and comparisons of it: as Alexander killed his friend Cleitus, being in his ales and his cups, so also Harry Monmouth, being in his right wits and his good judgments, turned away the fat knight with the great-belly doublet—he was full of jests, and gipes, and knaveries, and mocks; I have forgot his name.

Gower. Sir John Falstaff.

Fluellen. That is he: I'll tell you there is good men porn at Monmouth.

(IV, vii, 33–55)

Let's see—Henry killed his prisoners, the sort of thing Alexander would have done; and that reminds me, didn't he, also like Alexander though without the excuse of drink, effectively kill his best friend—what was the man's name? 'SIR JOHN FALSTAFF'. There he is once more—resurrected, by name, to, I think, devastating effect. The unavoidable implication of Fluellen's inspired concatenation is that this is a king who, when it comes to it, is willing to kill his enemies *and* his friends. And having just had an intimation that, beneath his rather stiffly maintained public exterior of piety, chivalry, regality (he is often described as 'puissant', as if he was turning himself into an archaic heraldic figure), Henry can be a man of 'rages, furies, wraths, cholers, moods'; we may register with a renewed sense of loss the impoverishingly depleting absence of Falstaff's 'jests, gipes, knaveries, and mocks'. Immediately following that exchange, Henry duly enters, indulging one of his rages:

> I was not angry since I came to France
> Until this instant. . . .
>   we'll cut the throats of those we have,
> And not a man of them that we shall take
> Shall taste our mercy.
>   (IV, vii, 57–8, 65–7)

In an earlier, calmer mood, Henry had declared: 'when lenity and cruelty play for a kingdom, the gentler gamester is the soonest winner' (III, vi, 117–18). 'Use lenity, sweet chuck!' (III, iii, 25) says Pistol, in one of the few possibly ironic echoes in the play. But the only 'lenity' actually shown, displayed is the better word, by Henry in the play, is to the bemused drunkard in Act II, and the sorely tricked, good soldier Williams in Act IV. This is cheap lenity indeed; or rather, no lenity at all. The proposition that these episodes are included to demonstrate Henry's 'magnanimity'—as I have seen advanced—is simply laughable. When the going gets serious, Henry is the very reverse of a 'gentle gamester'. 'O, 'tis a gallant king!'? However unintended, Gower's words have a hollow, ironic ring to them.

An important part of the legend of good King Harry was that he had the common touch, a gift of uncondescending familiarity with the people —presumably a residue of his tavern days. In the play, this is supposedly exemplified by Henry's moving among the soldiers on the night before the battle of Agincourt—though here again, Shakespeare rather complicates the matter. The scene is set by the choric introduction to Act IV, and this is perhaps a suitable point to say something about the Chorus in this play. Unlike any other play by Shakespeare, every Act is prefaced by a Chorus—or Prologue—plus an Epilogue. This choric framing has usually been seen as an attempt to make an *epic*-drama, with all the spaciousness and amplitude that that implies. But not quite so. A traditional chorus would help us to see the enacted events in a wider context, a longer perspective. But this triumphalist Chorus is more royalist than the King. I find a comment by Michael Goldman more to the point:

> Once it is recognized that the Chorus sounds very much like the King, much of the play's method becomes clear. Like Henry, the Chorus is a man whose job is to rouse his hearers to unusual effort. The straining note is struck from the start, and may well be the primary reason for the Chorus's existence, since none of the theories usually advanced to account for Shakespeare's unparalleled reliance on the device is satisfactory . . . nowhere else does he use it to call attention to the inadequacies of his stage, which is of course no more inadequate to this story than to the material of the other histories. Here, however, the notion of inadequacy is insisted upon, as is the effort we must put forth to make up for it . . . The playwright and the resources of his stage are deficient, but so are we, and we are asked to perform all kinds of brain-work to convert the work of actors into a convincing spectacle. . . As the Chorus says in his second appearance, the project we are engaged in is to 'force a play'.

'Force' suggests the necessity for unnatural effort; here, it can also mean 'stuff' (courtesy Dover Wilson), and, by definition, the thing that requires/invites 'stuffing' is previously empty. 'Work, Work', says the Chorus to his audience; 'On, on', says Henry to his soldiers. These comparable urgings suggest that they have poor, thin, reluctant material to work on and with. Desperately endeavouring to 'swell' the scene, the Chorus thereby implies that, without his efforts, we would be presented with but a famished, laggardly spectacle. And indeed, nearly all the *action* in the play —the movement (sailing, riding, fighting, running); the noises (boats, horses, voices, instruments); all the turbulent energy released in crowds and war—is in the *speech* of the Chorus (Shakespeare knows that words can do anything). What we *see* is more like a series of tableaux, often curiously still—indeed, stilted. The result of all this choric effort and dramatic inadequacy is more than a slight feeling of unreality. Perhaps—but of course, only perhaps—suggesting that the dramatic portrayal of the ideal, hero-saint King, is an almost impossible (unreal) task. Requiring too much 'forcing'.

And so to the choric introduction to Act IV.

> O, now, who will behold
> The royal captain of this ruined band
> Walking from watch to watch, from tent to tent,
> Let him cry, 'Praise and glory on his head!'
> For forth he goes and visits all his host,
> Bids them good morrow with a modest smile,
> And calls them brothers, friends, and countrymen.
> . . .
> That every wretch, pining and pale before,
> Beholding him, plucks comfort from his looks.
> A largess universal, like the sun,
> His liberal eye doth give to everyone,
> Thawing cold fear, that mean and gentle all
> Behold, as may unworthiness define,
> A little touch of Harry in the night.
>   (IV, Cho. 28–34, 41–7)

Which is fine, stirring, and heart-warming. The trouble is, that what we then go on to 'behold' is not remotely like this. For a start, Henry walks about the camp at night in disguise. (This has no basis whatsoever in the chronicles—Bullough suggests that Shakespeare took the idea from Tacitus's *Annals,* II, iii.) Thus, he does not appear as a 'sun' king, beaming rays of comfort and confidence on his sadly straitened soldiers. So far from that, he goes sniffing about for evidence of loyalty—or, probably more to the point, *dis*loyalty. He seems to be seeking the reassurance he should be offering. He gets the sort of (to us embarrassing) praise he wants from Pistol (of all people!). But he runs into a bit of trouble with Bates, Court, and Wil-

liams. Famously, he insists on the King's common humanity—'I think the
King is but a man, as I am . . . His ceremonies laid by, in his nakedness
he appears but a man' and so on (IV, i, 103–7). Bates gives the rather un-
promising reply that, whatever the King is, he wishes the King was standing up to his neck in the Thames 'and I by him, at all adventures, so we
were quit here' (IV, i, 119). The King then urges that we should be content to die in the King's company, 'his cause being just and his quarrel honorable'. To which Williams makes the utterly justified reply, 'That's more
than we know' (IV, i, 131)—and perhaps more than *we* know, too—going
on to say: 'I am afeard there are few die well that die in battle; for how can
they charitably dispose of anything when blood is their argument? Now, if
these men do not die well, it will be a black matter for the King that led
them to it; who to disobey, were against all proportion of subjection' (IV, i,
143–9). Henry makes an elaborate case for the innocence of the King in this
respect—which the men seem to accept. 'I do not desire he should answer
for me, and yet I determine to fight lustily for him,' says Bates (IV, i, 193–4).
This is loyalty enough, and the King should be satisfied. But he wants more,
and pushes too hard—thus:

> *King.* I myself heard the King say he would not be ransomed.
> *Williams.* Ay, he said so, to make us fight cheerfully; but when our throats
>   are cut, he may be ransomed, and we ne'er the wiser.
> *King.* If I live to see it, I will never trust his word after.
> *Williams.* You pay him then! That's a perilous shot out of an elder-gun, that
>   a poor and a private displeasure can do against a monarch! . . . You'll
>   never trust his word after! Gome, 'tis a foolish saying.
> *King.* Your reproof is something too round; I should be angry with you, if
>   the time were convenient.
> *Williams.* Let it be a quarrel between us, if you live.
> *King.* I embrace it.
> *Williams.* How shall I know thee again?
>   (IV, i, 195–212)

And so to the exchange of gloves, which the King will use to play a trick on
Williams after the battle. Henry is angry again (we have been warned about
these mean moods in *Henry IV* Part Two—'being incensed, he's flint;/ As
humorous as winter, and as sudden/ As flaws congealed in the spring of

day', IV, iv, 33–5); he hasn't got what he came for. But he gets, we must feel, nothing less than he deserves. Who would want a little touch of *this* Harry in the night?

Later, the trick is duly played on Williams; Henry reveals that the glove was, in fact his, and asks—'How canst thou make me satisfaction?'

> *Williams.* All offenses, my lord, come from the heart: never came any from
> mine that might offend your Majesty.
> *King.* It was ourself thou didst abuse.
> *Williams.* Your Majesty came not like yourself: you appeared to me but as a
> common man; witness the night, your garments, your lowliness. And
> what your Highness suffered under that shape, I beseech you take it for
> your own fault, and not mine; for had you been as I took you for, I made
> no offense. Therefore I beseech your Highness pardon me.
>   (IV, viii, 46–56)

Williams's position is unassailable, and his dignity unimpaired (he refuses the offer of a piddling tip from Fluellen)—the King was quite unfair, if not something worse, to practise on his soldiers, sufficiently under strain as they were, in this way—and it certainly *was* his own fault if he taxed some un-welcome truth-telling out of them. 'Your Majesty came not like yourself'—but he never did, he never has. Always Mercury, even when he looks like Perseus. Emily Dickinson's line, 'Ourself behind ourself concealed', might have been written for Henry. It is never certain when he *is* most 'like him-self'. When he is 'performing' the good king, as he does for much of this play? Perhaps. Or perhaps it is in those moments of cold fury ('as humor-ous as winter') when he breaks friends' hearts and cuts enemies' throats. With Henry, this Henry, you can just never know.

By convention, characters are most 'like themselves' in soliloquy; and Henry has only one, in this notably *un*inward-looking play. Characteristi-cally, it is not entirely clear what it reveals about him. It occurs on his night walk, when he has left the soldiers. Seemingly, it is a bitter lament for the burdens of high office, and the emptiness of 'Ceremony'.

>   What infinite heart's-ease
>   Must kings neglect that private men enjoy!
>   And what have kings that privates have not too,

> Save ceremony, save general ceremony?
> And what art thou, thou idol Ceremony?
> What kind of god art thou, that suffer'st more
> Of mortal griefs than do thy worshippers?
> What are thy rents? What are thy comings-in?
> O Ceremony, show me but thy worth!
> What is thy soul of adoration?
> Art thou aught else but place, degree, and form,
> Creating awe and fear in other men?
> Wherein thou art less happy, being feared,
> Than they in fearing.
>
> (IV, i, 241–54)

And much more—all seeming to underline the vanity and pointlessness of 'thrice-gorgeous ceremony'. It is as though the man, Henry, wants to distance, or at least distinguish himself from the ceremonial figure that he is having to become. But by personifying Ceremony, he in fact risks identifying himself *with* it. Because otherwise he is saying that he is simply a helpless creature of Ceremony, as though it had autonomous power. But the power is Henry's, and he *uses* all its ceremonial adjuncts and appurtenances. He may see through all these mystifying accessories, but he would never relinquish or discontinue them. The main burden of the speech is that the responsibilities of a king mean that he cannot sleep the sleep of—no, not the sleep of the just, as we say: the sleep of, to use Henry's preferred terms, the 'beggar', 'lackey', 'wretch', 'slave', all snoring contentedly away with 'body filled, and vacant mind'. This, it would appear, is how he really thinks of his subjects, among them those who, next day, will comprise 'we few, we happy few, we band of brothers'. Does this soliloquy 'come from the heart', as honest Williams would say? If so, then truly the man has a heart of winter.

The last Act wraps things up with France, as Henry's marriage to Katherine is settled (I will say nothing of Henry's 'courtship' of the poor, hapless Katherine—it is a peremptory business, crudely, and sometimes a little coarsely, done. The 'feminine' is effectively absent from this play.) Oaths are duly taken all round, and the last line of the actual play hopes 'may our oaths well kept and prosp'rous be!' (V, ii, 386). But, as Pistol told his wife— 'oaths are straws, men's faiths are wafer-cakes' (II, iii, 52). And as the Epilogue reminds us, the next king lost all that Henry had fought to win, and precipitated a civil war—'which oft our stage hath shown'. Shakespeare ends just where he began.

By which time, we can appreciate the aptness and force of W. B. Yeats's imaginative description of him:

> He meditated as Solomon, not as Bentham meditated, upon blind ambitions, untoward accidents, and capricious passions, and the world was almost as empty in his eyes as it must be in the eyes of God.

CODA

 ## HENRY VIII (1613)

> *Second Gentleman.* These are stars indeed.
> *First Gentleman.* And sometimes falling ones.
> *Second Gentleman.* No more of that.
>   (IV, i, 53–5)

1613: another *history* play—by *Shakespeare!* It seems somehow unfitting. When Prospero announced that he was breaking his staff and drowning his book, in *The Tempest,* most people have felt that this was Shakespeare's very own way of indicating that he was doing the same. And yet here it is— *Henry VIII,* included without any reservations in the first Folio of 1623 by Heminge and Condell (while they excluded works considered of more dubious Shakespearian status, such as *Pericles* and *The Two Noble Kinsmen*). However, in 1850 J. Spedding wrote an article entitled 'Who Wrote Shakespeare's *Henry VIII?*' in which he maintained, using plausible stylistic evidence, that parts of the play were almost certainly written by Fletcher. Debate and argument about this matter have continued ever since, with some learned scholars maintaining that there are good reasons for thinking that, in fact, Shakespeare wrote the lot, while others are equally sure that they can detect when Fletcher, as it were, takes over. I have nothing to add to this debate. That there are stylistic variations (and, if you will, dips into weakness) is undeniable; that there are lines which only Shakespeare could have written seems to me incontestable. That it is hardly a play, or 'drama', at all, is the proposition I shall try to advance.*

Why did Shakespeare write it (or part of it—but I shall leave this matter aside in this brief introduction, and simply refer to the play as a whole)? It is, by definition, an unanswerable question; and, more than that, surely no man's motives are less recuperable than Shakespeare's. But one reason is speculatively adduced, which I will simply transcribe. In February 1613, Princess Elizabeth, King James's daughter, was married to Prince Frederick, the Elector Palatine, a leader of the Protestant union in Germany. The wedding was the occasion for the most lavish celebrations—banquets, plays, masques, pageants, fireworks, etc.—and it is suggested that this firm Protestant alliance between Britain and a German power occasioned popular rejoicing as well as court festivities. There was still a slight Popish threat of a Spanish invasion and a second armada in 1613, and many old (patriotic) history plays were revived (see R. A. Foakes, Arden edition). The anti-Catholic implications of the marriage of this second *Elizabeth* was an occasion of great rejoicing; and a play celebrating both the downfall of the last great *Catholic* statesman in England (Wolsey), and the birth of the *first* Elizabeth (Protestant from birth), might have seemed both timely and appropriate. This, anyway, is what we have.

And, it might be said, that's *all* we have: downfall—downfall*s*, actually—and a birth. No rebellions, no usurpations, no invasions, no wars; no serious plotting, no really profound contestations, no irresolvable antagonisms—and no humour (just one—one!—ironic remark). It has been called, variously, 'a sort of historical masque or show-play' (Coleridge), a 'chronicle-

---

* Among those who believe in a shared authorship, the generally accepted division of labour is as follows:

> Prologue: Fletcher.
>
> Act One: i and ii: Shakespeare; iii and iv: Fletcher.
>
> Act Two: i and ii: Fletcher; iii and iv: Shakespeare.
>
> Act Three: i: Fletcher; ii: lines 1–203 Shakespeare, lines 204–459 Fletcher.
>
> Act Four: i and ii: Fletcher.
>
> Act Five: i: Shakespeare; ii, iii, iv: Fletcher.
>
> Epilogue: Fletcher.

pageant', a 'festive history'. And yet this was the reign in which England experienced what must have been the massive trauma of being suddenly, forcibly, violently changed from a Catholic to a Protestant country. About which, be it said, Shakespeare keeps very quiet (so that, to this day, people speculate about his possible Catholic sympathies, going through the plays considering whether unbearable Puritans come off worse than untrustable Catholics). Nothing of that trauma/drama gets into this play, though it ends exactly when it was taking place (in 1533, when Elizabeth was born). This is the court in peace time. We have four trials, three deaths, one marriage, one birth; we have politics, forensic casuistry, some off-the-cuff theology; and a lot of quite uncharacteristically detailed (in the stage directions) ceremony, ritual, and pageantry. We have no serious character development, but instead we have the largest cast of any of the histories. We have no real soliloquies from this King Henry; but, as an innovation, a number of nameless gentlemen who stroll in and out saying—did you hear this, everyone is saying that, and so on. There are three real griefs; but it is a resolutely public play, with everything tending to spectacle. Indeed, so 'spectacular' was the performance that, on one occasion, the discharge of 'chambers', at the King's entry to the masque, set fire to the Globe theatre, which burned down.

The play starts with a description of the famous meeting of Henry VIII and Francis I at the Field of the Cloth of Gold (1520)—a vast Renaissance tournament at which the kings vied to show off their magnificence. It ends with an extended depiction of the baptism of Elizabeth (1533), accompanied by a rapturous 'prophecy' by Cranmer of the glories she will bring to England (not so difficult to write, one might think, with the hindsight of 1613):

> This royal infant—heaven still move about her!—
> Though in her cradle, yet now promises
> Upon this land a thousand thousand blessings,
> Which time shall bring to ripeness.
> (V, v, 17–20)

'Thou speakest wonders' says the happy father-king, and that is the note the play ends on, a climax very suitable for a dramatic epithalamion in honour

of the just-married *Princess* Elizabeth, as Bullough points out. In between
we have, primarily the trial, fall, and death of, in turn, Buckingham, Katherine of Aragon, and Cardinal Wolsey; plus the (thwarted) trial and rise
of Archbishop Cranmer. Then—the ground clear—Henry's happy marriage to Anne Boleyn and the rapidly ensuing (historically, somewhat *too*
rapidly!) birth of Elizabeth. As usual, Shakespeare does some selecting and
rearranging and chronological collapsing. Henry did not marry Anne until
1532, but his meeting with her is placed before Buckingham's condemnation in 1521; while his marriage to Anne is placed before Wolsey's fall and
death, which in fact took place in 1530. Katherine of Aragon died in 1536,
but in the play this is made to occur before Princess Elizabeth is born (1533),
as is the plot against Cranmer, which probably took place in 1540. My details are, as usual, from Bullough, who gives his opinion that the reasons for
the changes were 'to give some illusion of enchainment or interconnection
to the incidents, and to suggest dramatic parallels or contrasts emergent in
a survey of the whole reign'. Cutting the action off where he does means
that Shakespeare does not oblige himself to (avoids having to) address the
darker and more problematical aspects of Henry's reign, and allows him
his triumphant, not to say triumphalist, conclusion, packed with happy auguries under a cloudless sky.

But whatever we make of this conclusion (and truncation), the predomi-
nant mood is one of sadness, as indeed the Prologue anticipates:

> I come no more to make you laugh. Things now
> That bear a weighty and a serious brow,
> Sad, high, and working, full of state and woe,
> Such noble scenes as draw the eye to flow,
> We now present. Those that can pity, here
> May, if they think it well, let fall a tear:
> The subject will deserve it . . .
> Be sad, as we would make ye. Think ye see
> The very persons of our noble story
> As they were living. Think you see them great,
> And followed with the general throng and sweat
> Of thousand friends. Then, in a moment, see
> How soon this mightiness meets misery;

And if you can be merry then, I'll say
A man may weep upon his wedding day.
(1–7, 25–32)

Sad—not tragic. Sad, rather in the way Hardy describes sadness. 'It is the ongoing—i.e. the becoming—of the world that produces its sadness. If the world stood still at a felicitous moment, there would be no sadness in it.' 'Becoming' also involves 'Be-going' (if I may be allowed the word), just as 'ongoing' must end in 'off-going', and it is the going off of greatness which produces the sadness of this play. 'My soul grows sad with troubles' (III, i, 1), says Queen Katherine, foreseeing her displacement and demise. 'And when you would say something that is sad,/Speak how I fell' (II, i, 135–6)—these are, effectively, Buckingham's last words. The word 'fall' tolls through the play. 'The Cardinal/Will have his will, and she must fall' (II, i, 167).

> I shall fall
> Like a bright exhalation in the evening,
> And no man see me more.
(III, ii, 225–7)

Wolsey rightly predicts. 'Press not a falling man too far' (III, ii, 333), says the compassionate Lord Chamberlain, echoed later by Cromwell—''tis a cruelty/To load a falling man' (V, iii, 76–7). 'These are stars indeed,' says the Second Gentleman, watching the Coronation procession of Henry and Anne. 'And sometimes falling ones,' rejoins the First Gentleman. He may intend a slight joke about the royal ladies' virtue; but, more generally, the play is, indeed, full of falling stars. 'No more of that,' adds the well-mannered Second Gentleman; and indeed, the play now puts the 'falls' behind, and concentrates on 'ongoing' and 'becoming'—marriage and birth. But the play as a whole has, unmistakably and inexpugnably, a dying fall. (The falls, incidentally, are more fully elaborated, and the 'stars' made more noble in their falling, than they are in Shakespeare's sources. Frank Kermode once described the play as 'an anthology of falls', and thought that it represented a return to the medieval conception of history as found in *The Mirror for Magistrates*.)

One of the falls is fully deserved; one is singularly unjust; and one is curiously indeterminate—but they have one feature in common. The one who falls is, initially, in some way 'chafed'—angry, rebellious, resistant: but they all come to accept their doom with dignity, 'patience', and forgiveness. And they approach their deaths in a state of 'calm of mind, all passion spent'. Reconciliation, both to one's lot, and with former enemies, accusers, opponents, is the order of the day. It is this that has led some critics to see the play as fully consonant with, even a continuation of, Shakespeare's more famous 'last plays'. I will come back to this view with which, while I understand it, I ultimately strongly disagree. But let us consider the fallen in their falling, for these are undoubtedly the most powerful moments, or scenes, in the play.

The play effectively starts with Buckingham in a temper about Wolsey's devious manipulations and ruthless self-advancement. Norfolk warns him against Wolsey's malice, potency, and 'high hatred':

> And let your reason with your choler question
> What 'tis you go about . . .
>   Anger is like
> A full hot horse who, being allowed his way,
> Self-mettle tires him . . .
> Heat not a furnace for your foe so hot
> That it do singe yourself. We may outrun
> By violent swiftness that which we run at,
> And lose by overrunning. Know you not
> The fire that mounts the liquor till't run o'er
> In seeming to augment it wastes it?
>   (I, i, 130–34, 140–45)

This sort of compression of thought and vigour of image is characteristic of parts, but only parts, of the play (and, of course, claimed for Shakespeare by those who want to give the somewhat more soft-focused, languid, even sentimental parts to Fletcher). This power often shows in Buckingham's angry speech; as, for instance, when he is blaming Wolsey for arranging the ruinously pompous expensive Field of the Cloth of Gold show—

> That swallowed so much treasure, and like a glass
> Did break i' th' wrenching.
>   (I, i, 166–7)

'Wrenching' is a dialect word for 'rinsing', and more strongly suggests a
powerful, even violent, physical act. In this, it is characteristic of many of
the images in the play which, as Caroline Spurgeon noted, evoke 'bodily action of almost every kind: walking, stepping, marching, running and leaping; crawling, hobbling, falling, carrying, climbing and perspiring; swimming, diving, flinging and peeping; crushing, shaking, trembling, sleeping,
stirring, and—especially and repeatedly—the picture of the body or back
bent and weighed down under a heavy burden'. At one point, after a distressed Cranmer has left the King, Henry comments:

> He has strangled
> His language in his tears.
>
> (V, i, 156–7)

That *is* a line, I venture to say, that only Shakespeare could have written.

Buckingham is soon caught in Wolsey's 'net', and betrayed by his 'false'
surveyor. Henry, about whom more later, unquestioningly believes the surveyor's slanderous evidence (that he heard Buckingham say he wanted to
kill the King), and we have another of those kingly speeches of horror at
the unforeseeable treachery of a trusted subject:

> This man so complete,
> Who was enrolled 'mongst wonders . . .
> Hath into monstrous habits put the graces
> That once were his, and is become as black
> As if besmeared in hell.
>
> (I, ii, 118–24)

Except that it is very far from clear whether Buckingham *is* guilty of anything approaching treason, while it is clear enough that the surveyor has
been put up to his lethal defamations by Wolsey. What is interesting, to me,
is that Buckingham doesn't seem to know whether he is guilty or not (I find
this entirely plausible—*did* I say that? Perhaps I did. But did I *mean* it?
Was I expressing an intention or releasing an anger? I could kill him—how
many unmurderous people have not said such a thing. And can a man ever
know the full extent of what he harbours in his heart? Even Holinshed is
not clear as to Buckingham's guilt—or innocence.) His last speeches are
those of a resigned and quiescent man, rather than a guilty one—indeed,

even while accepting the verdict against him, he refers to his 'guiltless blood':

> I have this day received a traitor's judgment,
> And by that name must die. Yet, heaven bear witness,
> And if I have a conscience, let it sink me
> Even as the ax falls, if I be not faithful!
> The law I bear no malice for my death:
> 'T has done, upon the premises, but justice.
> But those that sought it I could wish more Christians.
> Be what they will, I heartily forgive 'em.
>   (II, i, 58–66)

This strikes me as mild. But, in this play, finally mildness is all. The description of Buckingham, and his bearing, at the bar when he receives the dread sentence, in a way encapsulates the whole play:

> When he was brought again to th' bar, to hear
> His knell rung out, his judgment, he was stirred
> With such an agony he sweat extremely
> And something spoke in choler, ill and hasty.
> But he fell to himself again, and sweetly
> In all the rest showed a most noble patience.
>   (II, i, 31–6)

From sweat to sweetness; from choler to patience—and seemingly without effort or inner struggle, rather as if it was a miraculous conversion: this is the very stamp of the play. And so this 'noble ruined man' goes to 'the long divorce of steel', speaking of 'sweet sacrifice', 'angels', 'soul', 'heaven'—his nobility intact, indeed enhanced.

Justice, we feel, has not been done. But another 'divorce' is looming—here is the Second Gentleman:

> If the Duke [i.e. Buckingham] be guiltless
> 'Tis full of woe. Yet I can give you inkling
> Of an ensuing evil, if it fall,
> Greater than this.
>   (II, i, 139–42)

This 'evil' (strong word) is the rumour that the King is going to 'divorce', or rather set aside, Katherine, his wife for twenty years. We have already seen Henry helplessly attracted to Anne 'Bullen' at the masque, so that, despite the legal and theological debates which follow (concerning the 'separation' he clearly both wants and intends to have), we can have no doubts concerning Henry's real reason for wishing to have this separation somehow legitimized. Katherine's speeches, both at her 'trial', and thereafter, are the most moving of the play. She appeals to the King with a simple dignity:

> Alas, sir,
> In what have I offended you? What cause
> Hath my behavior given to your displeasure
> That thus you should proceed to put me off
> And take your good grace from me?
> (II, iv, 18–22)

But, remembering that she is a queen, she refrains from weeping, and 'my drops of tears/I'll turn to sparks of fire' (II, iv, 72–3). It is time for some very justifiable 'choler', and we duly get the 'sparks'—or rather, Wolsey does: 'your heart/Is crammed with arrogancy, spleen, and pride' (II, iv, 109–10) and more of the spirited same. She sweeps out of the Hall, saying 'They vex me past my patience' (II, iv, 130). She feels 'the last fit of my greatness' (III, i, 78). To Wolsey she says 'Ye turn me into nothing' (III, i, 114), and, while he rebukes her for her anger and stubbornness, she is tenacious of the rightness and justice of her position:

> I dare not make myself so guilty
> To give up willingly that noble title
> Your master wed me to. Nothing but death
> Shall e'er divorce my dignities.
> (III, i, 139–42)

As she fairly complains—'And am I thus rewarded? 'Tis not well, lords' (III, i, 133). Not—it is *not* well. 'Evil' was, I think, the Gentleman's word.

But, after 'choler'—'Patience, be near me still' (IV, ii, 76). This is addressed to her maid called Patience, but the larger implication is entirely apt. Although she does permit herself a rather tart remark when Griffith

brings her 'commendations' and 'comfort' from the King when she is effectively on her death-bed—''Tis like a pardon after execution' (IV, ii, 121)—
she dies in a spirit of reconciliation. She has a 'Vision' of 'Spirits of peace', in
which white-robed figures hold a garland over her head—*at which, as it
were by inspiration, she makes in her sleep signs of rejoicing, and holdeth up her
hands to heaven*'. Her last message to the King is:

> Remember me
> In all humility unto his Highness.
> Say his long trouble now is passing
> Out of this world. Tell him in death I blessed him,
> For so I will. Mine eyes grow dim. Farewell,
> My lord.
>
> (IV, ii, 161–5)

It is, one feels, somewhat better than Henry deserves. But that is, here, not
the point. She has had her vision, her 'good dreams' (another touch of miracle), and departs in peace—'unqueened', yet more royal than ever.

But it is the third fall—the absolutely just one—which is in many ways
the greatest, for Wolsey came from almost out of nowhere to reach dizzying heights of power, influence—and a sumptuous way of life. Wolsey is
the most marked and distinctive character in the play; evil (or ruthless ambition combined with insatiable pride), as ever, having a more complex and
dimensioned physiognomy than simple goodness, or even not-so-simple
fortitude and forbearance. He is not 'propped by ancestry' (he was a butcher's son), but, in one of Buckingham's images, he is a spider who has made
his own spectacular career 'out of his self-drawing web' (I, i, 63). This suggests a 'self-fashioning' of a distinctly venomous kind. We catch glimpses
of the range of his influence and power—hosting a banquet for the King,
commandeering a lord's horses which he covets ('He will have all, I think');
and we are given clear indications of his dominance and manipulation of
the King:

> He dives into the King's soul, and there scatters
> Dangers, doubts, wringing of the conscience,
> Fears and despairs . . .
>
> (II, ii, 26–8)

and—'he hath a witchcraft / Over the King in's tongue' (III, ii, 18–19). The lords both hate and fear him, not least they seem like helpless putty in his scheming hands:

> We had need pray,
> And heartily, for our deliverance,
> Or this imperious man will work us all
> From princes into pages. All men's honors
> Lie like one lump before him, to be fashioned
> Into what pitch he pleases.
>
> (II, ii, 44–9)

As Buckingham complains, Wolsey's ascent and mastery effectively proclaim 'there's difference in no persons' (I, i, 139). He threatens their rank, status, and distinction—seems, indeed, willing and able to subvert hierarchy itself to serve his purposes, and, more dangerously, to further his influence and alliance with Rome. To this end, he tries to delay the Papal dispensation for divorce which Henry initially seeks—because Wolsey wants Henry to marry, not Anne ('a spleeny Lutheran'), but his own choice—the Duchess of Alençon. And this is where he overreaches himself, and everything goes wrong.

> All his tricks founder, and he brings his physic
> After his patient's death: the King already
> Hath married the fair lady.
>
> (III, ii, 40–42)

Henry has already lost patience with the cardinals ('I abhor / This dilatory sloth and tricks of Rome' II, iv, 236–7) and called back his 'well-beloved servant, Cranmer' who has duly obliged in providing sound theological justification for the 'divorce' (this is the only oblique reference to the great break from Rome, and the Reformation). But, for Wolsey, it is not just a matter of a foiled plan. His letters to Rome 'miscarried, / And came to th' eye o' th' King' (III, ii, 30–31); even worse, by a slip so disastrous that it begs to be called 'Freudian', Wolsey includes in some state papers he sends to the King a 'schedule' of all the 'treasure' he has raked and heaped together for himself. 'What piles of wealth hath he accumulated / To his own portion! . . . it outspeaks / Possession of a subject' (III, ii, 107–8, 127–8) exclaims the by now angry King. He confronts Wolsey, and gives him the two incriminating papers, adding, grimly enough:

> Read o'er this;
> And after, this; and then to breakfast with
> What appetite you have.
>
> (II, ii, 201–3)

Wolsey knows that the game is up. With something of his old imperious pride, he tries to outface the nobles beginning to gloat over his impending disgrace and ruin. But, left alone, he confronts the truth, in the one powerful soliloquy of the play:

> Farewell! A long farewell to all my greatness!
> This is the state of man: today he puts forth
> The tender leaves of hopes; tomorrow blossoms,
> And bears his blushing honors thick upon him.
> The third day comes a frost, a killing frost,
> And, when he thinks, good easy man, full surely
> His greatness is aripening, nips his root,
> And then he falls, as I do.
>
> (III, ii, 351–8)

This occurs at about the middle of the play, and it may be taken as a central statement of its theme. But, almost immediately, the miraculous transformation or conversion begins:

> Vain pomp and glory of this world, I hate ye.
> I feel my heart new opened. O, how wretched
> Is that poor man that hangs on princes' favors!
> There is betwixt that smile we would aspire to,
> That sweet aspect of princes, and their ruin,
> More pangs and fears than wars or women have.
> And when he falls, he falls like Lucifer,
> Never to hope again.
>
> (III, ii, 365–72)

He tells his 'amazed' servant, Cromwell, that though he is 'fall'n indeed', he was 'never so truly happy', and goes on:

> I know myself now, and I feel within me
> A peace above all earthly dignities,
> A still and quiet conscience. The King hath cured me,
> I humbly thank his Grace; and from these shoulders,
> These ruined pillars, out of pity, taken
> A load would sink a navy—too much honor.
> O, 'tis a burden, Cromwell, 'tis a burden
> Too heavy for a man that hopes for heaven!
>   (III, ii, 378–85)

From his radically changed perspective, he gives Cromwell advice which runs exactly counter to his own life:

> Mark but my fall and that that ruined me.
> Cromwell, I charge thee, fling away ambition.
>   (III, ii, 439–40)

Cromwell's last advice is 'Good sir, have patience'; to which Wolsey replies, as do the other falling stars—'So I have.' He dies in 'peace', having 'found the blessedness of being little' (IV, ii, 66). It is in keeping with the generally benign, charitable, and forgiving atmosphere of the play that, when Griffith brings the news of Wolsey's death to the dying Katherine, while Katherine understandably recalls his 'evil manners':

> He would say untruths and be ever double
> Both in his words and meaning. He was never,
> But where he meant to ruin, pitiful.
>   (IV, ii, 38–40)

Griffith asks permission to 'speak his good', and proceeds to do so. So the last we hear of Wolsey is an account of his abilities and virtues: it is a moment of imaginative generosity to this detested Catholic not to be found in the Protestant chronicles.

But what of King Henry himself—the Henry of the play? It is hardly a very probing study, and, indeed, he speaks fewer than 450 lines. There is certainly nothing here of the profligate, the gourmand, the sensualist, the wife-killer of popular image. Bullough finds him 'generous and trusting until he realizes he has been deceived or that villainy is intended', and says that 'From being *Defensor Fidei* he becomes the Defender, not perhaps of Protestantism, but of the rights of the private conscience; and the enemy of divisions in Church and State.' The play, he says, 'sets forth a King who is no Prospero controlling all men and events in justice . . . who can be misled by self-seekers but who nevertheless does good in the main . . . growing (unhistorically) in wisdom and benevolence'. R. A. Foakes, the Arden editor, is even more positive. Of the three falls he asserts—'in no case is there any recrimination, or blame attached to Henry; the law operates in its normal course. . .' I find this an astonishing proposition. The play itself makes it clear that it is at least gullible of Henry to believe the deeply suspect surveyor rather than the everywhere respected Buckingham; that he wants to find legalistic reasons for getting rid of old-wife Katherine because he has fallen for Anne; and that he is responsible for allowing Wolsey's unconscionable sway over himself and the land. (Foakes allows that the one ironic exchange in the play does rather glance at Henry's dubious motives in wanting to 'divorce' Katherine:

> *Chamberlain.* It seems the marriage with his brother's wife
> Has crept too near his conscience.
> *Suffolk* [*Aside*]. No, his conscience
> Has crept too near another lady.
> (II, ii, 16–18)

—yet he still finds Henry 'blameless'! We will come to Henry's 'creeping' conscience.) But Foakes then makes a larger claim (and he is not alone in this): considering Henry's 'growth in spiritual stature' he contends 'when he administers the law himself, justice as of heaven operates, and in this assumption of control Henry may be compared to Prospero, for he seems to stand above fate, and in all accidents of fortune which befall other characters is praised and blessed . . . Like Prospero, he has a kind of vagueness, not a lack of solidity, but a lack of definition, as a representative of benevolent power acting upon others.' This is part of that attempt, which I mentioned, to recruit *Henry VIII* as another of Shakespeare's genuine 'last plays'—*The Tempest* continued in another key, as it were. As against all this rather hagiographic reading of Henry in the play, we may put this burst of uncompromising asperity from Hazlitt: 'The character of Henry VIII is drawn with great truth and spirit. It is like a very disagreeable portrait, sketched by the hand of a master. His gross appearance, his blustering demeanour, his vulgarity, his arrogance, his sensuality, his cruelty, his hypocrisy, his want of common decency and common humanity, are marked in strong lines.' You would hardly think that Foakes and Hazlitt had been to the same play, as it were! As it happens, Hazlitt's account is demonstrably more spirited than accurate; but, at that, hardly as misguided, I think, as the attempt to promote Henry to the status of a Prospero. Power, he has; but no magic.

The play does, admittedly, protect him to some extent; not only by stopping where it does, but in one or two little matters—for instance, by making Anne innocent, demure, totally unambitious, pitiful of Katherine, and clearly chaste; as opposed to the 'scapegrace' (Bullough) she apparently was, already Henry's mistress before the wedding, by which time she was pregnant. And in the matter of taxation. Queen Katherine warns him that the people are being taxed beyond endurance, by the orders of Wolsey, to the point that 'Tongues spit their duties out, and cold hearts freeze / Allegiance in them' (I, ii, 61–2). Henry (in the play) is shocked, and is prompted to one of those strong and vigorous Shakespearian images:

> Why, we take
> From every tree lop, bark, and part o' th' timber,
> And though we leave it with a root, *thus hacked,*
> *The air will drink the sap.*
>   (I, ii, 95–8, my italics)

He, benevolently, orders the tax to be rescinded, and, magnanimously, all those who refused to pay pardoned. But it was by historical Henry's order that the tax was levied in the first place! It is a small act of sanitization, but perhaps indicative of larger protective intentions.

But he clearly washes his hands of Buckingham:

> If he may
> Find mercy in the law, 'tis his; if none,
> Let him not seek't of us. By day and night!
> He's traitor to th' height.
>   (I, ii, 211–14)

His evidence for this is of the poorest, and this determined abjuration of 'mercy' does him no kingly credit. We also see him clearly making up to Anne—'O beauty,/Till now I never knew thee' (I, iv, 75–6), before we hear his accounts of his protracted struggles with his conscience (over having married his brother's widow—but, by any account, twenty years is a strangely long time to wait for a call of conscience!). Thus, when we hear him lament about Katherine:

> O, my lord,
> Would it not grieve an able man to leave
> So sweet a bedfellow? But, conscience, conscience!
> O, 'tis a tender place, and I must leave her.
>   (II, ii, 140–43)

we are bound to be sceptical and hear the words as hollow. Particularly as in the very next scene, when the so modest and demure Anne protests to her 'Old Lady' companion that 'I would not be a queen', the Old Lady (worldly, experienced) simply retorts 'so would you,/For all this spice of your hypocrisy', and goes on to refer to '(Saving your mincing) the capacity/Of your soft cheveril conscience' (II, iii, 25–6, 31–2). There is more than a 'spice of hypocrisy' in more than one part of this play, and Henry is capable of his own kind of 'mincing'. 'Cheveril' is kidskin, for high-quality gloves and such like, and the 'cheveril' of *Henry's* conscience is, as the play shows, of the softest and most stretchable. By the end, he is indeed in control, all oppositions and problems in one way or another dispersed; with Cranmer and Sir Thomas More safely installed, Cromwell about to begin his reliable work—and baby Elizabeth to crown it all. Still, the Court of King Henry VIII is a long way from Prospero's Isle.

The play ends with the dazzling Elizabethan sunrise. But that sun had set ten years before this play was put on. So what was it? An exercise in patriotic nostalgia? Larger claims have been made for it. '*Henry VIII* is a resplendent Finale, ritualistically expanding through conflict into grace and happy augury . . . there is suffering in the play, but the movement on the whole is towards the triumph of goodness, not through physical battle, as in *Richard II* and *Henry V,* but by dignified acceptance, by the strength of its own nature' (Bullough). Foakes sees the play as 'a whole of visionary power, culminating in a mood of joy and reconciliation, and a prospect of lasting peace and well-being'. Wilson Knight (another Henry as Prospero man) makes the largest possible claims for the play. 'The play is rich with both a grand royalism and a thrilling but solemn Christianity; orthodox religious colouring being present and powerful throughout far in excess of any previous play.' He admires its 'blending of national and religious prophecy', saying 'it is as though time and eternity were seen converging as the play unfurls'. His final verdict is: 'If in *The Tempest* Shakespeare gives us a comprehensive and inclusive statement of his furthest spiritual adventures, in *Henry VIII* he has gone yet further, directly relating those adventures to the religion of his day and the nation of his birth.' I think all these men are describing, not without some material justification, the play they would like it to be. But, despite the themes of reconciliation, resignation, and even miraculous conversion which are undoubtedly there, this is *not,* finally, assimilable to Shakespeare's other 'last plays' (one small piece of overlooked evidence, which *would* work for such critics, is the curiously frequent use of 'strange' in the play—'strange' is a very 'last play' word). For we must bear in mind the truth claims of the play. The Prologue claims that the audience 'may here find truth too'; and Sir Henry Wotton, who described the burning of the Globe theatre during one performance, tells us that the play was called *All is True* (possibly an alternative title). But, an audience of 1613, invited to watch the play as 'real' history and 'truth', would know very well that that truth included the following historical facts:

> that Henry was bitterly disappointed that Elizabeth was not a
>   male heir, and that, when Anne miscarried a deformed son, he
>   was convinced God had damned his second marriage, so he
>   destroyed Anne in a palace coup in 1536;
> that Henry went on to have a series of other wives, some also
>   violently removed;
> that Henry had Sir Thomas More beheaded in 1535, and Thomas
>   Cromwell beheaded in 1540;
> that Archbishop Thomas Cranmer was burnt at the stake by
>   Henry's daughter, Mary, in 1556.

You might keep all such matters out of the *play,* but there is no way you could keep them out of a 1613 audience's mind. It is hard to imagine that Shakespeare was unaware of the sheer irony of what was being depicted on stage. And, certainly, he does not give us a *drama* of the reign of Henry VIII, as he had done, one way or another, for his previous kingly subjects. There is simply no real drama *in* the play. So what is it? Festivity, celebration, nostalgia—a dream of history as it might-have-been, as it ought-to-be? Or is there a deep sadness and irony running inerasably through it all? I, myself, tend to register the sadness and irony; but there will always be individual variation (predisposition?), and presumably a Hazlitt and a Foakes would never agree. And why Shakespeare wrote it—to the extent that he did write it—is simply beyond the reach of informed conjecture.

MAJOR TRAGEDIES

Blood hath been shed ere now, i' th' olden time,
Ere humane statute purged the gentle weal;
(Macbeth, III, iv, 77–8)

Western tragedy opens with a troubled and apprehensive watchman or guard on the roof of the palace of King Agamemnon, watching and waiting for news and signals concerning the outcome of the Greek war against Troy. He conveys a sense of unease and disquiet. Something, which he dare not, or will not, or cannot, articulate is wrong within the palace or 'house' for which he is the watchman. It is nighttime and the atmosphere is ominous, full of dubiety and an incipient sense of festering secrets. The long drama of the *Oresteia* has begun. Some two thousand years later, *Hamlet,* the first indisputably great European tragedy since the time of the Greeks, will open in very much the same way—on 'A guard platform of the castle' (of Elsinore), at midnight, with a nervous, jittery guardsman—Barnado —asking apprehensive questions in the darkness, and revealing that, for unspecified reasons, he is 'sick at heart'. The similarity betokens no indebtedness of Shakespeare to Aeschylus (whose work he could not have known), but rather a profound similarity of apprehension as to what might constitute a source for tragic drama. Shakespeare does not start where Aeschylus left off: he starts where Aeschylus started. And the subject, which is to say the problem, which is to say the potentially—and actually— catastrophic issue which they both set out to explore in their plays—the drama they dramatized—centres on revenge.

The *Oresteia* is a trilogy and what the three plays dramatize is—to put it at its simplest—how do you effect the painful, difficult, but absolutely essential transition from the revenge code (vendetta)—blood will have blood, an eye for an eye—to the impersonalization and institutionalization of revenge by the setting up of courts of law (whereby, as we now say, the state has a monopoly of violence); just, exactly, the crucial transition described by Macbeth in the quotation at the start of this introduction. How—to put it starkly—do you, does the human race in whatever communal or aggregated form, 'legalize' murder. Or—to put it at its starkest—how does the group (house, tribe, city, state) handle, cope with, somehow control, the problem which, arguably, is THE problem for any community or would-be communality—the problem of violence.

René Girard has much to say about the problems the revenge code poses for the community in his book *Violence and the Sacred* (1977). 'Vengeance, then, is an interminable, infinitely repetitive process. Every time it turns up in some part of the community, it threatens to involve the whole social body. There is the risk that the act of vengeance will initiate a chain reaction whose consequences will quickly prove fatal to any society of modest size. The multiplication of reprisals instantaneously puts the very existence of a society in jeopardy, and that is why it is universally proscribed.' And, we might add, why Hamlet is thrown into such confusion when reprisal is very specifically prescribed for him. 'Vengeance is a vicious circle whose effect on primitive societies can only be surmised. For us the circle has been broken. We owe our good fortune to one of our social institutions above all: our judicial system, which serves to deflect the menace of vengeance.'

In a society in which a fully elaborated judicial system is not in place, Girard suggests, ritual sacrifice, by deflecting vengeance onto a surrogate victim, 'serves to protect the entire community from *its own violence;* it prompts the entire community to choose victims outside itself.' It thus serves to keep violence in check—which Girard sees as perhaps the profoundest need of any community. This is because violence is endlessly 'self-propagating'. At the same time, Girard reminds us that while it is essential to recognize and acknowledge the differences, both functional and mythical, between vengeance, sacrifice, and legal punishment, 'it is important to recognize their fundamental identity'. 'Murder most foul, as in the best it is'—as in the best revenge code, the best religion, the best legal system. With these words alone, the ghost of Hamlet's father renders the task he has set his son virtually impossible to execute. However the killing is ritualized or legalized, if we look hard enough 'we find ourselves face to face with the specter of reciprocal reprisal'. It is a disturbing sight. Nevertheless, using whatever sanctions, and they will usually be transcendental, a society must find a way of defining and justifying 'a violence that is holy, legal, and legitimate, successfully opposed to a violence that is unjust, illegal, and illegitimate'.

I think the problem of violence is central to tragedy and that, in some tentative sense, we can think of the tragic drama as a form of ritual sacrifice, and the tragic hero or protagonist who goes to his death as bearing some relationship to the figure of the scapegoat or surrogate victim. But, to emphasize what I take to be the importance of this matter, a final quotation from Girard. 'The mechanism of reciprocal violence can be described as a vicious circle. Once a community enters the circle, it is unable to extricate itself. We can define this circle in terms of vengeance and reprisals . . . In more general terms, the mimetic character of violence is so intense that once violence is installed in a community, it cannot burn itself out.' In the *Oresteia*, Aeschylus shows the House of Atreus to be hopelessly trapped within this vicious circle over generations. The question then becomes—how can the circle be broken? Who will take the first step out—and how?

When, in *The Libation Bearers,* the second play of the *Oresteia,* Orestes finally confronts his mother, Clytemnestra, and is about to kill her, she begs for pity from him as her son, reminding him that he drew milk from her breasts. And Orestes stops. There follows this exchange.*

> *Orestes.* What shall I do, Pylades? Be shamed to kill my mother?
> *Pylades.* What then becomes thereafter of the oracles
>   declared by Loxias at Pytho? What of sworn oaths?
>   Count all men hateful to you rather than the gods.
> *Orestes.* I judge that you win. Your advice is good.

This, I will make so bold as to say, is the most crucial moment in the whole trilogy—indeed, I will make bolder to say that it is a crucial moment in the emergence of western drama. Not just because with the authoritative pronouncement from Pylades we hear for the first time the voice of the famous 'third actor', marking a crucial further move away from the earlier choric-ritual form of tragedy. But, more importantly, because, in this brief moment, Orestes has introduced a break in the circle. He steps back from his ordained and premeditated act and, as it were, looks at it from the outside. He has opened up a gap in which, albeit briefly, reflection interrupts and defers action. He has, for that moment, stalled the imperatives of revenge and begun to raise matters of principle. It *is* terrible to kill your mother. 'What should I do?' It is the first time that question has been asked. Heretofore, wife killed husband, father killed daughter, uncle killed nephews, god killed offspring without any such reflective questioning or moment of

---

* Aeschylus quotation from the translation by Greene and Lattimore, *Greek Tragedies,* University of Chicago Press, 1960.

ethical uncertainty. They may, like animals, have had to wait to leap, but they never, like Orestes, stopped to think. What Orestes has done is to introduce or insert a 'pause' in which he 'scans' his imminent deed (meaning, looks at it before performing it). I use these two words because they are absolutely central to Shakespearean tragedy as I hope will emerge. We could say that, what for Orestes is a very short 'pause' and a very brief 'scan', becomes in *Hamlet* almost the whole of the play. Because, between Aeschylus and Shakespeare, something has taken place which permanently changed the western mind—namely, Christianity, and more particularly for the Elizabethans, the Reformation.

The earliest Elizabethan attempts at tragedy were mainly revenge plays, with Seneca as the model. The most important of them before *Hamlet,* is *The Spanish Tragedy* (probably 1586–7) by Thomas Kyd. He is said to have written the lost play of *Hamlet* (sometime before 1589), but that play has vanished without any real trace and nothing can be proved. There are certainly features of *The Spanish Tragedy* which can be seen as anticipating Shakespeare's play. There is a ghost demanding revenge. Hieronimo, called on to revenge the very brutal murder of his son, engages in soliloquies in which he goes over the problems of what he has to do. (At one point he quotes to himself 'Vengeance is mine saith the Lord', but he does it anyway.) Perhaps most crucially, he uses a play-within-the-play to effect his revenge. In this case literally, the supposed 'actors' step out and actually murder the guilty creatures sitting at *that* play. Hamlet's dramaturgy is a good deal more complicated.

But rather than these obvious similarities, I wish to draw attention to some lines spoken by Hieronimo, now seemingly, but perhaps only seemingly, mad (another anticipation of Hamlet):

> There is a path upon your left-hand side,
> That leadeth from a guilty conscience
> Unto a forest of distrust and fear,
> A darksome place and dangerous to pass:
> There shall you meet with melancholy thoughts,
> Whose baleful humours if you but uphold,
> It will conduct you to despair and death:
>
> (III, xi, 13–19)

What we have here is a landscape, as it were a topography, of a 'guilty conscience'. It would be too much to say that Christianity 'invented' conscience, but between the time of Augustine and Aquinas, the concept had been elaborated and expanded in an entirely new way. The Reformation served to give it even more centrality and prominence. The word seems to come into currency in English during the fourteenth century (the earliest usage cited by the OED is 1325), replacing the attractive Middle-English word 'inwit'. It is tempting but anachronistic to suggest that Orestes opened the gap of conscience in a world hitherto locked into a spiral of conscienceless action. The Greeks had much to say about guilt, but they had no word for 'conscience' and there is nothing like Hieronimo's speech in their drama. The Furies come from outside and are visibly there. Conscience—vast, frightening tracts of it—is all inside. As Brutus, Hamlet, and Macbeth will variously discover.

Here is a soliloquy by Brutus in *Julius Caesar* which is absolutely crucial in the evolution of Shakespearian tragedy:

> Since Cassius first did whet me against Caesar,
> I have not slept.
> Between the acting of a dreadful thing
> And the first motion, all the interim is
> Like a phantasma, or a hideous dream.
> The genius and the mortal instruments
> Are then in council, and the state of man,
> Like to a little kingdom, suffers then
> The nature of an insurrection.
>
> (II, i, 61–9)

Shakespearian tragedy takes place in and focuses on, exactly, the 'interim' between the first 'motion' (or prompting, or provocation, or incitement, or some stirring inclination) and 'the acting of a dreadful thing'. The 'motion' may be started by an ambiguous ghost (*Hamlet*), a scheming devil (*Othello*), or equivocating witches (*Macbeth*). The 'dreadful thing' is always murder—albeit in very different circumstances. The period in between is experienced by the protagonist as, in different ways, 'like a phantasma, or a hideous dream'. And that 'phantasma' is, among other things, the phantasmagoria of the conscience started, startled, into unprecedented activity. The experience takes all the tragic protagonists, in varying degrees, to the edge of madness. This period or 'interim' may be long or short. *Hamlet,* the longest and slowest of Shakespeare's tragedies, is almost all 'interim'. *Macbeth,* his shortest and fastest, concentrates on a man who, with increasing desperation, tries to shrink and indeed obliterate the 'interim'. These are the parameters of Shakespeare's major tragedies. And this is what they are about.

⚜ HAMLET (1600–1)

Why is *Hamlet* so long, and what do I mean by saying that it is nearly all 'interim'? It is, famously, a delaying play, a play about delay. Hamlet's procrastination, if that is what it is, has been endlessly discussed. At the simplest level there is the unassailable argument of 'no delay, no play', and certainly if Hamlet had hurried to dispatch Claudius as soon as the ghost had issued his imperative, or even if he had killed him when, by his own account, he might 'do it pat' shortly after the ambiguous success of his 'play', we would not have the 'play' we have. But mere dramaturgical expediency would not have made *Hamlet* the most famous and inexhaustible western tragedy of our modern era, and we must certainly enquire a bit more curiously than that. Here are some words from Claudius, inciting Laertes to revenge:

> That we would do
> We should do when we would, for this "would" changes,
> And hath abatements and delays as many
> As there are tongues, are hands, are accidents . . .
> (IV, vii, 118–21)

'Should' and 'would'; 'tongues' and 'hands'; intention and obligation; word and deed—the complex inter-relation and interaction between these things occupy much of the play. And 'accidents' turn out to be crucial. 'Abatements' covers weakenings and bluntings of resolve and general retardations, and these all contribute to the lengthening of the play. Once again, we are looking at the 'interim' between prompting or provocation—the 'first motion'—and performance—the 'dreadful deed'.

Let us just consider the matter of slowness and speed. When the ghost promises to tell Hamlet about his 'unnatural' murder (but is there such a thing as a *natural* murder?), Hamlet responds:

> Haste me to know't, that I, with wings as swift
> As meditation or the thoughts of love,
> May sweep to my revenge.
>
> (I, v, 29–31)

The analogies are startlingly but prophetically inapposite. As swift as *meditation?* It is precisely because Hamlet meditates so much—thinks 'too precisely on th'event', finds 'the native hue of resolution / Is sicklied o'er with the pale cast of thought'—that he can act so little. 'Sweep' to his revenge is very exactly the last thing he does. It is Claudius and his regime that move quickly. He and Gertrude married before the mourning for her husband was completed—as Hamlet comments:

> O, most *wicked speed,* to post
> With such dexterity to incestuous sheets.
> (I, ii, 156–7—my italics)

When Claudius perceives that Hamlet is becoming distinctly dangerous, he dispatches him to England 'with fiery quickness'. Hamlet knows very well that Rosencrantz and Guildenstern are the bearers of some plot against him: 'they must sweep my way / And marshal me to knavery' (III, iv, 205–6). Claudius and his gang are the 'sweepers' and work with 'wicked speed'. Hamlet's instincts—scholar that he is (i.e. given to the life contemplative)—are all the other way. When he is told about the ghost, but before he has heard his story, his reaction is—to do absolutely nothing:

> then sit still, my soul. Foul deeds will rise,
> Though all the earth o'erwhelm them, to men's eyes.
> (I, ii, 257–8)

Stillness is associated with virtue, as it was in the Elizabethan mind. As is made clear in the ghost's comment on his wife's hasty marriage to the brother who murdered him.

> But virtue, *as it never will be moved,*
> Though lewdness court it in a shape of heaven,
> So lust, though to a radiant angel linked,
> Will sate itself in a celestial bed
> And prey on garbage.
>   (I, v, 53–7—my italics)

The lustful are always on the move. How the meditative and would-be virtuous Hamlet can find an appropriate way to insert himself into, and to intervene in, a court, a society, for him a world, now given over to, taken over by, those who, to satisfy their appetites, act with 'fiery quickness' and 'wicked speed', is indeed the great prolonging problem of the play. No wonder there are 'abatements and delays'.

But before looking more carefully at this central problem, we might do well to consider another rather curious aspect of the play which certainly contributes to its length. In a word, there seem to be two of everything.* There are two kings (one dead, one alive); Hamlet has now two fathers (Claudius being now 'uncle-father'); there are two sons who have to avenge murdered fathers (Hamlet and Laertes—Fortinbras makes a third but I'll come back to that); Claudius sends two ambassadors to Norway—Cornelius and Voltimand; and there are his two tools, made almost comically indistinguishable—Rosencrantz and Guildenstern. The ghost appears to Hamlet twice; Laertes makes a double departure; Hamlet's play to catch the king is performed twice; Hamlet abuses two women; after the play he goes and speaks daggers to his mother and then, when it seems he has finished, he does it again.

But it is perhaps above all in the amazing language of the play that we most often encounter what seems like a compulsive doubling, as though Shakespeare will not use one word when he can think of two. I will run together a few examples: 'the sensible and true avouch of mine own eyes'; 'the

---

* On 'doubles' in *Hamlet,* see Frank Kermode's brilliant chapter, 'Cornelius and Voltemand', in *Forms of Attention,* University of Chicago Press, 1985.

gross and scope of my opinion'; 'this posthaste and romage in the land'; 'the extravagant and erring spirit'; 'the dead waste and middle of the night'; 'the perfume and suppliance of a minute'; 'the shot and danger of desire'; 'the pales and forts of reason'; 'the single and peculiar life'; 'the book and volume of my brain'; 'this encompassment and drift of question'; 'the flash and outbreak of a fiery mind'; 'the motive and cue for passion'; 'the hatch and the disclose'; 'the teeth and forehead of our faults'; 'the proof and bulwark against sense'; and so on.

This is not just Shakespeare exploring and exploiting the resources of the English language as he found it, as no one before (or since) had done—though it is gloriously that as well. On the one hand, Shakespeare continually confronts, or assails, us with strange couplings, unexpected conjunctions, at every turn, or in every speech. Either the pair is too similar—Rosencrantz and Guildenstern, 'book and volume'—or so different that you would expect them to be kept separate, not, that is, in the same clause—or in the same bed: 'perfume and suppliance'—Gertrude and Claudius. One of the things that all these varyingly odd doublings serves to point up is that the central rottenness of this out-of-joint society is an incestuous relationship grounded in murder. Murder and incest are the most graphic and violent or lustful ways of annihilating the differences and annulling the separations and distinctions on which any society depends. 'More than kin, and less than kind'—these are Hamlet's first words; only one letter separates 'kin' and 'kind'—similar indeed, almost echoic. But the difference is also important. We must know 'kin' from 'kind' (though we should be kind to all our 'kind'). Through Claudius' incestuous marriage, Hamlet has become at once too closely 'related' to him, and more distant and antipathetically alienated from him. Kin and kind are merging or falling apart in all sorts of ways throughout the play. Kinship terms have become oxymoronically muddled—'uncle-father and aunt-mother', 'my cousin and my son'; and the continuities effected by appropriate kinship relationships have been skewed off course—Claudius should not marry Gertrude, but he does; Hamlet should marry Ophelia but he does not (Ophelia is the most pathetic victim of this sick and perverted society). Something has gone wrong at the controlling centre. This feeling is only enhanced by what seems like the uncontrollable tendency towards redundancy and proliferation which, I have tried to suggest, characterizes the atmosphere of the play. I take it that a cancer is the uncontrollable multiplication

of cells to the mortal detriment of the housing organism. As the imagery of
the play constantly reminds us, the society in which Hamlet finds himself is
very sick indeed—'ulcerous', cancerous; and, among other things, the structure of the play enacts that condition.

In this polluted and poisoned atmosphere, Hamlet finds it very difficult
to know, to decide, how to act. Or whether to act. Indeed, what, exactly,
'acting' is. A traditional avenger would have no problem. As we are reminded by the reactions and behaviour of Laertes when he returns to Denmark and finds that *his* father has been murdered. Nothing makes *him*
hesitate and he has to be almost forcibly restrained from starting the killing
immediately.

> Conscience and grace to the profoundest pit!
> I dare damnation . . .
>   I'll be revenged
> Most thoroughly for my father.
>   (IV, v, 132–6)

I'll come back to 'conscience'. The point is that Laertes is an almost un-
thinking adherent to the old revenge code. What would he do to Hamlet?
—'cut his throat i' th' church!' Claudius (of course) approves—'Revenge
should have no bounds.' But this points the way back to chaos and old night.
As his effect on Denmark sufficiently indicates. According to a messenger:

> young Laertes, in a riotous head,
> O'erbears your officers. The rabble call him lord,
> And, as the world were now but to begin,
> Antiquity forgot, custom not known,
> The ratifiers and props of every word . . .
>   (IV, v, 101–5)

This is the nightmare which Aeschylus dramatized, and René Girard outlined, in which 'mere anarchy' and unending violence are loosed upon the
world which threatens to collapse back into its original confusion. Laertes
portends atavism and regression (he becomes a willing agent in the devious
and bloody plans of Claudius). Hamlet has evolved too much, or become
too complicated, to revert to that kind of response.

There is another avenger whose behaviour Hamlet can compare with what he himself takes to be his own culpable and incomprehensible dilatoriness. When the Players arrive, Hamlet asks one of them to recite a speech from a play in which Aeneas recounts the details of the slaughter of Priam by Pyrrhus. Pyrrhus is about to kill Priam when the 'hideous' noise of the collapse of Troy 'takes prisoner Pyrrhus' ear' (we'll come back to ears), and he stops.

> For lo, his sword,
> Which was declining on the milky head
> Of reverend Priam, seemed i'th'air to stick.
> So as a painted tyrant Pyrrhus stood,
> And like a neutral to his will and matter
> Did nothing.
> But as we often see, against some storm,
> A silence in the heavens, the rack stand still,
> The bold winds speechless, and the orb below
> As hush as death, anon the dreadful thunder
> Doth rend the region, so after Pyrrhus' *pause,*
> A roused vengeance sets him new awork,
> And never did the Cyclops' hammer fall
> On Mars's armor, forged for proof eterne,
> With less remorse than Pyrrhus' bleeding sword
> Now falls on Priam.
>   (II, ii, 488–503—my italics)

Hamlet himself is, at that moment, a 'neutral to his will and matter' (i.e. caught in a moment of suspended passivity between his intention and his task—between purpose and performance), and he too is doing nothing. But after a brief 'pause', Pyrrhus, with 'roused vengeance', sets remorselessly about his killing. But Hamlet's 'pause' lasts almost the whole play. Not because he is paralysed by possible 'remorse'—he detests Claudius, and he feels little remorse for killing Polonius and none for sending Rosencrantz and Guildenstern to their deaths. It is something else which is so extending the 'interim' between the 'first motion' and the 'dreadful deed'. 'The interim's mine,' he says, late in the play. He is referring to a specific period of time before the news of what has happened to Rosencrantz and Guildenstern will reach the Danish court. But, in a larger sense, he both creates and owns the 'interim' which is, effectively, the play.

Why is the 'interim'—which became the most influential drama in western Europe—so long? Although, like Orestes, he has no taste for the deed, Hamlet can kill allright—his claim 'Yet have I in me something dangerous' is amply borne out by the events. Yet it takes him the whole of the long play finally to close with Claudius. Macbeth will speak of 'the pauser, reason' (meaning that once you start thinking about a course of action, it 'gives you pause' as we say). Hamlet, the scholar, is much inclined to 'reason' about almost everything, so we can say that he has become, by nature, a 'pauser'. After his 'play' has disturbed the king, Hamlet comes across Claudius—praying. Not praying with any conviction, however, because as he says his 'guilt defeats my strong intent'. His next words are:

> And like a man to double business bound
> I stand in pause where I shall first begin,
> And both neglect.
>
> (III, iii, 41–3)

It is part of the atmosphere of the play, full of ricocheting analogies, that these words could have just as well been spoken by Hamlet, himself 'standing in pause'. But this seems a perfect opportunity to enact his too-long-deferred revenge.

> Now might I do it pat, now 'a is a-praying,
> And now I'll do't. And so 'a goes to heaven,
> And so am I revenged. *That would be scanned.*
> A villain kills my father, and for that
> I, his sole son, do this same villain send to heaven.
> Why, this is hire and salary, not revenge.
>
> (III, iii, 73–8—my italics)

Scan—to look something over carefully. As he is a great 'pauser' so Hamlet is a great 'scanner'—the one directly because of the other. Orestes opened up a very small pause for a very short scan of the matricidal deed required of him. Hamlet opens up an immeasurably larger gap in which, indeed, he seems to scan everything, moving from the problematical aspects of revenge out to the position of man, and woman, in the universe. In Shake-speare's hands, the old revenge play opens up to the spaces of metaphysics. And one of the faculties or organs responsible for the unprecedented dis-tension is—conscience. The word occurs seven times in the play. Hamlet concludes Act II with his plan: 'The play's the thing / Wherein I'll catch the conscience of the King.' Almost immediately after, in the next scene, when Polonius has quite innocently observed that 'with devotion's visage / And pious action we do sugar o'er / The devil himself, the King makes an aside:

> How smart a lash that speech doth give my conscience!
> The harlot's cheek, beautied with plast'ring art,
> Is not more ugly to the thing that helps it
> Than is my deed to my most painted word.
> (III, i, 50–53)

One of the poisonous effects of this festering guilty conscience at the centre of the realm is just this insidious separation of 'deeds' from 'painted words'. Very shortly after this, Hamlet gives this instruction to the Players: 'Suit the action to the word, the word to the action.' One of his own major problems is how somehow to effect a realignment of words and deeds. In the court of Claudius, saturated with intrigue, indirections, spying, this takes a long time.

But the 'conscience of the King' is something he wants and tries to keep 'plastered over'. There is Hamlet's 'conscience' as well, and this we see and hear at work, particularly in the great soliloquies. Shortly after the King's aside, in one of those soliloquies, Hamlet says:

> Thus conscience does make cowards of us all,
> And enterprises of great pitch and moment,
> With this regard their currents turn awry,
> And lose the name of action.
> (III, i, 83–8)

Specifically, he is talking about the fear of what might come after death, but we can from this generalize the 'pausing' power of 'conscience'. The word was drawing many senses into it during this period, and here we may say that it both includes the Christian sense of conscience, and the more inclusive faculty and disposition of introspection, reflection, self-consciousness. Hamlet is certainly no orthodox sort of a Christian. Having sent Rosencrantz and Guildenstern to their deaths, he says to Horatio—'They are not near my conscience'. Perhaps we should briefly consider just what sort of a Christian Hamlet is, what sort of a 'conscience' he has ('the widest consciousness in literature' Henry James called it).

It is hard to date with any certainty the action of the play. Clearly it is an early Renaissance court of some kind. The Hamlet story itself goes back to ancient Norse legend and archaic traces of this origin find their way into Shakespeare's play.* When referring to his father, Hamlet invokes Hyperion, Jove, Mercury, Mars, and Hercules; the ancient Rome of Julius Caesar is also invoked more than once. It is as though he is drawing effortlessly on precedents and memories of an earlier heroic, pagan age. On the other hand, when he encounters the 'questionable shape' of the ghost (capable of answering, but also dubious), he draws on a quite different lexicon.

> Angels and ministers of grace defend us!
> Be thou a spirit of health or goblin damned,
> Bring with thee airs from heaven or blasts from hell . . .
>
> (I, iv, 39–41)

When the ghost departs, Hamlet's first words are:

> O all you host of heaven! O earth! What else?
> And shall I couple hell?
>
> (I, v, 93–4)

And even up to the time he puts on his play he is entertaining this possibility—'The spirit that I have seen / May be a devil.' Hamlet, at the start, has just returned from studying in Wittenberg (whither he wishes to return, but is forbidden). Wittenberg, of course, was where Luther nailed his fa-

---

* In this compressed introduction I do not intend to go into Shakespeare's sources nor the ways he transformed them. The sources for the four tragedies in this volume are all most conveniently collected in Volume Seven of Geoffrey Bullough's majestic work—*Narrative and Dramatic Sources of Shakespeare,* Routledge and Kegan Paul, 1975.

mous *Theses* to the church door, thus effectively starting the Reformation in northern Europe. If he is not—detectably—a devout Protestant, nevertheless Hamlet's 'conscience', like his vocabulary, will be marked by Protestant thinking. For a Protestant, the Ghost would indeed have been regarded as a devil from hell (for a Catholic it could be a spirit from purgatory—the play seems to incline that way, but let us not get involved in fruitless speculations about Shakespeare's religious affiliations or allegiances). Perhaps more important, one of the main contentions of the Reformation thinkers was that 'justification' (salvation) could only be by faith, and not, not *at all*, by works as the Catholics maintained. Our fates were 'predestined', so it was folly to think any human effort could influence the divine plan. Taken to an extreme, this belief could see all attempts at significant salvational or restorative or corrective or expiatory action as, at best, futile, and more probably sinful. This, surely, is the theology which, among other things, Hamlet has been studying. Yet he is, most imperiously, called on to *act*.

Act as a good hero and soldier (following the models of Hercules, Mars, Pyrrhus); or act, by desisting from action, like a good Protestant (attending to the voice of Wittenberg)? Here again, the instructions or orders from the Ghost compound rather than simplify the problem. His first demand seems straightforward enough—(referring to himself as Hamlet's father) 'Revenge his foul and most unnatural murder.' (I will return to the problem of what is, or should be, 'natural'—central to Shakespearian tragedy— and whether there, could be such a thing as *natural* murder.) Here is the unambiguous old revenge code. But then:

> Murder most foul, as in the best it is,
> But this most foul, strange, and unnatural.
>
> (I, v, 27–8)

The Ghost has lost his point, even while trying to make it. His 'but' tries to introduce a distinction, but fails to. If murder is always 'most foul' (as in the best it is), his murder cannot be somehow more 'most foul' than any other. By definition, there cannot be comparatives within a superlative. The repetition of the phrase reveals the impossibility of making distinctions. The Ghost bewails and condemns a 'most foul' deed—and orders Hamlet to commit one. No wonder Hamlet goes into a spin. But even more puzzling:

But howsomever thou pursues this act,
Taint not thy mind, nor let thy soul contrive
Against thy mother aught. Leave her to heaven.
                                (I, v, 84–6)

'Soul', 'heaven'? This does not sound like the old revenge code. If that's the
way it is, why not leave Claudius to heaven too? (As Horatio—also from
Wittenberg—comments after the initial commotion caused by the appearance of the Ghost—'Heaven will direct it.' But will it? Hard to be sure in
this uncertain atmosphere. In the event, Hamlet becomes a secular kind of
'director'—he puts on a play.) Hamlet is to be a killer-avenger to the uncle-
father, but a forbearing Christian to his mother-aunt. The point, simple
enough perhaps but crucially generative for the play, is that Hamlet's mind,
his 'conscience', becomes a meeting-place, a battlefield, a forcing house, a
breeding ground, for the different codes, value systems, religions, cosmolo-
gies, which (with all due recognition of the prior influence of the Greek and
Jewish traditions) formed the modern European mind—ancient heroism,
Roman paganism, and Christian Reformation. And monarchial feudalism.

In a most interesting little book,* Carl Schmitt suggests that, rather than
situating *Hamlet* between the Renaissance and the Baroque as Walter Benjamin does, we might more profitably see the play as coming (and dramatizing) somewhere between the 'barbaric' and the 'political'. He explains
his terms. Summarizing and simplifying—the 'political' means the evolution and implementation of a state in which politics were separated from
religion. On the continent in the early seventeenth century, this was happening (Machiavelli was a crucial influence). The 'barbaric' connotes a society still dominated by what Schmitt calls 'pre-statal forms': it is feudal, and
religion and politics are still inter-involved. The sovereign state is a product
of the divorce between religion and politics; what this meant, among other
things, is that *power* is no longer mediated through (and thus sanctioned by)
God. It becomes mundane. But when a society is still in the 'barbaric' stage,
power is conceived as coming from (and thus sanctified and legitimated by)

---

* *Hamlet oder Hekuba,* Dusseldorf, 1956—to my knowledge, not translated into English. I wish to thank Nadia Fusini for introducing me to this work and helping me
with translating the contents, and for many helpful discussions concerning Shakespeare.

some trans-human source. As Schmitt sees it, the Stuarts remained unaware of the new movements on the continent, and were unable to detach themselves from the feudal and religious Middle Ages. James I (of England), for instance, still believed in the concept of 'the divine right of kings' although it was already an anachronistic notion by his time and would soon be done away with. It is notable that the articulation of this doctrine in *Hamlet* is given to the supremely hypocritical Claudius—('There's such divinity doth hedge a king' etc.—IV, v, 123–5). More, one feels by this time, of his desperate plastering over. The society or the world of *Hamlet* is still predominantly 'barbaric'. But it is sick, and falling to pieces.

It is not my intention to explore the contemporary historical background to Shakespeare's plays in this introduction. But Schmitt points out something so interesting, and probably constitutively crucial for the play, that I will summarize it here. He starts from the question of why the question of Gertrude's guilt and complicity in the murder of her husband is left unclear and unresolved. But she must not be touched. It is as though there is a taboo on dealing directly with the queen. Mary Stuart was married to Henry Lord Darnley who was assassinated by the Earl of Bothwell in February 1586. Very shortly after, in May of the same year, Mary married the assassin ('Thrift, thrift, Horatio'). It was a big scandal and the question of Mary's involvement in the murder was never settled. Perhaps needless to say, Protestants were convinced she instigated it. Queen Elizabeth died in 1603, the year of the first Quarto of *Hamlet*. This means that Shakespeare was writing his play when the question of the succession to Elizabeth was both unclear and increasingly pressing. Southampton and Essex supported James (Mary Stuart's son) for the succession, and Shakespeare and the Players supported them. Essex of course was executed (and his last words are said to be echoed in Horatio's farewell to the dying Hamlet), and Shakespeare and the Players temporarily had to leave London. James duly succeeded—Shakespeare and the Players came back to London. James was baptised a Catholic but brought up a Protestant—thus enabling him to succeed to the English throne (he also wrote a 'Demonology' in 1597 in which he discussed the question of the apparition of ghosts). He also honoured his mother and would hear no suggestion that she was involved in the murder of his father. The parallels to Shakespeare's play are too obvious to need spelling out—Schmitt calls it 'the potent eruption of historical reality in the play'. It would also provide a specific reason for why Shakespeare had to be so circumspect in his handling of the Queen. Schmitt is suggesting that, among many many other things, the figure and situation of Hamlet contain lineaments and echoes of those of James I. And thus, Hamlet's bestowal of Denmark to Fortinbras—making a man from another country the legitimate successor—could be seen as, before James' coronation, an augury and a hope; and after the coronation, a gesture of homage. In this instance, the contribution of contemporary history seems to me to be both powerful and incontestable. Which only makes it the more remarkable that, perhaps more than any other work, it has come to be felt to be a play for all time.

To place *Hamlet* in a period still in some ways 'barbaric' and feudal can be illuminating in another way. Here are some words from Hegel concerning tragedy. 'The Greek heroes make their appearance in an epoch anterior to legal enactment . . . so that right and social order, law and ethical custom, emanate from them'; by contrast, modern man acts 'within the bounds already marked out for him by legislative enactments in the social order . . . he is only a member of a fixed order of society and appears as such limited in his range rather then the vital representative and individual embodiment of society itself.' There are lawyers referred to (very disparagingly) in *Hamlet,* but not much sign of a legal system and 'legislative enactment'.* There is nothing of what Hegel calls 'the legalized fabric of modern society'. Hence the traces of the archaic, the barbaric, the heroic ages in the play. 'The time is out of joint' and Hamlet himself has to 'set it right': there are no police and law-courts to do it for him. Claudius knows right from wrong, but he makes his own laws, which Hamlet is powerless to obstruct (though it is clear that he has been 'illegally' dispossessed); and Hamlet will spend the whole play trying to find ways to circumvent and frustrate, repeal and replace, the power-backed edicts of a usurping king. Who still— an ultimate mockery—claims his power is God-given.

As we learn from Ophelia's encomium-lament (III, i, 153 *et seq.*), Hamlet is admired and looked up to as a courtier, soldier, and scholar—'Th' expectancy and rose of the fair state.' This is not, necessarily, an impossible trilogy of identities to maintain and roles to discharge (though I suppose there could be some friction between the impulses of the scholar and the soldier). But he is also, I have been trying to suggest, a rather more uneasy compound—a 'barbarian'-Christian. This is made clear even, or particularly, at

---

* *Hegel on Tragedy,* Doubleday, New York, 1962; pp. 100, 109, 111.

his death. Horatio—fellow-Wittenbergian—bids farewell to the Christian: 'flights of angels sing thee to thy rest'. Fortinbras, the warrior, pays his respects to the man of Mars:

> Let four captains
> Bear Hamlet like a soldier to the stage,
> For he was likely, had he been put on,
> To have proved most royal; and for his passage
> The soldier's music and the rite of war
> Speak loudly for him.
>
> (V, ii, 397–401)

Songs of angels and soldier's music—can they be harmonized? Or did Hamlet live out a life of perpetual dissonance—and that is what we have been watching?* And what can action, acting, mean and be for a courtier-soldier-scholar-barbarian-Christian? Hamlet indeed has much to 'scan'.

Fortinbras orders the captains to bear Hamlet 'to the stage' because, 'had he been put on', he was likely to have proved most royal. But Hamlet is already *on* a stage, and *Hamlet* has just *been* 'put on' (these are effectively the closing lines). A stage on a stage; a play within a play—what is Shakespeare doing? When an audience is presented with people who are already actors acting as 'actors' in a play staged within a play, it sets up ripples of ontological unease. This has been called the Pirandello effect. For where, one begins to wonder, does the acting stop? Are we not *all,* in one sense or another, 'guilty creatures sitting at a play'? Given that the Globe Theatre was indeed taken to be an image of the 'great globe' itself, and its symbolic façade represented the traditional cosmos, the feeling of the world as stage must have been very strong for an Elizabethan audience.† Hamlet persuades Claudius to watch a play containing a 'Player King'. But, an unlegitimated usurper, Claudius, is also a 'player king' (so two of these, too). We see him performing, acting the king, in Act I, scene ii, in which, with what looks like

---

* On this, and indeed on the whole play, see Nigel Alexander's admirable book, *Poison, Play and Duel,* Routledge and Kegan Paul, 1971.
† See *The Idea of a Theatre* by Francis Fergusson, Doubleday, New York, 1955, pp. 128–30. The whole long section on *Hamlet* in this book is seminal and extremely important.

authority, he issues orders, dispenses advice, grants requests in a manner which 'seems' authentically royal. It is, in fact, all 'show', and Claudius knows that, for his survival and success, the 'show' must go on. But Hamlet, from the very beginning, announces that he knows not '"seems"', and already has 'that within which passes show'. The trouble for Claudius will come from here—that we can anticipate. But it will not be easy. For in a court, a society, which seems saturated with 'seeming' and 'acting' of one kind or another, how establish or discover a more authentic mode of 'action'? And that, indeed, is what Hamlet and the play itself spend a good deal of time 'scanning'—simply, the problems and the meaning of 'action'.

In the graveyard scene (V, i), we see two clowns being very disrespectful of the dead. In this they are just like their so-called betters (cf. the treatment of Hamlet's father, Polonius, Ophelia) only somewhat coarser, or more direct. And one of them makes a most pertinent point, even while he seems to be mocking legal pedantry. They are discussing—*à propos* of the doubt hovering over Ophelia's death—suicide, and one of them says: 'For here lies the point: if I drown myself wittingly, it argues an act, and an act hath three branches—it is to act, to do, to perform' (V, i, 10–12). It is Hamlet's problem and task to work out the relations between acting, doing, and performing (but perhaps the distinctions are illusory?); to somehow recover or re-establish, to use his own phrase, 'the name of action'. When Claudius is trying to pray, after the play, he speaks with the clear-sightedness of a guilty conscience. In 'the corrupted currents of this world', he knows very well—from personal experience—that 'Offense's gilded hand may shove by justice' and that 'the wicked prize itself / Buys out the law.' The law is, as yet, helpless in the face of power, and is indeed too often easily purchasable by it.

> But 'tis not so above.
> There is no shuffling; there the action lies
> In his true nature
>
> (III, iii, 60–63)

Claudius presides over a 'shuffling' society; indeed he has created it. Trickery, spying, intrigue, lying and deception, everywhere. In this world, is it possible to find, or create, a place where 'action lies in his true nature' and thereby, we may infer, recovers its 'name'?

Hamlet contains a number of speeches alluding to, or describing, the fading of the will to act. I have quoted one by Claudius to Laertes concerning 'abatements and delays'. Here is part of another, by the Player King (the other one):

> But what we do determine oft we break
> Purpose is but the slave to memory . . .
>
> What to ourselves in passion we propose,
> The passion ending, doth the purpose lose . . .
>
> Our wills and fates do so contrary run
> That our devices still are overthrown;
> Our thoughts are ours, their ends none of our own.
>   (III, ii, 194–5, 200–201, 217–20)

Claudius's 'devices' are massively 'overthrown' in the climactic conclusion to the play, and I will come to that. Here we may note the pointing to the difficulty of, as it were, binding together passion, purpose, and performance. And this indeed is Hamlet's problem. After he has listened to the recital of the actor who has worked himself up 'in a fiction, in a dream of passion' he goes on to wonder;

>   What would he do
> Had he the motive and the cue for passion
> That I have?
>   (II, ii, 570–72)

After Fortinbras and his army have passed him, on their way to fight, and very likely die, for a piece of worthless land and 'a fantasy and trick of fame', again he scans and ponders his inaction:

>   I do not know
> Why yet I live to say, "This thing's to do,"
> Sith I have cause, and will, and strength, and means
> To do't.
>   (IV, iv, 43–6)

He has, then, the motive, the cue, the cause, the will, the strength, the means—yes, why *doesn't* he 'do't'?

At this point I want to return to his encounter with the Ghost. When he appeals to Hamlet to avenge him he says: 'If thou hast nature in thee, bear it not', and then proceeds to give Hamlet his directly contradictory imperatives—kill/do not kill—after he has already described his own murder as 'unnatural'. 'Nature' is perhaps the most ambiguous, or capacious, or problematical word in Shakespeare, and as we shall see, his tragedies time and again address themselves to the matter of what is nature, what is 'natural'? Here, the appeal to 'nature' can hardly help Hamlet. Will a 'natural' murder somehow avenge an 'unnatural' one? But is there such a thing? Aren't all murders 'most foul'? What I want to suggest is that the Ghost is effectively paralysing Hamlet even while goading him to action. Indeed, I would even say 'poisoning' him. Or rather, transmitting Claudius' poison to him. But to explain that I must turn to the matter of 'ears'.

The Ghost informs Hamlet that he was murdered by his brother who poured literal poison in his ear ('in the porches of my ear did pour / The leprous distillment'). But before this is told to Hamlet and the audience, we have heard this:

> And let us once again assail your ears,
> That are so fortified against our story
>
> (I, i, 31–2)

and this:

> Nor shall you do my ear that violence
> To make it truster of your own report
>
> (I, ii, 171–2)

and this:

> But this eternal blazon must not be
> To ears of flesh and blood
>
> (I, v, 21–2)

and this:

> So the whole ear of Denmark
> Is by a forged process of my death
> Rankly abused
>
> (I, v, 36–8)

And, after the Ghost's graphic account of the effect on his body of the 'leprous distillment', we will hear this:

> and with a hideous crash
> Takes prisoner Pyrrhus' ear
>
> (II, ii, 487–8)

and this:

> And I'll be placed, so please you, in the ear
> Of all their conference
>
> (III, i, 187–8)

and this:

> And wants not buzzers to infect his ear
> With pestilent speeches . . .
> Will nothing stick our person to arraign
> In ear and ear
>
> (IV, v, 90–91, 93–4)

—this from Claudius who, indeed, knows about infecting ears with pestilence.

And finally, though by no means exhaustively, this:

> I have words to speak in thine ear will make thee dumb
>
> (IV, vi, 25–6)

In *Othello,* Othello, explaining his 'enchantment' of Desdemona, says that she would come to listen to his exotic stories and 'with a greedy ear/Devour up my discourse' (I, ii, 148–9). Her father is sceptical: 'But words are words. I never yet did hear/That the bruised heart was pierced through the ear' (I, iii, 215–16). How wrong he is, the rest of the play will demonstrate as Iago sets about 'bruising' Othello's heart by 'abusing' his ear—'I'll pour this pestilence into his ear' (II, ii, 356). Not, this time, a 'leprous distillment', but insinuations of Desdemona's sexual infidelity and promiscuity. Deadly poison comes in many forms. In *King Lear* Edmund, who can produce false 'evidence' as diabolically as Iago, promises to afford Gloucester 'auricular assurance' of Edgar's treachery, another 'poison' which Gloucester catastrophically believes (I shall return to the matter of 'evidence' in Shakespeare). Lady Macbeth, who has already resolved that her husband will murder the king, can hardly wait for Macbeth's return: 'Hie thee hither,/That I may pour my spirits in thine ear' (I, v, 26–7)—and poisonous and 'unnatural' 'spirits' they are too.

In bringing all these quotations from the tragedies together, I am hoping to make an important point without belabouring the obvious. We can be mistaken in what we see (bent sticks in water, etc.), and we can hallucinate; we may be incorrect about the exact nature of something we touch; we may err in identifying a taste or a smell. But in no other sense are we so vulnerable as in our hearing. This is because (and this is where I risk being too obvious) it is through the ear that language enters the body. This is how and where we can be most 'rankly abused' and variously 'poisoned'. We may like to invoke Freud's point that it is through the ear that we internalize 'the family's *sounds* or *sayings,* the spoken or secret discourses, going on prior to the subject's arrival, within which he must make his way'.* Or we may be content with Montaigne's contention that the ears 'are the most dangerous instruments we have to receive violent and sudden impressions to trouble and alter us'. In the middle, literally, of his first really major tragedy (it happens almost exactly half way through, in the middle of Act III), the physical poisoning of the king's ear is re-enacted on the stage within the stage for all, if they are paying proper attention, to see—as if to make

---

* See an interesting comment on this in *Disowning Knowledge* by Stanley Cavell, Cambridge University Press, 1987, p. 189, though his reading of *Hamlet,* insofar as I follow it, strikes me as wild.

starkly visible what will everywhere else occur as an absolutely crucial metaphor. Crucial, because an abiding concern in the tragedies is—how and why do things (people, societies) go wrong? Where does the 'poison' come from? How does it spread? And what is the how and when of 'cure' or purgation? The Ghost, I want to suggest, 'poisons' Hamlet's ear with the truth of murder and incest—for there *are* truths which, to all intents and purposes, 'poison' the hearer. As the poison spreads to him, Hamlet is at once both enlightened and arrested—with the result that he must 'unpack my heart with words'. Macbeth compares the wounds of murdered Duncan to 'a breach in nature / For ruin's wasteful entrance'. How do ruin and waste—murder and poison—enter the world? What are the promptings, processes, and procedures of evil? And what—if anything—can be done about it? What are the chances—they may seem slim, they may turn out to be inexorable—of *re*paration, *re*stitution, *re*storation (as opposed to, simply, '*re*venge')? These are central concerns in all Shakespeare's tragedies, and of course they torment Hamlet's consciousness and conscience unrelentingly. With a vengeance, we might say. O cursed spite . . .

In the first scene of the play, the sentinel Francisco reports—'Not a mouse stirring.' Hamlet says his play is called '*The Mousetrap*'. After the performance of that play, and after Claudius has thereby been 'frighted with false fire', the mice start stirring. And the rats, too. Hamlet thinks he has killed one behind the arras in the Queen's closet ('How now? A rat? Dead for a ducat. . .'), but it turns out to be Polonius, who could, I suppose, be described as one of Claudius' mice. But King Rat, or the rat-King, will prove harder to pin down, and pin through, though Hamlet will, finally, manage it. How he manages it may be said to be problematical. He can scarcely claim that he has recovered 'the name of action' since, arguably, he himself initiates nothing. Indeed, it could be said that he settles for *re*action over action. Perhaps he has arrived at another name for action, action in another key. Although at the conclusion of his last soliloquy (IV, iv) he had resolved —'O, from this time forth, / My thoughts be bloody or be nothing worth', after his return from England—that is Act V—his mood, as everyone recognizes, has changed. No more 'whirling words', an end to 'antic disposition', self-tormenting soliloquies put behind him. His mood is more one of quiescence, acquiescence—this may be seen as religious resignation or stoic fatalism, or something of both. His language touches on various possibilities: 'There's a divinity that shapes our ends, / Rough-hew them how we

will'—'Why even in that was heaven ordinant'—'There is special providence in the fall of a sparrow': divinity, heaven, providence—none of them
capitalized. Hamlet thought his role was to be a 'scourge and minister', but
he finds a larger wisdom (or you could say, he finds the best way of being both), in just capitulating to the more mysterious, ineluctable processes
which he feels to be moving in and through the unfolding events—divinity? history? fate? undecidable; unknowable. His last words as he goes into
the final, fatal, fateful, scene, are simply—'Let be.' Shakespeare's incomparable dramatic poetry is never more piercing and powerful than when it
delivers itself in staccato monosyllables.

   In a characteristically original formulation, Walter Benjamin writes:
'Hamlet wants to breathe in the suffocating air of fate in one deep breath.
He wants to die by some accident, and as the fateful stage-properties gather
around him, as around their lord and master, the drama of fate flares up
in the conclusion of this *Trauerspiel,* as something that is contained, but of
course overcome in it.'* We may supplement this with a formulation by
Philip Brockbank: 'the play turns itself about. . . At the start . . . there is
apparent order in the macrocosm and disorder in the microcosm. But at
the play's end, the most memorable passages suggest quiescence and calm
within the mind of Hamlet while the spectacle presents total confusion
in the court of Claudius.'† As Brockbank goes on to say: 'Nothing in the
play goes according to plan, but everything happens by significant accident
when the time is ripe.' In almost his last speech, Horatio speaks:

----

* *The Origin of German Tragic Drama,* NLB, 1977, p. 137. This book contains many
pregnant thoughts about *Hamlet,* though I do not think the play can be contained
within the category of '*Trauerspiel*' (Mourning-play) in which Benjamin wishes to
place it.
† *On Shakespeare,* Blackwell, 1989, p. 170. Anyone teaching English for over thirty
years, as I have been doing, will inevitably have read a large number of books on
Shakespeare, and I cannot hope to trace all my influences nor acknowledge all my
debts. Where I can I have signalled specific sources. But I just single out the work of
Philip Brockbank. This, alas posthumous, collection of his essays on Shakespeare I regard as indispensable reading and is an identifiable influence on what I have to say.
But Philip Brockbank was also my supervisor when I was an undergraduate and I
think I learned, perhaps not always consciously, more from his fine, complex, ironic
humanism than from any subsequent influence.

Of accidental judgments, casual slaughters,
Of deaths put on by cunning and forced cause,
And, in this upshot, purposes mistook
Fall'n on th'inventors' heads.

(V, ii, 383–6)

This certainly covers the havoc, error, the confusion and ritual perversions (sporting duels which are murders, celebratory refreshments which are poisoned) of the last scene—without Hamlet planning it, planning anything, a purgation of the realm is effected, a clean succession ensured, a kind of justice done. (As well as stabbing the king with the 'envenomed point' of the treacherous sword—the poison of Claudius' court is everywhere now—Hamlet makes him drink the poisoned drink he had prepared for Hamlet which contains an 'union' (pearl). His last words to Claudius are 'Drink off this potion. Is thy union here? Follow my mother.' By a dramatic pun, Hamlet is forcing Claudius to swallow the incestuous 'union' with his mother which is part of the originating poison of the play.) It would seem as if you cannot, finally, 'take arms against a sea of troubles', but rather have to let the ultimately cleansing tides of providence and history 'sweep' you along, sweep you through, sweep you off. John Holloway has a helpful formulation: 'over and over in *Hamlet,* chance turns into a larger design, randomness becomes retribution'.* From the immediate, or contrived, bloody reprisals and mimetic violence of the revenge code, Shakespeare has moved to—'Let be.' In the process, he has transformed primitive revenge drama into metaphysical tragedy of enduringly awesome spaciousness, resonance, and reverberation.

OTHELLO (1603–4)

Hamlet could not have recourse to law. Othello, by contrast, is involved—embroiled is perhaps a better word—in law and legalism effectively from start to finish. The whole lexicon of 'justice' pervades the play: arraignment

---

* *The Story of the Night,* Routledge and Kegan Paul, 1961, p. 35. This is an interesting book on Shakespearian tragedy which should not be neglected.

and accusation; defence and pleading; testimony, evidence, and proof (crucial word); causes, vows, oaths; solicitors, imputations, and depositions—the law is, somehow, everywhere in the air. Since soldier Othello's discourse is—initially—almost entirely martial and exotic, he is bound to go astray in this fog of forensic terminology, and of course he disastrously does. The third scene sees him accused of bewitching and seducing Desdemona by her father, Brabantio, though we should note that this is not a formally constituted court of law but a sort of improvized hearing in front of the Duke of Venice which takes place, like much of the play, misleadingly at night. Improvized law, and finally the grossest perversion of 'justice', are to become major themes of the play.

We should also note that this scene has a double character or function. Othello is initially summoned to the Duke's council chamber because Venice has need of Othello—the great heroic warrior—against 'the general enemy Ottoman' who seems to be threatening to attack Cyprus (an important part of Venice's empire). Then Brabantio tries to use the occasion to indict Othello of criminal seduction and abduction. So Othello, in effectively his first appearance, is put in an ambiguous light—he is the military hero, essential to the defence of the state; but he might also be a sexual villain, racially un-Venetian and a deep threat to domestic order. On this occasion he is, of course, cleared of the 'crime' thanks to Desdemona's evidence. But at the end he will indeed appear in the dual role of soldier/criminal (Venetian/Turk), and play *all* the roles—accuser, penitent, judge, defendant, witness, jury and, finally, executioner—of himself, his Venetian part passing summary judgement on his Turkish part:

> And say besides that in Aleppo once,
> Where a malignant and a turbaned Turk
> Beat a Venetian and traduced the state
> I took by th'throat the circumcised dog
> And smote him—thus. [He stabs himself.]
>   (V, ii, 347–51)

There are no Turks in the play, only people who more or less 'turn Turk': we are perhaps not very comfortable with the implied racialism, but it has to be recognized that, in terms of this play and the Venetian lexicon which necessarily dominates it, the name 'Turk' stood for the barbarian, the heathen, the feared and savage Other. Iago is Venetian, but when he says to Desdemona 'Nay, it is true, or else I am a Turk' (II, i, 112) we should recognize one of his bitter ironies—what he says is, crucially, *not* true, and he *is*—in the terms of the play—a 'Turk', and turns people into Turks. When he organizes the drunken chaos of Othello's first night in Cyprus, Othello storms out of his house, asking angrily 'From whence ariseth this? Are we turned Turks?' (II, iii, 168–9). The double answer, which of course he cannot know yet, is that it ariseth from Iago, and *Othello himself is* about to 'turn Turk'. Iago is, exactly, the barbarian within—within Venice, finally within Othello.

I want to return to the third scene of the play, the improvized 'trial' of Othello. When Brabantio complains that his daughter has been 'abused, stol'n from me, and corrupted', the Duke promises him full recourse to, and support by, 'the bloody book of law' (I, iii, 67). It is a strange formulation. The *bloody* book of *law*? The bloody *book* of law? As I tried to suggest, 'law' was developed precisely to prevent bloodshed, at least as far as possible. Books (of rules and precedents) *instead* of blood; writing instead of fighting; law instead of private revenge; tribunals instead of murders; court-rooms instead of carnage. Of course, in its ultimate reaches the law *can* be 'bloody', but it is rather worrying to see law and blood thus conflated so early in the play, and by the ultimate source of authority in civilized Venice at that. It is, of course, unconsciously prophetic. In the course of the play law will drown in blood, or rather blood will take over law for its own bloody purposes. ''Sblood' is Iago's first word in the play (I, i, 3) and the word is often on his lips ('the blood and baseness of our natures'—I, iii, 332; 'lust of the blood'—I, iii, 339 etc.). Put very simply, what happens is that he transforms Othello—who as an important servant and protector of the state should be an instrument of law—into a man of blood, and introduces 'blood' into his mind and discourse until they are both awash with the word:

> My blood begins my safer guides to rule
> (II, iii, 205)

> O, blood, blood, blood!
> (III, iii, 451)

Even so my bloody thoughts, with violent pace,
Shall ne'er look back, ne'er ebb to humble love
                              (III, iii, 457–8)

I will be found most cunning in my patience;
But (dost thou hear?) most bloody
                              (IV, i, 91–2)

Thy bed, lust-stain'd, shall with lust's blood be spotted
                              (V, i, 36)

When he finally kills himself, Lodovico comments 'O bloody period!' (V, ii, 352). Given that the play is, among other things, about a constantly interrupted honeymoon in which the marriage is never properly consummated—or is consummated by murder (as we might say, the *wrong* form of 'dying'), and in which a good deal of the language traffics in sexuality—the increasing stress on blood, and the spilling or releasing of it, necessarily has an added specific resonance, glancing (without stating) at both menstruation and defloration. The crucial handkerchief which Desdemona drops and loses is, I will just note, 'spotted with strawberries' (III, iii, 432). Her marriage bed turns out to be her death-bed. 'O bloody period!'

Yet Othello manages to convince himself, or allows Iago to manage this managing, that he is, throughout, administering 'justice'. In Venice, the Duke is in charge of justice and, as we see, he dispenses it fairly. In the island outpost of Cyprus, Othello is the sole authority (with Iago the main manipulator), and 'justice' is increasingly, disastrously, perverted until, when Iago suggests that Othello should strangle Desdemona in her bed, Othello responds by saying with obvious pleasure—'The justice of it pleases' (IV, i, 222). Of course, by now the manifest *in*justice of it appals, and how Othello has so quickly arrived at this point of aberration constitutes the essence of the tragedy. The sensationally good soldier turns out to be a catastrophically bad judge. As things rapidly disintegrate into disorder and confusion in Cyprus (again at night—Iago works best in the dark), Othello thrashes around, interrogating, accusing, passing judgement, sentencing, in what becomes an increasingly ghastly black parody and simulation of proper judicial processes. What is happening is that the old blood-lust for revenge—for this, too, is a 'revenge' play though, as always with

Shakespeare, with a difference—subverts and then appropriates established legal procedures until the eruption and outbreak of a kind of insane
private violence can mask itself (at least, and indeed only, to itself) as the
impersonal administration of the law. When Othello comes to kill Desdemona, he tries to turn the bedroom into a court-room—a final bit of improvised 'legality'. He talks of 'the cause, the cause'—a word which recurs
throughout the play, first heard from the mouth of Brabantio complaining
of the abduction of Desdemona—'Mine's not an idle cause' (I, ii, 94). (In a
curious way, Brabantio foreshadows Othello. And Emilia is in the right of
it when she says to Desdemona—'They are not ever jealous for the cause,/
But jealous for they're jealous' (III, iv, 159–60). Othello likes the word—
it is what justifies you in going to law—but, in truth, he *has* no 'cause'.)
Othello accuses Desdemona, warns her of 'perjury', acts as her confessor,
passes judgement, then executes the sentence (V, ii). It is a kind of ultimate
nightmare—pure blind, brutal barbarity acting as if it were the acme of
civilized justice. Othello wants to think that what he is doing has the ritual
dignity of 'a sacrifice'—in fact, he knows it is 'a murder' (V, ii, 65). (Robert
Heilman describes the systematic degradation of justice in the play as moving through three stages from the opening scenes in Venice to the bedroom
murder: 'Justice: the imitation of justice: the negation of justice. Private
passion controlled by public form: private passion endeavouring to find
public form: private passion triumphant over public form.')*

How does this come about? How is it that within two nights of his marrying Desdemona, Othello is so eager to kill her? (for it *is* only two nights,
though I will come back to the strange time-scheme of the play). I will defer consideration of why Othello is even willing (eager?) to listen to the insinuating suggestions and calumnies concerning his new wife from his
lowly standard-bearer. Once he allows even the possibility of Desdemona's
infidelity to arise in his mind as an idea, he makes what is a fatal mistake in
Shakespearian tragedy—he starts asking for the wrong sort of 'evidence'—
in this way, 'ruin's wasteful entrance' is both enabled and assured. In this
connection, it is worth concentrating on the word 'proof'. The word first
occurs early in scene i when Iago is complaining to Roderigo that Othello
did not promote him to be his 'lieutenant', although 'his eyes had seen the

---

* *Magic in the Web,* University of Kentucky Press, 1956, pp. 134–5. This remains one of
the most sensitive and suggestive explorations of the play.

proof' of his valuable service (I, i, 25). Whether or not this is Iago's prime
motive in plotting against Othello is undecidable, perhaps irrelevant. But
Iago will dangle another kind of 'proof' in front of Othello's eyes which
will drive him mad. Othello might have been warned by the sensible words
of the Duke in response to Brabantio's wild accusations against Othello—
'To vouch this is no proof' (I, iii, 107), but in the event he will be persuaded
by less even than vouching. In Act III, scene iii, in the course of which
Othello—within the space of some four hundred lines—allows himself
to be persuaded of Desdemona's promiscuity and infidelity and dedicates
himself to 'a capable and wide revenge' (456), the notion of 'proof' becomes
crucial. The word occurs a number of times and I want to bring some in-
stances together.

> No, Iago;
> I'll see before I doubt; when I doubt, prove;
> And on the proof there is no more but this:
> Away at once with love or jealousy!
>
> (189–92)

Iago has just warned him of the misery experienced by the jealous lover
'who dotes, yet doubts' (170) and he is about to convert Othello from a doter
into a doubter with terrifying speed. Soon Othello is musing 'If I do prove
her haggard. . .' (259—i.e. a trained hawk which has gone wild again). Of
course, Iago has nothing resembling 'proof'; indeed he has no 'evidence'
against Desdemona at all. Indeed he cunningly seems to warn Othello
against believing in what he calls his 'scattering and unsure observance' (III,
iii, 151). But when Emilia gives Iago the precious handkerchief which Desdemona has dropped, Iago knows he has all he needs.

> Trifles light as air
> Are to the jealous confirmations strong
> As proofs of holy writ. This may do something.
>
> (319–21)

It does everything. Soon Othello is saying:

> Villain, be sure thou prove my love a whore!
> Be sure of it; give me the ocular proof . . .

> Make me to see't; or at the least so prove it . . .
> I'll have some proof.
>
> $$(356-7, 361, 383)$$

Ocular proof—of what? What kind of proof does he think he is after? What kind of proof could it be? As Iago very reasonably says—would you 'grossly gape on?/Behold her topped?' (392–3). People make love on their own in guarded privacy—'It is impossible you should see this' (399). What Iago offers instead is 'imputation and strong circumstances/Which lead directly to the door of truth' (III, iii, 403–4). But only *to* the door—which is why we are suspicious of what we call merely 'circumstantial evidence'. But by this time, Othello can hardly wait to push through the door so misleadingly pointed out for him by Iago. And what you *can* see is, for example, a handkerchief—almost the only prop and accessory which Iago needs for his suggestive theatricals. What you *cannot* see is—fidelity. As Iago very exactly phrases it (often diabolically speaking truths he knows will not be registered):

> Her honor is an essence that's not seen;
> They have it very oft that have it not.
> But for the handkerchief—
>
> $$(IV, i, 16-18)$$

Here is the play in little. You cannot *see* essences, in any empirical way—love, trust, honour, loyalty etc., there is no '*ocular*' proof' for these. (As the Bible perfectly states: 'Now faith is the substance of things hoped for, the *evidence of things not seen*' (Hebrews II—my italics). Othello has lost, misplaced, his 'faith'.) But for the handkerchief . . . Othello has entirely lost his hold on and apprehension of and belief and trust in 'essences' and handed himself and his vision (ocular not spiritual) over to the management and direction of a master of manipulable appearances. Here is 'vision' gone wrong indeed. No wonder most of the play takes place at night.

Problems involved in proper seeing—coming to see the true, the real—are often central to tragedy in which the process of arriving at true vision is often shown to be both horrendously difficult and fiercely resisted (Othello's period of true vision at the end lasts, arguably, for about thirty lines). In this play there are problems from the start. There is, for example, great uncertainty about the Turkish fleet. How many ships do they have? Which

island are they heading for? One Senator suspects trickery and deception—
''Tis a pageant to keep us in false gaze' (I, iii, 19). A storm takes care of the
Turkish fleet, but as the action shifts to the relatively domestic setting of a
peace-time garrison, we may say Iago keeps Othello (who could have handled Turks and fleets) in 'false gaze' with his 'pageants'. Iago is always directing Othello to mark this, behold that, look there, take note, see—and
all the time he is, of course, blinding him. A vital play on words indicates
how closely the two activities might appear. At the start, Othello promises
that marriage will not interfere with his soldiering; there will never, he is
sure, come a time 'when light-winged toys / Of feathered Cupid seel with
wanton dullness / My speculative and officed instrument' (I, iii, 263–5). He
is right. He is not in any danger from Cupid. But Iago will 'seel' his 'speculative instrument' more lethally than any Eros. When he is turning Othello
into a doubter, Iago reminds him that Desdemona deceived her father: 'She
that so young could give out such a seeming / To seel her father's eyes up
close as oak' (III, iii, 209–10).

Iago is a master of that slight shift which makes, literally, a world of difference—he can almost effortlessly transform doting into doubting; he can
make 'seeling' feel like 'seeing'. Indeed, he can run seeing and seeling and
seeming all together to the confusion of all and the destruction of some.
Lodovico's last words to Iago, pointing to the corpses on the bed, are: 'This
is thy work. The object poisons sight' (V, ii, 360). That is the triumph of evil
and one of the phenomena which tragedy is most involved in exploring—
the poisoning of sight.

We must take Desdemona to be of the essence, essential—one who 'in
th'essential vesture of creation / Does tire the ingener' (II, i, 64–5). In this
connection I wish to draw together three other words which play an important role in the play—'soul', 'jewel' (and other precious stones), and 'reputation' (or 'good name'). The word 'soul' occurs some thirty times—in a
play which Iago attempts to dominate with a strongly physical, corporeal,
material discourse. Othello himself refers to 'my perfect soul' (I, ii, 30) and
'mine eternal soul' (III, iii, 358), and there must be some question as to what
extent he might have lost that soul in having, as it were, switched his trust
(faith) from the essential Desdemona (she is much connected with 'soul') to
the rankly material Iago. There are literal jewels, which Roderigo wants
given to Desdemona and which Iago steals; and the metaphoric jewel, Des-

demona herself. Her father calls her his 'jewel' (I, ii, 193) which, as far as he is concerned, Othello has stolen. Othello himself, after he has robbed himself of Desdemona, compares her to 'one entire and perfect chyrsolite' (V, ii, 142) and realizes he has thrown 'a pearl away / Richer than all his tribe' (V, ii, 343–4). She, effectively, was his jewel-soul. Now this, in one of Iago's devastatingly truthful utterances with which he confuses Othello:

> Good name in man and woman, dear my lord,
> Is the immediate jewel of their souls.
> Who steals my purse steals trash; 'tis something, nothing;
> 'Twas mine, 'tis his, and has been slave to thousands;
> But he that filches from me my good name
> Robs me of that which not enriches him
> And makes me poor indeed.
>   (III, iii, 155–61)

Now Iago is supremely a 'purse' man ('put money in thy purse') as he is also the 'filcher' of jewels, and of 'good names' (Cassio's, Desdemona's). Perhaps he even manages to steal Othello's 'soul'. But what he says is a crucial truth of the play. 'Good name', 'reputation', like honour, like the soul, is an 'essence that's not seen'. And like them, it belongs to the realm of lasting values (thus a 'jewel') as opposed to the contingent world of the market in which prices rise and fall and purses endlessly circulate. Cassio realizes this when he falls into disgrace (engineered by Iago). He laments to Iago: 'Reputation, reputation, reputation! O, I have lost my reputation! I have lost the immortal part of myself, and what remains is bestial. My reputation, Iago, my reputation' (II, iii, 261–4).

He thus equates 'reputation' with 'soul'—more usually known as 'the immortal part'. Iago, on this occasion, is concerned to scotch and deride any such ideas. 'As I am an honest man, I had thought you had received some bodily wound. There is more sense in that than in reputation. Reputation is an idle and most false imposition oft got without merit and lost without deserving' (II, iii, 265–9). This is also true, another kind of truth. This is the truth of Iago who only believes in the body as in 'sense' (physical sensation), in that part of us which Cassio regards as 'bestial'. But no matter how vulnerable, how seemingly underminable, it is shown to be, the realm of 'soul' and 'reputation', imaged by jewels, must be registered as a reality which is ultimately—but *only* ultimately and after much destruction—out of Iago's reach. This is borne out by a most suggestive detail. Iago gives up speaking and 'seels' himself in silence *before* he is dead—'Demand me nothing. What you know, you know./From this time forth I never will speak word' (V, ii, 299–300); while the smothered Desdemona seems to speak *after* her death —'Nobody—I myself. Farewell./Commend me to my kind lord. O, farewell!' (V, ii, 123–4). Ever courteous, unaccusing and forgiving, charitable and 'heavenly true' (V, ii, 135), Desdemona—and all she embodies and stands for—*outlasts* Iago.*

One way of thinking about *Othello* is to see the play as a sort of collision or intersection between a Renaissance heroic procession and a medieval Morality play. I will draw on the work of Philip Brockbank to explain this. As he says, *Othello* is 'at the confluence of several theatrical and literary traditions, moral, heroic, comic and domestic, and therefore, also, of the corresponding traditions of human values'.† In particular, alongside the Morality play there developed in Tudor times the heroic play. This genre was related to the festive procession such as often comprised a part of the Lord Mayor's midsummer shows—processions in which an African often figured prominently. 'The evidence is in the account books. They tell us that a black, or tawny, soldier-hero was a figure in festivals long before he reached the Tudor stage. The 1519 accounts include what seems to be the first reference to a popular African pageant which was to become a regular feature of the annual shows and carnivals . . . Two years later, the King of the Moors and sixty 'morians' appeared in another extravagant procession . . . we can attribute to him a distant political significance, as a festive representative of power and sexual potency in the early stages of Tudor empire.'** Out of such events developed the processional and pageant theatre of *Tamburlaine,* an important precursor to *Othello* to which the later play seems almost implicitly to refer. That, clearly, is where the figure of Othello comes from.

Iago emerges from the Mystery and Morality plays, in which figures

---

* The point is nicely made by Heilman. 'Whatever disasters it causes, wit fails in the end: it cuts itself off in a demonic silence before death, while witchcraft—love—speaks after death.' op.cit., p. 225.

† Brockbank, op.cit., p. 198.

** ibid., p. 200.

called 'Youth' or 'Everyman' are tempted into sin and depravity by allegorical companions with names like 'Hypocrisy', 'Dissimulation', 'Fraud',
'Ambidexter' (Iago swears by double-faced Janus). Such figures are all related to the Morality devil and, like him, like Iago, enjoy what Brockbank
calls his 'satanic privilege of intimacy with the audience.'* Iago, like the
devil, comes forward and, with a slightly uncomfortable assumption of
sympathy if not complicity says, in effect—watch me confuse, mislead, and
then destroy this bombastic, gullible fool. The triumphal hero of the simple
procession suddenly finds himself in a bewilderingly complex moral area
which he cannot negotiate—and so, 'the warrior protagonist of the heroic
play is exposed to the Vice of Morality, in the black comedy of a garrison
town'. Shakespeare is thus testing 'the vitality of the heroic tradition and its
associated declamatory style of poetry'.† And whatever else he achieves,
Iago, as he promises, most certainly 'unpegs' Othello's 'music', reducing his
proud martial rhetoric to obscene gibberish—'Noses, ears, and lips?', 'goats
and monkeys!' (IV, i, 43; IV, i, 263).

It is perfectly to Shakespeare's purpose that in his source (Cinthio's *Gli
Hecatommithi,* 1565, which Shakespeare may have read in a French translation of 1584), the action is set in Cyprus, suspended as it were between
northern civilized-imperial Venice and southern barbarous-exotic Africa.
(Iago calls the marriage between Othello and Desdemona 'a frail vow betwixt an erring barbarian and supersubtle Venetian' (I, iii, 352); as it transpires, the Venetians in this play are straightforward and honest; Othello
'errs' all right, but led by the 'supersubtle' Iago who is, significantly, *not* a
Venetian and thus, effectively, an outsider—as Othello, much more obviously, also is.) Cyprus was of course the birthplace of Venus–Aphrodite and
the site of Paphos, the reputedly libidinous ancient city sacred to the goddess. It should, not to put it too crudely, at least augur well for the honeymoon and the as yet unconsummated marriage. When Othello greets Desdemona with the words 'Honey, you shall be well desired in Cyprus' (II, i,
202), one senses an anticipation of the sweet satisfactions of desire. In general there is a rather lubricious air about the whole place and, one way or
another, sexual references are effectively constant. But sexual desire goes
horribly wrong and turns into jealousy, nausea, madness, and violence.

---

* ibid., p. 201.
† ibid., pp. 199, 203.

Venice and Africa mate, and then meet in Cyprus. But the mating does not work, and their representatives are destroyed.

Iago is a Morality devil, directing his theatricals to trap the unwary. But he is more complex than that. He is, as we learn from his first speech, a disaffected and resentful soldier who has been passed over for promotion. He expected, and felt he deserved, to receive the post of 'lieutenant'. But the job went to Cassio and Iago is still Othello's 'ancient'. This is important (*every* detail seems important in Shakespeare). An 'ancient' was a standard-bearer who would advance in front of the troops with the flag—a lieutenant would direct manoeuvres from behind. So when shortly after this, Iago explains to Roderigo that he must simulate loyalty to Othello, with these words:

> Though I do hate him as I do hell-pains,
> Yet, for necessity of present life,
> I must show out a flag and sign of love,
> Which is indeed but sign.
>
> (I, i, 151–4)

we should be particularly alerted. Iago is the one who shows the flags—any flags he chooses. He has made himself master of 'signs' which are indeed but signs—divorced from and unrelated to things. Anyone who has become used to relying on and following his flags (and *everyone* in the play keeps referring to him as 'honest Iago') is a potential victim of his acquired ability to 'show out the sign'—any sign.

Why does he hate Othello? In his last speech in Act II, scene ii, he seems to be turning over some reasons including the unlikely one that Othello may have cuckolded him—Coleridge felicitously called this 'the motive hunting of motiveless malignity'. Shakespeare—unerringly I feel—leaves this area vague and undecidable. As Iago himself says—'What you know, you know.' And what you don't, you don't, and perhaps never can—for instance, what is the origin of that passion and energy for destructive evil which can erupt into the world through human agents. What *is* the whence and why of 'ruin's wasteful entrance'?

What we can say is that Iago is drawn to the idea of engendering—not new life; for such a sexual play it is curiously infertile—but 'the monstrous'. His relish is for negation and inversion—he likes to deepen darkness while pretending to bring light (on both nights, literally); he likes to introduce dirt into cleanliness and make white things 'grimy'; he enjoys administering poison while pretending to heal; he delights in causing madness while offering new mental clarifications. He is the flag-bearer to chaos and old night. He likes to reduce love to lust and when, to Roderigo, he says that before he would drown himself for love 'I would change my humanity with a baboon' (I, ii, 311), he indirectly reveals himself. For his special pleasure and intent *is* to transform men into beasts. (There are many references to animals in the play, most from the fouler end of the spectrum—monkeys, goats, dogs, toads, vipers.) When Othello says, too confidently, 'exchange me for a goat' (III, iii, 180) if I ever give in to jealousy, he is describing exactly what Iago is about to do to him, or effect in him. For Iago is a master of degenerative transformation—what we might call downward metamorphosis. Thus his supreme 'creative' act is the bringing forth of the monstrous:

> I have't! It is engendered! Hell and night
> Must bring this monstrous birth to the world's light.
> (I, iii, 394–5)

'Monster' derives from Latin *monstrum,* an omen portending the will of the gods, something supernatural, from *monere,* to warn. In being somehow 'out' of nature, 'the monstrous' is a strange category, or rather, it is that which threatens, disrupts and destroys categories, crossing and confusing taxonomic lines and confounding category differentiations. It is curiously related to tragedy, since one of the matters which tragedy explores is how or why or when does nature somehow engender and 'bring to birth' something seemingly 'unnatural', *anti*-nature. In Euripides' *Hippolytus,* a giant bull emerges from the sea to destroy Hippolytus. A bull from the *sea?* Monstrous! I shall have more to say about 'the monstrous' in connection with *King Lear.* But the emergence of the monstrous is crucial to *Othello.* There is a darkly ironic warning of what is to come when Othello, disturbed by the 'foul rout' which breaks out on the first night in Cyprus, says: "Tis monstrous. Iago, who began't?' (II, iii, 216). Iago began it, of course, and he is even now beginning his monstrous midwifery. When he begins his inexplicit insinuations about Cassio and Desdemona, Othello again sails much

closer to the truth than he can know, saying it is 'as if there were some monster in thy thought / Too hideous to be shown' (III, iii, 107–8). As indeed
there is. Simulating shock that he might be not telling the truth, Iago feeds
Othello the word; 'O monstrous world!' (III, iii, 374), and soon Othello is
gulping down his obscene evocations—'O monstrous! monstrous!' (III, iii,
424). The 'monster' is of course 'jealousy'—Emilia's definition cannot be
bettered: 'It is a monster / Beget upon itself, born on itself.' Unnatural; but
ruinously real. Once roused—once the unnatural beast is out of the sea—
the ramifying consequences can be devastating, as the final 'tragic loading
of this bed' (V, ii, 361)—murder and suicide—horribly demonstrate. Iago's
hideous child has been delivered.

   But why so quickly? Here we must address the notorious 'double-time'
scheme of the play. There is a time gap between Acts I and II to allow for
the voyage to Cyprus, but thereafter the action indisputably takes place
within two days, or rather two nights. As Bullough points out, this makes
many statements almost incomprehensible—at least in terms of literal
clock-time. Emilia says Iago 'hath a hundred times woo'd me to steal' Desdemona's handkerchief (III, iii, 292). When was that? Iago suggests to the
credulous Othello that Desdemona is tired of her husband. After two days?
He speaks of Cassio's and Desdemona's 'stolen hours of lust' (III, iii, 339).
When can that have been? Bianca accuses Cassio of neglecting her for a
week.* The crowning absurdity is Othello's pathetic and maddened cry
'Iago knows / That she with Cassio hath the act of shame / A thousand times
committed' (V, ii, 207–9). Say, once a day for three years. But of course we
are well past sanity and calendars by this time. In the source story, the action does indeed occur over some months. Shakespeare, who by now was—
incontestably as I see it—in total, indeed awesome control over his medium,
must have known what he was doing in thus impossibly conflating discrepant time schemes, so what was it? Arguments about ineptitude or careless-
ness (he never got round to intended revisions) hold no water. Shakespeare
being Shakespeare can make us forget the clocks and accept both Long and
Short time in the uninterruptedly accelerating tension and suspense of the
drama. Bullough has an entirely acceptable explanation. 'Thus Shakespeare
transcends external probabilities in a poetic vision of Iago's evil mind working with lightning rapidity to destroy the innocent, and of an agonized vic-

---

* op. cit., p. 229.

tim whose sense of past and present is increasingly confused under the stress of his jealousy.'* But in *two days?*

I think there is something else going on here. For a start, there is sufficient evidence to suggest that the marriage is not consummated. Othello himself says to Desdemona 'The profit's yet to come 'twixt me and you' (II, iii, 10). On the second night, Iago says 'He hath not yet made wanton the night with her' (II, ii, 16). When Othello goes to kill Desdemona the next night he says 'when I have pluck'd the rose, I cannot give it vital growth again' (V, ii, 13–14), which would seem to indicate that he has not yet 'pluck'd the rose' which would have been unambiguous enough for the Elizabethans. The interruptions of his two nights in bed with Desdemona are caused by street disturbances organized by Iago.† There is evidence that the interruptions are not entirely unwelcome. When the Duke of Venice tells Othello he must leave to fight the Turks, he uses an odd and rather unpleasant phrase—'you must therefore be content to slubber the gloss of your new fortunes with this more stubborn and boisterous expedition' (I, ii, 223–5). To 'slubber' is to besmear, and 'slubbering the gloss' will be Iago's occupation. But Othello is happy to go, saying that he finds the 'steel couch of war' the softest 'bed of down'. 'I do agnize [i.e. know in myself] / A natural and prompt alacrity / I find in hardness' (I, iii, 228–30). When a Senator

---

* ibid., p. 231.

† In his very interesting book, *Shakespeare's Festive World,* Cambridge University Press, 1991, François Laroque suggests that these raucous disturbances are linked to the old festive custom known as 'charivari' (or 'Skimmington riding') in which a couple were rudely woken in the night by some disturbance if the community disapproved of the marriage (it can be found in Thomas Hardy, *The Mayor of Casterbridge*). This makes Iago a sort of Lord of Misrule, 'Iago is the instigator of most of the popular traditions and scenarios evoked or indirectly suggested in the course of the play. He initiates a form of rough music, or charivari, in the dark streets of Venice to rouse Brabantio in the middle of the night; he engages in word-play and in a satirical portrait game with Desdemona in the tradition of Venetian *conversazione,* he sings merry drinking songs during the night of revels in Cyprus and possesses a whole repertoire of images of carnival customs. Iago . . . conjures up popular games and folk traditions only to pervert them to his own ends' (p. 287). Laroque also reminds us, as does Bullough, that a well-known Spanish saint of the time was Sant Iago Matarmos—San James, the killer of Moors (taken as winning the battle of Clavijo against the Moors in the eleventh century). I don't think we need to look further for the source of the name for Shakespeare's Moor-killer.

adds 'You must away tonight' Othello immediately and, one feels enthusiastically, replies—'With all my heart' (I, iii, 273). *All* his heart? No part of it
left for his new bride? Othello hardly seems an enthusiast for marriage.
One of Iago's first questions to him is 'Are you fast married?' (I, ii, 10) and
Othello, not quite giving a straight answer, goes on to say:

> For know, Iago,
> But that I love the gentle Desdemona,
> I would not my unhoused free condition
> Put into circumscription and confine
> For the sea's worth.
>
>   (I, ii, 23–7)

Othello, the great soldier, is used to great distances, vast space; foreign parts
and far-flung fighting-fields. He is certainly not prepared for circumscrip-
tion, confinement, and being 'housed'. But he is married—so it is said—
and thus 'housed'. This is a very domestic drama. And one thing it reveals
is that, while Othello the great warrior can easily cope with storms at sea,
he is, as we say, all at sea in a house. On the second day in Cyprus, after a
few of Iago's insinuations he is saying 'Why did I marry?' (III, iii, 242) and:

> O curse of marriage,
> That we can call these delicate creatures ours,
> And not their appetites! I had rather be a toad
> And live upon the vapor of a dungeon
> Than keep a corner in the thing I love
> For others' uses.
>
>   (III, iii, 267–71)

He speaks of Desdemona in terms of stone, 'monumental alabaster', snow—
never as warm living flesh and blood, corporeal and penetrable. In the
bedroom-murder scene, he kisses her as she is asleep and says, ominously
enough—'Be thus when thou art dead, and I will kill thee, / And love thee
after' (V, ii, 18–19). Does this mean that he can *only* love her when she is
asleep, stone, alabaster—dead?

When he enters the bedroom—in a rather trance-like, somnambulistic
state—he is holding a torch and, looking at Desdemona, says:

> Put out the light, and then put out the light.
> If I quench thee, thou flaming minister,
> I can thy former light restore,
> Should I repent me . . .
>
> (V, ii, 7–10)

he is of course addressing the torch, and goes on to say that if he puts out Desdemona's 'light' there will be nothing 'that can thy light relume'. Iago is Othello's 'flaming minister', constantly pretending to bring him 'illumination' as he leads him into ever-deeper darkness. *That* is the light he should have put out. But as it turns out, Othello, the peerless warrior, is curiously unable to kill his lowly 'ancient', even when he tries ('I bleed, sir, but not killed'—V, ii, 284). There is a touch of Satanic immortality about Iago. Can he *ever* be killed? Or is he, in his own evil way, another 'ancient of days'? Desdemona is true light and in smothering her, Othello simply, tragically, puts out the wrong light. Or does he?

'Yet I'll not shed her blood' (V, ii, 3)—these are Othello's words as he approaches his marriage bed for the third time. He is referring specifically to how he will kill Desdemona, but the words have, also, different implications. His wife is still a virgin and, not to put too fine a point on it, he *should* shed her blood (recall the practice of showing the blooded sheets after the first night of marriage—this is part of the suggestiveness of the red-spotted handkerchief which has 'magic in the web of it' and can subdue a husband 'entirely to her love'—II, iv, 60). But, if anything, Othello seems to dread the idea of the sexual act (he gives the impression that he regards copulation as something which loathsome toads do). We have seen his confident dismissal of the distractions of Cupid and heard of his 'prompt alacrity' for 'hardness'; heard, too, his rapid regret at having married. Part of him responds to the 'jewel' which is Desdemona, but not to the female, sexual body. His precipitate eagerness to trust and believe Iago's lubriciously vile, and quite incredible, scenarios—with a headlong speed which Shakespeare builds into the play at the risk of quotidian inconsistencies—reveal a positive *desire* to believe the false 'pageant' which holds him in 'false gaze'. Iago is indeed his reliable ensign, and (I want to suggest) in fact 'shows out' just the 'flags' which, by a profound and troubling paradox, a deep part of Othello wants to follow—certainly his late claim he was a man 'not easily jealous' who loved not wisely, but too well (V, ii, 341–2), is hardly justified by what we see in the play. What he 'loved' in Desdemona, remember, was the way she listened to his adventures and her 'pity' (I, iii, 167); it is not clear that he is, in fact, drawn to her sexually. I think there is quite a lot to Stanley Cavell's seemingly idiosyncratic contention that Othello, the immaculate soldier ('my perfect soul'), dreads sexual 'contamination'. 'I am claiming that we must understand Othello . . . to want to believe Iago, to be trying, against his knowledge, to believe him. Othello's eager insistence on Iago's honesty, his eager slaking of his thirst for knowledge with that poison, is not a sign of his stupidity in the presence of poison but of his devouring need for it.'*

Let me try to make the point in another way by asking the seemingly foolish question—to whom *is* Othello 'fast married'? As we have seen, he does not actually answer Iago's question, and there is this very suggestive exchange in the second scene of the play:

> *Iago.* He's married.
> *Cassio.* To whom?
> (*Enter Othello.*)
> *Iago.* Marry, to—Come captain, will you go?

Shakespeare does nothing by accident, so why should he not have given Iago one or two words more before Othello's entrance—just a second to say 'Desdemona' or 'Brabantio's daughter'? I think it is because he wants to introduce just that element of doubt about Othello's marriage. He is married 'to—'. We neither see nor hear anything of Othello's actual marriage—the legitimating ritual—to Desdemona. What we *do* see in the decisive Act III, scene iii, in the course of which Othello effectively hands himself over to Iago—follows all his flags—is the two of them kneeling down together making what Othello calls 'a sacred vow'. In the course of the scene they exchange vows. Othello says: 'I am bound to thee forever' (212), and Iago says: 'I am your own forever' (476). I allow that a priest is absent and they are not in church, but there is much improvized law in this play, and this— I submit—is the 'marriage' we *do* see. Ocular proof.

I am not suggesting any sort of homosexual relationship. The tragedy of this play turns on the tragic incompatibility of the heroic and the domestic,

---

* *Disowning Knowledge,* Cambridge University Press, 1987, p. 133.

the martial and the erotic (Othello prefers 'hardness' to 'honey'); Othello's
'occupation' is indeed 'gone', and in his new 'housed' situation he is so lost,
so out of control, that he needs what he too often insists is his 'honest' Iago
to show him the way, or—perhaps more desperately—the way out. That
there is a curious closeness between Iago and Othello has, of course, been
commented on. One of the most interesting essays on this relationship is by,
sadly the late, Joel Fineman.* He sees Iago as Othello's motivator, as it were
his first cause. He points to the two strange lines spoken by Iago in the first
scene: 'Were I the Moor, I would not be Iago' (55) and 'I am not what I am'
(62). If he is not what he is—*not* Iago—does it follow that somehow he *is*
the Moor? Fineman's suggestion is that Iago claims that he is non-identical
with himself 'and it is this principle—"I am not what I am"—. . . that, we
can say, Iago, as complementary opposite of a less complicated Othello, introduces to or into Othello in the course of the play . . . we can think of Iago,
because he is the motivator of Othello, as the inside of Othello, as a principle of disjunct being—"I am not what I am"—introduced into the smooth
and simple existence of an Othello who, at least at the beginning, is whatever else he is, surely what he is.'† Certainly, Othello goes from being 'all in
all sufficient' (IV, i, 265)—'my perfect soul'—to what Fineman calls 'an
empty shell of a hero'. After the murder and the realization of what he
has done, Othello announces to the Venetian officials 'That's he that was
Othello; Here I am' (V, ii, 280). Not exactly, 'I am not what I am' but certainly 'I am not what I *was*'—Iago has emptied him out; the hero is now
hollow.

It is in this connection that Fineman draws attention to the unusual prev-
alence of the sound of 'O' in the play. It is a common enough exclamation, but it pervades this play as it does no other. It's in pretty well all the
names. Not so surprising given they are Italians, you may say—but the
name 'Othello' is Shakespeare's invention, and while there is a Thorello in
Ben Jonson's *Every Man in his Humour,* Shakespeare clearly wants an 'O' at
the beginning and end of his name. But more than that, characters use it as
an exclamation at least one hundred times, by my counting. It would be
otiose to list all the occurrences, but for an example—in the first scene of

---

* 'The Sound of "O" in *Othello:* the Real of the Tragedy of Desire', in *The Subjectivity
Effect in Western Literary Tradition,* MIT Press, 1991, pp. 143–64.
† ibid., p. 148.

Act V it occurs twenty-two times. More notably, as Othello begins to be troubled by Emilia's vehement strictures ('O gull! O dolt! As ignorant as dirt!'—V, ii, 160–61), he falls on the bed crying—'O! O! O!' (V, ii, 194), and when he is finally penetrated by the no longer deniable truth, one of his last cries is 'O Desdemon! Dead Desdemon; dead. O! O!' (V, ii, 278). (These triple O's have an extra terrible irony when Othello makes the wild cry that Desdemona and Cassio have 'the act of shame a thousand times committed' (V, ii, 209)—for a thousand is precisely 1 and three O's. O! O! O!) An O is a circle and a nought. As a circle it can symbolize perfection ('my perfect soul'); as a nought it signifies—nothing ('That's he that was Othello'). The tragedy is the spectacle of Othello being transformed from one to the other. At one point, as Iago is getting Othello more and more worked up, and be-mused, Iago says to him:

> Marry patience;
> Or I shall say you're all in all in spleen,
> And nothing of a man.
>
> (IV, i, 91)

It is a veiled prediction—Iago will indeed serve to render Othello 'nothing of a man', though he has just enough of the heroic soldier left in him to pass judgement on the terrible zero he has become. O! O! O!

KING LEAR (1605–6)

'Now thou art an O without a figure'—this is the Fool, desperately trying to get Lear to realize the folly of what he has done: 'thou hast parted thy wit o' both sides and left nothing i' the middle . . . I am better than thou art now: I am a Fool, thou art nothing' (I, iv, 191–200). Under Iago's ministrations Othello became an 'O' in the course of the play. Lear makes himself 'nothing' at the start with no visible prompting or provocation. The play veritably starts with the eruption of, or into, nothingness and the word re-echoes throughout the opening scenes.

> *Cordelia.* Nothing, my lord.
> *Lear.* Nothing?

Cordelia. Nothing
Lear. Nothing will come of nothing.
(I, i, 90–93)

Lear repeats the word a number of times. Then Gloucester, very much a parallel figure for Lear, finds Edmund reading something. He asks him what it was.

Edmund. Nothing, my lord.
Gloucester. No? What needed then that terrible dispatch of it into your pocket? The quality of nothing hath not such need to hide itself. Let's see. Come, if it be nothing, I shall not need spectacles.
(I, ii, 32–5)

The play will be preoccupied with problems of seeing and right vision, and given what is to happen to his eyes, his words carry a terrible proleptic irony. Shortly after, Lear is repeating himself to the Fool who asks him 'Can you make no use of nothing, Nuncle?' 'Why, no, boy. Nothing can be made out of nothing' (I, iv, 135–6). When Edgar, a little later, decides to disguise himself as Poor Tom he says 'Edgar I nothing am' (II, iii, 21). The word becomes increasingly ominous and it is as if we are watching the world of the play being infiltrated with 'nothingness'—indeed, actively serving to install it, a world literally an-*nihil*-ating itself. It is a spectacle almost to freeze you—a world turning, returning, itself to 'nothing'.

There was a well-known Elizabethan Morality play called *The Three Ladies of London* (1584). The three ladies in question are—Conscience, Love, and Lucre, and they are variously beset and besought, importuned and rejected by characters such as—Dissimulation, Fraud, Simony, Simplicity, Usury, Hospitality, Sincerity, and so on. Lucre enjoys a good deal of success and boasts of turning Conscience out of house and home. In *King Lear*, too, we find many unjust banishings and harsh shuttings out. Sincerity has fallen on bad times for, as she complains, it is the flatterers who only love from the teeth forward who enjoy worldly success—and there could hardly be a better way to describe what Goneril and Regan are doing in their opening speeches to their father. Exactly like Cordelia, Sincerity prefers to 'see and say nothing' rather than attempt to match the dissimulators. Lucre's only gift to Sincerity is a Parsonage called St Nihil—and Nihil is nothing.

It is Lear's gift to Cordelia. It becomes pretty well the gift to Lear's family, and of his realm to itself.

I am not arguing for a specific source for the play.* Rather, I want to draw attention to the importance of the exchanges in the opening scene. Cordelia who is indeed Sincere and has a Conscience can only 'see and say nothing' in the presence of so much Dissimulation and Fraud. But how has this situation come about? Like Othello, Lear asks for the wrong sort of evidence; asks disastrously the wrong questions. He asks for 'auricular assurance' of his daughters' love as Othello had asked for 'ocular proof' of his wife's unfaithfulness. But you can no more 'hear' love than you can 'see' honour. Worse, he asks in terms of quantity. 'Which of you shall we say doth love us most?' (I, i, 54). He hands himself over to rhetoric and easily manufactured hyperboles. In the matter of how many knights he can bring with him to his daughters' houses, when Goneril says to him 'disquantity your train' (I, iv, 255) she is in fact speaking his language. He is still trying to quantify love when Regan wants to reduce his train by another half: he turns to Goneril—'Thy fifty yet doth double five-and twenty,/And thou art twice her love' (II, iv, 258–9). The sisters rapidly reduce his permitted train to zero. 'What need one?' says Regan, which provokes the searing response:

> O reason not the need! Our basest beggars
> Are in the poorest things superfluous.
> Allow not nature more than nature's needs,
> Man's life is cheap as beast's. Thou art a lady:
> If only to go warm were gorgeous,

---

* As I indicated, I do not intend to go into sources, but—briefly. There was an old folk tale in which a daughter tells her father that she loves him as much as salt. This makes him very angry until she explains that she means he is essential to her life. The story enters literature in the twelfth-century *History* of Geoffrey of Monmouth. In the sixteenth century it becomes part of British history and is told by John Higgins in the 1574 edition of *A Mirror for Magistrates,* by Warner in *Albion's England* (1586), by Holinshed, and by Spenser in Book II of *The Faerie Queene* (1590). Shakespeare probably knew all these. The most important thing to know, perhaps, is that in Holinshed Cordelia successfully restores her father to the throne and then succeeds him for five years—though she then commits suicide when imprisoned by her enemies. Only Shakespeare has Cordelia murdered.

> Why, nature needs not what thou gorgeous wear'st,
>
> Which scarcely keeps thee warm
>
> (II, iv, 264–9)

Many of the questions and preoccupations of the play are compacted in those lines, but let us return to the opening scene.

Lear's initial fault is exposed in Gloucester's opening words when he refers to 'the division of the kingdom' (I, i, 4). Almost immediately we see this made literal when Lear takes a map and divides the realm into three. It is a deed of horrifying irresponsibility and introduces 'division' into every unit of the society—family, court, realm. His explanation of what he is doing would have been even more shocking to the Elizabethans:

> Meantime we shall express our darker purpose.
>
> Give me the map there. Know that we have divided
>
> In three our kingdom; and 'tis our fast intent
>
> To shake all cares and business from our age,
>
> Conferring them on younger strengths, while we
>
> Unburthened crawl toward death . . .
>
> (Since now we will divest us both of rule,
>
> Interest of territory, cares of state)
>
> (I, i, 38–53)

By 'darker' he here means simply 'hidden' but it is an ominous word coming from a king, and, indeed, from this initial act there will spread a darkness over the realm until by the end 'all's cheerless, dark and deadly' (V, iii, 293). That a king, the great hub of the social wheel, the maintainer of unity and order, should suddenly express the wish to 'shake' off cares and 'crawl', like a child or a wounded animal, toward death, is almost terrifying if only because he should represent—indeed embody—stability, concord (not 'division'), the inexorable responsibilities involved in positions of power, and duties firmly discharged and unquestioningly upheld. He wants to keep the 'name' of king, but leave the 'execution' of his duties to others—a fatal attempt to divide word from thing. It is as though the linch-pin should withdraw itself from the wheel, the corner-stone rebel from its place in the structure of the church. No wonder the scene ends with a sense of dissolution and scattering. 'Kent *banished* thus? and France in choler *parted*? / And

the king *gone* tonight?' (I, ii, 24–5—emphasis added). The 'division' has
started, initiating an atmosphere marked by rapid, furtive, untimely, and
uncertain movement. The plotters turn up at odd times which surprise
even themselves—'out of season threading dark-eyed night'. Lear 'calls to
horse, but will I know not whither'. The French army creeps into England
'on secret feet'. Gloucester and Kent grope around the heath looking for
Lear. Everywhere there is a sense of midnight flight and fumbling which is
either conspiratorial or desperate. All seems uncertain and unnerved. 'The
images of revolt and flying off!' (II, iv, 88). Movement is no longer co-
ordinated, harmonious, ceremonially managed; rather it is madly centrifu-
gal—as though all things were being whirled off their right paths.

Shakespeare was clearly fascinated by what might happen if the great
central maintaining principle of social order was withdrawn, or withdrew
itself—he had tried the great experiment shortly before in *Measure for Measure*. It allows him to explore, dramatically, the question—what is human
nature when it is, as it were, unchecked in all directions: when all the bonds
have 'cracked' and the rats have bitten 'the holy cords atwain / Which are
too intrince t'unloose' (II, ii, 76)? Lear's sudden abdication leaves a vacuum
where there should be a majestic and irresistible principle of order, custom,
and degree. And in that vacuum, the deep realities of human nature are afforded a dark arena in which to play themselves out. Majesty has fallen to
folly, power has bowed to flattery, as Kent says—and indeed by the end of
the play Lear will have bowed, fallen, knelt, and crawled in dead earnest.
(It is a very sadistic play. People stumble, kneel, fall; are tripped, elbowed,
shoved, kicked, and tortured. I will just note here that, in this play, it is the
victims, the sufferers, the thrust-out and kicked-along, the blinded and
maddened who, at intolerable cost, achieve true vision. By contrast, the perception of the evil characters seem to shrink progressively until by the end
we have the image of Goneril and Regan 'squinting' at each other.) Wishing only to shake off his cares, shrug off his burdens, 'divest' himself of
rule, Lear discovers that there is no stopping the divesting, and he will be
stripped of his knights, his house, his clothes, his very reason—and finally
of Cordelia. His terrible fate lies coiled and nascent in his own opening
words.

'The King falls from the bias of nature,' says Gloucester (I, ii, 121). The
last time Shakespeare used that metaphor was in *Twelfth Night* when Se-

bastian tells Olivia: 'So comes it, lady, you have mistook;/But nature to her bias drew in that' (V, i, 259–60). The metaphor is from bowling and Sebastian is saying that, although Olivia was mistaken when she married him—because of course she thought she was marrying Cesario—she has in fact swerved back to nature's proper course in marrying him, because Cesario is, of course, a woman—Viola. For her to have married a woman would have been to 'fall from the bias of nature'. To be sure, Lear has not contracted a homosexual marriage, but, more generally, the image suggests that, in nature, there is a right way for things to go, and a wrong way, and Lear has taken the wrong way. How nature may 'err from itself' (to take an image from *Othello,* III, iii, 227) is a matter to which I will return. But Lear has fallen from the 'bias of nature' by his division of the realm, his abdication, and—worst of all—his disastrous misjudgement of Cordelia. To Burgundy he says 'her price is fallen' (more quantification—Lear is assessing her in Iagoish money terms whereas, like Desdemona, she is a jewel), and dismisses her as 'little seeming substance' (I, i, 199–200). He describes her as *un*natural ('a wretch whom nature is ashamed/Almost t'acknowledge hers'—I, i, 214), strips her of her dowry, and strangers her with an oath. He is not only completely wrong, but has totally inverted true values—Cordelia is all substance and no seeming, and is (along with Kent and Edgar and, for the most part, Albany) the most steadfastly 'natural' character in the play (there are problems in such an assertion to which I will return). No wonder Kent says 'See better, Lear' (I, i, 160). Lear is going to have to travel a hard and painful road to learn to penetrate the seeming and mere show of things and discern true reality—'the thing itself'. He will suffer greatly, indeed unendurably, before he draws back to 'the bias of nature'.

The King of France finds Lear's behaviour incredible, and finds it most strange that;

> The best, the dearest, should in this trice of time
> Commit a thing so monstrous to dismantle
> So many folds of favor . . .
>   (I, i, 219–20)

When he learns of what her 'fault' consisted, he is happy to take her as she stands—metaphorically naked, like traditional pictures of truth. I will return to 'monstrous', but want here to concentrate on that phrase—'dismantle so many folds of favor'. When Cordelia departs her last words are (to her sisters):

> The jewels of our father, with washed eyes
> Cordelia leaves you. I know you what you are . . .

More proleptic—by which I mean anticipatory—ironies. *Cordelia* is the 'jewel' of her father, and her 'washed eyes' and tears will be of extreme importance later in the play. Finally she says:

> Time shall unfold what plighted cunning hides,
> Who covers faults, at last shame them derides.
>   (I, i, 271–2, 282–3)

To this I must add the words of Isabella when she thinks she is not going to receive any justice at the hands of the Duke of Vienna (in *Measure for Measure*):

> Then, O you blessed ministers above,
> Keep me in patience, and with ripened time
> Unfold the evil which is here wrapp'd up
> In countenance.
>   (V, i, 115–18)

'Unfold' became a very important word for Shakespeare. It is one of the first verbs in *Hamlet:*

> *Barnado.* Who's there?
> *Francisco.* Nay, answer me. Stand and unfold yourself.

Thus the play opens, and it is a long 'unfolding' that is to come. In *Othello* it occurs at least four times. Desdemona says 'To my unfolding lend your prosperous ear' (I, iii, 245), and 'This honest creature doubtless/Sees and knows more, much more, than he unfolds' (III, iii, 242–3). Emilia, talking about her husband Iago, though she doesn't yet know it, says 'O heaven, that such companions thou'dst unfold,/And put in every honest hand a

whip/To lash the rascals naked through the world' (IV, i, 141–3). Iago himself, expert folder, has a worry—'the Moor may unfold me to him' (V, i, 21).
Cunning is 'plighted' (pleated, enfolded); evil is 'wrapped up', and, ultimately, only 'ripe time' (also used in this play) can do the unfolding (the
'blessed ministers' are hardly to be relied on). This suggests that once evil
has been released—made its 'wasteful entrance'—no human agent can arrest it, it must simply exhaust itself. In time. It is thus in this play where
even Edmund cannot stop the murder of Cordelia he himself ordered. He
is not—in time. Our acts get away from us. 'Unfolding' implies exposure,
revealing, revelation, and, as we say, the story 'unfolds' in front of our eyes
in the theatre. By the end of the play we too see them—all of them—'what
they are'.

But of course foldings and pleatings and wrappings directly evoke clothing and not for nothing are Goneril and Regan 'gourgeously' arrayed.
There is much changing of clothes in the play. Edgar abandons his court
clothes for a beggar's rags, then finally appears as a knight in armour. Cordelia dislikes Kent's necessary disguises. Lear himself sheds his crown, then
his clothes, marks his uttermost descent into sheer nature by dressing in
weeds, and is finally 'arrayed' in 'fresh garments' at Cordelia's command.
There is a feeling that while clothes change, people do not—'in nothing
am I changed/But in my garments' says Edgar to his father (IV, vi,
8–9)—though people can certainly regress and degenerate. Clothes can indeed cover evil and cunning, but clothes are also the very mark of the human, and the 'folds of favor' can be the signs of an achieved and function-
ing civilization. This play 'dismantles' these folds as well, and in addition to
exposing evil it lays bare the human body. Denudation is a deep theme of
the play. Let us call it the spectacle and exploration of the 'disaccommodation' of man. Literally—the Fool warns Lear of the folly of having given
away his crown, thus risking exposure. He calls him a 'shelled peascod' and
he is contrasted with the oyster and snail who at least have the wisdom to
carry their shells with them. In fury at the inhospitality of his daughters,
Lear says 'I abjure all roofs, and choose/To wage against the enmity o' th'
air' (II, iv, 207), and Act II ends with the sinisterly repeated order—'Shut
up your doors.' Directionless, Lear rushes wildly off into the heath where
nature itself is at its most naked—'For many miles about/There's scarce a
bush' (II, iv, 300–301). Stripped of crown, palace and followers—his 'folds
of favor'—Lear moves towards complete denudation. But the exposure

brings the beginning of insight. When he tells the Fool to precede him into the hovel, he calls him 'You houseless poverty' and follows this by considering—perhaps for the first time—'Poor naked wretches whereso'er you are', wondering

> How shall your houseless heads and unfed sides,
> Your looped and windowed raggedness, defend you
> From seasons such as these? O, *I have ta'en*
> *Too little care of this!*
>   (III, iv, 30–33—emphasis added)

Lear is becoming aware of basic, deprived conditions not thought about or cared for in the palace. But it is the sight of Edgar with his 'uncovered body' which provokes Lear to the final stripping.

> Is man no more than this? . . . Thou art the thing itself; *unaccommodated*
> *man* is no more but such a poor, bare, forked animal as thou art. Off, off
> you lendings! Come, unbutton here. [Tearing off his clothes]
>   (III, iv, 105–11—emphasis added)

The 'thing itself' was precisely what he could not see in the first scene, since he had put himself in the thrall of 'seeming'. Now we get the feeling that the terrible 'disaccommodation' which Lear has undergone has brought him—shatteringly—to true vision, even at the expense of what Edgar calls 'the safer sense' (i.e. sounder, saner—IV, vi, 81). Which is perhaps—in Lear's case—just what it costs. But in his 'madness', he breaks through to those piercing insights into and through the whole fabric of society—'a dog's obeyed in office' (IV, vi, 160):

> Through tattered clothes small vices do appear;
> Robes and furred gowns hide all . . .
>   (IV, vi, 166–7)

Lear has been brought to see through *all* the pleats and wraps and folds. Well might Edgar say wonderingly—'Reason in madness!' (IV, vi, 177).

France thinks Cordelia must have committed something 'monstrous' to 'dismantle so many folds of favor'. We shortly get an echo of this when

Gloucester, too credulously accepting Edmund's account of Edgar's treachery, says 'He cannot be such a monster' (I, ii, 101). The word occurs quite frequently, but most importantly in Albany's rebukes to Goneril.

> Thou changed and self-covered thing, for shame
> Be-monster not thy feature.
> (IV, ii, 62–3)

He calls her 'barbarous, degenerate' and says:

> If that the heavens do not their visible spirits
> Send quickly down to tame these vile offenses,
> It will come,
> Humanity must perforce prey on itself,
> Like monsters of the deep.
> (IV, ii, 46–50)

Heaven sends down no spirits, visible or invisible, in this play, and humanity—visibly—preys upon itself. Let me add this, from *Troilus and Cressida:*

> And appetite, a universal wolf,
> So doubly seconded with will and power,
> Must make perforce a universal prey,
> And last eat up himself.
> (I, iii, 121–4)

Just noting the recurrence of the word 'perforce', let us stay for a moment with the repeated word 'prey', usually used to refer to animals that hunt and kill other animals. The extraordinary proliferation of animal imagery and references to animals has often been noted. These references include— dog, cur, rats, monkeys, ant, eels, vulture, wolf, frog, toad, tadpole, newt, mice, foxes, cats, greyhound, worms, adders—this list is by no means exhaustive. The general feeling is that the human world is being rapidly taken over by animals—palaces seem to be repossessed by dogs and foxes and snakes and other low, mean, snapping and sliding animals. There is no sense of magnificent animal energy, rather of things that prowl and creep and slither—sharp-toothed yet devoid of valour and glamour. One of the horrors of the play is the sense of the fading away of the human while such animals scurry and leap and slip into the play from every side. But it is the humans who are reverting—degenerating—to animals. Goneril and Regan end up as 'adders' squinting at each other. Edmund turns out to be a 'foul-spotted toad'. The relapse, or regression, is, we feel, to some prior stage of evolution when things had but recently crawled out of the mud. These animals are not fine enough to be man's competitors; they are rather his mean ancestors. Yet how quickly they can repossess his world—how easily he can re-become them. So near is the ditch; so easy is the fall back into the slime. It is the copious listing of such encroaching and invading animals, or animalized humans, that gives such agonizing force to Lear's final complaint against the universe:

> Why should a dog, a horse, a rat, have life,
> And thou no breath at all. Thou'lt come no more,
> Never, never, never, never, never.
>   (V, iii, 308–10)

That last line must be the most appalling in literature. This is a world in which rats retain all their mean, scurrying activity while Cordelia is hanged in lonely squalor by a paid murderer. And will come no more. This is unbearable. Who would want to see as well, or as much, as this?

It is, indeed, monstrous, and there are a number of people in the play who effectively regress to the condition of preying animals or, worse, 'be-monster' themselves. As I have indicated, the 'monstrous' is the non-natural, and we are again confronted in this play, as never before so horrifyingly, with the profound and insoluble problem of how nature can produce the unnatural—anti-nature. Kent points to the problem:

> It is the stars,
> The stars above us, govern our conditions;
> Else one self mate and make could not beget
> Such different issues.
>   (IV, iii, 33–6)

Star-governed or not, how can Cordelia *and* Goneril and Regan issue from the same womb? (The play opens with the description of a pregnant belly

—'she grew round-wombed'—and the play will precipitate a deep exploration of just what the 'thick rotundity' of nature can bring forth.)
Why should one daughter draw to the bias of nature and the others fall
from it? And what *is* the bias of nature? This is what Albany says to
Goneril:

> I fear your disposition:
> That nature which contemns its origin
> Cannot be bordered certain in itself;
> She that herself will sliver and disbranch
> From her material sap, perforce must wither
> And come to deadly use.
>   (IV, ii, 31–6)

Again—*perforce:* by force, of necessity. It will happen whether we will it or
not, with or without visible or invisible spirits, irrespective of the stars. This
is the belief, or perhaps we should say—the hope. And note Albany's image. To 'sliver and disbranch' means to cut off from the main trunk, and
introduces the idea that Goneril has perversely, unnaturally, stripped herself away from the true source of life. In her treatment of her father, she
certainly 'contemns' her origin, and she *does* 'wither and came to deadly
use'. She, in her turn, has despised Albany's 'milky gentleness', and here
counters by calling him 'milk-livered man!' (IV, ii, 50). (In *Macbeth* we will
hear of the 'milk of human kindness'—there is a 'great abatement of kindness' in *King Lear*—and the 'sweet milk of concord'.) Milk and sap evoke
the nourishing, nurturing, generative and gentle aspects of nature. *Natural*
nature. Evil is often rendered or figured as a state of desiccation in Shakespeare; conversely, there is a beneficent, life-promoting—milk and sap—
force in nature which it is possible, indeed more natural, to remain attached
to and keep in touch with. It is often associated with a benign moistness,
and this is the importance of Cordelia's tears. They provoke an anonymous
Gentleman to a description of astonishing beauty:

> You have seen
> Sunshine and rain at once: her smiles and tears
> Were like a better way: those happy smilets
> That played on her ripe lip seemed not to know

> What guests were in her eyes, which parted thence
> As pearls from diamonds dropped.
>   (IV, iii, 18–24)

Rain, tears (and note that they are 'guests' in her eyes: when Cornwall and Regan put out Gloucester's eyes in his own house, among other things, they are hideously disfiguring and transgressing the sacred rules of hospitality and the guest–host relation, as Gloucester impotently complains); pearls, diamonds—here surely, irresistibly, are the true and enduring values. These are aligned with—spring from—the gentle and restorative virtues of nature—'our foster-mother of nature is repose', says the Doctor, indicating the nursing side of nature (IV, iv, 12)—which Cordelia invokes and summons as she seeks to cure and heal her mad father:

> All blest secrets
> All you unpublished virtues of the earth,
> Spring with my tears! be aidant and remediate
> In the good man's distress!
>   (IV, iv, 15–18)

These tears are, indeed, 'holy water from her heavenly eyes' (IV, iii, 81). The 'unpublished virtues of the earth' may mean, specifically here, secret remedial herbs, but the words have an infinitely larger resonance. After all the predatory cruelty and viciousness we have witnessed, Cordelia's tears demonstrate and remind us that there *is* 'a better way'. The earth does have 'virtues' even if it does produce monsters. Cordelia is not an angel or a divinely appointed agent of redemption. She is—we must feel this—the truly, uncorrupted human: dutiful, kind, honest, 'heavenly true', respectful of her origin and all the bonds and obligations that branch from it—nature *most* natural. But she is murdered and Lear is on a 'wheel of fire' of mental anguish and dies of unsustainable grief. What of 'nature' now? It is not visibly 'aidant and remediate'—not at all. And it is *Shakespeare* who murders Cordelia, which is more than legend and chronicle ever did.*

When Albany hears Lear cursing Goneril with terrible rage, he asks—

---

* Brockbank thinks Shakespeare does this to transform the play into a sacrifice: see '"Upon such sacrifices" . . . ' op. cit., pp. 220–43. The case is powerfully argued but, finally, I cannot see it that way.

'Now, gods that we adore, whereof comes this?'; to which Goneril replies
—'Never afflict yourself to know the cause' (I, iv, 297–8). Whereof comes a
father's maddened rage; whereof comes a daughter's cruelty and ingratitude; whereof comes whatever it is that drives a man to pull out another
man's eyes—whence 'ruin's wasteful entrance'? If we asked Iago such questions, we know what he would say, or rather what he wouldn't. Goneril's
last words offer an eerie echo of Iago's, though unlike him she exits to commit suicide. Confronting her with one of her treacherous letters, Albany
says 'read thine own evil . . . I perceive you know it'.

> *Goneril.* Say, if I do, the laws are mine not thine:
>   Who can arraign me for't?
> *Albany.*   Most monstrous! O!
>   Knowst thou this paper?
> *Goneril.*   Ask me not what I know. (*Exit.*)
>   (V, iii, 160–63)

'Demand me nothing.' 'Never afflict yourself to know the cause.' 'The
laws are mine.' Othello starts his long speech as he enters Desdemona's bedroom to kill her—'It is the cause, it is the cause' . . . he will not 'name' it, but
his repetition of the word is immensely suggestive. 'Cause' has, at least, two
senses. In natural science it is assumed that every 'effect' has a 'cause'. You
cannot actually *see* causes—they have to be inferred or deduced. This way
the laws of nature are discovered and established. The apple falls and the
cause is gravity. Of course there is scope here for any number of problems,
both scientific and philosophic. Causes may be multiple or untraceable: one
cause is the effect of a prior cause, and so on. But the word was also used to
refer to a matter (case, cause) which someone feels entitled to take to law. It
could be that in his entranced invocations, Othello is hoping (asserting) that
he has both natural and human law on his side. But we have seen how his
legal improvizations are a gross travesty of the law. Lear improvizes a grotesque parody of a courtroom, in the farmhouse where Gloucester leads
him from the heath.

> I will arraign them straight.
> [To Edgar] Come, sit thou here, most learned justice.
>   (III, vi, 21–2)

'Let us deal justly,' says Edgar, and Lear starts the proceedings. 'Arraign her first' (III, vi, 46)—meaning Goneril. Staying with the word 'arraign' for a moment, it is worth noting that it occurs in almost the last words of Goneril when she defies her husband, Albany: 'the laws are mine, not thine:/Who can arraign me for't?' (V, iii, 160–61). To 'arraign' is to bring to trial, and her words suggest a complete collapse of the legal structure. How law legitimates itself is always potentially a problem—is it simply a way of rationalizing and preserving the status quo, with all its inequalities? Goneril reveals here that she recognizes no law except her own—adapting a good phrase of Melville's, we can say that her conscience has become simply 'a lawyer to her will'. She is beyond 'arraigning'. Lear himself moves to a perception of the manifold injustices concealed by 'law': 'see how yon justice rails upon yon simple thief. Hark in thine ear: change places, and, handy-dandy, which is the justice, which is the thief?' (I, vi, 154–6). Back to the farmhouse and the imaginary 'trial'. Having arraigned Goneril in the form of a 'joint stool', Lear moves on to Regan: 'Then let them anatomize Regan. See what breeds about her heart. Is there any cause in nature that makes these hard hearts?' (III, vi, 75–7).

One could see this as *the* question of the play. Is there a cause *in* nature for the effect which is Regan's hard heart. Or is the effect *itself* the cause—hearts are causes, and her heart is like that because it is like that. Chilling. Lear spends a lot of the play aiming his deranged anger at his daughters—as though they are to blame for everything. Like many tragic heroes (like Othello in this), Lear resists and fights against self-knowledge until almost the end, and, it must be remembered, it was Lear's initial actions which permitted, arguably encouraged, the *emergence* and release of evil, even if it was already latently there, 'wrapped up in countenance'. To that extent, *he* is responsible. Only after he has been exposed to a maximum of inner and outer buffeting can he kneel and say to Cordelia—'I am a very foolish, fond old man' (IV, vii, 60). And then:

> I know you do not love me; for your sisters
> Have, as I do remember, done me wrong.
> You have some cause, they have not.
> *Cordelia.*   No cause, no cause.
>   (IV, vii, 72–5)

The calm, generous gentleness of Cordelia's words awaken thoughts of a side of nature which has been systematically and brutally erased in the course of the play, but which is serenely above arguments about causes. It is the cause, it is the cause? No cause, no cause. It is the better way. Let them anatomize Cordelia. See what breeds about *her* heart. Is there any cause in nature that makes these gentle hearts? I think we have to give the Emilia answer. They are not ever gentle for the cause, but gentle for they're gentle.

Edmund, of course, despises law from the start—'Fine word, "legitimate"' (I, ii, 18). Cornwall, determined to punish Gloucester, has an attitude to the law more like Goneril's.

> Though well we may not pass upon his life
> Without the form of justice, yet our power
> Shall do a court'sy to our wrath, which men
> May blame, but not control.
>   (III, vii, 25–8)

This is another way of saying—'the laws are mine'. He will twist the 'forms of justice' to satisfy his 'wrath', as he does in the horrifying improvized trial and torture scene that follows. There is a lot of anger in this play—Lear's rage, awesome in its excess, cosmic in its reach, as well as Cornwall's and Regan's sadistic wrath.

> To be in anger is impiety;
> But who is man that is not angry?
>   (III, v, 57)

Thus Timon of Athens. And there is another kind of anger—call it righteous indignation—which must be seen as justified and part of the fully human. As Kent says: 'anger hath a privilege'. When Cornwall is bent on putting out Gloucester's eye, *a servant*—one of those usually voiceless, deferential, obedient appendages of the court—says:

> Hold your hand, my lord!
> I have served you ever since I was a child;

> But better service have I never done you
> Than now to bid you hold.
>   (III, vii, 73–6)

Cornwall is incredulous at such insubordination, but the servant persists with the thrilling line—'Nay, then, come on, and take the chance of anger' (II, vii, 80), and although Regan stabs him in the back he has in fact killed Cornwall. The play starts with father turning against his child; then brother plots against brother; in due course husband and wife fall out (Albany and Goneril), and here the servant turns on his master. All the bonds are 'cracking'. But in this case it is a matter of the triumph of humanity over hierarchy. Evil has reached such a pitch that even the lowliest man—if he is still human—cannot stand idly by and watch. The cruelty of dukes can stir the anger of a serf. In a curious way, it is the hinge moment of the play. It occurs literally just about at mid-point, and in fact it marks the beginning of the end for the evil plotters. They have done much damage and will do more, but increasingly and in turn they 'come to deadly use'. Thus far, the tide of evil has gathered force and swept along unopposed. Now there is a physical reaction. Not words of horror but a deed of anger. And not by Albany, or Kent, or Edgar, but by an anonymous servant, a serf 'thrilled with remorse,/Opposed against the act' (V, ii, 723). That the agent who precipitates the turn, initiates the slow (too slow for Cordelia) self-correcting processes of nature, is part of the grim power of the play. Outraged reaction to, and taking preventative issue with evil, comes not from above, but from below, socially one of the lowest of the low.

This raises the question of whether there *is* anything or anyone above in this world. There are many references to divinities and the gods (always 'gods', generic and plural; there is no reference to 'God' as there is in *Macbeth*: there is no monotheism in this play).* We have invoked—Hecate, Apollo, Jupiter, Juno; we have 'heavens' with their 'visible spirits', 'the stars above', 'dearest gods', 'ever-gentle gods', Fortune, Jove, even 'fairies'. We are told 'the gods are just', 'the gods are clear' and pious references are made

---

* Not quite true. Lear says 'as if we were God's spies' (V, iii, 17). There is no knowing whether this was Shakespeare or the printer, but whoever capitalized the 'G', it is hardly evidence for an inchoate monotheism.

to 'gods that we adore'. When Albany hears of the servant's killing Cornwall his reaction is:

> This shows you are above,
> You justicers.
>
> (IV, ii, 78–9)

'Thou, Nature, art my goddess'—Edmund's opening words, of course (I, ii, 1). But when Lear curses his ungrateful daughters, he, too, divinizes Nature. 'Here, Nature, hear; dear Goddess hear' (I, iv, 282). What do these people believe? Are they pagans, pre-Christians, or what? (It is curiously hard to get a sense of the date and time of the action, even the place. No Elsinore, no Venice, no towns at all. In one of the oddest lines of the play the Fool says 'This prophecy Merlin shall make, for I live before his time' (III, ii, 95). It almost feels as though we are in pre-history.) Certainly, the very proliferation of divinities invoked makes it impossible to believe that these people live within any stable belief-system. There is a famous moment as the unbearable last scene comes to a climax:

> *Albany.* The gods defend her!
> (*Enter Lear, with Cordelia in his arms.*)

If these gods are 'justicers' it is of the most inscrutable sort. Russell Fraser wants to say—'The Gods dispense justice. But they do not dispense poetic justice.'* He fastens on the fleeting presence of a vocabulary of 'redemption' in the play:

> Thou hast one daughter
> Who redeems nature from the general curse
> Which twain have brought her to.
>
> (IV, vi, 208–10)

The 'twain' could be Goneril and Regan—or Adam and Eve. Robert Heilman finds some of Lear's late speeches 'permeated with Christian feeling'—

---

* See *Shakespeare's Poetics in relation to King Lear,* Routledge, 1962, p. 30. This is an excellent study of the play.

full of contrition, self-abasement, renunciation—and, in general, detects 'a pervading consciousness of deity . . . a largely unconscious, habitual reliance upon divine forces whose primacy is unquestioned'.* He points out that Edmund, Goneril, Regan, Cornwall, and Oswald never invoke gods (unless as public gesture) and never pray; while Cordelia, Kent, Albany, Edgar—and Lear—all pray. But Stephen Greenblatt thinks that, although people may pray, the gods never answer—which perhaps means there are no gods *to* answer. '*King Lear* is haunted by a sense of rituals and beliefs that are no longer efficacious, that have been *emptied out*. The characters appeal again and again to the pagan gods, but the gods are utterly silent. Nothing answers to human questions but human voices. . .'† These are not entirely unreconcilable positions. There seems to be a good deal of vague, instinctive piety—conventional? desperate?—in the play, but there is certainly not the slightest hint of divine response or intervention. If anything, Albany might have said 'This shows you are *below,* you justicers'—nature does seem slowly to correct and re-regulate itself, and it is thus appropriate that the first agent in this process is a figure with the lowliest social status in the play. There is also, perhaps, what Frank Kermode calls 'a self-limiting factor in the nature of evil'. If it happens that evil finally withers and exhausts itself, and that a few of the good characters are left alive—just— then it happens 'per-force' and not per-Jove or Jupiter or any other spirits or, indeed, fairies. As for the Christian feeling in Lear's speeches to Cordelia as they are despatched to prison:

> We two alone shall sing like birds i'th'cage
> When thou dost ask me blessing, I'll kneel down
> And ask of thee forgiveness . . .
>
> Upon such sacrifices, my Cordelia,
> The gods themselves throw incense.
> (V, iii, 9–11, 20–21)

these speeches do indeed seem to catch a glimpse of a world of calm and love, secure beyond the reach of the devouring anarchy of the present. But when Kent was in the stocks, he uttered the unforgettable line—'Nothing

---

* See *This Great Stage,* Washington Press, 1963—this is another magisterial study.
† *Shakespearian Negotiations,* California Press, 1988, p. 119.

almost sees miracles / But misery' (II, ii, 168–9), and I think we must regard Lear's vision of a 'heaven' (or is it a nursery?) as a miracle *almost* seen. There are no 'miracles' in this play, and Cordelia is hanged.

And it was Shakespeare who made it happen. This made the play unpopular for long periods, particularly in the eighteenth century. Dr Johnson could not sit through the last scenes. It was even re-written, with a happy ending. By common consent, it is all but unbearable. As to why Shakespeare should wish to take or bring his audience to this extreme point, one can only speculate. At one point Regan says to Lear: 'O, sir, you are old, / Nature in you stands on the very verge / Of his confine' (II, iv, 145–7). When Edgar brings Gloucester to the cliff, he tells him 'you are now within a foot / Of th'extreme verge' (IV, vi, 25–6). Dover cliffs are, in a sense, the 'extreme verge' of England; by extension, the extreme verge of the earth where it meets the sea, the element of flux and dissolution. Lear and Gloucester are indeed brought to the 'extreme verge' of all that living nature can bear, until, blessedly as we feel, they burst through the human 'confine'. I think Shakespeare wants to take us to that 'extreme verge'; to the point where, with Edgar, we feel 'I would not take this from report: it is, / And my heart breaks at it' (IV, vi, 143–4).

Except it is not, quite. When Edgar evokes for his father a vertiginous cliff with a monster standing at the top of it, we are watching Gloucester flopping and floundering about on a perfectly flat and empty stage. For his own purposes—to instil endurance—Edgar has conjured up a powerful 'image' of monsters and heights and depths. Which, we may say, is what Shakespeare, on a vaster scale, has done in *King Lear*. (A point also made by Greenblatt, albeit for a different purpose: 'Edgar does to Gloucester what the theatre usually does to the audience: he persuades his father to discount the evidence of his senses.')* It is as if Shakespeare is giving us 'the thing itself' *and* reminding us that we are watching an 'image' of it. As Lear stoops over the dead Cordelia, there is the following exchange between Kent and Edgar:

> Is this the promised end?
> Or image of that horror?

---

* op. cit., p. 118.

The promised end of the play—we are nearly there? Or the promised end
of the world—many Elizabethans thought they were nearly *there*? There
are many biblical echoes in the play and as well as Lear re-enacting, or re-
experiencing, the tribulations of Job, Revelation and its account of the last
days before final judgement is clearly in Shakespeare's mind. He is writing
in a period when many people regarded the world's end as imminent, and
an apocalyptic note is heard throughout the play. Although, at the end, Edgar and Albany are left to sustain 'the gored state' (V, ii, 322), there is no
sense of restoration, restitution, let alone of regeneration. There is nothing
'redemptive' here: instead, we are confronted with what A. P. Rossiter used
to call 'the alarmingness of the universe'. We have the sense of a few be-
numbed and cheerless survivors surrounded by the terrible harvest of the
released chaos and evil of the play. Albany speaks of 'this great decay' (V, iii,
299), and it *is* possible to feel that we are witnessing something approaching
the dark conclusion of things. Throughout, the play has seemed to be taking place in apocalyptic time rather than historical time. That we are also
reminded that the whole play is an 'image' in no way diminishes its terrible power. It is one of the features of great tragedy—Nietzsche wrote eloquently of this in *Birth of Tragedy*—that by exacting a vision of the very
worst that nature can do, tragedy, as theatre or ritual, sends out its audience
back into life with renewed energy and reinforced psychic strength. *We* are
the survivors. But, out of question, Shakespeare has taken us to the 'extreme verge' of what it is possible to endure in the theatre. When the howling Lear shows us the dead Cordelia, there seems to be no adequate or for-
mulable response. Except possibly to snatch at a piece of the Fool's nonsense
and say: 'So out went the candle, and we were left darkling' (I, iv, 223).

MACBETH (1606–7)

The candles go out in *Macbeth* as well. Act I ends with Macbeth having decided to 'do the deed' ('I am settled'). Act II opens with Banquo and his son
trying to find their way in the darkness round Macbeth's castle. Banquo remarks: 'There's husbandry in heaven./ Their candles are all out' (II, i, 4–5).
He is saying that the heavens are being frugal and not lighting up their
candles—there are no stars to guide or illumine. (There is a slight displaced
echo of the image in one of Macbeth's late speeches conveying a sense of terminal insentience and depletion—'Out, out, brief candle!' (V, v, 23) where

the candle is simply life itself.) The onset—summoned or suffered—of an ever-deepening darkness characterizes at least the first half of the play. As Macbeth feels the stirrings within himself of the murder he knows he is going to commit, he instinctively invokes the dark:

> Stars hide your fires;
> Let not light see my black and deep desires.
>
> (I, iv, 51–2)

The night of the murder of Duncan is 'unruly' ('the obscure bird/Clamored the livelong night' (II, iii, 61–2)) and the description by Ross points to the central question and struggle of the play:

> By the clock 'tis day,
> And yet dark night strangles the traveling lamp:
> Is't night's predominance or the day's shame,
> That darkness does the face of earth entomb,
> When living light should kiss it.
>
> (II, iv, 6–10)

We have the feeling that it is preternaturally dark and that the darkness is lasting an ominously long time. As though darkness itself had become a vicious agent in its own right, 'strangling' lights and lamps. The question 'Is't night's predominance or the day's shame'—is, in many ways, not only the central question of this play, but of tragedy itself. Whereof comes this? Is the light shamefully feebler than the dark? It is almost a Manichean worry. The possibility of 'night's predominance' is a nightmare indeed, and it is a possibility which tragedy must always at least canvass. Certainly, in this play Macbeth seems set on restoring or installing the empire of night. 'Come seeling night,' he says as he sets about planning the murder of Banquo and his son:

> Good things of day begin to droop and drowse,
> While night's black agents to their preys do rouse.
>
> (III, iii, 32–3)

Is it possible for those 'good things of day' to arouse themselves and resist 'night's black agents'? How? And if not—what then? We must feel the possibility of negative answers with growing alarm as the play unfolds. Almost exactly halfway through the play, Macbeth asks 'What is the night?' to which Lady Macbeth replies: 'Almost at odds with the morning, which is which' (III, iv, 128). 'At odds'—this means the morning and night are struggling with each other for supremacy. At this point it seems in the balance, the issue uncertain—'which is which'. It certainly is a struggle and the morning is a long time in coming—we have yet to see Lady Macduff and her children murdered. Ross says, rather helplessly, to Lady Macduff:

> Things at their worst will cease, or else climb upward
> To what they were before.
> (IV, ii, 24–5)

Do we have to wait 'even till destruction sicken' (IV, i, 60) and evil exhausts itself? Until 'things' somehow restore themselves to some previous order—'perforce'? Can the 'strangled' lamps be resurrected, reillumined? These are concerns raised by the play. When Malcolm affirms 'The night is long that never finds the day' we do feel that the dawn is slowly beginning to break. His conviction is the minimum assurance of the play. But the night has been long and the darkness deep.

   The atmosphere of the first part of the play—perhaps two-thirds of it—is perfectly summarized in the marvellously succinct description of oncoming dusk—'light thickens' (II, ii, 50). There is a pervasive sense of 'thickening': 'As thick as tale/Came post with post' (I, iii, 98), 'Come thick night,' says Lady Macbeth, so that 'heaven' may not 'peep through the blanket of the dark,/To cry "Hold, hold!"' (I, v, 54–5)—which, incidentally but crucially, is what the servant cried to Cornwall in *King Lear*. Lady Macbeth clearly articulates the what and why of her invocations:

> Make thick my blood,
> Stop up th'access and passage to remorse,
> That no compunctious visitings of nature
> Shake my fell purpose.
> (I, v, 44–7)

Appropriately, the Third Witch instructs: 'Make the gruel thick and slab' (i.e. viscous—IV, i, 32). This is an atmosphere in which it is becoming increasingly difficult to see things; in which the blood of human remorse and compunction is ceasing to flow, and nature itself seems almost to be thickening to a standstill. (In a famous essay, Thomas de Quincey interpreted the knocking on the gate in Act II as 'the pulses of life . . . beginning to beat again'.) Yet—it is not so much of a paradox as it might seem—the play is marked by extraordinary haste. As I have said, this is both the shortest and the fastest of Shakespeare's tragedies. We speak of things coming 'thick and fast' and that is exactly right for this play. A lot of the speed is literal: from the beginning people seem in a tremendous hurry. 'What a haste looks through his eyes!' says Lennox as Ross rushes in with news of the death of Cawdor (I, ii, 46). Messengers keep coming—'post with post' (I, in, 98). Duncan, in his gratitude, says to Macbeth:

> thou are so before
> That swiftest wing of recompense is slow
> To overtake thee.
>
> (I, iv, 16–18)

There the 'overtaking' is metaphorical, but almost immediately it becomes literal:

> Our thane is coming.
> One of my fellows had the speed of him
> Who, almost dead for breath, had scarcely more
> Than would make his message . . .
>
> (I, v, 35–8)

The King tries to reach Macbeth on the way to his castle:

> We coursed him at the heels, and had a purpose
> To be his purveyor: but he rides well,
> And his great love, sharp as his spur, hath holp him
> To his home before us.
>
> (I, vi, 21–4)

Indeed he does ride well. It seems that no one can either catch up or keep up with Macbeth. What his 'spur' is, we shall discover. It certainly is not 'love'. Macbeth's great problem and concern is whether, impossibly, he can outride himself. Something 'weird' (key word) is happening to time in this play. Macbeth sends letters to his wife about the prophecies of the 'weird sisters' and she tells him on his return:

> Thy letters have transported me beyond
> The ignorant present, and I feel now
> The future in an instant.
>
> (I, v, 57–9)

This unnatural displacement of the present by the future is the state that Macbeth, effectively, brings about in Scotland:

>   good men's lives
> Expire before the flowers in their caps,
> Dying or ere they sicken.
>
> (IV, ii, 170–3)

Good men dying *before* they sicken? Something is ominously wrong with time.

When, shortly after encountering the witches, Macbeth hears Duncan establish succession to the crown on Malcolm, his immediate reaction is 'That is a step/On which I must fall down, or else o'erleap' (I, v, 49). At the end of his absolutely critical soliloquy at the start of Act I, scene vii, he says:

>   I have no spur
> To prick the side of my intent, but only
> Vaulting ambition, which o'erleaps itself
> And falls on th' other—
>
> (I, vii, 25–8)

The other what? The other side, presumably. But the other side of *what?* Grammatically it should be 'itself', but how can anything jump over itself? Macbeth is accelerating dangerously, and at times it seems almost as if his *language* is trying to 'o'erleap itself'. The whole soliloquy is absolutely crucial and rather than quote it all I will attempt some summary of Macbeth's argument with himself. The opening words ('If it were done' etc.), whether

or not deliberately, echo Christ's words to Judas Iscariot—the great betrayer. It could well be a conscious allusion. Macbeth knows exactly what
his 'duties' are to his king and now that Duncan is in Macbeth's castle—
'he's here in double trust'. Macbeth is his kinsman, his subject, and now his
host—all relationships and bonds which entail sacred duties, responsibilities, and obligations. The absolute reverse of Othello and Lear (and to some
extent Hamlet), Macbeth sees with utmost clarity all the implications of the
deed he is contemplating, and the precise nature of its evil. He recognizes
Duncan's great 'virtues', and what would be 'the deep damnation of his
taking off'. His language touches on the theological and he refers to 'angels
trumpet-tongued' and 'heavens cherubin' who would damn and expose
his 'horrid deed'. He has been saying to himself that if the 'assassination'
could somehow catch and arrest ('trammel up') its own 'consequences'; if
his murder ('surcease') could immediately stop anything that might follow
(success); if, bluntly, 'this blow might be the be-all and end-all'—*if* all that,
then we might risk it and never mind eternity and the after-life ('we'd *jump*
the life to come'—emphasis added). *But*—and that's the point; there is
a but:

> But in these cases
> We still have judgment here; that we but teach
> Bloody instructions, which, being taught, return
> To plague th'inventor

Macbeth's intelligence and conscience are, alike, still in good order here. He
sees and recognizes the damnable nature of his meditated deed; the manifest goodness of the king; the inevitability of retribution; and the impossibility of blocking off, wrapping up, obliterating—try any metaphor—the
consequences of a 'dreadful deed'. He comes to the morally and intellectually correct conclusion and resolution—'We will proceed no further in this
business.' (I will note in passing that 'business' is invariably used in Shakespeare to refer to more or less unscrupulous scheming—it is the Regan–
Edmund word, Julius Caesar's word, and in this play it is both Lady Macbeth's—'This night's great business' (I, v, 69) and Hecate's, engaged in 'great
business' (III, v, 23).) What is particularly frightening in this play is that
within thirty lines of that eminently rational, sensible, honourable decision,
Macbeth is saying—'If we should fail?' (I, vii, 59). Disastrously, he has

shifted his ground from—it is wrong to do this; to—do you think we can get away with it? There is an alarming haste in this swerve from nature. From now on, Macbeth will stake everything on speed.

'We still have judgment here . . .' What Macbeth is trying to do as he goes faster and faster, is perfectly summed up in one of his own phrases: he is trying to 'outrun the pauser, reason' (II, iii, 113). In an important article, Frances Fergusson showed that the whole movement and action of the play are summed up in that phrase.* The 'pauser' as I have said before, is that within us which gives us 'pause';—conscience, reflection, reason, judgement. *Hamlet* is, effectively, one long pause, and it is very long. Macbeth is trying to get rid of that 'pause', trying to close the gap of conscience, to 'outrun' his own judgement—and his play is breathlessly short (almost exactly half the length of *Hamlet*). In connection with *Hamlet* I referred to Brutus' lines:

> Between the acting of a dreadful thing
> And the first motion, all the interim is
> Like a phantasma, or a hideous dream.

This is exactly Macbeth's experience—reality turns 'phantasmatic'. 'Are ye fantastical?'—to the witches; 'my thought, whose murder yet is but fantastical'—to himself. 'Is this a dagger which I see before me? . . . I have thee not, and yet I see thee still' (II, i, 33, 35). 'The time has been that . . . the man would die / And there an end; but now they rise again' (III, iv, 80–81)—as he sees Banquo's ghost. His world is rapidly becoming one in which it might well be said that 'nothing is, but what is not'. The 'interim'—and Macbeth uses the word (I, iv, 154)—has indeed become a 'hideous dream', and Macbeth becomes increasingly desperate to reduce it to nothing. He attempts to achieve this by speedy action. Let us take two quotations. After he has murdered 'the gracious Duncan' and thus, as with his customary clarity he realizes, given his 'eternal jewel' to the devil (Othello never arrives at such awful clearsightedness, for all his jewel-spangled talk), Macbeth follows the doomed logic to which he has committed himself: 'To be thus is nothing, but to be safely thus—' (III, i, 48). He arranges for Banquo and his son, Fleance, to be killed—the second of his 'secret murders'. With the

---

* See *The Human Image in Dramatic Literature,* Doubleday Anchor, 1957, pp. 115–25.

death of these two, Macbeth expects to be 'perfect'. He uses the Othello word twice, albeit with a different intention from his forerunner (there is, perhaps, an added ironic resonance in view of the biblical injunction 'Be ye therefore perfect'). Fleance escapes and Macbeth realizes he is embarked on an endless course of 'blood'—he can only 'wade' deeper and deeper. He does not go into details with his wife:

> Strange things I have in head that will to hand,
> Which must be acted ere they may be scanned.
> (III, v, 40–41)

Note first the tenses and modes of the verbs: have, will, must, may—present, future, imperative—and subjunctive (scanning is to be foregone—or outrun). 'Scan' is the Hamlet word—it is what you do in the 'pause'; it is the enquiring, assessing mental activity which at once creates and occupies the 'interim'. And Macbeth wants to anticipate, pre-empt, and avoid it. Thus he intends to go straight from the 'first motion' ('things I have in head') to the 'acting of a dreadful thing' ('will to hand'). The trouble is he can never go quite fast enough. As he realizes when Macduff escapes to England:

> The flighty purpose never is o'ertook
> Unless the deed go with it. From this moment
> The very firstlings of my heart shall be
> The firstlings of my hand. And even now,
> To crown my thoughts with acts, be it thought and done . . .
> This deed I'll do before this purpose cool . . .
> (IV, i, 145–9, 156)

He wants to bypass conscience and reflection entirely and translate impulse *immediately* into deed. This last is a recurring word in the play. Before the witches encounter Macbeth, the First Witch incants—'I'll do, I'll do, and I'll do' (I, iii, 10). It is to become Macbeth's motto—almost his blazon. 'Words to the heat of deeds too cold breath gives./I go, and it is done' (II, i, 61–2). Language itself is, of course, the prime 'pauser' or instrument of pausing. While you are talking (or writing) about it, you are not *doing* it. Words defer. Thinking persists. 'These deeds must not be thought/After

these ways,' says Lady Macbeth (II, ii, 32–3). *Deeds* must not be *thought* because then the risk is that 'function' (doing) will be 'smothered in surmise'
(thinking). Lady Macbeth refers to 'thoughts which should indeed have
died / With them they think on' (III, ii, 10–11)—but while kings may die,
thoughts live on. 'I have done the deed,' announces Macbeth after killing
the king. 'There shall be done a deed of dreadful note' (III, ii, 44), he promises, referring to the murder of Banquo. 'We are yet young in deed,' he says
ominously to his wife, a little later (III, iv, 145)—implying there are many
more deeds yet to be *done*. Thereafter, he seeks increasingly to live and
move entirely in the realm of 'deeds' and lose himself (blot out the interim)
in a life of unreflective action. Be it thoughtanddone—instantaneously, no
gaps or pauses. He seeks a sort of all-at-once-ness, the future and the present constanteous, the linear consequentiality of time annulled. But it is
not *quite* possible. 'We still have judgments here'—by the end, Macbeth has
effectively de-humanized himself and anaesthetized his conscience, but he
still knows very precisely the values—the 'good things of day'—he has lost:

> And that which should accompany old age,
> As honor, love, obedience, troops of friends,
> I must not look to have . . .
> (V, iii, 24–6)

But there is no going back, and he must go on doing the deed until his
death. By contrast, Macduff says that unless he encounters Macbeth, he will
sheathe his sword 'undeeded'—by this time that amazing neologism carries tremendous force.

Since Macbeth commits himself to an ever-accelerating life of action, we
might consider one of his first reactions to the witches' prophecies:

> If chance will have me king, why, chance may crown me,
> Without my stir.
> (I, iii, 143–4)

In *Troilus and Cressida,* Ulysses has the line: 'Since things in motion sooner
catch the eye / Than what stirs not' (II, iii, 182–3).

There is a strong Elizabethan feeling that virtue is associated with stillness (or slow, decorous movements). Think how little Desdemona and

Cordelia actually 'stir'. Evil was much more likely to result from 'things in motion', particularly the sort of unappeasable motion of a Macbeth which creates a fearful world in which all those around him or under his sway can only 'float upon a wild and violent sea/Each way and move' (IV, ii, 21–2). It is in the context of this vortex of violent motion created by Macbeth that one must understand the long, slow, seemingly pointlessly protracted scene between Macduff and Malcolm in England. As Fergusson very aptly describes it; 'the scene is like a slow eddy on the edge of a swift current'.* As Malcolm explains, he cannot trust anything or anyone emerging from Macbeth's darkened Scotland—'modest wisdom plucks me/From over-credulous haste' (IV, iii, 119–20). The play starts in 'haste' and seems to get ever vertiginously quicker. But here it is, laboriously, slowed down. The tide is beginning to turn.

'Know thyself'—this, surely, is one of the central, generative, admonitions in western culture. Most tragic heroes, from Oedipus on, have, for a variety of reasons, ever but slenderly known themselves, and when self-knowledge does finally break in, or through, it is invariably at ruinous cost. Hamlet, with his extraordinary ranging mind, doesn't know whether he knows himself or not (it is part of his self-paralysing intelligence). It is a moot point whether Othello ever *really* comes to know himself as, in his last speech, he embarks on an exotic flight in which self-condemnation is richly mixed with self-exculpation. Lear spends much of the play furiously fending off self-knowledge (always the daughters, the daughters). It breaks in or through only when he is himself broken (or, arguably, the breaking in of it breaks him). And then Macbeth. Who knows himself—perfectly; all the way down, as we say. Perhaps only Shakespeare could have moved directly from a Lear to a Macbeth. For Macbeth embarks on an exactly contrary journey—*away* from self-knowledge. In the process, he engages, long before Rimbaud, on a systematic 'déréglement' of the senses. He seems to separate out what he calls 'each corporal agent' (I, vii, 80) and set them at odds with each other, involving them in a mutually estranging or antagonistic activity. Let 'the eye wink at the hand' (I, iv, 52): 'bear welcome in your eye/Your hand, your tongue' (I, v, 65–6)—that is Lady Macbeth, but at this point they are two of a kind; 'false face must hide what false heart doth know' (I, vii, 82); 'Mine eyes are made the fools o'th'other sense/Or

---

* ibid., p. 124.

else worth all the rest' (II, i, 44–5); 'Present him eminence with eye and
tongue . . . And make our faces vizards to our hearts, / Disguising what they
are' (III, ii, 81, 84–5)—there are other examples of how he regards eyes,
hands, heart, tongue as separable agents to whom he can issue contradictory instructions. When, at the start, Duncan declares 'There's no art / To
find the mind's construction in the face' (I, iv, 11–12) he unwittingly pre-
pares us for the breathtaking feats of dissembling to be attempted by the
Macbeths. After her initial bout of truly demonic energy, Lady Macbeth
simply cracks up, and recedes into madness and suicide. Macbeth soldiers
on, as we may quite accurately say, but his senses are in sore disarray—they
are, to use Menteith's supremely apt word, 'pestered':

> Who then shall blame
> His pestered senses to recoil and start,
> When all that is within him does condemn
> Itself for being there?
>   (V, ii, 21–4)

The words bear pondering—how can such internal chaos and insurrection
come about? It is all the result of Macbeth's attempt knowingly to extin-
guish self-knowledge—an undertaking perhaps as impossible as jumping
over yourself. The most telling line in the whole play is:

> To know my deed, 'twere best not know myself.
>   (II, ii, 72)

Macbeth is the tragedy of man who goes to all lengths to o'erleap himself,
outrun himself, *not* know himself. It proves both impossible and utterly disastrous—and not for him alone.

Such an attempt at achieving complete self-alienation, self-estrangment,
is strange indeed, and 'strange' is one of the operative words of the play—
the play opens with 'strange images of death' and I will return to them. The
whole thing is overseen (precipitated?) by the *weird* sisters, and we had better look at them more closely. 'Weird' comes from Old English 'wyrd'—
fate, destiny; also 'werde'—death. But also from 'weorthan' and German
'werden'—to become. And also old Latin 'uortere' (or 'vertere')—to turn.
Thus, in the word 'weird' we have, in the words of Ann Lecercle, 'a becom-

ing that is a turning, a turning back, a reversal, a becoming that is a negation of becoming, epitomized in the chiasmus of the liminal proposition of
the play, "Fair is foul, and foul is fair."'* She maintains that 'It is no exaggeration to say that the entire structure of the work is contained in the word
"weird" and the perverse circularity that informs it.' But what is the, as they
say, ontological status of the 'weird sisters'? Supernatural solicitors? They
are clearly meant to be *there* for the people in the play—Banquo sees them
as well as Macbeth (by contrast only Macbeth sees Banquo's ghost). For the
contemporary audience and King James, reputedly watching the play at its
first performance, they would *not* have been simply 'fantastical'. Here we
do need some details about the antecedents and sources of the play; for, as
Bullough helpfully reminds us—'Of course Shakespeare could have invented everything, but he never liked to do that, preferring always to re-
make suitable existing material.'†

In 1605, when King James visited Oxford, he was greeted by three Sibyls
as the descendant of Banquo. This was part of the Stuart political legitimating myth, which sought to provide the Stuarts with a proper ancestry,
stretching back through Banquo to the first king, Kenneth Macalpine. On
this occasion a debate was conducted on 'whether the imagination can produce real effects'. With the accession of James to the throne, there was a
surge of interest in Scottish history. Bullough tells us that the story of Macbeth and Duncan goes back to the early eleventh century, when Scotland
had largely been unified and the ideas of nationality and kingship were
gradually developing. After killing Duncan, by all accounts a young and
unsatisfactory king, Macbeth, though a cruel man, reigned successfully, and
in many ways well, for *seventeen years*. Shakespeare collapses those years
into what must be a matter of weeks ('haste') and makes Duncan old and
venerable (thus, the deeper the damnation of his 'taking off'). In 1527, the
Scotorum Historiae of Hector Boethius (Boece) was published, translated in
1536. This was Holinshed's main source, as Holinshed was Shakespeare's.
In Boece Macbeth and Banquo meet three women referred to as 'thre weird
sisteris or wiches' and 'wiches' are mentioned several times. Also referred
to is Macbeth's 'innative cruelty'. In Holinshed, Banquo is involved in the

---

* In a brilliant article entitled 'Mannerist *Macbeth*' in *Miroirs de L'Être,* Toulouse, 1988.
† op. cit., p. 448. All the material that follows concerning sources is from the same volume, pp. 423–527.

murder of Duncan—Shakespeare decides to *contrast* the two men, starting with their instinctively different reaction to the witches. Holinshed also refers to 'weird sisters' and their prophecies, and 'witches' (and even 'wizzards') and Shakespeare combines these with the fantastic hags of current folk-lore and witch-hunts.

In 1597, James VI had published a book called *Daemonologie* in which he inveighed against witches and those who consulted them. Indeed, Bullough reminds us, his first Parliament passed an Act 'against Conjuration, Witchcraft, and dealing with evil and wicked spirits'. The King was much concerned with the existence and operations of demonic powers. He was also concerned about regicides. In the play 'the references to traitors and equivocation were obviously to the trials after the Gunpowder Plot, and especially to that of Father Garnet (March 1606), who after many of his denials had been countered, "fell into a large Discourse of defending *Equivocations, with many weak and frivolous Distinctions*".* ('Equivocation' was a Jesuit device by which a prisoner under interrogation might pervert the truth in order to avoid self-accusation.) When the Porter, 'porter of hell gate', imagines he is admitting people to the infernal regions of the damned—as, in a sense, he is—and says: 'Faith, here's an equivocator, that would swear in both the scales against either scale; who committed treason enough for God's sake, yet could not equivocate to heaven. O, come in, equivocator' (II, iii, 8–12)—there is a contemporary reference which the audience would have recognized. However, as he continues and goes on to talk about the effects of 'drink', his words begin to 'swarm upon' Macbeth, albeit proleptically: 'Lechery, sir, it provokes and unprovokes; it provokes the desire, but it takes away from the performance: therefore much drink may be said to be an equivocator with lechery: it makes him and it mars him; it sets him on and takes him off; it persuades him and disheartens him; makes him stand to and not stand to; in conclusion, equivocates him in a sleep, and giving him the lie, leaves him' (II, iii, 31–8). These last lines exactly describe the effect of the weird sisters' words—dangerous intoxicants?—upon Macbeth. They—the words—both make and mar him; set him on and take him off; persuade and dishearten him; give him the lie and leave him. Equivocate. To speak with equal and, by implication seemingly contradictory, voices. The play starts with the equivocations of the witches ('fair is foul'), and of

---

* ibid., p. 425.

the weather ('So foul and fair a day I have not seen' (I, iii, 38)). Nature, and perhaps supernature, is speaking with a double voice. By the end of the play, Macbeth, with his customary lucidity and searing accuracy of formulation, realizes what has been happening:

> I pull in resolution, and begin
> To doubt the equivocation of the fiend
> That lies like truth.
>
> (V, v, 42–4)

This is when he hears that Birnam wood seems to be approaching his castle. When Macduff tells him of his non-birth (ripped from the womb), Macbeth knows what has been done to him:

> And be these juggling fiends no more believed,
> That palter with us in a double sense . . .
>
> (V, viii, 19–20)

He has discovered from experience what Banquo suspected from the start:

> But 'tis strange:
> And oftentimes, to win us to our harm,
> The instruments of darkness tell us truths,
> Win us with honest trifles, to betray's
> In deepest consequence.
>
> (I, iii, 122–6)*

'Consequence' is something that Macbeth aspired to elude, outrun, block— 'trammel up'. What we watch are the 'consequences' of that impossible attempt.

---

* Frank Kermode very aptly compares Christ's accusation to Satan in Milton's *Paradise Regain'd*: 'That hath been thy craft,/By mixing somewhat true to vent more lies./But what have been thy answers, what but dark,/Ambiguous, and with double sense deluding?' (I, 432–5: Riverside Shakespeare, p. 1308). Milton could, of course, have known Shakespeare's play—but this double-dealing, double-saying, is a traditional attribute of the devil.

But is everything the fault of 'the fiend'? Would Macbeth never have embarked on his bloody, treasonable, damnable course, if he had not been provoked or inflamed by the witches' ambiguous prophecies? Nothing in the play makes us feel this, but we must look at the weird sisters again. Whether Shakespeare believed in witches and the fiend, is both undiscoverable and irrelevant. Such beliefs were much in the air at the time and must have been even more so in eleventh-century Scotland. You don't have to believe in witches to believe in a people that believed in witches. Shakespeare's witches habitually speak equivocally, in riddling ambiguities and seeming contradictions—'when the battle's lost and won' (I, i, 4); 'Lesser than Macbeth, and greater' (I, ii, 65). (This kind of equivocation—language doubling back on itself—infects other speakers: 'such welcome and unwelcome things at once,' says Macduff (IV, ii, 138); 'both more and less,' says Malcolm (V, v, 12), and so on). As figures, they are at once natural and unnatural, both in and out of nature—they 'look not like th'inhabitants o'th'earth,/ And yet are on't,' as Banquo very accurately says (I, iii, 41–2). The edges or limits of 'nature' were ragged, or murky, or indeterminable for the Elizabethans. It was imperfectly ascertainable where nature left off, as it were (reached the limits of its confine), and something else began to hold sway. After all, from one point of view, Goneril and Regan are themselves 'weird sisters'. In *Macbeth* the weird sisters are, they embody, something equivocal in nature itself—whether to be classed as 'supernatural' or 'fiendish' hardly matters. They neither bewitch or enchant, compel or persuade, Macbeth.

They do not need to. Their words simply touch and release into action ('performance') the 'black and deep desires' he already harbours. It might be helpful here to think of what some classical scholars refer to as the phenomenon of 'double motivation' in Greek epic and tragedy. This refers to the undeniable fact that, in Homer, in Aeschylus, gods and goddesses are continuously interfering in human affairs with varying irresistible, or un-negatable, imperatives—compelling to action, or constraining to abstinence. At the same time, we never feel that the human agents are mere automata, puppets in the hands of this or that angry or partial god or goddess. Their actions, though directed by—whatever, from—wherever, are their own. They *are* what they *do*. Their deeds, or refrainings, are, as it were, exactly in line with the divine propulsions or forbiddings. What the gods dictate or decree is curiously an echo, an identification, a premonition, a revelation, of the 'black and deep desires'—or (less often) the enlightened and elevated aspirations—of the human actors whose doings they seem to oversee. And so it is with Macbeth and the witches. Their tantalizing predictions 'provoke' a desire which was already stirring. Their 'fog[gy] and filthy' words, at one and of a piece with the 'air' in which they move and from which they seem to emanate, simply serve to speed Macbeth along a path which, we are made to feel, he is determined, destined, doomed, to follow. He knows it is 'against the use of nature' (I, iii, 137), but he is going to do it anyway.

And even that perverse compulsion-decision is somehow within the realm of 'nature'. But 'tis strange. Weird.

'Strangeness' is everywhere, and the play starts with 'strange images of death' (I, iii, 97). We may say that it ends with a strange image of birth ('Macduff was from his mother's womb / Untimely ripped'—V, viii, 15–16), but, in truth, strange images of birth have from the start been co-present with strange images of death, clinging together and, for a period, choking their art. I am here alluding to the Captain's account of Macbeth's victory in battle which, after the opening chorus by the three witches, effectively opens the play. The first words spoken (after the witches) form a question:

> What bloody man is this?

at this point it is the bleeding Captain, but in due course it will be Macbeth ('steeped in blood'), and that opening question becomes the question of the whole play—what bloody man is *that*? The Captain makes his bloody entry and I will just note here that a baby enters the world covered in blood. I hope the relevance of this will become clear. We need the Captain's opening speech:

> Doubtful it stood,
> As two spent swimmers, that do cling together
> And choke their art. The merciless Macdonwald—
> Worthy to be a rebel for to that
> The multiplying villainies of nature
> Do swarm upon him—from Western Isles
> Of kerns and gallowglasses is supplied;

And Fortune, on his damned quarrel smiling,
Showed like a rebel's whore: but all's too weak:
For brave Macbeth—well he deserves that name—
Disdaining Fortune, with his brandished steel,
Which smoked with bloody execution,
Like valor's minion carved out his passage
Till he fac'd the slave;
Which nev'r shook hands, nor bade farewell to him,
Till he unseamed him from the nave to th'chops,
And fixed his head upon our battlements.

(I, ii, 8–23)

I will come back to the importance of 'doubtful it stood'—it hangs over most of the play. The opening image seems strange in the context of war— spent swimmers clinging together suggests exhausted lovers rather more than entangled warriors ('spend', of course, was used by the Elizabethans to refer to orgasm). But lovers who 'choke their art' while clinging together suggest a barren, self-destructive sexuality (to be succinctly expressed by Lady Macbeth later in the play when she says bleakly: 'Noughts had, all's spent,/Where our desire is got without content'—II, ii, 4–5). Fortune is a 'whore' while Macbeth, incongruously, is a 'minion', a pampered favourite. In a speech shortly following he becomes 'Bellona's bridegroom' (I, ii, 54). Bellona is the goddess of War, and we can say at once that there is, from the start, some perverse mixing (stirring together we might say, in view of the witcherly activities obtaining) of the sexual and the lethal. Venus contending with Mars is a familiar Renaissance image, and Shakespeare elsewhere can show unusually close connections or similarities between the marital and the martial, as in the wonderfully erotic scene in *Antony and Cleopatra* in which armour becomes a site and adjunct of *amour.* In that play, the mixing makes for 'fairness': in Macbeth, it tends to 'foulness'. In the brilliant article I have referred to, Ann Lecercle comments: 'If foul is fair and fair is foul, battle is brothel and brothel battle.'* After the 'spent swimmers', we have 'the multiplying villainies of nature do swarm upon him'. *Swarm.* It is an incredibly powerful image. Bees swarm, and they swarm back to the

* op. cit. Our readings of the play coincide, but I certainly owe some of the following points to this arresting article.

Queen Bee in the hive. But the bees have become 'villainies' and the honey has turned to foulness. Something has gone wrong with nature's fecundity. (Lady Macbeth violently renounces all maternal feeling, while it is Hecate who has 'o'erteemed loins'.) The 'swarm' will shift from Macdonwald to his killer. And note the manner of his killing. Macbeth 'carve[s] out his passage'—there is a hint of the birth passage there—and then 'unseam[s]' the 'slave', from the navel upwards. This is pure, slaughterous violence, but it must have been a somewhat similar process and action when Macduff was 'ripped' from the womb. Only that was for the birth of life. Macbeth is delivering death into the world—and will continue to do so. The Captain's next speech serves to extend this feeling of strange births:

> As whence the sun 'gins his reflection
> Shipwracking storms and direful thunders break,
> So from that spring whence comfort seemed to come
> Discomfort swells.
>
> (II, ii, 25–8)

The witches plan shipwrecks: nature is pregnant—swelling—with 'discomfort'. (This will shortly be echoed when Macbeth says in an aside: 'Two truths are told,/As happy prologues to the *swelling* act/Of the imperial theme' (I, iii, 17–19—emphasis added). The deed will shortly reach its term.) At the end of his scene, the Captain is fainting and gasps—'my gashes cry for help'. It could, in a horribly distorted form, be the cry of a woman about to give birth. 'Gash' is a crucial word, and it anticipates a truly monstrous birth. There are hints of strange or aborted births throughout. When Macbeth writes to his wife, he refers to her as 'dearest partner of greatness' (he repeats the word) and Lady Macbeth is instantly 'great' with a deed that bleeds rather than a child which 'sucks'. One of the ingredients of the witches' cauldron is 'Finger of birth-strangled babe/Ditch delivered by a drab' (IV, i, 30–31), and for their second apparition for Macbeth's benefit, they bring forth (from the cauldron?) 'a Bloody Child' (IV, i, 77). As Duncan approaches Macbeth's castle, he thinks it is a 'pleasant seat' and that the air is 'gentle' (I, vi, 1–3). Banquo responds by saying that, indeed, 'heaven's breath/Smells wooingly here' and that the 'martlet' (martin) has 'made his pendent and procreant cradle/Where they most breed' (I, vi, 8–9). The proleptic ironies are dark. There is to be no wooing, no breeding, no 'procreant cradle' in this play (unless we feel that 'pity, like a newborn babe' does finally emerge). Macbeth has married murder, and the child is Death. He transforms Scotland into a country which 'cannot / Be called our mother but our grave' (IV, ii, 16). Lady Macbeth 'unsex[es]' herself.

The most important description of this perverted or inverted birthing is provided by Macbeth when he justifies his killing of the murdered king's servants:

> Here lay Duncan,
> His silver skin laced with his golden blood,
> And his gashed stabs look like a breach in nature
> For ruin's wasteful entrance: there, the murderers,
> Steeped in the colors of their trade, their daggers
> Unmannerly breeched with gore.
>   (II, iii, 113–18)

I have quoted this passage before, but now it must be more closely considered in the context I have been suggesting. The beautiful, the precious, the delicate (indeed the artistic)—silver 'laced' with gold—quickly gives way to the crude, the 'unmannerly', the gory. Fair turns into, turns out to be, foul. The sacred (suggestion of a sacred relic) degrades to the gross (suggestion of breeches). The body is 'gashed' as though it had, it was, 'a breach in nature' which could certainly suggest the entrance to the womb (a 'breach birth' is a difficult birth which often requires a Caesarian section, a 'ripping' or 'unseaming'). But what issues forth from this womb-wound is 'ruin', its entrance into the world 'wasteful'. Weird. A 'breach' is a break, a breaking, a breakage, and at this point nature itself seems to be broken. 'Breach', and 'breeched'. When things start to go wrong, begin to turn and swerve, Shakespeare likes to use apparently very different, even opposite, words which are very close in spelling and almost homophones. We have encountered seeing/seeling, and in this play there is surcease/success; highly/ holily; but most importantly—breach/breech. 'Breech'd with gore' suggests the daggers have been clothed in trousers of blood (to 'breech' a boy was to take him out of petticoats and put him into 'breeches'). 'Breech' comes from Latin *braca* which means, as the OED puts it, 'doubtful, double'. This, of course, is perfect for Shakespeare's play (it is entirely irrelevant to what extent he may consciously have intended it). '*Doubtful* it stood,' said the Captain: '*double, double,* toil and trouble,' say the witches (IV, i, 35). Through the 'breach' in nature, a very active 'ruin' has been born (Macbeth is at once bloody parent, butcher-midwife, and child Ruin himself); and this is ushering in a 'breech'd' world—breeched 'with gore' and also with doubt and doubleness. It will take another 'unnatural' child—'none of woman born' (IV, i, 80)—to confront, contest, and deliver *out* of the world, a child as monstrous as this.

Once again, we have witnessed nature awesomely—strangely, weirdly—engendering unnature. "'Tis unnatural/Even like the deed that's done,' says the Old Man of the strange climatic and animal disturbances which take place during the night of Duncan's murder (I, iv, 10–11). 'Unnatural deeds/Do breed unnatural troubles,' says the Doctor, commenting on the 'great perturbation in nature' manifest in Lady Macbeth's strange sleep-walking activities (V, i, 10, 75). He is the second doctor to appear in the play (it is, I think, the only play by Shakespeare to feature *two* doctors), and certainly the state of Scotland needs some drastic, if not miraculous, medicining and healing. The first doctor appears in the scene in England, in which he describes the royal ritual of curing the king's 'evil' (scrofula—but, in this play, the word seems fittingly generic for the disease spread by Macbeth):

> There are a crew of wretched souls
> That stay his cure: their malady convinces
> The great assay of art; but at this touch,
> Such sanctity hath heaven given his hand,
> They presently amend.
>
> (IV, iii, 141–5)

This, of course, adumbrates and forefigures the aid which the King of England will afford Malcolm as he embarks on his mission to restore to health the 'wretched souls'—his subjects—who 'stay his cure', and rid Scotland of its 'malady'. We should note that the English King is said to be 'full of grace', and his 'healing benediction' ('put on with holy prayers') deemed 'miraculous' (IV, iii, 159, 154, 147). In *King Lear* we were shown an image of the 'promised end', and at the murder of Duncan, Macduff says 'see/The great doom's image!' which means much the same thing (II, iii, 80). But whereas *King Lear* takes place in a miasma of uncertainty concerning what —if anything—obtains or operates in the supernatural world, in *Macbeth* there are unmistakable references to, and an assured belief in, a religious (and effectively Christian) order. From his vocabulary, it is clear that Macbeth believes in 'God', 'the devil', 'heaven' and 'hell', and the 'soul' ('Death of thy soul!' he shouts to the servant who brings him news of the approaching army—the words are terribly self-applicable—V, iii, 16). Lennox articulates what seems to be a general belief in, as well as a yearning for, 'angels' and 'blessings' ('Some holy angel/Fly to the court of England . . . that a swift blessing/May soon return to this our suffering country'—III, vi, 45–8). And Malcolm gives voice, in the darkest hour, to a belief that, somehow 'grace' remains itself and must persist:

> Angels are bright still, though the brightest fell:
> Though all things foul would wear the brows of grace,
> Yet grace must still look so.
>   (IV, iii, 22–4)

In his last speech, heralding the restoration of the health and order of the land, he promises;

> what needful else
> That calls upon us, by the grace of Grace
> We will perform in measure, time, and place . . .
>   (V, viii, 71–3)

'By the grace of Grace'—has Macbeth finally been defeated by divine intervention? Macbeth certainly becomes 'devilish Macbeth' and his 'fall' is as certain as Lucifer's. Yet though we are aware of an, at times almost despairing, faith ('the substance of things hoped for, the evidence of things not seen'), I do not think we sense the operation of divine retribution. I think we are aware of the working of natural cycles and rhythms—dawn must come *sometime* (anyone who lived through World War II will readily recognize the atmosphere of *Macbeth*); and once again, there is a sense of the unfolding and ripening of time. 'Time and the hour runs through the roughest day,' says Macbeth with his usual self-condemning accuracy (I, iii, 147). Thanks to him the day, or rather the night, is rough indeed. But time is running and at last runs through until, at the end, Macduff, holding Macbeth's head (an echo of what Macbeth did to Macdonwald at the start—more doubling), can proclaim—'The time is free.'

Then again, there is certainly the intimation that 'destruction sicken[s]' of its own proceedings and, somehow, runs into the sand. But human agency is crucial and indispensable. Doctors and doctoring kings certainly help. But the crucial thing is, I think, again 'anger'. Macduff never explains—'why in that rawness left you wife and child' (IV, iii, 26), and Lady Macduff's complaint that 'His flight was madness . . . the flight/So sins against all reason' (IV, ii, 3, 14–15) has always seemed to me unanswerable—certainly unanswered. But the slaughter of his family provides a motivation which serves to sharpen and shape him into the man who can confront Macbeth ('confronting' is important: it is what Macbeth does to the first Thane of Cawdor as he kills him (I, ii, 55); young Siward receives his mortal wounds 'on the front'—V, vii, 47). Malcolm exhorts him in these terms:

> Be this the whetstone of your sword. Let grief
> Convert to anger; blunt not the heart, enrage it.
> (IV, iii, 228–9)

Grief converting to anger perhaps runs parallel to night 'converting' to day. If things can turn ('vert') awry, they can, in time, turn back ('convert') to some (temporarily) lost or destroyed natural ordering and harmony. Perhaps by the grace of Grace: certainly with the aid of energy summoned up and directed by the enraged heart. The habitually 'undeedful' Macduff is the man to do the one indisputably necessary deed of ridding the world of Macbeth. Be it registered, grieved over, thought through, angered about, and then—in due time—*done*. This is the powerfully restorative, reconstitutive feeling at the conclusion of the last of Shakespeare's great tragedies. But the evil has been evil indeed.

These four plays were written one after the other in the relatively short period of 1598 to 1606.

It beggars belief.

GREEK AND
ROMAN PLAYS

Thou art a Roman, be not barbarous . . .

(*Titus Andronicus,* I, i, 379)

dost thou not perceive
That Rome is but a wilderness of tigers?

(ibid., III, i, 53–4)

When Shakespeare perused North's translation of Plutarch's *Lives* (1579)—which he did most carefully; the main source for the last four plays in this volume is North's translation—he would have read this:

To be short, it may be truly sayd, that the reading of histories, is the schole of wisedome, to facion mens understanding, by considering advisedly the state of the world that is past, and by marking diligently by what lawes, maners and discipline, Empires, Kingdomes and dominions, have in old time bene stablished and afterward maintayned and increased: or contrariwise changed, diminished and overthrown.

Just why the history of Rome was so important to the Elizabethans, and how and to what ends Shakespeare imaginatively deployed that history, will, I hope, be made a little clearer in the course of this introduction. But, from the outset, it is important to remember that although the following six plays are conventionally, and correctly, classified as tragedies, they are also histories. Indeed, to describe them, we can scarcely do better than avail ourselves of one of Polonius' felicitous, and too often wrongly mocked, compounds. These plays are 'tragical-historical'.

TITUS ANDRONICUS (1592–4)

Rome, Roman, Romans—the name of the imperial city echoes and re-echoes throughout the long opening scene (in varying forms, it occurs at least sixty times by my count). The play is certainly 'The most Lamentable

Romaine Tragedie of Titus Andronicus', as the quarto has it, but it is also, and inextricably, a play about Rome itself. More will emerge concerning this Elizabethan preoccupation with Rome, but at this point it will be helpful to have an authoritative statement from T. J. B. Spencer, who made a special study of the Roman plays.

> Roman history was used as the material for political lessons, because it was one of the few bodies of consistent and continuous historical material available. English national history, in spite of patriotic sentiment, was much more limited in scope and interest, and the historians were not nearly so good as the ancient Latin writers ... When Shakespeare turned from English history to Roman history as the subject of plays, he was touching upon grave and provocative problems of political morality ... Rome loomed much larger in the history of the world than it does to modern historians and writers; and the Roman Empire was much more important than the Roman Republic. The potentates elected as heads of the Holy Roman Empire were still numbered from Julius Caesar by Shakespeare's contemporaries. There were very few republics in sixteenth-century Europe, but there were plenty of aspiring Roman emperors; and it was therefore from the history of the growth of monarchical rule in Rome (the political events which allowed the rise and led to the fall of Julius Caesar and the conflict between Octavian and Mark Antony) that the most useful and relevant lessons could be learnt.
>
> (*Shakespeare: The Roman Plays,* p. 9)

The Rome of the opening scene displays all the panoply and adjuncts of a proud, imperial city. In the first speech we hear of 'noble patricians', 'the justice of my cause', 'the imperial diadem', 'my father's honors'. We hear of 'the gods of Rome', there are vows to heaven, priests with holy water, sacrificial rites, sacred monuments to the dead. There is a triumphal entry of the returning victorious general (Titus) along with his prisoners and spoils. We seem to be witnessing the confident ceremonies of the—very patriarchal—power of invincible Rome. But the scene starts with ferocious dispute about the imperial succession, and moves on to a brutal human sacrifice. This is followed by a disastrous mistake when Titus rejects election as Emperor and, being a believer in hereditary monarchy, bestows the title on the manifestly unscrupulous and ignoble Saturninus. Worse is to come when Titus kills one of his own sons who is courageously, and correctly, defending the

rights of his sister; then the new Emperor Saturninus impulsively—and
one infers lustfully—marries the captive Gothic Queen, Tamora. It was her
son whom Titus had sacrificed, so when she murmurs in an aside to her
new husband—'I'll find a day to massacre them all' (I, i, 451)—meaning
Titus and his family—it is clear that there is trouble ahead. Almost her last
words in this scene are

> Titus, I am incorporate in Rome,
> A Roman now adopted happily . . .
> (I, i, 463–4)

The Goth, the vengeful woman, is now '*incorporate*' in patriarchal Rome.
Whatever condition the 'body' of the state of Rome was in—and despite the
litany of 'just', 'noble', 'virtue', etc., it seems far from stable—that body is
now going to be threatened from within by an alien, savage, female agent.

'Kind Rome' (I, i, 165) says Titus at one point. But this Rome is visibly far
from 'kind'. The matter of the human sacrifice is particularly pertinent
here:

> Give us the proudest prisoner of the Goths,
> That we may hew his limbs, and on a pile
> *Ad manes fratrum* sacrifice his flesh . . .
> (I, i, 96–8)

Rome was a singularly brutal state, but it did *not* practise human sacrifice.
Spencer makes the point that, although Shakespeare's depiction of Rome
can be rather confused (at times it seems to be 'a free commonwealth, with
the characteristic mixture of patrician and plebeian institutions'), he does
seem to be trying to get Roman history 'right'. But then he deliberately inserts this archaic barbarity. As the 'barbarian' Goths note—'Was never
Scythia half so barbarous' (I, i, 131). It is as if, *from the very beginning*, Shakespeare wants to suggest that the conventional opposition of Rome–Barbarian simply will not hold. And we may note the words of Tamora, mother
of the sacrificed Goth, as she pleads that her son be spared:

> O, if to fight for king and commonweal
> Were piety in thine, it is in these.
> Andronicus, stain not thy tomb with blood.

> Wilt thou draw near the nature of the gods?
> Draw near them then in being merciful;
> Sweet mercy is nobility's true badge.
>
> (I, i, 114–19)

We may recall what Portia says of mercy in *The Merchant of Venice*—'it becomes / The throned monarch better than his crown' (IV, i, 189)—and feel that from every conceivable perspective Tamora is, here, humanly in the right of it. And Titus in the wrong. Tamora's comment, as the sacrifice is taking place—'O cruel, irreligious piety!' (I, i, 130)—inevitably becomes a comment on all the 'pieties' which noble, just, kind Rome regards as the distinguishing mark of its civilized state.

Titus is surely as equally in the wrong when he stabs his son Mutius who is honourably defending his sister Lavinia. As his brother Marcus—one of the few wise and temperate figures in the play—says to Titus, he has 'In a bad quarrel slain a virtuous son' (I, i, 343). The insensate rage of Titus at this point, his fury at any sign of filial insubordination, his willingness to destroy his own child, have suggested to a number of critics, rightly I think, that we can already detect here the early signs of a King Lear—a proleptic similarity enhanced when, as he is buffeted with grief after grief and atrocity after atrocity, it seems he must go mad ('my heart all mad with misery', 'no man should be mad but I'—III, ii, 9, 24). Like Lear, in this opening scene, Titus gets everything—the succession, the sacrifice, the treatment of his children—terribly, and as it will prove disastrously, wrong. (It might be added that some have also seen adumbrations of the figure of Othello in Titus—the great soldier living by a naive, martial code, who proves to be hopelessly vulnerable to the machinations of evil plotters when he moves from the battlefield to the city. In fact, in his courage, almost maniacal bravery, stubbornness, hardness, intemperate anger, and—yes—stupidity, the old warrior, an almost archaic pre-political figure, looks straight forward to Shakespeare's last Roman tragic hero, Coriolanus—whose desire to be revenged on Rome is referred to in this play—IV, iv, 69.)

Titus kills his son because he claims he has 'dishonored all our family' (I, i, 346). When his other sons plead that, since Mutius 'died in honor', he should be allowed a place in the family tomb, Titus most grudgingly allows it, but comments 'To be dishonored by my sons in Rome!' (I, i, 386). When the decent Bassianus attempts to defend Titus to the evil Saturninus, Titus stops him:

> leave to plead my deeds;
> 'Tis thou and those that have dishonored me.
> Rome and the righteous heavens be my judge,
> How I have loved and honored Saturnine!
>
> (I, i, 425–8)

Saturninus, hypocritically pretending that he has been robbed of Lavinia, has the gall to protest to Tamora:

> What, madam! Be dishonored openly,
> And basely put it up without revenge?
>
> (I, i, 433–4)

These Romans are everywhere and continuously invoking 'honor' (the word occurs at least seventeen times), not least when they are committing some cruel and ruthless deed. Contrariwise, any attempt at a decent or just deed is said by one man or other to 'dishonor' him. Clearly something has gone hopelessly wrong with the very concept of 'honor'; not only has it been devalued and emptied out of any positive value or meaning—it has been perverted, indeed at times inverted. It will not be long before Falstaff is famously asking 'what is this honor?' and we will be hearing much about 'honor' in later plays by Shakespeare. But, from the start, Roman honour is made to seem a twisted, deviant thing.

Act II starts with a shock—the black Aaron standing alone in front of the palace in Rome. We have seen the northern barbarian—the Goth—made 'incorporate' in Rome, and now here is the southern barbarian—the Moor—in the same city. He immediately announces his determination to 'wanton' with Tamora, the new queen of Rome, and cause the 'ship-wrack' of the whole state. Aaron, of course, is *the* villain—lustful, infinitely sadistic, delighting in the cruellest tricks and stratagems (for example, persuading Titus to cut off his hand in the deluded belief it will save the life of his son), incapable of remorse and completely committed to evil. Characteristically, he says such things as 'Aaron will have his soul black like his face' (III, i, 205) and:

> But, I have done a thousand dreadful things
> As willingly as one would kill a fly,

> And nothing grieves me heartily indeed,
> But that I cannot do ten thousand more.
>   (V, i, 141–4)

and

> If one good deed in all my life I did,
> I do repent it from my very soul . . .
>   (V, iii, 189–90)

We may find the racist implications disturbing, but Aaron's soul is meant to seem of the same 'hue' as his body—'Spotted, detested, and abominable' (II, iii, 74). He takes such a ghoulish pleasure in committing or arranging atrocities that some people have claimed to find him a comic figure—and indeed, faced with the horrors he contrives, that may be the more comfortable strategy. But I doubt that was how it struck the Elizabethan audience, and I'm not sure it should us. Certainly, he is an extreme and in some ways crudely outlined figure (probably owing something to Marlowe's Barabas), but as Titus is an early Lear, so Aaron foreshadows Iago (there is a premonitory hint of this when on one occasion he threatens 'I'll speak no more but "Vengeance rot you all!"'—V, i, 58). He is an embodiment of that phenomenon, awesome to Shakespeare, of almost motiveless and utterly uncontainable evil, though Shakespeare does add one rather surprising touch —Aaron's devotion to his illegitimate child by Tamora. There is no such blurring of the figure of Iago.

After the solo appearance of Aaron at the start of Act II, we move to 'A forest near Rome'. Shakespeare was to make much of the juxtaposition of the different realms of court and forest (or city and country), and in this play, where Rome was undoubtedly dominated by men and 'law' and ceremony, the forest offers the release of the barbarous—it is dominated by Tamora and Aaron, the woman and the savage, and is the place of lustful sexuality and the hunting of animals, literal and metaphorical. The occasion is a supposedly celebratory panther hunt. And here again, Shakespeare seems to be adding a deliberate anachronism, or non-historical incongruity, for his own purposes—there was no panther-hunting in ancient Rome. But it enables him to relate the literal pursuit of animals to all the sexual pursuit going on ('as if a double hunt were heard at once,' as Tamora says), and have them converge horribly on the 'doe', Lavinia, who is first ravished, then hideously mutilated. The forest is the ideal realm for Aaron's operations. As he says:

> The Emperor's court is like the House of Fame,
> The palace full of tongues, of eyes, and ears:
> The woods are ruthless, dreadful, deaf, and dull . . .
> (II, i, 126–8)

It is there he can 'wanton' with Tamora, and it is there he digs the pit which will fatally trap Quintus and Marcus. That pit itself becomes the image of frightening female sexuality, as is made tolerably explicit:

> What subtle hole is this,
> Whose mouth is covered with rude-growing briers,
> Upon whose leaves are drops of new-shed blood . . .
> (II, iii, 198–200)

It is also described as 'this detested, dark, blood-drinking pit' and 'this fell devouring receptacle' (II, 111, 224, 235); and while one part of the forest is full of animal life, in the dark part where there is the 'abhorred pit', as sexual and fecund Tamora says—'here nothing breeds' (II, iii, 96). That Shakespeare felt a nausea, a fear, at certain aspects of female sexuality becomes clear in later plays. But here, thus early, he identifies or equates this kind of ravenous, negative female sexuality—it 'devours' rather then 'breeds'—with treachery, murder, death.

Thus the forest is made to appear the complete opposite of the city. And yet, perhaps not quite so, either. The Capitol has its murders, and the palace has its 'wantonness' and irrational cruelties, as we have seen. Limbs are 'lopped' in Rome as they are, less 'ceremoniously', in the 'ruthless, vast, and gloomy woods', as Titus describes the forest (IV, i, 53). Confronted with the appalling spectacle of the tongueless, handless Lavinia, ravished and maimed in the dark part of the forest, the good Marcus asks:

> O, why should nature build so foul a den,
> Unless the gods delight in tragedies?
> (IV, i, 59–60)

But you cannot blame tragedy on terrain, and, as in *King Lear,* the invoked 'gods' are not remotely in evidence. It is *men* who 'foul' the den.

The rest of the play takes place in Rome, mainly in or near the house of Titus—though there is a scene on 'a plain near Rome'. We watch the intensification and acceleration of the horrors visited on Titus and his family (through the devices of Aaron and Tamora and the willing participation of Saturninus). We witness the apparent madness of Titus as the multiplication of atrocities passes way beyond the bearable. When he is confronted with his mutilated daughter, Lavinia, he reacts with powerful tropes:

> What fool hath added water to the sea,
> Or brought a faggot to bright-burning Troy?
> My grief was at the height before thou cam'st,
> And now like Nilus it disdaineth bounds.
>   (III, i, 68–71)

It is all, simply and literally, *too much*—Titus' grief is as uncontainable as Aaron's evil. Shakespeare was always drawn to the study of what 'disdaineth bounds'—excess of all kinds—and with the image of the rampant, overflowing Nile, we already have an adumbration of his greatest drama of excess—*Antony and Cleopatra.* Marcus, the balanced humane Marcus, laments that 'These miseries are more than may be borne!' (III, i, 243), and Titus' son Lucius refers to his father as 'The woefull'st man that ever lived in Rome!' (III, i, 289). Here again, this is where the tragedy prefigures *King Lear.* But another play, too, when Titus seems to go mad. He shoots arrows to the gods with letters attached, asking for justice and revenge ('There's not a god left unsolicited'). But there is method in his madness for, of course, the arrows and letters fall in Rome, as Saturninus recognizes, 'blazoning our unjustice everywhere . . . As who would say, in Rome no justice were' (IV, iv, 18–20). That is exactly what Titus is saying—he has already called Rome 'a wilderness of tigers', definitively confounding the conventional culture–nature distinctions. But if he is mad—deranged with grief —he is also steely sane. During Tamora's final, grotesque, attempt to trick him (pretending she is 'Revenge, sent from below'), in an aside Titus says:

> I knew them all, though they supposed me mad;
> And will o'erreach them in their own devices . . .
>   (V, ii, 142–3)

This anticipates Shakespeare's most famous character. *Titus Andronicus* is a 'revenge' play and shows some of the crudities of that genre, but by the time Shakespeare has finished transforming that genre, we will have *Hamlet*.

The final Act depicts Titus' revenge, as, in the last ghoulish incident in the play, he serves up to Tamora her sons baked in a pie ('Eating the flesh that she herself hath bred'—V, iii, 62)—a feast, incidentally, described by the unwitting Marcus as 'ordained to an honorable end,/For peace, for love, for league, and good to Rome' (V, iii, 22–3). Honorific terms are by now taking a hiding. The play ends in a rout of deaths and killings (but so does *Hamlet*—'This quarry cries on havoc,' exclaims Fortinbras). More interesting, perhaps, is the spectacle of what we may call the radical shift, or inversion, of allegiance. The great defender and saviour of Rome becomes its most implacable enemy as Titus' son, Lucius, goes off to raise an army of Goths to attack Rome. This, of course, is to be the great theme of Shakespeare's last Roman play, *Coriolanus*. But here it is, from the start. When Lucius is banished, Titus says:

> How happy art thou then,
> From these devourers to be banished!
> (III, i, 57)

Lucius himself has some rather Coriolanus-like lines:

> Lastly, myself unkindly banished,
> The gates shut on me, and turned weeping out,
> To beg relief among Rome's enemies . . .
> I am the turned-forth . . .
> (V, iii, 104–9)

What does it mean, what does it portend, when Rome 'turnsforth' its bravest and most illustrious defender-heroes? When a Goth can say:

> the great Andronicus,
> Whose name was once our terror, now our comfort,
> Whose high exploits and honorable deeds
> Ingrateful Rome requites with foul contempt . . .
> (V, i, 9–12)

Where is the authoritative voice now? With the Goths rather than the Romans? Can a 'terror' so quickly become a 'comfort'—and, presumably, *vice versa*? Here are problems of inversion, reversibility, even inter-changeability, to which Shakespeare was clearly extraordinarily well attuned. Now a Roman, now a Goth—handy-dandy, which is which?

This is not to say that Shakespeare erases all differences between the Romans and Goths, between the city and the forest. There is always the possibility—in patriarchal, cruel, and—yes—'barbarous' Rome—of law, order, stability, degree. Though if Saturninus is Emperor, one feels that Romans might as well head for the forest. But the forest offers *no* possibility of law. The emergence of the ravished and mutilated Lavinia from the forest is an apt image of what the realm encourages and permits. The continuous presence of Marcus—just, rational, decent, humane—is a reminder of what Rome can produce and what it might stand for. If—*if*—it can get the words right, it can, could, be the place and source of honour, virtue, nobility. *If*. At the end, Lucius is the new Emperor of Rome and seems to bespeak or promise a restoration of true justice and order:

> may I govern so,
> To heal Rome's harms and wipe away her woe!
> (V, iii, 147–8)

But the actual, and dramatic, ending has Rome disgorging itself of the body of the female Goth, Tamora, which had been so disastrously 'incorporated' into the city. Rome's ceremony ends here—there are to be no commemorative, funereal rites:

> But throw her forth to beasts and birds of prey.
> Her life was beastly and devoid of pity,
> And being dead, let birds on her take pity.
> (V, iii, 198–200)

But Rome has been shown to be 'devoid of pity'—where was 'mercy' in scene one? The issues are not clear cut, and Shakespeare makes very sure that we see that.

So what of the play as a whole? Famously, Edward Ravenscroft in 1687 described it as 'a heap of rubbish'. It has been described as black comedy, Grand Guignol, and melodrama (by H. B. Charlton, who found in the play no 'inner world' of the characters). Because the particularly horrifying episodes are quite explicitly 'quotations', as it were, from Ovid (Lavinia's mutilation repeats the story of Tereus and Philomena) and Seneca (the children in the pie comes from *Thyestes* out of Aeschylus), Muriel Bradbrook offered the opinion that '*Titus Andronicus* is a Senecal exercise; the horrors are all classical and quite unfelt, so that the violent tragedy is contradicted by the decorous imagery. The tone is cool and cultured in its effect.' I can understand this response, but do not share it. Modern readers will, of course, make up their own minds; but, while the play is marked by harsh oratory rather than the sinuous and subtle speech of psychological revelation, it seems to me to touch on issues of great moment—for the Elizabethans and for us. Not least—what does our Roman heritage—and we in the West are all inheritors of Rome—really comprise and stand for? And—is it possible, ever, to delimit and demarcate the 'barbarous'?

℣ TROILUS AND CRESSIDA (1601–2)

In *Titus Andronicus* 'our Troy, our Rome', are elided; Titus himself is referred to as the 'Roman Hector'. It was easy for Shakespeare to move from Rome to Troy as the two great cities—and their fates—were closely linked in the European imagination. Troy had a particular significance for western Europe since it traced its ancestry back to the Trojans, through Aeneas and Ascanius. According to the legend as recounted by Geoffrey of Monmouth, Brute, the great-grandson of Aeneas, founded London, which was New Troy. The legend of Troy was well known to Elizabethans: eight translations of Homer were available; there was plenty of Trojan material in Ovid's *Metamorphoses*, Chaucer's epic poem *Troilus and Criseyde* was well known, and Shakespeare would also almost certainly have known Henryson's *The Testament of Cresseid,* which offers itself as a sequel to Chaucer and traces out her pitiful life—and death—as a whore after Diomed has tired of her. Before considering the kind of drama Shakespeare made out of this familiar legend, it is important to bear in mind that the many medieval re-tellings of the legend of the Trojan war invariably debased it and degraded the participants. As Phillips puts it: 'the history of Troy in the middle ages is a history of degeneration and debasement' (*The State in Shakespeare,* p. 114). The Greeks in particular were invariably shown in a bad light—'merry Greek' was a pejorative, disparaging term. It is what Helen is called in Shakespeare's play. So it is perhaps not surprising that Shakespeare should choose to dramatize a moment in the war when demoralization and social disintegration—not to say corruption and rottenness—are heavy in the air. There are 'heroes', but heroism degenerates into squalid thuggery. There are 'lovers', but love deliquesces into lubricious promiscuity. The positive graces should be valour and devotion—but 'war and lechery confound all!' (II, iii, 77). Values are everywhere degraded—'soiled' in the language of the play. The root cause of the war is 'the soil of [Helen's] fair rape' (II, ii, 148), and this early oxymoron discolours the whole play, in which what seems fair invariably turns out to be soiled. The 'soilure' (IV, i, 56) of Helen permeates the play, so that even when Troilus maintains that it is a matter of honour for Troy to keep Helen, his metaphor partakes of the general contamination. 'We turn not back the silks upon the merchant/ When we have soiled them' (II, ii, 69–70).

The play starts, rather unusually, with an 'armed Prologue'. His last words are distinctly casual, nonchalant to the point of indifference:

> Like or find fault; do as your pleasures are;
> Now good or bad, 'tis but the chance of war.

In a way, this sets the tone of the play. In the first Act, Pandarus and Cressida are discussing whether or not Troilus has a 'brown'—dark—complexion:

> *Pandarus.* Faith, to say truth, brown and not brown.
> *Cressida.* To say the truth, true and not true.
> (I, ii, 97–8)

What it is to 'say the truth', and whether it is still possible, become matters of some moment. We seem to be tending, sliding, towards a situation, a world, in which things are indifferently 'good or bad', 'true and not true'. When Cressida asks Pandarus if Helenus can fight, his answer perfectly expresses this mood. 'No. Yes, he'll fight indifferent well' (I, ii, 228). A positive compounded with a negative producing—indifference. Good, bad; true, not true; yes, no. 'Tis but the chance of war.

The first scene in the Greek camp opens with Agamemnon summarizing and describing the current state of the army:

> Checks and disasters
> Grow in the veins of actions highest reared,
> As knots, by the conflux of meeting sap,
> Infects the sound pine and diverts his grain
> Tortive and errant from his course of growth.
>
> (I, iii, 5–9)

I will simply note that 'knots' is a word which occurs quite frequently—things, people, are constantly being blocked from following what might seem their natural course; but 'tortive and errant'—twisted and wandering in wrong directions—is a phrase that might fairly be said to apply to the whole play. When, shortly after, in his 'Degree' speech, Ulysses depicts the chaos that follows 'when the planets/In evil mixture to disorder wander', he says that the resultant 'commotion' serves to 'deracinate/The unity and married calm of states/Quite from their fixture' (I, iii, 94–5, 99–101). Troilus thinks that 'Never did young man fancy/With so eternal and so fixed a soul' (V, ii, 163). But there is no 'married calm' in the vortex, or wasteland, stemming from Helen's 'soilure', and nothing is 'fixed' any more in this world. At the very start of the play, we hear this. 'Hector, whose patience/Is as a virtue fixed, today was moved' (I, ii, 4–5). Even Hector. All are 'deracinated' in one way or another—Cressida most visibly, as she is brutally shifted from the Trojan to the Greek camp; but Hector as notably, as he suddenly shifts from one side to the other in the vital debate concerning the keeping or giving up of Helen. Too much of the movement (and thinking and feeling) in this play is 'tortive and errant'.

To return to Agamemnon's opening speech. He says that things have gone wrong ('bias and thwart') since the start of the siege, but that we should regard all these failures as:

> But the protractive trials of great Jove
> To find persistive constancy in men . . .
>
> (I, iii, 21–2)

Here indeed is a question raised by the play—is it possible to find any 'persistive constancy' in men? A constancy that would help to create and ensure stability and continuity—'unity and married calm'—both in individual relationships and the state? It is not to be found in this play, in which there is more discontinuity and instability of character than anywhere else in Shakespeare. Inconstancy is the norm. The one character who shows 'persistive constancy' is Thersites, and it is the constancy of virulent and scabrous negation. Agamemnon likens true constancy to a fine, rare metal. You will not find it if you leave it to Fortune—Fortune, he says, conflates and confounds all values. You need—it is an unusual personification—Distinction.

> Distinction, with a broad and powerful fan,
> Puffing at all, winnows the light away,
> And what hath mass or matter by itself
> Lies rich in virtue and unmingled.
>   (I, iii, 27–30)

Winnowing and straining or distilling are processes referred to more than once, and are connected to one of the great motivating questions of the play. If, in the name of 'Distinction', all the 'light' stuff, the chaff, the rubbish, is blown and winnowed away, will you be left with something solid and of unquestionable value—'rich in virtue and unmingled'? The question applies particularly to people, and one of the disquieting or dismaying—or displeasing—features of this play is the sense one has at the end of the main characters having been winnowed away to nothingness, as though none of them had the requisite 'mass or matter' to persist as on-goingly authentic, reliable human beings throughout the wasting and debilitating travails of the war. Thersites and Pandarus alone retain their original shape, remain what they were—'unmingled' perhaps, but hardly 'rich in virtue'.

Distinction—'distinguishableness', if I may gloss with an ugly but useful word—is visibly, audibly being lost. In his 'Degree' speech, Ulysses maintains:

> Take but degree away, untune that string,
> And hark what discord follows. Each thing meets
> In mere oppugnancy.
>   (I, iii, 109–11)

In the Quarto, 'meets' reads as 'melts' (to be a crucial word in *Antony and Cleopatra*)—I have no wish, and certainly no competence, to adjudicate between the readings. Indeed, ideally one would hear both words, for there is a sense in this play in which 'meeting' in oppugnancy becomes tantamount to 'melting'—it becomes hard to tell one thing from the other. Ulysses continues his vision of a world bereft of degree:

> Force should be right, or rather right and wrong—
> Between whose endless jar justice resides—
> Should lose their names, and so should justice too.
> Then everything include itself in power,
> Power into will, will into appetite,
> And appetite, an universal wolf,
> So doubly seconded with will and power,
> Must make perforce an universal prey
> And last eat up himself.
>
> (I, iii, 116–24)

Right and wrong and justice should lose their names ('Now good or bad, 'tis but the chance of war'), and everything be resolved, dissolved (melted) into the single matter of force, power, will, and self-devouring appetite. And not only ethical categories—most of the main characters effectively 'lose their names' as well, winnowed away by the long attritions of the war. Hector makes a comparable point in the Trojan camp when he answers the impetuous arguments offered by Troilus and Paris for continuing the war:

> The reasons you allege do more conduce
> To the hot passion of distempered blood
> Than to make up a free determination
> 'Twixt right and wrong; for pleasure and revenge
> Have ears more deaf than adders to the voice
> Of any true decision.
>
> (II, ii, 168–73)

In the atmosphere of this war, it no longer seems possible to make a true decision—'a free determination'—between right and wrong. And if this 'distinction' is gone, then clearly all distinctions are at risk.

Of course, differences remain. The Trojans—Hector certainly—seem to retain a vestige of the old heroic code and traces and shreds of a chivalric ideal; they are more courtly and courteous than their adversaries. As Thersites says—'the Grecians begin to proclaim barbarism, and policy grows into an ill opinion' (V, iv, 16–18). When Achilles calls on his gang of Myrmidons to fall on the unarmed Hector, we witness the ultimate debasement, or rather abandonment, of any and every code of conduct—martial or otherwise. Achilles' relish in the foulness of his act is sickening:

> Look, Hector, how the sun begins to set,
> How ugly night comes breathing at his heels.
> Even with the vail and dark'ning of the sun,
> To close the day up, Hector's life is done . . .
> The dragon wing of night o'erspreads the earth . . .
>   (V, viii, 5–8, 17)

It is as though night is falling—the curtain coming down (the play is nearly over)—on whatever values might have operated—in war, in love, in politics and government—in the pre-Christian classical world. Although Hector's magnanimity in sparing Greeks at his mercy—including Achilles—seems like the cherishable remnant of an older and better code, in the current atmosphere it is disparaged as a foolish anachronism. "Tis fair play,' he says to his brother Troilus, who replies—'Fool's play, by heaven, Hector'. Fair is soiled, fair is foolish—it has come to this.

In this great melt-down of distinctions and values, which the play both portends and enacts, questions of value and valuation become of paramount importance. What is this worth? How do you esteem that? What are your grounds for attributing this value, this worth, this price? Is it intrinsic, or in the eye of the beholder, the appraiser, the attributor, the reflector? Here, of course, the debate among the Trojans as to whether to send Helen back to the Greeks is central. Hector is very clear in his own mind—'Let Helen go'. He gives his reasons, and unanswerably good reasons they are. But Troilus invokes 'honor' and pours metaphoric contempt on 'reason'.

> You fur your gloves with reason . . .
> . . . Nay, if we talk of reason,
> Let's shut our gates and sleep! Manhood and honor
> Should have hare-hearts, would they but fat their thoughts
> With this crammed reason.
>   (II, ii, 38, 46–9)

Hector is too intelligent to be rebuffed and beclouded by metaphors, and simply, cogently replies:

> Brother, she is not worth what she doth cost
> The keeping.
>
> (II, ii, 51–2)

At which point, Troilus articulates the central question of the play: 'What's aught but as 'tis valued?' The question implies an extreme relativism in the realm of values (and we may remember that in *Hamlet,* written perhaps one year earlier, Hamlet had delivered himself of the opinion that 'There is nothing good or bad but thinking makes it so'). Troilus is saying, or implying, that there are no intrinsic values, only attributed ones. Coming from a young man who regards himself as exemplifying, as incorporating, an absolute standard of fidelity, this is somewhat inconsistent—but inconsistency prevails in this play. However, at this point, Hector deals firmly with his younger brother's casuistry:

> But value dwells not in particular will.
> It holds his estimate and dignity
> As well wherein 'tis precious of itself
> As in the prizer. 'Tis mad idolatry
> To make the service greater than the god;
> And the will dotes that is attributive
> To what infectiously itself affects,
> Without some image of th' affected merit.
>
> (II, ii, 53–60)

Difficult words (as so often in this tortive and errant play), but Hector is saying that many Trojans, like Troilus, have made 'the service' (of keeping Helen) 'greater than the god' (Helen's own worth). There is, he says, a lot of doting 'attributive' will around, which ascribes value without any objective sense of the thing or person thus evaluated. Mainly Hector wants to assert that something, someone, can be 'precious of itself/As in the prizer'. Simply, there are intrinsic, non-contingent values—values not dependent on the eye of the 'prizer' or appraiser. Things are *not* simply as they are valued. Hector is still capable of making a 'free determination' between right and wrong. Of course Helen should be given back to the Greeks:

> There is a law in each well-ordered nation
> To curb those raging appetites that are
> Most disobedient and refractory.
> If Helen, then, be wife to Sparta's king,
> As it is known she is, these moral laws
> Of nature and of nations speak aloud
> To have her back returned. Thus to persist
> In doing wrong extenuates not wrong,
> But makes it much more heavy. Hector's opinion
> Is this in way of truth.
>
> (II, ii, 180–89)

In way of truth. This is the absolutely crucial moment in the play—is it still possible to think, and speak, and winnow your way down and along to 'truth'? Or is everything now merely a matter of 'opinion'? This is a word which keeps occurring in the play, as if to mock the unitary pretensions of 'truth', until we realize the aptness and accuracy of Thersites' outburst—'A plague of opinion! A man may wear it on both sides like a leather jerkin' (III, iii, 265–6). There is opinion—lots of it—but so far from leading to the 'way of truth', it seems to lead, scatteringly, away from it. You can turn it this way and that way, inside and out; good–bad; right–wrong; true–false—either way, a reversible leather jerkin. Hector is still speaking out for the stabilities of truth against the unpredictable sways and surges of the errant tides of 'opinion'. But if we think we now have a 'fixed' point, we are about to be monumentally disappointed. Hector is about to reverse himself.

Following his statement that 'Hector's opinion / Is this in way of truth'—where for just one moment in the play opinion and truth are at one, identical—he announces:

> Yet ne'ertheless,
> My spritely brethren, I propend to you
> In resolution to keep Helen still . . .
>
> (II, ii, 189–91)

Having clearly perceived and delineated the 'way of truth', Hector suddenly abandons it, swerves away—he 'propends' to the others, a strange

word meaning leans or inclines, a tortive and errant movement and moment indeed. Cressida's rapid metamorphosis from chaste lover to one of
the 'daughters of the game'—under gruesome Grecian mass male pressure,
be it said—is not more swift or surprising than Hector's defection from the
'way of truth'. Of course, Shakespeare had made things impossibly difficult
for himself. He can write against the grain of history, as he often, dazzlingly, does. But even he could not rewrite history. Helen was not given
back, and Troy fell. No way round that. Hector's arguments cannot prevail
if the play is to remain within the plausible limits of the legend. What
Shakespeare can show in this extraordinary moment in which, for one last
time, truth is unanswerably articulated and asserted, and then haplessly
abandoned, is that truth, and a free determination of right and wrong, are
prime casualties of the war.

After this putting aside of 'truth' it is perhaps not surprising that things
and people are no longer regarded as 'precious of themselves' but only in
the eye of the 'prizer' or appraiser. There is much discussion—centred
on Achilles who hopes to keep his fame while refusing to fight—as to the
extent to which fame and value are essentially reflective. A man, says
Ulysses:

> Cannot make boast to have that which he hath
> Nor feels not what he owes but by reflection . . .
> (III, iii, 98–9)

Achilles takes the point:

> What the declined is
> He shall as soon read in the eyes of others
> As feel in his own fall . . .
> (III, iii, 76–8)

This means, of course, a complete externalization of value—it is completely
in the eye of the beholder, and for that eye to confer or withhold. And, indeed, an ephemeralization of value—'The present eye praises the present
object' (III, iii, 179). It is as if nothing (no one) can any longer be something
(someone) in and for itself. Through time. No wonder they are all winnowed away. Ulysses comments to Achilles:

> Nature, what things there are
> Most abject in regard and dear in use!
> What things again most dear in the esteem
> And poor in worth ...
>
> (III, iii, 127–30)

Abject, poor, dear—worth, esteem, use: this is the shifting value-lexicon of the play. At one end of the spectrum there is a lot of merchant talk (particularly among the Greeks) using terms concerned with prices, weights, measures—scruples, little characters, ounces, counters, spans, inches, fractions, orts, etc. At the other end, there is a more metaphysical language of truth and honour, but that language is as terribly under siege as Troy itself, and even sooner to be undermined. When Cressida is handed over to the Greeks, Troilus urges and warns Diomedes to value her in absolute, soaring terms. Diomedes replies: 'I'll answer to my lust ... To her own worth/She shall be prized' (IV, iv, 133–4). Once she is surrounded and serially kissed by the merchant-macho Greek 'prizers' (hints of a gang rape there), we can imagine what that 'worth' will be, and how it will be esteemed. Diomedes will answer to his lust. Ominous.

Troy–Greece; chivalry–barbarism; it looks, at the beginning, as if some such simple dualism and polarity is to be envisaged—and to an extent something of that remains. The Greeks, certainly, are the real bastards of the play. But there is, throughout, too much 'commixtion' to sustain any sense of simple divisions and oppositions. When, as the result of the rather foolish challenge to single combat, Hector is to confront Ajax, Trojan Aeneas says:

> This Ajax is half made of Hector's blood,
> In love whereof half Hector stays at home;
> Half heart, half hand, half Hector comes to seek
> This blended knight, half Troyan, and half Greek ...
>
> (IV, v, 83–6)

—blended, melted, it is difficult to sort things out into stable oppositional —Troy–Greece—categories. As Hector himself recognizes (speaking to Ajax):

The obligation of our blood forbids
A gory emulation 'twixt us twain.
Were thy commixtion Greek and Troyan so
That thou couldst say, 'This hand is Grecian all,
And this is Troyan; the sinews of this leg
All Greek, and this all Troy; my mother's blood
Runs on the dexter cheek, and this sinister
Bounds in my father's,' by Jove multipotent,
Thou shouldst not bear from me a Greekish member
Wherein my sword had not impressure made
Of our rank feud.

(IV, v, 121–31)

But it cannot be done. You cannot say of a person's body—or temperament, or being—that's the Trojan bit and that's the Greek bit. I'll reject this, save that. We are all, put it this way, Trojan–Greek compounds or 'commixtions', and, going by this play, not the much better off for it.

All of this makes the question of 'identity' a troubling matter (you may be as much of a Trojan as a Greek, but you have to take sides). People seem endlessly uncertain as to other people's identities. Who are you? Who is that? Is that so-and-so? Are you so-and so? Such questions are asked more in this play than in any other of Shakespeare's works. Even self-identity is in doubt. An early exchange:

Pandarus. Well, I say Troilus is Troilus

Cressida. Then you say as I say, for I am sure he is not Hector.

Pandarus. No, nor Hector is not Troilus in some degrees.

Cressida. 'Tis just to each of them; he is himself.

Pandarus. Himself? Alas, poor Troilus, I would he were.

Cressida. So he is.

Pandarus. Condition, I had gone barefoot to India.

Cressida. He is not Hector.

Pandarus. Himself? No, he's not himself. Would 'a were himself.

(I, ii, 66–78)

There is a good deal of splitting of the self in the play—these days we would, of course, refer to the divided self. A simple example is provided by warriors meeting during a truce. Aeneas greets Diomedes very courteously, but says—when we meet on the field, I will inflict all possible damage on you. That is absolutely all right by Diomedes:

> The one and other Diomed embraces.
> Our bloods are now in calm, and, so long, health!
> But when contention and occasion meet,
> By Jove, I'll play the hunter for thy life
> With all my force, pursuit, and policy.
>   (IV, i, 14–18)

Which encounter prompts Paris to comment:

> This is the most despiteful gentle greeting,
> The noblest hateful love, that e'er I heard of.
>   (IV, i, 32–4)

These are the oxymorons of war, and in the event it is the gentleness and nobleness that go under, while spite and hate triumph. But it is the splitting occasioned by this war—'the one and other'—I want briefly to stay with. And while all the main characters are split—divided, fractured, fragmented —in various ways, the crucial figure is Cressida.

This play is one of three by Shakespeare which has for its title the names of a pair of lovers (*Romeo and Juliet* and *Antony and Cleopatra* are the others). In fact, by the most generous estimate, barely one third of the play directly concerns the doomed lovers—and perhaps Shakespeare has not quite managed to make the private erotic affair fruitfully and illuminatingly coalesce with the public matters of the war—though clearly he wants to show love and war, or the erotic and martial, as inseparably intertwined. This is a play about the Trojan war, but still, the tragically split Cressida is central to the play, and she is aware of latent instabilities and divisions within herself, almost from the start:

> I have a kind of self resides with you;
> But an unkind self, that itself will leave
> To be another's fool. I would be gone.
> Where is my wit? I know not what I speak.
>   (III, ii, 149–52)

There is a kind of hapless honesty about Cressida. Secure in Troy, there is no reason to doubt that she would have been sincerely faithful to Troilus; but in a new, alien, context, with new pressures, fears, needs, importunities, other aspects of her self, or other selves, emerge (for which of us would that not be the case?). Troilus seems to have some intimation of possible danger ahead:

> But something may be done that we will not;
> And sometimes we are devils to ourselves
> When we will tempt the frailty of our powers,
> Presuming on their changeful potency.
>   (IV, iv, 94–7)

All this leads up to the crucial speech by Troilus when he actually witnesses Cressida being unfaithful with Diomedes:

> This she? No, this is Diomed's Cressida.
> If beauty have a soul, this is not she;
> If souls guide vows, if vows be sanctimonies . . .
> If there be rule in unity itself,
> This was not she. O madness of discourse,
> That cause sets up with and against itself:
> Bifold authority, where reason can revolt
> Without perdition, and loss assume all reason
> Without revolt. This is, and is not, Cressid.
> Within my soul there doth conduce a fight
> Of this strange nature that a thing inseparate
> Divides more wider than the sky and earth;
> And yet the spacious breadth of this division
> Admits no orifex for a point as subtle
> As Ariachne's broken woof to enter.
> Instance, O instance, strong as Pluto's gates;
> Cressid is mine, tied with the bonds of heaven.
> Instance, O instance, strong as heaven itself;
> The bonds of heaven are slipped, dissolved, and loosed,
> And with another knot, five-finger-tied,
> The fractions of her faith, orts of her love,

The fragments, scraps, the bits, and greasy relics
Of her o'ereaten faith, are given to Diomed.
                    (V, ii, 134–57)

There should be one Cressida—'a thing inseparate'—but she seems to
have 'divided' into Troilus' Cressida and Diomedes' Cressida. There should
be 'rule in unity' (i.e. one cannot equal two) but in the case of Cressida one
has become two. Hence Troilus finds himself pushed to the ontologically
impossible conclusion—'This is, and is not, Cressid.' As he experiences
it, there is a madness seeping into language itself: 'O madness of discourse,/That cause sets up with and against itself: Bifold authority'. Language seems to be going in opposite directions at the same time—with and
against itself; bifold authority—an authority which upholds and refutes at
the same time. Such is the double, self-contradictory, authority operative in
this play.

It is particularly horrifying and unacceptable to Troilus that the bonds
which tied Cressida to him and which should be absolute—'strong as
heaven itself'—'are slipped, dissolved, and loosed'. Bonds were holy things
for Shakespeare, too 'intrince t'unloose' (*Lear* II, ii, 77). If they do not hold,
nothing else holds. And in this play, nothing else does. It is notable that
Troilus, in his understandable nausea, thinks of Cressida's 'love' with
Diomedes in terms of unpleasant leftovers—'greasy relics of her o'ereaten
faith'. In a play in which rampant appetite is allowed free rein, it is hardly
surprising that so many of the activities and processes are likened to eating,
with taste constantly sickening over into distaste. From the start, love, or
rather sex, is made a kitchen matter—'He that will have a cake out of the
wheat must tarry the grinding' (I, i, 15). Reputation in war is, likewise, a
table matter: 'For here the Trojans taste our dear'st repute/With their fin'st
palate' (I, iii, 337–8). War is a ravenous glutton—'what else dear that is con-
sumed/In hot digestion of this cormorant war' (II, ii, 5–6). So is Time—
'A great-sized monster of ingratitudes./Those scraps are good deeds past,
which are devoured/As fast as they are made' (III, iii, 147–9). (In this play,
time is only and always 'injurious'—in other plays, 'mature' or 'ripe' time
can be an agent of restoration, regeneration, renewed continuities. It is what
always defeats evil when it seems that nothing else can. But in this play—it
is part of its bleakness—time is only a gobbler-up, a destroyer. 'What's past
and what's to come is strewed with husks/And formless ruin of obliv-

ion;/But in this extant moment...' (IV, v, 165–7). These Trojans and Greeks live only in the 'extant moment'—and it is desolating.) Agamemnon tells Achilles that virtues left unused 'like fair fruit in an unwholesome dish,/Are like to rot untasted' (II, iii, 122–3). But perhaps the most important food is honey, associated from the first with Helen, and by implication with the lubricious pleasures of sex. There is one scene in Priam's palace in which Helen ('honey-sweet'), Paris and Pandarus bandy innuendoes and the word 'sweet' is used seven times (II, i). By which time it has come to sound, and feel, distinctly sickly, sickening. One rather sympathizes with a later, spitting comment from Thersites—'"Sweet," quoth 'a! Sweet sink, sweet sewer' (V, i, 79). In the epilogue by Pandarus, added later, he refers to the time when a bee loses 'his honey and his sting' and 'Sweet honey and sweet notes together fail' (V, x, 45). As they have failed in this play. The play was to have ended with Troilus' line—'Hector is dead; there is no more to say' (V, x, 22). But Shakespeare decided there was just a little more to say, and he lets Pandarus say it. It is a speech about brothels, prostitution, venereal disease, and his own imminent death. No other play ends with such an unpleasant gesture to the audience:

> Till then I'll sweat and seek about for eases,
> And at that time bequeath you my diseases.
>
> (V, x, 55–6)

It is a strange play, and in many ways a sour and abrasive one. Any intimations of grace and a return to normal human life are ruthlessly excluded. It is easy to agree with Brockbank that there is 'no sense of betrayal of an heroic and chivalric tradition, for of that there were no glimpses', and his summing up seems apt: 'Love's infinity, heroic glory, and universal harmonies of state have only a transient visionary and verbal validity in a world that has lost touch with the values by which it pretends to live' (*On Shakespeare*, p. 10). There is little physical action in the play—Cressida goes to bed with Troilus, Hector is murdered. Most of the time, in both camps, is taken up with debate. Some scholars see this as supporting the theory that it was written for the Inns of Court, with its forensically sophisticated audience in mind. Certainly a lot of the rhetoric is strangely formal, intricate, hyperbolic. At the height of his anguish, Troilus uses words like 'recordation', 'esperance', 'deceptious' (V, ii, 113–21); wooing Cressida intensely he says things like—'What makes this pretty abruption? What too curious dreg espies my sweet lady in the fountain of our love?' (III, ii, 65–7)—which is oddly elaborate, to say the least. The language usage ranges from the smooth political orations of Ulysses (often founded on banalities, clichés, and tautologies), to the snarling, splenetic invective of Thersites—'all the argument is a whore and a cuckold' (II, iii, 75); '—nothing but lechery! All incontinent varlets!' (V, i, 103). We must allow Thersites the validity and consistency of his perspective, but he is too biliously predictable to merge as the reliable voice of the play. There is no such voice. Interestingly, Thersites and Ulysses never meet and confront each other. Perhaps these are two discourses which can just run on, uninterruptedly, forever. Perhaps too there is a sense in which the play is an experiment in language and its possibilities—certainly, the characters seem to stand a long way from us, and hardly engage us as characters in Shakespeare's other plays do. Nevertheless it is a disturbing and disconsolating experience as Shakespeare shows us, as only Shakespeare could, how war devours everything.

 JULIUS CAESAR (1599)

Plutarch's *Parallel Lives* of twenty-three Romans and twenty-three Greeks (as translated by North in 1579 from Amyot's French) was probably the most important book Shakespeare read from the point of view of his playwriting. (Terence Spencer reminds us that it was no easy undertaking—he would have had to pore over more than a thousand pages in a very large and heavy folio volume.) No play owes as much to Plutarch's *Lives* (*Life of Caesar, Life of Brutus, Life of Antonius*) as *Julius Caesar*—all the matters of substance, most of the events, many of the details, and indeed quite a number of lines, are transcribed directly from Plutarch. Of course, Shakespeare made additions, modifications, amplifications, and crucial shifts in interpretative emphasis, and in the event this play is one of his most searching dramatic explorations of the nature and processes of politics and power. But so close does the play seem to Plutarch that I want to start by quoting a number of passages from his work, as a prelude, perhaps, to appreciating what Shakespeare did with his source material.

Plutarch was a Greek philosopher, writing in the latter half of the first century AD. His preference was for republican ideals. In Spencer's words: 'The triumph of the monarchical principle was something that Plutarch, a Greek philosopher who looked back on the past of his own country and its brilliant small city-states with admiration and a kind of sentimental regret, detested although he saw its inevitability.' He regarded Caesar as the cause of the downfall of the Roman republic. And yet, many positive features emerge from his account of Caesar:

> the Romans, inclining to Caesar's prosperity and taking the bit in the mouth, supposing that to be ruled by one man alone, it would be a good mean for them *to take breath a little, after so many troubles and miseries as they had abidden in these civil wars, they chose him perpetual dictator* ... And now for himself, after he had ended his civil wars, he did so honorably behave himself, that there was no fault to be found in him ...

The italicized words apply exactly to the Elizabethans, worn out after the Wars of the Roses and the power-struggles of Catholics and Protestants under Edward VI and Mary, and glad to be 'ruled by one *woman* alone'. And we should remember that Brutus finds no actual fault with Caesar. Furthermore, Caesar treated the people with paternalistic fondness and respect:

> Now Caesar immediately won many men's good wills at Rome, through his eloquence in pleading of their causes, and the people loved him marvellously also, because of the courteous manner he had to speak to every man, and to use them gently, being more *ceremonius* therein than was looked for in one of his years. Furthermore, he ever kept a good board ...

Almost Caesar's first words are 'Set on, and leave no ceremony out' (I, ii, 11) and I shall be returning to the word I have italicized. We shall also catch a very significant glimpse of Caesar keeping that 'good board'.

So wherein did he offend? Well, there was the nature of his last 'triumph into Rome' (with which the play begins). A reminder of a little actual history might help here. Caesar had defeated Pompey at Pharsalus in 48 BC, and now he has returned from his final triumph over Pompey's sons in Spain in 45 BC. This made him sole dictator; more beneficially, it ended the factional strife which had marred and disturbed civil life under the Republic. But is it true that, with this victory and consolidation of Caesar as dictator, the citizens lost all their power and the Senatorial party lost much of its? Plutarch sees this as a bad moment. 'But the triumph he made into Rome for the same did as much offend the Romans, and more, than any thing that ever he had done before: because he had not overcome captains that were strangers, nor barbarous kings, but had destroyed the sons of the noblest man of Rome, whom fortune had overthrown.' But—for Plutarch —there was worse. 'But the chiefest cause that made him mortally hated was the covetous desire he had to be called king: which first gave the people just cause, and next his secret enemies honest colour, to bear him ill will . . . they could not abide the name of a king, detesting it as the utter destruction of their liberty.' Given his republican sympathies, Plutarch seems more on the side of Brutus, to whom he gives all the Roman virtues—he was noble minded, lowly, virtuous, valiant, and so on. He ascribes to him only the purest and highest of motives for killing Caesar. Yet Plutarch also gives us a troubled Brutus: 'when he was out of his house, he did so frame and *fashion* his countenance and looks that no man could discern he had anything to trouble his mind. But when night came that he was in his own house, then he was clean changed: for either care did wake him against his will when he would have slept, or else oftentimes of himself he fell into such deep thoughts of his enterprise, casting in his mind all the dangers that might happen: that his wife, lying by him, found that there was some marvellous great matter that troubled his mind. . .' (my italics). This is all Shakespeare needs to dramatize a crucial split in Brutus between the public and the private man—between the noble, idealistic, Roman, performer; and the tormented, introspecting, insomniac, individual. And he will make devastating use of that word 'fashion'. Plutarch certainly lends no nobility to the actual killing of Caesar—quite the reverse: 'Caesar . . . was hacked and mangled among them, as a wild beast taken of hunters.' In the play Brutus tries to make a 'sacrifice' out of the deed, but Plutarch's description is definitive. And after the assassination, in Plutarch's description, Caesar's 'great prosperity and good fortune that favoured him all his lifetime, did continue afterwards in the revenge of his death, pursuing the murtherers both by sea and land, till they had not left a man more to be executed, all of them that were actors or counsellers in the conspiracy of his death'. Only, in Shakespeare, it is not Caesar's 'good fortune' which 'did continue after-ward'—but his 'spirit'.

It has also to be remembered that, by Shakespeare's time, Caesar and Brutus had acquired symbolic identities in the popular imagination; they were seen as representative world-historical figures who embodied respec-tively—I simplify—the monarchical (and imperial) principle, and the re-publican ideal. It is undeniable that the numerous references to Caesar in Shakespeare's other plays treat him almost without exception with admira-tion, if not with something more. We may take one example, from *Hamlet* which refers to

> the most high and palmy state of Rome,
> A little ere the mightiest Julius fell . . .
>
> (I, i, 113–14)

—as if the time of Julius Caesar was regarded as the high point of Roman history. According to Spencer, 'Shakespeare's audience seem to have re-garded Caesar's death as one of the great crimes of history' (idem, p. 20). This is in line with Ernest Schanzer's contention in his essay on the play that 'a large part of the audience were in sympathy with the mediaeval apo-theosis of Caesar'. (And, of course, Dante put Brutus at the bottom of his Inferno.) In the same article however, Schanzer reminds us that during the Renaissance there were also divided and ambivalent readings of the two men—Caesar as boastful tyrant, Brutus as liberator and patriot. As we have seen, there are detectable ambivalences in Plutarch himself. It is certainly true that by the sixteenth century a number of writers openly admired Bru-tus, and his reputation seems to have increased after Shakespeare's time—understandable, perhaps, as the monarchical principle faded and waned. The period of Roman history from Julius Caesar to Augustus was of par-ticular importance for a number of Elizabethan and Renaissance political thinkers to confirm the argument in favour of monarchy. As Phillips puts it: 'In the stability which Caesar achieved under his dictatorship, in the civil strife which followed his assassination, and in the peace which returned un-der the imperial rule of Augustus, Tudor theorists found proof that under monarchy states flourish, under divided authority they decline' (op. cit., pp. 172–3). I hope all this gives some slight idea of the wealth and weight of material, and contradictoriness of opinion and interpretation, which Shakespeare could draw on when he turned to write the play he decided to call *Julius Caesar*.

I put it that way because, over the years, some commentators have questioned the appropriateness of naming a play after a character who has such a small part (some 130 lines out of 2,500), and who dies in the middle of the action. We may start from a consideration of this—quite accurate—point. Visibly, audibly, Caesar appears on stage for a shorter period than any other major Shakespearian protagonist. Yet his *name* occurs, re-echoes, throughout the play on *more* occasions than that of any other major protagonist: 211 times to Brutus' 130. This is a non-trivial point. The body goes: the name lives on. Caesar and Brutus both refer to themselves in the third person, as though it were possible to distinguish between, and separate, the self and the name (e.g. Caesar: 'I fear him not./Yet if my name were liable to fear. . .'—I, ii, 198–9). In the final battle at Philippi, for the defeated allies of Brutus it seems as though their names are all that remain to them—Cato: 'I will proclaim my name about the field' (V, iv, 4). Lucilius, to protect his leader, announces to the enemy soldiers—'And I am Brutus, Marcus Brutus, I;/Brutus, my country's friend; know me for Brutus!' (V, iv, 8–9). And, imprisoning the 'name', they think they have caught the man. Perhaps the most important speech in this connection comes from Cassius early on, when he is trying to 'seduce' Brutus to his murderous cause:

> Brutus and Caesar: what should be in that 'Caesar'?
> Why should that name be sounded more than yours?
> Write them together, yours is as fair a name;
> Sound them, it doth become the mouth as well;
> Weigh them, it is as heavy; conjure with 'em,
> 'Brutus' will start a spirit as soon as 'Caesar'.
>   (I, ii, 142–7)

Cassius is a materialist (at this point)—there is nothing in a name. But the mistake articulated in that last line is absolutely central to the play. 'Brutus' does *not* 'start' (raise) 'a spirit'—'Caesar' does. The possible divorce and discrepancy between the 'name' (the concept, the ideal, the image) and the actual thing (person, behaviour, event) is constantly coming to the fore. How lethal this divorce can be is vividly brought out in the short scene in which the plebeians kill Cinna the poet:

> *Cinna.* I am not Cinna the conspirator.
> *Fourth Plebeian.* It is no matter, his name's Cinna; pluck but his name out of his heart, and turn him going.
> (III, iii, 32–5)

Can you pluck out the name without plucking out the heart? No—says the play. The name of 'Rome' and 'Romans' are as constantly heard (seventy-two times) as in *Titus Andronicus,* and I will not try to better the comment of Foakes: 'There is a contrast between the Roman ideal and Romans in action, as is seen in the behaviour of the conspirators and the plebeians, similar to that between the ideal and the living person represented in Caesar and Brutus.' Perhaps the most telling and central dramatized illustration of this split between the bodily self and name (reputation, image) is provided by Antony's vivid evocation of the death of Caesar—of Caesar the man, that is:

> Then burst his mighty heart;
> And, in his mantle muffling up his face,
> Even at the base of Pompey's statue
> (Which all the while ran blood) great Caesar fell.
> O, what a fall was there, my countrymen!
> Then I, and you, and all of us fell down,
> Whilst bloody treason flourished over us.
> (III, ii, 188–94)

The bodily Caesar can fall—we have already had intimations of this in his 'falling sickness'. But while the body falls, the statues of previous great men (here Pompey the Great) stand erect after the death of those they commemorate. Monument, reputation, image, name—spirit—these are phenomena which can outlast corporeal terminations.

What do we gather of the living, speaking Caesar of the first two Acts and from his last speeches before the Capitol? Hazlitt—always a commentator to attend to—found the depiction disappointing. 'We do not much admire the representation here given of Julius Caesar, nor do we think it answers to the portrait given of him in his Commentaries. He makes several vapouring and rather pedantic speeches, and does nothing.' There is some vapour and pedantry in his speeches, but whether he 'does nothing' depends on your sense of action and agency. From one point of view, Caesar, or rather 'Caesar', does almost everything. The play opens with a street festival—Lupercal, a fertility festival which Shakespeare conflates with Caesar's triumph (which actually took place some five months earlier—there are numerous compressions and compactions in this play, a lot of history sometimes being dramatically squeezed into a single day). Apart from giving us our first glimpse of the people or 'commoners'—here quite effervescent and holiday-merry (later to turn mutinous and murderous)—this first scene is most important for the behaviour of the tribunes (representatives of the people and thus on guard against the Senate, never mind 'kings')—Flavius and Marullus. The people have festooned the images of Caesar in the city with 'trophies' (i.e. ornaments in honour of Caesar, not—here—spoils of war), and the tribunes go around stripping them:

> Disrobe the images,
> If you do find them decked with ceremonies.
> . . . let no images
> Be hung with Caesar's trophies.
> (I, i, 67–8, 71–2)

I have mentioned that almost Caesar's first words are 'leave no ceremony out', and after his death Brutus says 'we are contented Caesar shall / Have all true rites and lawful ceremonies' (III, i, 240–1). In these three uses of the word, it means, variously and not mutually exclusively, symbols of state and ritual observances. But the word is used on two other occasions with a different meaning. (The original Latin word—*caeromonia*—means reverence or dread, and in the plural form came to refer to the rituals by which people express or cope with these feelings; also it came to refer to the respect felt for dread-ful portents.) When Cassius expresses his doubt as to whether Caesar will go to the Capitol he says:

> For he is superstitious grown of late,
> Quite from the main opinion he held once
> Of fantasy, of dreams, and ceremonies.

Here the word means portents or omens. It is used in this sense in the next scene when Caesar's wife, Calphurnia, tries to persuade Caesar to remain at home because of her ominous dreams and the terrible prodigies seen in the city the previous night. 'Caesar, I never stood on ceremonies,/Yet now they fright me' (II, ii, 13–14). It is an important part of the movement and atmosphere of the play that Cassius himself, an extreme materialist in the Epicurus line, grows 'superstitious' as his end approaches:

> You know that I held Epicurus strong,
> And his opinion; now I change my mind,
> And partly credit things that do presage.
> (V, i, 76–8)

The play is full of superstition of all kinds—soothsayers, prophets or fortune-tellers, augurers, omens and portents and 'things that do presage'— the 'prodigies' seen during the storm on the night preceding the assassination which seem to show 'a civil strife in heaven', presaging, indeed, a civil strife on earth (most of the prodigies are from Plutarch, be it said), and of course the ghost of Caesar. In respect of this atmosphere of gathering portentousness, one may adopt the sharp, dismissive sanity of Cicero:

> Indeed, it is a strange-disposed time:
> But men may construe things after their fashion,
> Clean from the purpose of the things themselves.
> (I, iii, 33–5)

Or one may hover, awed and respectful, between belief and unbelief. After all, if Caesar had not defied augury and overcome his superstition with some rather bombastic self-grandiloquizing ('Danger knows full well/That Caesar is more dangerous than he . . . Caesar shall go forth'—II, ii, 45, 48) he might well have lived to fight—*and* be crowned—another day. Whether or not Shakespeare believed in ghosts, auguries, prodigies and so on, is nothing to the point. What he unerringly understood was that at a time when some crisis or catastrophic breakdown of the known social order seems or feels imminent, superstition floods the streets. We have seen it in our era in times of war, and it can be seen in California (in suitably ersatz form) any day of the week. That there *are* 'things that do presage'—straws in the wind, hints in the air, signs of things to come—Shakespeare, of course, knew was simply true.

From the start, then, Caesar is associated with 'ceremony'—rituals (with the troubling shadow-meaning of portents), images, symbols, trophies. These, indeed, can all be part of the panoply and mystique of power and hierarchy, but they can also help to maintain and reinforce order, civic regularity, peace—'after so many troubles and miseries as they had abidden in these civil wars'. Caesar is, in the exact Plutarch–North word—'ceremonious'. All these adornments and appurtenances can serve to make Caesar seem almost god-like, and there is no question but that Caesar is approaching this status at the start of the play. The ambiguous cheers of the crowd (reported in scene two) as Caesar is both offered and refuses the crown (*three* times is too loaded to pass unnoticed in a Christian culture), reveals something of Shakespeare's insight into mob psychology. It likes to create heroes, or kings, or gods—but, as we later see, it is as equally willing to tear them down.

The tribunes want to do away with ceremony, symbol, image, and strip Caesar down to the poor, forked, fallible, physical body he undoubtedly is. This is the republican–reductive drive at its crudest—no great men, please. (For their pains, they are 'put to silence'—in view of the brutal eliminations to come, it is worth noting that this may simply mean they lost their jobs as spokesmen for the people.) But we cannot—or at least should not—take the tribunes' view of Caesar. If you strip away *all* the 'ceremonies', it is not clear what might be left to hold the city—the state—together and in order. That Caesar is physically vulnerable even when he is at his most masterful —god-like and imperial—Shakespeare brings out in a little touch which, for once, he did not find in Plutarch. At the end of his wonderfully penetrating and acutely accurate analysis of Cassius, there is a sudden lapse into intimations of mortality:

> Such men as he be never at heart's ease
> Whiles they behold a greater than themselves,
> And therefore are they very dangerous.
> I rather tell thee what is to be feared
> Than what I fear; for always I am Caesar.
> Come on my right hand, for this ear is deaf . . .
>   (I, ii, 208–13)

The deafness is provided by Shakespeare—at our most potent and resplendent, we are already beginning to deteriorate and decay (as the Sonnets everywhere insist). But this is not a matter for contempt—the sort of contempt which Cassius expresses when he describes Caesar shaking like 'a sick girl' when he had a fever in Spain. It is hardly to Caesar's discredit that, whatever else he may be, he is unavoidably corporal and human. Just *what* Caesar is remains, perhaps, something of an enigma. There are various versions of Caesar, ranging from that of the mean and envious Cassius ('he doth bestride the narrow world/Like a Colossus'—I, ii, 135–6) to that of the loyal and loving Antony ('Thou art the ruins of the noblest man/That ever lived in the tide of times'—III, i, 256–7). And there is Caesar's version of himself, not to mention the crowd's Caesar. We only see him as he is constructed—*fashioned*, but I'll come back to that—by others, and by himself. In this connection, it is pertinent to acknowledge that a good deal of his speech (little enough though we hear of it), is self-aggrandizing and self-inflating, somewhat thrasonical and given to self-hyperbolizing. But to suggest that the arrogance of his last speech—

> Yet in the number I do know but one
> That unassailable holds on his rank,
> Unshaked of motion; and that I am he . . .
> (III, i, 68–70)

is sufficient justification for his assassination, as some critics have, seems to me to submit to conspiratorial homicidal intoxication, and identification with Cassius, that 'hot, choleric, and cruel man' (Plutarch). There is one little scene in Caesar's house on the morning of the murder which seems to me crucial—and here we come to what Plutarch called Caesar's 'good board'. Caesar is surrounded with, supposedly his good friends, actually those who will kill him. Before they set out for the Capitol, Caesar says:

> Good friends, go in and taste some wine with me,
> And we (like friends) will straightway go together.

To which, Brutus adds a concluding aside:

> That every like is not the same, O Caesar,
> The heart of Brutus earns to think upon.
>
> (II, ii, 126–9)

Shortly afterwards, in front of the Capitol, Brutus who, as these lines reveal, knows he is only a dissembling friend, says to Caesar—'I kiss thy hand, but not in flattery, Caesar' (III, i, 52). No, not in flattery—in betrayal. After the ceremonial communal wine of the Last Supper, the Judas kiss. At this point, the Elizabethans would surely have known what they were witnessing.

Brutus is a more complex figure. One reading sees him as a noble, idealistic, exemplary Roman who is 'seduced' into the conspiracy by the envious and bloody-minded Cassius (who knows very well that the 'work' he has 'in hand' is 'Most bloody, fiery, and most terrible'—I, iii, 130). Certainly he hopes that 'the great opinion / That Rome holds of his name' (I, ii, 319–20) will give honour and respectability to their enterprise. Just as Casca hopes that:

> that which would appear offense in us,
> His countenance, like richest alchemy,
> Will change to virtue and to worthiness . . .
>
> (I, iii, 158–60)

(In the event, Brutus proves to be a failed alchemist—he cannot transform 'butchery' into 'sacrifice', betrayal into virtue, murder into worthiness.) This view of Brutus was fostered by Plutarch, and Shakespeare is happy enough to take a Plutarchian line for Antony's panegyric over the dead Brutus:

> All the conspirators save only he
> Did that they did in envy of great Caesar;
> He, only in a general honest thought
> And common good to all, made one of them.
>
> (V, v, 69–71)

Did he, now? All Romans seemingly become 'noble' at their death. Brutus calls the vicious Cassius 'the last of all the Romans'; Antony dubs betrayer-murderer Brutus 'the noblest Roman of them all'; Octavius Caesar, in a later play, casts around for some appropriately respectful things to say about Antony whom he always regarded as a hopelessly debauched defector, but, as we shall see, he cannot even be bothered to finish. These encomiastic elegies are formulaic, Roman prescriptions which are, to all intents and purposes, interchangeable. Death can certainly bring dignity in Shakespeare, and it is appropriate at such a moment to let remembered virtues shine while flaws fade. But do not look for the truth of a man—and that includes Brutus—in these conventional orations and exequies.

From the very start, Brutus, by his own account, is 'with himself at war' (I, ii, 46). Cassius offers to be his 'glass', a mirror which:

> Will modestly discover to yourself
> That of yourself which you yet know not of.
>   (I, ii, 69–70)

He *does* know it, as we shall see, but he does not want to know that he knows it. Shakespeare is nowhere more brilliant in this play than in showing the operations and stratagems of self-deception. At the end of the scene, Cassius is content with his work:

> Well Brutus, thou art noble; yet I see
> Thy honorable *mettle* may be *wrought*
> From that it is disposed . . .
> For who so firm that cannot be seduced?
>   (I, ii, 308–10, 312: my italics)

There are a number of references to 'mettle' in the play (the people, not surprisingly, are regarded as 'the basest mettle') and there is always an implicit play on 'mettle' (disposition) and 'metal' (a material which can be 'wrought'). In this play, people can be sharp or blunt or dull, but, more importantly, they can be 'wrought'. The dictionary glosses that as meaning 'fashioned or formed'. It is the past participle of 'work'—another important word in the play. Crowds, of course, can be 'wrought'—now this shape, now that. And so can individuals, as when Brutus says of Caius Ligarius—'Send him but hither, and I'll fashion him' (II, i, 220). The vocabulary bespeaks a manipulative and instrumental—not to say materialistic—view of people, at the least. Perhaps Shakespeare thought this was very 'Roman'—though what price 'honour' and 'nobility' in such metallic people? But there is an even more insidious form of 'fashioning', as emerges in Brutus' first soliloquy. His first words to himself are—'It must be by his death'. That is, deep inside him the decision has been taken—Caesar, his best friend, is to be killed. Make no mistake, this Brutus is a murderer, though not the usual ambitious regicide of other Tudor plays. Now he has to find some reasons for the deed—political imperatives to mask the personal compulsion. Has to find them because—'for my part/I know no personal cause to spurn at him' and 'to speak truth of Caesar,/I have not known when his affections swayed/More than his reason' (II, 1, 10–11, 19–21). So he moves from the indicative tense—Caesar as he *is*—to the subjunctive and conditional, drawing hypothetical scenarios. *If* Caesar is crowned, he '*may* do danger'—'So Caesar *may*' (my italics). Always 'may' is allowed to supplant 'is'. Then this, which is decisive:

> And, since the quarrel
> Will bear no color for the thing he *is,*
> *Fashion* it thus: that what he is, augmented,
> *Would* run to these and these extremities;
> And therefore *think him as* a serpent's egg
> Which hatched, *would* as his kind grow mischievous,
> And kill him in the shell.
>   (II, i, 28–34: my italics)

Fashion it thus—words and arguments are like people, as far as Brutus is concerned; you can mould and shape them to suit, and justify, any ulterior intention. But this perverse substitution of the possible for the actual, is a step into anarchy—of self, and then of state. His own internal anarchy is revealed in a following soliloquy which starts: 'Since Cassius first did whet me against Caesar,/I have not slept' (II, i, 61–2). Note 'whet'—by which Brutus depicts himself as a tool which has been sharpened. He goes on—in a speech which anticipates Macbeth—to describe the 'phantasma' and nightmare inner world he is living in:

> The genius and the mortal instruments
> Are then in council, and the state of a man,

> Like to a little kingdom, suffers then
> The nature of an insurrection.
>
> (II, i, 66–9)

Brutus has been 'at war' with himself since the beginning, and what he effectively does is to extend that inner 'insurrection' to the state at large.

As the conspirators come in with their heads cloaked and concealed—as Portia says, they 'hide their faces / Even from darkness' (II, i, 277–8)—Brutus reveals, by his words, that he is well aware of the evil nature of the deed they are premeditating:

> O conspiracy
> Sham'st thou to show thy dang'rous brow by night,
> When evils are most free? O, then by day
> Where wilt thou find a cavern dark enough
> To mask thy monstrous visage? Seek none, conspiracy;
> Hide it in smiles and affability . . .
>
> (II, i, 77–82)

'Monstrous' is an important word for Shakespeare, indicating something which is in nature, since it is undeniably *there,* but also horribly *un*natural as well. Nature against itself. Brutus could hardly have chosen a more self-incriminating, self-damning, word. He also reveals a Machiavellian streak as he indicates the need for concealment, simulation and dissembling:

> And let our hearts, as subtle masters do,
> Stir up their servants to an act of rage,
> And after seem to chide 'em.
>
> (II, i, 175–7)

Calculated self-manipulation and strategic self-deception—let our hearts goad our hands to the act of murder, then afterwards, 'seem' to reproach them for doing it. What a splitting of the self! No wonder he can't sleep. But perhaps the key metaphor comes from the stage. As the conspirators are dispersing, Cassius says 'show yourselves true Romans', immediately followed by this exhortation from Brutus:

> Good gentlemen, look fresh and merrily.
> Let not our looks put on our purposes,
> But bear it as our Roman actors do,
> With untired spirits and formal constancy.
>   (II, 1, 224–7)

'False face must hide what the false heart doth know,' as Macbeth will say. We have had the stage mentioned before—while Caesar was dallying with the crown, the people, according to Casca, did 'clap him and hiss him, according as he pleased and displeased them, as they use to do the players in the theater' (I, ii, 259–60). After the assassination, in a strange self-conscious moment, Cassius says:

> How many ages hence
> Shall this our lofty scene be acted over
> In states unborn and accents yet unknown . . .

and Brutus: 'How many times shall Caesar bleed in sport' (III, i, 111–14). It seems as if 'true Romans' have to be 'Roman actors' and that public Rome—street, Capitol, Forum—is akin to theatre (Brutus, indeed, refers to 'our performance').

At this moment, in the theatre of Rome, Caesar is bleeding in dead earnest (although of course in the Globe Theatre he is even now bleeding 'in sport'). As the blood 'streams forth' from Caesar's 'wounds'—'rushing out of doors, to be resolved / If Brutus so unkindly knocked, or no,' as Antony remarkably puts it, stirring up the people (III, ii, 181–2)—we seem to have entered a blood storm: 'bloody men' with 'bloody hands' at their 'bleeding business', reducing Caesar to a 'bleeding piece of earth':

> Pardon me, Julius! Here wast thou bayed, brave hart;
> Here didst thou fall, and here thy hunters stand,
> Signed in thy spoil and crimsoned in thy lethe . . .
>   (III, i, 204–6)

and 'all the while' Pompey's statue 'ran blood'.

In the 'play' as Brutus plans it he will act the role of high priest and doctor of the republic—'Let's be sacrificers, but not butchers . . . purgers, not murderers' (II, i, 166, 180)—but Shakespeare knew that Plutarch's hunting image was the right one. Hunters and butchers. In the event, the conspirators fall on Caesar and 'hew him as a carcass fit for hounds' (II, i, 174). There will be blood everywhere—as if still streaming from Caesar's wounds—until the end of the ensuing civil war. As foretold by Antony:

> Over thy wounds now do I prophesy . . .
> Domestic fury and fierce civil strife
> Shall cumber all the parts of Italy;
> Blood and destruction shall be so in use . . .
> And Caesar's spirit, ranging for revenge,
> With Ate by his side come hot from hell,
> Shall in these confines with a monarch's voice
> Cry 'Havoc,' and let slip the dogs of war,
> That this foul deed shall smell above the earth
> With carrion men, groaning for burial.
>   (III, i, 259–75)

This pretty exactly describes the rest of the play, which will be dominated by Caesar's 'spirit', and in which Antony will prove to be one of the fiercest of the 'dogs of war' (his opening words in Act IV—'These many then shall die'—are as, if not more, ominous as Brutus' 'It must be by his death'. By the end, Brutus is more than justified in his comment—'Slaying is the word;/It is a deed in fashion' (V, v, 4–5).

Naively (to be generous), Brutus seems to think that after the assassination, it will be enough if they go into the streets and 'cry "Peace, freedom, and liberty!"' (III, i, 110), as if the republic would somehow run itself, without any structured authority. (However idealistic he may be, Brutus is a disastrously bad practical politician: he does not dispatch Antony; he lets Antony address the people; he insists on the wrong military tactics at Philippi—in all these matters, from a purely political point of view, Cassius is right. That they should quarrel after the assassination, and thus weaken their cause, seems almost inevitable—a case, as I see it, of rogues falling out.) Caesar kept, and represented, a central control of power. In killing him—as a 'tyrant'—Brutus merely releases chaos, anarchy, and civil war as different factions struggle for the masterless power let loose. Brutus has not purged the republic, but destroyed *all* government, and helped to usher in the new tyranny of the triumvirate, which will prove to be far more cruel, oppressive, and terrible than anything associated with the rule (if not reign) of Caesar. (The triumvirate, at first dominated by Antony, kill one hundred senators, including Cicero, and deliberately—nastily—including a number of each others' relatives—thus eliminating the senatorial party. Antony also tries to fiddle Caesar's will. Before Caesar's death, Antony appeared headstrong and passionately loyal—though Cassius knows him for a 'shrewd contriver'. Afterwards he becomes both greedy and barbarous. A dog of war indeed.)

Before the assassination, Brutus says to his fellow conspirators:

> We all stand up against the spirit of Caesar,
> And in the spirit of men there is no blood.
> O, that we then could come by Caesar's spirit,
> And not dismember Caesar! But, alas,
> Caesar must bleed for it.
>
> (II, i, 167–71)

They do dismember Caesar, and he certainly bleeds: but they do not 'come by' his spirit, which escapes and returns to haunt and hunt them—'ranging for revenge' as Antony predicts. Caesar seems to have a terrible posthumous power. Cassius and Brutus both commit suicide with his name on their lips, and Brutus comes to recognize that, indeed, they never did 'come by' his spirit:

> O Julius Caesar, thou art mighty yet!
> Thy spirit walks abroad, and turns our swords
> In our own proper entrails.
>
> (V, iii, 94–6)

'Spirit' is closely associated with 'fire' in this play:

> You are dull, Casca, and those sparks of life
> That should be in a Roman you do want . . .
>
> (I, iii, 57–8)

Cicero, on the other hand, has 'fiery eyes'. Cassius is glad 'That my weak words have struck but thus much show / Of fire from Brutus' (I, ii, 176–7).

During the night of prodigies there is 'a tempest dropping fire' and 'Men, all in fire, walk up and down the streets' (I, iii, 10, 25). It seems as if there is fire, flickering or flaming, all over the place. There are fires of portent; there is literal fire—the plebeians, incited by Antony, go for 'firebrands' crying 'Burn all', while Portia, who eats coals in Plutarch, here simply 'swallowed fire' (IV, iii, 155); and there is inner fire—'new-fired' hearts, the 'hasty spark' of anger, fiery spirits. Clearly, it is preferable to be 'fiery' with Cicero than 'dull' with Casca. But fire is the most dangerous element, spreading rapidly in unpredictable directions, and in this play there is a sense that it has become lethally out of control. And this loss of control is associated with the death of Caesar. After that, the fire rages and 'ranges' along with Caesar's spirit.

The source of fire is, ultimately the sun. There is an odd moment during the night-time meeting of the conspirators when three of them argue just where the sun is rising—'doth not the day break here?' No, there; both wrong, over there is where he 'first presents his fire' (II, i, 101, 110). It is as if they sense that they are standing on the threshold of a new dawn in Roman history, but are not quite sure, as it were, where the fire will be coming from. Nor, by the same token, the direction it will take. At the end, Titinius laments over dead Cassius:

> O setting sun,
> As in thy red rays thou dost sink to night,
> So in his red blood Cassius' day is set.
> The sun of Rome is set. Our day is gone . . .
> (V, iii, 60–63)

The bloody, fiery day of Roman history initiated by Brutus and his followers is over. But another sun is rising.

Octavius Caesar has very few lines in the play—about forty—and comes across as passionless, cold, detached. (It might be mentioned that much of the language in this play is cool, sparing of images, formal—perhaps because the play is dominated by Roman males.) But it is extraordinary how he makes his presence felt. Shakespeare did something very interesting here. In Plutarch, Octavius is sick and does not take part in the battle of Philippi. In Shakespeare, of course, he does; and there is this curiously telling exchange:

> *Antony.* Octavius, lead your battle softly on
>   Upon the left hand of the even field.
> *Octavius.* Upon the right hand I; keep thou the left.
> *Antony.* Why do you cross me in this exigent?
> *Octavius.* I do not cross you; but I will do so.
> (V, i, 16–20)

This calm assertive confidence, at once emotionless and assured, is rather chilling. You begin to realize, as perhaps Antony does—this man is going to run *everything!* Not for nothing does he, literally, have the last word of the play. Shakespeare will show Octavius' sun reach its zenith in his next Roman play. But the atmosphere in that play will be very different. For there we will have Egypt—and Cleopatra.

ANTONY AND CLEOPATRA (1607)

This, from North's translation of Plutarch's *Life of Antonius:* 'For they [Antony and Cleopatra] made an order between them, which they called AMIMETOBION (as much as to say, no life comparable and matcheable with it). Later, they invented another word—SYNAPOTHANUMENON (signifying the order and agreement of those that will die together).' They invented words. That is, from what was available they put together special terms which would apply to them alone—using language as a repository of possibilities, trying to transcend the limitations of the available formulations, re-rehearsing reality by stretching language in new directions and combinations. Shakespeare gloriously takes the hint. His Antony and Cleopatra seem intent on pre-empting language to establish new words to describe their love. New words, new worlds—this is the linguistic atmosphere of the play; ordinary language must be 'melted' (a key word) and reconstituted, so that new propositions and descriptions can be articulated to project and express their emotions. In their speech, everything tends towards hyperbole—i.e. 'excess, exaggeration'. Rhetorically this is related to *Super-*

latio, which a dictionary of rhetorical terms glosses as 'exaggerated or extravagant terms used for emphasis and not intended to be understood literally'. Of course, Antony and Cleopatra do not want to be understood 'literally'—they do not work, or play, or love, or live, by the 'letter'. It is precisely the 'letter', and all fixed alphabetical restrictions, that they talk, and love, to dissolve, so that, as it were, they can live and speak in a 'higher' language of their own inventing. For Antony, to burst his armour and his alphabet are, alike, related modes of energy moving towards transcendence.

In his introductory *Lectures on Philosophy,* Hegel wrote that 'alphabetic writing is in itself and for itself the most intelligent'; he also wrote 'everything oriental must be excluded from the history of philosophy'. Alphabetic writing is transparent, an instrument of clarity, it maintains the unity of consciousness; the oriental thus becomes an opaque script, another, more iconic, language altogether, another mode of writing and thus of being-in-the-world, which threatens to disturb and disrupt, even destroy, the alphabetic clarity of consciousness. We can apply this opposition to the play. Caesar is nothing if not 'alphabetic'. He instructs Taurus and his army as he hands out his written orders before the battle of Actium—'Do not exceed / The prescript of this scroll' (III, viii, 4–5). He never deviates from exact 'pre-scriptions'—the already written—and lives by and from within the orderings of his 'scroll'. Cleopatra, on the other hand, is quintessentially oriental—in Hegel's terms: her actions, like her temperament, are impossible to 'read' in any alphabetic way. She is, from Caesar's point of view, illegible; hardly to be 'read' in his Roman language. She is an ultimate opacity —from Rome's point of view—confounding all customary alphabetic descriptions and decodings. She is in no way 'prescribed' or prescribable, and can no more be held within Caesar's 'scroll' than she can be trapped by his plots and policies.

But first, let me turn to the question of armour, the steel second skin of the man, the soldier, the Roman. As so often in Shakespeare, the opening lines set up terms and problems which will reverberate throughout the play. Philo, a Roman soldier with Antony in Egypt, opens:

> Nay, but this dotage of our general's
> O'erflows the measure.

(I, i, 1–2)

The play, unlike any other by Shakespeare, opens with a negative. It thus implies the denial of a previous assertion—perhaps more affirmative—and his speech goes on to negate, or attempt to degrade and belittle, Antony's behaviour since he has been in Egypt. 'Overflowing the measure' immediately opposes the flooding Nile of Egypt to the concept of 'measure'—control, constraint, containment—which is the very language of Rome. The contest of the play is to be between overflow (excess) and measure (boundaries). Philo goes on to describe the transformation—or rather, in his terms, the deformation—of Antony the soldier into Antony the 'strumpet's fool', the victim of 'lust'. Philo always chooses the diminishing, pejorative word when referring to anything to do with Cleopatra and Egypt, anything which is not connected with Rome, Mars, and the 'office and devotion' of the warrior's code. Thus it is that he goes on to recall the great *soldier* Antony, to contrast him with the man who now serves Eros and Venus–Cleopatra. Again, his terms anticipate much that is to follow:

> His captain's heart
> Which in the scuffles of great fights hath burst
> The buckles on his breast, reneges all temper
> And is become the bellows and the fan
> To cool a gypsy's lust.
>
> (I, i, 6–10)

In battle, then, Antony could not be confined within his own armour; such was his force and energy that it broke out of his soldier's attire—it burst the buckles. Now his great heart 'reneges all temper'—renounces all restraint—but it is clear that it is not finally possible for Antony to be held within any 'temper', any restraints, or, indeed, any bonds. To be sure, he occasionally tries to stay within Roman rules; but in whatever he does—in war, in love—he is driven to burst whatever is 'buckling' him.

In Act IV, Antony is preparing for battle and calls for his armour. The aptly named Eros (as in Plutarch) brings it; but Cleopatra wants to help. She thus becomes, in Antony's words, 'the armourer of my heart' as she fastens the buckles and asks—'Is this not buckled well?' Antony:

> Rarely, rarely:
> He that unbuckles this, till we do please
> To daff't for our repose, shall hear a storm.

Thou fumblest, Eros, and my queen's a squire
More tight at this than thou.
                        (IV, iv, 11–15)

Armour—amour: there is no etymological connection, but phonetically the
words are close. And what we see here, with Cleopatra buckling Antony's
armour, almost while they are still in bed, is an overlaying of amour onto
armour, so that the armour is eroticized and sensualized—the *business* of
war (often referred to) here subsumed into the more all-embracing game of
love. (By contrast, we may say that any sensuality and physicality of love
and play is 'armoured' by Caesar and Rome: there the policy of war tries to
subsume love's body, making marriage and mating into mere instruments
of policy.) Antony's armour, erotically saturated by the hands of Cleopatra,
will not be taken off, he says, 'till we do please to daff't for our repose'. This
anticipates his death.

As he moves towards that death, Antony says to Eros:

Sometime we see a cloud that's dragonish,
A vapor sometime like a bear or lion . . .
. . . Thou hast seen these signs:
They are black vesper's pageants . . .
That which is now a horse, even with a thought
The rack dislimns, and makes it indistinct
As water is in water.
                        (IV, xiv, 2–11)

'Dis-limn'—that is, un-paint, efface—is Shakespeare's own invention; it is
part of the 'reversal' which is happening to Antony, whose role in the 'pageant' (which also meant a mobile play or stage) is nearly over. He is moving
towards 'indistinctness'—he, the man of the greatest 'distinction' in the
world: he is being physically 'dis-limned' (which sounds the homophone
'dislim*b*ed'), effaced by Caesar, by nature, by himself. (Cleopatra will 'paint'
him again after his death, but we will come to that dazzling act of retrieval
and recuperation.) Antony continues:

My good knave Eros, now thy captain is
Even such a body: here I am Antony,
Yet cannot hold this visible shape . . .
                        (IV, xiv, 12–14)

He is in fact moving towards physical invisibility, because Antony, the name, the individual, the specific and world-famous identity, can no longer 'hold' onto his bodily shape. He is moving out, moving through, moving beyond; melting, but also transcending the final barrier—the body itself. And so *he* takes his armour off, since he is indeed ready for 'repose':

> Unarm Eros. The long day's task is done,
> And we must sleep . . .
>   Off, pluck off:
> The sevenfold shield of Ajax cannot keep
> The battery from my heart. O, cleave, my sides!
> Heart, once be stronger than thy continent,
> Crack thy frail case! Apace, Eros, apace.
> No more a soldier. Bruised pieces, go;
> You have been nobly borne . . .
>   (IV, xiv, 35–43)

The armour is not broken or burst, but discarded; it is almost as though he is taking his body to pieces and throwing it away—'Bruised pieces, go' does seem almost to refer to the body as well, for it is that 'frail case' which he now wishes to burst free from. The body is the final boundary.

Boundary; bounty; bound; bond; band—these are words of varying importance in the play, but they all serve to set up a crucial series of echoes, half-echoes, indeed anti-echoes, if one can imagine such a thing. Rome is the place of bonds (Caesar: 'I know it for my bond'); and bounds ('He's bound unto Octavia,' the luckless messenger tells Cleopatra); and bands (Caesar says to Octavia—'prove such a wife . . . as my farthest band / Shall pass on thy aproof'). It is also the place of 'hoops' and 'knots' (in relation to the problem of what can bind Caesar and Antony together), and of 'squares', 'rules', and 'measures'. Antony tries to make a return to this Roman world, but no matter what 'bonds' he enters into, no matter how much he intends to try to live 'by the rule', it is, for him, finally not possible. This is not because he is a traitorous man, making and breaking promises for devious purposes. He simply cannot, as we say, be held 'within bounds'. When he is in Rome, in Caesar's house—in the heart of the heart of Rome, as it were—he seems to lose his natural strength and spirit and fortune. As his soothsayer tells him: 'If thou dost play with him at any game, / Thou art sure to lose; and of that natural luck / He beats thee 'gainst the odds' (II, iii, 26–8). And Antony recalls that this is indeed true; whatever game they play, with dice, cocks, quail etc., Caesar always wins. These details are all in Plutarch, but note the word that Shakespeare gives to Antony—'and his quails ever / Beat mine, inhooped, at odds' (II, iii, 38–9). 'Inhooped' refers to the game of putting the quails within a hoop so that they could not avoid fighting (apparently a very ancient sport, going back to China). But of course it is really Antony who is 'inhooped' in Rome, and within the hoop he cannot be himself, rendered almost impotent within the 'bounds' of Caesar's domain. Antony is most remarkable for his 'bounty', with all that that word suggests of generosity, an endless spending and giving of a superabundant nature. In North's Plutarch, this 'liberality' is often referred to—and with admiration, even when Plutarch is criticizing Antony for his riotous feasting and wasteful negligence. Antony, whatever else, is an example of '*magnanimitas*'.

In the play, this 'bounty' is constantly referred to and made manifest. I shall single out three notable occasions. On the night before the critical battle of Actium, Antony reasserts himself as 'Antony'. 'Come, / Let's have one other gaudy night: call to me / All my sad captains; fill our bowls once more', and Cleopatra joins in the spirit of the occasion, reasserting the *role* which in this case is the *reality,* of both of them: 'But since my lord / Is Antony again, I will be Cleopatra' (III, xiii, 182–7). They are most themselves when playing themselves. They are out-playing history, as I shall suggest later. But we then immediately go over to Caesar's camp and hear Caesar give *his* instructions on this important night: 'And feast the army; we have store to do't, / And they have earned the waste. Poor Antony!' (IV, i, 15–16). Then we are back in Cleopatra's palace, and hear Antony saying—'Be bounteous at our meal. . .' (IV, ii, 10). In the context and frame of Antony's 'bounty', Caesar's arid, quantifying speech seems like the utterance of a very small soul indeed—the epitome of cynical parsimony, so that 'feast' is translated into 'store', and then further degraded into 'waste'. Here is another absolutely basic opposition in the play, a confrontation and contestation of vocabularies so that what is 'feast' in one, is regarded as 'waste' in the other. Antony gives from bounty; Caesar works from inventories. 'Poor Antony!' —yes, from one point of view; from another he is rich Antony, since he gives unthinkingly from his spirit, while Caesar—poor Caesar—distributes carefully from his 'store'. 'Feast' celebrates excess: 'waste' defers to boundaries.

In North's Plutarch (and Shakespeare took almost as much from Plutarch for this play as he did for *Julius Caesar*) there is a little incident during the battle of Actium recorded thus:

> Furthermore, he dealt very friendly and courteously with Domitius, and against Cleopatra's mind. For, he being sick of an ague when he went and took a little boat to go to Caesar's camp, Antonius was very sorry for it, but yet he sent after him all his carriage, train, and men; and the same Domitius, as though he gave him to understand that he repented his open treason, he died immediately after.

Shakespeare amplifies this in his account of the defection and death of Enobarbus. Enobarbus, a good though cynical soldier, begins to feel that it is foolish to remain loyal to Antony in his visible decline:

> Mine honesty and I begin to square.
> The loyalty well held to fools does make
> Our faith mere folly: yet he that can endure
> To follow with allegiance a fall'n lord
> Does conquer him that did his master conquer,
> And earns a place 'i th' story.
>   (III, xiii, 41–6)

But shortly thereafter he leaves Antony and goes over to Caesar. Antony's reaction is immediate. He sends 'gentle adieus, and greetings', and soon a Roman soldier is telling Enobarbas:

>   Antony
> Hath after thee sent all thy treasure, with
> *His bounty overplus.*
>   (IV, vi, 20–23: my italics)

Bounty *overplus*—superabundant abundance, excessive excess. This is the mark of Antony. Enobarbus has no ague; but this act of bounty effectively kills him. His reaction:

> I am alone the villain of the earth,
> And feel I am so most. O Antony,

Thou mine of bounty, how wouldst thou have paid
My better service, when my turpitude
Thou dost so crown with gold! This blows my heart . . .
I fight against thee! No, I will go seek
Some ditch wherein to die: the foul'st best fits
My latter part of life.

> (IV, vi, 30–39)

His last words are:

O, Antony,
Nobler than my revolt is infamous,
Forgive me in thine own particular,
But let the world rank me in register
A master-leaver and a fugitive.
O, Antony! O, Antony!

> (IV, ix, 18–23)

Thus Enobarbus dies in a ditch—the lowest earth—untranscended; unlike Antony and Cleopatra, who move towards fire and air from the mud of the Nile. To be 'politic' with Caesar after being loyal to Antony, is a degenerative deformation which cannot be endured. And Enobarbus effectively 'loses his place in the story'—he cancels himself, writes himself out of the poetic termination of Antony's life, annihilates himself in a ditch. And his parting word is—not 'Poor Antony!'; but the far more expressive 'O, Antony!' This Antony is the measureless measure of all that Enobarbus has deserted. After such bounty—what forgiveness?

My third reference is to Cleopatra's imaginative re-creation and recuperation of Antony after his death. It takes place in the presence of Dolabella, and leads to one of the most crucial exchanges in the play. Cleopatra has her own oriental bounty, and she now speaks with an overflowing super-abundance of language which makes her final speeches perhaps the most poetically powerful and coruscating in the whole of Shakespeare. Her re-creation of Antony concludes:

For his bounty,
There was no winter in't: an autumn 'twas
That grew the more by reaping. His delights

Were dolphinlike, they show'd his back above
The element they lived in. In his livery
Walked crowns and crownets: realms and islands were
As plates dropped from his pocket.
                              (V, ii, 86–93)

Such a way of speaking, which goes beyond hyperbole into another realm
of 'truth', is too much for the Roman-practical-empirical Dolabella, who
interrupts her—'Cleopatra—'. To which she says:

Think you there was or might be such a man
As this I dreamt of?

Dolabella is sure—'Gentle madam, no'.

You lie, up to the hearing of the gods.
But if there be nor ever were one such,
It's past the size of dreaming; nature wants stuff
To vie strange forms with fancy, yet t'imagine
An Antony were nature's piece 'gainst fancy,
Condemning shadows quite.
                              (V, ii, 93–100)

Cleopatra's image of Antony out-imagines the imagination, out-dreams
dream. If you agree with Dolabella's Roman negative, the Roman deflationary perspective—the 'nay' which starts the play, then you deny Cleopatra's poetry and its power; deny Antony's bounty and *its* power. And you
are well in danger of 'losing a place in the story'. But that is hardly possible;
for by this stage, the soaring bounty of the imagination has passed beyond
the boundaries and circumscriptions of nature itself. This is the awesome,
magical excess which makes the world itself but a place of limits and limitations. Recall Antony and Cleopatra's opening words:

Cleopatra. If it be love indeed, tell me how much.
Antony. There's beggary in the love that can be reckoned.
Cleopatra. I'll set a bourn how far to be beloved.
Antony. Then must thou needs find out new heaven, new earth.
                              (I, i, 14–17)

Philo's 'lust' is immediately rephrased as 'love'. Cleopatra, playing, speaks temporarily in Roman terms—how much? (quantifying), and wanting to set a 'bourn' (boundary) on being loved. But Antony already points out the direction in which the play will move. For they do have to find out 'new heaven, new earth', a whole new world beyond quantifications and boundaries, until the 'truth' engendered by their love, their imagination, their dreaming, goes far beyond the restricted and impoverished realism of the Roman eye. By which point it simply *is* 'paltry to be Caesar'.

There is a great stress on 'time' in *Antony and Cleopatra,* and it is well to remember that this is a history play. The outcome of the events it dramatized was the so-called 'Augustan peace', during which Christ was born and the pagan Empire—which Virgil called the Empire without end—was established, according to later writers, as a divine preparation for the Christian Empire. Octavius Caesar, himself a pagan, unknowingly laid the way for the True City, so in Christian terms the struggles and battles in the play affect, not merely his society, but all human society, the *orbis terrae* of Augustine. The events of the play are indeed of 'world' importance—world-shattering, world-remaking (the word 'world' occurs at least forty-five times in the play). By the same token, an earlier pagan world is being silenced, extinguished, and history—as the audience would know—is on Caesar's side. He is in time with Time. Antony and Cleopatra are out of time, in more than one sense. Thus, at the beginning, when Antony decides that he must return to Rome, Cleopatra silences his apologies, referring to the time-out-of-time when they were together—'Eternity was in our lips and eyes'—while Antony, thinking Romanly for the moment, refers to 'the strong necessity of time'. Egypt, in this play, is a timeless present, which is to say an Eternity.

It can hardly escape our attention that the play is full of messengers from the start—two in the first scene, some thirty-five in all, with nearly every scene having a messenger of some kind. The play itself is extremely episodic, with some forty-two scenes (no scene breaks at all in the Folio), which makes for a very rapid sequence of change of place. There are nearly two hundred entrances and exits, all contributing to what Dr Johnson called the 'continual hurry' and 'quick succession' of events, which 'call the mind forward without intermission'. This can all be interpreted in different ways, but it certainly depicts a world in constant movement, in which time and place move and change so quickly that the whole world seems in a 'hurry' and in a state of flux—fluid, melting, re-forming. Messengers and messages bring information from the outside—they are interruptions, irruptions, precipitants of change. History is going on, and on, and at an ever accelerating pace. Yet the remarkable thing is that time seems somehow to stand still in Egypt—both within and without the reach of 'messages'; both vulnerable to history yet outside it. When Antony is away, Cleopatra simply wants to 'sleep out this great gap of time' (I, v, 6). (When she first approaches Antony in her 'barge', the city goes out to see her, leaving Antony alone 'Whistling to th' air; which, but for vacancy,/Had gone to gaze on Cleopatra too,/And made a gap in nature'—II, ii, 222–4. It is as if Cleopatra creates 'gaps'—gaps in time, gaps in nature.) For Rome, Egypt represents a great waste of time while the 'business' of history is going on. The word 'business', more often than not, carries pejorative connotations in Shakespeare. It is notable that Caesar interrupts his formulaic (as I hear it), elegiac 'praise' of the dead Antony because of—a messenger: 'The *business* of this man looks out of him;/We'll hear him what he says' (V, i, 50: my italics). He never completes the speech. Conversely, Cleopatra interrupts history to complete her poetic re-creation of Antony—from which no 'business' can distract her. From the Egyptian perspective, history itself is a 'gap of time', and Cleopatra, though growing physically older ('wrinkled deep in time'), seems to linger in Eternity, waiting for Antony to return from the trivial—though world-shattering—distractions of history.

As well as being a history play, *Antony and Cleopatra* contains within it traces of the outlines of a morality play—for by the early Renaissance the 'moral' of the story of the illustrious lovers was well established. We can find it in Spenser's *Fairie Queene,* Book V, Canto VIII:

> Nought under heaven so strongly doth allure
> The sence of man, and all his minde possesse,
> As beauties lovely baite, that doth procure,
> Great warriours oft their rigour to represse,
> And mighty hands forget their manlinesse . . .
> So also did that great Oetean Knight
> For his loves sake his Lions skin undight:

and

> so did warlike Antony neglect
> The worlds whole rule for Cleopatra's sight.

> Such wondrous powre hath womens fair aspect,
> To captive men, and make them all the world reject.

This 'moral' reading is there in Plutarch's version, in which Antony becomes 'effeminate' and made 'subject to a woman's will'. He is particularly critical of Antony's behaviour at the battle of Actium (when he followed the fleeing Cleopatra). 'There Antonius showed plainly, that he had not only lost the courage and heart of an Emperor, but also of a valiant man, and that he was not his own man . . . he has so carried away with the vain love of this woman, as if he had been glued unto her, and that she could not have removed without moving of him also.' In Spenser's terms, Antony 'rejected' the world for the mere love of a woman. Whether he found or made a better world is not, of course, considered. But, while Shakespeare's play does include these historical–morality elements (unquestionably, his glue-like relationship with Cleopatra ruins him as a politician and spoils him as a soldier, and, in worldly terms, she does—as he recognizes—lead him 'to the very heart of loss'—IV, xii, 29)—it complicates any ethical 'reading' of the story, so there can be no question of seeing it simply as another version of a good soldier losing his empire because of a bad woman. To understand this more clearly, we have to take into account another figure. For, if Octavius Caesar is related to the onward and inexorable movement of History, Antony is related to a god, Hercules.

This relationship is suggested in Plutarch who, however, relates Antony more closely to Bacchus. Shakespeare strengthens the association with Hercules. Hercules was famous for his anger, and so is Antony. As his anger begins to rise, Cleopatra says: 'Look, prithee, Charmian,/How this Herculean Roman does become/The carriage of his chafe' (I, iii, 84–5). Reacting in fury to Cleopatra's flight from the battle and what ensues, he cries out:

> The shirt of Nessus is upon me, teach me,
> Alcides, thou mine ancestor, thy rage.
>
> (IV, xii, 44–5)

Plutarch refers to Antony being deserted by a god: 'it is said that suddenly they heard a marvellous sweet harmony of sundry sorts of instruments of music . . . as they use in Bacchus feasts . . . Now, such as in reason sought the depth of the interpretation of this wonder, thought it was the god unto whom Antonius bare singular devotion to counterfeit and resemble him, that did forsake them.' Shakespeare takes the scene, and the interpretation, but makes one telling change. Late in the play, some soldiers hear 'Music i' th' air' and decide ''Tis the god Hercules, whom Antony loved,/Now leaves him' (IV, iii, 15–16). Where his Antony is concerned—despite his manifest taste for wine—Shakespeare wants us to think more of Hercules, less of Bacchus. Hercules was of course *the* hero—hero turned god—*par excellence.* There were many allegories concerning Hercules current by the Middle Ages. One (apparently from the Sophist, Prodicus), has Hercules as a young man arriving at a place where the road branches into two paths, one leading up a steep hill, the other into a pleasant glade. At the dividing point, two fair women meet him: one, modest and sober, urges him to take the steep path; the other, seductive if meretricious, uses her arts in an attempt to attract him into the glade. The hero, of course chooses the steep hill of Virtue over the beckoning glades of Pleasure. There were many medieval and Renaissance depictions of this struggle of Virtue and Pleasure over Hercules (there is a famous Dürer engraving of it—*Der Hercules*), with Pleasure, *hedone, voluptas,* sometimes associated with Venus. The implications, for us, are quite clear: if Antony is related to Hercules, Cleopatra is related to Venus. The key difference, of course, is that Hercules–Antony chooses Pleasure, pays heed to the solicitations of Venus—thus inverting the traditional moral of this allegory. According then to the accumulated traditional lore which had grown up around the much metamorphosed and allegorized figure of Hercules, Antony is indeed a version of Hercules, but one who, as it were, decided to take the wrong road—not up the steep hill of (Roman) virtue, but off the track into the (oriental) glades of pleasure.

There are other divinities in the play, and if Hercules deserts Antony, he in turn goes on to play Osiris to Cleopatra's Isis. The union of these divinities assures the fertility of Egypt: in Plutarch's study of the myth (well known in Shakespeare's time), Osiris is the Nile which floods and makes fertile the land—he is form, the seminal principle, and Isis is matter. From their union are bred not only crops, but animals, such as the serpents of the Nile. Typhon the crocodile, born of Nile mud, represents for Plutarch the irrational, bestial part of the soul by which Osiris is deceived and torn to pieces. There are, of course, numerous references to the Nile, its floods, its serpents, and so on, in the play, and Shakespeare clearly has this myth actively in mind. But it is not a stable or fixed incorporation. Cleopatra is Isis but also Antony's 'serpent of old Nile', and by a serpent of Nile will she die—a serpent by a serpent 'valiantly vanquished', as Antony–Osiris is 'a

Roman by a Roman valiantly vanquished' (that second Roman is more
Antony than Caesar—as Cleopatra says: 'Not Caesar's valor hath o'erthrown
Antony,/But Antony's hath triumphed on itself'—IV, xv, 14–15). The
monster-crocodile who destroys Antony is, in this play, Octavius Caesar—
though he is hardly seen in those terms. He is a disguised Typhon for Antony and Cleopatra, who are playing at being Osiris and Isis—but, really,
he is not in their self-mythologizing act, not in their 'play' at all. I use the
word 'play' advisedly and deliberately. Cleopatra is, of course, above all a
great actress. She can play with Antony to beguile him; she can play at being Isis, thus anticipating her own move towards transcendence; and she
can 'play' at her death, easily outplaying Caesar's crafty political deviousness. In this way, she completely transforms her desolate state, not submitting to the downward turn of Fortune, but inverting it into the occasion of
her own triumph of the imagination:

> My desolation does begin to make
> A better life. 'Tis paltry to be Caesar:
> Not being Fortune, he's but Fortune's knave,
> A minister of her will . . .
>
> > (V, ii, 1–4)

Cleopatra will be her *own* Fortune—a triumph of the 'will'.

She is aware that Caesar will display her in Rome, and that her life with
Antony will be 'staged' in a degraded form, in keeping with that tendency
of Roman rhetoric to devalue and translate downwards the life associated
with Egypt:

> The quick comedians
> Extemporally will stage us, and present
> Our Alexandrian revels: Antony
> Shall be brought drunken forth, and I shall see
> Some squeaking Cleopatra boy my greatness
> I' th' posture of a whore.
>
> > (V, ii, 216–21)

(Which, of course, exactly describes what is going on in the Elizabethan
theatre at that moment, with some boy 'squeaking' Cleopatra. This is not
Nabokovian self-reflexivity. Rather, it is effectively as if the drama is so in-

candescent that it is scorning its own resources, shedding the very medium which has served to put its poetry into flight. It is as though 'representation' is scorching itself away to reveal the thing itself—an electrifying moment of astonishing histrionic audacity and magic.) So—Cleopatra puts on her own play, on her own stage, with her own costume, speeches, and gestures:

> Now, Charmian!
> Show me, my women, like a queen: go fetch
> My best attires. I am again for Cydnus,
> To meet Mark Antony. Sirrah Iras, go . . .
> And when thou hast done this chare, I'll give thee leave
> To play till doomsday.—Bring our crown and all.
>   (V, ii, 227–32)

> My resolution's placed, and I have nothing
> Of woman in me: now from head to foot
> I am marble-constant: now the fleeting moon
> No planet is of mine.
>   (V, ii, 238–41)

She is moving beyond the body, beyond time, beyond the whole world of transcience and decay, beyond her own planet the moon, with all that it implies of tidal periodicity. The clown enters with his figs, which contain the serpent she will use for her suicide (at the beginning, Charmian says 'I love long life better than figs'—I, ii, 32—by the end this, like so much else, is reversed: Cleopatra likes figs better than long life). We move to her final self-apotheosis, played with great dignity and ceremony, at which Cleopatra is at once her own directress and her own priestess:

> Give me my robe, put on my crown, I have
> Immortal longings in me . . .
> . . . Husband, I come:
> Now to that name my courage prove my title!
> I am fire, and air; my other elements
> I give to baser life . . .
>   (V, ii, 280–90)

Out of the earth, mud, dung, water associated with the Nile and its fertility, she has distilled an essence composed only of the higher elements, air and fire. She is 'marble' for the duration of the performance; she is also, like Antony, 'melting', dissolving, but melting into a higher atmosphere. She gives a farewell kiss to Iras who falls down dead—perhaps from poison, perhaps from grief—and Cleopatra comments:

> Dost thou lie still?
> If thus thou vanishest, thou tell'st the world
> It is not worth leave-taking.
>
> (V, ii, 296–8)

To the snake she says:

> O, couldst thou speak,
> That I might hear thee call great Caesar ass
> Unpolicied!
>
> (V, ii, 306–8)

She has seen through Caesar's tricks and stratagems—'He words me, girls, he words me, that I should not / Be noble to myself' (V, ii, 191–2); she knows, too, that he uses language instrumentally, merely for devious political ends. And when Proculeus refers to Caesar's 'bounty', she knows that it is but a pitiful and transparent travesty of the real bounty of Antony. In her superbly performed death, we see the triumph of the 'oriental' imagination over the 'alphabetic' utilitarianism of Caesar. The world will indeed be his, and another kind of Empire inaugurated; but from the perspective of Cleopatra, and *just for the duration of the play,* it seems a world 'not worth leave-taking'. So her last words are an incomplete question: 'What should I stay—' as she passes out of language, body, world, altogether. There is no *staying* her now. Charmian completes her question with her own final speech:

> In this wild world? So, fare thee well.
> Now boast thee, death, in thy possession lies
> A lass unparalleled. Downy windows, close;
> And golden Phoebus never be beheld

Of eyes again so royal! Your crown's awry;
I'll mend it, and then play—

(V, ii, 314–19)

Thus Cleopatra, and her girls, play their way out of the reach of history, with an intensity of self-sustaining, self-validating poetry which does indeed eclipse the policies and purposes of Caesar. (There are some recent readings which see Antony and Cleopatra as failed politicians who turn to aesthetics to gloss over their mistakes and cheer themselves up with poetry. I can imagine such a play, but this one is not it.) Cleopatra was 'confined' in her monument, a prisoner of Caesar's force—apparently secure within the boundaries of his soldiers and his 'scroll'. It is by the unforgettable excess and bounty/beauty of her last 'Act' that she triumphs over all that would confine her, and turns death into 'play', *the* play that will take her into Eternity.

Let me return to the opposition between feast and waste. Feast derives from *festa*—holiday—and in one sense, Antony and Cleopatra turn life in Egypt into a perpetual holiday. 'Waste' is more interesting. Just as 'dirt' has been defined as 'matter out of place', so the idea of 'waste' presupposes a boundary or classification mark which enables one to draw a distinction between what is necessary, valuable, usable in some way, and what lies outside these categories—'waste'. Antony, we may say, recognizes no such boundary. Indeed, he 'wastes' himself, in the sense that he is endlessly prodigal of all he has and does not count the cost. From Antony's point of view, all life in Egypt can be seen as a feast; in Caesar's eyes—the Roman perspective—it is all 'waste'. From the etymology of the word (*uacare,* to be empty or vacant; *uanus,* hollow, vain; *uastus*, desolated, desert, vast; up to Old English *weste*—see Eric Partridge's *Origins*), we can say that there is a connection between vastness, vacancy, vanity, and waste. Antony is inhabiting a realm of vastness, vanity, vacancy—the 'great gap' named by Cleopatra (Caesar, indeed, refers to Antony's 'vacancy'). From Caesar's point of view, and those who see with the Roman eye, Antony is indeed 'empty' while Caesar is referred to as 'the fullest man'. Thus Enobarbus, commenting on Antony's challenge to Caesar to meet him in single battle: 'that he should dream,/Knowing all measures, the full Caesar will/Answer his emptiness!' Caesar is, from one point of view, *full*—full of history, of Fortune, of time. Antony is 'empty'—committed to vacancy, vanity, waste. The question implicitly posed is whether he and Cleopatra, and their way of life, are not 'full' of something quite outside of Caesar's discourse and his measurements, something which makes *him* the empty man. Caesar is full of politics, empty of poetry: Antony and Cleopatra reach a point where they are empty of politics, but full of poetry. Which is the real 'vacancy'? It depends where you are standing, how you are looking. But there is nothing 'vast' about Caesar: even if he conquers the whole world, everything is done with 'measure' and 'temper' (temperance). If Antony and Cleopatra melt and dissolve, it is into a 'vastness' which is the necessary space for their exceeding, their excess—'beyond the size of dreaming'. In this play, Shakespeare compels a complete revaluation of 'waste'. Historically, it was *not* paltry to be Caesar, certainly not this Caesar, who is insured of, and will ensure, a 'temperate' imperial future, during which time Christ would be born. This Caesar certainly has his place in the story of history. But in this play, his conquest is registered as a gradual diminishment as he—alphabetically—takes over the Orient, but in doing so merely imposes Roman 'prescriptions' on a vast world of pagan fecundity, spilled plenty, and an oriental magnificence which transforms 'waste' into 'bounty', and makes Caesar seem like the 'merchant' he is, a calculating Machiavel—an ass unpolicied.

Boundaries are, of course, of central importance for civilization. For Vico, in *The New Science,* civilized man is precisely one who creates and guards 'confines'—'for it was necessary to set up boundaries to the field in order to put a stop to the infamous promiscuity of things in the bestial state. On these boundaries were to be fixed the confines first of families, then of gentes or houses, later of peoples, and finally of nations.' There is much in Shakespeare which honours and defends the importance of recognizing the need for boundaries. But in this play, writing against the recorded, inexorable grain and movement of history, Shakespeare makes us re-value what might have been lost in the triumph of Caesar:

> O, see, my women,
> The crown o' th' earth doth melt. My lord!
> O, withered is the garland of the war,
> The soldier's pole is fall'n: young boys and girls
> Are level now with men. The odds is gone,

And there is nothing left remarkable
Beneath the visiting moon.

                                        (IV, xv, 62–8)

This is 'waste'? Rather, the fecundity, plenitude and bounty associated with
Egypt, and Antony in Egypt, have fed into and nourished Cleopatra's
speech, until she is speaking a kind of language of pure poetry about which
alphabetic man can have nothing to say. A whole pagan age is over; the future belongs to Caesar—and Christ. But confronted with this kind of transcendent poetry, which is indeed all 'excess', that future seems merely trivial, temporal, temperate. 'The road of excess leads to the Palace of Wisdom,'
wrote Blake. In this play, the poetry of excess leads to the unbounded, un-
boundaried, spaces of infinity. Saving leads to earthly empire: squandering
opens an avenue to Eternity. All air and fire—and poetry. Bounty overplus.

TIMON OF ATHENS (1607–8?)

'Bounty' figures prominently and plays a large role in what may, or may
not, be Shakespeare's next play—*Timon of Athens*. (It first finds print in the
Folio of 1623 where it occupies the place intended for *Troilus and Cressida*,
which had to be withdrawn because of copyright difficulties. On internal
evidence, it belongs to the 1605–9 period of Shakespeare's plays. But it
seems unfinished and could conceivably have been written later. I give the
conventionally agreed-on date.) Bounty, bounteous, bounteousness—the
words occur at least seventeen times by my count. But something has taken
a turn. This is the wrong kind of bounty, bounty gone wrong. We hear, in
the opening lines as the Poet, Painter, Jeweler, and Merchant enter Timon's
house (bent on hypocritical sycophancy and cynical exploitation): 'See,/
Magic of bounty, all these spirits thy power/Hath conjured to attend' (I, i,
5–7). But the 'magic' is irresponsible, discreative, ruinous, and all the 'spirits' it 'conjures to attend' turn out to be venal, heartless, 'monstrous'. As
well as the continuous acclaiming of Timon's 'bounty', there are some
warning lines:

'Tis pity bounty had not eyes behind,
That man might ne'er be wretched for his mind.
                                 (I, ii, 166–7)

'for his mind'—on account of his inclinations: this from Flavius, the loyal
and honest steward.

No villainous bounty yet hath passed my heart;
Unwisely, not ignobly, have I given.
                                 (II, ii, 183–4)

Thus Timon defends himself against the 'sermon' of his despairing steward. And it is the steward who, in response to Timon's expression of confidence that his friends will not let him 'sink', comments sadly:

I would I could not think it; that thought is bounty's foe.
Being free itself, it thinks all others so.
                                 (II, ii, 242–3)

Of course, Timon's friends are no friends at all—and first he 'sinks', and
then he dives.

Strange, unusual blood,
When man's worst sin is, he does too much good.
Who then dares to be half so kind again?
For bounty, that makes gods, do still mar men.
                                 (IV, ii, 38–41)

It is something of a question whether Timon is truly 'kind'—and how
much *good* he actually does. Dr Johnson maintained that the play 'is a warning against that ostentatious liberality which scatters bounty but confers no
benefits and buys flattery but no friendship'. Another eighteenth-century
writer, William Richardson, also judges Timon adversely. In this play, he
says, Shakespeare 'illustrates the consequences of that inconsiderate pro-
fusion which has the appearance of liberality and is supposed even by the
inconsiderate person himself to proceed from a generous principle, but

which, in reality, has its chief origin in the love of distinction'. As Richardson trenchantly points out, Timon 'is not so solicitous of alleviating the distress of obscure affliction . . . He is not represented as visiting the cottage of the fatherless and widow, but is wonderfully generous to men of high rank and character.' It would only be a little overstating the case to say that Timon's idea of 'bounty' is to lay on drunken orgies for his posh acquaintances. Witness Flavius:

> When all our offices have been oppressed
> With riotous feeders, when our vaults have wept
> With drunken spilth of wine, when every room
> Hath blazed with lights and brayed with minstrelsy,
> I have retired me to a wasteful cock,
> And set mine eyes at flow.
>
> (II, ii, 168–73)

('blazed with lights and brayed with minstrelsy'—this is Shakespeare at his most powerful). Aristotle states; 'he is liberal who spends according to his substance *and on the right objects;* and he who exceeds is prodigal' (my italics). Timon is not liberal: he is prodigal, culpably prodigal.

But certainly, his flatterers treat him, and possibly he regards himself, as a god. One of them says of his 'bounty':

> He pours it out. Plutus, the god of gold,
> Is but his steward . . .
>
> (I, i, 283–4)

We will come back to gods—and gold. Here it will serve to note that Timon's kind of 'bounty'—blind, indiscriminate, proud, self-deceiving, and terribly vulnerable—certainly 'mars the man'. Indeed, it could be said that Timon is never seen as a 'man' at all. When he can no longer go on playing 'god', he insists on being 'beast'—the two words recur, often in close proximity as if squeezing out, or foreclosing on, possible intermediate states. This is a play about extremes.

The main point about Timon's munificence is that it is as reckless, indiscriminate, and all-embracing, as his later invectives and denunciations are to be. All motives come mixed, but there is something distinctly impure in Timon's generosity. As the honest Flavius tells him:

> Great Timon, noble, worthy, royal Timon!
> Ah, when the means are gone that buy this praise,
> The breath is gone whereof this praise is made.
> Feast-won, fast-lost . . .
>
> (II, ii, 178–81)

Proud, ostentatious Timon has been buying praise and adulation—but, as Flavius well knows, all he purchases is empty words. He is indeed often called 'noble' and 'worthy', just as his 'bounty' is consistently referred to. But the words undergo what is sometimes referred to as devaluation through repetition (something similar happens to the word 'honourable' in Antony's famous speech over Caesar's body). When Flaminius goes to Lucullus to ask for money to help Timon, Lucullus, expecting another gift, asks him what he has under his cloak. 'Faith, nothing but an empty box, sir, which in my lord's behalf I come to entreat your honor to supply' (III, i, 16–19). But Lucullus has no 'honour' to 'supply' (fill) the box, so it remains empty. This is what happens to the honorific terms in the play. There is no longer anything to fill them; they are emptied out, and by the end, words like 'bounty' and 'noble' have a hollow ring. As with the key words, so with the main characters in this Athens—they are hollow, all 'outside', no inside. Timon commends painting because 'These penciled figures are / Even such as they give out' (I, i, 159–60). What you see is all there is. This is true of the characters who may, indeed, be said to be 'penciled'—outlined, sketched. They are just as hypocritical, mean, ungrateful as they appear. Most unusually for Shakespeare, they have no interiority (this very definitely includes Timon himself). Indeed, the play itself may be said to have no 'inside' and is, itself, something of an empty box.

Coleridge called this play an 'after vibration' of *King Lear,* and there are certainly distinctive echoes. These include the horror of ingratitude ('O see the monstrousness of man / When he looks out in an ungrateful shape'— III, ii, 77–8); Timon's denudation and reduction to an 'unhoused' condition in the wilderness outside the city walls; and the ominous reiteration of the word 'nothing' ('For these my present friends, as they are to me nothing, so

in nothing bless them, and to nothing are they welcome'—III, vi, 82–5).
But there is a very definite 'after vibration' of *Antony and Cleopatra* as well,
an after-echo which has a distressing or displeasing tendency towards satire
and even travesty, of a rather bleak kind. There is good reason to think that
Shakespeare wrote the two plays closely together (but no point in speculating as to the possible explanations for such a drastic change of mood and
tone). At times, Timon speaks lines reminiscent of Antony (e.g. 'Methinks
I could deal kingdoms to my friends'—I, ii, 228), but it is somehow not
the same. As in *Antony and Cleopatra* we have the regular use of the words
'bind', 'bond', 'bound'; but not only is 'bounty' revalued, or rather devalued, but 'feast' is rather horribly degraded, even, I shall suggest, to the
point of sacrilegious parody. In *Antony and Cleopatra*, 'feast' was opposed to
'waste'; in *Timon of Athens* 'feast' *is* 'waste'. The first feast in the play is a
veritable debauch, exemplifying Flavius' description of Timon's habitual
prodigal entertainment—amply justifying the question to Timon, 'What
needs these feasts, pomps, and vainglories?' (I, ii, 253–4). This is spoiled
ceremony, hospitality vulgarized, wasteful bounty. As a Senator comments:
'Still in motion/Of raging waste? It cannot hold, it will not' (II, i, 3–4).
Timon's bounty starts out as a flow of gold ('He pours it out'—I, i, 283);
it manifests itself as a 'flow of riot' (II, ii, 3); and soon becomes a 'flow
of debts' (II, ii, 152). Uncontrolled spillage. 'Feast-won, fast-lost,' as Flavius succinctly puts it. Trying to 'win' people with this kind of feasting, ensures that you will lose them. Timon's second 'feast', at which he serves water to his ungrateful 'friends' ('Uncover, dogs, and lap'), is a sort of anti-feast,
a complete negation at the opposite extreme from the earlier squandering. These are Timon's two, Timon's *only,* positions. 'One day he gives
us diamonds, next day stones' (III, vi, 121), says one of the lords as they
are driven away from the anti-feast. Diamonds or stones: nothing in between.

But something worse. At the first feast, there is the following exchange:

> *Timon.* You had rather be at a breakfast of enemies than a dinner of
>   friends.
> *Alcibiades.* So they were bleeding new, my lord, there's no meat like 'em; I
>   could wish my best friends at such a feast.
>   (I, ii, 76–80)

The exaggeration or jesting of a military man, perhaps. But there is more than a hint of cannibalism in this play in which flatterers are said to 'drink' men, and ladies to 'eat' lords. Timon, in his glory days, 'had the world as my confectionary' (IV, iii, 261), which suggests a too sickly-sweet meal, luxurious rather than nourishing. When, at the height of his hysterical revulsion, he scrabbles around in the wilds and finds a root, he says:

> That the whole life of Athens were in this!
> Thus would I eat it.
>> (IV, iii, 282–3)

Sweets, roots, Athenians—it is all 'eating'. This is a society in which, to the very edges of metaphor, people variously 'devour' each other. Feast as waste; feast as cannibalism. It is no wonder that, in this play, feasting leads to 'vomit' and what should be nourishment turns to 'poison'. And there is one more turn to this particular screw. Here is Apemantus, the scourge at the feast:

> O you gods! What a number of men eats Timon, and he sees 'em not! It grieves me to see so many dip their meat in one man's blood, and all the madness is, he cheers them up too.
> I wonder men dare trust themselves with men.
> Methinks they should invite them without knives:
> Good for their meat, and safer for their lives.
> There's much example for't; the fellow that sits next him, now parts bread with him, pledges the breath of him in a divided draught, is the readiest man to kill him.
>> (I, ii, 38–49)

Much example indeed—Jesus and Judas providing the most famous example of all. And here is the First Stranger—from outside Athens and revealed to be both dispassionate and compassionate:

> Who can call him his friend
> That dips in the same dish?
>> (III, ii, 70–71)

Honest Flavius refers to the 'glutt'nous maws' of the 'false masters [who] ate of my lord's meat' (III, iv, 50). And when Timon is set upon by the servants of ruthless creditors, he cries out: 'Tell out my blood . . . Tear me, take me, and the gods fall upon you' (III, iv, 94, 99). As you (his well-feasted 'friends') fall upon the god, taking and tearing his meat, his bread, his blood, his body. Of course, there are here deliberate echoes of the Last Supper, and Christian communion (and the eating of gods in general); it would be impossible to miss them. But to argue from this, as some have done (most famously Wilson Knight), that this makes of Timon something of a Christ figure, seems to me badly to misread, misapprehend, the tone and atmosphere of the play. Certainly, Timon disports himself as a god, and is willing to be treated (or addressed) as one by his flatterers, who readily comply as long as his 'grace' and beneficence is flowing their way. Tear, take, eat: this is my blood, this is my body. And so they do. But this is no *sparagmos* and *omophagia,* in the ancient sense; or, to the extent that it is, it has been sordidly translated into financial terms. Nor is it even analogous to the Christian communion. There is no hint of the sacred here; not a touch of ritual observance. What we *do* have is a blasphemous, empty, parody or travesty of sacrificial rites which have elsewhere and at other times been dignifying, meaningful, perhaps redeeming. But not here, not now—not in *this* Athens.

Timon of Athens is a very schematic play. It is composed of two starkly contrasting halves (the first half clearly more finished than the second). It is very static, the second half consisting of a series of interviews. Characterization is cursory, 'penciled', thin to the point of impersonality and abstraction. It seems more like an allegory or morality play (or even a folk tale—three false friends, loyal servant, etc.) than a fully developed drama. For the first ninety-four lines none of the speakers is named—they are types. (At line ninety-four, Timon enters and his first word is 'Imprisoned'—anticipating his own imprisonment, in his own house, his debts, but most of all in his temperament—for he, too, proves to be a fixed 'type'.) The play has been seen as more of a bitter satire than a tragedy, and certainly there is none of the dramatic conflict and sense of inexorable progress (or development and movement) that we experience in Shakespeare's great tragedies (just compare *Macbeth*). Perhaps more to the point, there is no development in the 'characters', particularly of Timon. There is no halting but growing self-awareness, no bruising stumbling to an initially resisted self-knowledge. In his soliloquies, Timon exhibits none of the meditative inwardness and

deepening self-exploration of Hamlet. When he stops giving, he starts cursing. Having postured and dispensed like a god, he turns to crawling and
snarling like a beast. Where Hamlet really thinks, Timon mainly rants.
This is not to deny the undoubted power of some of his furious and nauseated outbursts (see, for example, the speech beginning 'O blessed breeding
sun, draw from the earth/Rotten humidity'—IV, iii, 1 *et seq.;* or his address
to the bandits starting 'I'll example you with thievery'—IV, iii, 442 *et seq.;*
both worthy of Lear himself). But like his 'generosity', his hatred is indiscriminate, all-inclusive. At times, he is reduced—if that is the word—to
lists:

> Piety, and fear,
> Religion to the gods, peace, justice, truth,
> Domestic awe, night-rest, and neighborhood,
> Instruction, manners, mysteries, and trades,
> Degrees, observances, customs, and laws,
> Decline to your confounding contraries,
> And let confusion live.
>
> (IV, i, 15–21)

In other words, *everything* that makes human, civilized life possible—damn
and confound the lot. Having instantly arrived at, jumped or inverted to,
this state of terminal misanthropic nihilism, there is no way in which Timon can change or develop—he can only reiterate, and die. The dramatic
possibilities of such a figure are strictly limited, and perhaps that is why
Shakespeare left the play unfinished and moved on to more fruitful fields.

Apemantus, the Cynic (i.e. 'dog'—the word re-echoes through the play),
has some cogent insights into Timon during their climactic exchange in
Act IV:

> Thou'dst courtier be again
> Wert thou not beggar.
>
> (IV, iii, 242–3)

> The middle of humanity thou never knewest, but the extremity of both
> ends.
>
> (IV, iii, 301–2)

God, or beast—this extremism was familiar to the Elizabethans from the well-known saying of Aristotle that 'that man which cannot live in civil company either he is a god or a beast, seeing only God is sufficient of himself, and a solitary life agreeth with a beast' (this is, of course, very relevant for *Coriolanus* as well). Whatever we think of Apemantus, a descendant of Jacques and Thersites, we may take William Richardson's felicitous formulation—'his invectives are bitter, but his remarks are true'.

The god who really *does* rule and dominate in the play is—gold:

> What a god's gold, that he is worshiped
> In a baser temple than where swine feed!
> (V, i, 49–50)

Thus Timon, as people come flocking to him in the wilderness, trying to ease, or flatter, out of him his new-found gold. As a 'god' himself, he had 'poured' out gold in Athens; now he distributes it freely again, with, of course, a directly opposite motive:

> Thou visible god,
> That sold'rest close impossibilities
> And mak'st them kiss; that speak'st with every tongue
> To every purpose. O thou touch of hearts,
> Think thy slave man rebels, and by thy virtue
> Set them into confounding odds, that beasts
> May have the world in empire.
> (IV, iii, 391–7)

May the god gold turn all humans to beasts (again, the words appear in close proximity as if to occlude intermediary possibilities). And if the announced position of the two prostitutes is anything to go by—'we'll do anything for gold' (IV, iii, 151)—his hope may well be realized. Perhaps it has been realized already, given Apemantus' declaration—'The commonwealth of Athens is become a forest of beasts.' (Incidentally, the Greek word *time* or *timos* means both honour and price, thus pointing to the equivocal nature of true 'value'. Timon's initial belief in the 'honour' of his friends, switches to an unshakable conviction that money rules all. He carries his fate in his name.)

But the Athenians are not, not quite, *all* beasts. Lowly figures often play a vital role in Shakespeare—for instance the unnamed servant who turns on his master, Cornwall, and kills him—refusing to stand and watch his cruelty—and it is a very important part of this play that Timon's steward, Flavius, also unnamed in the early part of the folio version, is truly loyal and loving to his master, Timon. (Flaminius and Timon's other servants are also loyal, and disgusted at the base and cruel rapacity of their so-called 'betters'.) In the first half of the play, Flavius agonizes over the irresponsible waste he is helpless to prevent—'I bleed inwardly for my lord' (I, ii, 210). And when the impoverished Timon takes to the wilds, Flavius seeks him out, loyal as ever:

> O you gods!
> Is yond despised and ruinous man my lord?
> Full of decay and failing? ...
> ... I will present
> My honest grief unto him, and as my lord
> Still serve him with my life. My dearest master.
> (IV, iii, 467–9, 477–9)

In the face of Timon's suspicions as to his motives for seeking him out—having trusted everyone he will, of course, henceforth trust no one—Flavius protests:

> That which I show, heaven knows, is merely love,
> Duty and zeal to your unmatched mind ...
> (IV, iii, 524–5)

We may blink at that 'unmatched mind', of which we have seen precious little evidence (similarly it strains credulity when the Senators come and beg him to take over the captaincy of the city as being the only man who can save Athens from the threatened attack of Alcibiades—one senses Timon would be hardly a better strategist than he is an economist); but —'merely love'. With the crucial exception of Flavius' unwavering devotion, this non-commercial 'commodity' is *entirely* absent from the play. And this is, certainly, intimately connected to another absence—the absence of women, apart from two prostitutes (who, like the Athenian men, will 'do anything for gold') and the Amazons in the masque (hardly representative of 'the female'). When Flavius announces himself to the misanthrope Timon as 'an honest poor servant of yours', Timon feigns non-recognition:

> Then I know thee not.
> I never had honest man about me, I; *all*
> I kept were knaves . . .
>   (IV, iii, 485–7: my italics)

As he had cried out at the end of his 'anti-feast'—'henceforth hated be/Of Timon man and *all* humanity' (III, vi, 105–6). Given Timon's particular mentality and temperament, it always has to be 'all'—or 'nothing', of course. But with 'humanity', you never can say 'all', whether in this direction or that. With tears, Flavius protests the genuineness of his honest compassion—'Nev'r did poor steward wear a truer grief/For his undone lord than mine eyes for you' (IV, iii, 489–90). What follows is a key speech by Timon:

> What, dost thou weep? Come nearer. Then I love thee
> Because thou art a woman, and disclaim'st
> Flinty mankind, whose eyes do never give
> But thorough lust and laughter. Pity's sleeping.
>   (IV, iii, 491–4)

No one who remembers Cordelia's tears will need reminding of the importance of weeping in Shakespeare. It is associated—certainly not exclusively, but predominantly—with women, and true compassion and devotion. Pity is certainly sleeping among the Athenian men in this play (Flavius and other servants apart). And it is a powerful reminder of the absence of 'true women' from this play that Timon should identify Flavius as 'a woman' simply on account of his manifesting 'pity'—as though that makes him an anomaly among men. Timon continues:

> Had I a steward
> So true, so just, and now so comfortable?
> It almost turns my dangerous nature *mild*.
> . . .

> Forgive my general and exceptless rashness,
> You perpetual-sober gods. I do proclaim
> One honest man. Mistake me not, *but one.*
> No more I pray—and he's a steward.
> How fain would I have hated *all* mankind,
> And thou redeem'st thyself. But *all* save thee
> I fell with curses.
>
> > (IV, iii, 499–510: my italics)

'and he's a steward'—so he *almost* doesn't count. But of course he does. Enormously. Because once an exception is admitted to a totalizing general-ization, once absolutism is punctured, the protective shell of '*all*' is broken. One, two—who *knows* how many there may be? Potentially, Timon would not be able to staunch a leak of his own conceding.

Perhaps this is the point of including Alcibiades and his story in the play (a point that has been queried by some commentators). He, too, is most un-gratefully treated by an Athens which he has valiantly defended. The Sen-ate is determined to execute a brave fellow-soldier who has been involved in some civic violence. In a speech reminiscent of the 'mercy' speeches of Portia (*The Merchant of Venice*), and Isabella (*Measure for Measure*), and, come to that, Tamora (*Titus Andronicus*), Alcibiades pleads for his friends:

> For pity is the virtue of the law,
> And none but tyrants use it cruelly.
>
> > (III, v, 8–9)

The Senators abjure 'mercy' and, unmoved and unmovable, identify with the supreme rigour of the 'law'. 'We are for law. He dies' (III, v, 86). As the admirably humane 'First Stranger' comments: 'But I perceive / Men must learn now with pity to dispense, / For policy sits above conscience' (III, ii, 91–3). Alcibiades vows revenge against Athens (which is why, in Plutarch, Timon makes much of him; and why, in the play, he gives him gold). At the end of the play, he is indeed marching on Athens. Having failed to secure Timon's apparently indispensable help, the Senators can only plead with Alcibiades who is approaching their city 'like a boar too savage' (V, i, 166—it would be otiose to point out how often men are referred to as animals in this 'beastly' play). And their case is, to a rational person, unassailable:

> We were not all unkind, nor all deserve
> The common stroke of war.
>
> (V, iv, 21–2)

> All have not offended.
> For those that were, it is not square to take
> On those that are, revenge.
>
> (V, iv, 35–7)

We were not *all* unkind . . . *all* have not offended . . . those that are, are not the same as those that were. Times change; one generation yields to another; it is not an absolute world. Unlike Timon, Alcibiades accepts this, and exchanges vengeance for that mercy which he himself had once pleaded for. In a rather perfunctory conclusion, he takes on the role of a Richmond, a Malcolm, a Fortinbras, restoring peace and order to the city-state:

> And I will use the olive with my sword,
> Make war breed peace . . .
>
> (V, iv, 82–3)

This is the sort of change or modification of attitude which is impossible for Timon, who can only live in, and by, extremes. The only 'action' he is capable of in the second half is negative speech, and when he gives that up— 'Lips, let four words go by and language end' (V, i, 221)—he can only die, under two—just to make sure—characteristically venomous and nihilistic epitaphs. Arguably, death has been his real aim:

> My long sickness
> Of health and living now begins to mend,
> And nothing brings me all things.
>
> (V, i, 187–9)

And all things bring him nothing. These lines offer a curious, distant echo of Cleopatra's 'My desolation does begin to make / A better life'; yet, as is fitting in a play in which, indeed, 'all's obliquy'—twisted, crooked, awry— they are utterly unlike them as well, Again, Shakespeare seems to be exploring, experimenting with, a completely negative version of some of the drives and values, and poetic achievements, of *Antony and Cleopatra.* In that play, I suggested, we could appreciate the meaning of Blake's assertion that 'the road of excess leads to the palace of wisdom'. In *Timon of Athens,* the road of excess leads to nothing—nothing at all. Shortly after writing his most glorious play, it seems that Shakespeare wrote his bitterest. Who knows why?

CORIOLANUS (1608)

Timon was *first* a god—or 'godded' by his sycophantic friends (to use an apt and striking noun-verb from *Coriolanus*)—and *then* a beast. Coriolanus, in what appears to be the last of Shakespeare's Roman plays (and thus, arguably, his last tragedy), seems to move inexorably towards becoming both at the same time. Both, and more besides. More and less. But here again, as, once more and for the last time, Shakespeare turns to Plutarch for the main outlines of his hero and the events of his play, it signally helps to have some of North's version of Plutarch before us:

> Caius Martius, whose life we intend now to write, . . . was brought up under his mother a widow . . . This man also is a good proof to confirm men's opinions, that a rare and excellent wit, untaught, doth bring forth many good and evil things together . . . For this Martius' natural wit and great heart did marvelously stir up his courage to do and attempt notable acts. But on the other side, for lack of education, he was so choleric and impatient, that he would yield to no living creature, which made him churlish, uncivil, and altogether unfit for any man's conversation. Yet men marveling much at his constancy, that he was never overcome with pleasure nor money and how he would endure easily all manner of pains and travails, thereupon they well liked and commended his stoutness and temperancy. But for all that, they could not be acquainted with him, as one citizen useth to be with another in the city. His behaviour was so unpleasant to them by reason of a certain insolent and stern manner he had, which, because he was too lordly, was disliked. And to say truly, the greatest benefit that learning bringeth unto men is this: that it teachest men that be rude and rough of nature, by compass and rule of reason, to be civil and courteous, and to like better the mean state than the higher. Now

in those days, valiantness was honored in Rome above all other virtues, which they call *virtus,* by the name of virtue itself, as including in that general name all other special virtues besides. So that *virtus* in the Latin was as much as valiantness. But Martius, being more inclined to the wars than any other gentleman of his time, began from his childhood to give himself to handle weapons . . .

As we shall see, 'handle weapons' is what Shakespeare's Coriolanus does from very first to very last. But first, one more amplification of his character from Plutarch:

> For he was a man too full of passion and choler, and too much given over to self-will and opinion, as one of a high mind and great courage that lacked the gravity and affability that is gotten with judgment of learning and reason, which only is to be looked for in a *governor of state:* and that remembered not how willfulness is the thing of the world, which a *governor of a commonwealth,* for pleasing should shun, being that which Plato called 'solitariness,' as in the end, all men that are willfully given to a self-opinion and obstinate mind, and who will never yield to others' reason but to their own, remain without company and forsaken of all men.
>   (My italics)

During the Renaissance there was much discussion concerning the proper education, duties, and responsibilities of the good prince or governor—what qualified a person to exercise 'the speciality of rule'. As Plutarch stresses, it is precisely these qualifications which Coriolanus so signally lacks: he is a prime example of what Renaissance thinkers regarded as the ill-educated prince, a man from the governing classes who is, by nature, temperament, and upbringing, unfitted and unfit to rule. Magnificent as a soldier, he is disastrous as a politician. Shakespeare takes the latent tensions between martial and civic (and domestic) values, between the battlefield and the city, between—in the play's terms—the 'casque' (a helmet) and the 'cushion' (indicating a seat in the Senate), and screws these tensions up to breaking point, dramatically exposing, in the process, not just their perennially potential incompatibility, but—*in extremis*—their very actual and active explosive oppugnancy. The problem—a permanent one—baldly stated is as simple as this. You certainly could not found, much less renew and prolong, any form of civil society on such figures as Coriolanus. But it is debatable whether you could defend and thus preserve any such society *without* such men. (Having banished Coriolanus, the tribunes complacently say 'Rome/sits safe and still without him'—IV, vi, 37. They could not be more wrong, nor was Rome ever more vulnerable.) Society cannot do *without* the sort of '*virtus*-valiantness' embodied in Coriolanus; but, given its uncontainable explosiveness, it cannot very well do *with* it either. Shakespeare never took hold of a more enduring and intractable social problem. This is one of the most violent of Shakespeare's plays, with tremendous and terrible powers released to do their 'mammocking' and 'mangling' work (two apt words—from the play—for the wrecking forces let loose). And, when Coriolanus is savagely cut down, we feel awed at what Bradley eloquently called 'the instantaneous cessation of enormous energy'.

The legendary history of Coriolanus dates from the fifth century BC, and refers to the creation of the tribunate of 494 BC and the corn riots three years later (Shakespeare, for more urgent impact, conflates these events). Phillips summarizes the importance of this period of Roman history for the Elizabethans. 'The consular government which had supplanted the earlier monarchy underwent further modification in the direction of popular rule when economic unrest forced the Senate to grant political representation to citizens of Rome. One result of this concession was conflict between the democratic and aristocratic elements within the republic. In the turbulent history of Rome in this period Tudor theorists who argued in defence of monarchy and the hierarchy of degrees found a convincing demonstration of the dangers of democratic government' (op. cit., p. 147). There was no previous play about Coriolanus, and his story was only occasionally referred to by political writers as illustrative of the dangers of popular riot, or of civic ingratitude. Shakespeare certainly uses Plutarch, but the play is all his own. He makes it a very 'Roman'-feeling play. Four of the early Roman kings are referred to (Numa, Tullus, Ancus Martius, and Tarquin), and there are references to political and religious customs and the Roman mythology and pantheon. Dryden thought that there was something in the play 'that is truly great and truly Roman'—though, as always in Shakespeare, Rome and the Romans appear in a far from unequivocal light. But there are also Greek, Homeric, echoes. Hector is twice named in connection with Coriolanus (and Virgilia is 'another Penelope'). Plutarch mentions Homer as well, and he also names Achilles. Curiously, that name is absent from

Shakespeare's play; yet, given the well-known epic theme of the wrath of Achilles, this would seem a more appropriate name to invoke than that of the more moderate, temperate Hector—for Coriolanus is nothing if not 'choleric'. Perhaps, by withholding the obvious name, but reminding us of Greek heroes, Shakespeare is prompting us to see Coriolanus as an Achilles in a Roman context. (Achilles also had a mother, Thetis, who made him almost, but not quite, invulnerable—a point certainly not lost on Shakespeare.) Certainly, Coriolanus is another of Shakespeare's great warriors, embodying an almost archaic heroic code, who gets hopelessly, disastrously confused when he is removed from the relative simplicities of the battlefield, and forced to negotiate the more complicated political world of the *polis* (I am thinking of, in particular, Titus Andronicus and Othello). Coriolanus cannot, or will not, see that words and conduct which are most fitting and efficacious on the battlefield might be ruinously inappropriate in the city. The fearless and undefeatable soldier may, using the same code, sound politically like an intolerant and unacceptable tyrant. You can't, in this case, make a cushion out of a casque.

The god invoked by Coriolanus himself is, understandably enough, Mars —'Now, Mars, I prithee, make us quick in work' (I, iv, 10). Then, effectively, he *becomes* Mars—'thou Mars' (IV, v, 122)—thus Aufidius addresses him when he goes over to the Volscians. Indeed, as Cominius says, 'He is their god' (IV, vi, 91). But this is not a god of mercy ('there is no more mercy in him than there is milk in a male tiger'—V, iv, 28–30), but an angry god:

> You speak o' th' people,
> As if you were a god, to punish, not
> A man of their infirmity.
>   (III, i, 80–82)

By the end, his harsh and uncompromising demeanour moves Menenius to declare: 'He wants nothing of a god but eternity and a heaven to throne in' (V, iv, 24–5). (A Volscian soldier gives the not very different opinion that 'He's the devil'—I, x, 17.) But, if a god, also a beast, and a very particular beast. He is once an eagle, once a tiger, once a horse, but three times a 'dragon'. First, by his own designation, after being banished—'I go alone,/ Like to a lonely dragon, that his fen/Makes feared and talked of more than seen' (IV, i, 29–31). For the Volscians, he fights 'dragon-like' (IV, vii, 23).

After he has switched his allegiance, his old Roman friend Menenius comments:

> There is a difficency between a grub and a butterfly; yet your butterfly
> was a grub. This Marcius is grown from man to dragon: he has wings;
> he's more than a creeping thing.
>   (V, iv, 11–14)

In post St-George times, knights are obliged to kill dragons; this ancient pre-Christian, and decidedly *un*Christian, proto-knight is metamorphosing *into* a dragon. (This late reference to butterflies of course echoes the early account of Coriolanus' son's characteristic conduct: 'I saw him run after a gilded butterfly; and when he caught it, he let it go again . . . catched it again; or whether his fall enraged him, or how 'twas, he did so set his teeth, and tear it. O, I warrant, how he mammocked it!'. Volumnia's comment 'One on's father's moods'—I, iii, 63–70—might well prepare us for Coriolanus' subsequent behaviour. Butterflies for boys: dragons, or dragonish behaviour, for men.)

God, and beast, he is also described as a 'planet' and an 'engine'. Always more or less than human. And perhaps the most decisive pointer to his inhumanity, non-humanity, is the number of times he is referred to simply as a 'thing':

>   from face to foot
>   He was a thing of blood, whose every motion
>   Was timed with dying cries.
>   (II, ii, 110–11)

>   He sits in his state as a thing made for Alexander.
>   (V, iv, 22)

He also becomes 'a kind of *nothing*' (V, i, 13: my italics). Talk of reification, or self-reification, is perhaps superegatory; we all know, more or less, what it implies to call a person a 'thing'. Whether, and how, we can witness the 'tragedy' of a 'thing'—or a 'no-thing'—is a matter to which we will have to return.

More specifically, Coriolanus is closely identified with his sword. It is often referred to, usually 'smoking' with slaughter. One comes to feel that he is seldom happy, or quite at ease with himself, when it is out of his hand. Like his little son, he 'had rather see the swords and hear a drum than look upon his schoolmaster' (I, iii, 58–9). His ambitions are entirely military and not, indeed, remotely 'scholastic', nor even—in truth—political. He is happy with, and perhaps only with, the casque. And the sword. One of his earliest interventions in the row precipitated by the 'mutinous citizens' is:

> And let me use my sword, I'd make a quarry
> With thousands of these quartered slaves . . .
>   (I, i, 199–200)

His very last words are 'To use my lawful sword' (V, vi, 129)—his sword is full of law, *is* the law as far as he is concerned. But civic society depends on having laws *instead* of swords. In his younger days he 'lurched all swords of the garland' (II, ii, 102), and at Corioles 'His sword, death's stamp,/Where it did mark, it took' (II, ii, 108–9). Lartius pays him a rather curious compliment:

> O noble fellow!
> Who sensibly outdares his senseless sword,
> And when it bows stand'st up!
>   (I, iv, 53–5)

This seems to suggest that Coriolanus himself remains erect, even when his sword droops. I think there is an entirely appropriate phallic hint there. Effectively, *all* his energy and appetite and drive—in sum, a colossal force—have been directed (displaced, if you will) into his fearful, 'smoking', instrument of death—Eros 'bowing' to the stand-up work of Thanatos. When his soldiers lift him up in their arms (presumably carrying him on their shoulders), after his exploits at Corioles, Coriolanus cries out, not unhappily one feels—'Make you a sword of me?' (I, vi, 76). He is, indeed, to all intents and purposes, *the* sword of the city. The deeper truth is that he has made a sword out of himself.

This engine, this thing, this sword, this man of steel (let us say)—it is hard to see what could break or bend, deflect or deter, him. Yet that, of course, is just what happens at the climax of the play. After his victory at

Corioles, Marcius (soon to be named 'Coriolanus'), in a speech refusing praise and flattery, says:

> When steel grows soft as the parasite's silk,
> Let him be made a coverture for th' wars!
>   (I, ix, 45–6)

This is a much disputed and debated passage, marked by that harsh, over-compacted meaning so characteristic of the play. Take one possible meaning as—when the army turns soft, use silk for armour. The power of the image lies, of course, in the idea of steel growing soft as silk. Impossible. Yet steel Coriolanus does turn, briefly, fatally, as soft as silk, when he capitulates to the intercessionary pleas to spare Rome. Aufidius picks up the image for us, after the capitulation:

> Breaking his oath and resolution, like
> A twist of rotten silk; never admitting
> Counsel o' th' war; but at his nurse's tears
> He whined and roared away your victory . . .
>   (V, vi, 95–8)

Man of steel to man of silk (rotten silk to the critical)—part of the tragic power of the play surely lies in this sudden transformation, and we must inquire a little as to how it comes about.

The crucial factor, or influence, is of course his mother, Volumnia. Plutarch–North has this to say concerning the relationship between Marcius (later Coriolanus) and his mother:

> the only thing that made him to love honor was the joy he saw his mother did take of him. For he thought nothing made him so happy and honorable, as that his mother might hear everybody praise and commend him, that she might always see him return with a crown upon his head . . . thinking all due to his mother . . . at her desire [he] took a wife also, by whom he had two young children, and yet *never left his mother's house therefore.*
>
>   (My italics)

There is not much more concerning Volumnia in Plutarch, apart from the crucial intercessionary scene when she dissuades her son from sacking his native city, Rome. All the other scenes involving Volumnia in the play are Shakespeare's invention, and, with powerful dramatic economy, they serve to reveal how—psychologically and emotionally—Coriolanus, indeed, never leaves 'his mother's house'. Whatever else he is or becomes—sword, engine, dragon, planet, god—he remains, ineradicably, a *mother's-boy*. These two words are central and crucial to the play.

Volumnia embodies, and articulates, the martial values of Rome. In her first speech, she celebrates that shift of affect, and affection, from the cushion to the casque—or rather, from the bed to the battlefield—we have already noted as a 'Roman' predisposition:

> If my son were my husband, I should freelier rejoice in that absence wherein he won honor than in the embracements of his bed where he would show most love.
>
> (I, iii, 3–5)

Better an absent honour than a present embrace—that's Rome. Or, at least, Volumnia's Rome. Virgilia, the wife of Coriolanus, is given no words by Plutarch, though he makes nothing of the fact. Shakespeare's Virgilia is, as it were, audibly silent. 'My gracious silence, hail!' (II, i, 181) is about as amorous as Coriolanus gets in exchanges with his wife—but though she is almost entirely effaced and displaced by the extremely vociferous Volumnia, there *is* grace in Virgilia's silence. Ruskin found her 'perhaps the loveliest of Shakespeare's female characters', and, while that doubtless tells us something about Ruskin, as always he has a point. Most of the speech in this play is, one way or another, pretty unpleasant. In the circumstances, there is, as it were, much to be said for not speaking. Such *very* few words as she does speak (Desdemona and Cordelia are loquacious by comparison), are either modestly decorous, or right against the Roman grain. For example, when Volumnia voluptuously wallows in the thought of her son's 'bloody brow' in battle, Virgilia's involuntary interjection is 'O Jupiter, no blood!' (I, iii, 41). Virgilia is, in Volumnia's terms, very distinctly *not* a 'Roman' woman—and more power to her!

Having made him what he is—'Thy valiantness was mine, thou suck'st it from me' (III, ii, 129)—Volumnia, on two crucial occasions, uses her influence to persuade him, against his better judgement (or steely, intransigent resolve), to go right against the rigid martial inclinations and instincts which she herself nurtured in him. It is she who launches the idea that he should stand for consulship—'There's one thing wanting, which I doubt not but/Our Rome will cast upon thee.' Knowing that that will involve having to ingratiate himself with the common people, whom he quite intemperately and viscerally loathes, Coriolanus, rightly, senses immediately that such a role is not for him—'Know, good mother,/I had rather be their servant in my way/Than sway with them in theirs' (II, i, 207–10). In particular, he shrinks in aversion from the prospect of having to put off his armour and don the 'vesture of humility' and then going to stand in the market-place, showing his wounds and begging for votes. Such a parade of pseudo-humility ill becomes a man who is uncorruptibly a total soldier—a butcher-soldier perhaps, but with his martial integrity intact. Quite simply, he won't do it:

> I do beseech you
> Let me o'erleap that custom, for I cannot
> Put on the gown, stand naked, and entreat them,
> For my wounds' sake, to give their suffrage. Please you
> That I may pass this doing.
>   (II, ii, 136–40)

More pertinently—'It is a part/That I shall blush in acting' (II, ii, 145–6). Coriolanus is a soldier who can, emphatically, do *deeds* (there is much stress on this), but who cannot act parts. But Volumnia is a mother who always gets her way. So he tries, though not without some heavy irony concerning the self-falsification it involves. 'I will practice the insinuating nod, and be off to them most counterfeitly; that is, sir, I will counterfeit the bewitchment of some popular man' (II, iii, 103–6). Though his instinct is all the other way. 'Rather than fool it so,/Let the high office and the honor go' (II, iii, 126–7). After his session in the market-place, he cannot wait to 'change these garments'—thereby 'knowing myself again' (II, iii, 153). He seems to have the people's 'voice', but then the tribunes agitate the crowd and it turns against Coriolanus. Coriolanus lets the tribunes know what he thinks of 'the mutable, rank-scented meiny [crowd]' (III, i, 66), and as his anger mounts his words concerning the people (Hydra-headed mob etc.) become more bilious and choleric, until the tribunes can say he has 'spoken like a

traitor' (III, i, 162) and urge his execution. Coriolanus draws his sword—
knowing himself again—and the people are beaten back. He intends to be
uncompromisingly defiant, uncompromisingly himself, come what may—
'yet will I still / Be thus to them' (III, ii, 5–6). But he has reckoned without
his mother—and her maternal desires and ambitions. She wants to be able
to say 'my son the consul' as well as 'my son the soldier'. Coriolanus is confused. His mother had taught him *always* to despise the people:

> I muse my mother
> Does not approve me further, who was wont
> To call them woolen vassals, things created
> To buy and sell with groats . . .
> [Volumnia enters]
> I talk of you:
> Why did you wish me milder—Would you have me
> False to my nature? Rather say I play
> The man I am.
>
> (III, ii, 7–16)

But she, with some clever if partly specious arguments, urges him to play
the man he is *not:*

> You are too absolute;
> Though therein you can never be too noble
> But when extremities speak. I have heard you say,
> Honor and policy, like unsevered friends,
> I' th' war do grow together. Grant that, and tell me
> In peace what each of them by th' other lose
> That they combine not there.
>
> (III, ii, 39–45)

Coriolanus' response is a rather helpless 'Tush, tush!', as well it might be,
since the point is a tricky one, though one that touches on the problem at
the centre of the play. All's fair, certainly in war, and there it is not incompatible with 'honour' to outwit your enemy with 'politic' stratagems. So
why not in peacetime? Why not trick the plebeians, for the honour of a
consulship? Coriolanus knows, or rather *feels,* that there is an important

difference, but he is quite unable to argue it through. No man is less a sophist than Coriolanus. Just what his 'nature' is, and what being true or false
to it might entail, we must consider later. Here, his mother—'I would dissemble with my nature . . . I should do so in honor'—asserts herself as his
instructor-director:

> speak
> To th' people, not by your own instruction,
> Nor by th' matter which your heart prompts you,
> But with such words that are but roted in
> Your tongue, though but bastards and syllables
> Of no allowance to your bosom's truth.
>
> (III, ii, 52–7)

We have only recently heard Coriolanus' old friend Menenius say of him—
'His heart's his mouth:/What his breast forges, that his tongue must vent'
(III, i, 256–7), and we should recognize that, with their theatrical instructions—'perform a part', 'come, we'll prompt you' (Cominius)—his mother
and the supporting Roman nobles are making an impossible demand of
Coriolanus. Cornered, the intellectually unresourceful Coriolanus can only
capitulate, though not without a good deal of foot-dragging and something
like a tantrum of protest at the self-division, self-dispersal, indeed self-
dissolution, which is being asked of him:

> Well, I will do't . . .
> You have put me now to such a part which never
> I shall discharge to th' life.
>
> (III, ii, 101–6)

Be like a harlot, eunuch, virgin, knave, schoolboy, beggar?—why can't I
just be a soldier? Why should I make my mind and body play false to each
other? No, damn it, I *won't* go through with it! At which, his mother turns
from him, as if giving up on a child in a particularly fretful and tiresome
mood. 'At thy choice then.' As much as to say—well, if you are going to
be *that* difficult! And Coriolanus wilts back into her scolded, remorseful
little boy.

> Pray, be content:
> Mother, I am going to the marketplace;
> Chide me no more . . .
>
>   (III, ii, 130–32)

And, though we do not know it yet, there will indeed be some 'boy's tears' to follow. This mother will be the death of him.

Coriolanus leaves for the market-place, attended by the hopeless injunction—'mildly' (repeated five times). 'Well, mildly be it then—mildly' (III, ii, 145). 'Mildness' is certainly *not* in his nature, whatever that nature might be; and, as the tribunes well know, it will take little to make him 'play the man I am':

> Being once chafed, he cannot
> Be reined again to temperance; then he speaks
> What's in his heart, and that is there which looks
> With us to break his neck.
>
>   (III, iii, 27–30)

Coriolanus is nothing if not honest, and once the tribunes have 'chafed' him by calling him 'traitor' (the word is not in Plutarch), he lets fly at the people with such vitriolic fury that by communal (or rather, mob) agreement, he is banished. His response is, we may say, predictable:

> You common cry of curs, whose breath I hate
> As reek o' th' rotten fens, whose loves I prize
> As the dead carcasses of unburied men
> That do corrupt my air, I banish you.
> . . . Despising
> For you the city, thus I turn my back.
> There is a world elsewhere.
>
>   (III, iii, 120–35)

Brave and powerful talk; and we can surely still respond to a something heroic in Coriolanus' 'absolute' and unyielding refusal of compromise, his furious and contemptuous rejection of the mass, the masses, the world *here*.

The question the remainder of the play will explore is whether it is finally possible for Coriolanus to 'banish' Rome—his city, his class, his friends, his family, his *mother*. Or—put it another way—can there finally be, for a Roman, 'a world elsewhere'?

Coriolanus has always appeared as single, singular; sharply outlined and standing out against the rest. He is 'constant', 'absolute', *adamant* we might say. During the war against the Volscians, he is locked, trapped, within the enemy's gates on his own—as a soldier says: 'He is himself alone,/ To answer all the city' (I, iv, 52–3). This description holds good whether the city is Corioli or Rome. 'O me alone!' he cries, after his one-man victory (I, vii, 76)—and the cry reverberates throughout the play. After his banishment from Rome, he goes—instantly—over to the enemy. As in the case of Timon, it seems that 'absolutists' are either rigidly 'constant', or must *totally* invert their commitments. As we have seen, Shakespeare is very interested in these sudden switches of allegiance whereby a passionate Roman becomes a virulent anti-Roman (I am thinking of Lucius in *Titus Andronicus* and Alcibiades in *Timon of Athens*)—on the spot, as it were. In what is arguably his only soliloquy (as with Timon, there is no inwardness in the depiction of Coriolanus, none of the wracked, intelligent, conscience-searching of a Macbeth: Coriolanus is all outside, all deed, all sword), Coriolanus says:

> O world, thy slippery turns! Friends now fast sworn . . .
> On a dissension of a doit, break out
> To bitterest enmity . . .
> . . . So with me:
> My birthplace hate I, and my love's upon
> This enemy town.
>
> (IV, iv, 12–24)

Well, it might be—and Shakespeare could be exploring the unstable and changeable foundations of what we fondly take to be our our most immovably fixed commitments, allegiances, and loyalties. But Coriolanus might not be so rid of his 'birthplace', so cleanly and hatefully disengaged from Rome, as he thinks. It is notable that, after his banishment, he is seen entering the enemy town of Actium 'in mean apparel, disguised and muffled'.

This detail, unremarked, is in Plutarch. But Shakespeare would surely have seen an added irony in Coriolanus having recourse to almost the same 'dissembling' strategies he had so furiously repudiated in Rome. Has he learnt theatricals in spite of himself? Is he going to 'play' the dragon, 'act' the vengeful god, 'counterfeit' the ireful anti-Roman? If so, he may well not prove as impregnable as he has hitherto seemed, for a time could come when the 'acting' has to stop. Not that he gives signs of dissembling. His determined disavowal and rejection of Rome seems absolutely resolute and total. His single imperative to his old friend, Menenius, who comes to plead with him on Rome's behalf, summarizes the stance of denial and dismissal he has adopted—'Away!' He spells it out:

> Wife, mother, child, I know not. My affairs
> Are servanted to others . . .
> Therefore be gone.
>
> (V, ii, 83–4, 88)

Away *every* Roman; away even his own Roman self. Cominius receives as much of a brush-off as Menenius:

> Coriolanus
> He would not answer to; forbad all names;
> He was a kind of nothing, titleless,
> Till he had forged himself a name o' th' fire
> Of burning Rome.
>
> (V, i, 11–15)

I will come to the importance of 'names' in the play. Here we may note his attempt entirely to erase and disown all traces of his Roman identity, rendering himself—certainly from the Roman point of view—'a kind of nothing'. Just as swords are 'forged', so he will forge a new name in the fire of burning Rome.

   To my knowledge, it was Bradley who first pointed out how references to fire and burning Rome (not mentioned in Plutarch), suddenly start and then proliferate in Acts IV and V, as the not-Coriolanus, the anonymous, titleless 'nothing', starts to move inexorably—all engine-beast-god now—against the city of his birth. This dragon is breathing fire. Territories are being 'consumed with fire'; there is terrified talk of burned temples and houses put to 'the brand'. Menenius gives his opinion:

> If he could burn us all into one coal,
> We have deserved it.
>
> (IV, vi, 138–9)

Volscian soldiers, talking to downcast Romans, refer gleefully to 'the intended fire your city is ready to flame in' (V, ii, 47), and Menenius, trying to get through to the alienated and no-longer Coriolanus, haplessly recognizes—'Thou art preparing fire for us' (V, ii, 72). It is all summed up in Cominius' description of the oncoming avenger:

> I tell you he does sit in gold, his eye
> Red as 'twould burn Rome, and his injury
> The jailer to his pity.
>
> (V, i, 63–5)

Fire consumes everything and leaves, effectively, nothing. A total razing and cleansing. This is not so much revenge as an intended eradication, obliteration, annihilation. This unnamable and omnipotent figure is, indeed, absolute—'too absolute'.

The nightmare prospect behind all this, is the destruction, the 'unbuilding', the 'unroofing', or the 'melting', of the city—THE city. Rome. When things come to crisis point between the plebeians and the tribunes, and Coriolanus and the nobles, Cominius cries out:

> That is the way to lay the city flat,
> To bring the roof to the foundation,
> And bury all which yet distinctly ranges,
> In heaps and piles of ruin.
>
> (III, i, 203–6)

For Rome, the 'city' simply *was* the available civilization (no matter what its internal impairments might be), and whatever was outside the city was uncontainable and unformulable (out of language, out of bounds), potentially 'monstrous'—dragons clawing their way towards the city walls. But there was a nightmare within the nightmare—pointed to when, in the internal crisis, Menenius beseechingly cries out:

> Proceed by process [i.e. by law, the cement of the city];
> Lest parties (as he is beloved) break out,
> *And sack great Rome with Romans.*
>   (III, i, 312–14: my italics)

From the start of Shakespeare's Roman plays, we have seen that Rome could be 'barbarous', Romans barbarians (as in this play the plebeians are to Coriolanus—'I would they were barbarians, as they are,/Though in Rome littered'—III, i, 237–8—though no one, on his day, more 'barbaric' than Coriolanus). That could be handled, contained, perhaps worked out. The city would still stand. But if Rome should self-destructively turn on itself; not just a Roman by a Roman 'valiantly' vanquished, but *Rome* by Romans . . . if the city tears *itself* to pieces, what price *any* hope for civilization and order then? We must be clear about this. Shakespeare is very far, *very* far, from being an uncritical admirer of the Roman world as he conceived it, or at least as he dramatized his version of it. It is a hard, brutal, militarized, legalistic, excessively male world, with women and domestic values and virtues—procreative eroticism, love, gentleness, mildness, pity—marginalized to the point of near-extinction. But Rome—arid, unimaginative, unbounteous, politic and cruel Rome—was the alternative to chaos, the (badly faulted) prototype of civilized (problematic, question-begging word, as Shakespeare well knew) societies in the western world. Shakespeare being Shakespeare, he lent some of his finest poetry to a final elegiac efflorescent flaring of an Egyptian world that was inevitably superseded. For good or bad, good *and* bad, Rome was the future, and the future was to be—*mutatis, mutandis*—Roman.

The Rome of *Coriolanus* is a noisy place; more specifically it is a city of 'voices'. Since most plays are comprised of speakers, I must attempt to avoid a fatuity here. But the word 'voice' (or 'voices') occurs over forty times, far more often than in any other Shakespeare play. And the voices are, preeminently, the voices of the people. In this play, the people (or mob, or rabble, or children, or slaves—according to their behaviour and your point of view) are, certainly, volatile, fickle, too—easily swayable, and, when pressed too hard or deprived too far, dangerously dissentious and mutinous. (They are probably 'stinking' too—the working classes are the sweating classes, and doubtless, their food is none of the best either.) But the play makes clear that many of their grievances are justified, while the behaviour of the supposedly responsible, 'paternalistic' patricians, leaves a lot to be desired. Coriolanus is only the *most* obscenely contemptuous of the common people among his class—it is a matter of degree, not kind. Menenius is as willing to call them 'rats' as Coriolanus is determined to call them 'curs'. The use by Menenius of the tired allegory of the body politic to placate the mob in the first scene, is really a piece of gross effrontery. Smugly and complacently, he allows the Belly (= the Senators) to explain to the 'mutinous members' (= the people) that they 'From me receive that natural competency/ Whereby they live'. A 'natural competency' is just exactly what these famished citizens–plebeians lack, and, indeed, all they ask for. Later in the play, Menenius says how 'supple' we are 'when we have stuffed/These pipes and these conveyances of our blood/With wine and feeding' (V, i, 53–5). Clearly, he speaks from experience, and the earlier, hostile case against the Belly–Senate—

> it did remain
> I' th' midst o' th' body, idle and unactive,
> Still cupboarding the viand, never bearing
> Like labor with the rest . . .
>
> (I, i, 99–102)

—would seem to fit him, and who knows how many other Senators, perfectly. The voice and 'voices' of the people, then; to which we should add the unusually large number of references to mouth(s), tongue(s), breath(s). There is the heroic-martial Coriolanian world of swordly doings and deeds; and the people's world of voices, or mouthly deeds. Coriolanus is an 'engine', but the voice of the people is an instrument, too. Voices are votes (as in some Elizabethan elections, during this period in Rome the elected were chosen by vocal acclaim, or 'shouting'), and it is having to supplicate for the people's 'voices' in the market-place which is anathema to Coriolanus. But —'the people/Must have their voices' (II, ii, 140–41), and if Coriolanus cannot finally bring himself to ask for them 'kindly', the voices will turn on him. In the event, he will be 'Whooped out of Rome' by, as he sees it, 'th' voice of slaves' (IV, v, 81–2). (For all his gnashing vituperations, Coriolanus is not really at ease using tongue, mouth, voice. When Cominius describes how Coriolanus dismissed him 'with his speechless hand'—V, i, 67—we have the essential man in all his silent physicality.) But the voices which 'did hoot him out o' th' city' might well 'roar him in again' (IV, vi, 124–5). When it is learned that Coriolanus will spare Rome, a Senator exhorts the city, impossibly as it sounds, to 'Unshout the noise that banished Marcius' (V, v, 4). Shouting, whooping, hooting, roaring—this civic noise sounds ugly. And there is not much to redeem it in the rhetoric of the patricians, either. Gordon would seem to be justified in his pessimistic summing up of the play (in his essay 'Name to Fame'):

> It is a show of civil life. The city must stand and continue, for outside it there is the monstrous, or the nothing. But within the walls absolutes turn out to be instrumental; the words that identify and bind become words that debase and destroy: whoops, or hoots, curses, lies, flatteries, voices, stinking breath . . . In this city to speak is to be guilty.

No wonder Virgilia prefers to remain silent.

'Voices' are also intimately connected with 'fame' and 'name'—two more words which often recur. Gordon again: 'Name is Fame, is Honour, and is won by deeds—in Rome, by deeds in war' (ibid. p. 60). Fame depends on 'praise', 'renown', 'applause and clamor', 'good report'—all more or less dependent on 'voice'. Volumnia, explaining to Virgilia how she brought up her son, says: 'I, considering how honor would become such a person—that it was no better than picture-like to hang by th' wall, if *renown made it not stir*—was pleased to let him seek danger where he was like to find *fame*' (I, iii, 10–14: my italics). To acquire 'name' and 'fame', Coriolanus will need 'voices' in a more than electoral sense. (In ancient Greece, the word for 'truth'—'*aletheia*'—meant, literally, *not* forgetting, or forgotten. The epic singers and reciters were so important just because they prevented the silent deeds of heroic warriors from falling into an eternal, soundless, oblivion. They preserved and perpetuated the 'renown', exactly by *re*knowing, *re*naming. This keeps the honour 'stirring'.) Caius Marcus of course wins fame and name after his exploits at Corioli:

> from this time,
> For what he did before Corioles, call him,
> With all th' applause and clamor of the host,

Caius Marcius Coriolanus.
Bear th' addition nobly ever!

(I, ix, 62–6)

Or, as the Herald announces it:

he hath won,
With fame, a name to Caius Marcius; these
In honor follows Coriolanus.

(II, i, 169–71)

As his mother proudly says—he is 'By deed-achieving honor newly named'
(II, i, 179).

But if name and fame depend upon voice, mouth, breath, their possible
persistingness is always vulnerable, precarious. Voices can be withheld, or
—just like that—shout the other way. (It is notable that only once does
Coriolanus think of *writing* as possibly a proper preservative of fame—and
I will come to that moment.) Of course, when Coriolanus leaves Rome to
join the Volscians, he makes a point of trying to shed and disown all his
previous names, both family-given and war-won ('forbad all names'). This
attempt by Coriolanus to reject or leave behind his names is highlighted by
Shakespeare (but not Plutarch) when the disguised and prevaricating Coriolanus first arrives in Antium, and Aufidius has to ask him *five times*—
'what is thy name?' At last, Coriolanus has to answer. His attempt at an act
of willed dis-nomination proves finally to be impossible. And when Aufidius at the end refuses to call his Roman ally by 'thy stol'n name / Coriolanus'
(V, vi, 89), it is, to be exact, the last but one straw. Perhaps the most poignant
episode illustrating both the cardinal importance and the ephemeral for-
gettability of names, occurs after the first battle with the Volscians. Victorious Coriolanus asks a modest, and indeed honourable, favour of his com-
mander Cominius:

I sometimes lay here in Corioles
At a poor man's house; he used me kindly.
He cried to me; I saw him prisoner;
. . . I request you
To give my poor host freedom.

(I, ix, 82–7)

Cominius is more than happy to comply. All they need is 'his name'.

> By Jupiter, forgot!
> I am weary; yea, my memory is tired.
> Have we no wine here?
>   (I, ix, 90–92)

So easily can a 'name' be 'lost'. In Plutarch, the kindly 'enemy' host is wealthy, and there is no mention of his name having been forgotten by Coriolanus. You can decide what kind of a point Shakespeare was making with his changes. But, clearly, some amnesias are lethal, and the forgetting of a person's name may cost the forgotten one not less than everything. Coriolanus himself will effectively give up his life in one last desperate attempt to secure fitting and appropriate remembrance.

When his mother and family approach, to plead for Rome, he tries to stiffen his resolve:

> But out, affection!
> All bond and privilege of nature, break!
> Let it be virtuous to be obstinate.
>   (V, iii, 24–6)

But, even at the sight of them (particularly his mother), he is beginning to crack (he is too brittle, too 'forged', to bend):

> I melt, and am not
> Of stronger earth than others. My mother bows,
> . . . and my young boy
> Hath an aspect of intercession which
> Great Nature cries 'Deny not.' Let the Volsces
> Plough Rome, and harrow Italy! I'll never
> Be such a gosling to obey instinct, but stand
> As if a man were author of himself
> And knew no other kin.
>   (V, iii, 28–37)

He is trying to hold on to his inflexible intransigence, regain that unshakable, immovable erectness he so admires—'Like a great sea-mark, standing
every flaw' (V, iii, 74). But he is wobbling, 'melting' (he even speaks of kissing his wife), slipping from steel to silk. Coriolanus is discovering that he
cannot 'stand' as if he were 'author of himself', some 'unnatural' partheno-
genetic freak; discovering that there are some bonds of nature which cannot be broken, some imperatives of 'Great Nature' which cannot be refused.
He *will* be a 'gosling' and 'obey instinct', before reasserting his lost identity
as an 'eagle'. But, even as he is capitulating to nature, he feels he is also being untrue to his *own* nature. Coriolanus is being torn apart by contradictions in nature, contradictions *of* nature. We have heard much of his na-
ture—he cannot help his nature, his nature is too noble for this world, 'his
nature/In that's no changeling' (IV, vii, 10–11), and so on. Aufidius has the
most searching speech about Coriolanus, when explaining to his lieutenant
why Rome banished him:

> Whether 'twas pride,
> Which out of daily fortune ever taints
> The happy man; whether defect of judgment,
> To fail in the disposing of those chances
> Which he was lord of; or whether *nature,*
> *Not to be other than one thing, not moving*
> *From th' casque to th' cushion,* but commanding peace
> Even with the same austerity and garb
> As he controlled the war; but one of these—
> As he hath spices of them all . . .
> . . . made him feared,
> So hated, and so banished.
>   (IV, vii, 37–48: my italics)

The tragedy which Coriolanus experiences and enacts is the discovered impossibility for a man 'not to be other than one thing'. He tries, more ferociously than any other of Shakespeare's heroes. He can certainly dispense
with the 'cushion'—never wanted it, anyway. But he cannot defy or deny
his mother. It is not, finally, in his 'nature'. Whatever that nature is. We
hear and see quite a lot of his *un*nature, too, best summed up in Cominius'
description of him as he marches on Rome with the Volscians:

> he leads them like a thing
> Made by some other deity than Nature,
> That shapes men better . . .
>
> (IV, vi, 91–3)

To his mother, in the final scene, still trying to stave off her influence, he cries out:

> Tell me not
> Wherein I seem unnatural. Desire not
> T' allay my rages and revenges with
> Your colder reasons.
>
> (V, iii, 83–6)

It is perhaps his truest nature to *be* unnatural? In which case, when he capitulates and obeys 'Great Nature', is he finally maturing into a new, recognized, and accepted humanity (as some have thought)? Or is he succumbing to an internal splitting which will destroy whatever integrity of identity he may have—helplessly regressing to the enfeebled status of 'mother's boy'? You can see it in either way; though I think it is better, somehow, to try to see it as both.

As he feels his resolve slipping in front of his family, he says:

> Like a dull actor now,
> I have forgot my part and I am out,
> Even to a full disgrace.
>
> (V, iii, 40–43)

When he was asked to stop being a soldier and at least pretend he was a politician, he discovered it just wasn't in him to act a part. But this speech seems to imply that he is being discomfited out of his 'part' of the adamantine warrior. Or does he just mean that being confronted with his mother again gives him the equivalent of stage-fright? Is he losing his grip on what, exactly, he is as a man? The arguments and appeals with which his mother works on him need not be summarized here. He is effectively lost when she kneels to him—'What's this? / Your knees to me? To your corrected son?' (V, iii, 55–6); it horrifies him as if it were some chaotic inversion in nature.

She inevitably has her way with her 'corrected son'. But there is a barb in the words that recognize her triumph:

> O mother, mother!
> What have you done? Behold, the heavens do ope,
> The gods look down, and this unnatural scene
> They laugh at. O my mother, mother! O!
> You have won a happy victory to Rome;
> But, for your son—believe it, O, believe it!—
> Most dangerously you have with him prevailed,
> If not most mortal to him. But let it come.
>
> (V, iii, 182–9)

What *has* she done? She has saved Rome: but in the case of her son, she has both made and marred him; taught him immutability and made him change; 'manned' him and unmanned him. Made him steel, turned him silk. As Aufidius says:

> He bowed his nature, never known before
> But to be rough, unswayable, and free
>
> (V, vi, 25–6)

For Plutarch, the moment when Coriolanus gives in is all 'nature'. 'And nature so wrought with him that the tears fell from his eyes and . . . [he] yielded to the affection of his blood.' It is Shakespeare who makes Coriolanus deem it an '*unnatural* scene'. At the very least, we can say that one 'nature' has been undermined by another, and while that is undoubtedly good for Rome (and perhaps humanity), Coriolanus is clearly right in sensing that it will prove disastrous for him. Much of the rest of his speech is in Plutarch—but not those last four words. 'But let it come.' This, as Brockbank remarked, is directly reminiscent of Hamlet's 'Let be.' It is as if he recognizes that, by what had just happened, an inexorable process has been set in train, the outcome of which is at once unforeseeable and ineluctable. It amounts to a recognition and acceptance of the tragic workings of nature.

After this, it is easy for Aufidius to goad Coriolanus to a self-destructive fury. He calls him 'traitor'—as Rome did; denies him his 'stol'n' name; and,

when Coriolanus invokes Mars, delivers the final taunt which he knows
will drive him completely out of control: 'Name not the god, thou boy of
tears!' (V, vi, 101). This makes Coriolanus explode:

> Measureless liar, thou hast made my heart
> Too great for what contains it.
>
>   (V, vi, 103–4)

and he calls down the knives:

> Cut me to pieces, Volsces, men and lads,
> Stain all your edges on me. 'Boy'! False hound!
> If you have writ your annals true, 'tis there,
> That, like an eagle in a dovecote, I
> Fluttered your Volscians in Corioles.
> Alone I did it. 'Boy'?

In a sense, Aufidius is absolutely correct (sometimes, nothing wounds like
the truth)—Coriolanus *did* regress to being a 'boy of tears' in front of his
mother. (Though, of course, there could be a less denigrating, more generous way of describing his transformation.) But if he goes down as 'Boy', he
wants once more to assert his old martial-eagle identity of the matchless
warrior who could take a city 'alone'. And he wants to think of this identity
and exploit set down and preserved in the immutability of writing (not
trusting to the vagaries of voice). 'Annals' are the distinctively Roman form
of history, primarily associated with Tacitus (it is the only time Shakespeare
used the word). Having employed the heroized Coriolanus, banished and
then besought him, Rome will continue without him, finding other soldiers
for other wars. That is why Coriolanus wants what he has been and done to
be written '*true*' and written '*there*'. So ends the last great tragedy written
for the English stage.

ROMANCES

feigned nowhere acts

> (Thomas Nashe)

Did you ever dream of such a thing?

> (*Pericles,* IV, v, 5)

The dream's here still. Even when I wake it is
Without me, as within me; not imagined, felt.

> (*Cymbeline,* IV, ii, 306–7)

Your actions are my dreams.

> (*The Winter's Tale,* III, ii, 80)

And rather like a dream than an assurance

> (*The Tempest,* I, ii, 45)

The imagination may be compared to Adam's dream—he awoke and
found it truth.

> (John Keats, *Letters*)

Trying to differentiate and distinguish the characteristic features of 'romance' and 'realism', Henry James came up with a characteristically surprising image:

> The real represents to my perception the things we cannot possibly *not*
> know, sooner or later, one way or another; it being but one of the acci-
> dents of our hampered state . . . that particular instances have not come
> our way. The romantic stands, on the other hand, for the things that, with
> all the facilities in the world, all the wealth and all the courage and all the
> wit and all the adventure, we never *can* directly know; the things that can

reach us only through the beautiful circuit and subterfuge of our thought
and our desire . . . The only *general* attribute of projected romance that I
can see, the only one that fits all its cases, is the fact of the kind of experience with which it deals—experience liberated, so to speak; experience
disengaged, disembroiled, disencumbered, exempt from the conditions
that we usually know attach to it. . . The balloon of experience is in fact of
course tied to the earth, and under that necessity we swing, thanks to a
rope of remarkable length, in the more or less commodious car of the
imagination; but it is by the rope that we know where we are, and from
the moment that cable is cut we are at large and unrelated: we only swing
apart from the globe—though remaining as exhilarated, naturally, as we
like, especially when all goes well. The art of the romancer is 'for the fun
of it' insidiously to cut the cable.

Attempting to work out the implications of the extended metaphor, we
might offer something like this—the imagination can travel a long way
from the surface of reality, i.e. the earth. In a 'romance', sometimes we feel
we are still in touch, however remotely, with the earth, and sometimes we
sense we no longer are. That 'rope' would seem to be something like our
sense of relative plausibility—'our general sense of the way things happen'
in James's own words. But it may be a very tenuous rope, and, still following the image, it may prove difficult to say whether the rope is cut or not.
As James recognized with another image. 'It is as difficult . . . to trace the
dividing-line between the real and the romantic as to plant a milestone between north and south. . .' It is, of course, not difficult to plant that milestone between north and south; it is impossible. Or rather such an act of
demarcation is arbitrary, and decreed and controlled by convention; either
imposed by authority, or agreed by consensus. To be *really* real, James discovers, the novel must incorporate 'romance'.

James was writing as a late nineteenth-century novelist. Not so very many
years before this, in the 1870s, another Victorian, Edward Dowden, was the
first to designate Shakespeare's Last Plays as 'Romances'.* By then the word

---

* The first person to use 'romantic' in connection with Shakespeare seems to have been
Coleridge. '*The Tempest*, I repeat, has been selected as a specimen of the romantic
drama; i.e. of a drama, the interests of which are independent of all historical facts and
associations, and arise from their fitness to that faculty of our nature, the imagination I

had acquired a lot of semantically blurred luggage since the time it simply meant a tale in a vernacular Romanic language—'Isn't it romantic?' is not the sort of question worth going into here. The Elizabethans and Jacobeans used the word of stories but not of dramas. Shakespeare never used the word at all—not of plays, not of anything. Yet, bearing in mind the contemporary Jacobean uses of the word, Dowden's classification is an astute and helpful one. And James's tentative definition of generic romance as dealing with experience 'liberated . . . disengaged, disembroiled, disencumbered, exempt from the conditions that we *usually* know attach to it' (my italics) is appropriate to bear in mind as we approach these last plays by Shakespeare, dealing as they do with the *un*usual and extraordinary—even the seemingly 'miraculous'—in human experience. But we should also bear in mind James's recognition that you cannot *finally* demarcate 'romance' from 'the literally true'—and perhaps also Mervyn Peake's brave affirmation from the depths of great suffering that 'to live at all is miracle enough'. 'Wonders will never cease' is a popular saying; and that's literally true in Shakespeare's Romances, in which an almost unceasing wonder comes to prevail. It may be that the rope to that Jamesian balloon is both always cut and never permanently severed.

But, eschewing further paradox, let us be more, relatively speaking, mundane. Here is Dr Johnson to keep our feet, and our balloons, on the ground. 'In romance, when the wide field of possibility lies open to invention, the incidents may easily be more numerous.' In other words—anything can happen, endlessly. The romance tale permitted, or rather encouraged, a copious abundance of incident, with little or no concern for verisimilitude, plausible links of cause and effect, or clear continuity. A romance invariably concerns the course of true love running very rough indeed. It comes out all right *in the end*—poetic justice is always, satisfactorily, done and seen to be done. But before that, *anything* can happen—distressed damsels in danger

---

mean, which owes no allegiance to time and place—a species of drama, therefore, in which errors of chronology and geography, no mortal sins in any species, are venial, or count for nothing.' And this is Edward Dowden in his *Shakespeare* (1877): 'He seems to have learned the secret of life, and while taking his share in it, to be yet disengaged from it . . . In these "Romances" . . . a supernatural element is present . . . Shakespeare's faith seems to have been that there is something without and around our human lives, of which we know little, yet which we know to be beneficent and divine.' I owe this footnote to Ian Donaldson.

and heroic knights in armour, losings in the forest and findings in the court, shipwrecks and pirates, traps and escapes, evil queens and beneficent magicians, death and resuscitation, danger and rescue, desolation and comfort, disguise and recognition, enigmas from oracles and salvation by gods. And, as Nabokov would say, much, much more.

The Elizabethans did not employ the word 'romance' much, though the noun had been around since the thirteenth century (the adjective 'romantic' arrives in the seventeenth century). Yet there were at least two incalculably influential Elizabethan romances—Sidney's *Arcadia* (of which more in a moment), and Spenser's *The Faerie Queene*. And, crucially for our present interest (and Shakespeare's plays), there had been a series of translations of early Greek romances from the middle of the sixteenth century onwards. These romances date from the second and third centuries AD. They are episodic, processional 'quest' stories, involving perilous journeys and final recognitions and reunions. We find in them the origin of the heroine figure, such as she appears in Shakespeare's Last Plays. Too much detail would distract us unnecessarily here and I will allow a scholar in the field to summarize. Here is Carol Gesner:

> In Greek romance the 'quest' usually is begun when a pair of youthful lovers—frequently married—are separated. Their desire for reunion usually motivates the journey. The minor episodic adventures frequently include storm and shipwreck, followed by various combinations of brigands, pirates, brothel keepers, poisoners, and kidnappers. Usually the hero and heroine experience imprisonment, slavery, and attempted seduction. The great crisis frequently comes to the heroine rather than to the hero: as a result of some misfortune she falls into an unconsciousness so deep that it is mistaken for death. Eventually she is restored to the hero, most often at the conclusion of the romance in a trial-like recognition scene in which all mysteries and mistakes are explained and all loose threads are knitted up again.

The most important of them are—the *Babylonica* of Iamblichus (the motif of apparent death occurs four times); *Chaereas and Callirrhoe* of Chariton of Aphrodisia (in which the resourceful heroine is so beautiful she is mistaken for a goddess—like Pastorella in *The Faerie Queene,* the prototype for some of Shakespeare's heroines); *Apollonius of Tyre,* known to us only through a sixth-century Latin translation (this provides almost the entire plot of *Pericles*); the *Aethiopica* of Heliodorus of Emesa (which has a wicked stepmother, oracular dreams, grief over a dead body mistakenly thought to be that of a beloved, insistence on the heroine's virginity—immemorially associated with magic power and central for Shakespeare); *Daphnis and Chloe* by Longus (crucial for its pastoral setting); *Leucippe and Cleitophon* by Achilles Tatius (apparent death and resurrection, oracular dreams, emphasis on the heroine's virginity, and so on). It can be seen at once how many of the themes and motifs of these early prose romances turn up in Shakespeare's Last Plays either through direct appropriation or by refraction through the work of others—though some of them are, of course, as old as folk tale itself. And what Shakespeare makes of them is itself a wonder.

The romance world is one of extremes—the good are very good, the evil very evil; the noble are beautiful, the bad are ugly. Frank Kermode aptly describes this as 'an extension of platonic realities into the phenomenal world'. There is small concern for psychological and narrative plausibility—the attention is turned, rather, to the mysterious more-than-human forces and powers which seem to shape and determine human fates, rough hew them how we will. These may be Chance, Fortune, an inscrutable Providence, or even Divinity itself, and there is often a tendency towards theodicy, even theophany whereby the gods not only look down but come down (note that Shakespeare's deities appear *in dreams*—which I suppose you could call hedging his bets). This should not be regarded as showing an inclination to illustrate and reinforce an orthodox religion (which would produce allegory, at best,)* but rather a desire to grasp and display those

---

* I will just note here that until quite recently, there was a persistent drive to 'explain' the Last Plays in terms of—or perhaps co-opt them for—anthropology or religion. I quote some wise words of John Danby. 'The first of these has been based on *The Golden Bough* and the fertility cycle and rebirth. The second has been similarly based on the Christian conception of regeneration and resurrection. Neither, I think, is as satisfactory as the contemporary and conventional scheme which Shakespeare used. Anthropology does not take us far enough. By its insidious precipitations it tends to silt over the clear and sharp contours of the Renaissance moral world. The second explaining system errs in the opposite direction. It carries us too far and too fast. It particularizes in a field of meaning beyond Shakespeare's intention—though Shakespeare, I have no doubt, would know St Paul and the burial service, and accepted the New Testament. To theologize the Last Plays, however, is to distort them. Though patience as

times and events in life when it *seems* that something transcendent gleams through the usually less radiant texture of sublunary human doings and affairs. But it *is* important to bear in mind that the English humanist romancers were all Protestants, and for Protestants, as Howard Felperin pointed out, life itself was a matter of continuous trial and tribulation, so that the tests and trials in, say, *The Faerie Queene* and *Arcadia* inevitably have some relation to, and flavour of, the tests and trials of an exemplary Christian life. (As Felperin remarks, the Christian epic itself—paradise, the fall, expulsion, the wanderings and buffetings of history, salvation, paradise regained or heaven—was the canonical romance of both medieval and Renaissance culture, so there was bound to be a strong pull for secular romances to adopt something of its ethical and eschatalogical system.) And here I must say a little about Sidney's *Arcadia*.

Deprecated today ('a monument of dullness'—T. S. Eliot, one of his less happy pronouncements), this was 'for a century and a half the best-loved book in the English language' (John Buxton). Between 1590 and 1638 there were seventeen issues. But although it contains just about every adjunct, accessory and feature of romance tales, down to marauding bears and revealing birthmarks, it is arguably more important for the philosophy and spirit which informs it. And this 'is something gravely moral, Christian, and Renaissance, in spite of its Greek names and pre-Christian terminology'. I quote John Danby. He has written very illuminatingly on the *Arcadia,* showing that it was Sidney's project to bring classical, romance and chivalric themes 'within the orbit of an instructed Renaissance Christianity'. Danby discerns four interlocking spheres in Sidney's romance world.

> There is first the sphere of virtue and attained perfection; then the sphere of human imperfection, political and passionate, surrounding and likely at any minute to threaten the first; around these again, the sphere of non-human accident, chance, or misfortune, the sphere of the sea and storms;

Shakespeare conceives it implies St Paul and the New Testament, patience as Shakespeare realizes it in the Last Plays is a familiar and well-walked parish in a wider diocese. Nor is the parish presided over by the Fisher King, and in it St Paul is taken for granted but not allegorized in every Whitsun pastoral.' And Philip Edwards: 'It is a disservice to Shakespeare to pretend that one is adding to his profundity by discovering that his plots are symbolic vehicles for ideas which are, for the most part, banal, trite and colourless'.

and finally, enclosing all, the sphere of the transcendent, guaranteeing after the 'storm or other hard plights' that the ending will be a happy one—
given patience.

'Patience'—the Christian virtue (Christus Patiens), not classical Stoic fist-
clenched passivity—Danby sees as vital for Sidney (as it is to be for Shakespeare). He quotes Milton deploring the conventional notions of heroical
poetry, indicating his loftier intention:

> Warrs, hitherto the onely Argument
> Heroic deem'd, chief maistrie to dissect
> With long and tedious havoc fabled Knights
> In Battels feign'd; the better fortitude
> Of Patience and Heroic martyrdom
> Unsung.
>
> *(Paradise Lost* XI, 28–33)

Sidney himself, writing of the *Odyssey,* said: 'Well may you see Ulisses in a
storme, and in other hard plights; but they are but exercises of patience and
magnanimitie, to make them shine the more in the neere-following pros-
peritie.' The usual adversities which characterize the romance tale, for Sidney have a purpose. Danby: 'Fortune is the school of Patience. It leans on
and demands the transcendent. It is the point at which the human discovers the divine.' In Sidney's work there is, of course, the external world of
events—the realm of endangered heroines and heroic courage; but there
is also the inner world of 'the passive and possibly unrewarded virtues—
singleness, constancy, devotion, command over one's will and one's possible
self-division'. Virtues are as important as fortunes. In line with this new
importance of the inner world, it is important to note some of the literal
components of romance moving into metaphor. Thus, for example, there is
no more recurrent feature of the romance than danger at sea—for Sidney,
and Shakespeare too. But, in the *Arcadia,* when Pyrocles leaves Musidorus,
the latter exclaims: 'Pyrocles, what means this alteration? . . . Heretofore
I have accused the sea, condemned the pirates, and hated my evil fortune
that deprived me of thee; but now thyself is the sea which drowns my comfort. . .' Again, Sidney describes Antiphilus as being 'suddenly borne into
an ocean of absolute power, he was swayed withal, he knew not how, as
every wind of passion puffed him'. The terms of romance now apply to

the inner environment as well; and in this topography the most important qualities are Christian patience allied with Aristotelian magnanimity. This is as true for Shakespeare as it is for Sidney.

'Nothing almost sees miracles/But misery' says Kent in the stocks (*King Lear* II, ii, 168–9). That tragedy stresses the *almost*—heart-breakingly. The Last Plays delete it. It is as if we, and the characters, *do* see miracles. There is a new mood of enhanced wonder and an intensified lyricism of reconciliation in Shakespeare's last four plays which sets them apart from the problem comedies and outright tragedies which preceded them; though we should remember that there are all sorts of adumbrations and foreshadowings—preparations for, gestures towards, tentative anticipations of—the materials and themes of these last romances throughout Shakespeare's work—from the beginning indeed, starting with *The Comedy of Errors*. We might briefly consider them as a group.

I start with a quotation from Philip Brockbank:

> We may say of Shakespeare's Last Plays that each is about the renewal of
> creative life in an afflicted state of society. In each a miraculous provi-
> dence works, through different agencies, to saving purpose. But in each
> an element of self-confessed artifice qualifies the auspicious outcome to
> remind us that the ultimately reassuring moral order that can be dis-
> played to us in the theatre is indeed theatre; it cannot be transposed too
> promptly into 'fact'—the verity of it is under suspicion.

That 'element of self-confessed artifice' is crucial. Wilson Knight writes with customary thrilled eloquence of these plays as being 'myths of immortality' and one can see what he means. At the same time, we must recognize that they offer little or no reassurance of life after death, or survival in the life-ever-after to come. The miracles and resurrections are staged, sometimes doubly so, as when Paulina, in *The Winter's Tale*, arranges a theatrical coup (a 'statue' starting to move), a performance which is itself Shakespeare's *coup de théâtre*. Which is not to deny that the plays are in themselves 'miracles' (literally—wonderful things, objects of wonder).

Brockbank's point may be reinforced in another way by John Danby:

> Shakespeare during the last period is comparatively relaxed. He makes a
> toy of thought . . . we might describe the plays of the final period as works

in which formula, and schema, and intelligent manipulation, are the
dominant things. Up to 1606 Shakespeare was growing. His works are an
existential record of his growth. After that time all his work seems to be
that of a man who has got things finally clear and is no longer worried.
Not only are things clear, they are almost cut and dried. Shakespeare now
can engage or disengage himself just as far as he wishes. He can be unanx-
ious, he can even be careless. All the time, certainly, he can preserve that
attitude which Sidney Greville called *ironia* . . . I have myself no doubt
that the last plays are less serious than those of the tragic period . . . we
are taken by beauty continually. The last plays are the fancies of a Lear
dreaming of Cordelia refound. They exist at a remove from reality. They
give us a schema for life rather than the life itself.

I will come back to 'dreaming'. Of course, in all this periodizing of Shakespeare's life, it behoves us to remember that it is quite undiscoverable
whether Shakespeare himself knew that these *were* his 'last' plays: he might
simply have been embarking on new experiments in the medium of which
he was, by now, complete master. (The idea that he was trying to imitate
the younger and successful Beaumont and Fletcher is both unverifiable and
unconvincing—by this stage in his career Shakespeare had no need to copy
anyone. Similarly, there is no evidence that he was adapting to new conditions obtaining in the indoor theatre, Blackfriars, taken over by Shakespeare's company in 1608.) But he does seem to have 'sailed into a calm'
with the writing of these plays.

At the same time, there is much that is harsh and painful—anti-
romantic—in these last plays; something more than the wind and the rain
that were gathering in the later comedies. Jaques and Touchstone ironize
and mock the Duke's benign vision of life in the Forest of Arden, but they
do not threaten it in the way Antonio and Caliban do Prospero's island. It is
good for Leontes and Hermione to be reunited and reconciled after sixteen
years; but they have lost, irreparably, irrecoverably, perhaps the best years
of their lives. There is always some residual bitterness in the sweetness.
These last plays 'subsume tragedy in the process of transcending it', as Felperin puts it. The suffering and loss of Pericles remind us of Lear; in the
insanely furious jealousy of Leontes we hear again Othello; the humiliation
of Imogen and Hermione is only just less fatal than the treatment meted
out to Desdemona and Cordelia. Felperin: 'side by side with the magical

speech-music exist the harshest cacophonies of the tortured soul familiar from the great tragedies'. And there is a major difference from the comedies. There, the obstacles to felicity which have to be circumvented are erected by paternal interdiction, bad law, or some perverse individual. In the Romances, while there are certainly evil agents, one feels that there is something in the very nature of things which can work to obstruct, interrupt, and delay human happiness.

But also something which can work to restore it. The deep feeling that after winter comes the spring runs throughout these plays. The key mythic figure here is Proserpina, specifically invoked by Perdita who effectively becomes her. Marina is Proserpina from the sea, while Proserpina's mother, Ceres, is summoned to bless Miranda. We are back with Ovid. 'The Rape of Proserpine' is told in *Metamorphoses,* Book V. Prior to her abduction by Pluto, we are told that it is 'always spring', which means the Golden Age— 'Springtime it was, always, for ever spring'. The rape of Proserpina, and her return from Hades for six months of the year, effectively marks the start of the Silver Age which saw the coming of the seasons and agriculture:

> Then Jupiter
> Curtailed the pristine spring and led the year
> Through winter, summer, autumn's varying days
> . . .
> Then in long furrows first were set the seeds
> Of grain and oxen groaned beneath the yoke.

While we are with the Ages, we might note that in the last, 'hard' Age of Iron, when 'all evil straight broke out', for the first time 'men sailed the sea'. Given the importance of voyages, and shipwrecks—not to mention the very hard presence of evil—in the Last Plays, we might think of them as showing an Iron Age world finally blessed with a Silver Age restoration. Proserpina returns to earth.

Just as, in Jonathan Bate's words, 'Ovid returns to the surface of the drama.' He points out that one of the effects of Perdita on the winter court was—'Who was most marble there changed color' (*The Winter's Tale* V, ii, 96–7), which alludes to what is perhaps Ovid's 'most celebrated story of artistic creation'—that of Pygmalion, who somehow coaxes and caresses his statue of a beautiful girl into life (Book X). As Bate points out, there are some dark aspects of the story which Shakespeare omits, concentrating instead 'on three positive aspects of the story: the power of the imagination or wish-fulfilment, the magic of the awakening, and, crucially, the art that outdoes nature'. Nature restoring nature, and art outdoing nature, are two potencies everywhere under consideration in the Last Plays: it would not be wrong to think of them as, in some way, presided over by the spirits of Proserpina and Pygmalion. And Diana, 'the tutelary goddess of the Last Plays' in Danby's view. Chastity—and virginity—play a vital role in these plays. Proserpina returning figures fertility, and fertility requires seedings and couplings. The Last Plays are, indeed, centrally concerned with love, and the triumphs of love. But it is a very chaste, chastened love—there is little trace of the erotic here (Venus is explicitly banished in the masque in *The Tempest*). For instance, the act by which Pericles begat Marina is occluded, or idealized, by choric Gower:

> Hymen hath brought the bride to bed,
> Where by the loss of maidenhead
> A babe is molded.
>   (III, Gower 9–11)

The point was neatly made by Carol Neely, who also noted that, in the Romances, on the one hand raw male sexual power tends to be blunted or transmuted into benign forms, while, on the other hand, 'mothers are not merely absent but are explicitly dead or else die or apparently die in the course of the play'. This allows female sexuality to be represented by the chaste innocence of younger daughters, with a resultant shift of emotional and dramatic emphasis to father–daughter bonds. With the exception of Imogen, already a wife (albeit a very chaste one), the heroines, aged between fourteen and sixteen, are noticeably younger than Shakespeare's other heroines, apart from Juliet. In comparison with Marina, Perdita and Miranda, Portia, Beatrice, Rosalind, Viola and Helena, while chaste enough, seem positively worldly-wise, and quite capable of engaging in a certain amount of controlled sexual banter and innuendo unthinkable in their innocent young successors. These totally virtuous, idealized, even conventionalized, beautiful young figures, more universal than individual, merit Sidney's description of his Arcadian Philoclea. Adversity, and indeed anything else, 'could no more imperfect her perfections than a die any way cast could lose its squareness'.

Shakespeare was never one to concern himself over-much with the unities of time and place, and he was certainly never concerned, as a neoclassical dramatist like Ben Jonson was, to make time passing on the stage the same as time passing for the audience. But in the Last Plays (with the curious exception of *The Tempest*), he plays fast and loose with time and place as never before: the action in *Pericles* takes place 'dispersedly in various Countries', and there are scenes in six different cities; while we have a fourteen-year gap here, a sixteen-year interval there—in these plays, Time, as they say, *flies*. And even appears on stage, to let us know it.

> *Enter Time, the Chorus.*
> I that please some, try all, both joy and terror
> Of good and bad; that makes and unfolds error,
> Now take upon me, in the name of Time,
> To use my wings. Impute it not a crime
> To me, or my swift passage, that I slide
> O'er sixteen years, and leave the growth untried
> Of that wide gap, since it is in my pow'r
> To o'erthrow law, and in one self-born hour
> To plant, and o'erwhelm custom. Let me pass;
> The same I am, ere ancient'st order was
> Or what is now received.
> . . .
> Your patience this allowing,
> I turn my glass, and give my scene such growing
> As you had slept between.
>   (*The Winter's Tale*, IV, i, 1–17)

We have had devouring time, injurious time, 'envious and calumniating time'; and we have seen how the 'unfolding' power of time became increasingly important for Shakespeare, a mysterious, invisible, inexorable process by which 'error' and evil were finally exposed. Now, with Time standing on the stage, chatting to the audience while amiably turning his glass, he is beginning to look suspiciously like Shakespeare himself, saying to the spectators: with your permission, I can do anything. Time has become wax in his hands. He can even make us feel we have been asleep.

A recurrent feature of the Last Plays is characters experiencing what Brockbank called 'a rapture of recognition'. Northrop Frye remarked that this 'spirit of reconciliation . . . is not to be ascribed to some personal attitude of his own, but to his impersonal concentration on the laws of comic form'; quoting this, Kermode comments: 'In the Romances, this act of concentration was focused on the recognition, which was to be studied with a new intensity and thoroughness in relation to romance-plots; for it has a special force in these extensive tales of sundered families, wandering kings, and lost princesses'. In a not very helpful way it could be said that simply to read a book is to enact a recognition scene of one kind or another (the Greek words are close: 'anagnostes' = reader, 'anagnorisis' = recognition). But given the special importance of 'recognition' in the Romances, it might be worth saying a little about its more general centrality for literature (here I must recommend Terence Cave's fine book *Recognitions,* from which I am taking some material). Early recognition scenes invariably involved the revelation of true identity and the re-establishment of kin. The Ur figures, or paradigms, are Oedipus and Odysseus. Odysseus knows who he is and who are his, and becomes a witting imposter to regain his own; while Oedipus is an unwitting imposter who has to find out who he is and who his own really are. Odysseus occults his identity until he can be safely recognized by his wife; Oedipus is after the occulted facts about his parents. Either way, the recognition—felicitous or tragic—is of kin. There were always possible extensions to these motifs. For instance in New Comedy, which is dependent on disguises, secrets and confusions, as well as false identities, the recognition is a disclosure to all of 'what has been done', and is not limited to the emergence of unforeseen or hidden kinship relations. (We have seen Shakespeare making use of these devices in his early comedies.) Clearly the notion of 'recognition' may be extended, or attenuated, so that the object recognized may be a relation, a state of affairs, a fact, a higher order, a hidden law, a truth about Being, a truth about self, or something so elusive that you lose it in the act of trying to find and speak it.

But Cave points to a potentially more complicated and disturbing aspect of 'recognition'. He calls recognition a 'scandal', not only because recognition plots are often about a scandal (incest, murder, adultery), but also because they represent 'a shift into the implausible'. What emerges is 'a sense of a means of knowing which is different from rational cognition. It operates surreptitiously, randomly, elliptically and often perversely, seizing on precisely those details that from a rational point of view seem trivial.' From Aristotle on there has been an attempt to differentiate a 'low' sort of recognition plot, involving birthmarks and scars and rings and what-not, and a 'high' kind, registering the discovery of order, causality, harmony, truth. And, as Cave brilliantly shows, it can't be done. The higher recognition seems to celebrate an order and offers a sense of security, while the lower suggests that we are laughably, worryingly, appallingly, at the mercy of randomness and contingency, bits of matter which happen to turn up, or fail to. But the distinction will not hold and the higher is always infected with traces or hints of the lower. For no evidence is absolutely conclusive, no proof is total. Can Penelope be *absolutely* sure that the man she goes to bed with is Odysseus? A recognition scene thus affords a not-quite-complete reassurance.

> The recognition scene shows that the beast can be caught—or at least that *a* beast can be caught: but the magic has to be constantly repeated to exorcize all the times it hasn't worked and *we haven't noticed:* the hanging of the innocent man, the survival of the impostor, the adultery or incest that continues concealed and unchecked, the bastard brought up as the rightful heir.

Thus, Cave suggests, a residual unease and anxiety can be traced in even the most triumphant and satisfying recognition scenes.

I want to make one more general point about the Last Plays. The epigraphs I used for this section indicate that all these plays in some way participate in the 'nowhere' realm of dreaming. In this connection Allardyce Nicoll has an interesting point to make concerning the Court Masque. Shakespeare knew about masques of course, and used them. However, Nicoll discounts claims sometimes made, that Shakespeare was directly, even heavily, influenced by the Jacobean masque as it was ushered in at Whitehall by Ben Jonson's *The Masque of Blackness* on 1 January 1605. The appeal of these masques was new, and Inigo Jones's dazzling contributions must have been part of the novel attraction. And, suggests Nicoll, there was one feature which very probably *did* influence Shakespeare—'the fundamental novelty of Jones's method—the changeability of his scenes'. Palaces, temples, towers 'dissolve' suddenly into each other, and delicate cloud-work contributes to the sense of an 'insubstantial pageant'. Nicoll points us to

Prospero's most famous speech, and, as an example, he cites *The Vision of the Twelve Goddesses* by Samuel Daniel (1604). This masque starts with Night waking up her son, sleeping, sleepy Somnus, and asking him to provide some 'pleasing novelties' for the expectant audience:

> And make their slumber to beget strange sights,
> Strange visions and unusual properties,
> Unseen of latter ages, wrapp'd up in mysteries.

Somnus complies:

> Dear mother Night, I your commandment
> Obey, and dreams t' interpret dreams will make
> As waking curiosity is wont
> . . .
> Be this a temple, there Sibylla stand,
> Preparing reverent rites with holy hand,
> And so, bright visions, go, and entertain
> All round about whilst I'll go to sleep again.

Iris, 'the daughter of wonder' (note), appears in a 'fair Temple of Peace' and announces 'the coming of a celestial presence of Goddesses' to an amazed Sibylla. And as the goddesses duly appear (they include Ceres and Proserpina, and silvery Diana who will also appear in *Pericles*—the 'goddess argentine'), Sibylla's wonder-struck reaction could almost have come from one of Shakespeare's Last Plays:

> What have I seen? where am I, or do I see at all? or am I anywhere? was this Iris . . . or else but a phantasm or imagination? . . . what perspective is this? or what shall I herein see? O admirable Powers! What sights are these?

'Dreams to interpret dreams' could be one, fruitful, way of thinking about Shakespeare's Last Plays. And the, apparently magically produced, changing fleeting spectacles of these later masques could well have contributed significantly to the atmosphere of Shakespeare's Last Plays, in which, says Nicoll, we often 'have the impression that we are floating away into a realm of the spirit and are coming very close to the world of the gods'. I myself think, rather, that we tend to feel 'wrapped up in mysteries'—as we do when we are at the mercy of our own dreams. Only here, Shakespeare is master of the dreams. As he was, of course, in the in some ways anticipatory *A Midsummer Night's Dream.*

The most memorable actual dream in Shakespeare is Clarence's dream in prison, in *Richard III.*

> Methought that Gloucester stumbled, and in falling
> Struck me (that thought to stay him) overboard
> Into the tumbling billows of the main.
> O Lord, methought what pain it was to drown!
> What dreadful noise of water in mine ears!
> What sights of ugly death within mine eyes!
> Methought I saw a thousand fearful wracks;
> A thousand men that fishes gnawed upon;
> Wedges of gold, great anchors, heaps of pearl,
> Inestimable stones, unvalued jewels,
> All scatt'red in the bottom of the sea.
> Some lay in dead men's skulls, and in the holes
> Where eyes did once inhabit there were crept,
> As 'twere in scorn of eyes, reflecting gems
> That wooed the slimy bottom of the deep
> And mocked the dead bones that lay scatt'red by.
>   (I, iv, 18–33)

All the time, his soul is trying to find 'the empty, vast, and wand'ring air' (I, iv, 39); but it is a bad dream and he is drowned, and passes over into 'the kingdom of perpetual night' (I, iv, 47). This strange, rich, undersea realm of wrecks and treasures, where drowned men seem to be being magically transmuted into priceless precious things, is an imaginative world away from the constricted arid land where Richard pursues his grim and grue-some political ends. But it is distinctly closer to the worlds of *Pericles* and *The Tempest,* and more generally to the sense of wonder out of wreck-age which pervades the Last Plays. Those 'reflecting gems' which, marvel-lously, *woo* the bottom of the deep 'in scorn of eyes', *as 'twere,* anticipate

'Those are pearls that were his eyes'. But—*are*. The magic has become literal. The dream is the play.

 PERICLES (1608)

> What seas what shores what grey rocks and what islands
> What water lapping the bow
> And scent of pine and the woodthrush singing in the fog
> What images return
> O my daughter.
> > (T. S. Eliot, *Marina*)

> Did you not name a tempest,
> A birth and death?
> > (V, iii, 33–4)

> Gentlemen,
> This queen will live
> > (III, ii, 93–4)

The play opens with the appearance on stage of a single figure who announces that he is the fourteenth-century poet, John Gower. There was a Chorus in *Henry V,* but to have a long-dead poet coming on to announce (and effectively to direct) the play is something entirely new in Shakespeare. Let's consider what he says:

> To sing a song that old was sung,
> From ashes ancient Gower is come,
> Assuming man's infirmities,
> To glad your ear, and please your eyes.
> It hath been sung at festivals,
> On ember-eves and holidays,
> And lords and ladies in their lives
> Have read it for restoratives.
> The purchase is to make men glorious;
> *Et bonum quo antiquius eo melius.*

If you, born in those latter times,

When wit's more ripe, accept my rhymes,

And that to hear an old man sing

May to your wishes pleasure bring,

I life would wish, and that I might

Waste it for you, like taper-light.

(I, 1–16)

An *old* song, sung by an *ancient* poet—so, for the audience, it is doubly old. Gower has risen from ashes—a miraculous Phoenix-like *resurrection*. He is going to address the *ears* and the *eyes*—he will tell, and he will show. The song is habitually performed at festivals, pre-fasting evenings, and holidays—a customary part of public, communal celebrations. It has been read for its *restorative* power. The 'purchase' (gain or benefit) is to make men 'glorious'—a strange line, to which I will return: followed by the apparent *non sequitur* in Latin, meaning—the more ancient a good thing is the better. Then a final rather self-deprecating, indeed self-sacrificing (wasting), apologetic hope that these wittier 'latter times' will accept his inevitably rather old-fashioned presentations. We have heard this acknowledgment of generational difference before, with the sense that the smart young things no longer have time for the older pieties, as in the King of France's quoting of the late Count Rousillon's feeling of alienation from 'younger spirits, whose apprehensive senses/All but new things disdain' (*All's Well that Ends Well* I, ii, 60–61). The fundamentals of the play's form and content are, in fact, adumbrated or pre-figured in these lines (my italics act as rather crude pointers), and what we are about to watch and listen to will be emphatically an *old* tale—'like an old tale . . . like an old tale still', as the wondering Gentlemen in *The Winter's Tale* keep reiterating (V, ii, 30, 65).

Why this stress on the oldness of the tale (or 'song')? Why is 'ancient Gower' there at all? For a start, it *is* a very old tale, probably from an ancient Greek romance concerning Apollonius (= Shakespeare's Pericles) of Tyre. It survived in a Latin version of the sixth century AD, and it entered the *Gesta Romanorum* (a Latin collection of tales from the thirteenth century—this was the 153rd story), and was disseminated in versions all over Europe. It is the main story in Book VIII (which treats of 'Unlawful love') of John Gower's *Confessio Amantis* (1393), which was Shakespeare's main source—so Gower's appearance as the presiding impresario is very proper.

There was also a prose version by Laurence Twine, *The Patterne of Paine-full Adventures* (1576 and 1607), which Shakespeare undoubtedly drew on. The adventures of Pyrocles (*sic*) in Sidney's *Arcadia* (1590) might also have been in Shakespeare's mind—shipwrecks, chests from the sea, helping shepherds, found armour, pirates, and so on—though all this may simply argue a common older source. Also relevant are legends of Christian saints, particularly that of St Agnes (again known in many versions from the seventh century onwards). Among other features of her life, she was sent naked to a brothel where an angel protected her life, much to the consternation of the brothel regulars; she also revives an apparently dead Roman. So—yes; old, old, old. ('Some mouldy tale like *Pericles*'—Ben Jonson.)

Just why this particular story should have exerted such a hold on the European imagination (and be it said, going by contemporary evidence, *Pericles* was by some way the most popular of Shakespeare's plays before the theatres were closed in 1642), can only be a matter of speculation—conceivably, it has something to do with the worrying proximity, and the felicitous avoidance, of incest (of all taboos, apparently the most universal). An old tale, then, being again retold. (It may also be an old play rewritten. I will not address the unresolvable question of whether the first two acts are wholly, or partly, by Shakespeare; or not by him at all. The writing there is certainly not in Shakespeare's mature style—Geoffrey Bullough thinks it 'jejune and rigid'—but whether Shakespeare was building on the cruder efforts of a now unknown minor dramatist, or rather taking up one of his own earlier abandoned beginnings and seeing it through to a richer conclusion, is undecidable. But he had shown an interest in this old tale in his very first play and, having alerted readers to alternative theories, I shall treat the whole of *Pericles* as Shakespeare's play.) Shakespeare duly gives his play an 'atmosphere of the antique', as Bullough says, with Gower using obsolete words and forms and having recourse to old-fashioned devices—pageant, ceremonial scenes, *tableau*-like dumb shows, and so on. This makes it all seem curiously distant—violent deeds muffled by frames and long perspectives. But this archaic feel and flavour is hardly gratuitous or diversionary. The implication is, surely, that some old and abiding truths are best displayed in an avowedly archaic ('mouldy') mode, leaving the audience undistracted by innovational technical flair. Brockbank has a more general suggestion: 'It happened at the beginning of the seventeenth century, and would happen again at the end of the eighteenth, that a society with a highly complex and civilized literary culture looked back to old tales and to the Middle Ages in search of rich simplicities, expressed in innocent speech and show.' Shakespeare is de-sophisticating his audience.

'To make men glorious'—Gower's announced intention—was the aim of the medieval legends of the saints and of the miracle plays derived from them (these plays were called simply 'miracles', so if you saw one you could indeed say that you had 'seen a miracle'—relevant for Shakespeare's audience). It was F. D. Hoeniger who first persuasively argued that *Pericles* closely parallels the structure of certain miracle or saints' plays. Such plays (performed all over England from around 1100 to 1580) depicted events and stages in the lives of saints and martyrs, and were like holy romances, showing happiness (or triumph, beatification, salvation—some heavenly reward) after long suffering. You could see romance as a secularized 'miracle'. Here is Hoeniger:

> All that was needed in *Pericles* was to carry one step further the process of secularization, already much in evidence in some of the later miracle plays: to replace God or Christ by Diana or Neptune, and the Christian saint or apocryphal character by a prince or princess; for there is no greater difference between the saints' legends and the romance of Apollonius of Tyre. They are both biographical romances. The fate of Pericles, like that of St Andrew or Mary Magdalene or Tobit, is governed by Providence. Like them, he undergoes manifold adventures, which bring upon him great suffering. Like them, he is lifted out of despair by a miraculous-seeming intervention of a god—a Christ or a Diana.

This, then, is the sort of thing that Gower is going to put on for us. By as it were handing over the presentation of the play to Gower, Shakespeare ensures that it is almost entirely undramatic. Gower habitually *tells* (narrates, reports, summarizes) and *then* shows (leaves 'to the judgement of your eye'); the acted scenes are more like illustrations or demonstrations than agonistic discoveries. This means that whatever else the audience experiences, it is seldom suspense, until the final act, when showing effectively overtakes, supplants, and relegates telling, and we are left to witness what T. S. Eliot called 'the finest of the "recognition scenes"'.

An old tale, then; but in fact a very new kind of play which involves evoking and invoking more archaic modes, both of thinking and depicting, of telling and showing. The tale itself is of a prince who leaves his city to seek a bride. A renowned beauty attracts him, but to gain her he must solve a riddle—or forfeit his life. He sees that the answer to the riddle is that the beautiful princess is committing incest with her father, the king. The Prince flees in horror and, after shipwreck, finds himself in a happier kingdom where he wins a fitting bride. Marriage is swiftly followed by pregnancy and, with auguries of felicity, the couple set sail for the Prince's own kingdom. There is another shipwreck, in which the mother apparently dies in childbirth and is buried at sea. The devastated Prince takes the baby girl to another country where seeming friends promise to bring her up alongside their own daughter. Some sixteen years later this traitorous couple plan the murder of the girl, because her many perfections are serving to eclipse their own daughter. The scheme is foiled, and the girl is abducted by pirates, who sell her to a brothel in another country. Just at this time, the Prince (now King) arrives to take his now grown-up daughter back, only to be told that, sadly, she has died. Prostrate with grief, the King enters what seems to be a terminal silence, refusing all human communication. The daughter meanwhile has miraculously chastened the brothel world, and become a renowned and accomplished teacher of the arts. Her father's ship unwittingly puts in at the very port city where she practises her skills. Told of the King's aphasic melancholy, the local ruler suggests that the amazing young girl should be allowed to try out her 'sacred physic' on him. The King initially rebuffs her (in Twine, he kicks her in the face and she falls bleeding; in Gower he punches her; Shakespeare, habitually more sparing of visible violence, has him simply push her away). She persists and recognition follows in due course. An oracular vision reveals that the mother is still alive, having in fact been saved after her sea burial. An ecstatically happy reunion ensues in the temple of Diana, and the profound, simple (archaic) romance pattern of love, loss, and restoration, is completed. Bonds thought severed are rejoined, and the wretchedly scattered and miserably separated family is finally reassembled and at one.

Even thus crudely summarized, the story shows itself to be totally unamenable to neat, tight plotting. There are so many cities; so many spaces and gaps; so much wind-driven hither-and-thithering; so much storm and 'tempest'; such blank stretches of time; such various magics; so much that is utterly, almost unutterably, extra-ordinary—and everywhere the sea, the sea. The climactic recognition scene takes place on board a ship riding at anchor off Mytilene; we actually see Pericles 'on shipboard' helplessly remonstrating with the fierce storm during which his wife (apparently) dies, while at the end he succumbs gratefully to 'this great sea of joys rushing upon me' (V, i, 195); and two key scenes take place on the seashore, that bottomlessly, endlessly suggestive liminal area where our constitutive elements meet, and the firm gives way to the flowing—with Pericles emerging from the sea, and Marina (so named by Shakespeare because she was 'born at sea'), as it were, returning to it. There is, indeed, a very 'elemental' feeling to the play—where we come from, what we are exposed to, to which we will return.

> The river is within us, the sea is all about us;
> The sea is the land's edge also, the granite
> Into which it reaches, the beaches where it tosses,
> Its hints of earlier and other creation
>   ('The Dry Salvages')

T. S. Eliot's lines are particularly apt for this play.

The dislocated, apparent randomness of events; the prevailing feeling of man being adrift in floods and tides of unchartable, unplottable contingency; the sense, indeed, of human helplessness, is poignantly expressed in Marina's opening speech:

> Ay me, poor maid,
> Born in a tempest, when my mother died,
> This world to me is as a lasting storm,
> Whirring me from my friends.
>   (IV, i, 17–20)

'Whir' is not, not properly, a transitive verb; but of course, once Shakespeare has used it in this way—as he does only this once—we are stunned by its rightness, and realize that no other word would do. We have entered an actively 'whirring' world. It is a question whether there is any supervising, supervening power controlling or directing this fragmented, tempestuously unpredictable world. 'The gods' are very frequently invoked, with Jove, Juno, Apollo, Aesculapius and Priapus named, and Diana actually appearing, albeit in a dream, in Shakespeare's first theophany, which takes place during an annual celebration of Neptune—we are certainly in a pagan world. But 'the gods' were invoked in *King Lear,* and much help they were there. Are these all just helpless gestures to an empty sky?

That is not quite the feeling here. Wilson Knight thinks these are more active and potent gods: 'there is a greater sense of their reality, beneficence, and intervention'. He senses an increasing 'religious reverence' and maintains that 'Shakespeare's drama is aspiring towards the eternal harmony and the eternal pattern'. More generally, Bullough thinks that the 'old tale' of Apollonius with its oracular vision and final temple scene 'helped to revive in Shakespeare the sense of an overriding benevolent Providence which he had rejected in *Lear* and ignored in *Coriolanus,* and to evoke the note of healing and forgiveness which he was to seek in the last three romances'. Many commentators agree that, while the play is undoubtedly secular in both content and intention, it has *some* Christian relevance—a classical world with biblical resonances (as one might see Pericles now as a pagan prince, now as Job or Everyman). The old tale itself, says Hoeniger, presents 'a pattern of the course of human life partly analogous to the biblical one', the basic similarity being that man has to suffer much before he will see and understand God's purposes. 'Shakespeare conceived the significance of the tragicomic pattern of the story of Apollonius of Tyre more deeply than did Gower or Twine . . . he was led to a view of the place of suffering in a great man's life more like that of another profound view, the Christian one.' The stress should be on '*analogous*'—the play is in no way an adjunct to orthodox Christianity. But you could certainly say that in both the Bible and the play, God/gods move(s) in a mysterious way His/their wonders to perform. And wonders there certainly are, however brought about.

That being said, as Gower tells it, it is always Fortune that is responsible for events. 'Providence' is never mentioned (Shakespeare only used the word half a dozen times, and we have to wait until *The Tempest* for 'Providence divine'), while we hear of Fortune on some eighteen occasions. And a pretty rough-handed Fortune it is:

> Till fortune, tired with doing bad,
> Threw him ashore
>
> (II, Gower 37–8)

Let Pericles believe his daughter's dead
And bear his courses to be ordered
By Lady Fortune
                              (IV, iv, 46–8)

Marina is placed in a brothel ('this sty') by 'most ungentle fortune' (IV, vi, 102), and Gower's fortune is never less than 'fierce and keen' (V, iii, 87). So what brings about the miraculous dénouement—has the harsh old Wheel of Fortune ameliorated into a benign Wheel of Providence, as some suggest? Do the gods finally intervene as they so conspicuously did not in *King Lear*? Or is it all up to inscrutable Chance—miraculous luck *finally* balancing out atrocious luck, but don't bank on it? People will respond in different ways. Certainly we sense the presence of something mysterious and wonderful in the enraptured unfoldings of the last act. I think the prevailing feeling is that fortune has suddenly, inexplicably, begun to exercise a calming, self-rectifying influence on events—confusion yields to coherence, and the tempest gives way to music. But the experience is theatrical, not theological, and none the less valuable for that. '*Pericles* offers its reassurance, creating a world in which death is an illusion and the dream of immortality is appeased without the postulate of an afterlife' (Brockbank).

The only unity this whirring, scattering play has—apart from Gower standing there pointing, narrating, and moralizing—is the fact that all the incidents bear directly on the weal and woe of Pericles and his daughter, Marina. The minor characters are relatively undeveloped, often nearer to types than individuals. And Pericles is an unusual sort of hero in that he is completely passive. He initiates almost nothing on his own behalf (he brings relief to a starving city). He travels in search of a wife, and wins one in a medieval tournament rather fascinatingly being held in ancient Greece, but he is far from being a passion-driven lover. Mainly we see him escaping or departing. He does not, like many heroes, take things (or people) by the scruff of the neck, one way or another, and try to shape them to his desires or aspirations—rather, things happen *to* him. He simply endures the slings and arrows—and finally the gifts—of outrageous Fortune. He is not the maker, and certainly not the master, of his fate. We see no moral failings, no struggling with conflicting emotions—no mistakes or errors, in fact. He certainly does nothing to deserve or to bring down the calamitous suffering visited on him; considerations of tragic flaws or hubris are irrelevant here.

As put on by Gower, the man is wholly good (and thus, as a character, almost wholly uninteresting). The fact that he has no meaningful or revealing relation to his destiny increases the sense that accident rules all—call it Fortune, call it gods. In his next two romances, Shakespeare shows the hero initially guilty of wicked mistakes and thus to a large extent responsible for the events thereby set in train; in his last romance, the hero has been the victim of wickedness. Either way, the old tale of restoration and recognition is given an ethical meaning. This is accomplished, as Kenneth Muir succinctly puts it, 'by replacing the workings of an arbitrary providence by the operations of sin and forgiveness'. Meanwhile, Pericles simply suffers in self-imposed silence.

He is thereby sometimes held up to be demonstrating an exemplary Christian-type patience, even piety. It is pointed out that whereas Lear rages at the angry elements on the stormy heath, Pericles almost respectfully submits to them:

> Wind, rain, and thunder, remember, earthly man
> Is but a substance that must yield to you;
> And I, as fits my nature, do obey you.
>
> (II, i, 2–4)

Shortly thereafter, the elements, as he thinks, take his wife's life. He is often enjoined to 'Patience', yet he scarcely seems to need such exhortations. Again:

> We cannot but
> Obey the powers above us. Could I rage
> And roar as doth the sea she lies in, yet
> The end must be as 'tis.
>
> (III, iii, 9–12)

'O, sir, things must be as they may', as the First Fisherman says to him on the beach (II, i, 119). This sounds more like stoicism, or just fatalism, than Christian humility. It has been suggested that Shakespeare took the name 'Pericles' from Plutarch's life of an Athenian with that name and whose great patience is stressed; but I think Ernest Schanzer is right to discount this and point instead to the Pyrocles in Sidney's *Arcadia* with whom Shakespeare's Pericles shares many qualities and accomplishments. Now, the only defect in Pyrocles' knightly perfection is a *lack* of patience in adversity, which might seem to spoil the fit. On the contrary, says Schanzer, it clinches it.

'He shuts himself away from all human society, and when Marina visits him, he has not spoken to a living soul for three months. Can Shakespeare really have thought that this is the way in which exemplars of patience accept the blows of fortune?' Schanzer finds support for this view in a prose narrative by one George Wilkins, entitled *The Painfull Adventures of Pericles Prince of Tyre,* published in 1608 and almost certainly based on viewings of Shakespeare's play. The Quarto of the play, published in 1609, is a notoriously bad one, and the reporter(s) who offered this reconstruction of the play certainly got things wrong and possibly left things out. Be that as it may, in Wilkins' version, Lysimachus comments on Pericles' behaviour thus: 'though his misfortunes have beene great, and by which he hath great cause for this sorrow, it is great pity he should continue thus perverse and obstinate', while Marina comments that 'it was most foule in him to misgoverne himself. Put it this way: if you are plunged into near-unbearable grief by the death of a loved one, and if you had a strong tendency to extreme reactions, you might try to kill yourself by beating your head against the wall, as Sidney's Pyrocles does when he thinks his beloved Philoclea is dead; or you might simply die to the world, petrifying yourself into a sealed-up vessel of unassuagable cosmic fury—which is perhaps what Pericles does when he thinks his beloved Marina is dead. Perhaps he is warned so often to be patient because those who know him are aware of a proclivity for the opposite. (There is at least a hint of this in his first reaction to the loss of his wife at sea: 'O you gods!/Why do you make us love your goodly gifts,/And snatch them straight away? We here below/Recall not what we give, and therein may/Vie honor with you' (III, i, 22–6). As who should say—'You *bastards!*') True patience *is* extremely important in all these late romances, and I will come back to this. Here we may just note that Marina *does* show real, positive endurance and patience in her very extreme adversity, not retreating into a helpless grief but entering and engaging with the world as an admired teacher of artistic skills. Remember Milton's 'I cannot praise a fugitive and cloistered virtue', which seemed apposite for Isabella in *Measure for Measure*. Perhaps Shakespeare also deprecated a 'fugitive and cloistered' grief as well, no matter how understandable. Arguably, we are meant to see a *contrast* between the reactions and behaviour of the father and the daughter. In the last act, the man is manifestly psychically ill—he is indeed called 'a kingly patient' (V, i, 72), the noun *not* the adjective—and Marina has to engage him in a long session of therapy.

The play is very definitely about the father *and* the daughter, and their very different lives up to the time of their strange reunion in the last act. The title page of the first Quarto makes this very clear (it also makes it clear that it was staged primarily at the Globe and not Blackfriars):

> THE LATE, and much admired Play, Called Pericles, Prince of Tyre. With the true Relation of the whole Historie, adventures, and fortunes of the said Prince: As also, The no lesse strange, and worthy accidents, in the Birth and Life, of his Daughter MARINA, As it hath been divers and sundry times acted by his Maiesties Servants, at the Globe on the Banck-side. By William Shakespeare.

This dual focus, or double plot, is something new in Shakespeare's plays, and it occurs in three of the last romances. The sort of love interest which drove most of the earlier comedies is reduced or vestigial. The emphasis and interest has moved to familial relationships, particularly that of father and daughter. In this play, the proposed marriage between Lysimachus and Marina is arranged in a peremptory three lines (V, i, 262–4), and Marina is never heard to assent to it—her last words are for her rediscovered mother. And the whole play moves, in its disjunctive, episodic way, from the bad incest between father and daughter of the opening act, to what we may call the good 'incest' of the last act.

Gower starts by telling us of the incest of Antiochus and his daughter, a relationship Antiochus protects with a riddle which his daughter's suitors never solve and thus pay the penalty of losing their lives—'as yon grim looks do testify' says Gower, pointing to a row of heads displayed on the palace walls. ('Yon' is used frequently, as is the imperative 'see' or 'behold'. There is a lot of pointing in the play, as there is of moralizing—a sort of ethical pointing.) We then see the King and his daughter, with Pericles enthusiastically praising her virtues and beauty. He has recourse to a standard trope:

See where she comes, appareled like the spring,

. . .

Her face the book of praises, where is read
Nothing but curious pleasures

(I, i, 13–16)

She turns out to be a false spring (Marina will be the true one), and Pericles misreads the book ('curious' then meant 'exquisite', as any edition will tell you; but our more common meaning of strange or odd was emerging in the seventeenth century, and it turns out that her pleasures *are* 'curious'—curiouser and curiouser, as you might say). Willing to 'hazard' his life, Pericles asks for the riddle, which concludes:

I sought a husband, in which labor
I found that kindness in a father.
He's father, son, and husband mild;
I mother, wife, and yet his child.
How they may be, and yet in two,
As you will live, resolve it you.

(I, i, 67–72)

We might note that the riddle is somewhat different in the sources, where the answer is Antiochus himself. Moreover, only Shakespeare has the daughter present while Pericles is reading the riddle in front of her father —he wants to foreground daughters—and of course here *she* is the answer. As in the sources, the daughter remains nameless. In Twine's version, confessing to her nurse that her father has 'violently forced her', the daughter laments 'O my beloved nurse . . . even nowe two noble names were lost within this chamber . . . Where is my father? For if you well undestoode the matter, the name of Father is lost in me, so that I can have no remedie now but death onely.' The dread of incest must have something to do with the threatened loss of distinct identity; for if, like Oedipus in the most famous incest legend, you can become at once son, husband, father, and brother (to your own children), then all generational differences and demarcated kinship roles have collapsed into each other and individuation is lost. Most societies stigmatize and taboo incestuous sexuality as perverse:

perhaps, as used to be surmised, because it distinguishes us from animals who seem to be indifferent about the matter; perhaps because it destroys the family, and endangers the future—for a father 'forcing' his daughter is the past devouring the future. Daughters are to be exchanged, and given in marriage *out* of the family. Antiochus' daughter is right; she has lost her name—and her future.

Pericles has no trouble with *this* text, and it makes him 'pale to read it' (I, i, 76). His shocked realization—a constantly recurring one in Shakespeare—is that appearances cannot be trusted; the beautiful girl is a 'casket stored with ill' (I, i, 78). Realizing that if he answers the riddle correctly and thus reveals that he knows their guilty secret he will be killed, Pericles asks the King's permission to remain silent—and does so with an elaborate image which I find extraordinary but have never seen commented on:

> All love the womb that their first being bred;
> Then give my tongue like leave to love my head.
>
> (I, i, 108–9)

This conjoining—strong to the point of near identification—of the child in the womb and the tongue in the head, is somehow deeply suggestive in a play about a lost child and her dumb-struck father. More seriously, if loving the womb wherein your being is bred were to be translated into an adult activity, it would indeed be the ultimate Oedipal incest. With his image, Pericles—no doubt unconsciously—could be pleading for far more than the right to silence. Antiochus realizes that Pericles has discovered his secret, but feigns courtesy and friendship while planning murder. But Pericles has learned the lesson of deceptive Antioch—'How courtesy would seem to cover sin' (I, i, 122), and duly makes his escape.

Back in Tyre, he worries lest the powerful Antiochus will have him pursued, and falls prey to a barely explicable 'dull-eyed melancholy' (I, ii, 3) —not the first Shakespearian hero to whom that happens. Setting out on his destinationless travels, he arrives at the famine-struck city of Tharsus. There we hear the Governor Cleon reveal that the people are close to cannibalism: 'mothers . . . are ready now/To eat those little darlings whom they loved' (I, iv, 42–4). Part of the riddle of the daughter of Antiochus was 'I am no viper, yet I feed/On mother's flesh, which did me breed' (I, i, 65–6). Cannibalism is perhaps the most ancient taboo of all, and is curiously linked with incest as part of some primal confusion—'chaos and old night'—out of which human society emerged. Saturn devouring his children looms in the misty antecedents to the first Greek tragedy, which indeed dramatized this emergence (the *Oresteia* of Aeschylus). Intrafamilial—incestuous—cannibalism is the ultimate negation of the family and the transmissive separation of generations. Again, the future is ingested. This has not, in fact, yet happened in Tharsus when Pericles arrives with his timely aid of corn. But it is curious that the travels of Pericles should start with dangerous brushes with these two most ancient of dreads —curious, and perhaps part of the enduring and ubiquitous appeal of this 'old tale'. Setting sail again, he is shipwrecked, and thrown up on an unknown beach. It is as though his identity has been washed away in the storm—'What I have been I have forgot to know' (II, i, 75); but with the help of local fishermen, and his 'rusty armor' which they have netted, he reassembles himself as a knight and duly wins a local tournament and the king's daughter who, unlike his previous choice, is a glorious casket stored with *good*. In another reversal, her father pretends to be angry, but is really pleased. Such bad/good inversions are characteristic of fairy tales and old romances, and such is the atmosphere of the first two acts.

Act III finds Pericles in the middle of a terrible storm at sea, and also finds Shakespeare beginning to write in his recognizably late style. Pericles gains a daughter in these impossible conditions:

> Now, mild may be thy life!
> For a more blusterous birth had never babe;
> Quiet and gentle thy conditions! For
> Thou art the rudeliest welcome to this world
> That ever was prince's child. Happy what follows!
> Thou hast as chiding a nativity
> As fire, air, water, earth and heaven can make,
> To herald thee from the womb.
>   (III, i, 27–34)

Having welcomed a daughter, he has (as he thinks) to bury a wife—the close conjunction of things dying with things newborn is a distinguishing feature of the atmosphere of the Last Plays.

A terrible childbed hast thou had, my dear;
No light, no fire. Th' unfriendly elements
Forgot thee utterly; nor have I time
To give thee hallowed to thy grave, but straight
Must cast thee, scarcely coffined, in the ooze;
Where, for a monument upon thy bones,
And e'er-remaining lamps, the belching whale
And humming water must o'erwhelm thy corpse,
Lying with simple shells. O Lychorida,
Bid Nestor bring me spices, ink and paper,
My casket and my jewels

(III, i, 57–67)

It is a beautiful exequy—touchingly intimate and solicitous ('my dear'); awed, at the bleak indifference of the elements; somehow tranquillizing, with the 'humming water'; and finally mysteriously peaceful, with his wife at rest 'lying with simple shells'. The undersea world seemingly has its own placating processes—to which Pericles will despatch his wife, suitably accompanied by spices and jewels. Disaster has been turned into ritual.

We shortly see him leaving the new-born Marina with Cleon and Dionyza at Tharsus (they owe him a favour since he relieved their starving city) who promise to bring her up like their own daughter. But before that, there is a strange scene with Lord Cerimon which affords us perhaps the first certain intimation that we have entered the world of Shakespeare's late romances. Cerimon is a master of 'secret art':

'Tis known, I ever
Have studied physic, through which secret art,
By turning o'er authorities, I have,
Together with my practice, made familiar
To me and to my aid the blest infusions
That dwells in vegetives, in metals, stones;
And I can speak of the disturbances
That nature works, and of her cures

(III, ii, 31–8)

We have met herbalists and apothecaries before; and, seeking to allay the
suffering of her father, Cordelia prays:

> All bless'd secrets,
> All you unpublished virtues of the earth,
> Spring with my tears! be aidant and remediate
> In the good man's distress!
>
> *(King Lear,* IV, iv, 15–18)

Her 'blest secrets' are Cerimon's 'blest infusions', and his 'vegetives' are her
'virtues of the earth' (= medicinal plants). Shakespeare has already shown
an interest in good or white magic, and mysterious remedies; you may recall Helena's dead father (in *All's Well*) 'whose skill was *almost* as great as his
honesty; *had* it stretched so far, *would have* made nature immortal' (I, i, 20–
22, my italics). But it didn't—though he handed on some powerful secret
recipes to his daughter. Just what 'aidant and remediate' powers man's art
may draw out of nature to cure 'disturbances' which nature herself 'works',
is an increasing concern for Shakespeare. Marina is successfully 'aidant and
remediate' to her father in this play in a way which is debarred to Cordelia
in the intractably bleak world she moves through. And remember that, as
Gower indicated at the start, the whole story is intended to serve as a 'restorative'—for all of us.

   Cerimon values 'cunning' (skill) more than 'riches' because 'immortality
attends the former, / Making a man a god' (III, ii, 30–31); and it does indeed
come to seem that he has attained the skill that Helena's father just fell
short of. When some gentlemen bring in the casket/coffin containing the
'corpse' of Thaisa, he calls for his 'boxes', a fire, and some 'still and woeful
music', saying:

> Death may usurp on nature many hours,
> And yet the fire of life kindle again
> The o'erpressed spirits. [I have read
> Of some Egyptians, who after four hours' death
> Have raised impoverished bodies, like to this,
> Unto their former health.]
>
> (III, ii, 82–7)

(The lines in brackets are hopelessly garbled in the Quarto, and the much clearer words from Wilkins' prose narrative have been inserted.) Cerimon, it seems, has learned the 'secret art' of resurrection. Thus his triumphant speech:

> The music there! I pray you, give her air.
> Gentlemen,
> This queen will live: nature awakes; a warmth
> Breathes out of her. She hath not been entranced
> Above five hours. See how she 'gins to blow
> Into life's flower again!
>
> (III, ii, 92–7)

And Thaisa wakes—as if returned from the grave:

> Where am I? Where's my lord? What world is this?
> (III, ii, 107)

A resurrection! It is, as the amazed watching Gentlemen declare, 'most strange!', 'most rare!' Cerimon is, as Wilson Knight long ago pointed out, an early sketch for Prospero.

Right, says Gower, imagine Pericles back at Tyre, and Thaisa gone to Ephesus to be a votaress in Diana's temple. 'Now to Marina bend your mind'. She has, he tells us, 'gained/Of education all the grace' which has made her 'the heart and place/Of general wonder' (IV Gower 5, 8–9, 10–11). To keep us fully informed in advance, he tells us we will see envious Dionyza planning her murder—which immediately we do. Marina then enters with flowers—exactly like Ovid's Proserpina—lamenting her dead nurse:

> No, I will rob Tellus of her weed
> To strew thy green with flowers; the yellows, blues,
> The purple violets, and marigolds,
> Shall as a carpet hang upon thy grave,
> While summer days doth last.
>
> (IV, i, 13–17)

'Tellus' is a female personification of the earth, and Marina 'robbing' Tellus is a gentle reminder that, in some important way, this play is concerned with the meeting-point, and interpenetration, of sea and land. The scene takes place on the seashore. Taken down the beach by her appointed murderer, she is brusquely abducted by some pirates who suddenly appear. Like Proserpina she is taken off to an infernal underworld—in her case a brothel in Mytilene; of which, again like Proserpina, she will become effectively queen.

Moving to the brothel, we are back, briefly, in the world of *Measure for Measure*. (The Last Plays often contain echoes and short reprises of features of earlier plays. In this play, for example, the relation between the murderous Dionyza and appalled, weak Cleon is Goneril and Albany, in little, all over again.) With the brothel scenes, Shakespeare elaborates considerably on his story material for the first time. Pander, Bawd and Boult are all his own. Their low talk outside the brothel reflects the rankness and rottenness which comes with their trade. They sorely need a fresh wench, and to that end they buy Marina from the pirates. They gather gloatingly round her. Boult is told that, since he 'bargained for the joint', he will be allowed to 'cut a morsel off the spit' (IV, ii, 136–7). He in turn promises that he will inflame the lusts of the regular customers with his descriptions: 'I warrant you, mistress, thunder shall not so awake the beds of eels as my giving out her beauty stirs up the lewdly inclined' (IV, ii, 149–51). It is all nastily lubricious and concupiscent. Marina calls on Diana to help her preserve her 'virgin knot'—but 'What have we to do with Diana?' says the old Bawd, as they lead Marina into the brothel. She seems doomed to be forced into whoredom.

Two intervening scenes show Pericles brought to the supposed tomb of Marina, erected by Cleon and Dionyza to conceal the fact she was, as they think, murdered. In dumb show '*Pericles makes lamentation, puts on sack-cloth, and in a mighty passion departs.*' Then we are back in front of the brothel, and apparently something strange has been happening. Two regulars are hurrying away:

> Did you ever hear the like?
> No, nor never shall do in such a place as this, she being once gone.
> But to have divinity preached there! Did you ever dream of such a thing?

No, no. Come, I am for no more bawdy houses. Shall's go hear the vestals sing?

(IV, v, 1–7)

However she did it (and it is interesting that Shakespeare chooses *not* to show us *this* miracle), she has somehow talked or preached the customers out of their lusts, and kept her virginity intact. Inside the brothel, Pander, Bawd and Boult are discussing their problem. 'Fie, fie upon her! She's able to freeze the god Priapus, and undo a whole generation. We must either get her ravished or be rid of her . . . she would make a puritan of the devil' (IV, vi, 3–5, 9). But it seems that ravishing Marina is easier said than done—her 'virginal fencing' seems undefeatable. Then there follows a rather curious episode. Lysimachus, who is in fact the Governor of Mytilene, comes in disguised, apparently bent on some of what is usually on offer. 'How now! How a dozen of virginities?' (IV, vi, 21). Left alone with Marina, he first addresses her as he might a prostitute, then, when she explains that all she wants is to be 'free from this unhallowed place' (IV, vi, 106), he says:

> Had I brought hither a corrupted mind,
> Thy speech had altered it. Hold, here's gold for thee:
> Persever in that clear way thou goest,
> And the gods strengthen thee!
>> (IV, vi, 110–13—my italics)

And he leaves. But if he didn't come with 'a corrupted mind', what on earth was he doing disguised in a brothel in the first place? Here again, the reporter seems to have gone wrong. In the Wilkins version, Lysimachus goes to the brothel for the very reason you might expect a man to go to a brothel, and is converted by Marina's passionate pleading and telling reproaches ('virginal fencing' taken to a high art). He admits as much: 'I hither came with thoughtes intemperate, foule and deformed, the which your paines so well have laved, that they are now white.' She has done it again—another one 'sent away as cold as a snowball' (IV, vi, 145). This is more plausible than the weird version which stands in the (pirated) Quarto.

Angrier than ever—'She makes our profession as it were to stink afore the face of the gods' (IV, vi, 141–2)—Bawd and Boult determine to 'have your maidenhead taken off' and 'crack the glass of her virginity'—'she

shall be ploughed' (IV, vi, 133, 148, 151). But, left alone with Boult, she assails him with blistering reproaches about his occupation, until he says in
self-defence:

> What would you have me do? Go to the wars, would you? Where a man
> may serve seven years for the loss of a leg, and have not money enough in
> the end to buy him a wooden one?
>
> (IV, vi, 175–8)

Danby says that Boult is the only person in the play to ask an awkward
question, and suggests that it is out of place here. Certainly it sounds an odd
note of realism which we might expect more readily in, say, one of the history plays. Marina soon conquers him with her eloquence, and persuades
him that he will be better off if he promotes her as a teacher:

> If that thy master would gain by me,
> Proclaim that I can sing, weave, sew, and dance,
> With other virtues which I'll keep from boast;
> And I will undertake all these to teach.
>
> (IV, vi, 187–90)

Marina—Mistress of the Arts.

This is what Gower emphasizes at the start of the last act. In her dancing,
singing, learning, she is '*like* one immortal', 'goddess*like*' (my italics), and
her needle composes:

> Nature's own shape of bud, bird, branch, or berry,
> That even her art sisters the natural roses
>
> (V, Gower 6–7)

where 'sisters' is used for the only time by Shakespeare as a verb. 'Absolute
Marina' indeed (IV Gower 31). These last plays are much concerned with
familial relations, and an art actively serving as a 'sister' to nature is as important as a daughter who can act like a mother to her father—as we are
about to see. And for once, Gower does not tell us what is to happen, taking
us back to Pericles, now on his ship, and leaving us with—'what is done in
action . . . Shall be discovered. Please you, sit and hark' (V Gower 23–4).

What follows will be 'discovery' rather than illustration—for the characters, but also for the audience. And indeed, after Gower has drawn the curtain for the act to begin, almost immediately we have a character drawing another curtain to reveal the prostrate, seemingly petrified Pericles—a spectacle within a spectacle. (There will be other curtains to be drawn, veils to be lifted.) It is almost as if Pericles is becoming an abstract exemplar of a condition, a fate. This feeling of characters becoming like figures in allegory—'allegorized' as it were—is an important part of the atmosphere of the extraordinary scene to follow.

> Behold him. This was a goodly person
> Till the disaster that, one mortal night,
> Drove him to this.
>
> (V, i, 35–7)

Helicanus is about to tell the story of Pericles to Lysimachus—the play is full of narrators, narratives, narration, when—

> Sit, sir I will recount it to you.
> But see, I am prevented.
>
> (V, i, 63–4)

Marina enters. She will both stop, and come before, the spoken narrative, as though to give us the unmediated thing itself—'better than reportingly'.

She is asked to draw on her 'sacred physic' to cure Pericles, and promises to 'use / My utmost skill in his recovery' (V, i, 76–7). But as she attempts to address Pericles, he rudely pushes her away. Her reaction starts the cure—and the magic.

> I am a maid,
> My lord, that ne'er before invited eyes,
> But have been gazed on like a comet. She speaks,
> My lord, that, may be, hath endured a grief
> Might equal yours, if both were justly weighed.
> Though wayward fortune did malign my state,
> My derivation was from ancestors
> Who stood equivalent with mighty kings:

> But time hath rooted out my parentage,
> And to the world and awkward casualties
> Bound me in servitude.
>   (V, i, 86–96)

The scene that ensues is peculiarly moving because we are all the time in possession of a knowledge towards which we watch the main characters falteringly, incredulously, and finally ecstatically move. Pericles is the main beneficiary; Marina, with her apparently scarce-credible stories, draws him back into speech, and brings him psychic healing. Her opening, gently reproachful, speech cracks his aphasia, and, as if awakening from a death (for this is another resurrection), he gropes disjointedly for words:

> My fortunes—parentage—good parentage—
> To equal mine—was it not thus? What say you?
>   (V, i, 99–100)

Her answer, given what we know to be their actual relationship, is exquisitely poignant:

> I said, my lord, if you did know my parentage,
> You would not do me violence.
>   (V, i, 101–2)

He starts to press her with questions—a dormant mind galvanized into activity—'what countrywoman? / Here of these shores?' (V, i, 103–4). She answers with a riddle (like Helena in this, as in her healing gifts):

> No, nor of any shores.
> Yet I was mortally brought forth, and am
> No other than I appear.
>   (V, i, 105–7)

Those last six words are of crucial importance both for the play, and for Shakespeare as a whole. Many more Shakespearian characters than Duncan have found that 'there's no art to find the mind's construction in the face' (*Macbeth* I, iv, 11–12), a discovery made to their pain, if not their horror (as when Pericles realizes that the 'glorious casket' of the daughter is 'stor'd with ill'). Evil people are not what they *seem*—the word which echoes and re-echoes throughout the whole of Shakespeare. It is one of the felicities afforded by romance that the good people *are* as they 'appear' (while the evil figures, here Antiochus and his daughter, Cleon and Dionyza, duly come to a bad end). If this play does act as a 'restorative', it is perhaps in part because it restores our faith in at least some appearances. Marina can make you want to trust the world again.

The mounting urgency of Pericles as he moves closer to what, for him, is an entirely impossible truth, communicates itself to us, even though we are 'in the know', and the wonder begins to rise. It is a seamless process, but two ways he addresses Marina deserve special note:

> Falseness cannot come from thee; for thou lookest
> Modest as Justice, and thou seemest a palace
> For the crowned Truth to dwell in.
> (V, i, 122–4)

and

> yet thou dost look
> Like Patience gazing on kings' graves, and smiling
> Extremity out of act.
> (V, i, 140–42)

He is seeing Marina, not yet as a daughter, but allegorically—almost abstractly—as Justice and Truth personified; and architecturally—a palace, and a funerary statue of Patience 'gazing', in effect, on *his* grave. For, lying there unwashed, hairy, and dumb, Pericles must resemble, at the start, an unburied corpse. And this is the Patience which really matters. We have encountered it before:

> She sat like Patience on a monument,
> Smiling at grief
> (*Twelfth Night*, II, iv, 115–16)

His face still combating with tears and smiles,
The badges of his grief and patience
                    (*Richard II*, V, ii, 32–3)

       patience and sorrow strove
   Who should express her goodliest
                    (*King Lear*, IV, iii, 17–18)

Viola, Richard II, Cordelia—there is something of all of them in Marina.
The figure of Patience is an image found in tomb sculpture and other art,
as well as in emblem books. Claire Preston has written admirably and en-
lighteningly about how 'the culture of emblems and their dialectic of word
and figure'—emblems contained a picture and, underneath, an epigram-
matic moral to be drawn from it—helps to explain some of the unusual and
distinctive features of the play, its 'stasis, formality, and inaction'. In connection with Pericles' words to Marina, Preston comments: 'The exterior
emblem motto implied by the play as a whole and by this scene especially is
something like "*Patientia vincit omnia*"'. 'Extremity' we may take to cover
every sort of calamity (including the extreme act of suicide). Shakespeare
uses the word quite frequently, but only here with a capital E, thus personifying it into an actual entity to be confronted and somehow bested. This
play, like other Last Plays, certainly contains 'a sea of troubles' but, rather
than taking arms against them, Marina—Patientia 'smiles' them away—a
beautiful image which perfectly embodies the irenic, even beatific, atmosphere the Last Plays manage to distil.

As Pericles' memory begins to stir, he breaks out of his catatonic de-
pression, and frozen feelings begin to flow again, finally bursting into full
flood:

   O Helicanus, strike me, honored sir!
   Give me a gash, put me to present pain;
   Lest this great sea of joys rushing upon me
   O'erbear the shores of my mortality
                    (V, i, 193–6)

The 'tempest' has turned 'kind', and metamorphosed into a metaphor for
joy. The restoration of Pericles both to his daughter and to psychic sanity is

accompanied by a request for 'fresh garments' and the playing of music (as in *King Lear,* but where the cure is short-lived). Only Pericles can hear the music—'rarest sounds!'—and he declares it to be 'the music of the spheres' (V, i, 232). It puts him into 'thick slumber', during which he has his vision of Diana. While listening to Marina's seemingly impossible story, Pericles declared:

> This is the rarest dream that e'er dulled sleep
> Did mock sad fools withal. This cannot be . . .
> (V, i, 164–5)

Now, he dreams a goddess, who finally instructs him—'Awake, and tell thy dream' (V, i, 251). In this atmosphere, the dream to be told is true, and 'cannot be' gives way to 'has to be'. Accelerating unstoppably towards the total revelation and completed miracle of the conclusion, the play finally reunites father and daughter with the wife and mother, Thaisa, 'supposed dead and drowned' (V, iii, 35). Wonder on wonder.

The central restoration is that of the proper relationship between father and daughter, so monstrously inverted at the start of the play. When Pericles is finally convinced that Marina *is* his long-lost, thought-dead, daughter, he cries:

> O, come hither,
> Thou that beget'st him that did thee beget
> (V, i, 197–8)

Anthropologists tell us that incest and riddles are closely associated, perhaps the apparently impossible (the riddle) standing in for the actually unthinkable (incest). Here, with the image of his daughter giving him (new) life, as he once gave her life, Pericles is pointing to a metaphorically good 'incest' which puts the family to rights. And that is very satisfying and reassuring. Though there is possibly a shadow of the story *not* told, or avoided —the Oedipal story of a man who sets out on his travels to *avoid* incest, only to discover that that has been his destination. Widowed Pericles—another travelling man—might have married the gifted nurse in a foreign land who cured him, if the unimaginable truth had not emerged. It is, arguably, a close thing. Terence Cave calls this 'the hidden other face of recognition'.

And there *is* just the faintest shadow of something else, which I think is an important part of the play's rich conclusion. At one point, as the weepingly incredulous Pericles is listening to her story, Marina, tentative and reticent throughout, says 'It may be / You think me an impostor' (V, i, 180–81). It is a word Shakespeare seldom used, and, interestingly, the only other person who defends herself against the possible imputation is Helena, another daughter with miraculous-seeming healing powers—'I am not an impostor' (*All's Well* II, i, 157). Of course Marina is the true Marina; *of course* she is. However, perhaps just a little bit more evidence:

> this is Marina!
> What was thy mother's name? Tell me but that,
> *For truth can never be confirmed enough,*
> Though doubts did ever sleep.
> (V, i, 202–5—my italics)

She names Thaisa and he is convinced. But the italicized line cuts exactly two ways—you can never have too much confirmation; but on the other hand, you can never have *enough* confirmation. This is also just hinted in the reunion of Pericles and Thaisa. He is following the instructions of a goddess, and when Thaisa names herself he gratefully acknowledges 'Immortal Dian' (V, iii, 36). However, it's just that bit more reassuring when she recognizes his ring as a gift of her father. 'This, this! No more,' he cries out happily (V, iii, 39). Well, perhaps just a little more. This man coming in—

> Can you remember what I called the man?
> I have named him oft.
> (V, iii, 51–2)

She names him correctly—names have an almost talismanic quality in this play, and it is important to get them right—and Pericles is even more pleased—'Still confirmation' (V, iii, 53). Shakespeare is certainly not suggesting in any way that Marina and Thaisa are impostors. He is just blinking once at the fact that they just, *just,* could be. In these matters there never can be perfect proof, complete 'confirmation', absolutely certain knowledge. And in this play there are so many 'gaps'. Indeed one of Gower's functions is to 'stand i' th' gaps to teach you/The stages of our story' (IV, iv, 8–9). Put another way (and I suppose this is Cave's point), a chancey recognition scene—and nothing more chancey-looking than the reunion of Pericles and Marina—might awaken in us a dim sense of all that we (they) might *not* have recognized: unexposed impostors, or undetected incest. Rather than decreasing our sense of wonder at the end of this play, such considerations, stirring only at the very periphery of thought, should enhance it. It might so easily have all been otherwise.

The theologian, Richard Hooker, writing in the 1590s, said of the celebration of the birth of Christ at Christmas: 'The love and mercy of God towards man which this way are become a spectacle as neither men nor angels can behold without a kind of heavenly astonishment.' Intending no disrespect for Hooker's theology, I wish to borrow a phrase from him for a more secular occasion; since I think we can hardly do better than to say that we behold Shakespeare's spectacle, too, with 'a kind of heavenly astonishment'.

CYMBELINE (1610)

> I see before me, man. Nor here, nor here,
> Nor what ensues, but have a fog in them
> That I cannot look through.
>> (III, ii, 79–81)

> It is no act of common passage, but
> A strain of rareness
>> (III, iv, 93–4)

> Fortune brings in some boats that are not steered.
>> (IV, iii, 46)

'You do not meet a man but frowns.' So begins this extraordinary play, classifiable, if at all, rather helplessly as a tragical-comical-historical-pastoral-political romance. There are more frowns to come—frowns of worry, frowns of anger, but mainly frowns of incomprehension as, increasingly, 'perplexity' overcomes the participants in the myriad, mixed actions. The 'fog' which centrally engulfs the heroine, Imogen, settles variously on them all, until they cannot see to see—to borrow Emily Dickinson's powerful formulation. In no other play do so many characters seem so blind. 'I am amazed with matter' cries the bemused King (IV, iii, 28): 'I remain perplexed in all' laments a bewildered servant. There is a bit of a war in the play (there is a bit of everything in this play), during which:

> friends kill friends, and the disorder's such
> As War were hoodwinked.
>   (V, ii, 15–16)

When War is blundering around blindfolded, and disorder itself seems to be, as it were, losing its grip, then you have a mess indeed. 'Confusion thick'—and thickening, seems to be the order–disorder of the day (V, iii, 41). 'How comes these staggers on me?' cries out Posthumus, near the end (V, v, 233), and by this time everyone, including the audience, is feeling dizzy. If ever a conclusion was calculated to affect all concerned with a thrilling vertigo, it is the astonishing last scene of this play—compositionally one of Shakespeare's greatest *tours de force*—during which (according to a critic with a head for numbers) no less than twenty-five plot complications are untied in less than five hundred lines. There is nothing else like it.

And so much the better, Dr Johnson would have said.

> To remark the folly of the fiction, the absurdity of the conduct, the confusion of the names, and manners of different times, and the impossibility of the events in any system of life, were to waste criticism upon unresisting imbecility, upon faults too evident for detection, and too gross for aggravation.

There is the eighteenth century in full throat. But neo-classicism's geese are romance's swans, and the lamentable vices denounced with such juridical relish by the great Doctor can turn into radiant virtues when looked at with a—dare one say it—less blinkered eye. Certainly the play plunges ever more deeply into anarchy, and seems to court the risk of a collapse into chaos. With seemingly quite unrelated plots starting at different points and at different times in Roman Britain, Renaissance Italy and primitive Wales, and the fragmented events spinning centrifugally out of control, it becomes increasingly difficult to see how any of the agents involved might take over the direction of things, or impose some kind of order and inter-relatedness. There is no Duke Vincentio, no Prospero to hand; indeed there is no artificer or organizer (baleful or benign) in sight. Just thickening fog. And yet, in what seems like the last few minutes of this very long play, everything is resolved, clarified, unified, without a loose end left behind. Never was a more dazzling feat of tidying-up. Do we thank Jupiter, who puts in a rather bad-tempered, belated appearance; or rather marvel at Shakespeare, who by now clearly does know every trick in the theatrical book—and then some? But if he is pushing back the boundaries of his art—to what end?

The play is extremely rich in material, and some extravagant claims have been made, not unjustifiably, for the historical and religious significance manifestly attaching to some of its themes. Wilson Knight was right to point out that it exceeds any other play by Shakespeare in the fecundity of its classical and mythological reference—it is a work, he says, 'saturated with religious suggestion'—and right, too, to maintain that at least part of the purpose of the play is to emphasize the importance of ancient Rome in Britain's history. These are major matters and I will return to them. But I want to start by trying to suggest something of the distinctive atmosphere of this unique play. Shakespeare is by now a past master at exploiting what Bertrand Evans calls 'discrepant awareness', whereby the audience knows more than some or all of the characters for some or all of the time. We can thus watch them wading ever more deeply into error, or arriving, slowly or suddenly, at true knowledge, with the relevant attendant emotions of horror and joy, anxiety and relief. But in no play do the audience know more, and the participants less, than in *Cymbeline*. One way to make sure an audience is in the know is for a main plotter, through asides or soliloquies, to keep us informed of his (or her) devices and intentions. Whomsoever else Richard III and Iago trick and bamboozle, they have no surprises for us and, effectively, no secrets from us. For a wonder, this is exactly *not* the case with the one Iago*ish* plotter in this play, who gives us our one pure surprise—more of which later. For the rest, neither the play nor the people in it seem inclined to keep any secrets from *us;* from each other is a different matter. This results in some curious effects, of which I will give three examples.

The unnamed Queen—she is just a generic Bad Queen—asks her physician, Cornelius, to prepare a 'strange ling'ring poison' for experimental purposes. In a long aside, effectively to us, he says (I summarize): 'I can see through this wicked Queen, but I have tricked her. She thinks I have given her a deadly poison. Little does she know that it's a harmless sleeping draught. I've made a fool of her' (I, v, 33–44). Now this is the sort of stage effect most of us will have experienced in pantomime, and one result is to drain the figure of the Queen immediately of all real threat and menace. However nasty she is (very—torturing animals and so on), we know that ultimately she can do no lasting harm. You never feel that about Lady Macbeth. When the male-disguised Imogen is taken by the Romans, she gives the name of the corpse (which she thinks is Posthumus) as Richard du Champ, then offers this aside (I summarize): 'Actually, I'm lying a bit here, but it's harmless enough. I do hope the gods will understand—that is, if they are listening' (IV, ii, 377–9). Other Shakespearian heroines make no such apologetic asides about their resourceful inventiveness. Here, it slightly lowers the tension, and makes us a bit more aware of the theatricality of what we are watching. When Posthumus finds himself back in Britain, supposedly obliged to fight on the side of the Italians, he says in soliloquy: 'Therefore, good heavens/Hear patiently my purpose' (V, i, 21–2). This is really for our benefit as he goes on to explain that he will take off his Italian clothes, dress up as a British peasant, and at least fight for Imogen's side. This is really rather back-stage stuff, and, again, it makes us aware that, in various little ways, Shakespeare keeps giving us glimpses of the reverse side of the tapestry.

But if we are, if anything, over-informed, the characters suffer from pitifully partial knowledge. True, everyone knows *something,* his or her little patch as it were; but nobody knows much. As the play progresses, we acquire more and more secrets, while watching the varying ignorance of the participants grow and grow. The character who suffers most from this process is Imogen, as we see from the first act. Firmly defying her blusteringly tyrannous father; coolly taking the measure of her treacherous stepmother ('Dissembling courtesy!'); treating Iachimo's insinuations and overtures with superb, well-bred contempt—Princess Imogen is not only by a long stretch the most intelligent (not to say the most attractive) character in the play; she shows herself well qualified to join the ranks of those masterful, independent spirits, Portia and Rosalind. But she isn't given a chance. Whereas they actively decided to assume male roles, both to give themselves access to areas of experience usually debarred to women, and to work to revitalize and restore a social order which has gone wrong, the Princess Imogen is advised *by her servant* to abandon her female identity ('You must forget to be a woman', III, iv, 156), and she never masters or makes much of her male role (in the Welsh mountains, she is happiest singing and cooking). Leah Scragg makes the relevant point succinctly: 'previously a change of identity affords the opportunity to enter the play world on a new footing. In *Cymbeline* by contrast the opposite is the case, in that the heroine adopts a disguise in order to leave her world rather then enter it.' Completely in control in the opening scenes until the departure of banished Posthumus, Imogen is thereafter never again fully the mistress of her situation, nor is she a partner in our awareness. She seems to get further and further from us as she enters deeper and deeper into the fog. I might just add here that the phenomenon of things passing out of sight into distances of *air* (key word)—ships, birds—is another delicate motif, contributing to the atmosphere of the play. As in Imogen's exquisite lines about how she would have tried to 'after-eye' Posthumus's departing vessel:

> I would have broke mine eyestrings, cracked them but
> To look upon him till the diminution
> Of space had pointed him sharp as a needle;
> Nay, followed him till he had melted from
> The smallness of a gnat to air
>   (I, iii, 17–21)

'Diminution of space' has an added resonance in a play which brings ancient Britain, Renaissance Italy and wild Wales together in the same spot. And I have a quite unjustifiable sense that Shakespeare would like us to experience this play as somehow taking place at the very periphery of vision, where lands and times and events merge together—and the gnat melts to air.

Imogen, then, is unique in her pitiable plight. Marina experienced life as 'a lasting storm'; but she pretty quickly masters the brothel, and what she knows she knows, as Pynchon would say. Imogen, to all intents and purposes, knows nothing; and, once she has fled from the hostile court, is entirely at the (honourable) mercy of Welsh outlaws and Roman invaders. 'No heroine in the comedies is cast in such a role,' writes Bertrand Evans, 'kept unaware so long, ignorant of so many secrets, abused by so many practices, endangered from so many quarters.' None of which, needless to say, reflects on the character or capacities of Imogen herself. It is just the nature of the world in which she, unhappily, finds herself. She has no one to guide her, as Vincentio looks out for Isabella (Portia and Rosalind simply take over the show). In this world, there don't seem to *be* any guides (Pisanio does a loyal servant's limited best; Philario is sensible, and ignored, in Rome). Finally it is only Imogen's own quick 'eyestrings' less than four hundred lines before the end—'I see a thing / Bitter to me as death' (V, v, 103–4), i.e. her ring on Iachimo's finger—which set in train the tumble of revelations and recognitions which so 'staggeringly' conclude the play. Of this final scene Evans writes: 'For us, the experience of the closing scene is that of witnessing the revelation of secrets that have been locked in our minds, and of observing the effects of their revelation upon the persons who have been ignorant of them and to whom they are of most concern . . . The release of each secret accomplishes a welcome reduction, degree by degree, of the pressure that has been mounting in our minds since error first began to pile on error; one effect of the scene, thus, is the relief of overmuch understanding, painful because it has been unsharable.' This is part of the special experience of *Cymbeline*.

It is perhaps most helpful to identify three potentially quite separate stories which Shakespeare has most cannily interwoven. They involve, respectively, a newly married but separated couple (mainly romance); a disrupted dynasty (which involves both pastoral and something close to fairy tale); and an international dispute (history and pseudo-history). The marriage between Imogen and Posthumus must have been a 'handfast' (I, v, 78—a word used only once again by Shakespeare; curiously in his very next play, *The Winter's Tale*). This was an old form of irregular or probationary marriage contracted by the parties joining hands and agreeing to live as man and wife—for a princess to agree to such an unceremonious bonding does indeed reveal 'a strain of rareness', as Imogen claims. It was a marriage but not yet a legal finality, which is presumably why, out of her innate 'pudency' (lovely word, and used only this once, for this rarest of heroines—II, v, 11), 'Me of my lawful pleasure she restrained' (II, v, 9), as Posthumus bitterly complains, insanely convinced that Imogen has afforded Iachimo what she refused him. That it was this sort of unsanctified marriage would seem to be born out by the simple fact that the boorish Cloten still thinks he can win her, denying the validity of her 'contract'; and she, while doing everything possible to repulse him, never simply says—you're wasting your time, I'm already married.

It is this recent, secret, away-from-court 'marriage'—to a commoner, at that—which so enrages her father, King Cymbeline (in this way the play starts rather like *Othello*), who instantly separates them by banishing Posthumus. In this, he plays the traditional role (in comedy) of the obstructing, prohibiting father who seeks to block young love. Here, he literally 'comes between' the lovers.

> or ere I could
> Give him that parting kiss which I had set
> Betwixt two charming words—comes in my father,
> And like the tyrannous breathing of the north
> Shakes all our buds from growing.
>
> (I, iii, 33–7)

Wrathful, foolish, *'imperceivant'* King Cymbeline (the italicized word only appears this once in Shakespeare—Cloten ludicrously misapplies it to Imogen, but it will do very nicely for Cymbeline, and indeed many others in this fog-bound play) has indeed sunk his court and realm into a 'winter's state' (II, 4, 5). He has disrupted the due processes of nature ('shakes all our buds from growing'); he has somehow lost his two sons (the legitimate heirs), alienated his one remaining true child (Imogen), and effectively handed power over to a poisonous, poisoning second queen and her monstrous son, so the feeling of sterility is strong in the air. It will require the enactment of an apparent 'death' and rebirth, or resurrection—as in some primitive fertility rite—to re-establish the proper cycle of the seasons, and bring the fruit back to the trees.

Cymbeline was a king of ancient Britain when the Romans still held sway over it, and I will return to this. But following the banished Posthumus, we find ourselves in Renaissance Rome—a curiously easy modulation—and here the romance story starts. It is based—closely—on a story in Boccaccio's *Decameron* (Day 2, Novella 9), which is, in turn, a relatively sophisticated version of a widespread folk tale involving the wager on a virtuous wife. The husband who bets on his wife's virtue is invariably tricked by false evidence into believing that she has betrayed him, and orders her death. She escapes, often in male disguise, and is finally enabled to reveal the truth.

She is reunited with her contrite husband, and the villain is punished. Boccaccio's version, involving Italian merchants, is decidedly middle-class; Shakespeare prefers to set it at the level of the court, since that way he can make it intermesh with the historical–political material which will later come into prominence—but he retains much of the mercantile talk of coins, prices, values, weights, measures etc. Boccaccio has his wronged wife, Ginevra, escape, as a young man, into the Oriental and Moslem world of the eastern Mediterranean, where (s)he rises to high office under the Sultan of Alexandria. This was no use to Shakespeare, who needed to restrict his already sufficiently disparate material to Britain and Italy, so, in Bullough's words, 'he substituted the popular medieval theme by which the ill-used woman wanders in search of her man into a pastoral setting and there finds solace and help until she can be reinstated'. Thus, instead of the Orient—Wales. Also, in Boccaccio the convicted villain who faked the evidence is fiendishly tortured to death (impaled on a stake, covered in honey, devoured by flies, wasps, and hornets). Shakespeare, *Titus Andronicus* aside, the least ghoulish of writers, prefers to have him forgiven—though he may have a specific reason for this, as well.

The story involving dynastic disruption only starts to emerge in the first scene set in Wales (III, iii). Here we meet Belarius who combines two conventional roles in pastoral romance—the rusticated courtier, and the shepherd father. We learn that he was unjustly banished—Cymbeline's angry mistakes go a long way back—and that he abducted the two baby princes (fearing the corrupting influence of Cymbeline's disastrous court), so that the lost royal children (who don't know their true parentage) have grown up in the wild Welsh mountains. When the starving Imogen stumbles into their cave, it is the beginning of a process which will in time knit them into the swelling master-narrative accommodating them all. Shakespeare could have found material for the interlude in Wales in a number of Greek romances. (In this connection Carol Gesner makes an interesting observation: the motif of the hero striking the unrecognized heroine at a trial-like public occasion, as Posthumus does Imogen, is standard and recurrent in Greek romance. It never advances the plot, so it must be there for another reason. It is certainly the most *painful,* literally shocking, moment in Shakespeare's play.) Shakespeare also almost certainly borrowed from an anonymous play, *Love and Friendship* (acted 1582). This play contains, for instance, a fleeing heroine named Fidelia (cf. Imogen's pseudonym Fidele) who finds ref-

uge with a hermit in a cave. Shakespeare added the folk-tale motif of the
Wicked Stepmother, eager to advance her own, hideous child. But there
was almost certainly a more substantial reason for choosing Wales as the
setting for this part of the play. The summer of 1610 saw the investiture of
Prince Henry as Prince of Wales, to great rejoicings and many entertainments—one of which may well have been *Cymbeline*. The use of Milford
Haven as the landing place for Posthumus and the Romans would certainly
resonate for the contemporary audience, since it was there that Henry, Earl
of Richmond, landed when he came to save England from Richard III. He
became Henry VII, the Tudor ancestor through whom the current James I
could be connected with the Tudor mythology of the descent from the Trojan Brut. Wales plays a special part in the legends and myths concerned
with the founding of England. And this looks towards the third, international story.

What exactly is the 'name and birth' of that Posthumus who has just married Imogen? asks the somewhat bemused Second Gentleman in the busy,
frowning first scene of the play. First Gentleman:

> I cannot delve him to the root. His father
> Was called Sicilius, who did join his honor
> Against the Romans with Cassibelan,
> But had his titles by Tenantius, whom
> He served with glory and admired success,
> So gained the sur-addition Leonatus
>   (I, i, 28–33)

Shakespeare and his contemporaries were interested in origins and in delv-
ing their nation 'to the root'—Troy? Rome? Lud? Brutan? Britain?—but
if they strained their eyestrings to see where the gnat of early Tudor history melted into the air of the unseeably previous, they would find themselves in the, well, fog of ungraspable legend—Geoffrey of Monmouth's
History of the Kings of Britain; Holinshed's early Chronicles. Shakespeare
certainly turned again to Holinshed, not this time for the historically an-
chored Tudor material, but to glance at the insecurely drifting Brutan material (Brut was supposedly descended from 'Aeneas the Trojan', legendary founder of Rome, and was said to have founded Britain). There he
would have found those British–Latin names—Sicilius, Tenantius, Cassi-

belan; not to mention Posthumus, Innogen (possibly what Shakespeare intended), Guiderius and Arviragus, Cloton and, of course, 'Kymbeline or Cimbeline'.

> Kymbeline or Cimbeline the sonne of Theomantius was of the Britains
> made king after the deceasse of his father. . . This man (as some write)
> was brought up at Rome, and there made knight by Augustus Caesar,
> under whome he served in the warres, and was in such favour with him,
> that he was at libertie to pay his tribute or not. Little other mention is
> made of his doings, except that during his reigne, the Saviour of the world
> our Lord Jesus Christ the onelie sonne of God was borne of a virgine,
> about the 23 yeare of the reigne of this Kymbeline . . . some writers doo
> varie, but the best approved affirme, that he reigned 35 years and then
> died, and was buried at Londonn, leaving behind him two sonnes, Guide-
> rius and Arviragus.

Holinshed notes that there was some subsequent dispute between Britain and Rome over tribute money, with the Romans planning (at last) to invade. He thinks it was the son, Guiderius, who 'gave occasion to breach of peace betwixt the Britains and the Romans, denieing to pay them tribute':

> But whether this controversie which appeareth to fall forth betwixt the
> Britains and Augustus was occasioned by Kymbeline, or some other
> prince of the Britains, I have not to avouch: for that by our writers it is
> reported that Kymbeline, being brought up in Rome, and knighted in the
> court of Augustus, ever shewed himselfe a friend to the Romans, and
> chieflie was loth to breake with them, because the youth of the Britaine
> nation should not be deprived of the benefit to be trained and brought up
> among the Romans, whereby they might learne both to behave them-
> selves like civill men, and to atteine to the knowledge of feates of warre.

From these hints Shakespeare drew out the international theme of the play, the rising tension between Rome and Britain. This third action starts properly in III, i, with the arrival of the Roman ambassador, Lucius, though we have had preparatory hints concerning the paying of Roman tribute in II, iii and iv. Shakespeare, in fact, makes it Cymbeline who refuses to pay the tribute—not his son. He could have taken this idea from Spenser's *Faerie*

Queene (which he certainly knew). This is from the 'chronicle of Briton kings' (Book II, Canto 10):

> Next him *Tenantius* raigned, then *Kimbeline,*
> What time th'eternall Lord in fleshly slime
> Enwombed was, from wretched *Adams* line
> To purge away the guilt of sinfull crime:
> O joyous memorie of happy time,
> That heavenly grace so plenteously displayd;
> (O too high ditty for my simple rime.)
> Soon after this the *Romanes* him warrayed;
> For that their tribute he refused to let be pay'd.

The most important feature of the remote and misty reign of Cymbeline was that it coincided with the reign of Caesar Augustus in Rome and the birth of Christ. This, understandably, has been used to suggest that there is a larger, more significant action going on here, a play we can't see behind the play we can. Thus Northrop Frye: 'The sense of a large change in human fortunes taking place off stage has to be read into *Cymbeline*'. And Francis Yates: 'The universal imperial *justitia* and *pax* was sanctified through that birth, and through the interpretation of the prophecy in Virgil's Fourth Eclogue as applying both to the peace and justice of the Augustan golden age, and to the birth of Christ, the Prince of Peace, in that age.' Thus was the Empire Christianized. 'The interpretation of the reign of Cymbeline as contemporary with the reign of Augustus, in which Christ was born, gave it an atmosphere of the sacred; it approximated the British sacred reign to the sacred reign of Augustus Caesar; it drew together British imperial and Roman imperial sacred legend in some new fusion of Britain and Rome. This is exactly what happens in *Cymbeline* which is dominated by a vision of a Romano-British imperial eagle.' Shakespeare certainly knew all about the sacred importance of the Augustan Peace. The increasingly dominant Octavius Caesar confidently predicts, near the end of *Antony and Cleopatra,* 'The time of universal peace is near' (IV, vi, 5). There is, perhaps, a just comparable moment in this play, when the 'curiously oracular jailer' (Frye) says, after the freeing of Posthumus: 'I would we were all of one mind, and one mind good. O, there were desolation of jailers and gallowses' (V, iv, 175–6). But I hardly think that this, or indeed anything else in the play, points to what Felperin calls 'a momentous change for the better in the fortunes of the entire human community'.

Felperin offers what might be called an eschatalogical reading of the play. 'The incarnation represents a turning point within Christian history from the eras of nature and law to a new era of grace. The former are character-ized by wrath and justice—motives associated with tragical history [= the first four acts of *Cymbeline*]; the latter by love and mercy, motives associated with romantic comedy [= Act V of *Cymbeline*].' He could hardly be more confident: 'Jupiter is a divine lame duck whose term of office is about to expire and the ending of the play has more to do with the doctrine of an-other deity whose reign is about to begin . . . The Roman gives way to the Christian not only within the action as a whole but within each character, the tragical history gives way to romance.' (I imagine that this far from even-tempered Jupiter would be surprised to hear of his imminent redun-dancy, and might well feel inclined to pay Felperin one of his sulphurous visits—but I stray from the real world.) This is all very satisfyingly neat and cut-and-dried; and the evidence for such a reading is—just about—there, if you care to isolate it and, as I think, exaggerate it. But it risks turning the play into something of a tract, albeit of a high order (Felperin is a very sub-tle reader). Many intelligent people read the play along these lines, and it is only appropriate to place this version before readers of this introduction. But the play just doesn't *feel* like this to me. I think we need something with a bit more of a 'stagger' in it.

One other aspect of the Roman material in the play should be mentioned. Caius Lucius, the Roman ambassador and general, is 'honourable' and 'holy'; he is also courteous, gracious, kind and reasonable. All of which, the King of Britain—on the evidence we see—is notably *not*. Yet, we recall from Holinshed, Cymbeline was knighted in the court of Augustus Caesar, and wanted the youth of Britain to be brought up among Romans so that they would learn to behave 'like civill men' and acquire the martial virtues. In a word, for Britain, Rome—and this was felt to be historically true—was *the* civilizing influence. The strident, sneering nationalism of Cloten and the Queen when they refuse and reject Lucius (III, i) should be registered as a jarring and inappropriate isolationism—football-terrace stuff (admit-tedly, in a different kind of history play, it might pass for rough-tongued patriotism). Cymbeline's final, willing reconciliation with Rome signals his release from thraldom to the wicked Queen, and a return to the larger civilizing forces of the world.

But if Lucius is one (ancient) Roman, Iachimo is another (Renaissance) Italian, closer to Machiavelli than to Augustus Caesar. In him the civilized virtues have run to super-subtly smooth manners and a refined self-satisfying aestheticism (he certainly seems to appreciate Imogen's physical beauty more than Posthumus does). Posthumus, despite the hyperbolically good report we hear of him in the first scene, emerges as neither particularly refined, nor conspicuously elegant of manner. His first appearance in Italy shows him prickly and quarrelsome, while his subsequent behaviour, however we finally take it, is hardly that of a truly civilized man. There is a national point here, concerned with Britain's ancestral strengths and weaknesses, which certainly interested Shakespeare. Brockbank quotes a contemporary *Description of Britain* in which the dullness of the British—'men of great strength and little policie, much courage and small shift'—is contrasted with the 'craftinesse, subtile practises, doubleness, and hollow behaviour' of the ingratiatingly polite Italians. As a straightforward, honest, literal-minded British lad, Posthumus is hopelessly out of his depth in Rome (there is a hint of the bull in the china shop). But, while Iachimo simply crumbles in battle, Posthumus's heroism turns the day for Britain, and there is no doubt that his basic virtues and strengths are vindicated—having been, though, not only sorely tried, but all too easily abused.

The enlarged inter-national (and thus, as it were, inter-spatial, inter-temporal) dimension is absolutely vital; but the core and main thread of the play is the romance story concerning the (recently married) lovers, just as Imogen is herself the linking 'strain of rareness' that runs through its more 'common passages'. The first two acts dramatize the testing of that love, with, as is invariably the case in Shakespeare, the man failing the test while the woman remains constant. Forced apart in the bustling, scattering first scene, Imogen and Posthumus barely have time to swear their love ('I did not take my leave of him, but had/Most pretty things to say'—Imogen's sweet words, I, iii, 25–6), and plight their troth with the exchange of a ring and a bracelet (and how important these little *things* prove to be; how deeply involved we are with our merely material adjuncts and accessories!). But she has, as it were, barely finished her incomplete farewell to her paragon and 'jewel', when we are in Rome in the company of assorted foreign gen-

tlemen expressing degrees of scepticism about the growing reputation of
this British Posthumus, who is about to arrive to spend his banishment with
his friend Philario.

The leading sneerer is Iachimo—he clearly finds his pleasure in disparaging and belittling—and he reveals an important aspect of his mentality in
his opening remarks. I think I saw the man once: 'But I could then have
looked upon him without the help of admiration, though the catalogue of
his endowments had been tabled by his side and I do peruse him by items'
(I, iv, 4–7). He will, in due course, peruse by items, catalogue, and tabulate
the sleeping body of Posthumus's wife, though of course no one can know
that yet—except Shakespeare, who is giving us an early clue as to how Iachimo's mind works. He thinks in inventories. As far as he is concerned, a
man—and a woman—is *exactly* the sum of his, or her, isolatable and item-
izable parts. What he can't peruse and catalogue—as might be, devotion,
loyalty—isn't there. A sharp eye, but a hard eye—and a cold one. He is the
last person for the rather hot-headed young Briton, now *dépaysé* (out of his
country, thus disoriented), to tangle with; but that is what Posthumus im-
petuously does.

He allows himself to get involved in a quite improper and degrading
wager about the physical virtue of his absent wife, foolishly—and arguably
offensively—boasting her to be more chaste, more virtuous, more everything, than any other woman of any country. Cunningly, Iachimo starts to
play on the comparable and relative values of the diamond ring on Posthumus's hand, and the wife who gave it to him—both no doubt excellent, but
you cannot be sure that either is the absolute best. Posthumus maintains
that he 'rates' them just as he has said, maintaining a difference. The exchange which follows is crucial:

> The one may be sold or given, or if there were wealth enough for the pur-
>   chase or merit for the gift. The other is not a thing for sale, and only the
>   gift of the gods
> *Iachimo.* Which the gods have given you?
> *Posthumus.* Which by their graces I will keep.
> *Iachimo.* You may wear her in title yours, but you know strange fowl light
>   upon neighboring ponds. Your ring may be stol'n too. So your brace of
>   unprizable estimations, the one is but frail and the other casual. A cun-

ning thief, or a that-way-accomplished courtier, would hazard the winning of first and last.

(I, iv, 87–99)

Iachimo wants to bring Imogen down from the gods and into the market—
and to his great shame, Posthumus lets him. He seems to have a grasp of the
crucial difference between the ring, which indeed must remain, at least the-
oretically, within the realm of the purchasable; and his wife, who is, as he
correctly says, 'not for sale'. The ring is a symbol of their love; Imogen is
love itself. But for Iachimo, a woman, any woman, *is* simply another 'ring'
(the obscenity intended), so he can speak mockingly to Posthumus of his
'*brace* of unprizable estimations', and refer indifferently to 'she your jewel,
this your jewel' (I, iv, 159), as much as to say—six of one, half a dozen of the
other. And notice how Iachimo draws seemingly casual traces of suggestive
insinuation in front of the less urbane young Briton: 'you know strange
fowl light upon neighboring ponds'. If he doesn't take the hint and make
the application, Posthumus might well register this as a meaningless irrele-
vance. But when the grosser parts of his imagination have been stirred, it
will be a different matter. (In the next play, Leontes will give himself the
nightmare of imagining how any man may have 'his pond fished by his
next neighbor'—*The Winter's Tale* I, ii, 195.) Iachimo wants matters of value
and worth to be measured in ducats, and when Posthumus agrees to remove his ring (when she gave it him, Imogen abjured him to keep it on till
'Imogen is dead', I, i, 114—she will, duly, 'die') to match the gold which has
been staked on Imogen's seducibility, he effectively hands her over to Iachimo, who promises to bring him '*sufficient testimony* that I have enjoyed
the dearest bodily part of your mistress' (I, iv, 155–6, my italics). Posthumus enters wholeheartedly into the business of 'articles', 'covenants', 'lawful counsel' whereby the disgraceful wager is given specious respectability. Only the sensible Philario 'will have it no lay' (I, iv, 153); 'Gentlemen,
enough of this. It came in too suddenly; let it die as it was born . . .' (I, iv,
126–7). Things coming in 'too suddenly'—eruptive violence—is often the
mark of tragedy, and, at the moment, that's the way this play is tending.
The wager, once 'born', will not 'die', and there will have to be other deaths
before there are other births.

There follows a strange little scene, back in Britain, which looks rather pastoral—the Queen and her ladies gathering flowers—violets, cowslips, primroses. For distilling fragrances, you might think. But the Queen has graduated from perfumes to poisons, and she's after a real killer—only to be tricked by her virtuous physician, as we have seen. There is something pantomimic in this scene; but we might recall that a dumb-show of a sleeping king having literal poison poured into his ear was at the centre of Shakespeare's first tragedy; and while the Queen's efforts are rather fee-fi-fo-fum, there are always subtler poisons for the unsuspecting (or too suspicious) ear in Shakespeare. As loyal Pisanio instantly recognizes when he incredulously reads the letter from his master, describing Imogen's adultery and ordering her murder.

> Leonatus,
> O master, what a strange infection
> Is fall'n into thy ear! What false Italian,
> As poisonous-tongued as handed, hath prevailed
> On thy too ready hearing?
> (III, ii, 2–6)

Spot on—and, as so often in Shakespeare, it is a pity that a master can't see what is instantly clear to his servant. But that's the play. The poisonous-tongued *and* poisonous-handed (both—quite right, Pisanio) 'false Italian' is, of course, Iachimo; and after the wager scene we see him working his poison.

Or failing to. Obviously, his first destination is the court of King Cymbeline, where he can try out his assorted wiles on Princess Imogen. He arrives with flattering letters of introduction from Posthumus (part of the wager), but as soon as he sees her, he knows he has an impossible task.

> All of her that is out of door most rich!
> If she be furnished with a mind so rare,
> She is alone th' Arabian bird, and I
> Have lost the wager.
> (I, vi, 15–18)

The relationship between what a person looks like on the outside ('out of door') and his internal 'furnishing'—misleading discrepancy and contradiction, or honourable congruence and continuity—is a concern, and a dramatically exploitable resource, in almost all of Shakespeare's plays. Here, there are quite a number of references to 'without/within', but they are fairly relaxed—'less without and more within' says Posthumus amiably enough, as he pulls on a peasant's smock prior to plunging into battle—and possible discrepancies do not seem to occasion much concern. Cymbeline is every inch a bloody fool, and shows it; Imogen is as virtuous as she is fair; Cloten is reliably boorish *all* the way down, and so on. Iachimo is quite a smooth ingratiator, but he is manifestly not a man to go on a tiger hunt with. If anyone, Posthumus is the big letdown: 'so fair an outward and such stuff within' says the eulogizing First Gentleman in the first scene (I, i, 23). But some of that 'stuff within' turns out to be rather nasty.

Recognizing that he will never win the wager in the sense in which it was made, Iachimo invokes 'boldness' and 'audacity', and first he tries something he is good at—filthy sexual innuendo, murmured with courtly disgust as if in a half-aside. The line is—how could any man, with such a peerless woman, want to go after trash?

> Sluttery, to such neat excellence opposed,
> Should make desire vomit emptiness,
> Not so allured to feed . . .
> . . . The cloyed will—
> That satiate yet unsatisfied desire, that tub
> Both filled and running—ravening first the lamb,
> Longs after garbage.
>
> (I, vi, 44–9)

These are very powerful speeches, and the very *idea* of uncontrolled sexual lust (since that is all this is) seems always enough to call forth Shakespeare's strongest, indeed most *disgusted* language—that tub both filled and running seems to have stood permanently somewhere in the grounds of his imagination. Sane Imogen simply thinks Iachimo is mad; so, abandoning the oblique approach, he more straightforwardly describes Posthumus as living a wild, debauched life in Rome, in terms taken from the extreme reaches of lasciviousness and foulness. Clean Imogen simply hears it with sadness, and tells him to desist. 'My lord, I fear / Has forgot Britain . . . Let me hear no more' (I, vi, 112, 117). Iachimo then makes a perhaps despa-

rate, certainly disastrous, attempt to incite Imogen to take her revenge—
with him:

> Should he make me
> Live like Diana's priest betwixt cold sheets,
> Whiles he is vaulting variable ramps,
> In your despite, upon your purse? Revenge it.
> I dedicate myself to your sweet pleasure . . .
>   (I, vi, 132–6)

at which point Imogen promptly calls for the police—or rather Pisanio and,
by implication, the palace guards, telling him to report to the King that a
'saucy stranger' is using his court 'to expound his beastly mind to us' (I, vi,
151–3). Not, certainly, a good day for Iachimo. But, never without a stratagem, he recoups by congratulating Imogen on her performance, and felici-
tating Posthumus in having such a faithful wife—he was just *testing* her. By
nature given to trust, Imogen believes and forgives him, and indeed offers
hospitality. But no, he must leave on the morrow, only asking as a favour
that she will afford a trunk full of precious gifts for the Emperor 'safe stow-
age'. Of course—'I will keep them / In my bedchamber' (I, vi, 195–6). 'Send
your trunk to me'—so she concludes the first act (I, vi, 209); how ominously,
we have yet to learn.

   This confrontation of Iachimo and Imogen is one of Shakespeare's great
scenes—never more piquant adversaries, with such different resources to
draw on! Never mind the looming war between Rome and Britain, *this*—
however you care to name its contesting qualities or virtues or skills or
powers—is the battle at the soul of the play, to be shortly followed by what
must be a unique scene in Shakespeare. Imogen is in her bed, attended by a
lady, about to go to sleep: she turns down the page of the book she has been
reading, asks for her taper to be left burning, dismisses her lady, and prays
to the gods to protect her from fairies and 'the tempters of the night' (II, ii,
9). She sleeps; all is peace: and then *Iachimo comes from the trunk* (which of
course was there for safe-keeping). This is the one totally opaque deed in
the play, and it should take us, the audience, *completely* by surprise. This is
unusual, particularly in this play where people are given to announcing
their intentions. Cunning, plotting villains in particular in Shakespeare, invariably let the audience know what they are planning, perhaps thus to in-

volve us in the somewhat guilty complicit pleasure of enjoying the uninformed discomfiture of their victims. But Iachimo has not dropped us a word nor tipped us a wink. We should be as surprised as Imogen—except that Imogen is asleep, so now we know something she doesn't know. But that spectacle of the figure of Iachimo silently emerging from the trunk in the nocturnal bedroom may be sufficiently troubling; who knows *what* comes out at night, within us and without us? It is, at the same time, rather comic—not exactly Box-and-Cox, but that way inclined. We should bear this mixed tonality in mind—particularly, as it happens, in another scene involving another 'trunk'.

Iachimo's forty-line soliloquy over the sleeping Imogen is amazing. Everything about the setting and situation suggests and presages rape. Imogen has been reading about the rape of Philomel by Tereus in Ovid's *Metamorphoses* (Iachimo finds the book with the page at which she stopped turned down—Shakespeare showing one of the key sources for his own art on stage, another glimpse into the works, as it were); while Iachimo, in a moment of misplaced solidarity, invokes '*Our* Tarquin', whose rape of Lucrece Shakespeare himself had, of course, written about. These were two of the most violent rapes in mythology or history, and they set dire precedents. But Iachimo is gentleness itself, speaking with a hushed reverence and awed appreciation that bespeak a finer sensibility than—so the feeling sometimes goes—an oily little Italian seducer has any right to. He seems initially to be, as it were, stunned into poetry; his first dozen lines are exquisite, quite transcending his usual cynical manipulation of discourse. It seems another voice, from:

> The crickets sing, and man's o'erlabored sense
> Repairs itself by rest.

to:

> The flame o' th' taper
> Bows towards her and would underpeep her lids
> To see th' enclosèd lights, now canopied
> Under these windows, white and azure-laced
> With blue of heaven's own tinct.
>
> (II, ii, 11–12, 19–23)

But this sort of entirely non-prurient wonder won't get the job done—as he realizes. 'But my design'. And he sets about his 'inventory'—'I will write all down'—proceeding to itemize the contents of the room and, as far as he can (a mole on the left breast), the details of Imogen's body. His penetrations and appropriations are entirely ocular. 'That I might touch!' he sighs at one point: but he can't-mustn't-won't. The Tarquin he invoked differed exactly here:

> His rage of lust by gazing qualified;
> Slacked, not suppressed; for, standing by her side
> . . .
> His drumming heart cheers up his burning eye,
> His eye commends the leading to his hand;
> His hand, as proud of such a dignity,
> Soaking with pride, marched on, to make his stand
> On her bare breast, the heart of all her land . . .
>   (*The Rape of Lucrece*)

Iachimo can only use his hands to steal Imogen's bracelet—a symbolic violation of her chastity, if you will, but still a scopic one. Because, of course, he has come, not for direct sex, but for indirect 'evidence': the bracelet—'this will *witness outwardly,* / As strongly as the conscience does *within,* / To th' madding of her lord'; the mole—'Here's a *voucher* / Stronger than ever law could make' (II, ii, 35–7, 39–40—my italics). With these, plus his 'inventory'—'I have enough' (II, ii, 46)—he returns to the trunk, with the uncharacteristically unconfident lines—'I lodge in fear. / Though this a heavenly angel, hell is here' (II, ii, 49–50). Hell is where? In the bedroom? In the trunk? Perhaps in Iachimo himself? Not clear—but certainly, a sudden shiver. The whole astonishing, voyeuristic episode is one which it can be both gripping and unsettling to participate in—as we, fellow intruders in the bedroom, inevitably do.

After a short scene, allowing a break for his return to Italy, Iachimo is back in Rome, boasting to Posthumus of an easy triumph—'the ring is won', and he means both of them (II, iv, 45). His demonstration that he has 'knowledge of your mistress' (II, iv, 51)—meaning carnal knowledge—falls into two parts. First, drawing no doubt on his 'inventory', he meticulously

describes the decorations on the walls of her bedroom, on the chimney or
fireplace, and on the ceiling. The main subjects—in tapestry and in sculpture—are Cleopatra meeting Antony on the swelling Nile, and 'Chaste
Dian bathing' (throw in two silver andirons in the form of 'two winking
Cupids')—as if the room is brimming with rising eroticism and an entic-
ingly displayed and vulnerable chastity (the golden cherubims on the ceiling seem to come from somewhere else, though I suppose they would be
fairly Cupid-like). The main feature, though, is the striking life-likeness of
the art:

> a piece of work
> So bravely done, so rich, that it did strive
> In workmanship and value; which I wondered
> Could be so rarely and exactly wrought,
> Since the true life on't was
>
> (II, iv, 72–6)

and

> Never saw I figures
> So likely to report themselves. The cutter
> Was as another Nature, dumb; outwent her,
> Motion and breath left out.
>
> (II, iv, 82–5)

Forget the sex—look at the art-work. At the start of *Timon of Athens,* the
Poet says to the Painter of one of his works:

> I will say of it,
> It tutors nature; artificial strife
> Lives in these touches, livelier than life.
>
> (I, i, 37–9)

It was a common enough contemporary figure; here it is probably a piece of
rank flattery, and thus absurdly exaggerated. But the idea of an art that,
as it were, steals a march on nature, goes one better, outdoes or outskills

it, clearly haunts or delights Shakespeare during the writing of these last plays, when he must have felt that he had more tricks up his sleeve than life itself. As it is his pleasure to demonstrate to us.

These details of the decorations are what Iachimo calls his 'circumstances' which, he says to Posthumus 'must first induce you to believe' (II, iv, 61, 63). The word means 'details' or 'particulars', but it is particularly appropriate since all this is what we would now call (merely) 'circumstantial evidence', *not* proof. Posthumus, rightly, sees it in this way, too. Iachimo could have found out these details in any number of ways without even coming near the person of Imogen, and as far as Posthumus is concerned, Iachimo has lost the wager. Then Iachimo produces the bracelet. Within ten lines Posthumus hands over the ring given to him by Imogen—completely assured, just like that, of Imogen's infidelity.

> The vows of women
> Of no more bondage be to where they are made
> Than they are to their virtues, which is nothing.
> O, above measure false!
> (II, iv, 110–13)

Philario again tries, vainly, to introduce a little sense—hang on man, bracelets can be lost or stolen. Posthumus pauses, but Iachimo only has to repeat that 'I had it from her arm' (as indeed he did) for Posthumus to revert—eagerly, as one feels—to his conviction of Imogen's 'incontinency':

> No, he hath enjoyed her.
> The cognizance of her incontinency
> Is this. She hath bought the name of whore thus dearly.
> (II, iv, 126–8)

Philario—'this is not strong enough to be believed' (II, i, 131)—is wasting his time. 'Never talk on't./She hath been colted by him' (II, iv, 132–3). One feels Posthumus's perverse pleasure in using coarse language about his wife. Just to make sure—or just to turn the knife—Iachimo describes how much he enjoyed kissing the mole under Imogen's breast. That *really* does the trick.

Spare your arithmetic; never count the turns.
Once and a million!

(II, iv, 142–3)

O that I had her here, to tear her limb-meal!

(II, iv, 147)

We have seen before in Shakespeare how men will explode into the crudest, most deranged form of sexual jealousy on the smallest amount of (obviously) manufactured 'evidence'—which Posthumus will swear amounts to 'testimonies . . . proof as strong as grief' (III, iv, 22–4), while Iachimo later admits it was just 'simular (simulated) proof' (V, v, 200)—and we are to see it one more, shattering, time, in the next play. As a phenomenon it clearly fascinated Shakespeare; and, as clearly, he saw that there could be in men a deep, masochistic pleasure in the self-torturing thought of infinite ('once and a million') sexual betrayal. It is a deeply worrying male proclivity which could have—Shakespeare is often at pains to show—endlessly ramifying destructive consequences.

And now Posthumus is all over the place, having abandoned his better self which was invested in his love for (and trust of) Imogen. He is given a long, incoherent soliloquy, full of gross sexual fantasizing:

Perchance he spoke not, but,
Like a full-acorned boar, a German one,
Cried 'O!' and mounted

(II, v, 15–17)

and spluttering, uncontrolled misogyny:

For there's no motion
That tends to vice in man but I affirm
It is the woman's part . . .
All faults that have a name, nay, that hell knows,
Why, hers, in part or all, but rather all.
. . . I'll write against them,
Detest them, curse them.

(II, v, 20–22, 27–8, 32–3)

That should settle their hash! This, of course, is all furious, flailing foolishness—a tantrum. Posthumus has become stupid, coarse, out of control. He has nowhere to go, and he disappears from the play. Interestingly though, the next two acts will be plagued by a man who is—stupid, coarse, out of control; and I can assure you that something funny *is* going on here.

The third act sees the opening up of the action to the growing row between Rome and Britain and its extension to the new area of Wales, where we meet the long-banished Belarius and the King's two lost sons, Guiderius and Arviragus. Imogen, following her 'longing' ('mine's beyond beyond', III, ii, 57), is deceived into setting out for Milford Haven (which is in Wales) by a letter from Posthumus, where he has ordered Pisanio to murder her. It is at this point that Imogen enters the fog. The scenes in the Welsh mountains allow Shakespeare to open up pastoral issues concerning the differing claims and gifts of nature and nurture, and the various dispositions of natural man—thus, Cloten is a born savage made worse by civilization, while Guiderius and Arviragus are brought up as *enfants sauvages* yet reveal innately royal blood:

> How hard it is to hide the sparks of nature!
> These boys know little they are sons to th' King
> . . .
> I' th' cave wherein they bow, their thoughts do hit
> The roofs of palaces, and Nature prompts them
> In simple and low things to prince it much
> Beyond the trick of others.
> (III, iii, 79–80, 83–6)

Belarius, understandably perhaps, given his bad experiences at court, extols the superior nobility of their simple, primitive life in the wild nature of the mountains. But for the young boys it is 'a cell of ignorance . . . a prison':

> Out of your proof you speak. We poor unfledged
> Have never winged from view o' th' nest, nor know not
> What air's from home . . .
> We have seen nothing,
> We are beastly: subtle as the fox for prey,

Like warlike as the wolf for what we eat.
Our valor is to chase what flies.
                    (III, iii, 27–9, 39–42)

Now, this very aerial play—heights and distances, good and bad air to
breathe—is full of birds, both mean and proud: puttock, crows (lots of
them), jay, raven—most nobly, the eagle; and, supremely, the phoenix. Belarius reveals something about his cowed (not coward) state when he sends
the boys racing up to the heights of the hills, telling them to look down on
him with a bird's-eye view—'I'll tread these flats' (III, iii, 11). He thinks
that they will thereby learn a lesson of caution, seeing:

    The sharded beetle in a safer hold
    Than is the full-winged eagle.
                    (III, iii, 20–21)

A defeated and disappointed man, Belarius has become a convinced hugger
of the earth. But princes will needs be airborne, and warrior eagles rather
than creeping beetles will command the concluding spaces of the play. And
the Welsh mountain retreat is a far from safe refuge—as becomes apparent
when the war threatens to engulf them all. Pastoral dreams cannot with-
stand the rigours of history; and the play refuses to sentimentalize life in the
mountain wastes.

   When Imogen learns, from the letter to Pisanio, that Posthumus has convicted her of adultery and ordered her death, she perceives a terrible danger
which, potentially, threatens society itself.

        All good seeming,
    By thy revolt, O husband, shall be thought
    Put on for villainy, not born where't grows,
    But worn a bait for ladies.
    . . .
    Goodly and gallant shall be false and perjured
    From thy great fail.
                    (III, iv, 55–8, 64–5)

The world is full of bad seeming which takes in good people—Shakespeare has no more constant theme. But what happens when people will not believe in '*good* seeming'—then *nothing* and no one will be trusted, and good-bye all the virtues. It is, indeed, a 'great fail'. Somehow, the play will have to work to rehabilitate 'good seeming'. But not before there has been some more 'seeming' of, let's say, an indeterminate kind, not least in the form of two disguisings (Pisanio provides both sets of clothes—visibly, the wardrobe man). The first is nothing new in Shakespeare. Imogen, who is now 'dead to my husband' (III, iv, 132—since Pisanio is supposed to have killed her), dresses up as a boy and sets out to seek service with the 'noble' Roman, Lucius, who is advancing towards Milford Haven. She is thus the last, and it has to be said least high-spirited, of Shakespeare's epicene heroines. One little aspect of this disguising is worth noting. The wondrous whiteness of Imogen's skin has been noted, and Pisanio regrets that she must expose it to 'the greedy touch/Of common-kissing Titan' (III, iv, 164–5), i.e. get sunburned ('Titan' is a name applied to the sun by both Virgil and Ovid). Belarius and the princes worship the sun and 'heaven' (the boys are referred to as 'hot summer's tanlings', IV, iv, 29, and you won't be surprised to learn that they are the only 'tanlings'—little tanned ones—in Shakespeare, or indeed anywhere else!), and when Imogen stumbles, as it were, into their territory, she has exchanged the court for life under the open sky—the larger point being that the play is overseen by Jupiter, ruler of the heavens.

I will come back to Imogen's Welsh interlude. But the other disguising—of Cloten—is something else again. I must go back to a short scene in the second act when Cloten was urging his exceedingly unpleasant and unwelcome attentions upon Imogen. She tries to remain courteous in her rebuffs, but when Cloten dismisses Posthumus as 'base slave', she flares out:

> His meanest garment
> That ever hath but clipped his body is dearer
> In my respect than all the hairs above thee,
> Were they all made such men.
> (II, iii, 135–8)

All Cloten can do is to stand there repeating incredulously 'His meanest garment?'—four times! Some critics have wondered at this—Frank Kermode, for example, found it excessive. But surely the impression we should get is that of a record that has got stuck. I register Cloten as a kind of automaton—an assemblage of all the conventional stage properties used to identify the villain. He makes all the most horrible and obnoxious villain-like noises—that is what the machine is geared up to do. But he is never intended to come across as a *human* being. Bizarrely enough, in one of my very few appearances on the school stage, I played Guiderius, and when I walked on with Cloten's head, saying:

> This Cloten was a fool, an empty purse;
> There was no money in't. Not Hercules
> Could have knocked out his brains, for he had none
>   (IV, ii, 113–15)

I was invariably met with gales of laughter. This was doubtless occasioned by my own inherent, undisguisable ridiculousness, but even then I dimly perceived that there was no known histrionic art which could render this entry anything but comic. Brockbank is surely right in suggesting that, with these lines, the 'clotpole' stage head would have been displayed as a hollow property. Very well, it might be said; but what is the point in confronting us with this noisy, hollow contrivance? This takes us to his disguising.

When Cloten hears that Imogen has fled from court, he is sure that she has gone to meet Posthumus, and he determines to follow. First, he bullies Pisanio into helping him, as now he has Posthumus's servant. He tells Pisanio to bring him a set of Posthumus's garments, and it so happens that Pisanio has 'the same suit he wore when he took leave of my lady' (III, v, 125–6). While waiting for the clothes, Cloten runs over his planned revenge.

> She said upon a time—the bitterness of it I now belch from my heart—
> that she held the very garment of Posthumus in more respect than my
> noble and natural person, together with the adornment of my qualities.
> With that suit upon my back will I ravish her; first kill him, and in her
> eyes. There shall she see my valor, which will then be a torment to her
> contempt. He on the ground, my speech of insultment ended on his dead
> body, and when my lust hath dined—which, as I say, to vex her I will ex-
> ecute in the clothes that she so praised—to the court I'll knock her back,

foot her home again. She hath despised me rejoicingly, and I'll be merry
in my revenge.

(III, v, 134–47)

The brutality machine is turned up to full volume (automata which seem to
be alive may look comic, but they can also be very frightening). Pisanio
brings the clothes, and Cloten is off.

We next see him wandering around in Wales, well pleased with his disguise—'How fit his garments serve me!' (IV, i, 2–3): they are suitable—and
they fit. He is still relishing his coming revenge—'Posthumus, thy head,
which now is growing upon thy shoulders, shall within this hour be off'
(IV, i, 16–17). As luck, and the play, would have it, it is *his* head which is off
within the hour, he having run into Guiderius and made the mistake of
treating him contemptuously as some sort of outlaw mountain criminal. At
which provocation, the rightful heir to the throne quite fittingly despatches
and then decapitates the vile pretender. Which in turn leads to what must
be the strangest scene in Shakespeare. Imogen is thought dead (she has
taken Pisanio's potion which is, in fact, a safe sleeping draught), and the
two young princes lay her out for what seems like some sort of Celtic, pre-
Christian burial—the body on the earth, strewn with herbs and flowers. At
the instigation of Belarius—'He was a queen's son, boys' (IV, ii, 244)—they
bury the body of Cloten in the same way, laying it next to Imogen. They
leave—and, of course, Imogen soon wakes up, understandably dazed, still
half in a dream. But then she sees the body.

> A headless man? The garments of Posthumus?
> I know the shape of's leg; this is his hand,
> His foot Mercurial, his Martial thigh,
> The brawns of Hercules; but his Jovial face—

(IV, ii, 308–11)

except, of course, there isn't a face. 'How? 'Tis gone.' Where's the head?
Where on earth is the head? The killer might at least have left the head?—
one imagines her casting around. (Whatever else this is, it cannot entirely
exclude the comical.) Then, with more laments, and execrations for Pisanio
and Cloten who, Imogen is sure, have killed Posthumus, she falls on

the body, as for one last embrace—'O my lord, my lord!' (IV, ii, 332). The Romans approach, Lucius talking to his Soothsayer, when the spectacle makes him stop—'Soft, ho, what trunk is here? / Without his top?' (IV, ii, 353–4). I think this brings us close to one, at least, of the centres of this strange play.

Let's go over the moment. A somewhat dazed, half-awake Imogen finds herself lying next to a headless body wearing Posthumus's clothes. She not only assumes that it is Posthumus, but identifies the body, part by part, as that of her beloved—yet it is the body of the figure she most abhorred, on which she proceeds to throw herself. What is this telling us? Is it the head alone (= quality of mind, refinement of intelligence and understanding) which differentiates man from man? (cf. Imogen just previously:

> But clay and clay differs in dignity,
> Whose dust is both alike.
>
> (IV, ii, 4–5)

—*how* does living clay differ in dignity?) Take off the heads or 'tops', and is there then no difference between Posthumus and Cloten? *And* didn't we see Posthumus effectively 'lose his head' in Rome, succumbing figuratively to what has overtaken Cloten literally? This point was nicely made by Robert Hunter, who suggested that, since we see the insanely jealous Posthumus adopting the mindless savagery of Cloten, during Posthumus's two-act absence Cloten provides us with a present parody of him. Others have suggested that the execution of Cloten in Posthumus's clothes acts as a vicarious or symbolic (or substitute) death of Posthumus's bad self. However you take it, there is certainly an odd continuity between Posthumus and Cloten; and, despite what looks like their all too obvious oppositeness, a curious kind of heads-and-tails identity. They are never on stage together; and their only reported encounter is a very slight skirmish in which neither is hurt (they 'play' rather than 'fight'). The relationship is, I think, more than parodic—though it may well include the warning that if a man loses his grasp on his best self, he may easily relapse into a *parody* of a human being. Not so different as you might think. And Imogen has been unwittingly involved with an inappropriate 'trunk' before—the one containing Iachimo which she ordered to be brought to her bedroom. Thus the poor woman has, variously, spent the night with, and lovingly embraced, the two male 'trunks' which were most hateful to her. Can you ever be really sure who, what, you are embracing—what is in anyone's 'trunk'?

Imogen also has a potentially troubling relationship with the two young princes in the Welsh mountains. Of course, the exiles treat 'him' (she is now Fidele) with all the rural courtesy which displaced courtiers usually encounter—to their surprise—in their pastoral interludes:

> These are kind creatures. Gods, what lies I have heard!
> Our courtiers say all's savage but at court.
> Experience, O, thou disprov'st report!
> (IV, ii, 32–4)

So far, this is, conventionally, as it should be. Fidele acts, gratefully, as their 'housewife' (they are the *hunters*), sings to them like an 'angel', and turns out to be a wonderful cook (the point is emphasized—'But his neat cookery!', IV, ii, 49—Shakespeare had no need of the 'culinary triangle' of Levi-Strauss to appreciate the importance of cooking methods in signalling culture). This is all domestically harmonious. But the young princes find Fidele *very* attractive. Belarius reacts to him as 'an earthly paragon'— 'Behold divineness / No elder than a boy' (III, vi, 43–4)—not the first time a Shakespearian heroine is taken for a divinity. The boys react, as it were, more physically:

> Were you a woman, youth,
> I should woo hard but be your groom in honesty.
> I'ld bid for you as I do buy.
>
> I'll make't my comfort
> He is a man. I'll love him as my brother . . .
> (III, vi, 68–71)

Just as their bearing is royal without their knowing they are princes, so here, their behaviour is fraternal without their knowing they are brothers—such are the pleasing ironies of romance. But the certain implication is, that *if* Fidele was a girl—as of course s/he *is*—their attentions would be a good deal closer. Once again, we have a light skirting, flirting with the pos-

sibility of incest. Not, I think, gratuitously, and certainly not pruriently—
there is not a hint of any untoward behaviour; quite the reverse. But Shakespeare is clearly interested in the imponderable ways in which the sexual
impulses are involved in those all important drives which make for family
bonds and bondings. If you want to think of sublimation (though the concept seems too crude)—the transforming of the sexual drive into something
finer—you may find it in the beautiful dirge the boys speak at Fidele's 'funeral':

> Fear no more more the heat o' th' sun
>> Nor the furious winter's rages
>
> . . .
>
> Fear no more the frown o' th' great;
>> Thou are past the tyrant's stroke . . .
>>> (IV, ii, 258–65 on to 281)

Though in fact there is more heat, and sun, and frowning still to come for
the not-dead Fidele; and tyranny has not yet essayed its last stroke. This is
not the Forest of Arden.

Indeed it is not; for soon the area is engulfed in the war between the
newly-landed Romans and the Britons—'the noise is round about us' (IV,
iv, 1). Characteristically, Belarius wants to hide in the mountains; but
Guiderius and Arviragus want to 'look on blood' and try themselves in battle—for royal blood is also knightly-warrior blood—and they all make towards the war. The fog now is at its thickest, and the next person to loom
out of it is Posthumus (he has come over as part of the Italian contingent).
The Cloten-part of his identity has, as it were, been ritually killed off, so
it is not surprising that we see and hear his better self re-emerging. He
now bitterly regrets the 'death' of Imogen (he has a bloody handkerchief—
Pisanio's 'proof' that he carried out his fatal instructions), shows contrition,
and blames himself. Evidence of recovered sanity comes in his remark:

> You married ones,
> If each of you should take this course, how many
> Must murder wives much better than themselves
> For wrying but a little!
>> (V, i, 2–5)

'Wrying but a little'—just deviating a little from the straight and narrow—
shows he has gained a sense of proportion; you don't kill a wife on account
of a little loose sex. Note that Posthumus still believes that Iachimo *did* pleasure himself with Imogen. This is important, not only because it reveals
that he has learned to forgive her; but also because, in the brief fragment
of the war which next occurs in dumb-show, Posthumus, now dressed as
a British peasant, actually encounters Iachimo (fighting for the Romans).
And '*He vanquisheth and disarmeth Iachimo and then leaves him*' (V, ii, directions). As Hunter points out, this means that we actually *see* Posthumus
effectively forgiving Iachimo, whom he would certainly recognize, and
whom war would allow him legitimately to despatch. This briefly glimpsed
moment adumbrates the mood at the end of the play when Posthumus will
be able to say to an abjectly repentant Iachimo:

> The pow'r that I have on you is to spare you;
> The malice towards you to forgive you. Live,
> And deal with others better.
>   (V, v, 418–20)

At the sight of which, the inanely choleric old Cymbeline, who goes on
wildly trying to hand out death sentences up to the last moment, finally gets
the point:

> We'll learn our freeness of a son-in-law:
> Pardon's the word to all.
>   (V, v, 421–2)

These merciful gestures have been seen as constituting the specifically
Christian turn to the otherwise pagan play; but while there is a deal of
Christian terminology in the play (free play is made with the word 'election' in reference to lovers' choices, for example), it seems to me more in
keeping with the mood of reconciliation, reunion, recognition (often ne-
cessitating contrition and forgiveness) which Shakespeare works to bring
about at the conclusions of these last plays. And if Shakespeare has no trouble in putting Renaissance Italy and Celtic Wales in ancient Britain (or vice
versa), he certainly won't think twice about having them all in Christen-
dom—even with Jupiter still reigning under his 'radiant roof' (V, iv, 91).

Shakespeare's theatre is much more capacious than theology. The atmosphere or mood at the end of the play is neither firmly pagan nor distinctly
Christian—it is simply Shakespearian; neither very definitely here, nor unmistakably there: rather—'beyond beyond'.

The last act recounts the brutal confusions of war ('lolling the tongue
with slaught'ring'—as graphic as *Guernica*: V, iii, 8), the heroic exploits of
Posthumus and the triumphant trio of Belarius, Guiderius and Arviragus.
Britain and Cymbeline are saved by the virtues and efforts of those whom
the King had so stupidly and blindly banished. Careless of life (still thinking he is guilty of Imogen's death), Posthumus allows himself to be wrongfully imprisoned and sentenced to death (well, 'fear no more—tavern bills'
says the rather jocular Jailer—surely, as Brockbank suggested, a lightly
comic echo of the earlier dirge: V, iv, 129–30), and it is in prison that his
parents and Jupiter appear to him in a dream. Jupiter is given what is often
taken to be a crucial speech (he is answering the family ghosts who are both
reproaching him, as men have always reproached their gods, along the lines
of—why do you let such atrociously unjust things happen? and asking his
help—'Peep through thy marble mansion', V, iv, 60):

> Be not with mortal accidents opprest.
> > No care of yours it is; you know 'tis ours.
> Whom best I love I cross; to make my gift,
> > The more delayed, delighted . . .
> > > > (V, iv, 69–72)

This is more or less how gods have always answered men, when they deign
to talk to them at all. God moves in a mysterious way—and don't ask questions. This is, as it were, the bottom line of religion. Jupiter's announcement
of himself and his ways is little more than a theological platitude, and the
idea that this manifestly stagey theophany is an electrifying revelation of
godhead among mortals seems to me misconceived. Jupiter then makes
what must have been a tricky theatrical exit—'Mount, eagle, to my palace
crystalline' (V, iv, 83).

Against this, we may put the relatively unillumined human perspective
of Pisanio: 'Fortune brings in some boats that are not steered' (IV, iii, 46).
There's the question—is there a god, any god, overseeing, directing, 'steer-
ing' all? Is there any kind of Providence 'shaping' our rough-hewn man-

glings? Does a divinity 'peep through' marble mansions, blankets of dark, whatever? ('Peep' is the perfect, modest word—for whatever the state of our unbelief, there are times when most of us have a sense, a glimpse, that something more than us might just have an eye for what is going on down here.) Is there a Jupiter—or is there just a Shakespeare, using the god's name to put his signature deifically on the play? Or should we defer to Fortune, more or less tidying things up? The questions manifestly cannot be resolved (unless we are sure we know the answers all along), and I'm not sure that it greatly matters when it comes to responding to the play. What Shakespeare *does,* having brought matters to an unholy state of utter confusion (he has thrown in an oracular text, found by Posthumus when he wakes in prison, to further confound matters and add to the growingly-felt need for explanations), is, effectively, to invite us to wonder at how quickly the fog can be burned off. As it does in the remaining scene, in an explosive series of revelations and recognitions which can hardly be kept pace with, so that the audience is dazzled while the characters stagger. The peak, and cracking point, comes when Posthumus strikes the as-yet-unrecognized Imogen to the ground. At this, it is as if, not only we, but the play itself cannot take any more, and it rushes unpausingly to a conclusion with a torrent of clarifications and recognitions. 'Does the world go round?' asks the dizzied King (V, v, 232). Yes it does; bringing in its changes and its restorations, time's revenges (Cloten and the Queen are dead) and the season's rebirths and renewals. The fruit is back on the tree, and the lovers are in one another's arms. 'Hang there like fruit, my soul, / Till the tree die' (V, v, 263–4) says Posthumus to Imogen as she embraces him—all error cleared—in a line that brought tears to Tennyson's eyes. The Phoenix has risen from its ashes (Imogen, 'th' Arabian bird'); the Roman eagle is 'on wing soaring aloft', united to the 'radiant Cymbeline'; the 'majestic cedar' of Britain has been 'revived'. And now—'such a peace' (the last words). All clear. All settled. All over.

   Shakespeare has taken an assortment of the most disparate, incongruous, intractable material imaginable, all concerning important matters—sexual, familial, dynastic, political, imperial; and proceeds to show with what a light touch it can be handled. He allows it to puddle and fog together to the point of hopeless chaos, and then—whoosh! it's all significantly related and cleared up. And suddenly the play seems to have been like Imogen's dream:

> 'Twas but a bolt of nothing, shot at nothing,
>
> Which the brain makes of fumes.
>
> (IV, ii, 300–301)

Our pleasure should be tragical-historical-comical-pastoral-romantical; and also, theatrical-magical. *Cymbeline,* it seems to me, is the most *extraordinary* play that Shakespeare ever wrote. How does he do it? Staggering!

 THE WINTER'S TALE (1611)

> Who was most marble there changed color
>
> (V, ii, 96–7)

> warm life,
>
> As now it coldly stands
>
> (V, iii, 35–6)

Thunder from a clear sky. For the ancient Greeks, it bespoke the gods— was the gods speaking. It is the sign given to Odysseus before he re-enters his home. Oedipus knows the gods are calling him to his mysterious death by 'harsh and constant thunder'. It is heard again in this play by Cleomenes and Dion on their visit to the oracle:

> the burst
>
> And the ear-deaf'ning voice o' th' oracle,
>
> Kin to Jove's thunder
>
> (III, i, 8–10)

But there is thunder out of a clear sky among mortals, too. Leontes' sudden jealousy is not animated, motivated, precipitated by anything at all —not even the insinuations of a Iago or the goadings of a Iachimo. Nothing. It just erupts, explodes, bursts—thunder from a clear sky. E. M. W. Tillyard refers to the 'god-sent lunacies' of the Greeks—Ajax, Heracles. This is apt enough, but Shakespeare makes it clear that there is *no* influence working on Leontes outside his own sick mind and 'pestered' senses. His destructive outburst is another 'great fail'—perhaps the greatest one in

Shakespeare. What might be involved in effecting any kind of restoration after the damage he has caused (not least to himself) occupies the rest of the play.

As in *Pericles* we have three acts showing the destruction and scattering of a royal family; a fourth act centring on the long-lost daughter; and a final act dedicated to recognitions and family reunion. But Pericles was quite blameless for what befalls him and his family; whereas Leontes is the absolute author of, and exclusively responsible for, the disasters that destroy his house. Not that Shakespeare is offering a dramatization of the etiology of jealousy, a psychological tracing of its inception and its workings. He simply starts with the final explosion, and an incredible feeling of out-of-nowhere-ness. It is instructive to compare this opening with that of his main source for the play, the romance *Pandosto* by Robert Greene. (In part, Shakespeare follows Greene very closely—there are more echoes of his source than in any other play; but he makes some absolutely crucial changes, to which I will come.)

Greene starts his tale with a long paragraph moralizing on the dangers of jealousy: 'Among all the passions wherewith human mindes are perplexed, there is none that so galleth with restlesse despight, as the infectious soare of jealousy', and so on. The story starts with a description of the growing affectionate friendship between Bellaria (Hermione) and Egistus (Polixenes), beloved friend of Pandosto (Leontes). Bellaria is very friendly indeed with Egistus, 'oftentimes comming her selfe into his bed chamber, to see that nothing should be amiss to dislike him'. There is never a hint that this is other than chaste courtesy, though I suppose there are quite a few husbands who might raise the shade of one eyebrow at such demonstrative concern. Their intimacy develops—long walks together, 'private and pleasant devices'—until 'a certaine melancholy passion entring the minde of Pandosto, drave him into sundry and doubtefull thoughts'.

> First, he called to minde the beauty of his wife Bellaria, the comeliness and braverie of his friend Egistus, thinking that Love was above all Lawes, and therefore to be staied with no Law: that it was hard to put fire and flaxe together without burning; that their open pleasures might breede his secrete displeasure. He considered with himselfe that Egistus was a man, and must needes love: that his wife was a woman, and therefore subject unto love, and that where fancy forced, friendship was of no force.

> These and such like doubtfull thoughtes *a long time* smoothering in
> his stomacke, beganne *at last* to kindle in his minde a secret mistrust,
> which increased by suspition, grewe *at last* to be a flaming Jealousie, that
> so tormented him as he could take no rest. (my italics)

And now the story gets under way. Pandosto's jealousy is very reprehensible, no doubt, and he pays for it. But it is prepared for, explained if not excused, and given a relatively long incubation period before it grows at last
to be a 'flaming Jealousie'. In Shakespeare's play there is none of this—we
are confronted with spontaneous combustion.

There are two other major changes Shakespeare makes to his source
which it is worth noting before we consider the play. When the oracle pro-
claiming Bellaria's (Hermione's) innocence is read out, Pandosto (unlike
the more deranged Leontes) *instantly* accepts it, and is ashamed, repentant,
apologetic—though it's too late, of course. His son dies, and then Bellaria
dies, and dies in good earnest. Shakespeare, or rather Paulina, keeps Hermione alive in secret—*but,* and this is unique in Shakespeare in relation to
such a key bit of information, the secret is kept from the audience, as well as
from the King and court. The original audience of the play, many of whom
would have read the popular *Pandosto,* would certainly have been sure that
Hermione was truly dead at the end of Act III—and so, ideally (but now
impossibly), should we.

In the concluding part of the story, when Dorastus (Florizel) arrives at
Pandosto's court with Fawnia (Perdita), Pandosto is so taken with Fawnia's
beauty that he feels a sudden overwhelming lust for her. He has Dorastus
thrown into prison (and 'heavie Irons') to get him out of the way, and,
'broyling at the heat of unlawful lust', trys to persuade Fawnia to submit
to his 'hot desire', threatening to use his 'power' to compel her 'by force'
if necessary. When he is thwarted in his base intention, he says she will be
put to death. He discovers that she is his daughter by the same plot moves
that operate in Shakespeare, but his reaction is very different from that of
Leontes.

> Pandosto (calling to mind how first he betraied his friend Egistus, how
> his jealousie was the cause of Bellaria's death, and that contrarie to the
> law of nature hee had lusted after his owne daughter) moved with these
> desperate thoughts, he fell into a melancholie fit, and to close up the
> Comedie with a Tragicall stratageme, he slewe himselfe . . .

The incest possibility is only fleetingly glimpsed at in *The Winter's Tale*. Leontes expresses a momentary desire to have Perdita for himself; but, under
correction from the ever vigilant Paulina, hastily says that all he meant was
that she reminded him of his 'dead' wife—as indeed, well she might since
she is her daughter. As in the previous two plays, Shakespeare allows the
merest whiff of incest to linger briefly in the air. But he has other business in hand, and a quite other conclusion in mind. He will close up his
almost-tragedy with a comic 'stratageme' which nobody else could have
dreamed of.

The Winter's Tale opens in Sicilia, and this marks another, smaller, change
which Shakespeare makes to his source. The play moves from Sicilia to Bohemia; in Greene, it is the other way round. (Though Shakespeare gives
Bohemia a coast—probably because he wants a shipwreck: it doesn't matter, any more than it matters that in a play set in a pre-Christian era there
are references to an Emperor of Russia, a Puritan, a Renaissance artist,
Whitsun pastorals, the betrayal of Christ. This is romance.) Sicilian and
Bohemian lords are discussing the very close relationship and amity that
exists between their two kings:

> *Camillo.* They were trained together in their childhoods; and there rooted
>   betwixt them then such an affection, which cannot choose but branch
>   now. Since their more mature dignities and royal necessities made sepa-
>   ration of their society . . . they have seemed to be together, though absent:
>   shook hands, as over a vast; and embraced as it were from the ends of
>   opposed winds. The heavens continue their loves!
> *Archidamus.* I think there is not in the world either malice or matter to
>   alter it.
>
>   (I, i, 23–35)

They conclude by emphasizing the importance of the child, Prince Mamil-
lius, Leontes' son and heir. The emphasis is both on the two boys' closeness
and near inseparability; and on the inevitable separation occasioned by their
'more mature dignities and royal necessities'. What these mature necessities
amounted to is indicated by the consequent discussion of the child. Kings
must marry and breed. The 'malice and matter' which will indeed 'alter'
the two men's loving relationship is going to stem from that simple fact.

The second scene opens with Polixenes saying that 'Nine changes of the
wat'ry star' have passed since his arrival. Here, he mentions the fact to lend

force to his insistence that it is high time he returned to his own kingdom. It will soon take on much more importance, since a sojourn of nine months will afford Leontes some 'matter' to back up his paranoid insistence that Hermione's new-born child was fathered by Polixenes. This detail is not in Greene but it is in Ovid in a very different, but perhaps not unrelated context. *Metamorphoses* includes the story of one of Diana's nymphs, Callisto, who was raped by Jove. After 'nine times the crescent moon had filled her orb' she gives birth, and Diana—thinking Callisto was a willing partner to her unchaste act—is so furious she turns Callisto into a bear. 'She was a bear, but kept her woman's heart.' She is always having to flee from hunters, and is nearly killed by her own son out hunting—Jove intervenes and turns them into stars. It wouldn't do to make too much of this; but there *is* an important bear in Shakespeare's play (probably also being hunted when he kills Antigonus), and I think Bate has a point when he says that both Callisto and Hermione are wrongfully accused of conceiving a child out of their own wantonness and lust. Shakespeare uses the bear, but he turns Hermione into something else.

As if to emphasize the importance of breeding, Queen Hermione enters, visibly pregnant. There have been a few pregnant women in Shakespeare's previous plays: Tamora must be pregnant at one stage in *Titus Andronicus;* Jaquenetta is mentioned as pregnant in *Love's Labor's Lost;* we are told that a babe has been 'molded' in Thaisa, in *Pericles;* and it is the evidence of sexual activity 'grossly writ' on the almost completely silent Juliet that prompts Angelo to initiate his reign of terror in *Measure for Measure.* But there is nothing like the central focus that there is on the pregnant Hermione who, we soon hear, 'rounds apace' and 'is spread of late into a goodly bulk' (II, i, 16, 20). That growing, unborn babe is, and will provide, vital 'matter'—in every sense. 'Birth' is what Carol Neely calls 'the play's central miracle'. The word 'issue' occurs fourteen times, far more than in any other play; and, as it happens, seven times it refers more specifically to children, and seven times more generally to outcome—though, of course, it invariably glances at both. As Cleomenes and Dion return with the 'sealed up' oracle, they hope that when the contents come out—

> something rare
> Even then will rush to knowledge . . .
> And gracious be the issue!
>
> (III, i, 20–22)

The 'something rare' will turn out to be the knowledge of Hermione's innocence, *and* the birth of her daughter Perdita—both come in a 'rush'; and
the overall 'issue' will, *finally,* prove to be 'gracious'. 'Thou met'st with
things dying, I with things new born' (III, iii, 112–13) is, rightly, a famous
and memorable line, but the whole lexicon of pregnancy, birth, breeding,
delivery—used literally and metaphorically—is pervasive. The birth of the
baby, Perdita, is described in a way which, potentially, generalizes it enormously.

> This child was prisoner to the womb and is
> By law and process of great Nature thence
> Freed, and enfranchised
>
> (II, ii, 58–60)

The 'law and process of great Nature' will have to do a great deal of freeing
and enfranchising, outside the nursery as well. The final 'enfranchisement'
will be the liberation of Hermione from stone, a process which, Neely suggests, imitates labour and delivery. Neely writes well of the importance of
the whole vocabulary of birth in the play. 'The metaphors emphasize the
fundamental components of the process of reproduction; union and fullness, labour and separation, creation and loss, risk and fulfilment, enclosure
and enfranchisement.' Certainly, the reproductive repair of the damage
caused by the two kings is entirely dependent on three women—Hermione,
Paulina and Perdita.

The scene proceeds with courtly courtesy as the Queen is enlisted by
Leontes to persuade Polixenes to defer his departure. Hermione takes
Polixenes back to his childhood relationship with her husband—'You were
pretty lordlings then?'

> We were, fair Queen,
> Two lads that thought there was no more behind
> But such a day tomorrow as today,
> And to be boy eternal.
>
> (I, ii, 62–5)

Psychoanalysts—not that I'm eager to draw them in—recognize what they
indeed call a *'puer eternus'* syndrome, the arrested mental and emotional

condition of a man who wishes to remain 'boy eternal' and avoid growing up with its attendant responsibilities. Leontes and Polixenes clearly have some of that disposition. Polixenes looks longingly back to when 'we were as twinned lambs' and only changed 'innocence for innocence'; and if, he says, our spirits had 'ne'er been higher reared/With stronger blood' we would have remained untainted by original sin (I, ii, 67–74). Hermione is quick to see the implication—'By this we gather/You have tripped since', 'tripped' being a nicely polite way of saying 'fallen'. The exchange which follows is conducted at the level of decorous banter—but, in retrospect it is heavily ominous.

> *Polixenes.*   O my most sacred lady,
> Temptations have since then been born to's, for
> In those unfledged days was my wife a girl;
> Your precious self had not then crossed the eyes
> Of my young playfellow.
>
> *Hermione.*   Grace to boot!
> Of this make no conclusion, lest you say
> Your queen and I are devils. Yet go on,
> Th' offenses we have made you do we'll answer . . .
>   (I, ii, 75–83)

By Eve man fell—so the Good Book says. Polixenes is blaming the irresistible temptations and compulsions of sex (that 'stronger blood' that comes with growth) for the loss of his and Leontes' 'innocence' and their consequent separation, eternal boys no longer. Hermione laughingly points out the damning implications for the two Queens in this line of thinking. This is all courtly playfulness—the sort of poised and witty courtesy appropriate in a regal group. But Hermione *is* about to be turned into a 'devil'; and both she and her daughter will be made to 'answer' for imaginary offences attributed to their sexuality, or rather their sex. For somewhere in these boy-kings, there is a fear of woman as such—a fear which can turn to loathing, as Leontes is about to demonstrate (Leontes is, of course, the guiltiest in this respect, but Polixenes is not exempt, as a later outburst to Perdita will reveal).

Hermione 'grace-fully'—and she is, and will prove to be a figure of

'Grace'—persuades Polixenes to stay, and Leontes is well pleased. And then, quite suddenly, he is something else.

> [*Aside*] Too hot, too hot!
> To mingle friendship far is mingling bloods.
> I have tremor cordis on me; my heart dances,
> But not for joy, not joy.
>
> (I, ii, 108–11)

Just what his heart *is* dancing for is hard to define. His next three speeches, and then his soliloquy after Hermione and Polixenes have left to walk in the garden, are among the most extraordinary that Shakespeare ever wrote. I know nothing else in literature which so tellingly dramatizes a mind procuring its own unease. At times seeming to talk to his uncomprehending young son, but really talking semi-coherently to himself in what Tillyard called 'hot and twisted words', Leontes is diving into the unfathomable depths of self-generated jealousy, the perverse, male, masochistic relish of imagined sexual betrayal which Shakespeare has keenly eyed in previous plays. To Leontes' wilfully disordered perception, courteous and friendly exchanges become 'paddling palms and pinching fingers' (I, ii, 115). Having lodged the sick-sweet thought in his mind that his wife is betraying him, Leontes scratches the sore and tongues the wound.

> Inch-thick, knee-deep, o'er head and ears a forked one!
> Go play, boy, play: thy mother plays, and I
> Play too—but so disgraced a part, whose issue
> Will hiss me to my grave
>
> (I, ii, 186–9)

Children's play, sexual play, theatrical play—Leontes' overheated and distempered imagination is melting everything into a scorchingly self-tormenting synthesis. Sexual nausea is fuelling the fire:

> And many a man there is, even at this present,
> Now, while I speak this, holds his wife by th'arm,
> That little thinks she has been sluiced in's absence,
> And his pond fished by his next neighbor, by

>   Sir Smile, his neighbor . . .
>   Physic for't there's none;
>   It is a bawdy planet . . .
>   Be it concluded,
>   No barricado for a belly. Know't
>   It will let in and out the enemy,
>   With bag and baggage.
>   (I, ii, 192–206)

Foul, unspeakably foul; but what a *pleasure* to spit out the words—sluiced, fished, belly, in and out, bag and baggage. Who can understand the mind's, and the mouth's, strange self-mortifying satisfactions? The larger, unspoken question is—what do we do about, how do we cope with, our inescapable sexuality? Shakespeare really is going for the big 'issues'.

As can happen in the broken and disjunctive self-picking mutterings of an erstwhile sane (majestic) mind, the murmured roving ravings of Leontes happen on an enigmatically and confusedly illuminating core.

>   Can thy dam, may't be?
>   Affection! Thy intention stabs the center.
>   Thou dost make possible things not so held,
>   Communicat'st with dreams—how can this be?—
>   With what's unreal thou coactive art,
>   And fellow'st nothing. Then 'tis very credent
>   Thou mayst co-join with something, and thou dost,
>   And that beyond commission, and I find it,
>   And that to the infection of my brains,
>   And hardening of my brows.
>   (I, ii, 138–46)

Starting by considering whether his son's mother could possibly be unfaithful, he embarks on a semi-unintelligible yet curiously revealing musing on the power of lustful passion ('affection'): it 'stabs the center'—of women, certainly; but also of a man's heart; perhaps it goes to the heart of the world itself. It makes it possible for people to dream of impossible (prohibited) things (sexual acts), and then to make the dream seem real. So when there *is* something (someone) real there, it is easy to believe that lust will actually commit unthinkable things—as it is doing now, and it's driving me mad as I feel myself becoming a cuckold. That—filling in the lacunae left or jumped over by his inconsequent thinking—is one sort of sense. But if you hear it as Leontes (unconsciously) saying that *my* passion is coactive with unrealities, is communicating with dreams, and is peopling a vacancy—he is revealing no less than the deep truth. His brain is *self*-infected, and his head is hardening indeed.

Now determined beyond doubt that his wife is 'slippery', he speaks of her in foul terms to Camillo, who bravely responds—'You never spoke what did become you less/Than this' (I, ii, 282–3). But, for Leontes, the 'evidence' is now so obvious and overwhelming—how fertile is a fixated mind!—that anyone who cannot see it, or attempts to gainsay it, is a liar and an enemy. Ordered to poison Polixenes, Camillo—seeing that Leontes is now beyond reach in an insanely distorted world of his own making—instead tells Polixenes of Leontes' grotesque delusion, which occasions a telling exchange:

> *Polixenes.*   How should this grow?
> *Camillo.* I know not: but I am sure 'tis safer to
> Avoid what's grown than question how 'tis born.
>   (I, ii, 432–4)

This is, at present, the best wisdom at court. They make a stealthy departure for Bohemia.

Their flight is proof on proof to Leontes: 'How blest am I/In my just censure, in my true opinion' (II, i, 36–7). He then develops at some length a surprisingly coherent image:

>   There may be in the cup
> A spider steeped, and one may drink, depart,
> And yet partake no venom, for his knowledge
> Is not infected; but if one present
> Th' abhorred ingredient to his eye, make known
> How he hath drunk, he cracks his gorge, his sides,
> With violent hefts. I have drunk, and seen the spider.
>   (II, i, 39–45)

So much was common superstition (that spiders were only venomous in food and drink if you saw them). For Leontes, the figure fits his case perfectly—you detect the self-pitying self-dramatization in the last line. What is becoming clearer, and more worrying, is that he *needs* to see the spider, he *likes* to see the spider, there *must be* a spider! Hence the following unbelievably gross speeches to his wife. He calls her, in front of the court, 'adult'ress', 'bed-swerver', 'traitor', and announces that Polixenes 'has made thee swell thus' (II, i, 61). With truly regal dignity and restraint, Hermione makes a memorable response:

> When you shall come to clearer knowledge . . .
> > Gentle my lord,
> You scarce can right me throughly then to say
> You did mistake.
> > > (II, i, 97–100)

Leontes orders her son to be removed from her, and has her imprisoned. As often happens, subsidiary figures keep their sanity and still see clearly. Antigonus says:

> You are abused, and by some putter-on
> That will be damned for't. Would I knew the villain
> > (II, i, 141–2)

Posthumus was 'abused' by 'putter-on' Iachimo. Here, of course, the 'villain' is Leontes abusing Leontes. It takes Shakespeare to show us how a man can be a 'putter-on' to himself.

Nobody can reach him, or, as we say, get through to him now. 'The matter, [that word again]/The loss, the gain, the ord'ring on't/Is all properly ours', he announces (II, i, 168–70). This is a true claim, though not in the sense he intends it. He is asserting his royal 'prerogative'; but, in effect, he *is* ordering—disordering—'the matter', disposing of the material and arranging the 'reality', to suit and fit his own determinations. And, like jealous characters before him, he is absolutely certain of his evidence. He refers again to the sexual relationship between Hermione and Polixenes—

> Which was as gross as ever touched conjecture,
> That lacks sight only, naught for approbation
> But only seeing, all other circumstances
> Made up to th' deed
>
> (II, i, 176–9)

'Approbation' is 'proof', and Leontes is sure he has all he needs. He lacks what Othello asked for—*ocular* proof'; but, as Iago reasonably enough pointed out, it is in the nature of the deed that this kind of proof is effectively unobtainable. Instead, Iago proffers 'imputation and strong circumstances' (*Othello* III, iii, 403); these are enough for Othello, and they are enough for Leontes, though he has preferred them to himself. He relies on 'circumstances' and 'conjectures' (in the Induction to 2 *Henry IV* 15–16, 'Rumor is a pipe'/Blown by surmises, jealousies, conjectures'). That all this is no evidence at all but rather the reverse, hardly needs stressing. But Leontes is King, and he has the power, and thus the ordering of the matter—if he says that it is so, then, to all intents and purposes, it *is* so. But only for a while. He reveals that he has sent Cleomenes and Dion to the oracle of Apollo (which, like Greene, Shakespeare mistakenly thought was at Delphos) 'for a greater confirmation' and he is confident that 'from the oracle/They will bring all' (II, i, 180, 185–6). Indeed they will.

Paulina (Shakespeare's creation) now enters the play. Hermione has given birth to a daughter in prison, and Paulina determines to take the baby to the King, confidently breaking through the lords who would prevent her unwanted approach with the promise:

> I
> Do come with words as medicinal as true,
> Honest as either, to purge him of that humor
> That presses him from sleep.
>
> (II, iii, 35–8)

Medicine and purgation the sick King certainly needs, but an outspokenly reproachful woman carrying what he takes to be the illegitimate child of his wife is the last thing he wants. It drives him into a mad fury. While Paulina resolutely points out the baby's likeness to the King (eye, nose, lip, forehead, chin, cheek—body parts are important in this play), thanking 'good goddess Nature, which hast made it/So like to him that got it' (II, iii, 102–3), Leontes is frantically ordering his men to 'take up the bastard', burn the bastard, dash the bastard's brains out—he says the word at least eight times, much as he kept calling Hermione 'adultress', as if mere reiteration provides some assuaging satisfaction, or perverse profaning pleasure. Of the many subsequent ironies prepared for in this abusive repetition of 'bastard', none extends further than this—

> Shall I live on to see this bastard kneel
> And call me father?
>
> (II, iii, 153–4)

Only if you are very lucky, very penitent, very blessed by 'great goddess Nature'. But, for now Leontes orders that this 'female bastard' should be taken to 'some remote and desert place' and abandoned (II, iii, 174).

The short opening scene of Act III is literally a breath of fresh air, reminding us how unpleasantly heated, fetid and claustrophobic the court has become. Out on the open road, Cleomenes and Dion are marvelling in retrospect at the atmosphere on the temple-island of the oracle—'The climate's delicate, the air most sweet,/Fertile the isle' (III, i, 1–2)—bringing home to us the indelicacy, foulness, and sterility (children dead and thrown out) which have prevailed in the preceding scenes. Dion says:

> I shall report,
> For most it caught me, the *celestial* habits
> (Methinks I so should term them) and the *reverence*
> Of the *grave* wearers. O, the sacrifice,
> How *ceremonious, solemn, and unearthly*
> It was i' th' off'ring!
>
> (III, i, 3–8—my italics)

The italicized words remind us of all the positive, civilized qualities and dignities which Leontes has abandoned or destroyed in his own court, where, truly, all the 'ceremonies of innocence' have been drowned. Oh for a cup of this island air—one might fairly yearn. But we are instantly plunged back into the inverted, deranged world that Leontes is creating around him. We are in what Leontes calls 'a court of justice'. It is, of course, quite monstrously the reverse.

We have, more than once in Shakespeare, seen ruthless characters appropriate the language and procedures of the law, and subvert, *per*vert, them to serve, and seemingly justify, their own wilful and dastardly purposes— Othello and Angelo come to mind, but the phenomenon is widespread. It is, of course, a standard practice of all tyrants; and in trying to clear himself of such a charge, Leontes simply draws attention to its truth and applicability.

> Let us be cleared
> Of being tyrannous, since we so openly
> Proceed in justice, which shall have due course,
> Even to the guilt or the purgation.
>   (III, ii, 4–7)

Oh no it won't; or rather, in the end it *will,* but not through the agency of Leontes.

He continues with his unevidenced accusations, and Hermione's three long speeches in her own defence are models of dignity, decorum and poise. As she so accurately says:

> if I shall be condemned
> Upon surmises, all proofs sleeping else
> But what your jealousies awake, I tell you
> 'Tis rigor, and not law.
>   (III, ii, 109–12)

Shakespeare often speaks of the 'rigor' *of* the law; Leontes has substituted it *for* the law. It seems a too moderate word for his behaviour. Hermione appeals to a higher court:

> if powers divine
> Behold our human actions—as they do—
> I doubt not then, but Innocence shall make
> False Accusation blush, and Tyranny
> Tremble at Patience.
>   (III, ii, 27–31)

The personifications bring in something of the atmosphere of a morality play—appropriately enough, since Leontes has become the embodiment of Tyranny, while Hermione will prove herself the quintessence of Patience—that indispensable virtue in these late plays. Hermione rests her case, as it were:

> Your honors all,
> I do refer me to the oracle:
> Apollo be my judge!
>
> (III, ii, 112–14)

Leontes gives the order—'Break up the seals and read.' And now Apollo delivers some of *his* thunder:

> 'Hermione is chaste, Polixenes blameless, Camillo a true subject, Leontes
> a jealous tyrant, his innocent babe truly begotten, and the King shall live
> without an heir, if that which is lost be not found.'
>
> (III, ii, 130–33)

Leontes tries to dismiss it—a last hopeless madness:

> There is no truth i' th' oracle,
> The sessions shall proceed; this is mere falsehood.
>
> (III, ii, 137–8)

But then things start to happen quickly.

He is told his son has died, and Leontes realizes that the gods are angry:

> Apollo, pardon
> My great profaneness 'gainst thine oracle.
> I'll reconcile me to Polixenes,
> New woo my queen, recall the good Camillo
>
> (III, ii, 150–53)

—and everything will be fine again. But rectification, reparation and restoration are not so easily achieved or arrived at—not by a very long way. Paulina then enters with the news that the Queen is dead, and it is now that

Paulina comes into her own and takes on a dominant role. She is the deliberately tactless and abrasive voice of accusation and reproach and even 'vengeance'. In modern parlance, she gives Leontes a tongue-lashing; she says all the things that the 'dead' Hermione would be all too justified in saying—indeed, Paulina effectively stands in for the Queen during her long absence. She calls Leontes a lot of unkingly names in a most uncourtly manner. Think of all the tyrannous, damnable things you have done, she tells him, 'And then run mad indeed, stark mad' (III, ii, 181). Leontes cowers before her, concedes the justice of what she says, and agrees to follow the course of penitence and repentance she lays down. Effectively, she becomes the custodian of his conscience. One of her speeches is prophetic—and not, I feel, without a degree of calculation. She insists that Hermione is dead:

> I say she's dead; I'll swear it. If word nor oath
> Prevail not, go and see; if you can bring
> Tincture or luster in her lip, her eye,
> *Heat* outwardly or *breath* within, I'll serve you
> As I would do the gods. But, O thou tyrant
> Do not repent these things, for they are heavier
> Than all thy woes can *stir;* therefore betake thee
> To nothing but despair.
>   (III, ii, 201–8—my italics)

Now, not that anybody else knows it, including the audience, but this is simply not true. Hermione is not dead. This is artifice (or lying with a positive purpose); and I sense that Paulina already has her long-term plot in mind, since this speech anticipates the final scene in which 'heat', 'breath', and 'stir' will prove to be the crucial, climactic words and phenomena. But of course, everyone from the King down believes Paulina; and as far as the audience is concerned the action has come to a tragic conclusion. But it's only the end of Act III. What will Shakespeare do now?

There is, in fact, one more scene to Act III, and it serves as a bridge between the court of Sicilia and rural Bohemia. Set on the famously nonexistent sea-coast of Bohemia, it shows Lord Antigonus depositing the dead Queen's rejected child in a deserted spot, as ordered by the King. Antigonus is convinced that Hermione is dead because he has had a particularly vivid dream. He says to the babe that he is sure he has seen her dead mother's spirit:

> thy mother
> Appeared to me last night; for ne'er was dream
> So like awaking.
>   (III, iii, 16–18)

There is a greater 'awaking'-dream yet to come. In this one, Hermione has seemingly returned to instruct Antigonus:

> In pure white robes,
> Like very sanctity, she did approach
> My cabin where I lay; thrice bowed before me,
> And, gasping to begin some speech, her eyes
> Became two spouts; the fury spent, anon
> Did this break from her: 'Good Antigonus,
> Since fate, against thy better disposition,
> Hath made thy person for the thrower-out
> Of my poor babe, according to thy oath,
> Places remote enough are in Bohemia,
> There weep, and leave it crying; and for the babe
> Is counted lost forever, Perdita
> I prithee call't . . .'
>   (III, iii, 21–33)

In this apparitional form, Hermione appears as something of a goddess (and something of a fury), rather like Diana ordering Pericles in a dream; she has taken on an unearthly, holy authority. Something, some power, seems to be intervening to direct things. (In *Pandosto* the baby is abandoned in a boat in the sea and arrives at the island of Sicilia by chance.)

Antigonus of course obeys; and here is laying Perdita down in a remote part of Bohemia. Stormy weather threatens; the day darkens ominously— 'A savage clamor' (III, iii, 55). He exits 'pursued by a bear'. Incontestably a comical stage direction looked at flat. But, in context, it is not funny. The bear, itself probably either starving or being hunted and frightened into attack (Callisto), like the storm at sea which wrecks the ship while the bear is tearing Antigonus to pieces, is part of the 'savage' side of nature which seems to have been activated and released in relation or response—in some obscure way—to the savage and unnatural acts of Leontes.

Then a shepherd enters—and we are in a different world. It is not just that he speaks in prose, which we have not heard since the gentlemanly chatting of the opening scene—though of course that does have the effect of slackening the tension. The voice is also so down-to-earth, of-the-earth; in touch, as one feels, with what Whitman called the 'primal sanities of nature'. The Shepherd talks easily of 'country matters'—hunting and herding, stealing and fighting, browsing and wenching (he is notably relaxed about sex). Here, one feels, is a clear-sighted, sober-minded realist. After hearing Leontes raving round his Sicilian court, it makes a change. Finding little Perdita, the Shepherd instinctively takes her up—'for pity'. Similarly, his son Clown (in the original sense of rustic), goes off to bury the remains of Antigonus—'That's a good deed' says his father approvingly (III, iii, 132). Between them, they take care of 'things new born' *and* 'things dying'. This is not to idealize or sentimentalize our country cousins. Simply, they are people with sound instincts still in place—perhaps, indeed, partly because they have never had to negotiate the complex power relations, the hierarchical rituals and ceremonial deferences, the bribes and threats, of court. Shepherd and Clown remain nameless—they are generic, even telluric, and long may the earth continue to produce them.

At the start of Act IV, Time comes forward himself and whisks away sixteen years, inviting us to turn our attention to the children of the Kings: Prince Florizel, and Perdita 'now grown in grace/Equal with wond'ring' (IV, i, 24–5). This effortless 'sliding' over 'wide gaps' of time is entirely appropriate in a romance. But it must not be thought that the omitted time leaves no traces—just as it is the time which permits Perdita to grow to beauty, so it is the time which will bring wrinkles to her mother's face. As Time says, he is responsible for the bringing in of the 'freshest things'; but he will also 'make stale/The glistering of this present' (IV, i, 12–14). He allows 'errors' to be made; but ensures that matters will, in due course, be 'unfolded'. He ruins, and reveals; erases and renews. As Kermode has pointed out, Shakespeare's attitude to Time is comparable to Spenser's as expressed in the Mutabilitie Cantos:

> All things steadfastness do hate
> And changed be: yet being rightly weighed
> They are not changed from their first estate,
> But by their change their being do dilate,
> And turning to themselves at length again,
> Do work their own perfection so by fate.

The subtitle of *Pandosto* is: 'The Triumph of Time. Wherein is discovered by a pleasant Historie, that although by the meanes of sinister fortune, Truth may be concealed yet by Time in spight of fortune it is most manifestly revealed.' Shakespeare prefers more compact, pregnant formulations, but the feeling is shared.

Then a short scene which reveals Polixenes' concern that his son is spending a lot of time away from the court at the house of a shepherd who is reported to have 'a daughter of most rare note' (IV, ii, 45). Polixenes intends that he and Camillo should visit the place, in disguise. Then we meet another figure created by Shakespeare for this play (though drawing on Greene's *The Art of Conny-Catching* pamphlets—informed accounts of devices of thieving and gulling)—Autolycus. He announces his ancestry:

> My father named me Autolycus, who being, as I am, littered under Mercury, was likewise a snapper-up of unconsidered trifles.
>
> (IV, iii, 24–6)

In fact, he was sired by Ovid:

> And to the wing-foot god [Mercury] a wily brat
> Was born, Autolycus, adept at tricks
> Of every kind, well used to make black white,
> White black, a son who kept his father's skill.

His brother, born to Chione from Phoebus, was Philemon, 'famed alike for song and lyre'. In the play, Autolycus takes on both roles—he tricks and sings. Bate says that the appearance of Autolycus 'confirms that the play is shifting into the register of myth'. Yes and no. The rest of this act is full of contemporary rural realities, and as Wilson Knight suggested you can, as it

were, find as much Hardy as Ovid in this world—it is the coalescence of
the classical and folkloric which generates the quite special atmosphere.

Autolycus enters singing:

> When daffodils begin to peer,
> With heigh the doxy over the dale,
> Why, then comes in the sweet o' the year,
> For the red blood reigns in the winter's pale.
>   (IV, iii, 1–4)

The winter's pale(ness) is a reflection of the winter's tale which, effectively,
was told and dramatized in the first three acts. Good red blood (not the bad
hot blood of Leontes' sick imagining) is rising to flush it out. The sourness
of the court is about to give way to the sweetness of the country. The daffo-
dils beginning to 'peer' anticipates the entry of Perdita in the next scene,
looking like 'Flora,/Peering in April's front' (IV, iv, 2–3). The word 'peer'
occurs quite frequently in Shakespeare, invariably referring to what we
would now call members of the House of Lords. Its—infrequent—use as a
verb, as far as I can find, always denotes something positive: the sun peers,
honour peers, proud rivers peer, perhaps gods peer, and life peers ('through
the hollow eyes of death', *Richard II* II, i, 270–71). Perdita–Flora–spring
peers; and her mother, we later learn, 'lived peerless' (V, iii, 14). (Antony
and Cleopatra 'stand up peerless', *Antony and Cleopatra* I, i, 40—it is a word
for rare and special, and Shakespeare uses it sparingly of people.) After the
cold and wintry sterility of Leontes' court, new life is beginning to 'peer'
('to look out keenly or with difficulty; peep out; come into view, appear'—
OED: all meanings apply here), and Shakespeare signals this in the first
line of the first song of the play (no singing at Leontes' court, but there will
be music in Paulina's chapel at the end).

Switching to his other skill, Autolycus, pretending he has been beaten
and robbed, picks the pocket of the too trusting Clown who is going shopping for the sheep-shearing feast (he runs through what he has to get—saffron, pies, mace, dates, nutmegs, ginger, prunes, raisins; such listing and
itemizing, out of place in the placeless idealities of conventional pastoral,
help to give a thick sense of the local, the real). Unaware of his loss, Clown
offers to give Autolycus what 'little money' he has. Autolycus is a rogue
(not the dark and evil figure some tremulous critics have found him), and

his rogueries, along with his singing and ballads and peddling, liven up this whole act, just as they animate the whole sheep-shearing feast and the little rural community. But Clown's instinctive little gesture of kindness and compassion means that he 'glisters' through Autolycus's 'rust'—as Leontes admitted that Camillo did through the royal rust (III, ii, 167–8). It is surely not insignificant that Autolycus boasts he has spent time at court—where he no doubt learned to refine his skills of deception. But, as the Shepherd wearily accepted, stealing was as much a part of country life as wenching; and the roving energy and 'snapping-up' activities of the amorally opportunistic, though invariably merry, Autolycus (a touch of the *picaro* here) adds a realistic saltiness (how appropriate that he breaks into a list of spices!) to a scene which might have become *too* 'sweet'. I do not intend to track the comings-and-goings of Autolycus, but one of his ballads is worth noting. It is a ballad supposedly sung by a lamenting fish which appeared off the coast: 'It was thought she was a woman, and was turned into a cold fish for she would not exchange flesh with one that loved her. The ballad is very pitiful, and as true' (IV, iv, 280–83). It's like a distant, distorted echo from another world—where a king turned himself into a cold tyrant because he did not trust one that loved him and thought that she had exchanged flesh with someone else; where a king turned a woman into a cold corpse because he ceased to love her. Can these cold fish live?

The feast at the Shepherd's cottage opens with the first appearance of Perdita, whom *Flori*zel has dressed up as *Flor*a (revealing his merging intentions?). Flora was the Roman goddess of *flowers,* and there is no scene in Shakespeare as full of flowers as the one that follows. Prince Florizel is playing at classical pastoral:

> This your sheep-shearing
> Is as a meeting of the petty gods,
> And you the Queen on't.
>
> (IV, iv, 3–5)

Perdita is, though, uneasy that he has 'obscured' his 'high self' with 'a swain's wearing; and me, poor lowly maid,/Most goddesslike pranked up' (IV, iv, 7–10)—and she is right to be uneasy at being thus 'pranked up' (Shakespeare's only use of the word). No matter how sincere his love, Florizel is playing a dangerous pastoral 'prank' on her. There is certainly myth in the air. Florizel invokes the gods 'humbling their deities to love', and cites the 'transformations' of Jupiter to a bull, Neptune to a ram, Apollo to a swain—though even he realizes that these metamorphoses are not particularly happy auguries as far as a woman is concerned, and he hastens to distinguish his own honourable 'desire' from their hot, unchaste 'lusts'. But as well as myth, there are more insistent proximate realities, some of them unpastorally harsh and cruel, as the scene will bear out. The old Shepherd (now, supposedly her father) immediately comments on the inappropriateness of her dress (he says she looks like 'a feasted one, and not / The hostess', IV, iv, 63–4), and gives a picture of the more ungoddess-like behaviour and deportment required in this setting:

> Fie daughter! When my old wife lived, upon
> This day, she was both pantler, butler, cook;
> Both dame and servant; welcomed all, served all;
> Would sing her song, and dance her turn . . .
>   (IV, iv, 55–8)

and so on—affording a vivid cameo of an actual rural festival.

The whole prolonged episode serves to show the kind of world Perdita grew up in—not her royal birth but her rural nurturing. It is not a brief interlude in the 'green world', nor does it take place in a magic wood. It is an extended scene—at some nine hundred lines it must be the longest in Shakespeare (there is none of this in Greene, simply half a dozen lines referring to a 'meeting of all the Farmers Daughters in Sycilia' where Fawnia appears as 'mistres of the feast'), and through it all there is an accumulating sense of the realities of country life. After three oppessive, sterile acts in the court of Sicilia, we need a good long dose, or draft, of the freedoms and fertilities of rural Bohemia—if only to make us feel that this world has sufficient weight and reality to counterbalance Sicilia's winter-world.

With the arrival of the guests to the feast (including the disguised Polixenes and Camillo), Perdita commences her obligations as hostess—by giving everyone flowers. She starts by handing rosemary and rue to the unknown visitors, and Polixenes comments that these 'flow'rs of winter' fit well 'our ages' (IV, iv, 78–9). Here we may just note that there is what must be a deliberate indeterminacy about the time of year this is taking place.

Sheep-shearing would be in mid-June, and there is certainly a feeling of late-spring burgeoning in the air. Yet Perdita replies to Polixenes:

> Sir, the year growing ancient,
> Not yet on summer's death, nor on the birth
> Of trembling winter . . .
>
> (IV, iv, 79–81)

which suggests the near approach of autumn. The reason for this, I suggest, is that while Perdita is certainly a Proserpina-like figure of returning spring, her mother will of necessity be in the autumn of her life at the time of the reunion which this scene is preparing for. I think Shakespeare wants to mix or merge a sense both of rising sap and mature ripening—the non-wintry phases of creative life.

Perdita continues her speech to Polixenes:

> the fairest flow'rs o' th' season,
> Are our carnations, and streaked gillyvors [pinks],
> Which some call Nature's bastards: of that kind
> Our rustic garden's barren; and I care not
> To get slips of them.
>
> (IV, iv, 81–5)

This precipitates what has been called the 'great debate', and it certainly leads to a major exchange, when Polixenes asks Perdita why she 'neglects' such flowers:

> *Perdita.*   For I have heard it said,
> There is an art, which in their piedness shares
> With great creating nature.
>
> *Polixenes.*   Say there be;
> Yet Nature is made better by no mean
> But Nature makes that mean; so over that art,
> Which you say adds to Nature, is an art,
> That Nature makes. You see, sweet maid, we marry

A gentler scion to the wildest stock,
And make conceive a bark of baser kind
By bud of nobler race. This is an art
Which does mend Nature, change it rather; but
The art itself is Nature.
                         (IV, iv, 87–97)

The Elizabethans loved discussing the relationship between Art and Nature, and throughout his work Shakespeare found many occasions and formulations to deepen and further that discussion. There is nothing particularly original in Polixenes' argument, which from one point of view is unassailable—Nature that made the carpenter, made the house, as Emerson succinctly put it. Compare this, from Puttenham's *The Arte of English Poesie* (1589): 'In some cases we say arte is an ayde and coadiutor to nature, or peradventure a meane to supply her wants . . . In another respect arte is not only an aide and coadiutor to nature in all her actions, but an alterer of them, and in some sort a surmounter of her skill. . .', a description which fits nicely with what Shakespeare is doing as a playwright. But it was also felt that men, with their 'artificiall devises', had in some ways corrupted and 'bastardized' 'our great and puissant mother Nature' (see Montaigne's essay 'Of the Cannibales'—Florio's translation appeared in 1603). The grafting and cross-breeding of plants, in which there was much contemporary interest, offered a fine focus to such discussions—as it does here. It could be said that they are both 'right', inasmuch as Perdita is deprecating (bad) artificiality, while Polixenes is defending (good) art. The more general point is that the whole matter of the relations between nature and art is both vital and endless—is itself generative. 'Piedness' (from the miscellaneous objects jumbled together by the magpie) here means the multi-coloured results achieved by crossbreeding flowers, and Perdita feels that there is something unnatural about it (how nature can produce something felt to be 'unnatural' occupies Shakespeare from start to finish).

The more immediate dramatic effect of the scene is of a profound irony, partly retrospective, partly proleptic. We heard the baby Perdita many times execrated as a 'bastard' by Leontes, and she was cast out as one—yet here she is taking a principled stand against bastardy. While Polixenes here argues positively in favour of the practice whereby 'we marry / A gentler scion to the wildest stock'; but when it comes to grafting the (supposedly) base-born Perdita onto his own noble twig ('scion') Florizel (which *is,* after all, what Perdita is hoping for, despite opposition to graftings), his horticultural approval vanishes in a fury of rejection. For the moment, Perdita continues to distribute flowers—hot lavender, mints, savory, marjoram, marigolds, 'these are the flow'rs/Of middle summer' (IV, iv, 106–7). She specifically regrets that she lacks 'some flow'rs o' th' spring' which would be more fitting, both for Florizel and the shepherdesses—virgins all. But, in the poetry of her regret she effectively brings in spring:

> Daffodils,
> That come before the swallow dares, and take
> The winds of March with beauty; violets, dim,
> But sweeter than the lids of Juno's eyes,
> Or Cytherea's breath; pale primroses,
> That die unmarried ere they can behold
> Bright Phoebus in his strength . . .
>   (IV, iv, 118–24)

Nothing else could evoke an actual English spring more immediately than those quite astonishingly lovely opening lines. At the same time, the young maid's fancy lightly turns to myth; and Juno, Cytherea and Phoebus are somehow hovering over the flowers. It is in this speech that Perdita specifically invokes Proserpina, and the flowers she let fall 'from Dis's wagon' (IV, iv, 118), and of course the Ceres–Proserpina relationship is the most important mythic enlargement of the central drama of the mother and the daughter in *The Winter's Tale*. It is perhaps because Shakespeare wanted to strengthen this enriching analogy that he switched the geography, thereby having Perdita born in Sicily which was the birthplace of Proserpina and from whence she was abducted. This is the story from Ovid with the most influence on the play. I hardly need rehearse it here in full, but one detail is worth noting. When Ceres learns from Arethusa that her daughter is now a queen in hell—

> The mother heard in horror, thunderstruck
> It seemed and turned to stone.

The mother is 'turned to stone' in Shakespeare's play as well, though in quite different circumstances and to quite different ends.

Florizel is, understandably, enchanted by the demeanour and words of Perdita, and he is moved to this ardent hymn of appreciation:

> What you do
> Still betters what is done. When you speak, sweet,
> I'd have you do it ever; when you sing,
> I'd have you buy and sell so; so give alms,
> Pray so; and for the ord'ring your affairs,
> To sing them too. When you do dance, I wish you
> A wave o' th' sea, that you might ever do
> Nothing but that—move still, still so,
> And own no other function. Each your doing,
> So singular in each particular,
> Crowns what you are doing in the present deeds,
> That all your acts are queens.
>   (IV, iv, 135–46)

The poetry of this, and of Perdita's immediately preceding speeches, is at times blindingly beautiful—there is hardly a more regal compliment in the whole of Shakespeare than that last one; and—among other things—it contributes greatly to our sense of Perdita's very special beauty. This, it has to be said, is her most important quality: she has none of the wit and sparkle and intelligence of Beatrice, Viola and Rosalind (she is more like Pastorella in Spenser's *Fairie Queene*), and she is, indeed, effectively a mute for the whole of the last act. But in this play her preternatural beauty is everything; she is, as it were, the almost divine representative of great creating Nature herself.

But Florizel's speech also touches on a deeper longing that runs through the play—that the beauties of life should last; here, that youth's blooming grace and loveliness should be somehow perpetuated and preserved—not once and gone, but now and 'ever'. That nature, which is forever moving, indeed 'dancing', should also, somehow, be 'still'. Shakespeare, of course, fastens on just that phenomenon in nature which seems to enact that contradictory condition—a wave, which, as it moves towards the shore is always and never the same. Shakespeare catches this with marvellous economy—'move still, still so': movement and stillness, movement *in* stillness,

stillness moving—these four words anticipate the climax of the play. But it is and can be only *seems*. The wave must break on the shore; Perdita must acquire her mother's wrinkles, and her spring will pass away into winter. But the yearning and striving for eternity—the desire that the mutable natural should yield the unchanging eternal—is a profound one, and Shakespeare taps more deeply into it in this play than ever before. Shakespeare knows as well as every other human being that things pass away, that even a memory cannot be made to last forever; that 'thy grave [must] give way to what's seen now', as Paulina says to the supposedly dead Hermione (V, i, 97–8). But just there we stop. Paulina has seen to it that Hermione has *not* passed away, and, until the final stunning surprise, it appears that she has been preserved in and through art. Shakespeare, being Shakespeare, has one further step to take. Of course, when Hermione steps out of art into life, she is still in theatre. But Shakespeare gives play to the great and unending question of to what extent art can appease or satisfy man's desire for what Yeats called 'monuments of unageing intellect', whether it can provide, or substitute for, or act as 'the artifice of eternity'. Yeats articulates and explores this desire in 'Sailing to Byzantium', and again in 'Byzantium' where the 'glory of changeless metal' and the 'marbles of the dancing floor' seem to offer an immutable value, as opposed to 'the fury and the mire of human veins' and the 'dolphin-torn' sea. Art, it might be, allows life to produce 'monuments of its own magnificence' ('Sailing to Byzantium'). All these matters come to a head in the concluding moments of the play.

The rural pleasures continue for some time, and the amorousness of the young lovers rises to the point where they wish to formally commit themselves to each other, and Florizel asks the unknown visitors to act as witnesses to 'mark our contract'. 'Mark your divorce' says his furious father, now dropping his disguise (IV, iv, 421). Polixenes has been so courteous, and so appreciative of Perdita's beauty and seemingly innate nobility, that when he now starts spewing hatred, anger and cruel threats around, it is as sudden and frightening as Leontes' earlier incomprehensible eruption. Perdita becomes a 'piece of excellent witchcraft', his own son a 'royal fool', while the old Shepherd he will have hanged. The viciousness with which he turns on Perdita is truly shocking:

> I'll have thy beauty scratched with briers and made
> More homely than thy state.
>
> (IV, iv, 429–30)

As children Leontes and Polixenes were 'as twinned lambs'; as adults they
are as twinned—what? wolves, maddened bears? Polixenes has brought a
Sicilian winter to the Bohemian country, and what was so promisingly in
the bud seems blighted. Perdita was right to be apprehensive—some intimation of the potentially dark behaviour of father–kings must have been
born in her blood. The rest of the act is taken up with the plotting and
arrangements which will bring all those involved back to Sicilia. Perdita
doesn't know it, but she is going home.

Back in Sicilia, in the first scene of the last act, the whole issue of 'issue' is
becoming increasingly urgent. After sixteen years of, as one gathers, pretty
stiff penance, Leontes still has no heir. His courtiers are pressing him to
marry again, but Paulina—still acting as the uncompromising voice of conscience and the sleepless guardian of memory—reminds the King that the
wife he killed was 'unparalleled', and repeats the oracle's prophecy that he
will have no heir 'Till his lost child be found' (V, i, 40). Leave it to the gods:

> Care not for issue,
> The crown will find an heir.
>> (V, i, 46–7)

As for his marrying again—never; unless another 'As like Hermione as is
her picture' appears. Paulina makes a binding request of the King:

> give me the office
> To choose you a queen; she shall not be so young
> As was your former, but she shall be such
> As walked your first queen's ghost, it should take joy
> To see her in your arms.
>> (V, i, 73–81)

Not that Leontes, or we, should have an inkling of the fact, but Paulina is
preparing her ground. A final exchange emphasizes what will be a crucial
word:

> *Leontes.*   My true Paulina,
> We shall not marry till thou bidd'st us.
> *Paulina.*   That

Shall be when your first queen's again *in breath;*
Never till then.

(V, i, 81–4—my italics)

Then Florizel makes his entrance with Perdita, presented as a princess from Libya. To Leontes, she looks a 'goddess' (V, i, 131), and he invokes blessings upon the pair:

The blessèd gods
Purge all infection from our air whilst you
Do climate here!

(V, i, 168–70)

In fact it is they who will be the disinfecting agents of the Sicilian climate, purging an air poisoned and made sterile by Leontes. But when a lord announces the arrival of a furious Polixenes, threatening 'divers deaths in death' (V, i, 202—which means tortures) to poor Shepherd and Clown, and hell-bent on catching the young couple and preventing their marriage, it seems that winter has come again and infection returned to the air.

All the more surprising, then, that the next scene brings us a series of excited gentlemen telling of royal recognitions and reunions. Suddenly, the air is clear, all anger lost in grateful celebration.

Nothing but bonfires. The oracle is fulfilled; the King's daughter is found; such a deal of wonder is broken out within this hour that ballad-makers cannot be able to express it.

(V, ii, 24–7)

The identity of Perdita is revealed, though the whole matter strains credulity.

This news, which is called true, is so like an old tale that the verity of it is in strong suspicion. Has the King found his heir?

(V, ii, 29–32)

Again that problem—can it really be *proved?* The confident Third Gentleman answers with an arresting image:

> Most true, if ever truth were pregnant by circumstance; that which you
> hear you'll swear you see, there is such unity in the proofs.
>
> (V, ii, 33–5)

The usual gloss on the opening image is 'if ever truth was made convincing by evidence'; but, as we have seen, pregnancy and birth are at the centre of this play, and we can look a little closer than that. 'Circumstance' is circumstances, and circumstantial evidence. This news is true *if* these have ever made truth pregnant, swelled it out (note that it is 'by', not 'with'). Truth will then presumably deliver, in time, a child of truth; or, as here, a true child. But it has to be prefaced by that conditional 'if'. The 'proofs' and 'many other evidences' (V, ii, 41) certainly seem conclusive, and no one would wish to doubt them. We, of course, have been privileged to see enough to know that it *is* true. But for the gentlemen of Sicilia, and for the King, the 'evidences' can only be 'circumstance', circumstantial—a jewel, a mantle, some letters, (handkerchief and rings to establish the fate of Antigonus), a facial resemblance; again, the 'proof' depends on materialities. Here, it seems overwhelming, and the wonder is only temporarily laced with doubt ('the verity of it is in strong suspicion'). But Posthumus thought the 'evidences' presented to him by Iachimo were overwhelming as well. Shakespeare is not trying to spread scepticism. There is, it seems to me, simply an unspoken reminder that, no matter how great our hunger for certainties, there is a point when trust must take over. 'Proofs' can only go so far; love must go further.

Third Gentleman asks Second if he saw the meeting of the two kings. He did not. 'Then have you lost a sight which was to be seen, cannot be spoken of' (V, ii, 45–6). Nevertheless, speak of it is what he does, at length and to enthralling effect. As he promised, 'that which you hear you'll swear you see'. First Gentleman has described the meeting of Leontes and Camillo— 'There was speech in their dumbness, language in their very gesture' (V, ii, 14–15). A speaking dumbness and the language of gesture—this applies to the main participants in the great scene of reunion. But why does not Shakespeare give us the scene direct? Why these, entirely amiable, chattering gentlemen? Why narration, rather than drama—or let us say, narration *as* drama? Why can't *we* see the meeting of the kings? It is quite instructive, even amusing, to see the explanations which have been offered. The usual line is that Shakespeare must have felt that he had done the father–daughter

reunion in *Pericles,* so here he relegated it in order to highlight the reunion
of the husband and the wife. But Shakespeare is surely a more resourceful
and imaginative playwright than that. If he fills the stage with breathless
talk for a whole scene, prior to a scene which will centre on stone, silence
and sight, you may be sure he is after a particular effect. As far as I am concerned, only Leonard Barkan has appreciated what Shakespeare is doing.

> The lack of dramatic three-dimensionality here sets the stage for the
> scene in which the three-dimensional medium of sculpture becomes that
> of drama by metamorphosis. The speech-without-drama of this scene is
> contrasted with the statue-with-silence of the following scene. The verbal
> without the visual is empty, while the visual without the verbal is frozen.
> Only Shakespeare's medium can effect the marriage.

Exactly.

In fact, the gentlemen refer to the statue of Hermione (it is the first we
have heard of it) just before they leave. The reference is perfectly placed. It
comes immediately after Third has described the moving moment when
Perdita learned the details of her mother's death and wept, with a dolorous 'Alas'. 'I am sure my heart wept blood. Who was most marble there
changed color, some swooned, all sorrowed' (V, ii, 95–7). He then proceeds
to tell them that Perdita has gone to see 'her mother's statue, which is in the
keeping of Paulina':

> a piece many years in doing and now newly performed by that rare Ital-
> ian master, Julio Romano, who, had he himself eternity and could put
> breath into his work, would beguile Nature of her custom, so perfectly he
> is her ape: he so near to Hermione hath done Hermione, that they say one
> would speak to her and stand in hope of answer.
>
> (V, ii, 101–9)

With hindsight, one may say that this is preparing us for the final scene. But
there is a lot more going on than that.

With the return of Perdita—let us say—the people of the Sicilian court
who have been, effectively, turned to marble through the disastrous life-
destroying nihilism of Leontes, are flushed with life-returning blood again.
Her mother, most regrettably, was terminally frozen out of life by Leontes.

But, it appears, she has been memorialized, monumentalized, as a statue—turned to marble in another sense. And by Julio Romano. Now it is not often that Shakespeare refers to an actual Renaissance artist by name in his plays, so this departure from practice invites our attention. Never mind that it is another unashamed anachronism (Romano's dates are 1492–1546), it must be signalling something directly relevant to the play at this stage. By common agreement, Shakespeare's most likely source for the name, and his reason for using it, lies in Vasari's *Lives* (published in 1550). There he would have found—in Latin—a transcription of the epitaph on Giulio Romano's tomb, which, translated, is:

> Jupiter saw sculpted and painted bodies breathe and the earthly buildings made equal to those in heaven by the skill of Giulio Romano. Thus angered he then summoned a council of all the gods, and he removed that man from the earth, lest he be exposed, conquered, or equalled by an earth-born man.

Sculpted bodies that seem to breathe; works of art which rival (and thus threaten) divine powers of creation—Shakespeare is further preparing for his last act, which, among other things, effects perhaps his most profound plumbing of the provenance, the power, the privilege, and finally the limitations, of art, in miraculously compacted form.

To get some sense of how much lies behind this short final scene, it will help to have before us passages from two stories in Ovid's *Metamorphoses*. I have mentioned the general importance of the Pygmalion story for late Shakespeare; now, some of the details become particularly pertinent. They concern the actual period of transition when Pygmalion's master-work passes from ivory to flesh and blood, and the statue moves into life.

> It seemed to be alive,
> Its face to be a real girl's, a girl
> Who wished to *move* . . .
> . . .   is it flesh
> Or ivory? Not ivory still, he's sure!
> . . .
> And he kissed her as she lay, and she seemed *warm*
> . . . beneath his touch the flesh

Grew *soft,* its ivory hardness vanishing
. . .

His heart was torn wonder and misgiving,
Delight and terror that it was not true
. . .

She was alive! The *pulse* beat in her veins!
. . .   she . . . shyly raised
Her eyes to his and saw the world and him.
(my italics)

The other story is that of Deucalion, curiously enough referred to earlier (for only the second time in Shakespeare) by Polixenes in an entirely different context. Shakespeare leaves his traces in unexpected places. Deucalion and his wife Pyrrha are the sole survivors of the great Deluge visited by an irate Jupiter on an impious people. Facing a desolate, unpeopled world after the waters subside, Deucalion longs for some of his father's (Prometheus) magic to 'restore/Mankind again and in the moulded clay/Breathe life'. Consulting the oracle of Themis as to how to repair the loss of mankind, they are instructed—'cast behind you your great mother's bones'. Initially baffled, they decide that this can only refer to the stones which lie around them on the ground, and they duly throw them over their shoulders.

Those stones (who would believe did ancient lore
Not testify the truth?) gave up their hardness;
Their rigidness grew slowly soft, and, softened,
Assumed a shape, and as they grew and felt
A gentler nature's touch, a semblance seemed
To appear, still indistinct, of human form,
Like the first rough-hewn marble of a statue,
Scarce modelled, or old old uncouth images.
The earthy part, damp with some trace of moisture
Was turned to flesh; what was inflexible
And solid changed to bone; what in the stones
Had been the veins retained the name of veins.
In a brief while, by Heaven's mysterious power,
The stones the man had thrown were formed as men,
Those from the woman's hand reshaped as women.

Hence we are hard, we children of the earth,
And in our lives of toil we prove our birth.

These two 'magic' moments of stone gradually giving way to/becoming
life—moments which should give us what Thomas Mann referred to as
'the archaic shudder of myth'—the hard becoming soft, the cold acquiring
warmth, stillness beginning to move—these moments are vital for Shakespeare. And the gradualness is important: these are not sudden jumps—
now stone; hey presto, now life. Rather, the one almost imperceptibly gives
way to the other, so that it would be very difficult to mark a point at which
the actual transformation took place, albeit that the time it takes is 'brief'.

When the last scene opens in the chapel in Paulina's house, a remark from
Leontes makes it clear that they—which means all the main characters and
some courtiers—have already spent some time looking at works of art—
'Your gallery/Have we passed through, not without much content/In
many singularities' (V, iii, 10–12). They have, as it were, had a preliminary
immersion in the realm of aesthetic artefacts. And *now* Paulina *'draws a
curtain and discovers Hermione standing like a statue'*; or, for the onlookers
and the audience, we should, at this point, more accurately say—a statue
standing like Hermione. We are to take it that they all stand still and silent—rapt, is perhaps the word. (Paulina—'I like your silence; it the more
shows off your wonder', V, iii, 21–2.) It is then that Leontes remarks that
his Hermione was not so wrinkled, which Paulina turns into a further
compliment to the artist who 'makes her/As she lived now' (V, iii, 31–2).
The artifices of eternity must somehow incorporate the inexorabilities of
time.

Leontes addresses the 'statue'; indirectly (you don't talk to stone), and
then directly (you may if it seems to be the life it images):

Oh, thus she stood,
Even with such life of majesty—warm life,
As now it coldly stands—when first I wooed her.
I am ashamed: does not the stone rebuke me,
For being more stone than it? O royal piece!
There's magic in thy majesty, which has
My evils conjured to remembrance, and

From thy admiring daughter took the spirits,
Standing like stone with thee.
                                    (V, iii, 34–42)

This is a peak moment, before the scene begins to move on. We are to imagine Perdita standing next to the 'statue' of her mother—in her almost divine beauty, she represents 'perfection of the life'; while the mother, through the almost divine art of the maker, represents 'perfection of the work' (the terms are again from Yeats). Art and life, for one impossible tremblingly arrested moment, seem momentarily identical, indistinguishable, at one. While Leontes realizes that the statue forces him to confront the question —who, in their relationship, was *really* the 'stone' one? Penance and time have brought softening (as well as wrinkles), and it is time for some frozen hearts to melt.

For a while, Leontes wants to prolong the arrested moment—'Do not draw the curtain . . . Let be, let be!' (V, iii, 59, 61)—'gazing on this sphinx-like boundary between art and life' as Wilson Knight has it. He permits himself what, at this stage, must seem like Pygmalion-esque fantasies:

See, my lord,
Would you not deem it *breathed*? And that those *veins*
Did verily bear blood?
Polixenes.   Masterly done!
The very life seems *warm* upon her *lip*.
Leontes. The fixure of her *eye* has *motion* in 't,
As we are mocked with art.
                                    (V, iii, 63–8—my italics)

His now positive and appreciative gaze seems almost to be reassembling his wife's body part by part, conferring warmth on what he had once frozen into stone. Paulina purports to be anxious that Leontes will soon be 'so far transported that/He'll think anon it lives' (V, iii, 68–9), and Leontes replies that he would like to live in that delusion (that the stone seems to be hovering on the brink of life) indefinitely—'Make me to think so twenty years together' (V, iii, 71). Then he pushes his fantasy to the limit—'methinks,/ There is an air comes from her' (the 'it' of the statue has become 'her'):

'What fine chisel/Could ever yet cut breath?' (V, iii, 77–8). Romano's genius was that he carved statues that seemed to breathe (lifelikeness was the
supreme merit of art for the ancients). Leontes determines to take this literally and he moves to put flesh on stone—'Let no man mock me,/For I will
kiss her' (V, iii, 79–80). At which point Paulina, now curator, director and
priestess all together, makes her final move; and remember that this should
be as much of a shock and surprise to us as it is to the people gathered in the
chapel.

> Either forbear,
> Quit presently the chapel, or resolve you
> For more amazement. If you can behold it,
> I'll make the statue move indeed, descend,
> And take you by the hand—but then you'll think,
> Which I protest against, I am assisted
> By wicked powers.
>   (V, iii, 85–91)

Black magic, white magic? We are in a 'chapel', which suggests Christian
transforming grace; but we are in pre-Christian times, foregrounding pagan metamorphosing power. Leontes is content to accept any new miracles
Paulina can effect with the Hermione–statue, 'for 'tis as easy/To make her
speak, as move' (V, iii, 94–5). Here is the moment which marks and acknowledges the essential difference—art can do *almost* anything; but only
(human) life can breathe, and speak, and move. Paulina (telling anyone
who thinks 'it is unlawful business I am about' to leave—no one moves, the
onlookers have become statuesque: V, iii, 95–7) makes her master-stroke
and works her (white) magic.

> Music awake her: strike.
> 'Tis time, descend; be stone no more; approach;
> Strike all that look upon with marvel; come;
> I'll fill your grave up. *Stir;* nay come away;
> Bequeath to death your numbness, for from him
> Dear life redeems you. You perceive she *stirs.*
>   (V, iii, 98–103—my italics)

There it is, the key word: everything that had been stilled, frozen, arrested into a long sterile winter now 'stirs' as '*Hermione comes down*'. As she steps out of art back into life—and time—it is as if Hermione had simply been standing still for sixteen years in a state of suspended animation (Barkan's term). In this, she also stands for—embodies, figures—the kingdom of Sicilia of which she is Queen. But Perdita has returned. And it is to her, and only to her, that Hermione addresses her one speech (not one word for Leontes):

> You gods look down,
> And from your sacred vials pour your graces
> Upon my daughter's head
> . . .
>
> thou shalt hear that I,
> Knowing by Paulina that the oracle
> Gave hope thou wast in being, have preserved
> Myself to see the issue.
>
> (V, iii, 121–8)

Ceres and Proserpina are reunited. Perdita is the 'issue' in every sense.

When Hermione steps down, Leontes gasps:

> Oh, she's warm!
> If this be magic, let it be an art
> Lawful as eating.
>
> (V, iii, 109–11)

It may seem strange to invoke 'eating' at this point, but then we recognize just how apposite it is. Eating is what every living body has to do, if it is to stay 'warm' with circulating blood. A magic as lawful as eating has nothing supernatural about it. There has been no divine—much less nefarious—intervention. Hermione's body has been a living body throughout, only arrested and concealed for sixteen long, barren years. The only 'magic' is Paulina's 'art', and her thaumaturgy is that of a dramatist. The last scene, with its stunning *coup de théâtre,* is stage-managed by Paulina (note the importance of music). Shakespeare is quite self-consciously putting his own

art on stage—Paulina's chapel is Shakespeare's theatre in little. 'If you can
behold it,/I'll make the statue move' (V, iii, 87–8)—Shakespeare is effectively speaking to his own audience through Paulina. When Leontes first
sees the statue, he asks, in amazement—'What was he that did make it?'
(V, iii, 63). For that moment, Hermione is at once a statue, a woman and an
actor. So how should we answer Leontes' question? Julio Romano? Shakespeare? Great creating nature? or . . . But no—finally it is *the* unanswerable
question.

When the First Gentleman describes the meeting of Leontes and Camillo
he says:

> they looked as they had heard of a world ransomed, or one destroyed. A
> notable passion of wonder appeared in them . . .
>
> (V, ii, 15–18)

or one destroyed: there are some phenomena—events, spectacles—which
cause a response in which the wonderful is indistinguishable from the terrible. There is a description of Tolstoy's face while he listened to great music—an expression of *horror* came into it. Just so with this play. It does not
merely please and entertain. It should leave us *aghast,* uncertain of just what
sort of extraordinary thing it is we have just witnessed. In these last plays
Shakespeare is touching on ultimate matters in quite amazing ways. Indeed, he might even have surprised himself.

THE TEMPEST (1611)

> those infortunate (yet fortunate) Ilands
> (*The True Declaration of the Estate of the Colonie in Virginia,* anon., 1610)

> I might call him
> A thing divine; for nothing natural
> I ever saw so noble.
>
> (I, ii, 418–20)

> That a monster should be such a natural!
>
> (III, ii, 34–5)

> These are not natural events; they strengthen
> From strange to stranger.
>
> (V, i, 227–8)

Where are we? In the three previous plays we have adjusted ourselves, imaginatively, to the worlds of classical antiquity, Roman Britain, and pre-Christian Sicily. But here there are no offered orientations. Most unusually, the Folio has a written indication of locality—'An un-inhabited Island'—though this may have been added by a scrivener, Ralph Crane, who worked for Shakespeare's company and perhaps made the transcript. Whoever wrote it, it is an indication pointing to nowhere, or no-known-where I should say. Coleridge had it right when he wrote 'in this play Shakespeare did not appeal to any sensuous impression of time and place but to the imagination'. It opens in the middle of what seems like an Atlantic storm and shipwreck, on what turns out to be a Mediterranean island, though by the end we must feel that we have passed out of geography altogether.

In a strange, late essay on the play, Henry James maintained that 'The story in *the Tempest* is a thing of naught, for any story will provide a remote island, a shipwreck and a coincidence.' Well! But this is not as breath-takingly dismissive as it sounds. James stresses, rather, the final triumph of Shakespeare's *style*—'its rich simplicity and its free elegance . . . its re-finement of power . . . It renders the poverties and obscurities of our world in the dazzling terms of a richer and better.' He, rightly, admires the wonderful economy of this (surprisingly short) play—'the economy not of poverty, but of wealth *a little weary of congestion*' (my italics). That too feels right, for there is a sense in this play of sorting things out, summarizing essentials, eschewing the distractions of life's plenitudes. James says that the play reflects Shakespeare's 'charged inspiration and clarified experience', and 'clarified' is just the appropriate word. At the same time, no play is more blurring and blurred. I shall try to explain this, only apparent, contradiction.

To be sure, *The Tempest* has many of the features we associate with the Last Plays—an initial outbreak of disruptive evil and discord (in this play recounted, not shown); ensuing separations and voyages; miraculous salvation from shipwreck; reconciliations and reunions; and the coming together of almost divinely beautiful royal children who finally unite in a marriage presaging future harmony and renewal. What was *lost*—kingdoms, children—is found; though, as always, lost years cannot be retrieved. But, somehow, it's all very different. Recognitions and reconciliations are almost passionless and automatic; there is almost no repentance and what there is is off-hand, minimal; the forgiveness is brusque and unconvincing; there is no sense of regeneration, renewal, restoration—certainly not of redemption. Patience is mentioned, but only as not being practised. There is no sense of the seasonal replenishment afforded by 'great creating nature' —it is figured in a masque, but made to seem unbelievably insubstantial, a diaphanous sketch at two or three removes from reality. In fact, *everything* seems faint and somehow far away. The verse carries very few metaphors such as usually bring powerful extra life and presence to the words and set off cascades of meanings in the mind. The beat of the iambic lines is so unemphatic as to be almost inaudible. Indeed, I would venture another paradox and suggest that in a curious way it is almost as though we don't distinctly hear the words at all but rather a strange, almost hypnotic 'humming' such as Gonzalo hears while sleeping on the island. I say this in the full knowledge that the word 'roar' (and cognates) occurs more often here than in any other play. For there is a 'roaring' (a strange, semantically empty, hollow-throated word) which is a kind of silence—like the hissing, humming, 'oh-ing' noise you hear on the radio when the programmes are over. It's what you hear in sea-shells; and when you have been too long under water.

The story which for James was 'a thing of naught' was a thing of many romances, and many folk and fairy tales with a recurrent theme of a magician living in solitude and bringing up a daughter—on an island, or even under the sea (note). As with the play in some ways most closely related to it, *A Midsummer Night's Dream,* there is no specific source for *The Tempest.* Shakespeare has made his own mix wherein the genres blend into each other so that the play is, variously and at once, a romance, a pastoral, a tragicomedy, a morality, an allegorical history, a comedy influenced by *commedia dell'arte,* and a masque. Or, if you like, none of the above but something else again. But, beyond all reasonable doubt, a number of contemporary documents acted as some sort of immediate triggering influence. These were what have become known as the Bermuda Pamphlets, and here I must recount what, for some, might be a familiar story. From the time of 1582, when Richard Hakluyt the elder published *Divers Voyages touching the Discovery of America*—which starts 'I marvel not a little that since the first discovery of America (which is now full four-score-and-ten years), after so great conquest and plantings of the Spaniards and Portugals there, that we of England could never have the grace to set fast footing in such fertile and temperate places as are left as yet unpossessed by them'—the Elizabethans grew increasingly excited at the idea of settling North America. Hawkins investigated the coast of Florida, Drake found his way to California, and in 1585 Ralegh sent out his first colony to Virginia (so named to honour Elizabeth) under the command of Sir Richard Grenville. For various reasons this colony did not take and the failed and much-reduced colonists were taken home by Drake in the following year. But the hunt was irreversibly on, and in 1607 another colony was settled in Virginia at the now appropriately named Jamestown. Interest in reports sent or brought back from the New World (containing details of the voyages, the local flora and fauna, the indigenous natives, and the many difficulties and problems among the colonizers) was at a peak in the early years of the seventeenth century—just, of course, when Shakespeare was writing his play (which is his only play to contain the word 'plantation').

More immediately, an expedition to Virginia in 1609 led by Sir Thomas Gates had disappeared at sea. But he returned safely from Virginia in 1610, with a tale to tell of a terrible storm and shipwreck in the Bermudas; an almost miraculous escape to land; a period of surprisingly easy survival on a strange island; and finally the troubling state of the Virginian settlement when he managed to get there. The story occasioned various accounts by actual survivors and others, including a long letter by William Strachey giving '*A True Repertory of the Wracke and Redemption of Sir Thomas Gates . . . the Ilands of the Bermudas: his comming to Virginia, and the estate of that Colonie. . .*', which was not published until 1625 but which Shakespeare must have read (he had many friends on the Virginian Council, for whom the letter was written). It is on these pamphlets and this letter that Shakespeare draws for his play, though, as always, submitting the material to his own alchemy. I will quote a series of extracts which, I think, throw an interesting light on the play and, more importantly, on the alchemy.

And first, from that *True Repertory*—'a most dreadfull Tempest'.

> A dreadfull storme and hideous began to blow from out the Northeast,
> which swelling, and roaring as it were by fits . . . at length did beate all
> light from heaven . . . so much the more fuller of horror, as in such cases

horror and feare use to overrunne the troubled, and overmastered sences
of all which (taken up with amazement) the eares lay so sensible to the
terrible cries, and murmurs of the windes, and distraction of our Company . . . our clamours drownd in the windes, and the windes in thunder
. . . Windes and Seas were as mad, as fury and rage could make them . . .
there was not a moment in which the sodaine splitting, or instant over-
setting of the Shippe was not expected . . . For my part I thought her al-
readie in the bottome of the Sea . . .

which is perhaps where the play takes place; but more of that in time. You
will recognize the details of Shakespeare's own tempest with which the play
opens; and here is the origin of Ariel's fire:

an apparition of a little round light, like a faint Starre, trembling, and
streaming along with a sparkling blaze, halfe the height upon the Maine
Mast, and shooting sometimes from Shroud to Shroud . . .

Then, the providential escape or salvation:

it wanted little . . . to have shut up hatches, and commending our sinfull
soules to God, committed the Shippe to the mercy of the Sea . . . but see
the goodnesse and sweet introduction of better hope, by our mercifull
God given unto us. Sir George Summers, when no man dreamed of such
happinesse, had discovered, and cried Land.

(As they seem to be foundering, Gonzalo cries out a longing 'for an acre of
barren ground—long heath, brown furze, anything', I, i, 65–6.)

Indeede the morning now three quarters spent, had wonne a little cleere-
nesse from the dayes before, and it being better surveyed, the very trees
were seene to move with the winde upon the shoare side—and by the
mercy of God unto us, making out our Boates, we had ere night brought
all our men, women, and children, about the number of one hundred and
fifty, safe unto the Iland.

(In another pamphlet, *A Discovery of the Barmudas, otherwise called the Ile
of Divels,* Sylvester Jourdain expresses more wonder: 'But our delivery was

not more strange, in falling so opportunely and happily upon the land, as our feeding and preservation was beyond our hopes and all men's expectations most admirable.')

The island turns out not to be as rumour, or seamen's superstition, has it.

> We found it to be the dangerous and dreaded Iland, or rather Ilands of the Bermudas . . . they be called commonly, The Devils Ilands, and are feared and avoyded of all sea travellers alive, above any other place in the world. Yet it pleased our mercifull God, to make even this hideous and hated place, both the place of our safetie, and meanes of our deliverance.
>
> And hereby also, I hope to deliver the world from a foule and generall errour: it being counted of most, that they can be no habitation for Men, but rather given over to Devils and wicked Spirits; whereas indeed wee find them now by experience, to bee as habitable and commodious as most Countries of the same climate and situation.

(Jourdain, who says the island is reputed to be an 'enchanted' place, is even more enthusiastic: 'Wherefore my opinion is that whereas it hath been and is still accounted the most dangerous, infortunate, and most forlorn place of the world, it is in truth the richest, healthfullest, and pleasing land . . . and merely natural, as ever man set foot upon.')

Strachey goes on to list all the trees, berries, fruits, birds, fish, crustaceans and other animals the island affords—including a 'reasonable toothsom (some say) Tortoyse' (Prospero calls Caliban a 'tortoise'). There are no rivers or springs; you have to dig to find 'certaine gushings and soft burblings' of water (Caliban can show you where). He notes the absence of 'any venemous thing'—certainly, he never saw a snake; which is somehow appropriate in this somewhat anamorphic version of Paradise. And all the venom on Prospero's island is secreted by men. These observations are apt for Shakespeare's own ambiguous and enchanted island. But we should remember that, in the play, the Bermudas are mentioned just once—fleetingly, peripherally: Ariel was once sent by Prospero 'to fetch dew / From the still-vexed Bermoothes' (I, ii, 228–9). The action is a long way elsewhere.

There are two more sections in the letter, both having relevance for the play. Once they were all safely landed and the danger was over, the men started to fall out and go wrong, as men will unless they are properly 'governed' by some good authority, however legitimated or derived. (The prospect of mobs of 'masterless men' was a nightmare for the Elizabethans and Jacobeans.) 'Loe, what are our affections and passions, if not rightly squared? . . . some dangerous and secret discontents nourished amongst us, had like to have bin the parents of bloudy issues and mischiefes . . . a conspiracy was discovered [led by] a mutinous and dissembling Imposter.'

> In these dangers and divellish disquiets (whilest the almighty God wrought for us, and sent us miraculously delivered from the calamities of the Sea, all blessings upon the shoare, to content and binde us to gratefulnesse) thus inraged amongst our selves, to the destruction each of other, into what a mischiefe and misery had wee bin given up, had wee not had a Governour with his authority, to have suppressed the same? Yet was there a worse practise, faction, and conjuration a foote, deadly and bloudy, in which the life of our Governour, with many others were threatened, and could not but miscarry in his fall . . . But as all giddy and lawlesse attempts, have always something of imperfection, and that as well by the property of the action, which holdeth of disobedience and rebellion . . . as through the ignorance of the devisers themselves . . .

Just so: this plot collapsed and came to nothing; as will a similar 'foul conspiracy' against Governor Prospero's life, hopelessly botched by Stephano and Trinculo, 'giddy and lawlesse' with drink.

They finally reach the Jamestown colony in Virginia, and find it to be 'full of misery and misgovernment'. In the absence of good government, 'the headlesse multitude' had fallen into 'wastful courses' and 'Idleness'. There was 'no husbandry'; they couldn't even be bothered 'to sowe Corne for their owne bellies'. Captain John Smith, writing about Virginia in 1608, describes how difficult it was to get the settlers to do any of the necessary plantation work. Neglecting agriculture and carpentry, all they wanted to do was look for non-existent gold. (A lot of these greedy, lazy wastrels were young gallants hoping for easy riches, not honest labourers.) Thus Strachey: 'Unto such calamity can sloath, riot and vanity, bring the most setled and plentifull estate.' Another contemporary anonymous pamphlet about Virginia makes the same point even more vigorously. 'So that, if it bee considered that without industry no land is sufficient to the Inhabitants: and that the trade to which they trusted, betrayed them to loose the opportunity of

seed-time, and so to rust and weare out themselves.' Yet another anonymous pamphlet known as *The True Declaration of the Estate of the Colonie in
Virginia* (1610) makes a definitive statement:

> The ground of all those miseries, was the permissive providence of God,
> who, in the fore-mentioned violent storme, separated the head from the
> bodie, all the vital powers of regiment being exiled with *Sir Thomas Gates*
> in those infortunate (yet fortunate) Hands. The broken remainder of
> those supplies made a greater shipwrack in the continent of *Virginia,* by
> the tempest of dissension: every man overvaluing his own worth, would
> be a Commander: every man underprizing an others value, denied to be
> commanded . . . it is no wonder that so many in our colony perished: it is a
> wonder, that all were not devoured.

More than one kind of shipwreck; more than one kind of tempest. The importance of work, and agriculture and husbandry; and the whole question
of good and necessary 'government', and 'the vitall powers of regiment'—
these are central matters in Shakespeare's play. One more quotation from
the *True Declaration:*

> The next Fountaine of woes was secure negligence, and improvidence,
> when every man sharked for his present bootie, but was altogether care-
> lesse of succeeding penurie. Now, I demand whether Sicilia, or Sardinia
> could hope for increase without manuring? A Colony is therefore de-
> nominated, because they should be Coloni, the Tillers of the Earth, and
> Stewards of fertilitie: our mutinous Loyterers would not sow with provi-
> dence, and therefore they reaped the fruits of too deeere bought Repen-
> tance.

You will hardly find a better phrase for Stephano and Trinculo than 'mutinous Loyterers' sharking for booty (Caliban is something else). Shakespeare's play is not a study of imperialism and colonialism as currently understood. But it does engage with basic issues concerning what is involved
in being proper *coloni* and in establishing 'plantations' in the New World.
On this matter, a final quotation from a later essay by Francis Bacon entitled 'Of Plantations' (1625):

> It is a shameful and unblessed thing to take the scum of people, and
> wicked condemned men, to be the people with whom you plant: and not
> only so, but it spoileth the plantation; for they will ever live like rogues,
> and not fall to work, but be lazy, and do mischief, and spend victuals, and
> be quickly weary, and then certify over to their country to the discredit of
> the plantation . . . For government, let it be in the hands of one, assisted
> with some counsel . . . And above all, let men make that profit of being
> in the wilderness, as they have God always, and his service, before their
> eyes.

With extraordinary economy, Shakespeare's play encompasses, or glances
at, all these matters.

The Strachey letter was published in 1625 in *Purchas His Pilgrimes* with
marginal notes by Samuel Purchas. I have not yet mentioned any of the remarks made by the commentators on Virginia concerning the indigenous
inhabitants, the miscalled Indians. Suffice it to say that they were found to
be credulous and adoring (treating the colonizers as gods); helpful (many of
the colonies were completely dependent on the natives for food and instruction about the terrain, in their early years); and treacherous (there are some
terrible massacres, often *but not always* provoked by the disgraceful behaviour of the colonists)—sometimes in that order. You will readily see that
this exactly describes the range of responses that Caliban goes through with
regard to Prospero. Strachey describes an episode of treachery on the part
of the Indians, suddenly turned hostile. Purchas adds a marginal comment:
'Can a Leopard change his spots? Can a Savage remayning a Savage be
civill? Were not wee our selves made and not borne civill in our Progeni-
tors days? and were not Caesars Britaines as brutish as Virginians? The
Romane swords were best teachers of civilitie to this & other Countries
neere us.'

This last point, you may remember, was taken up in *Cymbeline*. More
generally, it can be readily understood that the discovery of apparently totally uncivilized and 'primitive' (= first of its kind) natives in the New
World lent enormous new impetus to that favourite Elizabethan topic of
debate, and a concern central to all Shakespeare's drama—the relationship
of savagery to civility, of nature to nurture; indeed, the *nature* of Nature
itself. When Prospero describes Caliban as 'a born devil, on whose na-
ture/Nurture can never stick' (IV, i, 188–9), he is raising all the questions.

(We should not, incidentally, take Prospero's statements and definitions as veridical and definitive. It would be a mistake to assume that Shakespeare's view of Caliban is coextensive with Prospero's.) Leaving aside Caliban's role in the play for a moment—he is in a way the pivot; the figure against whom all the others are measured—we can see that he incorporates attributes associated with, at least, the European figure of the wild or 'salvage' man (of the woods) and the native of the New World. About this native, travellers' reports were continuously ambiguous—he was innocent, essentially uncorrupted, naturally happy; he was a cannibal, truly savage, naturally brutal. In Spenser's *Fairie Queene* Books IV and V, there is 'a wilde and salvage man', a cannibalistic monster, who lecherously abducts Amoret; but there is also a gentle 'wilde man' who, though without human speech, takes pity on Serena and saves her. Just so. Caliban has his lecherousness and murderousness; but he also has his sensitivities and delicacies (even though Prospero reserves that word exclusively for Ariel). His name is, effectively, an anagram of 'cannibal'; it might owe something to the Romany word for blackness—*cauliban;* it could refer to the Caribbean. Whatever he is—born devil; monster (nature *un*natural); enslaved native; or just 'natural man' (man *in* a state of nature)—it is of particular interest that Prospero *needs* him.

> We cannot miss him. He does make our fire,
> Fetch in our wood, and serves in offices
> That profit us.
>
> (I, ii, 311–13)

(It is perhaps worth noting that the one task we see imposed on him, and after him on Ferdinand, namely 'fetching wood', was exactly the work which the insubordinate settlers initially refused to do for Sir Thomas Gates—though he wanted the wood to build a boat to escape from the island, where the mutinous loiterers preferred to remain in idleness.) You would have thought that a magician with Prospero's so potent powers (he can raise the dead!) would have been able to whisk a bit of firewood into his 'cell' at the flick of a wand. But no—Shakespeare wants to mark a curious and perhaps significant reliance and dependence. This is not a reprehensible implausibility, but a matter to think on.

Columbus himself was sure he had encountered cannibals in the Caribbean, and he contrasted them with the 'meke and humayne people' on other islands—'they seeme to lyve in that goulden worlde of the whiche owlde wryters speake so much; wherein men lyved simplye and innocentlye without enforcement of lawes, without quarrelling Judges and libelles, content onely to satisfy nature. . ." It was reports like this which helped to inspire Montaigne's essay 'Of the Cannibales' (John Florio's translation of the *Essais* was published in 1603—a work which Shakespeare certainly knew and whose copy is almost certainly even now in the British Museum). I will quote some relevant passage; and you can see a tolerant and provocative relativism creeping in which surely appealed to the ironic Shakespeare.

> I finde (as farre as I have been informed) there is nothing in that nation [the newly discovered America], that is either barbarous or savage, unlesse man call that barbarisme which is not common to them [point taken!] . . .They are even savage, as we call those fruits wilde, which nature of her selfe, and of her ordinarie progresse hath produced: whereas indeed, they are those which our selves have altered by our artificiall devices, and diverted from their common order, we should rather terme savage [well, all right—an agreeable and refreshing inversion and oxymoron; the product, of course, of civilized casuistry] . . . me seemeth that what in those nations we see by experience, doth not only exceed all the pictures wherewith licentious Poesie hath proudly imbellished the golden age and all her quaint inventions to faine a happy condition of man, but also the conception and desire of Philosophy [a nod there to the 'Golden Age' as described by 'licentious' Ovid] . . . It is a nation, would I answer Plato, that hath no kinde of traffike, no knowledge of Letters, no intelligence of numbers, no name of magistrate, nor of politike superioritie; no use of service, of riches or of povertie; no contracts, no successions, no partitions, no occupation but idle; no respect of kindred, but common, no apparell but naturall, no manuring of lands, no use of wine, corne, or mettle . . .

And as for cannibalism, continues Montaigne, compared to the indescribable tortures we 'civilized' people inflict on living bodies, the eating of a dead body is infinitely less 'barbarous'—and we can take that point, too. Shakespeare, of course, allows the good Gonzalo to articulate much of this passage from Montaigne (see II, i, 148–73), making it clear that his wist-

ful evocation of the 'Golden Age' is full of impossible contradictions, easily pounced on by the sneering, worldly derision of Antonio and Sebastian.
But where Gonzalo's confused and unrealizable fantasy is benign ('holy
Gonzalo, honorable man'), the jeering malice of Antonio and Sebastian
does them little credit, trenchant and telling though it is. As Coleridge very
rightly observed: 'Shakespeare never puts habitual scorn into the mouths of
other than bad men.'

But Ovid's Golden Age can hardly be squared with, or mapped on to, the
'New Land like unto That of the Golden Age', as one contemporary traveller described America. For one thing, there was no voyaging in it ('man
knew no shores except their own'); for another, the sowing and farming
necessary for plantation survival (even if some of those work-shy early settlers did try to regress to a Golden Age idleness) are innovations of the Silver Age ('then in long furrows first were set the seeds'); and for a third, not
only voyaging ('men sailed the sea'), but also all the evil of 'deceit and
treachery / And violence and wicked greed' and the 'hands of blood' which
the travellers bring with them to the island, are the distinctive features of
the Age of Iron. The 'brave new world' which Miranda so innocently wonders at is in fact the varyingly corrupt old world of Europe. Even Sycorax
was from Algiers, and Caliban is not an indigenous native, not a Virginian
or a Caribbean savage. From this point of view, the island *is* 'uninhabited'
(the implication being, perhaps, that the only golden worlds are unpeopled
ones), and whether Caliban is innately disposed to evil or was corrupted by
his encounter and enforced servitude with Prospero, all the malign and infecting influences in the world of this play are importations, sourced elsewhere—wherever it *is* that evil is sourced; on this point Antonio is as un-
yieldingly silent as Iago.

So, while his opening shipwreck and aftermath has something more than
echoes of the Atlantic adventure of Sir Thomas Gates and his crew, Shakespeare locates his island squarely in the Mediterranean, as we gather between Naples and Tunis. Italy, for Shakespeare and the Elizabethans,
meant the glories of Renaissance civilization (here figured as Prospero's
'liberal arts without a parallel'), and the horrors of unscrupulous Machiavellian politics (Antonio's ruthless usurpation of Prospero's dukedom). Tunis, from where they are returning after what was clearly a completely
political marriage of Alonso's daughter to the Tunisian king (the play's
alertness to the importance to royal families of astute dynastic marriages

may have some contemporary relevance), allows a backward reference to Carthage and some seemingly pointless banter about 'Widow Dido' and 'Widower Aeneas'. Carthage may be allowed to evoke a memory of the lost civilization of the ancient world ('Delenda est Carthago'), while Aeneas is, of course, the most famous founder of Empire of all. There are small echoes of the *Aeneid* in the play, and these have a quiet, marginal relevance. But the exiled Prospero is not an empire builder, no matter how relevant the settlement of Virginia is to his background in the play. It is the more general resonance gained by suspending this mysterious island between, or off, a sort of palimpsest of European civilization which is more cardinally suggestive.

Thus far, I have stood somewhat outside the play, identifying rather aridly possible thematic concerns; but, as we feel our way gently into the mysteries of the play, all this material, like Ferdinand's father (and much else), 'doth suffer a sea change/Into something rich and strange' (I, ii, 401–2). The opening scene of the storm and wreck shows confusion and disorder: the angry sea makes social hierarchy irrelevant ('What cares these roarers for the name of king?'—(I, i, 16–17), and it is no longer clear who is 'the master'. The overworked Boatswain, annoyed at the useless courtiers in his way, sounds a note of insubordination, saying to Gonzalo 'if you can command these elements . . . use your authority' (I, i, 22–4). Straight away questions of mastery and authority and command—and mutiny and insurrection—are raised which will recur in a different form on the island, where Prospero 'commands the elements' in his own special way, and where the roaring sea will merge into Prospero's anger. There is desperate talk of 'sinking', a literal downward movement which, again transmuted, will affect figures in scenes to come. Furious, unpleasant Antonio shouts at the Boatswain 'would thou mightst lie drowning/The washing of ten tides!' (I, i, 57–8). Pirates were hanged on the beach and left there until they had been covered by three tides. The sea has much more work than that to do in this play, and the tidal washing continues, in various forms, throughout. For as well as being capable of stormy 'roarers', this is a cleansing and a 'clarifying' sea. And, in a curious way, it is as if the characters from the wreck *do* 'lie drowning' (not drown*ed,* note) during the play. This entirely realistic little scene ushers in what is to be the 'strangest' play Shakespeare ever wrote.

The second scene, it seems to me, marks an absolute alteration in mood and atmosphere, rather like the sudden change you experience if you are swimming in a noisy pool and suddenly duck your head down into submarine silence. Miranda refers to 'the wild waters in this roar' (I, ii, 2), but I don't think we can hear them. The world has gone quiet—the magisterial figure of Prospero is in complete command. It is indeed almost as if the play is taking place under the sea (as someone once remarked to Philip Brockbank); certainly there is something 'unearthly' about this island, and we soon learn that we have left the world of known and recognizable actualities behind. Miranda immediately reveals her 'piteous heart' by her instinctive sympathy with the shipwrecked men—'I have suffered / With those that I saw suffer' (I, ii, 5–6). This pity must be innate since there is no one to teach it her, no 'piteous' precedent to learn from on this island. Miranda's compassion is absolutely vital; it bespeaks her inherent 'nobility', and is part of her 'better nature' which is essential to offset and compensate for the bad nature which will soon be abroad on the island (and is perhaps incorporate in Caliban). From what we see of him, the austere and imperious Prospero is given more to anger than to pity, though pity is a lesson he will have to learn.

Prospero embarks on his long account of what befell him in Milan, the treacherous conspiracy against him, and how they were bundled into a boat and abandoned:

> To cry to th' sea that roared to us; to sigh
> To th' winds, whose pity, sighing back again,
> Did us but loving wrong.
>
> (I, ii, 149–51)

This sea always seems to be 'roaring', but within the tumult there is a wind sighing with pity—so the elements *can* set 'piteous' precedents. The apparent oxymoron of 'loving wrong' (which will be distortedly echoed by Caliban when he yearns for 'good mischief', by which he means the murder of Prospero: IV, i, 217) is important to the atmosphere and resolution of the play. When Miranda asks her father whether their coming to the island was 'foul play' or 'blessed' he replies:

> Both, both, my girl!
> By foul play, as thou say'st, were we heaved thence,
> But blessedly holp hither.
>
> (I, ii, 61–4)

When, near the end, Ferdinand is reunited with the father he thought drowned, he exclaims:

> Though the seas threaten, they are merciful.
> I have cursed them without cause.
>   (V, i, 178–9)

This is a restatement of Viola's 'Tempests are kind, and salt waves fresh with love!' (*Twelfth Night,* III, iv, 396), though in a somehow more sombre key. In this play, Nature *can* 'bless', as is clearly figured in the masque when Ceres says to Miranda and Ferdinand 'Ceres' blessing so is on you' (IV, i, 117), and more generally by the seemingly miraculous rescues and restorations on the island. But the word 'foul' occurs much more often; more often indeed than in any other play apart from *King Lear.* This is very much a Nature of 'both, both' with ultimately, as it were, no sure and lasting winner. As long (but only as long) as Prospero has his magic, the 'blessing' will seem to triumph. It is as if he works with the elements to bring about the mental renewal or spiritual cleansing of the errant courtiers. As he releases them from their charmed state, he comments:

> Their understanding
> Begins to swell, and the approaching tide
> Will shortly fill the reasonable shore,
> That now lies foul and muddy.
>   (V, i, 79–82)

The cleansing sea has entered their very being. But not all the foulness can be washed away, as the mutely, contemptuously unrepentant Antonio sufficiently reminds us. And who can say what might yet happen to Prospero back in Milan—without his magic and, as it were, as vulnerable as the next man to the abiding foulness of the world.

As Prospero begins to recount their history, he announces 'The hour's now come'; most unusually, we are told exactly what time the play takes place (between 2.00 and 6.00 pm), and, for only the second time in Shakespeare, the duration of the action is the same as the length of the play (the other is *The Comedy of Errors*). Something is coming to a head; and the words spoken later by Antonio to Sebastian, with reference to his plan to murder Alonso, might more fittingly have been said by Prospero to Miranda:

> We all were sea-swallowed, though some cast again,
> And, by that destiny, to perform an act
> Whereof what's past is prologue, what to come,
> In yours and my discharge.
>
> (II, i, 255–8)

The past which is prologue to Prospero's final 'performance' reveals that he was foully treated by his usurping brother, but also that he was not without some responsibility for what happened. We have encountered the figure of the negligent or absconding ruler before (most notably in *Measure for Measure*), and, by his own account, Prospero was guilty of an irresponsible dereliction of duty while he pursued his 'liberal arts'.

> Those being all my study,
> The government I cast upon my brother
> And to my state grew stranger, being transported
> And rapt in secret studies.
>
> (I, ii, 74–7)

Not 'good government', whatever else it was. In a roundabout way, Prospero actually admits his responsibility:

> *I* thus neglecting worldly ends, all dedicated
> To closeness and the bettering of my mind—
> . . .   in my false brother
> *Awaked an evil nature,* and my trust,
> Like a good parent, did beget of him
> A falsehood in its contrary as great
> As my trust was, which had indeed no limit,
> A confidence sans bound.
>
> (I, ii; 89–97—my italics)

So *he* did the 'awaking' of an evil latent in nature; just as his trust did the 'begetting' of falsehood. (I note in passing that for trust to be constructively operative it should not be limitless, any more than confidence should be simply boundless—to the extent that they are, they become indistinguishable from indifference.) A lot of things go by their 'contraries' in this play: there's a good father and a bad mother (Sycorax. Miranda's mother has one indirect reference which leaves her entirely without presence); a good brother and a bad brother; a noble child and a 'monstrous' child; a holy courtier and a foul one; a good servant and a bad servant; white magic and black magic. These contraries do not all remain stable and clear-cut—they wouldn't in Shakespeare; but there's a curious sense in which things somehow 'beget' their seeming opposites, a not-to-be-explained feeling that, say, Caliban is there because Ariel is there, that we have Sycorax because we have Prospero—or vice versa. As though people engender and awaken shadow selves. It is a very strange island.

One of Prospero's many complaints about the conduct of his brother is the way in which he used the power Prospero had allowed him to win Prospero's own followers over to him; but the way Prospero describes this treacherous feat points to a larger mystery:

> new-created
> The creatures that were mine, I say—or changed 'em,
> Or else new-formed 'em
>
> (I, ii, 81–3)

New-created, new-formed, changed creatures—this is what we have been watching throughout Shakespeare's comedies, and here the mysteries of metamorphosis and change are an essential part of the island's atmosphere. Antonio changed creatures for the worse; Prospero seeks to new-create and new-form them for the better—in a Nature of 'both', people can always go either way. Prospero emerges as the better maker (as T. S. Eliot called Ezra Pound—*il miglior fabbro*), though his instructive failures with Caliban and Antonio mark a limit to his magic.

Nearing the end of his account, Prospero says:

> Now I arise.
> Sit still, and hear the last of our sea sorrow.
>
> (I, ii, 169–70)

Perhaps he stands up; but more importantly, he senses the approach of his 'zenith', and this starts the ascending movement, with a slight resurrectionary air, which counters the prevalent sinking tendency in the play. The 'sea sorrow' is over, and the 'roarers' will soon convert to music. Prospero is now in every sense the Governor. It is notable that he ascribes his sea-salvation to 'providence divine', and the propitious conditions for his coming triumph to 'bountiful Fortune'.

> By accident most strange, bountiful Fortune
> (Now my dear lady) hath mine enemies
> Brought to this shore; and by my prescience
> I find my zenith doth depend upon
> A most auspicious star, whose influence
> If now I court not, but omit, my fortunes
> Will ever after droop.
>
> (I, ii, 178–84)

Destiny, Providence, Fortune, accidents, stars, his own 'prescience' (not to mention his science)—it is impossible to fix just who or what runs things, where the shaping and determining powers come from. But everything is somehow at work, and things are coming together.

Prospero starts his long narration by asking what images Miranda 'hath kept with thy remembrance' (I, ii, 44). The words 'remember', 'remembrance' occur more often in this play than elsewhere, and there is a great deal of retrospective peering into 'the dark backward and abysm of time' (I, ii, 50). The most of life, one feels, was back there. Here, Prospero has to educate Miranda's memory (as later he will Ariel's and Caliban's) since for her it is as if it all happened in another world.

> 'Tis far off,
> And rather like a dream than an assurance
> That my remembrance warrants.
>
> (I, ii, 44–6)

This dream-like quality pervades the play; even as Prospero recounts the real, waking world of Italian history to Miranda, it seems to have a narcotic, even hypnotic effect on her (thus his repeated jogging of her attention as she, presumably, keeps dropping off—'The strangeness of your story put/ Heaviness in me', I, ii, 306–7). Finishing his account he concludes:

> Thou art inclined to sleep. 'Tis a good dullness,
> And give it way. I know thou canst not choose. [*Miranda sleeps.*]
> (I, ii, 185–6)

This particular dormition cannot have required a very strong spell. This is not a facetious point. The island is full of sleep, could itself be asleep and dreaming. A 'strange drowsiness', 'wondrous heavy' (II, i, 202–3) is everywhere. Many scenes end in sleep or trance ('They fell together all . . . they dropped as by a thunderstroke', II, i, 207–8), and by the end you feel the difference between waking and dreaming is terminally blurred. Can you any longer be sure which is which? Thus Sebastian to Antonio:

> What? Art thou waking?
> *Antonio.* Do you not hear me speak?
> *Sebastian.*   I do; and surely
> It is a sleepy language, and thou speak'st
> Out of thy sleep. What is it thou didst say?
> This is a strange repose, to be asleep
> With eyes wide open; standing, speaking, moving
> And yet so fast asleep.
> (II, i, 213–19)

As it happens, the murderously plotting, and the slothfully biddable, two courtiers are wickedly awake; yet Sebastian's words aptly evoke the curious liminal state the characters seem to find themselves in, speaking a 'sleepy language', falling into a 'strange repose'. When the Boatswain appears in the final scene, he tells how they were 'dead of sleep'; then 'awaked' (with more 'roaring' sounds); then 'even in a dream . . . brought moping [dulled] hither' (V, i, 230–39). By this time, the characters hardly know if they are asleep or awake, or suspended in some waking dream. And nor do we. We (and they) might, by the same token, wonder if they are alive or dead, or in some sort of transitional limbo between the two states. Nobody dies in this play. Unless, that is, they are all dead already, all 'sea-swallowed' from the start. As Brockbank so pertinently commented, 'there is no death after death'.

While Miranda is asleep, Prospero summons Ariel (nobody apart from Prospero ever 'sees' Ariel, which makes him a very different kind of presence from the grossly corporeal Caliban, unpleasingly visible to all). Throughout this scene Prospero constantly addresses Ariel as 'spirit', another word occurring far more often in this play than elsewhere (twenty-nine times); and clearly enough he (I don't know if spirits are gendered, but 'it' sounds rude) represents some kind of elemental opposite to Caliban, who is invariably associated with (and even addressed as) 'earth'. However, it soon becomes clear that Ariel is quicksilvery volatile, at ease in all the elements. In the air, of the air, obviously; but also doing Prospero's 'business in the veins o' th' earth / When it is baked with frost' (I, ii, 255–6). Of course he can fly, and swim, and 'ride on the curled clouds' (I, ii, 192); he can also 'dive into the fire', and on the King's ship 'I flamed amazement' (I, ii, 198). I am not sure that we need to know that he has the qualities allowed to Intelligences in medieval theology; or that in some angelogy he is one of the planetry spirits—superhuman but lower than the angels; or that he is 'a rational Platonic demon'. He has some of the fairy qualities of Puck, and while he is clearly under the control of Prospero, he seems to enjoy and exercise a certain degree of moral autonomy, acting responsibly as Prospero's agent.

But when Prospero tells him there is more work to do and he exhibits signs of reluctance—'Is there more toil?' (I, ii, 242)—Prospero turns on him in fury, calling him 'malignant thing' and, tellingly, 'my slave' (I, ii, 257, 270). Since Prospero also calls Caliban his 'slave', we have to bear in mind that, whatever their extreme manifest differences, Ariel and Caliban have at least that status in common. Ariel wants 'my liberty' from Prospero; while Caliban, severely intoxicated by Stephano, deliriously, though utterly mistakenly, celebrates his new-found 'Freedom, high day, freedom!' (I, ii, 245; II, ii, 195). It wouldn't do to make too much of the fact that a number of Elizabethans had already made fortunes by introducing slavery into the West Indies, though it may well be relevant; and, given the horror that slavery in the New World was to become, we might wish to allow Shakespeare a disturbing prescience. But more relevant for the play is the fact that Shakespeare is reactivating, and of course richly transforming, a situation and theme from the old world of classical Plautine comedy. Bernard Knox has written an important article on this subject, and I can do no better than summarize his contribution.

Classical comedy derives a good deal of its humour from exploiting the absolute difference, crucial in the society of the time, between the free man and the slave (for Aristotle they were different natures). However callous we may find it, the crude activities and base proclivities of the slave were phenomena to be laughed at. But there were, for the purposes of the comedies, two kinds of slave: the stupid, sullen, cursing, drunken, lecherous, thievish, cowardly—let us say 'foul'—slave, who makes clumsy attempts to rebel, and is humiliated and punished; but there was also the clever, adroit, intelligent—let us say 'delicate'—slave, who would actually help his master and solve his problems, thereby gaining his freedom. The master in these comedies was invariably an irascible and rough-tongued *senex,* or old man, who turns out in the end to be good-hearted and generous. You can see what Shakespeare has done with these crude stereotypes in the infinitely richer and more complex figures of Caliban, Ariel and Prospero. And in some of the comedies there could be an ironic twist whereby free men show themselves as thinking and acting like slaves, while a slave might prove superior to his master in intelligence, taste, and emotion. We have an echo of this in a crucial moment at the beginning of the last act (Prospero's last act—as Prospero—in every sense). Prospero's former foes are now completely in his power—'At this hour/Lies at my mercy all mine enemies' (IV, i, 262–3). The long-awaited, long-prepared-for moment has come and the hour has struck. Prospero asks Ariel (now again addressed as 'my spirit') how the King and his followers are faring: 'all prisoners, sir . . . They cannot budge till your release.' The three guilty men are still 'distracted', while the others are mourning bemusedly over them (V, i, 9–13). Then Ariel continues:

> Your charm so strongly works 'em,
> That if you now beheld them, your affections
> Would become tender.
> *Prospero.*   Dost thou think so, spirit?
> *Ariel.* Mine would, sir, were I human.
> *Prospero.*   And mine shall.
> Hast thou, which art but air, a touch, a feeling
> Of their afflictions, and shall not myself,

One of their kind, that relish all as sharply,
Passion as they, be kindlier moved than thou art?
Though with their high wrongs I am struck to th' quick,
Yet with my nobler reason 'gainst my fury
Do I take part. The rarer action is
In virtue than in vengeance.

(V, i, 17–28)

This is a key moment in Shakespeare, first to last—vengeance is abjured or transcended; pity and forgiveness prevail. Some critics have spent fruitless time speculating whether angry old Prospero was intending to give his 'enemies' a good stiff dose of their own malignant medicine, before Ariel's irresistibly cadenced intercession. Maybe he was, and maybe he wasn't. Be content that Shakespeare has made sure we can never know. What he *does* show us is the supposedly non-human servant tentatively presuming to give his master a lesson in humanity. It is another 'rare' moment on this enchanted island.

Venting his fury on the hapless Ariel, Prospero reminds him that he was previously enslaved by the 'damned witch Sycorax' who had been banished to the island from 'Argier' (I, ii, 263). Because Ariel was 'a spirit too *delicate* / To act her *earthy* and abhorred commands' (I, ii, 272–3, my italics), he refused to obey her orders; as punishment

she did confine thee,
By help of her more potent ministers
And in her most unmitigable rage,
Into a cloven pine

(I, ii, 274–7)

and left him there until she died. It was only Prospero's 'art' which released him. And if Ariel goes on showing a disinclination to follow Prospero's instructions—'I will rend an oak / And peg thee in his knotty entrails till / Thou hast howled away twelve winters' (I, ii, 294–6). Ariel is reduced to the abject pleas for mercy of a cowed slave threatened with a whipping. Prospero, the majestic Italian mage and royal magician, master of high Renaissance Arts, whose daughter is a 'wonder', must seem a kind of absolute opposite to Sycorax, the disgraced North African 'hag', 'damned witch' and

wicked sorceress, whose offspring is a 'monster'. Of course we are prompted
to say—white magic opposed to black magic. But they are both banished
figures; they both depend on slaves and 'ministers'; and Prospero in *his*
'most unmitigable rage' threatens a rebellious Ariel with a punishment almost identical to the one visited on him by Sycorax (for, as between being
confined in a cloven pine and pegged in an oak's entrails, it must be very
much a case of six of one, half a dozen of the other). Prospero's 'Art' (always
with a capital A in the First Folio) is constantly stressed—it is *another* word
used more frequently in this play than elsewhere; and it is registered as being akin to an occult mystic science, while Sycorax dabbled diabolically in
the merest witchery. Yet in his final invocation of all his 'elves' and 'demi-
puppets', prior to abjuring his special powers, Prospero is made to echo, in
detail, the invocation of Medea in Ovid's *Metamorphoses* (V, i, 33–50). Now
it is true that on this occasion Medea wants some magic to restore the youth
of Jason's aged father, Aeson. But this is perhaps the only occasion on which
she uses her strange skills for re-creative purposes. Even though she does
finish up in pagan heaven, her life is littered with dismembered or otherwise butchered corpses, including those of her own children. Understandably, Medea came to be the prototypical name for the witch of terrifying,
dark destructive power. And if, as it were, Prospero draws on some of her
spells and recipes, we must at least wonder whether his 'rough magic' contains some elements from the Medea brew. Of course Prospero and Sycorax
are very different; but worrying similarities begin to appear, and what
looked like a separation and a clarification—white here, black there—turns
out to be a proximity and a blurring.

After Ariel, of course Caliban, as night follows day. He, too, shows a reluctance to respond to Prospero's orders (on the not unreasonable grounds
that (a) 'There's enough wood within', and (b) 'I must eat my dinner', I, ii,
314, 330). Clearly it is a day for slaves to be recalcitrant, and Prospero is in
what might be called a 'foul' temper. First, he promises Caliban a pretty
painful night of cramps and stinging pinches (the punishments Prospero
metes out sound sort of fairy-folksy, but, if read carefully, they would seem
to be, not exactly tortures, but at least 'cruel and unusual'; for instance, being wound round with adders which 'hiss me into madness', II, ii, 14).
Then, as with Miranda and Ariel, he reminds Caliban of the past. 'I have
used thee (filth as thou art)'—always the kind word—'with humane care'
(I, ii, 345–6), trying to educate him, as he was educating his own child.

Miranda, indeed, reminds Caliban, in some uncharacteristically harsh words (she sounds like her father—'abhorred slave' and so on), that she taught him language. This continued 'till thou didst seek to violate/The honor of my child' (I, ii, 347–8)—'O ho, O ho! Would't had been done!' cries Caliban, revealing the unrepentant lechery of the savage (I, ii, 349)—at which point the 'humane care' very promptly stopped, and Caliban was 'confined into this rock'—another of Prospero's prisoners.

Caliban has another view of what happened:

> This island's mine by Sycorax my mother,
> Which thou tak'st from me.
>   (I, ii, 331–2)

Disregarding the fact that all talk of 'property rights' on this 'uninhabited island' seems faintly absurd, Caliban's claim to, as it were, legitimate ownership is dubious. It will not do to see him as representing the expropriated native of shameful colonial history. The banished Sycorax (with child) has no more 'right' to the island than the exiled Prospero (with child). They are both alien interlopers (call them witches, call them settlers) on a land hitherto outside of history. Admittedly she was there first; but he seems to have made a better fist of things. What *is* certain is that Caliban—however he was while running wild and free—is *considerably* worse off as the solitary 'subject' under (usurping?) 'king' Prospero. Caliban's famous retort on being reminded of what we call the 'gift' of language is unanswerably compact—'You taught me language, and my profit on't/Is, I know how to curse' (I, ii, 363–4). So he does; and so he curses, inventively and volubly, throughout. But his cursing is, must be, some kind of derivative of the abominable language of execration, disgust and vilification regularly bestowed on him by his ferocious-sounding master. Prospero may be many things, and I will come to that; but, here, let us notice one little detail. Shakespeare had a particular feeling for dogs' names, and when Ariel and Prospero finally set the *'divers Spirits in the shape of dogs and hounds'* on doomed, drunken and thieving Stephano, Trinculo and Caliban, the dogs summoned by Ariel are 'Mountain' and 'Silver'—which seems appropriate enough since Ariel is equally at home in shining light and 'heavy' earth; while the dogs called up by Prospero are 'Fury' and 'Tyrant' (IV, i, 255–7). Point taken—ask Ariel and Caliban.

Caliban also reveals that, initially, Prospero was kind or, at least, conciliatory in his treatment of him—'Thou strok'st me and made much of me' (I, ii, 333); though perhaps this is rather as one might pet a dog of uncertain temper. In response 'I loved thee/And showed thee all the qualities o' th' isle,/The fresh springs, brine pits, barren place and fertile' (I, ii, 336–8). Just as the native Indians were indispensable to the first settlers. And notice that the island is barren *and* fertile. Both. You can read it either way, according to your temperament and predisposition—holy Gonzalo and good Adrian see the fertility ('see how lush and lusty the grass looks', etc.); rank-minded and sour-souled Antonio and Sebastian stress the fen-like barrenness ('the ground indeed is tawny', etc.—see II, i, 37–60). The island as a whole says different things to different people, who duly experience it in different ways.

It is notable that Caliban reveals himself as capable of 'love'; for the rest, the talk of love is, rightly enough, exclusively between Ferdinand and Miranda—except for a curiously touching moment shortly before the end when Ariel quite unexpectedly asks Prospero, 'Do you love me, master? No?' ('Dearly, my delicate Ariel'—Prospero's response is perhaps his tenderest utterance in the play, IV, i, 48–9.) It seems that there is a surprising capacity for 'love' in these non-human, or sub-human, slaves that you will look for in vain in worldly-wise, worldly-withered courtiers like Antonio and Sebastian. Caliban has had this 'love' whipped out of him ('lying slave,/Whom stripes may move, not kindness!', I, ii, 344–5); but we see him pathetically eager to transfer it to Stephano. It will not do to interpret this as some sort of instinctive, animal-like, tail-wagging servility. The need and desire to love is the very mark of the human. And as well as the (acquired— thank you Prospero and Miranda) ability to curse, Caliban also reveals an (innate) sensitivity, which manifests itself in one of the most beautiful speeches in the play—not, surely, something that Shakespeare would have given him if he wanted us to share the unqualifiedly negative Prospero view of Caliban.

> Be not afeard; the isle is full of noises,
> Sounds and sweet airs that give delight and hurt not.
> Sometimes a thousand twanging instruments
> Will hum about mine ears; and sometimes voices
> That, if I then had waked after long sleep,

Will make me sleep again; and then, in dreaming,
The clouds methought would open and show riches
Ready to drop upon me, that, when I waked,
I cried to dream again.
                              (III, ii, 140–48)

It is a moment of 'rare' sensibility.

I have no desire to sentimentalize Caliban; there is clearly much of the savage about him, and there was that sexual attempt on Miranda (not that *that* makes him sub-human, alas!). But it simply will not do to see Prospero as embodying or representing Art, civility, law and order, the most advanced western civilized thought and skill, having to bring to heel raw, recalcitrant wild nature in the misshapen shape of the 'beast', Caliban. *Something* of that, certainly; but, as I have intimated, in this play all such schematic, diagrammatic clarifications are, finally, out. Caliban is called 'monster' often (it is yet another word which occurs more frequently than elsewhere), but only by Stephano and Trinculo (they also compare him to 'a dead Indian', II, ii, 34—which *may* be a Virginian hint)—never by Prospero, who stays with 'beast'. And Stephano and Trinculo are pickled silly most of the time; certainly not qualified to pronounce on the more or less monstrous in man or nature. They reveal an inferiority to Caliban when they allow themselves to be distracted from their plot by the useless finery set out to snare them. 'Let it alone, thou fool! It is but trash' (IV, i, 224) says unacquisitive Caliban. He is primitive; they are degenerate. The real 'monsters' on the island are, of course Sebastian and, particularly, Antonio. They are both effectively speechless and notably unrepentant during the final reconciliation scene. Antonio really *is* an utterly recalcitrant piece of degraded nature; impervious to, and contemptuous of, any grace or kindness. He may have the bearing of a courtier, but in him we see nature *de*natured, the last humanizing flicker extinguished. There are worse things in heaven and earth than Caliban. True, he does instigate the plot to kill Prospero, thus initiating the parodic version of Antonio's planned regicide which, in turn, is a repetition, this time thwarted, of the distant usurpation of Prospero. (Unlike Scott Fitzgerald's Gatsby, Prospero *can* repeat the past—and change it.) Certainly, you should not assassinate Governors, and we must never forget the importance of 'the vital power of regiment'; but one has heard of justified, or at least justifiable, slave revolts. Just how much 'nurture' will, or can, 'stick' on Caliban's 'nature' remains an open question. Clearly there are some natures on which it won't—one of the mysteries we live amongst. At the end, Caliban seems resolved to have another go—'I'll be wise hereafter,/And seek for grace' (V, i, 295–6). At the same time, Prospero acknowledges some sort of responsibility for Caliban which remains terminally ambiguous—'this thing of darkness I/Acknowledge mine' (V, i, 275–6). Why his?

If I have not wanted to promote Caliban as a version of the mythical 'noble savage', I have, by the same token, no desire to *de*mote Prospero into an *ig*noble slave-driver. 'Nobility'—and it is very important—in this play appertains exclusively to the Italian courts, and Prospero must be registered as noble, even though disquietingly prone to anger. As Miranda watches, as she thinks, the ship go down, she instinctively guesses that it 'had no doubt some noble creature in her' (I, ii, 7); and so it does—Ferdinand:

> I might call him
> A thing divine; for nothing natural
> I ever saw so noble.
>   (I, ii, 418–20)

This is Miranda's response to her first sight of him (she in turn will be thought a 'goddess' by Ferdinand's father; this is par for romance, and together they make a 'noble' pair). Just as nature can produce monsters, so it can engender nobles. Though, to define true nobility (when it doesn't just mean rank or title) may be said to be an ongoing matter, always to be explored in Shakespeare's plays. Certainly, some of the 'goodly creatures' that Miranda wonders at when the courtiers are assembled at the end, are neither so good, nor indeed so 'beauteous', as she generously assumes (V, i, 182–3).

But Ferdinand is presented as genuinely noble (this is demonstrated in his courteous and chivalric courting of Miranda, enduring the test of penal servitude for her sake). Like Caliban, he also hears some of the 'sounds and sweet airs' of the isle, which again prompt some beautiful lines:

> Where should this music be? I' th' air or th' earth?
> It sounds no more; and sure it waits upon
> Some god o' th' island. Sitting on a bank,

> Weeping again the King my father's wrack,
> This music crept by me upon the waters,
> Allaying both their fury and my passion
> With its sweet air.
>
> (I, ii, 388–94)

The last word nicely elides air–oxygen with air–melody; the sounds are Ariel's, but it is as if Ferdinand is breathing in the music of the elements— earth, air, waters. And the grammar allows the music to be weeping with Ferdinand. The threatening roaring of the sea has modulated to a consoling, placating singing. A second song effectively distils the atmosphere and process of the whole play.

> Full fathom five thy father lies;
>   Of his bones are coral made;
> Those are pearls that were his eyes;
>   Nothing of him that doth fade
> But doth suffer a sea change
> Into something rich and strange.
>
> (I, ii, 397–402)

This is the magical metamorphosis which seems to spread through the play.

Ariel also makes sounds specially for Alonso, Antonio and Sebastian— this time, a moral indictment:

> You are three men of sin, whom destiny—
> That hath to instrument this lower world
> And what is in't—the never-surfeited sea
> Hath caused to belch up you and on this island,
> Where man doth not inhabit—
>
> (III, iii, 53–7)

It is as if these indigestible sinners have caused the very sea to vomit them out. Ariel reminds them of their 'great guilt' and their treatment of Prospero—

> for which foul deed
> The pow'rs, delaying, not forgetting, have
> Incensed the seas and shores, yea, all the creatures,
> Against your peace.
>
> (III, iii, 72–5)

'The powers'—unspecified; it is as if they were under the supervision of the seas and shores, which are 'instrumenting' this 'lower world'. To Alonso, it is as if the sea had spoken:

> O, it is monstrous, monstrous!
> Methought the billows spoke and told me of it;
> The winds did sing it to me; and the thunder,
> That deep and dreadful organ pipe, pronounced
> The name of Prosper; it did bass my trespass.
> Therefore my son i' th' ooze is bedded; and
> I'll seek him deeper than e'er plummet sounded
> And with him there lie mudded.
>
> (III, iii, 95–102)

The elements of nature, mediated by Prospero, refracted through Ariel, yield a moral music.

When Ferdinand has passed his test and is honourably betrothed to Miranda, Prospero, through Ariel, puts on a masque for them, which he calls 'some vanity of my art' (IV, i, 41); and much of his art is, indeed, theatrical. Ceres and Juno appear to bestow 'Honor, riches, marriage blessing' (IV, i, 106) on the pair, and Ceres invokes the seasonal bounty of great creating Nature:

> Earth's increase, foison plenty,
> Barns and garners never empty
> Vines with clust'ring branches growing,
> Plants with goodly burden bowing,
> Spring come to you at the farthest
> In the very end of harvest.
>
> (IV, i, 110–15)

It is important that Venus is kept away, since virginity is essential for a royal marriage; and this is a marriage Prospero very much wants (so that his child's children will inherit Milan *and* Naples). Hence his stress on the necessity for 'all sanctimonious ceremonies' and his almost hysterical hands-off warnings to Ferdinand. The masque does celebrate a more familiar pastoral nature; but it is as if in a dream within a dream. And it ends suddenly with '*a strange, hollow, and confused noise*' as the dancing Nymphs and Reapers '*heavily vanish*' (more 'hollowness' and 'heaviness' on the isle). He has foiled one plot, but he has another to deal with. 'I had forgot that foul conspiracy / Of the beast Caliban and his confederates / Against my life. The minute of their plot / Is almost come' (IV, i, 139–42). He must go carefully by the clock, and can't really afford much dalliance with pastoral illusionism. But the thought of Caliban's malevolence brings back his old fury, and Ferdinand and Miranda are dismayed to see him 'with anger so distempered' (IV, i, 145). He seeks to reassure them with what is, I suppose, the most famous speech in Shakespeare:

> be cheerful, sir.
> Our revels now are ended. These our actors,
> As I foretold you, were all spirits and
> Are melted into air, into thin air;
> And, like the baseless fabric of this vision,
> The cloud-capped towers, the gorgeous palaces,
> The solemn temples, the great globe itself,
> Yea, all which it inherit, shall dissolve,
> And, like this insubstantial pageant faded,
> Leave not a rack behind. We are such stuff
> As dreams are made on, and our little life
> Is rounded with a sleep. Sir, I am vexed.
> Bear with my weakness; my old brain is troubled.
> Be not disturbed with my infirmity . . .
>   (IV, i, 147–60)

This was how masques 'dissolved', and Shakespeare had seen a number. Here it leads easily on to a vision of cosmic dissolution. Prospero is a magician; but he is also a vexed old man, with his thoughts turning towards the grave. (People have understandably wondered whether this is also Shakespeare, not so old—forty-seven—and, as one hopes, not so vexed, with his thoughts turning towards retirement.)

From now on his 'project doth gather to a head' (V, i, 1). The King and courtiers are drawn into a circle where they '*stand charmed*', 'spell-stopped' (V, i, 61). They have indeed been 'justled from your senses' (V, i, 158), but now Prospero commences the breaking of the spell and the clearing of the mind.

> The charm dissolves apace;
> And as the morning steals upon the night,
> Melting the darkness, so their rising senses
> Begin to chase the ignorant fumes that mantle
> The clearer reason . . .
>
> (V, i, 64–8)

The senses are rising, the understanding is swelling—the refreshing tide of renewed sanity is coming in. The reconciliations, reunions and restorations are perfunctorily managed, and a quick forgiveness is dispensed. (Even to 'unnatural' Antonio, though with some asperity and quite a touch of the old temper—'For you, most wicked sir, whom to call brother / Would even infect my mouth, I do forgive / Thy rankest fault—all of them', V, i, 130–32. He gets no reply.) It is as if Shakespeare through Prospero is saying—these are the familiar conventions of the genre; let's just quickly run through them. Time is running out—and the absconding playwright shows his hand through the retiring Governor. Good Gonzalo, always positive, is the most appreciative:

> O, rejoice
> Beyond a common joy, and set it down
> With gold on lasting pillars. In one voyage
> Did Claribel her husband find at Tunis,
> And Ferdinand her brother found a wife
> Where he himself was lost; Prospero his dukedom
> In a poor isle; and all of us ourselves
> When no man was his own.
>
> (V, i, 206–13)

Truly to 'find' yourself is the best benefit afforded by this island.

But they can still 'taste/Some subtleties o' th' isle, that will not let you/ Believe things certain' (V, i, 123–5), and as seeming miracle follows seeming miracle—a curtain drawn revealing Ferdinand and Miranda playing chess (more theatrics); the news that the wrecked ship is, in fact, as good as new —it is the sheer 'strangeness' of the whole experience which overwhelms them.

> These are not natural events; they strengthen
> From strange to stranger.
> (V, i, 227–8)

> This is as strange a maze as e'er men trod,
> And there is more in this business than nature
> Was ever conduct of.
> (V, i, 242–4)

'Strange to stranger'—to strangest (appropriately enough, 'strange' is yet another word which occurs more often in this play than elsewhere—the last one I will mention); what cannot happen here? These are, indeed, not 'natural' events—they are theatrical events. Which brings us to Prospero and Shakespeare.

The inclination to identify Prospero and his creator goes back a long way. In 1838 Thomas Campbell wrote of *The Tempest* that it 'has a sort of sacredness as the last work of the mighty workman. Shakespeare, as if conscious that it would be his last, and as if to typify himself, has made its hero a natural, a dignified, a benevolent magician.' This view of Prospero prevailed at least up to and including Frank Kermode's landmark, and still indispensable, Arden edition of 1954 (few editions have weathered the years so well). But more recent commentaries have knocked quite a few spots off that dignity and benevolence, and a second look has been taken at Prospero's magic. This seems to me to be correct; though when he is made out to be a megalomaniacal fascist imperialist, one begins to yearn for the old sanities. Prospero is a complex character in his own right, and we must leave him firmly embedded in the play rather than trying to transport him to Stratford. Having said that, there are some clear parallels between Prospero and Shakespeare, just as there is an unmistakable sense of concludingness in the

famous lines of relinquishment, and in the generally penumbral air of the
last scene, which is at once a new dawn and an old dusk (both).

> I'll break my staff,
> Bury it certain fathoms in the earth,
> And deeper than did ever plummet sound
> I'll drown my book.
>
>   (V, i, 54–7)

Marlowe's Doctor Faustus promises to 'burn my books' in his very last
words, and there is surely, here, a distant echo: but Shakespeare's is, rather,
a drowned and drowning play; though it is worth noting that Faustus also
prayed that his soul should be:

> changed into little water-drops,
> And fall into the ocean, ne'er to be found!
>
>   (*Doctor Faustus*, V, ii, 118–19)

Prospero's 'project' and Shakespeare's play last exactly the same length of
time because, finally, they are one and the same thing. At the end, Prospero
must put on his Milanese clothes, leave his island, and return to his un-
magical ducal daily duties in Italy; just so, playwright and audience must
leave the theatre and return to their less bewitching, 'real' lives. Even
Shakespeare's magic can only work in the theatre and for so long. That is
why Prospero (and there is a nice legend that Shakespeare played the role)
comes forward to speak the Epilogue; post-play, minus magic, in the hands
of God—and the audience.

> Now my charms are all o'erthrown,
> And what strength I have's mine own,
> Which is most faint.
> . . .   Now I want
> Spirits to enforce, art to enchant;
> And my ending is despair
> Unless I be relieved by prayer.
>
>   (1–3, 13–16)

Prospero can put on spectacular, spell-binding shows, he can 'justle' the senses this way and that; but, if you remember, his 'art' cannot get the daily chores done (like bringing in the wood), and it cannot convert the unconvertible (Antonio). And, we have to say, that goes for Shakespeare and his art, too. (He, too, can wake 'sleepers' from their graves by *his* 'so potent art', V, i, 50—Theseus, Caesar, Cleopatra, Henry V—you name it.) It is irrelevant, and certainly undiscoverable, whether Shakespeare was here consciously saying goodbye to the theatre. But he was, by this time, far too self-conscious an artist for it not to be the case that in depicting and delimiting Prospero's magic he was both displaying and examining his own art. There has never been an art like it, before or since.

When I started to write these introductions, I made a point of acknowledging the enduring influence of the man who taught me how to read Shakespeare at Cambridge (and, in effect, for the rest of my life), the late Philip Brockbank. As a very small concluding piety I want to let him answer my opening question, and have the last word on the last play.

> Where is the island of *The Tempest*? The final answer to this question must be, 'in the theatre' . . . Every Shakespearian play is 'islanded' from the flux of life to which the epilogue returns us at the end of *The Tempest,* and having left the island–theatre we know that the fuller significance of our lost lives was there brought home to us.

ABOUT THE AUTHOR

Tony Tanner (1935–1998) was a Fellow of King's College, Cambridge, and Professor of English and American Literature in the University of Cambridge. He travelled extensively and taught in many universities in the United States and across the world. His many books include *The Reign of Wonder: Naivety and Reality in American Literature* (1965), *City of Words: American Fiction, 1950–70* (1970), *Jane Austen* (1986), *Scenes of Nature, Signs of Men* (1987), *Venice Desired* (1992), *Henry James and the Art of Non-Fiction* (1995), and the posthumous collection of essays *The American Mystery: American Literature from Emerson to DeLillo* (2000). His last great critical project was the set of introductions to the Everyman's Library edition of Shakespeare (1992–1996).